—————— MIND MATTERS ——————

Minds, Brains and Machines

───── MIND MATTERS ─────

Series editor: Judith Hughes

In the same series

minds, brains and machines

GEOFFREY BROWN

PUBLISHED BY BRISTOL CLASSICAL PRESS

Printed in Great Britain

First published in 1989 by:

Bristol Classical Press,
226 North Street,
Bedminster,
Bristol BS3 1JD.

British Library Cataloguing in Publication Data

Brown, Geoffrey
Minds, Brains and Machines. – (Mind Matters)
1. Mind – Philosophical perspectives
I. Title II. Series
128'.2

ISBN 1-85399-012-4
ISBN 1-85399-013-2 Pbk

to my family

contents

foreword

'A philosophical problem has the form *I don't know my way about*,' said Wittgenstein. These problems are not the ones where we need information, but those where we are lost for lack of adequate signposts and landmarks. Finding our way – making sense out of the current confusions and becoming able to map things both for ourselves and for others – is doing successful philosophy. This is not quite what the lady meant who told me when I was seven that I ought to have more philosophy, because philosophy was eating up your cabbage and not making a fuss about it. But that lady *was* right to suggest that there were some useful skills here.

Philosophizing, then, is not just a form of highbrow chess for postgraduate students; it is becoming conscious of the shape of our lives, and anybody may need to do it. Our culture contains an ancient tradition which is rich in helpful ways of doing so, and in Europe they study that tradition at school. Here, that study is at present being squeezed out even from university courses. But that cannot stop us doing it if we want to. This series contains excellent guide-books for people who do want to, guide-books which are clear, but which are not superficial surveys. They are themselves pieces of real philosophy, directed at specific problems which are likely to concern all of us. Read them.

MARY MIDGLEY

preface

Philosophers are very good at talking to one another. Some of them are also good at talking with other people. In the market-places of Athens, the cafés of Paris, and lately, in the pubs of London, philosophers have always found a public bursting with its own ideas and keen to discuss them with others. The need to ask and attempt to answer philosophical questions is in us all and is prompted sometimes by particular events in our personal lives and sometimes by a more general unease about wider social or political or scientific issues. At such times there is always a popular demand for philosophers to explain themselves and the views of their illustrious forebears in ways which others can understand and question and use.

It is not an easy thing to do because Philosophy is not easy, though its central insights, like those in the sciences, are often startingly simple. To gain those insights we all have to follow the paths of reasoning for ourselves. Signposts have been left for us by the great philosophers of the past, and deciphering some of them is part of the business of this series.

'Mind Matters' is not 'Philosophy Made Easy' but rather 'Philosophy Made Intelligible', and the authors in this series have been chosen for more than their philosophical knowledge. Some of them are also experts in other fields such as medicine, computing or biology. All are people who recognise and try to practise the art of writing in an accessible and clear manner, believing that philosophical thought which is not understandable is best kept to oneself. Many have acquired this ability in the harsh discipline of adult education where students bring their own knowledge and puzzles to the subject and demand real explanations of relevant issues.

Each book in this series begins with a perplexing question that we may ask ourselves without, perhaps, realising that we are 'philosophising': Do computers have minds? Can a pile of bricks be a work of art? Should we hold pathological killers responsible for their crimes? Such questions are considered and new questions raised with frequent reference to the views of major philosophers. The authors go further than this, however. It is not their intention to produce a potted history of philosophical ideas. They also make their own contributions to the subject, suggesting different avenues of thought to explore. The result is a collection of original writings on a wide range of topics produced for all those who find Philosophy as fascinating and compelling as they do.

Whether or not machines can think is the stuff of which dreams and nightmares are made. Geoffrey Brown lives in this world, however, and his expertise in computing engineering gives him a down-to-earth view of the present complexity and future possibilities of the machines which appear to control much of our lives.

But he is also a philosopher who sees that the question demands careful consideration of some fundamental issues. What do we mean by 'think'? Is machine 'thinking' like human 'thinking'? What does it mean to be conscious? And in answering these questions we reach the heart of what is called the philosophy of mind.

JUDITH HUGHES

acknowledgements

I am happy to express my thanks to the Catholic University of Leuven, Belgium, for the fellowship during the course of which this book was written, and to all the members of the Institute of Philosophy who gave me help and encouragement, especially Herman De Dijn and Herman Roelants. Special thanks are also due to Frank Bock for assistance in innumerable ways. I am grateful for many useful discussions with Geoffrey Midgley and for helpful suggestions from Mary Midgley and from David Bell. I am grateful also to my wife Valerie for her help and support.

introduction

'Can a machine think – that is, really think in the same sense that human beings really think?' This is a question which most people are by now quite used to hearing from various quarters. It is not just an obscure 'philosopher's question', in the sense of a question which is of interest only to a small and specialised bunch of academics – though it is indeed a philosophical question, and our treatment of it will be an exercise in Philosophy. Nor is such a question of interest purely to those whose work lies in the field now known as Artificial Intelligence. Today a large and ever increasing number of people come into contact with highly sophisticated machines, either in the course of their job or of a pastime. People make use of them, interrogate them, compete with them in games, talk to them, and often love them or hate them – or even both.

It is hardly surprising, therefore, that the question should arise for people of how far these machines can be, or ought to be, treated as actually thinking, genuinely intelligent, creatures. For it is clear that they are capable of many of the same intellectual tasks that human beings are able to perform. Furthermore, if someone is unable to believe that genuine thought is going on inside his common-or-garden desktop computer, do there not exist machines many times more powerful and complex, to which real thought could nevertheless be attributed? And if even this doesn't look too promising, the way has now been opened for him to ask the question: 'Could any man-made machine ever, in principle, be said to be thinking in the full sense?'

1

People interrogate them, compete with them in games...

Now once a question of this kind really takes hold of us, once we have really understood its implications, it tends to hang around in our minds and refuse to leave until it gets an answer. This, it might be said, is characteristic of a philosophical problem, or perhaps of a philosopher. A relatively unreflective person will typically throw at it the first answer that comes into his head: 'Of course they can't — they could never do this-that-or-the-other'; 'Obviously they can, they already do such-and-such far faster than the human brain!' We have probably all heard these glib responses. It may be said here that if anyone thinks the question posed above is indeed a trivial or stupid one, or that it can be answered in a few words only, then he had better stop reading at this point, unless he is prepared to consider that things might be otherwise. For it is ultimately with this question that we shall be concerned throughout this book.

There are at least two ways of going about getting to a chosen destination (in this case, an answer to the question). One is simply to make a bee-line for it, ignoring everything else in sight, and possibly thereby missing a great many landmarks that might have been of use. Another is to approach it in a more leisurely and open-minded fashion, stopping where there is something of interest, viewing the scenery and noting the intersections with adjacent routes, and maybe even asking ourselves occasionally whether the original destination was where we should really have aimed at in the first place. It is something like this latter approach which will be adopted in what follows. The reader must not, therefore, be put off if some of the ground covered seems at the time to be only loosely connected with the topic in hand, or even downright irrelevant. It is hard to know in advance what considerations will prove relevant to solving a philosophical problem, for it is also fairly typical of a philosophical question that there is some unclarity regarding what sort of a question it actually is. Is it, for example, a matter of observation and experience, of calculation, of pure reasoning, or perhaps merely of definition?

Moreover, philosophical questions tend to need a context. Such questions do not come simply 'out of the blue'. And the context of the particular question which we have set ourselves here, is the whole tradition of what is called the Philosophy of Mind, at least in the modern period, which by general consent is reckoned as dating from the seventeenth century. It is therefore part of the purpose of the book to convey to the reader something, though it will be a small taste only, of the flavour of that tradition.

Having said a little about the nature of philosophical questions, we may now consider briefly how philosophical questions are answered. The activity of philosophy does not consist, as some academic pursuits do, in the collecting of facts, or the presentation merely of pieces of information. A philosophical problem can only properly be approached by conducting an argument; that is, by seeing how a number of considerations, which may in themselves be quite mundane and familiar, are connected. Argument, in this sense, need not necessarily mean arguing against anyone, or the taking of sides in a disagreement. All that is necessary is the existence of a conceptual problem, and the ability to make out a reasoned case in favour of one particular answer, or type of answer, to it.

With this in mind, let us run briefly through the way in which the argument will proceed in the remainder of this book.

After some initial clarification in *chapter 1*, we will go on in *chapter 2* to discuss the ways in which the presence or absence of thought can be recognised in general – as much in human beings as in machines. We will find that this raises some awkward questions about the evidence for other minds.

In *chapter 3* the Problem of Other Minds (what makes one think that anything, apart from oneself, has real thoughts?) will be met head-on. Attempts to solve the problem on the part of various previous philosophers will be discussed, but no definitive solution will be offered at this stage.

A solution of a kind will, however, be presented in *chapter 4*, in which we look at the philosophy of Ludwig Wittgenstein, and in particular the celebrated 'Private Language Argument'. This will, we shall find, throw light also on the kind of symptoms of genuine thought for which we should be looking.

In *chapter 5* the topic of communication in relation to the capacity for thought will be discussed, and we will be looking at one or two examples of the ways in which computers can be made to interact with people in something like the same way that human beings do.

Chapters 6, 7 and *8* will be devoted to examining a range of traditional approaches to the 'Mind-Body Problem' – that is, the philosophical problem concerning the relationship between the physical and mental features of human beings. Only by doing this can we get a clear picture of what we think the relationship would be, if any, between a machine's ability to think, and its physical make-up.

Continuing from there, *chapter 9* will go into a little more technical detail (though not too much) regarding both computers and the human brain, and will ask the question: are there enough significant similarities to make us suspect that real thought in one may imply real thought in the other?

In *chapter 10*, some arguments will be presented concerning the relations between a cluster of concepts which we will by then have encountered: thought, conceptualization, rule-following, purposiveness, autonomy, and consciousness.

Finally, *chapter 11* will embody such conclusions as we are able to reach in the course of this short and introductory treatment.

We must bear in mind first of all, however, that a significant aspect of philosophy lies in examining our questions themselves, lest we should get into difficulties by attempting precipitately to answer misleading, ill-formed, or badly-understood questions. It is for this reason that chapter 1 is devoted to a discussion of the question posed above, and to this we will now turn.

1: asking the right question

We (reflective human beings, I mean) divide things in the world into two categories – those which think, and those which do not. People, and probably monkeys, cats and dogs, think. Bricks and biscuits, and probably plants, on the other hand, do not think. In some cases, such as flies and earthworms, most people are unsure what to say. Thus we seem to have two sets of things, with a somewhat fuzzy no-man's land between them.

This distinction is by no means symmetrical. Firstly, those things which think do not *always* think – for example, they are (most people would accept) without thoughts during much of the time when they are asleep. Things which do not think, however, are without thoughts *all* of the time: there are no lapses into thoughtfulness! The distinction is, then, between those things which *sometimes* think and those which *never* think; between those things which are capable of thought and those which are incapable of it.

Secondly, it is clear that at least some of the things which think are capable of making this very distinction, whilst none of those things which do not think are capable of doing so. We are dealing, therefore, with a distinction imposed from the only side of the divide capable of making distinctions of any sort. Nor could there, even in principle, be any 'objective' arbiter who could make such a distinction from a position of neutrality, since the categories Thinking Being and Non-Thinking Being are obviously jointly exhaustive – everything falls into one and only one of them.

All of this sounds, on the face of it, very straightforward, though, as we shall see, it is not. It is, however, a great deal more straightforward than what comes next. So far, we have noticed that human beings are unhesitatingly regarded as thinking beings, and that as we go through the animal kingdom in what used to be called the direction of 'down', we are increasingly less inclined to ascribe thought to the creatures we encounter. When we reach plants, all but the very unorthodox are certain that no real thinking is going on. And when we come to to inanimate things – those which are not even *alive* – we are all agreed on its absence. Or are we?

There is one special case, which for obvious reasons has only come to serious attention in recent decades. This is the case of the 'intelligent' machine. It has been suggested by quite a lot of more-or-less influential people, that it would be possible to build a computer which not only behaves as a simple tool, like an hour-glass or an abacus, but which *really thinks*, in the sense in which you and I really think. Some have gone further and hinted that certain of our existing machines may have this property. It will be the task of the remainder of this book to examine claims of these kinds. Can computers really think or can't they? And if they can't, could they perhaps if they were only a little more complex? Or a *lot* more? Or could they never do so, however sophisticated we made them? Let us (as befits reflective human beings) reflect.

knowing what we mean
If the question were even as simple as it seems, this book would probably be a great deal shorter. As it is, I am going to begin by playing what many will see as a typical philosopher's trick, and say, 'It depends what you mean by "really think".' Like most such questions, this looks odd at first sight. When someone says, 'Be quiet, I'm thinking', or 'Aunt Ethel is thinking about Iceland again', we stand in need of no clarification regarding the meaning of the word 'thinking'. In our present context, however, a more searching analysis is called for; not so much because these everyday uses are vague or ambiguous, but because the question we are considering is not merely to do with recognizing well-understood central cases of thinking, or

even with particular instances at all, but with what we might call the 'essence' of thought. This grand-sounding phrase really only means that we are concerned with what does and does not count as thinking. For this reason, it will be useful to attempt some sort of characterization of what we mean by 'really think' when we ask whether a computer could really think. In the rest of this chapter, it is important to remember that we are not merely casting about for a stipulative definition – a question that can be settled by definition is not a philosophical question at all. Rather, we have identified a question which actually arises for some people, and which genuinely puzzles them; and we want to pin down that question, that source of puzzlement, in such a way that we do not end up by offering an answer to the wrong question.

thinking as intelligence

We have already seen that the question of whether machines can think tends to arise in connection with those machines which are described as 'intelligent'. It makes sense, then, to begin by asking whether being capable of thought is the same thing as being, in this sense, intelligent.

Intelligent machines are machines which have (a) a store of residual knowledge, and (b) some sophisticated means of applying it in a given case. This means that the machine in some way incorporates or has access to a data base (a store of facts), and also carries some quite complex software for handling new cases and relating them to what it already 'knows'. Since these are not strictly part of the machine itself, the whole set-up is usually known as an 'intelligent system'. Now is this the type of intelligence which we might want to identify with thought in the fullest sense?

One reason for *not* making this simple equation is the merely quantitative nature of the criterion which we would be applying were we to do so. One thing which impresses people about 'intelligent systems' is the amount of information they can store. A typical data base can hold many thousands of times more facts than any human being could hope to remember. Another is the speed at which they can search through this data and respond to interrogation, and the vast multiplicity of possible responses which they are capable of making. Yet all this differs only in degree from, say, a word processor with a built-in spelling checker. True, we must be wary of writing off enormous differences of complexity as 'mere' differences of degree – the ability of human beings to think no doubt has *something* to do with their degree of complexity. Yet it cannot surely be a matter of just more facts, more combinations of facts, quicker access to facts, and so on: somewhere along the line, the capacity for thought must depend on the *kind* of complexity involved. No sheer degree of capacity or speed can be actually *identified* with real thought. And the same goes even when we take into account some of the more impressive things which such systems can do, such as drawing inferences, or distinguishing between relevant and irrelevant information.

Whilst these 'mechanical' kinds of ability are no doubt *necessary* for genuine thought, it is highly implausible to suggest that they are *sufficient*. That is to say, whilst anything which genuinely thinks must be able to perform to some extent the sort of tricks which an 'intelligent system' can do, it by no means follows that anything which does these tricks is thereby capable of genuine thought. We have to conclude that the concept of thought in the fullest sense cannot be just the same as that of intelligence, in the sense in which machines can be 'intelligent'. This is not, of course, to pre-judge the issue against the view that machines can think: it simply means that the person who suspects that the computer might be 'really thinking' must be being tempted to attribute something extra to it, *over and above* (though possibly arising out of) its sheer capacity and complexity of data-handling.

If real thought were the same thing as this mechanical sort of intelligence, our task would be an easy one: of course some machines are intelligent – they can work out square roots, direct space rockets, and so on – therefore by definition they think. Unfortunately, this too-easy equation falls to bits as soon as we start to prod at it a little, and we will have to look further in order to discover what that 'extra' ingredient referred to above could be.

thinking as creativity

One possible candidate is *creativity*. A promising sign is that this is *par excellence* one of those attributes about which disagreement is rife when it comes to attributing it to machines: some people maintain that no machine could ever exhibit creativity, whilst others tell us that creative machines are already in existence.

The trouble here, of course, is pinning down the meaning of 'creativity' itself. The first trap which we must avoid is that of regarding creativity as exclusively the province of gifted artists, musicians and the like. It may be that the everyday human characteristic of creativity is better developed in such persons, but for our purposes we require nothing very highflown. If creativity is an essential component of genuine thought, then it must be a kind of creativity exemplified, to a greater or lesser extent, by everyone.   The sorts of things we will have in mind

Others tell us that creative machines are already in existence.

here are, we might suggest, (a) the ability to come up with new solutions to problems, that is, solutions which are not part of a repertoire which has been explicitly taught to the person or thing in question, and (b) the propensity to initiate interest in some topic or activity without having been overtly directed to it by a controlling agency: in other words, to act with some degree of *autonomy*. This idea of autonomy is very important, and we shall be returning to it in chapter 10. What, then, of these two features?

Certainly a thing which instantiates these characteristics will be a better candidate for 'really thinking' than one which does not. Yet there are drawbacks here also. Take firstly the idea of creativity as the ability to generate new solutions. It will be claimed that there exist machines already which can do this. However, when we look at the way in which they do it, we find that they have, naturally, been programmed to do so, and to do so by carrying out a predetermined, mechanical, procedure. And we have already noted, in the last section, that such 'mechanical' abilities, whilst they might in some way *support* real thinking, cannot be *identified* with it. The ability to generate original solutions does not, then, seem to have brought with it what we were looking for – the characteristic or ingredient which makes the difference between mere data-juggling and genuine thought.

And if we take the second feature which we associated with creativity – the ability to initiate interest in something – we will find that it gets us little further. Suppose we have a system which is somehow so advanced that when I instruct it to play a game of chess with me it sometimes says, 'No, I'm getting more interested in bridge just at the moment'. How did it arrive at this response? Surely there are only two possibilities: either that was the only thing it *could* have done, because it was programmed to do that, or it was totally mysterious how it arrived at the answer. But worse is to come. For if we accept this, why should we accept anything different when it comes to human beings? If a friend gives me the same response, how do we explain how *he* arrived at it? Of course, it is not utterly mysterious to us how other people come to have the interests which they do – in a sense, we know quite a lot about it. We commonly explain this sort of thing by reference to such factors as the choices available to a person at a given time, the extent of that person's knowledge, the current influences on him, and so on. And in the case of explaining the interests of a *person*, we would refer to *reasons* as well as *causes*: that is, we would regard some of the relevant antecedents as things which may have been taken into rational consideration by the person in question, as opposed to forces acting 'blindly' on him. The trouble is that the 'ingredient' of human beings which makes it appropriate to ascribe reasons as well as causes to them, is itself something of a philosophical puzzle: we find ourselves unsure of what it is, even in ourselves, which distinguishes authentic 'creativity' in this sense from some purely mechanical process. We will return to this topic later. It is enough here to recognise that the difference between simply obeying a 'program' and being truly creative, is proving as hard to nail down as the original distinction between 'real' and merely 'apparent' thought, which it was meant to illuminate.

creatures with minds

This is perhaps the appropriate point at which to try out a more general concept, and one with a very long history. This is the idea of 'the mind', as opposed to the purely physical aspect or component of a thing. One way, at least, of registering the fact that human beings actually *think* is to say that besides or because of, or as a feature of the kind of physical make-up which we have, we can also be said to have *minds*. We found in the last section that the notion of creativity raised at least as many problems as it was meant to solve, and it will almost certainly turn out to be the same with the concept of the mind. However, it will be found worthwhile going into this approach, since it does appear to bring us closer to what people commonly think of when they attempt to articulate what it is that char- acterizes thinking beings as opposed to those with merely mechanical or calculative abilities. The problems raised by the idea of having a 'mind' will be tackled in more detail in a later chapter, when we come to look at the variety of existing approaches to this subject. It will be sufficient at this stage to introduce a further concept, which has normally been taken as central to the idea of 'the mind'. This is the notion of *consciousness*, which will be of cardinal importance to much of what follows in this book.

thinking as consciousness

When we ask whether or not a thing – an organism or machine or whatever – is conscious, we are asking much more than whether it is able to carry out this or that task, however 'clever' or complex the task may be. What we are asking is: *does it have a point of view?* Or, to express the same thing another way: *does it have an 'inside' as well as an 'outside'?* Some people may find no oddity at all in this question. Others may find it hoplessly abstract and, in the most ominous sense of the word, 'philosophical'. Let us try to sharpen it up a little.

One reason for not believing that a brick can think, is that the question 'What would it be like to be a brick?' strikes us as making very little sense. It isn't just that we have no way of telling what the experience of bricks is like; if we thought that bricks had experiences we could always say something like, 'Well, people get hold of you and cement you to walls'. Rather, we are not inclined to think that being a brick is like anything at all, for we are not tempted to believe that bricks have experiences of any kind. It is in this sense that a brick presents itself to us as something with an 'outside' but no 'inside': something which has no viewpoint of its own on the world, although some things in the world, of course, have a viewpoint on *it*. To put it as its crudest and also, perhaps, its vaguest, we do not feel, in considering the brick, that there is 'anyone at home' there.

We noticed earlier in this chapter that those things which think nevertheless do not think *all* of the time, whilst non-thinking things *never* think. We may now make the point that a *conscious* being is one which has that feature which you and I have when we are awake, but lack when we are asleep. Conscious beings (beings capable of consciousness) are not necessarily always conscious, whilst the other sort never are.

It is probably the concept of consciousness above all, which is at the bottom of the distinction between 'real' or 'genuine' thought, and that kind of intelligence, or whatever, of which some machines are obviously capable. A creature which actually thinks is one which 'knows what it is doing', in the richest possible sense of 'knows'. It is one which has its own point of view – or, if we like, has 'its own world'; one which is not just an extension of its creator, designer or programmer.

When we have said this, it must by no means be thought that our problems in this direction are over. On the contrary, they are only just beginning; for we have so far done little more than gesture at the idea which we are trying to capture. However, it does seem as though we have arrived at a workable approach to what people have in mind when they wonder whether a computer might be 'really thinking'. It is chiefly to this idea which we shall be addressing ourselves in subsequent chapters.

some apparent confusions

Unfortunately, things are not so straightforward as might appear from the foregoing. For the ideas of 'genuine thought' and 'consciousness' do not by any means refer to just the same thing. There is, for example, good reason for believing that many of the lower animals are conscious, in the sense that they have sensations, see and hear, feel pain, heat and cold and so on: yet we would certainly hesitate before calling what they do 'thinking'. Thinking suggests the kind of abilities to form concepts, to make judgements, and to reason, which such creatures clearly lack. On the other hand (and more dubiously), some people are inclined to attribute thought in the absence of consciousness, especially in the case of machines: one hears it said, for example, that the question of whether machines can think does not depend on whether or not they have conscious mental states. It is true that psychologists often talk of activities which we would normally call thinking, as taking place subconsciously, or even *un*consciously. However, a significant difference between unconscious thought on the part of human beings, and the non-conscious 'thinking' of machines, is that human beings are *sometimes* conscious; and the possibility of unconscious thinking seems to depend on the existence of at least some conscious experience.

To avoid these apparent confusions and to capture what is intended to be our topic, we shall speak of 'conscious thought' as referring to the intersection of the two features – that is, those cases which are both cases of consciousness and of thinking. Later on, in chapter 10, some arguments will be presented to the effect that there is in fact a fairly tight logical connection between the two things. For now, however, we will move on to look at the notion of consciousness in more detail, and also, in the process, to uncover a further obstacle to our enquiry.

2: symptoms of consciousness

So far, we have done no more than to formulate a rather loose idea of what it is that we are asking when we ask if a machine can, or could, *really* think. We have still gone no way towards giving an answer to the question thus formulated. It is to this task that we now turn.

How, then, can we begin to tell whether a given machine, or a machine of a given type and degree of complexity, is conscious? How, for that matter, can we tell in general whether anything is conscious or not? It will be best to begin by discussing human beings, since we are, presumably, more certain that they are sometimes conscious than we are in the case of other things around us.

how to tell whether someone is conscious
On the face of it, it's fairly simple to discover whether a person is conscious at a given time or not. When people are conscious, they tend to move, talk, and respond to external stimuli such as kicks, pricks, pinches and punches. When people are *un*conscious, they tend to remain stationary and relatively quiet, they don't respond, at least in the normal way, to external stimuli, they fall over when forcibly propped against walls, and so on. We can only say 'tend to' since there are grey areas like sleepwalking or daydreaming. But these do not alter the fact that there are many cases in which no doubt is involved, and some symptoms of consciousness which are overwhelmingly reliable. In no sense are we always, or even often, in the dark about whether a human being is conscious.

But let us now ask: what status does this certainty have? At this point, we must remind ourselves of an important distinction between two ways in which the word 'certain' is used. In one way of using it, the certainty lies in the mind of the person who is certain of the thing in question. For example, I am certain that I have a pipe in my jacket pocket, though I recognize that it is *possible* that I am mistaken. My turning out to be mistaken would not convince me that I had not really been certain of it at all. In the other way of using it, the certainty lies in the fact itself: it is certain because it *could not be otherwise*. For example, we may say that it is certain that animals which eat meat are carnivores. This is not equivalent to saying that this or that person, or even everybody, is 'certain in their mind' that this is the case. What is meant is, rather, that it is certain in the sense that it is *logically* true: once we know that something eats meat, it follows without any possible doubt that it is carnivorous. It is not like the certainty of the whereabouts of my pipe, since once I recognize the connection, in this latter case, I cannot entertain the possibility that it might turn out to be otherwise, for to suppose this will make no sense. Also, unlike the 'certain in the mind' use of 'certain', if it turns out that I *have* somehow made a mistake, for example about the meanings of the words, then I have to accept, not just that it is not the case, but that there never was any certainty of this kind about it at all.

Now in which sense are we certain, at least in the clearest, most central cases, that if people talk, respond, move about without bumping into things etc., then they are in fact conscious? It seems that it cannot be the latter, stronger, sense, since it is *possible* (i.e. involves no contradiction) to imagine just such physical creatures which do all these things and yet are not conscious, have no point of view on the world, have an 'outside' but no 'inside'. We can imagine, in other words, all these kinds of behaviour being exhibited without there being 'anybody at home'.

But if we must accept that our certainty that other people are conscious is only a matter of being 'certain in our own minds', then there is a logical gap between the premise (the fact that such behaviour is exhibited) and the conclusion (that consciousness is present). And if there is such a gap between the evidence and what it is evidence for, then, it may be argued, there is room for doubt. And if there is room for doubt, then surely we must not regard as totally unreasonable, a person who seriously thinks there are no other minds in the world than his own – who really believes that other people are merely automata whose characteristics are exhausted by the physical aspect they present, or could present, to him. A person who takes this view is called a *solipsist*. It might be worth issuing a warning here that there are more and less sophisticated types of solipsism, and that what has been outlined above is only a very crude form.

Of course, *how* reasonable we think the solipsist's position to be must depend on how good we think the evidence is for the consciousness of other people. If we think that the evidence is, under the circumstances, quite poor, then the solipsist's conclusion will present a genuine threat; but if we believe the evidence to be still pretty sound, then the solipsist will emerge as a person obstinately embracing a position for no better reason than that it can't be shown to be false (and perhaps also that it appeals to him). Yet this doesn't somehow seem good enough. Is there not something wrong with the position which we have got ourselves into, of having to take seriously *at all* the idea that even other people, let alone computers, don't really think? Before exploring what might have gone wrong, we will look at an even stronger argument for the solipsist, to the effect that the 'evidence' for other people's consciousness is not just inconclusive, but is really no evidence at all. But first, let us return for a moment to our central topic, the relation between computers and thought.

machines aren't like people

Another thing which might be troubling us in the above discussion of the evidence for human consciousness, is that it seems to suggest a misleading model for the evidence of machine consciousness. For it appears to suggest that the way to tell whether a machine is conscious is to watch it and see whether it jumps around, responds to stimuli and so on. Two things must make us wary of this approach. The first is that many of the kinds of machines to which people are tempted to attribute consciousness do *not* do these things. The sorts of machine which do move around in a vaguely human-like way tend largely to be ones like manufacturing robots which, far from being capable of independent thought, are typically designed for a simple task such as screwing nuts on to bolts, and go haywire in a very 'thing-like' way when faced with a comparatively trivial difficulty such as being given a washer instead of a nut. On the other hand, the 'intelligent' machines which some suspect of real thought are usually ones which just sit there receiving data and giving answers. Only if the producing of text on a screen can be counted as fully 'responding' can such machines be said to respond in the same sense that people do.

Secondly, building a machine which simulates at least *some* of the things a human person can do like moving about, saying 'good morning' and so on, is not difficult at all. In short, (i) it doesn't seem that a machine has to be animate in order for it to come under suspicion of doing some genuine thinking, and (ii) it *does* seem, at least superficially, that almost any fool can build a machine which is in some sense animate, though no one would suspect *it* of conscious thought simply on account of its animation. All this clearly raises problems in the light of what has been said earlier in this chapter about everyday 'symptoms of consciousness'. We will come back to these problems in a later chapter. First, however, let us look at the stronger argument for solipsism mentioned above – an argument which also casts doubts on the relevance of the argument from everyday symptoms as evidence of consciousness.

the solipsist's (apparent) trump card
The trump card which the solipsist is able to play lies in the following consideration. Although we have so far proceeded on the assumption that certain things count as evidence of a sort for consciousness in others, it can easily be argued that the onus is squarely on the believer in other minds to show how

this 'evidence' can be evidence at all, let alone conclusive or even persuasive evidence. For the stubborn fact which the solipsist is always able to fall back on, is that there is no demonstrable connection between the kind of 'symptoms' in question, and the presence of real mentality. Whereas in some other contexts we can argue the presence of B from that of A on the basis of their having appeared in conjunction in all, or most, known instances, the case of other minds is different in that there are no available manifest instances of such a conjunction, since other minds by their nature cannot be directly accessible. The only conscious thought to which any given person has first hand access, is his own. And to argue from the fact that the 'symptoms' are accompanied by genuine mentality in oneself, to the conclusion that the same symptoms are likely to be accompanied by it in others, seems, at first sight, to be a very weak sort of argument indeed, since it draws a conclusion about a whole great class of instances on the basis of a consideration of only one of them! This point will be discussed in the next chapter, when we come to deal explicitly with the 'Argument from Analogy' for other minds. The problem to bear in mind here is that an upholder of the solipsistic position can, it seems, put the ball in his opponent's court by simply pointing to the fact that mental states are private (which is undoubtedly true). If it seems that this argument is too crude to do the job for which it is intended, let us be patient and attend to what follows.

It appears that what we lack is certainly not *prima facie* evidence but, as it were, evidence that this *prima facie* evidence is indeed evidence at all; that is, a justification for treating these very obvious 'symptoms' as symptoms of anything in the first place. This, then, is the result, for our present discussion, of the fact that mental states are essentially private. It must not be thought, from the above, that the reader is being invited to entertain seriously the solipsist position. Indeed, someone who seriously did adopt it would in fact be a psychopath rather than a philosopher (though Bertrand Russell is said to have received a letter from a lady who affirmed that she was a convinced solipsist, and could not understand why everybody else wasn't!). However, the real philosophical issue is not so much an open-ended enquiry into the question of whether other people have minds or not, as a puzzle concerning what can have gone wrong for us to find ourselves in this position in the first place. If solipsism is, in practice, untenable, then the arguments which seem to place the onus on the critic of it must have been in some way invalid or misleading in the first place. We will move on, in the next chapter, to look at some of the philosophical positions which have been adopted in response to this difficulty, which in modern philosophy goes under the name of the 'Problem of Other Minds'.

3: the problem of other minds

We now seem to have reasoned ourselves into an even more absurd position than previously. For it appears not just that there is room for the sceptic about other minds to hold his position if he wishes to, but that the onus is on the *believer* in other minds to show that there is anything in his favour at all! In order, then, to get our discussion into logical order, we must tackle head-on the question of how other-minds scepticism can be answered. That is, before deciding whether to attribute minds to things other than human beings, we must be sure that we know that we can, and *why* we can, attribute minds even to other human beings.

We will begin by looking at the views of a modern writer, Richard Rorty, who presents us with a good starting point since he argues, in effect, that there is, or need be, no problem of other minds at all. If we can go along with all that Rorty says, it will obviously save us a lot of unnecessary trouble.

Rorty's rejection of the 'mirror of nature'
Among Rorty's avowed aims in his writing on this topic are 'to undermine the reader's confidence in "the mind" as something about which there ought to be a "theory"'. It is only to be expected, then, that he himself does not have a theory about our knowledge of other minds, in the sense that many other philosophers have had. Assuming that we already have some confidence to undermine, let us see how Rorty goes about attempting to do this.

Central to Rorty's position is the idea that much of the

traditional Western philosophy of mind rests on, not exactly a mistake, but on philosophers' having been under the spell of a particular set of pictures, or metaphors, concerning our mental life. The chief among these is the idea of man as having a 'glassy essence' (a phrase coined by Shakespeare), of possessing a mind which is the 'mirror of nature'. To unpack the metaphors a bit, this means it has traditionally been regarded as characteristic of man that he is capable of mental states which are at least sometimes like 'reflections' of things in the physical world – for every physical thing of which I am aware, there is a sort of mental counterpart in me, existing in a 'non-material medium'. These are not, however, on the traditional view, the only contents of the mind: there are also such things as beliefs, desires, intentions, and 'raw feels' (such as pains, and uninterpreted sensations such as young babies have). Of these, it is perhaps the 'raw feels' which are the hardest to have doubts about, since it is with these that we are most immediately acquainted.

This immediacy of acquaintance with at least some of the contents of our minds is, Rorty argues, partly what lies at the bottom of the confusion which he sees in traditional philosophy of mind. For according to him, it results in a temptation to 'deduce' from the fact that we know our own minds better than anything else, that we could still know the contents of our own minds even if we knew *nothing* else (i.e. that things could still be the same in our minds even if the solipsist were correct). And further, to draw the conclusion that knowing whether something has a mind involves knowing it *as well as it knows itself*. If this latter is true, then it is easy to see how total other-minds scepticism results. For, in this sense, I *cannot* know another person as well as that person knows himself, since I cannot have his experiences.

why I can't have your experiences
Here, let us interrupt the discussion of Rorty for a moment, to get something clear. Some may doubt, at first, the impossibility of having someone else's experiences. If so, then ask what would *count as* having the experiences of another person.

Clearly it cannot just be a matter of seeing, hearing, touching, the same *things*: for although there may be a single flower which is the flower that you and I are both looking at, there are undoubtedly *two* experiences (however qualitatively similar) of the flower – yours and mine. Suppose, though, that only you were actually seeing the flower, but that my brain was somehow wired up to yours in such a way that the experience was transmitted 'directly' from your brain to mine. Would I then be having *your* experience? We must still say that I wouldn't, since it remains possible to talk about 'my' experience of the episode and 'your' experience of it; and, as a result, to doubt whether they are in fact qualitatively identical. The fact that such doubt could occur is sufficient to show that there is no strict identity between your experience and mine. If we had actual identity (i.e. one thing and not two) no question could arise about how far A is similar to B, provided we understood them properly, since 'A' and 'B' would be just two ways of referring to the same thing. The reason why I can never have your experience is, at bottom, a *logical* one: if we *both* experience something, then there are two experiences of it and not one. Only if we were one person and not two people, would it count as one experience and not two – but then nobody would be having the experience of *another* person!

self-knowledge as observation

To return to Rorty's argument, he rejects the piece of reasoning which seems to lead to the (impossible) requirement that we must know something as well as it knows itself – i.e. 'from the inside' – if we are to know whether it has a mind or not. (Of course, it will only *have* an inside if it has a mind, since the two things are the same.) The apparent plausibility of the reasoning is, he believes, a result of the model (which he attributes to Descartes) of self-knowledge as akin to *observation*. What does this mean?

Consider what happens when someone, let's say, asks you whether you have a headache, and that you reply sincerely, 'Yes'. Was any *observation* going on prior to your answering? Did you have the feeling of spying on some secret realm known only to yourself and concealed from everyone else? Rorty would want to say something like the following. It's certainly true that nobody else could have answered the question with the certainty that you could. But doesn't the very immediacy of the experience itself rule out the idea that you needed to make an observation in order to answer the question? Surely the headache wasn't something which you *came to know* by self-observation ('introspection', as philosophers sometimes call it) and subsequently *reported*, but something which you simply *had*, and just *expressed* faithfully by your answer much as the young child expresses the same thing by crying, only in a more sophisticated and conventional fashion. In fact, Rorty goes further than this, and says that 'the way in which the pre-linguistic infant knows that it has a pain is the way in which the record-changer knows the spindle is empty'. This is undoubtedly controversial, since people have usually considered that an infant, however pre-linguistic, has 'feels' in a way which the record-changer does not. Equally clearly, this has important implications for our own concern with the relation between the 'minds' of people and the 'minds' of machines.

Rorty and the aliens
In connection with this, Rorty asks us to consider a hypothetical race of people on another planet, who don't possess the concept of a mental state at all. They use words corresponding to 'believe', 'intend' and the like, though they don't know what is meant by calling these 'states of mind'. On the other hand, they do not have the concepts of 'idea', 'perception', or 'mental representation'. In other words, all those mentalistic concepts which refer to what 'represents' or 'mirrors' things in the world, and can be *immediately present* to the person who has them, are unknown to them. Furthermore, he asks us to suppose that these people, instead of talking about mental states, talk only of *neurological states* (since neurology and biochemistry are what they are best at). Thus, when a child is in danger of burning itself, on that planet, the mother will say, 'Be careful – you'll stimulate your C-fibres!' (the neurological state corresponding to being in pain).

Now we are invited to speculate on what will happen when a group of philosophers from Earth try to discover whether these people actually have minds or not, whether they are 'really' conscious. This they take to be equivalent to, or to depend crucially on, the question: do they have sensations, or 'raw feels' (the most basic mental item) or not? The next point is of great importance, and shows us why 'raw feels' are what the mentalist philosopher most wants to insist on. It is that our knowledge (if that is what it is) of these items is *incorrigible*. Take the case of pain. The distinctive thing about a sensation such as a pain, is that I cannot be in any doubt whether I am having it or not. For it to *seem* to me as if I were in pain would be the same as *being* in pain, as is brought out ironically in the well-worn limerick:

> There was a faith-healer from Beale
> Who said 'Although pain isn't real,
> When I sit on a pin
> And it punctures my skin,
> I dislike what I *fancy* I feel!'

Now what will our aliens say about all this? Suppose they know of a neural state, which they call state T-435, that corresponds to its *seeming as though* the C-fibres are stimulated (i.e. as though one were in the neural state associated with pain); suppose further, that sometimes one of them is in state T-435 though it turns out that his C-fibres are not stimulated. From this it will be clear that it is possible for these people to be mistaken about whether they are in the neural state corresponding to pain. We can then ask if they can be wrong about whether they are in a neural state T-435, and once again they might say, 'Yes, it sometimes happens'. Thus they can even be wrong about whether they are in the neural state associated with the seeming-to-be-in-the-pain-type-state. The point is that none of this is going to tell us whether or not they have sensations ('raw feels') about which they *cannot* be wrong. Nothing at all that we can discover about them seems to be relevant to whether these raw feels are present – and furthermore, they themselves do not, we will remember, possess the concepts of such feels and sensations at all. The feels and sensations just seem to drop out of the question altogether.

This gets us back to Rorty's rejection of the idea of a mental world accessible only to the person whose world it is. The aliens can't *tell* us anything relevant to deciding whether or not they have a mental life, so if we still want to ask the question, we must be talking about something which is, in principle, *incommunicable*. But if the fact that someone really is, for example, in pain (has the raw feel, and not just the outward behaviour) is incommunicable to others, then it can have nothing to do with the use of the *word* 'pain' or what it means. For our language concerning sensations, pains and so on, is clearly a means of communication, and anything which it might be *about* is of course communicable. Thus, whatever we are talking about, in talking about 'raw feels' or 'sensations', it seems that it cannot be what is referred to by what we regard as our sensation vocabulary ('pain', 'feeling' etc.)! In making this kind of point, Rorty is influenced by the earlier twentieth-century philosopher Wittgenstein, some of whose views we will be considering later. Rorty concludes that scepticism about other minds is, properly understood, philosophically uninteresting, in much the same way as scepticism about the external world is (he says) uninteresting. We cannot *know* or *prove* that tables and chairs exist when they are not being observed, but what we do know is that, if they don't, their absence makes no difference to anything. Nothing depends on it, for a world in which they don't is, for *all* purposes, the same as a world in which they do; and much the same is true, Rorty suggests, of other minds.

Not surprisingly, many people do not accept this view, and would rather stick firmly to the idea that other minds do make a difference, and that other-minds scepticism needs to be met head-on rather than (as they see it) brushed under the carpet. Before looking at an example of the head-on approach, we will briefly consider a view of other minds which is in some ways like, and in other ways unlike, Rorty's.

consciousness as a status

Rorty, whilst arguing that the 'problem of other minds' is no longer philosophically interesting once its origins are understood properly, still accepts the existence, in some sense, of states of consciousness which are irreducibly mental. Some philosophers, however, have taken a slightly different tack (which Rorty himself could easily have taken but does not), and maintained that genuine thought, or consciousness, is more like a *status* which we *ascribe* to another person than a property which they actually independently possess.

In order to make clearer what is meant here by 'ascribing a status', let us look first of all at a three-way distinction which has been made by the present-day American philosopher Daniel Dennett. He talks of three possible 'stances' which we might take in dealing with some object such as a machine. These are, firstly the *physical stance*, secondly the *design stance*, and lastly the *intentional stance*. Note that 'intentional' here is a bit of philosophers' jargon, and does not mean what we mean by it in ordinary language. The concept of 'intentionality' was largely developed by the philosophers Franz Brentano (1838-1917) and Edmund Husserl (1859-1938). It refers to the feature of 'directedness', or 'having an object', i.e. being *about* something, which they regarded as the characteristic mark of conscious thought.

What, then, do these three stances involve? Suppose you want to explain *why* some machine does a particular thing which it does. Take first of all a simple machine like a catapult, and ask why the stone gets thrown at a given time. The explanation which we would all give is a purely physical one such as, 'The lever gets thrust forward by a sudden release of the torsion on a bow of coiled rope, and stopped by a wooden butt, thus releasing the missile'. Now take a more complex kind of device, like a modern washing machine. Why, we may ask, does it empty itself part way through the cycle and pour fresh water over the contents? Here, we will not be likely to give an explanation in terms of purely mechanical workings of the machine, but rather in terms of the purposes of the designer. We will say something like, 'It's meant to rinse the clothes and wash the soap away'. Here, we have passed from the physical stance, which is what we adopted in the case of the catapault, to the design stance. The characteristic thing about the design stance is that, although we refer not to the physical make-up of the machine, but to some motives, intentions, purposes etc. (i.e. mental kinds of things), they are not ascribed to the machine itself, but to the person who designed it.

Now thirdly, take an even more sophisticated machine, such as a chess-playing machine. What kind of reply do we give when asked a question like 'Why did it retract that knight?'? The chances are that the explanation we give will be neither in terms of mechanics nor of design. The internal workings of the machine and the details of the chess-playing software will be too complex for almost anyone to hold in their head thoroughly enough to explain the knight's move by reference to them. Furthermore, an explanation involving the designer's purposes will be almost as hard to give. The exact way in which the general strategy which the programmer intended the software to embody, such as to avoid loss of pieces or to try to gain control of the centre of the board, connects with the fact that this particular move was made at this point in the game, is probably so remote and tortuous that it is opaque even to the programmer herself. The way we will almost certainly go about explaining it is to talk as though this machine (or this program, or this-machine-in-the-control-of-this-program) has purposes *of its own*. That is, we will say something like, 'It doesn't want to risk losing the knight to your king's rook', or 'It's trying to block your queen's advance'. Of course we won't, deep down, regard the machine as actually thinking. We know, at the back of our mind, that behind the intentional-type behaviour of the machine lies a design, and behind the design lie some 'brute' physical facts about its make-up. In other words, we know that it would be possible *in principle* to give an explanation in more fundamental terms than we do; it is just simpler and more natural to describe the behaviour of so sophisticated a machine in mentalistic language.

the circularity of the 'status' view

It is this very consideration, however, which has led some philosophers to wonder whether the same might not be true of the way in which we use mental concepts when talking about each other. (Here we must not include Dennett, whose own views are considerably less simple.) The idea is that there is no 'fact of the matter' about whether other people are conscious. This claim can be supported, if necessary, by some of the considerations we saw in looking at Rorty. Rather, we simply cannot avoid taking a mentalistic, intentional stance towards them, since the details of their physical make-up are, despite Rorty's aliens, far too complex to refer to all the time, and we don't regard them as being designed for a purpose in the sense that machines are. This view has a good deal of initial appeal, since it simplifies the world in the kind of way a good theory should. Both people and machines are 'really' just physical things, and all their actions are *in principle* capable of explanation on the purely physical level. But when a thing gets too sophisticated to handle by reference to physics, or the purposes of a designer, we respond to it by the use of mentalistic concepts.

Unfortunately, or perhaps fortunately, things are not so straightforward. How, we may ask, can this view explain the fact that anything can *ascribe* consciousness to anything else, or take up any stance *towards* it? Remember that in the case of the machine we are supposed to bear in mind that it's not *really* thinking – we just talk *as though* it were. Now if human beings are in some sense in the same position, then who is doing the ascribing? Who is it that is genuinely taking up a stance towards something else? The answer seems to be 'No one'. For if intentionality, that is the capacity to think about something, is not an independent property a thing has, but always, even in the case of human beings, only a concept which *others* use about *it*, then the situation seems to be as follows. Not only will the capacity for 'real thought' be ascribed rather than independently existing, but the *ability to ascribe thought* will itself be only ascribed. But this is surely circular. No one can be the first to acquire the feature in question, for possessing the feature depends on having it attributed by someone who already has it.

Rather than pursue this point further, we will now go on to look at a view which is far removed from those we have seen so far in this chapter. It comes from the philosopher Thomas Nagel, and may serve to sharpen up some of our reservations about the theses described above.

Nagel and the bats

Thomas Nagel, although a well-known writer in various areas of philosophy, is probably best known for his famous question 'What is it like to be a bat?', the title of an essay in which it occurs. The important thing is not so much answering the question, as noticing that it makes sense to ask it. Nagel chooses bats for the example since they are high enough up the evolutionary tree for us to have little doubt that they have conscious experience and yet at the same time their activities are sufficiently different from ours to make them distinctly alien to us. The point of the question 'What is it like to be a bat?' is that, in Nagel's view, the essence of our belief that bats have experience is that *there is something that it is like to be a bat*. More generally, he says 'the fact that an organism has conscious experience...means, basically, that there is something it is like to *be* that organism'. What he has done here is to give some substantive content to the abstractions which we have discussed so far, such as 'consciousness' and 'experience'. To say that there is something it is like to be a particular thing, also gives us more to go on, philosophically, than the metaphors with which this topic was introduced in the first chapter, such as having 'an inside as well as an outside', or there being 'someone at home'.

Even more importantly, what Nagel seems to have done by posing the question in this way, is to give us a new starting point in the problem of other minds, by providing a means of expressing what it is that we are saying about other creatures when we attribute minds, or consciousness, to them. A means, also, which seems to be free of the drawbacks which afflict talk of 'sensations', 'feels' and so on. For in the case of these latter, all that could count as evidence in favour of their presence, seems nevertheless to be consistent with their absence. And this includes any avowals which a person might make, of having conscious experience: the words 'I am really in pain' are just a piece of behaviour like any other, and the pain *itself* drops out of the picture through sheer incommunicability.

How does Nagel's approach help us here? Well, unlike saying that a thing has sensations or feels, saying that there is 'something it is like' to be that thing is to make a statement which could not be true unless its internal, shadowy counterpart really did exist. We saw that words like 'pain' and 'sensation' could operate just as they do, in the absence of the 'raw feels' to which we are tempted to think that they refer. Nagel's formulation is not like this; indeed, it could have no meaning at all unless there were some way in which it can at least sometimes have an answer. To explain this a little more: there is no way in which Nagel's question can still have meaning, if our mental vocabulary is really only about outward behaviour, and not about 'internal' states. And it *does* seem to us that the question makes sense.

However, as many philosophers will be glad to remind us, the fact that a form of words *seems* to have a sense, is no guarantee that it does. Might not this apparently straight-forward question in fact be a piece of disguised nonsense produced by misguided philosophical speculation? For all that has been said so far, it might. For if the 'raw feels' of experience are somehow incommunicable, then it may turn out to be, strictly speaking, a piece of nonsense, on the grounds that to speak of what is incommunicable is nonsensical. But the significant thing about Nagel's formulation is not that it guaran-tees its own meaningfulness (Nagel simply *assumes* that we know what it means alright – and we feel that we do), but that it encapsulates what it is that we want to ask about other creatures, without the possibility of the question itself being 'defused' by the anti-mentalist through being construed in some apparently harmless way. Nagel does, however, make a remark which points us in the direction of a defence of the question as a real and meaningful one. To understand the following, we must bear in mind that the word 'phenomenological' means something like 'how an experience feels *to the person experiencing it*', or maybe rather 'the experience *as it feels to* the person experiencing it'. Nagel says:

> There is a sense in which phenomenological facts are perfectly objective: one person can know or say of another what the quality of the other's experience is. They are subjective, however, in the sense that even this objective ascription of experience is possible only for someone sufficiently similar to the object of the ascription to be able to adopt this point of view – to understand the ascription in the first person as well as in the third, so to speak.

How is being 'sufficiently similar' to a creature supposed to help us in knowing what the quality of that creature's experience is? How can it even help us in knowing that the creature has experiences at all, unless we mean by it 'similar in having the same sort of experiences'? And even then there would be a problem about how we *know* this. To find any answers in this direction, we must go far beyond any mere reformulation of the question, however helpful. And the obvious place to begin is with the 'argument from analogy' which was mentioned in the last chapter.

Russell and the argument from analogy
We saw that the solipsist appears to hold a trump card which he is always able to play against non-solipsists. This is the fact that none of us have, or can have, *direct* evidence for the existence of other minds. However physically like us other people may be, however psychologically plausible their behaviour, there always exists the logical possibility that they are no more than mindless automata. And worse still, if no *direct* evidence exists, it seems that *all* the evidence is rendered worthless, giving us apparently *no* reason to believe in other minds at all.

The argument which these considerations are meant to counter is the 'argument from analogy'; that is, in outline, the argument that people who are like me in *some* respects are probably like me also in possessing consciousness – that the external likeness gives me reason to think that there is 'something it is like to be' them, just as there is something it is like to be me. We will examine briefly two formulations of the argument, one by Bertrand Russell, and the other (a defence of the argument against certain criticisms) by A.J. Ayer.

To take Russell first, he begins by considering the simplest kind of argument from analogy, and showing why it will not hold water. The simplest form is as follows. I know that, for example, when I jump around and rub my foot, it is because of a sensation of pain which I feel in that foot. I therefore conclude that when other people jump around similarly, it is because they have a pain in their foot – a genuine sensation – also. This I do on the grounds that *like causes produce like effects*. What is wrong with this argument as it stands is, Russell points out, that we need to assume, not only that if A causes B on one occasion then A will always cause B, but also that *only* A ever causes B. In other words, we must (illicitly) suppose that if a pain in the foot causes behaviour of a certain kind in me, then whenever behaviour of that kind occurs, it is produced by the same cause – a pain in the foot. But to argue in this way is to neglect the fact that the same behaviour in another person may be caused by a different sensation or by something which is not a sensation at all (i.e. there is no conscious experience of any kind occurring).

To get over this, we need some justification for the above assumption. This Russell finds in the *complexity* of human responses. When an event is of a simple kind like, for example, a loud bang, it is usually the case that it could have been caused in a number of different ways: an explosion, someone dropping a heavy object, a clap of thunder, and so on. But the more complex the event, Russell argues, the less likely it is that it will be subject to multiple causes, since every detail of it will be a result of some particular feature of the cause. Russell sums up his version of the argument from analogy as follows:

> From subjective observation I know that A, which is a thought or feeling, causes B, which is a bodily act, e.g. a statement. I know also that, whenever B is an act of my own body, A is its cause. I now observe an act of the kind B in a body not my own,

and I am having no thought or feeling of the kind A. But I still believe, on the basis of self-observation, that only A can cause B; I therefore infer that there was an A which caused B, though it was not an A that I could observe. On this ground I infer that other people's bodies are associated with minds, which resemble mine in proportion as their bodily behaviour resembles my own.

Will the argument, as formulated by Russell, work? We may notice several things in it to which critics would take exception, such as the notion of 'self-observation' and the idea that one *mind* can 'resemble' another to a measurable degree. For the moment, however, we will pick on one particular line of objection to it. Although Russell seems to have shored up the argument from analogy against the objection from multiple causes, he seems to have done nothing to allay the suspicions of those who attach importance to the fact that we can never have *direct* experience of other people's thoughts, feelings etc. which could reassure us that we are on the right lines in the *indirect* (i.e. analogical) cases. For an attempt at overcoming this obstacle, we must turn to Ayer.

Ayer's defence of the analogy argument

Now Ayer clearly recognizes that there is a case to answer against the sceptic who argues from the above position. And he equally recognizes the nature of the challenge: how can an argument from analogy work, when the conclusion is of a kind which can *never* be *directly* substantiated? In the case of a more usual type of argument from analogy, this is not so. For example, I see shadows on the blind, and infer that there are people in the room, on the grounds that this connection has always been observed to hold in the past. The difference is that I can, if I wish, go into the room and check whether the inference was correct; indeed I probably have done so in the past, and this is what gives me the right to argue from past cases to the present one. But in the case of other minds, there is no such thing as checking whether the analogy holds or not: I cannot argue from the fact that two things are externally alike *plus the fact that the external likeness has been observed to go along with a further likeness in the past*, but only from the fact that the two things are externally alike. How, then, are we justified in assuming that the required analogy, from external likeness to 'inner' likeness, holds at all?

Ayer's response to this is subtle. He begins by comparing the apparent handicap of being logically denied access to another's mental states, with other similar handicaps. For example, I cannot logically have direct access to facts about the past. Nor can I check directly on facts about any region of space where I do not happen to be, since I cannot be both here and somewhere else at the same time. Once we start making these comparisions we are, Ayer thinks, perhaps less tempted to consider that there is something uniquely mysterious about other *minds* as opposed to other times or places which prevents us from knowing *anything* about them. We do not normally think that there is a 'problem of other places', so why should we be worried about the supposed 'problem of other minds'?

But is this argument not too simple? Surely there is a difference between the sense in which I cannot be *somewhere* else, and that in which I cannot be *somebody* else. For the former seems to be merely a physical constraint (I could have been somewhere else if I had wanted to be), whereas the latter is a *logical* contraint (I could not be *someone* else however much I wanted to be).

Ayer has an answer to this, which will be paraphrased rather than reproduced in detail here. Take first of all the idea that I could possibly be somewhere other than where I am. In one sense it is patently false, for no one can be in more than one place at once – the statement 'I am somewhere else' (i.e. somewhere other than where I am) cannot be true when said by anyone, in the same way that the statement, 'I am here' is always true whoever says it. In another sense, however, it is obviously correct, since it is by no means impossible that I should have been at this moment in Brussels, or Leeds, or Istanbul, rather than where I happen to be. Now doesn't the same hold for the idea that I could be *somebody* else? For whilst 'I am somebody else' (i.e. somebody other than the person I am) simply cannot be true, the statement 'I am Joan Collins' is one which *happens* to be false when uttered by me, but *could* have been true. How can this be?

Most of us have a fairly good grip on what it means to say that I could have been somewhere else, but only a hazy idea of what it means to say that I could have been a different person from who I am. Or do we? Most of us surely have had thoughts such as 'How would it have been if I had been born five years earlier?' or, more imaginatively, 'What would it have been like if I had been a woman and not a man?' Once again, the important thing is not how we would go about answering such questions, but the fact that they appear to make perfectly good sense. And if this is true, then I *can* give some meaning to the idea that I could have fitted other descriptions (descriptions which I don't in fact fit) *whilst being the same person that I am*. Of course, if I take very outlandish descriptions (could I have been a caveman, or a butterfly, or a prime number?) we run into difficulties about what 'I' is supposed to mean. As Ayer puts it, there are 'no fixed rules for determining what properties are essential to a person's being the person that he is'. But if we stick to the people around us – the people with respect to whom the problem of other minds arises in the first place – there is, Ayer argues, some sense in which I could have been, though I am not, any one of these other people. Furthermore, when it is stated that someone other than myself has an experience of a given sort, *it is no part of what is being asserted, that the experience belongs to someone else and not to me*; all that is being said is that it is the experience of someone *fitting a particular description*, a description which I logically *could* have fitted, but in fact do not. In this way, the argument from analogy can be defended against the original charge that other minds differ from e.g. other places, in that they can't be inspected. If we accept Ayer's reasoning, it seems that we are no more logically trapped in our own selves than we are trapped in our own period: we *could have* inspected another person's mind, if we had been that person (fitted the same descriptions), just as we *could have* inspected another place, had we been there.

Should this put our minds at rest and defeat the sceptic?

Three things suggest that it should not be seen as a final cure. The first concerns Ayer's insistence on the fitting of descriptions as being what constitutes personal identity; many philosophers (following Saul Kripke) would now disagree with the underlying assumptions made by Ayer, but this would get us into a rather technical area of philosophy, and we will not pursue it here.

The second is that, glancing back at the starting point of this enquiry, nothing which Ayer says has altered the fact that it is apparently logically possible that nobody except myself has any conscious experiences. What Ayer has done is to remove some of the obstacles to accepting observable facts about other people as evidence of their consciousness. But our original problem was that such evidence, however good of its kind, can never be shown to be *conclusive*, and that this has the effect of forcing us into the seemingly absurd position of having to take the solipsist seriously.

The third reservation which we may have about Ayer's formulation of the argument, is that it is little consolation to be told that statements about other minds are no worse off than statements about other times or other places, if, like the more radical type of solipsist, we are tempted to doubt these latter as well! For the solipsist can easily reply that, not only does he have no evidence that there are other minds apart from his own, but that he equally has no evidence that there are any states of affairs at all, which are not really just states of his own mind.

We may be beginning to suspect that the solipsist does indeed possess a trump card, and that no amount of argument can force him to budge from his original sceptical position. Indeed, there is something about scepticism of all kinds which at first presents this aspect. The sceptic apparently cannot be defeated so long as, in response to every reply we make to him, he simply says 'How do you know?' In the next chapter, however, we will look at a very different approach from that of the analogy argument, though it will be seen to have close connections with the views of Rorty, and the 'mentalistic stance' idea, explained earlier in this chapter.

4: Wittgenstein and the private language argument

The approach which will be outlined in this chapter is that suggested by some of the work of Ludwig Wittgenstein (1889-1951), an Austrian-born philosopher who spent most of his philosophical career in England. Wittgenstein has probably been the greatest single influence on British and American philosophy in the latter part of this century. His earlier philosophy is encapsulated in the *Tractatus Logico-Philosophicus* (1921), and the best-known work of his later period is the *Philosophical Investigations* (published posthumously in 1953). It is with the later work that we shall be concerned here, and especially with a few passages in the *Investigations* which have come to be known collectively as the Private Language Argument, for reasons which will become clear. These passages were probably not originally intended by Wittgenstein as a response to the problem of other minds, but the argument, if accepted, is very rich in its ramifications, and extends to this topic among others. There are also many different interpretations of the passages in question, though it is neither possible nor desirable to discuss them all here. What will be presented, then, is a fairly orthodox account of the argument, giving prominence to those aspects of it which are most relevant to our purposes. For this reason, the argument will be paraphrased rather than given in Wittgenstein's own words.

using language and making judgements
To begin, we recognize the way in which the making of *judge-*

ments depends on our being able to use *language*. Ours is, it seems, the only species capable of using language, in the full sense. By saying 'in the full sense' we mean that human beings can employ a connected system of conventional signs to communicate. It may be true that some other animals communicate by signs, such as screeching when some danger is present. Why should we not call this real language? The two words 'connected' and 'conventional' supply the answer. 'Conventional' means that the signs used have no natural connection with the thing being talked about. The word 'water', for example, is in no way *essentially* connected with the liquid stuff to which it refers. The French use the word *eau* and the Germans *Wasser*, and none of these words is any more correct or accurate than another: the word has no *intrinsic* meaning. This is unlike, for example, the way in which I might indicate the presence of water by making wavy motions with my hand, or show that I have a headache by grimacing and pointing to my head. It is also unlike the example of screeching to warn of danger: screeching is natural as opposed to conventional, not through being intrinsically connected with what it refers to, but because it is a spontaneous reaction rather than part of a learned and agreed code. By 'connected', we mean that language as used by human beings is a complex arrangement of signs which can be used in an unlimited variety of combinations with each other. We can distinguish, for example, between different *kinds* of danger: an earthquake, a large earthquake, a mad bull, a mad black bull, a black bull with large horns, a white bull with large horns, a black bull with small horns, and so on. This endless possibility of making distinctions and forming combinations of them using different parts of speech and grammatical constructions, is the other thing which seems to characterize genuine language and distinguish it from more primitive forms of communication. This difference between 'real' language and these primitive forms may, of course, be at bottom only one of degree, but it is none the less real for that.

What has this got to do with the possibility of making judgements? The important thing to recognise here is that a creature without language cannot, strictly speaking, be either right or wrong about something's being the case. This may sound odd at first, for cannot a cat, for example, spring at a leaf mistaking it for a mouse, and then walk away disappointed? Well, certainly a cat can make a mistake, but what is being claimed is that this is not a mistake *about something's being the case*. To make a mistake about what is the case, a mistake of fact, is to apply the wrong concept in a particular situation, and the cat cannot be said to possess the *concept* of a mouse in general, though it is usually able to recognise one in a given instance. We may say that the cat knows *how* to recognize a mouse, but not that it knows *that* such-and-such a thing is a mouse.

To make this clearer, let's take another example. I know *how* to ride a bicycle, though I do not know *that* certain things are the case concerning the way it is done. When the bicycle threatens to fall over in one direction, I turn the handlebars the opposite way, though I have never (until this moment) reflected that this is what I do. And when this happens, I am not making a judgement about what is the case: I just *do* it. If I fail to right the bicycle and it topples over, I have not made a mistake *of fact*, though I have of course made a mistake. Now I might, if I did enough research into it, be able to come up with a set of principles which would allow me to make judgements of fact concerning what is going on in such a situation. Then, if I were sufficiently quick thinking, I could say, 'Ah, the bicycle is leaning to the left at an angle of sixty degrees to the horizontal, on a fifteen degree adverse camber, with a radius of twenty yards, so it requires a five-eighths clockwise turn of the handlebars to right it'. And if I still toppled over I might say, 'Oh dear, it should have been *seven*-eighths!' In other words, I can now accuse myself of having made an error regarding a matter of fact, as opposed to just having done something foolish. The point is that my new-found ability to make a judgement of fact here depends on my having acquired the appropriate concepts, and this in turn depends on having mastered the use of certain linguistic terms such as 'degrees', 'clockwise', and 'adverse camber'.

If we are still not convinced that making judgements of fact is dependent on being a language user, consider finally the familiar word 'red'. Could I possess the concept of redness without knowing how to use the word 'red'? In one sense I obviously could, since a Frenchman certainly possesses the concept of redness, though he may never have heard the word 'red': this is because the word 'rouge' expresses the very same concept. But what about someone who had *no* word for what we understand by 'red'?

If we are tempted to think that he might nevertheless possess the concept of redness, secretly and incommunicably, let us ask how, even in his own terms, he could be right or wrong in employing the concept. In the case of our public concept which manifests itself in the use of the word 'red', we have a pretty good idea of what range of the colour spectrum constitutes the extension of the concept. At the borderlines we may disagree with each other, saying 'No, that's brown', or 'I'd call that orange'. Far from casting doubt on our grasp of the concept, this is actually one way in which the concept gains such sharpness as it has. For the boundaries, and the way in which it connects, in terms of differences and similarities, with surrounding concepts, are what give it its point. Hence our insistence on language being conventional, the result of an agreement to use signs in a particular way, and systematically connected, which is to say that words, and thereby concepts, gain their significance from the way they fit into a system of interrelated signs and concepts. A person who lacked the word 'red' could not possess the concept which we signify by it, for the reason that there could be no sense in describing her as either right or wrong about what colour an object, let's say an apple, is: all that her 'judgement' would boil down to, would be the idea that the apple 'is the colour that it is' (i.e. whatever colour she sees when she looks at it). And this is no judgement at all, since it is a mere truism, which *cannot* be false.

Of course, she might regard herself as making the 'judgement' that the apple is the same colour as the one she saw yesterday. But what can she suppose herself to mean by 'the same'? How alike in colour do two apples have to be in order to be 'the same colour' in her book? The answer surely is that since she has not learned when and when not to apply the word, the concept has no genuine extension for her – she cannot say where its application begins and ends, and therefore nothing will count as her being right or wrong in a given case, so nothing will count as her making a judgement about it. For the same reason, nothing will count as a right or wrong way of portraying something by gestures, or of emitting a spontaneous screech. We may regard as borderline the case of an intelligent animal which has been trained to respond in a given way to all and only those things which we call red. This brings us to the next stage in the argument.

the impossibility of a private language
Having seen how the making of judgements depends on our using language, we may now ask: what, apart from the right sort of brain structure etc., which we will look at in chapter 9, is necessary in order for one to be able to possess a language? And one answer which Wittgenstein gives is: the company of other language users. To see why this might be so, let us ask what it might mean to say that someone had a *private language*.

Many crude theories about how we acquire language suggest that it is, at bottom, a matter of mentally 'pinning labels' on things. The labels happen, of course, to be words in the language with which we have been brought up. But, according to this crude account, there is no logical reason why we should not do it in the absence of any other language users, merely by inventing our own labels. Now some versions of this rather naive theory involve thinking that the logically primary use of language is in labelling *one's own experiences* (private feelings, sensations, etc.), and that it is only secondarily that we can talk about external, public objects, by 'constructing' them out of the basic, uninterpreted experiences. On first sight, all this looks very straightforward and plausible: the development of understanding, according to this picture, is from simple to complex, from inner to outer, from oneself to other things. This is, however, roughly the reverse of the logical order of things as Wittgenstein teaches us to see them.

Notice, first of all, the difference between the weaker and the stronger forms of the naive view sketched above. The version which only says that language learning could be done in the absence of other language users, presupposes that you could, in such a case, invent a 'private language' known to you alone, with your own words for the objects around you. Having done this, you would then be in a position to teach that language to others. There are reasons for thinking that constructing such a private language would in fact be almost impossibly hard, unless you didn't already know *something* about language and languages. We need not go into these here. What is important is that, if you *did* succeed in inventing the language, it would be just a language like other languages, which could be learned and taught by other people. Consider, however, the stronger form which says that language is ultimately about our own sensations and suchlike. If I speak a language in which the words refer to private experiences of mine, it follows that this language is not teachable to anybody else, since the objects to which the basic terms of the language refer are not accessible to anyone other than myself. Ask, for example, how you could go about teaching another person the meaning of the word 'red', if 'red' functioned as a name for a certain quality of a patch in your own private visual field. There would be no way in which you could point out a red thing to that person, since private sensations are not the kind of thing at which you can point. In this way, a language which functioned like this would be *essentially private*: nobody else could *possibly* learn it. And if ordinary languages like English do function in this way, there must be a sense in which we each have our own language: a sense in which there must be as many 'English languages' as there are speakers of English. This is a tenable view, provided we can make sense of the idea of a private language in the first place. And this is precisely what Wittgenstein denied.

We will remember from the last section how the use of language is important for thought, because of the way in which it allows us to *fix the extension* of concepts: to agree on which cases are instances of them and which are not, and on what it is that makes the difference between something's being and not being an instance. This aspect of language Wittgenstein considers as an example of 'rule following'. Following a rule is the opposite of such things as acting in a purely instinctive way, as most animals do. Rule-governed activities are ones which involve acting according to some principle which tells us which things count as following the rule and which things count as going against it; which gives us an idea of what the difference consists in, between something's according with or not according with the rule. The rules of grammar are like this, and so perhaps are the rules of mathematics. So also are the rules which connect words in the language with things in the world – the semantic rules.

Now what would it be like to have only *private rules?* *Wittgenstein considers this hypothetical situation:*

> Let us imagine the following case. I want to keep a diary about the recurrence of a certain sensation. To this end I associate it with the sign 'S' and write this sign in a calender for every day on which I have the sensation. – I will remark first of all that a definition of the sign cannot be formulated. – But I can still give myself a kind of ostensive definition. – How? Can I point to the sensation? Not in the ordinry sense. But I speak, or write the sign down, and at the same time I concentrate my attention on the sensation – and so, as it were, point to it inwardly. – But what is this ceremony for? For that is all it seems to be! A definition surely serves to establish the meaning of a sign. Well, that is done precisely by the concentration of my attention; for in this way I impress on myself the connexion between the sign and the sensation. – But 'I impress it upon myself' can only mean: this process brings it about that I remember the connexion *right* in the future. But in the present case I have no criterion of correctness. One would like to say: whatever is going to seem right to me is right. And that only means that here we can't talk about 'right'.

This insistence on the fact that, in genuine rule following, there must be a distinction between what is right following of the rule, and what merely *seems* right, is typical of Wittgenstein during this period, and is crucial for the understanding of the Private Language Argument. If I find myself attempting to follow a rule which is mine alone, how do I tell whether I am following it correctly? On the one hand, I am the tutee who is learning how to recognize which cases do accord with the rule and which do not; on the other hand, I am also the authority of whether a given case is a genuine instance or not. This is paradoxical.

Wittgenstein's response to this is to claim that a private rule is no rule at all – that in order to engage in genuinely rule-governed activity, we need to be members of a *community* which upholds that rule and which is the authority on what makes the difference between following it and departing from it. Here, it is important to note that a 'rule', in this sense, does not mean something like a *law*, or *regulation* – it is not something which is enforced, which tells us *what to do*, but a principle which tells us *how to do* something. We will see more of this distinction in chapter 10. There are two aspects to the insistence on the need for a community of rule followers. One is the fact that, in a community, there exists the possibility of a *public check* on one's own understanding of the rule. The need for such a check arises out of the fact that unorthodox interpretations of any given rule are always possible. And this is to be understood in the strict logical sense: we can never be fully certain that another person understands a particular rule in the way that we do.

Suppose, for example, that we teach someone a rule by showing him a sequence which begins

2,4,6,8...

and then encourage him to continue the sequence in the same way. He will probably go on

10,12,14,16...

which suggests that he has understood the rule as corresponding to the instruction 'Add 2 at each step'. But he may, for instance, continue with

10,14,18,22...

If we point out to him that he is not continuing in the same way, he might reply that he took the rule to correspond to 'Add 2 up to 10, and after that add 4', and that he had been applying this rule all along. Thus, what counts as 'doing the same' is itself going to depend on what rule is being applied. So we cannot appeal to the notion of sameness to explain how we are following the same rule. Now since any such rule will have a potentially infinite number of instances, and we can only ever present someone with a finite selection of them, it follows that we can never be wholly certain that someone understands the rule in the same way that we do: there will always be an infinite number of cases in which his interpretation could diverge from ours.

At this point, some people will be tempted to say, 'But surely he can simply *tell* us what he understands the rule to be'. Can he not, for example, just say 'I'm adding two at each step', or 'I'm adding two until I get to ten, and after that four'? And since this is possible, why can't we merely do the obvious thing, which is to reach a verbal agreement on which rule we are using on any given occasion? The reason why this is no solution illustrates how deep the Wittgensteinian notion of rule following goes. For the verbal behaviour involved in telling someone which rule one is following, is also a rule-governed activity. And if we choose to be sceptical about whether two people are following the same mathematical rule, in order to be consistent we must be equally sceptical about whether they are using the same linguistic rules when they discuss which rule is being meant. How, then, can we ever be certain that any of us are following the same rule as one another? Or for that matter, how can a person ever be sure what rule *he himself* is following? For none of us can have considered every possible case of any such rule which he claims to follow. Of course, in practice we have no problem: on the whole, our interpretations tend to coincide with each other in those instances which we actually encounter. And where they do not, we can nearly always make the appropriate adjustments. Herein lies one possible solution to the problem of what has come to be known as 'rule scepticism'.

We may conclude that what it is for a number of people to be following the same rule is, not for each of them to have the same inner, private (and undiscovered even to the person in question) *interpretation*, but simply for them to *agree in practice*: this is the importance of the possibility of a 'public check'. Philosophers who call themselves Wittgensteinians tend to differ on the amount of weight which they place on the idea of a public check; and some are prepared to go further than others in regarding the community of agreement as all there is to having a genuine rule.

As indicated above, there is, however, another aspect to the need for other language users as a pre-condition for the acquisition of language. If we accept the impossibility of making a rule fully explicit, even to oneself, then there must come a point at which we can offer no further explanation of the rule in question, except by giving examples of what counts as following that rule in a certain (finite) number of cases. In a famous passage, Wittgenstein says:

> This was our paradox: no course of action could be determined by a rule, because every course of action be made out to accord with the rule. The answer was: if everything can be made to accord with the rule, then it can also be made out to conflict with it. And so there would be neither accord nor conflict here. It can be seen that there is a misunderstanding here from the mere fact that in the course of our argument we give one interpretation after another; as if each one contented us for at least a moment, until we thought of yet another standing behind it. What this shows is that there is a way of grasping a rule which is *not* an *interpretation*, but which is exhibited in what we call 'obeying a rule' and 'going against it' in actual cases.

The emphasis on the rule as manifested in actual cases is very much what we saw above. When Wittgenstein says that there must be a way of grasping a rule which is not an interpretation, a further point is being made. We cannot know what counts as following a rule in *all* its instances, since we cannot possibly consider all of them. Yet we are tempted to think that in some way when we grasp a rule, all the instances of it are in a sense already fixed. Wittgenstein explains this in the following way:

> 'All the steps are already taken' means: I no longer have any choice. The rule, once stamped with a particular meaning, traces the lines along which it is to be followed through the whole of space. – But if something of this sort really were the case, how would it help? No; my description only made sense if it were to be understood symbolically. – I should have said: *This is how it strikes me*. When I obey a rule, I do not choose. I obey the rule *blindly*.

A way of grasping a rule which is 'not an interpretation' is, then, a matter of following 'blindly'. When we come to the point at which we can give no further explanation of the rule, all that is left is to appeal to what comes naturally. And the reason why we can do this, is because of the habits which have been instilled into us by our *training* in rule following. This appeal to training brings out an aspect of what is necessary for genuine rule following, which goes even beyond the idea that we require our applications of a rule to be checked by a community of rule followers. What it suggests is that we have no real claim to grasp rules at all, unless there is some way in which we initially internalized them: some way, that is, in which we could be said to have learned, to have acquired, the rule in question. And making it up oneself is not, in this sense, an authentic way of acquiring a rule: for in such a case one would have to invent not just a rule itself, as though it could be captured in its entirety by a single mental act, but what is to count as an instance of it in *every* given case.

Training in rule following is not possible, if we accept the above, for an isolated individual. If what has been said is true, the use of language, properly speaking, is a collective and social phenomenon. What repercussions does this have for the original question which motivated this discussion of Wittgenstein?

the case against solipsism

We are now in a position to see why it has been claimed by some that the Private Language Argument, if we accept it, shows that solipsism cannot be correct. For if the making of judgements depends on being able to use language, and if language, as a rule-governed activity, requires a public check and training in the following of a rule, then the absence of other people means that, despite appearances, one could not be genuinely making judgements if one were the only intelligence in the world. Try to imagine such a world: a world of which oneself is the only genuine occupant. Of course, all the other people will be there also, at least in appearance; but they will be merely empty shells with an 'outside' but no 'inside'. Only oneself has an 'inside'. In such a position, how would one ever know the meaning of a word or symbol?

This is a serious question. There would be no difference between following a rule and merely *thinking* one was following a rule; no difference, as Wittgenstein puts it, between something's *being* right and *seeming* right. The idea of there being any 'right' collapses, through its being indistinguishable from whatever would seem right to oneself at a given time. Judgements will, then, be impossible; for there being no difference between applying a concept rightly and applying it wrongly, in other words no difference between making a correct and an incorrect judgement, destroys what is central to the whole idea of a judgement.

The upshot of all this, is that *if* it is true that you are really thinking, making genuine judgements, having coherent thoughts, *then* solipsism is false. But why need one accept the first statement – that one really is genuinely thinking? Could one not be sceptical and agnostic about both of them? The answer is that one could not. For even to suspect or consider the notion that solipsism *might* be true is to make a coherent judgement. On this account, even to take solipsism seriously is to be in a muddle about what one can and can't, logically speaking, take seriously. It is very like the idea of judging oneself to be mad – not as a real madman might in a rare moment of lucidity, but judging oneself to be totally insane whilst one is making the judgement itself. It is an impossible judgement to make, precisely because if it were true, it would follow that it was not a genuine judgement (provided we understand 'totally insane' to entail 'not able to make judgements').

This, then, is the case which a certain brand of Wittgensteinian philosopher might offer to us about solipsism. What are we to say of it? First of all, how sure are we that the notion of a public check on our use of concepts, and our training in the use of them, do really require there to be other conscious people. Will not the empty shells of the solipsist's world do just as well? After all, if I cannot distinguish a world in which the other people are real and have 'insides', from one in which they are mere automata and only have 'outsides', what difference could it possibly make to anything? The answer to this, is that the question of whether any genuine rule following is going on is not an empirical one, that is, not one which can be settled by an further *experiences,* but a logical one. And, if the Private Language Argument is correct, then rule following in one person entails that there is some rule following going on elsewhere. Unfortunately, this has a slightly embarrassing consequence for the Wittgensteinian, since it commits us to the view that *at least one other person* is conscious, and therefore to maintaining simply that the total number of conscious beings in the world is at least *two*! Fortunately, however, the existence of one other conscious being bodes quite well for the rest of them, for the very reason that two is somehow an inherently unlikely number. In any case, it tells us that solipsism is not open to us, and this is what we first started out to settle. Later, in chapter 10, an argument will be made out for the view that rule following demands consciousness, which was the weak link here.

In the meantime, should we be convinced by the Private Language Argument itself? One can imagine an objection to it which goes something like this. A single individual trying to follow a rule all by herself will never be in a position to know whether she is following the rule correctly or not, for there will never be any public verification. But how is an entire community in a better position? For since we are considering logical possibilities (things which are possible since they are not self-contradictory, but which may be extremely improbable), could not a whole community be misled about the rule, and in the exact same way, so that the divergence could not be detected? And if so, doesn't this show that one man would, from a logical point of view, have been as good as a million in the first place?

This is a tempting objection, but it arises out of having missed the point of the Private Language Argument. For the argument is *not* to the effect that one person could be mistaken about how he applies the rule, whilst a number of people are more likely to be correct. Its point is that *the whole idea of correctness* becomes meaningless when applied to the case of a lone individual. The difference between there being one consciousness and more than one is not just that two heads are better than one; it is the difference between being able to make a distinction between what *is* right and what *seems* right, and not being able to make it.

Before leaving the topic of the Private Language Argument, let us go back to what was said above about the fact that the argument demands the premise that we really are, in fact, capable of making judgements. In other words, the argument is *conditional* in form: it says '*If* there are any real judgements being made, *then* solipsism is false. We noticed that it is impossible to deny the first statement, since to do so would itself be to make a judgement. But there is something fishy about this. It is true that *I* cannot doubt that *I* am making judgements. But I *can* doubt whether someone else is doing so, and he can doubt that I am. The reason for this is simply that there is no logical guarantee that *any given* person is really thinking, even oneself. The proposition 'It is impossible for me to doubt that I am making judgements' does not add up to the conclusion 'Therefore I must be making judgements'. One knows perfectly well what it is for someone such as a lunatic not really to be making judgements. And one therefore knows *what it would be* for this to be the case with oneself – maybe at some future time, for example. Thus, one knows what would be being asked by the question 'Am I really making judgements?', and therefore one knows in a sense what is meant by supposing that one might not be. Thus the argument still remains conditional in form: the conclusion that solipsism cannot be true continues to rest on the unverified premise that one is genuinely using concepts and making judgements. As premises go, however, this might be thought to be quite a strong one. At any rate, we know, if we accept Wittgenstein's argument, that there is no point in questioning it: we are stuck with it for all practical purposes, and therefore with that which follows from it.

An argument which has this kind of structure is often known as a *transcendental argument*. A transcendental argument says, in essence: 'We must suppose A to be the case; and if A is the case then B must be also, in order to make A possible'. Attention was drawn to transcendental arguments in the eighteenth century by the philosopher Immanuel Kant. We will be seeing more of Kant in chapter 8.

5: communication and interaction

The problem with which we began was: could a machine ever be capable of genuine conscious thought, and if so, how could we tell? We then recognized that there was a problem not just about how we can tell in the case of machines, but about how we know other *people* are conscious: and not just some borderline cases, like the badly brain damaged or comatose, but *all* other people. Now if Wittgensteinian philosophers are cor- rect, who make out a case of the sort discussed in the last chapter, then we seem to have a transcendental argument to the effect that solipsism is false, and one has no choice but to accept that other people have conscious thoughts in just the way one does oneself. No one has a privileged status in this respect, just by virtue of being 'number one' as far as *he* is concerned. But where does this get us as regards our original question? How can the Wittgensteinian position help us in deciding what kind of thing might lead us to suspect that a *machine* might be having thoughts in just the way we do?

animation and the Turing test
It was pointed out in chapter 2, that the kind of machines to which people are often tempted to attribute consciousness are ones which just sit somewhere handling data, and which are not animate in any real sense. It was also noticed, that it is animation which gives us the clue to when a human being is conscious and when not. However, in chapter 2 we concluded that it would be an easy matter to build a machine which

jumped around and suchlike, but to which no one would have the least temptation to attribute consciousness. It must now be recognized that this was much too short a way with the point about animation. For there is more to genuine animation than simply doing what a jack-in-a-box or 'nodding dog' does. And what is required over and above mere movement and simple responses, we have seen in discussing Wittgenstein. It is the ability to *communicate*: to enter into a dialogue, or into a shared practice with other creatures.

One thing, then, which might quite rightly lead us to suspect that there was some real thinking going on in a machine, would be if we found ourselves reacting to the machine as though it were a conscious being, due to the likeness of *its* responses to those of a human person. If, that is, we found ourselves entering into what seemed like real communication with it. In particular, if we found it impossible to distinguish between communicating with the machine and communication with a human being, this tendency would be at its strongest. This was, in fact, the test suggested by the pioneer of computing, Alan Turing, in 1950. Recognizing that questions about whether machines can think are apt to raise the spectre of solipsism, and recognizing also that even those who completely reject the idea that machines can think nonetheless wish to avoid the solipsist position, Turing concluded that there must be some *test* for whether a thing is really thinking or not – a test which most humans beings pass, and which most, if not all, machines don't.

The test which Turing came up with was precisely that of finding out whether communication with the machine was indistinguishable from communication with a human being – whether a person could be 'fooled' by a machine. Of course, if you really wanted to carry out the test, you would need to have both a computer and a human being able to communicate with a second human being in the same way, for example via a series of questions and answers on a terminal, with the second human being having to guess which was which. But the point of the test is primarily theoretical: it is meant to establish the *principle* that the criterion of when something is really thinking, is whether or not that thing can communicate, answer questions and so on, in a way which is indistinguishable from that of a human person.

One passage from Turing's writing is well known in this respect. He is replying to the arguments of Sir Geoffrey Jefferson, a critic of artificial intelligence, who said in 1949:

> Not until a machine can write a sonnet or compose a concerto because of thoughts and emotions felt, and not by the chance fall of symbols, could we agree that machine equals brain – that is, not only write it but know it had written it. No mechanism could feel (and not merely artificially signal, an easy con- trivance) pleasure at its successes, grief...be warmed by flattery, be made miserable by its mistakes, be charmed by sex, be angry or depressed when it cannot get what it wants.

Turing first asks how Jefferson himself would tell whether another human being really had certain abilities, or only the semblance of them. He says:

> I am sure that Professor Jefferson does not want to adopt the extreme and solipsist point of view. Probably he would be quite willing to adopt the imitation game as a test. The game...is frequently used in practice under the name of *viva voce* to discover whether someone really understands something or has 'learnt it parrot fashion'.

Turing goes on to give an example of an exchange between an 'interrogator' and a 'witness', in which the interrogator is attempting to establish whether some lines written by the witness were written with genuine understanding or not. The gist of the argument is that if, in a situation like this, the interrogator cannot distinguish between a machine as 'witness' and a human being, then there are no grounds for holding the machine's intelligence to be less a case of genuine thought than that of a human person. He concludes:

> In short, then, I think that most of those who support the argument from consciousness could be persuaded to abandon it rather than be forced into the solipsist position. They will then probably be willing to accept our test. I do not wish to give the impression that I think there is no mystery about con- sciousness...But I do not think these mysteries necessarily need to be solved before we can answer the question with which we are concerned in this paper.

The question with which Turing actually began the paper was simply 'Can machines think?' However, he considered this question so obscure that he proposed to 'replace' it with the question of whether a machine could fool people consistently in the above way. From the final remarks in the passage, it is clear that Turing is not one of those who reject the concept of consciousness entirely. He does, however, want to divorce it from the notion of thinking. We shall be looking, in chapters 10 and 11, at some reasons for thinking that this cannot be done. We may consider here, however, that Turing's reason for wishing to make this move is one which we have already rejected. It is that in Turing's view the insistence on consciousness as the important element goes hand-in-hand with the view that the only way of telling whether a creature thinks is to *be* that creature. For Turing, the person who interprets the above question as asking 'Are machines *conscious*?' is forced into a solipsistic position. Here Turing's reasoning is weak. For there can be evidence of consciousness – the symptoms we talked of above – which do not rely at all on *being* the thing or person in question. Some of them are, in fact, precisely those captured by the Turing Test itself.

It is quite reasonable, therefore, for those who want to insist on consciousness as the crucial element in 'real' thought, to adopt the Turing Test as suggested: but not as a replacement for the harder question about consciousness. Rather, as an indication of the answer to that question in a given case. We may, of course, want to insist on other ingredients besides those pointed to by Turing. For example, there is the question of animation, which was discussed in chapter 2, and earlier in this chapter. We shall see later that sentience must also be considered important in any candidate for consciousness. Symptoms, then, there are a-plenty. And Wittgenstein has shown us a way of connecting the symptoms with the condition of which they are symptoms. For what the Wittgensteinian argument demonstrates, if it is correct, is that the fact that no amount of these symptoms *logically add up to* the conclusion that a given creature is conscious does *not* mean that we are seriously threatened with solipsism. It is time now to look further at some of the symptoms themselves, and at some of the human inventions which may be thought to exhibit them.

programs that talk to us

Inevitably, attempts have been made to create computer programs which are capable of passing a test such as the Turing Test: programs which will cause a machine to converse with someone in a believably human way. Many of the early language-using programs involved no more than a question-and-answer type situation. They merely answered a very large number of questions on a given topic, such as football, or geography, or whatever. Naturally, no one could be fooled into thinking that such a thing was human – change the subject and they are lost completely! Others, however, were broader and more advanced.

One of these became well known as a just credible human substitute. It has actually been known to fool an employee of the company where it was developed. This program is called ELIZA, after Eliza Doolittle, the heroine of Shaw's *Pygmalion*, who was taught to speak 'good' English. The reason why ELIZA is able to create, up to a point, the illusion of genuine interaction, is that in place of having a data base of facts on a given topic, or even on general knowledge, it takes its material from the conversation of the other person, the user. A program which merely used its own information would soon be 'found out' when the interlocutor suddenly changed the subject, or alluded to one of those trivial but universally shared items in our culture which are hard to pin down in a data base. The beauty of ELIZA is that *it* asks the questions, and talks about whatever the user wants to talk about.

An example of the beginning of a real conversation with ELIZA is the following (ELIZA's responses are in capital letters):

> HELLO. PLEASE TELL ME ABOUT YOUR PROBLEM.
> I keep getting headaches.
> YOU SAY YOU KEEP GETTING HEADACHES.
> I think it's because of my job.
> YOUR JOB?

Yes.
PLEASE TELL ME MORE.
I get a lot of trouble from customers.
CAN'T YOU ELABORATE ON THAT?
They make a lot of demands on me.
I AM NOT SURE I UNDERSTAND YOU FULLY.
They cause lots of stress.
PLEASE GO ON.
I think I need a holiday.
WHAT WOULD IT MEAN TO YOU IF YOU GOT A HOLIDAY?
It would give me a rest.
WHAT DOES THAT SUGGEST TO YOU?
I work too hard.
......etc.

It will be noticed that ELIZA's conversation resembles that of a psychiatrist talking to a patient. It is significant that this was the intention with which the program was written, since the

psychiatrist-patient situation is one in which it is normal for one party, the psychiatrist, to make conversation which centres entirely on the other party's topics. Such an interview also tends to keep off 'hard facts' and revolve more around feelings and reactions, so that a detailed knowledge of actual things (as opposed to what the patient feels or thinks about them) is unnecessary.

But when we turn to general conversation, of the kind which usually leads us to believe that we have encountered a conscious human being, the results are much worse, often to the point of being comical. Consider another actual conversation with ELIZA, in which the user did not play the part of a disturbed person anxious to talk about his own feelings, but that of a normal person looking for a conversation:

> HELLO. PLEASE TELL ME YOUR PROBLEM.
> I can't find a bottle opener.
> HOW DO YOU KNOW YOU CAN'T FIND A BOTTLE OPENER?
> I've looked for half an hour.
> I AM NOT SURE I UNDERSTAND YOU FULLY.
> I have looked for the bloody bottle opener for the past half hour.
> YOU SAY YOU HAVE LOOKED FOR THE BLOODY BOTTLE OPENER FOR THE PAST HALF HOUR.
> Yes.
> PLEASE GO ON.
> ....etc.

As Professor Margaret Boden has put it:

> such 'speaking machines' do not behave like someone conversing in her native language. Rather, they resemble a person resorting to trickery and semantic sleight-of-hand in order to hide her own lack of understanding of a foreign tongue.

There is, of course, no reason *in principle* why a combination of this sort of interrogation of the user, with a phenomenally large data base of everyday facts, should not produce something realistic. But 'in principle' is a very big qualification to make.

nuts and bolts

Although it might be possible, in principle, to write a program which will really allow a machine to simulate the linguistic and other behaviour of a human being, there is another factor which might make us want to hesitate before accepting that such a machine would really be thinking. This is the curious fact that the temptation to regard a machine as really thinking tends to go away once we know in detail how it works – once we get down to the 'nuts and bolts'. One reason, in fact, why so many people really do suspect that computers might be consciously thinking, is that their circuitry is electronic, hidden, and not understood by most people. If it worked by clockwork, or wind power, or water power, probably no one would be interested in making this claim at all. But to someone who actually does know how a computer is put together, how a 'talking program' is written, there arises, at least as yet, no question of attributing conscious thought to it. Nor is it likely to in the foreseeable future. Of course, to some journalists, we are always on the brink of some breakthrough which is going to be the 'great leap forward'; computer scientists and artificial intelligence workers are, on the whole, more cautious in their optimism.

Herein lies a curious anomaly. For we appear not even to apply the same standards of evidence to human beings as we do to artifacts. Whereas knowing in detail how a machine works is likely to make us less inclined to suspect it of anything like conscious thought, the same is not true as regards people. The discoveries of medical science concerning the functioning of the human body do not have the effect of making us more sceptical about other minds. Here, of course, the Argument from Analogy does have some purchase, which explains the anomaly: for the knowledge that at least one physical mechanism put together in our shape is capable of consciousness does remove any feeling of inherent unlikelihood with regard to the possibility of such mechanisms supporting conscious thought in general. But if the analogy argument can get us this far, it still does not follow immediately that we are entitled to attribute consciousness to other physical mechanisms just insofar as they resemble ourselves. For this, we require some further argument.

It ought now to be obvious that one aspect of this will lie in the question of what it is for a creature to be actually understanding what it is doing, and in particular understanding the language it uses. The kinds of systems we glanced at above are not such that one would suspect them of genuinely attaching meaning to the utterances they produce, however sophisticated these utterences might look on the surface. To put this another way, systems of this type have no real *semantics*: the meanings of their utterances are only meanings imposed by us, the creators and users of them, and not meanings to the machine or system itself. And one reason why the vast majority of artifacts cannot seriously be suspected of possessing any semantics, is that they do not interact in the relevant ways with the 'outside' world. They cannot pin meanings on words in the way that we can, because they do not have genuine access to the things which the words *stand for* in the way that we do. We shall see more of this later, especially in chapter 10.

For the moment, however, we will need to embark on another extended detour. For before beginning to draw sweeping conclusions about what conditions are necessary and/or sufficient for conscious thought, we really ought to ask what, in general, is supposed to be the relation between a physical organism such as a human being, and the conscious thought of which it is capable. And this, as many readers will probably have already realised, is none other than the traditional 'Mind-Body Problem': the question of the relation between the mental and physical aspects of a person. In the next three chapters, therefore, we will be looking at some common approaches to this philosophical problem. If, at some points, it begins to look as though this detour is in danger of rendering the issue less rather than more clear, it is important (as always) to bear with the argument until it is possible to see in what direction it leads.

6: mind and matter

If the criteria for consciousness are something to do with the behaviour which a thing exhibits to other creatures, and its interactions with them, what significance we actually give to these things will depend to a large extent on the view which we take of the precise nature of the relation between mind and body, or between mind and outward behaviour. In other words, it is all very well to say that there are 'criteria' for recognizing the presence of consciousness; but what we understand by this rather loose term will be determined by our general view of (to put it first of all in a deliberately traditional way) the connection between mind and matter. This is, of course, an enormously old philosophical problem, or cluster of problems, which originally arose only with regard to human beings and the way in which their mental features relate to their bodies, physical make-up and bodily behaviour. Only by seeing how the matter stands when dealing with human beings, then, will we be likely to throw light on how it stands when we come to deal with machines.

In order to understand what choice of views is available here, and how the different views would fit into the question about minds and machines, let us look (though we will only be scratching the surface) at the chief theories which have been propounded. We will divide them into two groups, the first corresponding to what are known as *dualist* theories, and the second to what are called *monist* theories. Roughly speaking, dualist theories see mind and matter as two fundamentally separate things, whereas monist theories hold that there is really only *one* thing – either mind, or matter, or something of which both mind and matter are aspects. We begin with the dualist theories, leaving monist accounts for the following two chapters.

Cartesian dualism

The most obvious, and in some ways the simplest, dualist theory is that of the French philosopher René Descartes (1596 –1650). When the word 'dualism' is mentioned to a phil-osophically trained person, the name of Descartes is the one which probably springs first to mind.

At the heart of Descartes' theory is the idea that the body and the mind are two quite different, though in some way connected, things. They are, to put it in the language of his time, different 'substances'. Descartes' central argument for this is as simple as it is initially appealing. Close your eyes, shut off your ears and other sense organs, and try to imagine yourself without a body. Suppose for a moment that nothing physical, nothing material, exists, and concentrate purely on your own consciousness. If you can do this, then Descartes thinks it follows that it is logically possible (i.e. involves no contra-diction) that *you* should exist, even in the absence of your body, or indeed of any other physical thing. What remains is the immaterial, incorporeal *mind*.

In fact, we did not even need to close our eyes. For, as Descartes' initial position of scepticism (suspension of belief) emphasises, the *apparently* physical things around me which I see, hear, and so on, could themselves possibly be only ideas or illusions in my mind! And if this is how things stand, then we cannot escape the conclusion that the mind is a totally different and independent thing from the body. If the 'man in the street' knows anything at all about Descartes, he probably knows the famous phrase 'I think, therefore I am'. This is Descartes' way of saying that the one thing which I cannot doubt is my own existence, for the very act of doubting itself inevitably involves the existence of the person doing the doubting. Thus, I am first of all aware that I am conscious, that I have a *mind*, and only subsequently am I aware, by using my mind, that I have a body – that is, that there are physical items in the world which are uniquely and directly under my control, and are of special concern to me.

As we recognized earlier, Descartes does, of course, accept the existence of a connection between the mind and the body: naturally the mind must be able to control the bodily movements which are subject to our will, and the body must in turn be able to affect the mind, since much of what we know in our minds has to originate with the sense organs of the body. Rather quaintly to us, Descartes locates the chief intersection between the mind and the body in the pineal gland, a small organ in the brain. Whilst nobody now would take seriously this glandular explanation, there are many who are tempted – and it is not hard to see why, on first sight – by a Cartesian or neo-Cartesian form of dualism. Most philosophers these days, however, reject Descartes' account. Why?

Firstly, Descartes' case, at least as stated above, rests on a premise which is not fully articulated in his writing. This may be expressed as the assumption that wherever one thing, call it A, can be imagined without simultaneously imagining another thing B, then A and B must be different entities, with A not being dependent on B for its existence. Do we have to accept this? Take a simpler, though perhaps rather imperfect, example. Can you imagine fire without the presence of oxygen? In some sense, most of us probably can. Primitive man, when he imagined fire, would certainly not have imagined it as entailing the presence of oxygen, though obviously he could not have thought of it as oxygen-less either. Does it follow from this that fire and oxygen are two separate things, and that fire is in no way dependent for its existence on oxygen? Surely not, for we now know that fire in fact *is* burning oxygen. We cannot pretend that this brief argument constitutes any sort of final refutation of Descartes – his defenders would have much to say in reply. In order to follow this up, however, one would have to go to a specialist book or journal on the subject. All that has been done here is to sketch one possible approach to a rejection of Descartes' reasoning.

Malebranche and occasionalism

Now if we want to retain the idea that mind and matter are two separate things, and yet cannot bring ourselves to believe in some Cartesian-type mechanism whereby they interact, an obvious move would be to deny that they interact at all. This is the view taken by Nicolas Malebranche (1638-1715), who was himself greatly influenced by Descartes. The problem for the defender of such a view is, of course, to explain the *apparent* interaction of mind and body: in particular, the correspondence between our mental desires and volitions, and the physical effects which they seem to produce in our bodies. For example, I decide to pick up an apple which I see in front of me, because I want to eat it. This mental occurrence results in the movement of my arm as I reach out for it. Is there not surely something like a causal connection between the mental act of decision and the physical movement of the arm?

Malebranche says there is not; indeed he denies the existence of *any* causation in the sense in which most of us understand it. The apparent connection, according to him, is to be explained by the fact that God, noting my decision, brings it about that my arm moves. God, on Malebranche's view, directly brings about all those things which we normally think of as being caused by other things or events in the world. What we naturally regard as being the cause of an event is not, he maintains, the *true* cause at all, but only what he refers to as the *occasional* cause (the occasion of God's acting), hence the name given to his theory – occasionalism.

Malebranche has a clever, if not entirely convincing, argument for his thesis that we do not really cause our own bodily movements. He points out that if we did cause them ourselves, we would have to know *how* to do so. And from this it follows, on his account, that we would have to know about the workings of the human brain, the nerves, the muscles, and all that goes into producing the action. Clearly we do not know all this, and yet are somehow capable of performing considerable feats of dexterity. Therefore, he concludes, we cannot be directly responsible for these actions ourselves – they are brought about not by us, but by God acting 'on our behalf'. Conversely, the apparent causal effects which physical objects exert on our minds can be explained along the same lines. The regularity of the apparent 'laws' linking mental and physical occurrences can be accounted for by the fact that God has indeed laid down laws, though these only have the status of resolutions on His part to act in certain regular and predictable ways.

One obvious drawback which people find with occasionalism is that it requires us to bring in God to explain some quite familiar facts about the world, and that the explanation itself is highly counterintuitive. Malebranche, of course, would point out that reason requires us to believe that things happen in the way he describes, since any other way is logically ruled out by his argument. Yet the argument, as presented here, is not at all as watertight as he considered it to be. The best point at which to attack it would probably be the step from knowing how to perform an action to knowing some facts about human physiology. Philosophers today would, on the whole, be inclined to see a sharper distinction between knowing *how* (to do something) and knowing *that* (something is the case), and to hesitate before concluding that the former always implies the latter. Remember, in this connection, the bicycle example in chapter 4. However this may be, we will move on now to consider a rival theory of the relation between mind and body, propounded by a critic of Malebranche.

Leibniz and the pre-established harmony

This critic is Gottfried Leibniz (1646-1716). Leibniz both admired, and found fault with, the systems of Descartes and of Malebranche. He considered that Descartes had simply 'abandoned the struggle' when it came to explaining how mind and body can ever interact. And his view of Malebranche was that the latter had shown what could *not* be the case, without having explained what in fact *is*. That is, he accepted Malebranche's thesis that our bodily movements are not truly caused by our own mental acts of will, but found himself unable to agree with Malebranche's occasionalist explanation, according to which God must somehow step in at every point to salvage the appearance of genuine connection between things.

There is neither space nor necessity here to go into the whole of Leibniz's philosophy, even as regards the mind, but the outline of his theory concerning the relation between mind and body goes like this. The mental occurrences which make up the experience of the mind, arise entirely from its own nature and constitution. Similarly, the physical happenings which form the life of the body, are part of *its* nature, and come about only by physical laws. The apparent causal interaction between mind and body is brought about not, as Malebranche had argued, by the direct intervention of God on each occasion of ostensible interaction, but by a 'pre-established harmony' between the two processes. Whereas Malebranche regarded the 'laws' governing the coincidence of mental and physical events as merely resolutions on God's part to act on each individual occasion in a given way, Leibniz saw them as principles which God had set in motion and, having done so, could leave alone to fulfil their intended purposes, much as a watchmaker winds up a watch and leaves it to run, without constantly having to set it at the correct time.

Leibniz himself uses the analogy of two clocks to explain his view. If, he points out, two clocks are both so accurately made and so perfectly adjusted that they neither gain or lose at all, then both of them will always be doing corresponding things at the same time. One will be chiming eight just when the cuckoo is coming out of the other one eight times. This, Leibniz believes, is the real position regarding mind and body. Both are originally set in motion in such a way that they keep in perfect accord with each other. Thus, just at the time when I am resolving to eat an apple, my arm reaches out and picks one up – not because I actually cause it to do so, but because things are so divinely ordered that the two events coincide perfectly in time, with the result that we are tempted to attribute some further connection to them.

What can we say about Leibniz's theory? First of all, like Malebranche's it requires us not only to believe in God, but to believe that many ordinary facts about the world can only be explained by granting to God a special role in our scientific methodology. Leibniz argues, in effect, that his view is a neater, more elegant one than that of Malebranche. He says that the system he describes is 'more worthy' of God, and in this he is right. What we may doubt, however, is whether the thinkers of the period we have so far been considering were correct in seeing such a radical difficulty in explaining how unlike 'substances' can interact. And, even more fundamentally, whether they were right to think of mind and matter as two equally real and independent substances (types of thing) at all. These questions are of too great a scope for the present work, though some light might be shed on them by comparing the theories we have seen so far with some more recent ones which do not embody the same kinds of assumptions. The final theory which we shall consider in this chapter brings us much nearer to the present day, and certainly has a less theological flavour about it.

Huxley's epiphenomenalism

Although it sounds rather daunting, 'epiphenomenalism' just means the theory that mental events, although real, do not function as *causes*. We began by seeing how Descartes considered that mind and matter could *interact*, i.e. act *on each other*. Now whilst Malebranche and Leibniz both denied that any genuine interaction was going on, the nineteenth century English writer T.H. Huxley took the course of accepting the existence of causal interaction *in one direction only*. Although he regarded both matter and mind as real, in a sense matter was for him the 'more real', for he saw it as causing mental events, whereas mental events did not, he argued, cause physical ones.

Mental phenomena, then, according to Huxley, are 'epiphenomena', mere concomitants of physical action, with no causal power of their own. When it seems to us that a mental event, such as a conscious intention to put my hat on, is the cause of a physical event, namely the putting on of my hat, what actually happens is that the physical event is brought about, not by the conscious intention, but by the *physical counterpart*, in the brain or wherever, of the conscious intention. Thus, according to the epiphenomenalist, the man in the street tends to regard a mental event as being the cause of a physical event, whereas in fact a quite different physical event is the cause of them both. When this understandable confusion is remedied, we see that mind, or consciousness, is no more than a kind of ineffective froth given off by the more fundamental physical processes. In Huxley's words:

> It seems to me that in man, as in the brutes, there is no proof that any state of consciousness is the cause of change in the motion of the matter of the organism...it follows that our mental conditions are simply the symbols in consciousness of the changes which take place automatically in the organism; and that, to take an extreme illustration, the feeling which we call volition is not the cause of a voluntary act, but the symbol of that state of the brain which is the immediate cause of the act. We are conscious automata, endowed with free will in the only intelligible sense of that much-abused term – inasmuch as in many respects we are able to do as we like – but none the less parts of the great series of causes and effects...

It is worth spending a little time on a discussion of epiphenomenalism, since it is at first sight a very plausible theory, and is likely to have a good deal more initial appeal than the accounts discussed in this chapter so far. One aspect of it which attracts many people is its seemingly 'scientific' character, being able to do justice to the existence of conscious experience, whilst avoiding any ghostly or spiritual substance or mechanism.

What kind of objection, then, may be argued against epiphenomenalism? One is quite obvious, when it is pointed out: it certainly seems, in our, experience, that things turn out differently when we put conscious thought into them, from how they turn out without it. If I walk around the house without having my mind on it, or in my sleep, I tend to fall over, bump into things, and so on. Surely, the epiphenomenalist will say, but for all you know, it could just as easily be that you actually do things more efficiently when you have *that physical feature which gives rise to* the conscious feeling of wakefulness, attentiveness, etc.

This is, of course, a move which the epiphenomenalist can make with regard to any mental state which threatens to be causally efficacious. There are reasons, however, for hesitating before accepting it. Firstly, it must be remembered that if we accept this account of how things are, we pay as heavy a price for it as we do if we accept occasionalism or the pre-established harmony, in terms of the number of everyday beliefs we have to give up. Not only will my intention to put on my hat not be what brings it about that I put it on, but nobody will truly be said to have a drink because they feel thirsty, go to college because they want to learn French, or get married because they are in love: inverted commas will have to go round nearly everything.

Secondly, psycho-physical events present themselves to us in such a way that, not only is it the case that a conscious intention is invariably found to be followed (all other things being equal) by the physical action of which it was the intention; but further, that there is an intimate relationship between the two – what philosophers call an internal relation – one which is not just accidental but which somehow follows from the nature of the related things themselves. This is borne out by a matter of logic: the action, say, of 'waving to the woman next door' would not count as being this particular action, without the context provided by my intention. It might count as some other physically identical action, such as trying to swat a fly or fanning myself to keep cool, or it might not count as an action at all, if, for example, it was the result of a nervous tic. The nature of the resulting action, and therefore its (according to Huxley, physical) explanation will depend on the intention – *and on the intention itself, not its alleged physical counterpart*, since it simply makes no sense to suppose that the appropriate context could be provided by physical counterparts.

Of course, this does not prove that there are causes which are non-physical; but it does show at the very least that there are explanations which are not causal. These non-causal explanations may, like the one in the example above, be of a *contextual* kind, and it is this sort of explanation which cannot be handled by the epiphenomenalist, since he can neither accept it as it stands, since it is not a physical explanation, nor give an equivalent description of it in purely physical terms. It is not so much that we need mental events as causes, distinct from the physical events which they cause; it is rather that the character of the event cannot be properly understood without some reference to the fact that it has a mental, as well as a physical, side to it (i.e. some reference, not to the intention as the cause of the action in the sense that a stone may cause a broken window, but to the intention *with which the action was performed*, as making it the action which it is).

This should perhaps suggest to us that in dealing with an apparent case of mental cause giving rise to physical effect, we might be misleading ourselves by talking about *two* things and debating whether and how they interact. An internal relation such as that between intention and action is too close to admit of 'interaction' (the premises and conclusion of an argument don't *interact*, neither do the size and shape of a box). Should we perhaps not be looking in the direction of regarding an event such as an intentionally-performed action as a single thing rather than two things welded insecurely together? It is to this line of enquiry that we turn in the next chapter.

7: just one thing: monism

As we saw in the last chapter, the alternative to a dualist account of the relation between mind and body is a *monist* account. A monist holds the opinion that there are not *really* two things – mind and body – but only one thing which somehow presents itself as a duality, or encourages us to see a duality where there is none. Monist views may be divided into categories, according to what they consider the one thing in question to be. We may start by separating them into just three categories, depending on whether they regard the one 'real' substance as (a) mental, (b) physical, or (c) neither.

We may ameliorate the task ahead of us by dealing with the first category very briefly. A mental monist believes the only reality to be ultimately mental, and the physical world to consist only of *ideas* in the mind. For this reason, the mental form of monism is usually called *idealism*. The earliest of the idealists we need mention is George Berkeley (1685-1753), an (Anglican) Irish bishop who, beginning from *empiricist* principles (i.e. from a theory which puts *experience* prior to all else), developed a view according to which things only exist insofar as they are perceived by an observer. A theory which conforms in part with Berkeley's is that of J.G. Fichte (1762-1814), one of the German idealists; for Fichte, however, it is the 'moral will' which is the ultimate reality and which creates its own objects. The culmination of German idealism comes with G.W.F. Hegel (1770-1831). Hegel's views are many and complex, and it will suffice here to say that, for Hegel, what is ultimately real is the Absolute, or divine Idea.

This does not pretend to be a full, or even an adequate, treatment of idealist approaches to the mind-body problem. Its purpose is merely to reveal why we do not need to concern ourselves with idealism here. For one thing, there are very few people today who take idealism seriously; a better reason for leaving it aside, however, is that it is irrelevant to our central purpose. This purpose is to throw light on the relation between minds and machines. Now if the idealist were correct, the answer to our question would be trivial and uninteresting: machines would be no more than ideas in the mind, like everything else. This does not, of course, mean that idealism is wrong, but simply that anyone who is seriously wedded to idealism may as well stop reading at this point. After this clarification, we will begin by looking at the position which stands at the opposite extreme to idealism – materialism.

the materialism of Armstrong and Smart
Two modern philosophers who take the extreme position of actually *identifying* the mental with the physical, are D.M. Armstrong and J.J.C. Smart. The essence of Armstrong's thesis is simple, though his defence of it is not. He believes that mental states simply *are* physical states of the organism's central nervous system. His definition of a mental state is in terms of its typical causes (stimuli) and effects (behaviour of the organism). He then presents the hypothesis that these causes and effects are 'contingently identical' with states of the central nervous system. For this reason, the kind of materialism propounded by Armstrong and Smart is often called Central State Materialism, though it is also known as Eliminative Materialism and the Mind-Body Identity Theory. To say that A is *contingently* identical with B, is to say that A is *in fact* one and the same with B, though it *might not have been*, i.e. it is not a logical truth that it is. In other words, Armstrong wants to regard it as a scientific discovery, and not just a matter of conceptual reasoning, that states of mind and states of the central nervous system are identical. What makes this thesis materialist is that he also regards the physical side of the equation as the more fundamental, and as that in terms of

which the mental side is to be explained. This account is normally referred to as *reductivist*. Any theory is reductivist if it takes one kind of thing and 'reduces' it to another; that is, if it attempts to show that it is 'really no more than' the latter. Materialism in this way attempts to reduce the mental to the physical.

The problem for the materialist is to show how the apparently mental states or events such as the 'feels' and 'sensations' which we have seen earlier, can *really* be physical states of the organism. How, for example, is she to explain the apparently irreducible fact that a particular object *looks* the way it does to me, that there is something it is *like* to be me in this instance, to adopt Nagel's formulation discussed previously? Armstrong's answer is to identify perception with the acquisition, or possible acquistion, of beliefs about the world including our own bodies; and subsequently to give a *behavioural* account of the beliefs – that is, to identify the beliefs with their behavioural manifestations.

For all its apparent simplicity, Armstrong's theory has turned out to be in many ways a rather confused one. For it never becomes clear what it is that is supposed to be being 'reduced' to the physical, if mental states are to be *defined* in the way Armstrong suggests. The confusion shows itself in the fact that Armstrong himself seems never to be sure whether the 'inner' mental states are a kind of myth or delusion on our part, or whether they are real enough, but properly to be explained in terms of the nervous system. If the former, then his own writing is vitiated by constant reference to them; and if the latter, then it is hard to see why their supposed identity with physical states shows the physical states to be the only 'real' ones – except, perhaps, by being causally prior to the mental ones, though even this gives us no reason to think the pain less real than the kick!

This dilemma is implicitly dealt with by Smart, who is concerned to answer a certain kind of objection to his form of Armstrong-type materialism. Suppose, he says, someone accepts his thesis that sensations simply *are* physical states, and yet sees no reason to deny that these physical states have *irreducibly mental properties*. His response to this challenge is to treat the concepts which are claimed to be irreducibly mental (sensation concepts, etc.) in a way which involves no commitment to their being either mental or physical concepts. This analysis of them he calls a 'topic-neutral analysis'. In outline, what he suggests is that they be understood in terms of the 'inputs' and 'outputs' of the states in question. The concept of pain is not to be thought of as being about an 'inner' mental sensation, but rather in terms of typical stimulus (damage to body tissue, stimulation of nerves and so on), and typical response (crying out, rubbing the affected part, and suchlike). This refinement will not be discussed further just here, since it has something in common with both behaviourism, which will be dealt with in the next section, and with functionalism, which will be treated in the one following.

behaviourism: Watson, Skinner and Ryle

Behaviourism is a kind of theory which began life as a revolutionary methodology in psychology. Its founder was the American psychologist J.B. Watson, who first laid down its principles in a paper published in 1913, since when it has enjoyed much influence, even with many who would not go so far as to call themselves behaviourists. As a psychological methodology, behaviourism involves concentrating on the outward and observable behaviour of an organism, whilst attaching little importance to its own feelings and sensations. This elevation of the public and verifiable, whilst devaluing the mental and subjective, was held by many psychologists to place psychology on a more objective and scientific footing than that provided, for example, by introspection (observation of one's own mind). These behaviourists did not altogether deny the existence of introspectable sensations and feelings; they merely believed that from a scientific point of view they could safely drop out of the picture (cf. the views of Wittgenstein and Rorty, discussed earlier, on the mental 'dropping out' of the picture).

How, if these items are allowed to exist, can they possibly be ignored by psychologists, of all people? The answer lies in the *stimulus-response* explanation of human behaviour.

According to the behaviourist, human action has causes, and these causes are themselves outward and physical. For example, suppose we want to make an animal in a laboratory eat a certain kind of food which it is reluctant to eat. One thing we may do is to deprive it of other food until it becomes hungry and will eat what is available. Here we have a chain of events

deprivation ------> hunger ------> eating

which seems to be causally linked: the deprivation causes the hunger, and the hunger subsequently causes the eating. But if this is the case, given that the relation of causality is transitive, we can ignore the inner, unsurveyable hunger, and talk as though the deprivation directly causes the eating.

Behaviourists have since developed sophisticated theories and concepts to do with the nature and variety of conditioning. An example is the notion of 'operant conditioning', which is the kind of conditioning that requires the experimental subject to perform some task, such as pressing a lever, before receiving a reward. A well-known instrument of operant conditioning is the Skinner Box, a device used by the American psychologist B.F. Skinner (b.1904). Skinner, besides doing experimental research in psychology, has also conducted a campaign in recent years to defend behaviourism from its critics. In this way, he has become probably the best-known present-day behaviourist. His works include a novel, *Walden Two*, in which Skinner tries to demonstrate, by using the example of a fictional society, how mankind could live in a happier and more rational way if we would only agree to accept the idea that we are governed by conditioning, and yield to the more beneficial forms of it instead of holding out for mistaken ideals such as 'liberty'. This is also the thesis of Skinner's philosophical work *Beyond Freedom and Dignity.*

From the above, it will be clear that there is plenty to object to in the behaviourist program, should we be inclined to do so. However, from the point of view of our present concerns, the significant facts are that, whilst some behaviourist psychologists simply considered that the mental aspects 'drop out' of the question, or can be ignored, certain of the more extreme exponents actually argued that, due to their lack of objectivity, they cannot be regarded as real items in the world at all. This view influenced a number of anti-mentalist philosophers, who also came to be known as behaviourists. The best-known of these has been the English philosopher Gilbert Ryle (1900-1976). Ryle, whilst perhaps not being entirely happy with the label 'behaviourist', accepted that it might 'harmlessly' be applied to him. He is certainly the leading exponent of philosophy in the behaviourist spirit, though his version of it is a good deal more sophisticated than some.

Ryle's chief single work, in which he expounds this view, is his book *The Concept of Mind* (1949). In some ways it is difficult to sum up Ryle's own theory of the mind, since most of the book is devoted to attacking the accounts with which he disagrees. These are, he argues, systematically connected, since they have in common a misleading assumption about the mind, which Ryle regards as so pervasive that he calls it 'the official doctrine'. The official doctrine is, roughly speaking, the tradition of mind-body dualism which comes down from Descartes. It maintains that a person has, or is, two things, a mind and a body, and that there are mental entities, events and processes just as there are physical ones. It is this doctrine, Ryle says, which has perpetuated what he refers to as 'the myth of the ghost in the machine' – the idea of the person as a physical, mechanical thing, but inhabited by a ghostly, spiritual agent.

Well, as Ryle freely admits, we all constantly use language which seems to embody the idea of the ghost in the machine, or something like it. We not only say things like 'in my own mind', and 'a feeling inside me', but a host of other concepts, such as desires, beliefs, motives, intentions, seem to refer to inner and (to others) unobservable items. How can Ryle account for this?

The chief method which he uses to render these concepts harmless, is the *dispositional analysis* of the terms in question. Rather than seeing these psychological words as referring to things which are private to the subject of them, he analyses them as referring to *dispositions* on the part of people to engage in certain kinds of outward behaviour. Thus to say that a person *believes* something is not to say that he has an unobservable mental state of belief, but that he will act in particular ways under given circumstances: the belief that it is raining outside can be cashed in terms of a disposition to take an umbrella, etc. Similarly, to say that someone has a *desire* for a drink is to say that he will take steps to get a drink if possible, will not refuse one when offered, will tend to head for the bar, and so on.

This brings us to Ryle's characterization of the 'official doctrine' as a *category mistake*. In order to see what a category mistake involves, consider the example which Ryle gives to illustrate the notion. A visitor to England is shown round Oxford University: he is shown the colleges, libraries, laboratories and playing-fields, and then he asks, 'But where is the University?' His mistake was a category mistake in that he thought the University was something of the same *type* as colleges, libraries, etc., instead of something made up of them. In the same way, Ryle thinks that philosophers and others have been mistaken in thinking of the mind as something different from, but of the same type as, the body, in the sense that it has been thought proper to say that people have a mind *and* a body. Rather, Ryle argues, the mind is something constructed out of observable bodily behaviour and the dispositions which it displays.

What, then, of the existence of feelings and sensations, that chief bastion of the mentalist? Surely we cannot settle for a dispositional account of these, for are they not *par excellence* the mental items which are inaccesible to all but the person possessing them? To this, Ryle replies that the talk about such things is a product of the way in which language has been misused by mentalistic philosophers. What I observe at first hand, he says, are ordinary public objects in the world, not my own sensations or feelings. Like Watson, he seeks no reason to bring in a private, mental entity to stand between the physical stimulus and the physical response. Indeed he claims that, if we understood the issue properly:

> We have no employment for such expressions as 'objects of sense', 'sensible object', 'sensum', 'sense datum', 'sense content', 'sense field' and 'sensibilia'... They commemorate nothing more than the attempt to give the concepts of sensation the jobs of concepts of observation, an attempt which inexorably ended in the postulation of sense data as counterparts of the common objects of observation. It also follows that we need no private stages for these postulated extra objects, nor puzzle our heads to describe the indescribable relations between these postulated entities and everyday things.

Now in some respects, Ryle has been clearly recognized as correct. 'Sense data', the supposed *immediate* objects of perception (which might or might not correspond to real objects in the world) cannot be discussed and described in the way that public, physical objects can, for we have no public language in which to discuss them (remember Wittgenstein and the Private Language Argument). Nor should they be spoken of as though they were extra objects in the world, alongside the public and physical ones. Yet none of this alters the fact that there is such a thing as *the way in which things appear* to a person: there is *something it is like* to be him when observing a particular object, over and above what can be reported of him by another observer. The fact that this is so, and that we have no common language for talking of our private sensations, is the reason why we cannot make headway with such questions as 'Do other people see colours the way I see them?' Nor, despite what some philosophers have said, does there seem to be good reason for thinking this is not a proper question.

Here, Ryle seems to waver, for he sometimes seems to be denying this, and sometimes not. As the philosopher Stuart Hampshire has put it:

> ...Ryle has not decided whether he is saying (a) that no mental concepts 'stand for' imperceptible (=ghostly) processes or states: all 'designate' some perceptible or nearly perceptible (e.g. 'silent colliloquies) patterns of behaviour: or less drastically (b) that all statements involving mental concepts are in principle testable, directly or indirectly and in various degrees, by observation of the behaviour of the persons concerned.

It seems we must conclude that if what he is saying is the latter, then his method has not entirely succeeded in exorcising the 'ghost in the machine', and that if it is the former, then more argument is surely necessary. For how, on any ordinary under-standing, can we actually *equate*, for example, the belief that it is raining with the disposition to carry an umbrella? Even if we make the disposition more sophisticated, including also such things as wearing a hat, saying 'It's raining' and so on, there is still a logical gap between the behaviour and the belief; is it not still possible (as some people have suggested) that the person in question is a 'perfect actor' who, for reasons of his own, wants us to *think* he believes it is raining? The behaviourist can, perhaps, elaborate his account of the disposition even further, including the proviso that the person should not be intending to deceive, where the notion of *intending* is likewise cashed out in dispositional terms. Yet there seems to be more than a whiff of circularity about this. Furthermore, it is unlikely to satisfy us when it comes to feels and sensations: no amount of outward behaviour and dispositions is going to add up to a pain, to the pain *itself*. We will now move on, as promised, to consider an account of the mind which has links with both materialism and behaviourism: functionalism.

functionalism and Turing machines

A currently popular, though not always well-understood, ap-proach to the philosophy of mind is known as functionalism. The best way to go about understanding the family of views which come under this heading, is by considering some criticisms of materialism and behaviourism, both of which sets of criticism helped to give rise to the acceptance of functionalism. What makes some people hesitate before accepting a straightforwardly materialist position is the following consideration. It seems very unlikely that the physical state of the brain or whatever, which corresponds to, say, pain in a human being, is exactly the same physical state which corresponds to pain in another animal such as a squirrel. Thus to say that to be in pain *is* to be in this physical state begins to look implausible. What deters many people from accepting a behaviourist position, is their recognition that the inputs and outputs of mental states need not be always physical states – they might be themselves mental states. Worry gives rise to depression, and not just to nail-biting. Functionalism, at least on first sight, promises to remedy both of these difficulties.

According to the functionalist, mental states are functional states. That is to say, if an organism is in a given mental state, this state can be defined in terms of its causal roles. Thus the state of feeling thirst is that feature which is characterized by being caused by dehydration, and by causing the action of drinking. This is what thirst in one creature, or kind of creature, has in common with thirst in another, which makes them both cases of thirst and not something else (hence apparently overcoming the objection to materialism). Furthermore, we can say that thirst may cause not only drinking, which is a physical thing, but also, for example, thoughts of water, which are mental (thus seemingly solving one of the problems about behaviourism, which is that a single 'mental state' does not always have only physical inputs and outputs). Some functionalists trace the origin of this view back to Aristotle, though in the form which it now takes it is relatively recent.

It is interesting for our purposes that a quite popular form of functionalism involves comparing the mental states of an organism to the states of a machine. The most common machine version of functionalism is called Turing Machine Functionalism. A Turing machine is the simplest kind of computational machine, and is named after its inventor Alan Turing, whom we came across in chapter 5. A Turing machine is a *theoretical machine* in the sense that we don't need physically to build the machine in order to reap the benefits of the concept of such a machine, for its purpose is itself essentially theoretical. The original set of problems which the Turing machine idea was meant to illuminate were to do with the notion of calculability in general, and the usefulness of the Turing machine idea lay in the fact that it allows us to reduce all methods of calculation to a single, basic, underlying set of operations. A Turing machine may be thought of as having a number of *machine states*, and as reading symbols from squares along an endless tape. Some of the squares may be blank. The basic operations are performed by the machine in response to the combination of (a) the machine state it is in, and (b) the symbol it is reading in the current square. The *table* for the machine is what tells it what to do in a given situation, rather like the program of an ordinary computer. A machine table may look something like this:

S1, 1, R, S2
S1, 2, R, S3
S2, 1, R, S3
S2, 2, 3, S2
S2, 3, R, S1
S3, 1, 3, S3
S3, 2, 4, S3
S3, 3, R, S1
S3, 4, R, S1

The first line says that if the machine is in state S1 and is reading a 1, then it is to move one square to the right and go to state S2. The second line says that if the machine is in state S1 and is reading a 2, then it is to move a square to the right and go into state S3. The third line tells us that if it is in state S2 and is reading a 1, then it must move right a square and go into state S3. The fourth line says that if it finds itself in S2 and reading a 2, it is to print a 3 (erasing the 2) and remain in S2. The meaning of the remaining lines should be obvious. To illustrate the idea, let us take the fifth line and show how the machine deals with it.

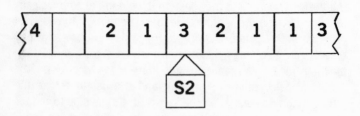

Figure 1

Figure 1 shows the situation just *before* the action has taken place. The machine is in state S2 (as indicated under the triangular head which 'reads' the tape), and is confronted with a 3 on the tape.

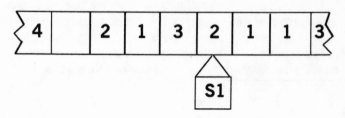

Figure 2

In Figure 2, we see how things look *after* the machine has obeyed the instruction. Having found itself in state S2 and scanning a 3, it has moved one square to the right and gone into state S1. (As an exercise, work out from the table what it will do *next*.) These two figures show what would be happening

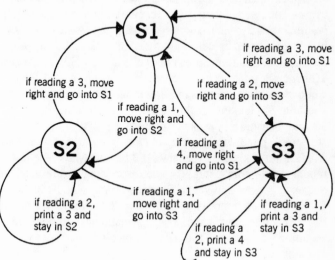

Figure 3

with the Turing machine if we actually built such a machine. A more abstract diagram, however, will allow us to depict the whole repertoire of the machine, i.e. all the actions prescribed by the nine instructions in the table. This is given in Figure 3.

After all this, it might be reasonable to ask: what is all this *for*? What good is a theoretical machine which obeys an withabstract set of rules laid out in a mathematical table? To begin to answer this, let us consider one, among many, of the things which this abstract specification of a machine may be taken to represent. Imagine a machine which dispenses cups of tea at a price of 15 pence per cup, and which accepts either 5 pence or 10 pence pieces. Whilst nobody is using the machine, it remains in its 'waiting state'. Let us take this to be state S1 in Figure 3. Now let the insertion of 5 pence correspond to reading a 1, and the insertion of 10 pence to reading a 2. It will be seen that on receiving 5 pence the machine moves to the right, which might be regarded as equivalent to 'waiting for the next coin', and goes into state S2, which therefore corresponds to 'waiting for 10 pence'. If, however, the machine receives 10 pence, it moves right and goes into state S3, which can be seen as 'waiting for 5 pence'. Now if it is in state S2 (waiting for 10 pence) and it receives a 5, then it moves right (waiting for the next coin) and goes into state S3, i.e. waiting for 5 pence. If, on the other hand, it is in state S2 and receives 10 pence, it prints a 3 (which we may interpret as dispensing a cup of tea) and remains in S2, whereupon it moves right and goes into S1, waiting for things to start all over again. If it is in S3 and receives a 5, it likewise prints a 3 (gives a cup of tea), stays in S3, and subsequently moves right and goes back into S1. But if it is in S3 and receives 10 pence, it has 5 pence too much; it therefore prints a 4 (corresponding to the action of dispensing-a-tea-and-giving-5 pence-change) and remains in S3, after which it moves right and goes back to S1, waiting for the process to start again. The tea machine described above therefore *instantiates* the Turing machine whose table was given above.

Now what the Turing machine functionalist suggests is that mental states can be seen as like the states (S1, S2 and S3 in the above example) of the theoretical machine. It will not then matter *how* the states are in fact instantiated (what the states physically *are*) – the same states can have different physical instantiations in different types of creature. For example, thirst in a camel will go along with a different physical state from thirst in a human being. What they have in common, however, which makes them both cases of thirst, is that they occupy the same role in the system; in the same way that what counts as a tea machine of the above kind being in state S3 is its relations with states S1 and S2. What that state *is*, is characterized by when and how it derives from S2 and results in S1 (or in remaining in the same state S3). Thus we may *build* the machine in electronic, hydraulic, steam-driven, or any other form: but what makes all cases of S3 cases of S3 is the functional role they perform – their causal relations with other states in the machine, including inputs and outputs. So whilst the materialist says that what all cases of thirst have in common is the physical thing, and the behaviourist claims that what they have in common is a behavioural feature, the functionalist says that the feature they have in common is *functional* – a common causal role. And the machine version of functionalism holds that this can be described in terms of a table for a theoretical machine such as the Turing machine.

the varieties of functionalism
Unfortunately, not all functionalists agree on what follows from this. Some functionalists are also materialists, and think that functionalism supports materialism (Armstrong and Smart, for instance, both agree with a certain version of functionalism). Others believe that functionalism entails the *falsity* of materialism. For example, David Lewis, who is on the side of Smart and Armstrong, argues that since it is in fact a physical state in all known cases which occupies the causal role corresponding to a functional state such as 'pain', the functional view must lead us to believe that pains are physical things. On the other hand, the non-materialist functionalists such as Jerry Fodor and Hilary Putnam point to the fact that the occupant of that causal role *need not necessarily* be physical: at least it

does not follow from the principles of functionalism as such, that it has to be. They stop short of *identifying* each functional state with a physical state, and regard the functional state as merely that which all pains, for example, have in common, which makes them pains rather than something else.

When someone claims that all instances of functional state such-and-such are in fact physical states with common physical characteristics (e.g. that every individual pain is a physical state with the same properties), he is known as a *token identity theorist* – a 'token' being an 'instance'. On the other hand, when a person holds merely that pain in general is physical though its embodiment may be different in different creatures, he is said to be a *type identity theorist*, which in a sense is a weaker position – he claims only to explain what type of thing pain is, and not what each individual pain is.

The fact that functionalism allows us, as we saw above, to characterize mental states in terms of other mental states does not, therefore, mean that the functionalist has to accept mental states as ineliminable. All it means is that we cannot eliminate Mental states one at a time. That is, we cannot give a reductive analysis of a single, isolated mental state; otherwise we end up being unable to give an account of some others. For example, if 'thirst' is typified by the fact that it gives rise to 'thoughts of water', then the 'thoughts of water' cannot be explained away, they cannot be eliminated, without making the concept of thirst unintelligible. A move which the functionalist can make, however, is to claim that mental states as a whole are eliminable; that is, that they are eliminable provided we eliminate them *all at once*. Thus, we cannot eliminate them singly by saying 'Mental state such-and-such is really only something-or-other', but we can do it by saying 'Mental states in general are really only this-that-and-the-other'. This leaves room for the functionalist to be also a materialist. But at the same time it leaves it open for the non-materialist to embrace functionalism. The fact is, that the materialist and non-materialist functionalists tend to understand functionalism in different ways. The materialists take themselves to be talking about actual states which occupy particular functional roles, whilst the non-materialists understand themselves as only saying something about what it is to be a state of a particular type.

This ambiguity helps us to show up how functionalism falls short of doing the job which we hoped it might do – of elucidating the connection between mental and physical states. For functionalism, broadly understood, is compatible with too many different points of view concerning this relation. In some of its forms, it is merely a version of Central State Materialism; in other forms, it is so non-committal about what *actual* mental states are, that it sidesteps the central question in which we are interested. For the broad-minded functionalist, the same causal role could, in principle, be filled by a physical state, an irreducibly mental state or 'spiritual' state, or indeed by some other kind of state of which we have no conception.

Despite the apparently promising connection, then, which some functionalists draw between human thinking and machine behaviour, it turns out that the merely theoretical character of the machine in question (its independence of any specific implementation) deprives it of the explanatory power which it appeared at first sight to possess.

Now before going on to discuss less extreme forms of monism, we will consider a relatively modern defence of the doctrine of materialism, but one which is essentially different from the kinds outlined above.

Davidson's anomalous monism

This mysterious-sounding theory is, in fact, a version of materialism, though not along the lines which we have seen earlier. It was propounded by the American philosopher Donald Davidson in an article published in 1970. Davidson's reasoning differs from that of, say, Armstrong and Smart, not so much in its conclusion as in its starting point. A typical materialist is likely to have, as one of his reasons for being a materialist, the fact that he believes there to be law-like correlations between certain physical events and certain events of the sort commonly called mental. For example, he will regard it is a 'law of nature' that when a particular event occurs in the brain, a given 'mental state' will be present in the person whose brain it is. Davidson's case depends, however, on the alleged *absence* of psycho-physical laws. Our correlation of mental and physical happenings is, he says, only a matter of rough generalization:

> ...if an event of a certain mental sort has usually been accompanied by an event of a certain physical sort, this often is a good reason to expect other cases to follow suit...The generalizations that embody such practical wisdom are assumed to be only roughly true, or they are explicitly stated in probabilistic terms, or they are insulated from counterexamples by generous escape clauses. Their importance lies mainly in the support they lend singular causal claims and related explanations of particular events. The support derives from the fact that such a generalization, however crude and vague, may provide good reason to believe that underlying the particular case there is a regularity that could be formulated sharply and without caveat.

What sort of regularity? Well, Davidson agrees, mental events are at least sometimes the causes and effects of physical events. And if two things are connected as cause and event, then this causal relation must be an instance of a *law*. But since there are no laws connecting mental and physical events, one of these must be reducible to the other, in order that we can preserve the idea of causal interaction. The one which must be reduced, Davidson argues, is the mental, since it does not constitute a 'closed system', whereas the physical does. What this means is that we can, in principle, find a physical cause for every physical event (there may also appear to be a mental one, but there will at least be some physical cause – a brain event perhaps); but we cannot find a mental cause for every mental event (the cause of a pain, for example, is usually a physical cause, and there is often no further mental event which causes *it*).

Two things should make us wary of accepting this position too readily. First, how seriously should we take the fact that detailed psycho-physical laws seem not to be forthcoming? Might it not simply be that establishing the appropriate correlations is too difficult owing to the enormous open-ended variety of physical and mental behaviour, when compared with the behaviour of inanimate objects? And why, anyway, is

Davidson so certain that every physical event can be ascribed a physical cause? It cannot be shown from experience, any more than can psychophysical correlations, and what is more, many modern quantum physicists actually reject it!

The second objection is more subtle, and concerns the fact that, if Davidson is right, some events will have both a physical and a mental *description* though they will 'really' be physical events. Now since, according to him, physical events all stand in causal relations, and therefore instantiate laws, and since he thinks mental events *don't* stand in law-like relations with physical ones, it follows that on his view some events are instances of a law under one description but not under another. But his starting-point was that mental events are sometimes causes and effects of physical ones. Yet his own theory dictates that mental events can be causes of physical ones only under their physical description, whereas it is fairly clear that the initial premise is attractive only if it is the *mental* descriptions of these events which is in question. We are surely more certain that stubbing your toe causes the feeling of pain, than we are that it causes such-and-such a brain state.

In the next chapter we will be looking at some other forms of monism, and also asking where the present part of the discussion is leading as regards our central topic.

8: more about monism

The monist-type positions which we glanced at in the last chapter were largely of a materialist or functionalist kind. Continuing to explore the many permutations of monism, we will at this point leave all forms of materialism and functionalism behind, and first of all look at a philosophical position which takes its starting point from a very different angle.

Strawson and the concept of a person

This is the view laid out in Peter Strawson's book *Individuals* (1959). Strawson's approach to the mind-body problem differs radically from any that we have looked at so far, in that he adopts the idea of a *person* as the central, primitive notion, rather than that of either mind or body as such. Once we have the concept of a person we can, according to Strawson, then go on to attribute mental as well as physical properties to persons. But it is first of all essential to our concept of a person that persons should be the kind of thing we can identify and reidentify. We must, in other words, be able to tell, in principle, which person is which: to tell one person from another, and be able to recognize a person as being the same from one occasion to another. This is because our concept of a person is a concept of an *individual* thing and not, for example, of a property or of a substance. Now minds, conceived of as purely immaterial, or abstract, things, are *not* such that they can be reidentified in this sense: if people *only* had minds, we would be literally unable to distinguish one person from another. It is the physical body which makes reidentification possible, and which therefore serves as the 'anchor' for our concept of a person. In Strawson's words:

> The concept of a person is logically prior to that of an individual consciousness. The concept of a person is not to be analysed as that of an animated body or an embodied anima. This is not to say that the concept of a pure individual consciousness might not have a logically secondary existence, if one thinks, or finds, it desirable. We speak of a dead person – a body – and in the same secondary way we might at least think of a disembodied person. A person is not an embodied ego, but an ego might be a disembodied person, retaining the logical benefit of individuality from having been a person.

Strawson goes even further, however, and claims that the possibility of attributing mental properties to ourselves depends on our being prepared, at least sometimes, to attribute them to other people. It will be noticed that this is an inversion of the traditional way of approaching the problem of other minds (which we discussed in chapters 2 and 3). It perhaps has more in common with the philosophy of Wittgenstein, in this respect, than have most other accounts. The traditional approach takes as primary the ability to attribute mental states to ourselves, and regards the possibility of attributing them to others as depending on it. Strawson, however, argues that since it was outward bodily behaviour which provides the anchor for our concept of a person, and therefore for our concept of a mind, it is by observing others that we acquire the concept, and not from observing ourselves. I don't actually *observe* my own behaviour, though I might be *aware* of it: I am the agent, and not a spectator. Only then, on Strawson's view, are we able to attribute mental properties to ourselves. He says:

> If, in identifying the things to which states of consciousness are to be ascribed, private experiences are to be all one has to go on, then, just for the very same reason as that for which there is, from one's own point of view, no question of telling that a private experience is one's own, there is also no telling that a private experience is another's...One can ascribe states of consciousness to oneself only if one can ascribe them to others. One can ascribe them to others only if one can identify other subjects of experience. And one cannot identify others if one can identify them *only* as subjects of experience, possessors of

states of consciousness.

The result of all this is an account of the relation between mind and body, according to which they are such that there is just one kind of thing – a person – to which *both* physical and mental properties are applicable, though persons are reidentified through the reidentification of their bodies, which is to give some precedence to the physical over the mental concepts.

It is perhaps difficult to tell, in forming an opinion of Strawson's view, whether he is standing the traditional problem of other minds on its head, or whether he is putting it back on its feet after its having been turned upside-down by earlier philosophers. One trouble with the Strawsonian account is that the reasons given for it do not really add up to a logically strict defence. He says that the mental cannot consist merely of private experiences, which is precisely what most people *do* think the mental consists of, since, if 'private experiences are all one has to go on', we would be unable in all cases to say *whose* experience the experience was. But to say that private experiences are what mental things *are*, is not the same as to say that private experiences are 'all we have to go on'. As we saw in earlier chapters, it is quite possible to believe in private, inner experiences, which nonetheless have public and outward *symptoms*. To point out that we could not form the *concept* of mind if we did not have other people's outward behaviour to go on, does not actually imply anything at all about the nature of mind *itself*. The nature of the thing which the word 'mind' refers to, if it does refer to a thing at all, is not guaranteed to be exhausted by the nature of those things by which we originally learned how to use the word. And it is with the nature of the mental itself with which we are concerned.

Of course, Strawson does not go so far as to deny that there is *any* 'inner' experience. The problem is, that he does not really give us an account of *its* relation to the physical world: to say that there is just one kind of thing to which both mental and physical properties are attributable, and that mental concepts are learned through observing physical behaviour, does not by any means add up to a theory of the relation between the mental and the physical.

It is, however, a move in a certain direction, and that is the direction in which we are going. For one aspect of Strawson's view is that it displaces both mind and matter from the centre of the stage, in favour of a concept which is neither exactly mental nor physical. Now at the time when Strawson was writing there was already a theory in existence which went further in this direction – the theory known as 'neutral monism'. Its most famous exponent was Bertrand Russell, and it is to his account of it that we now turn.

Russell's neutral monism
The theory of neutral monism comes originally from the American psychologist William James (1842-1910). Russell adopted it during a significant period of his career though he took some time to be convinced of it, and later abandoned it. It is called 'neutral' for the reason that it neither makes the mental secondary to the physical, nor vice versa. Rather, the neutral monist sees all mental and physical things as *constructed* out of something more basic, but something which is in itself neither physical nor mental. Russell sums up the outlines of neutral monism very succinctly in a well-known passage, and we will let him speak for himself:

> 'Neutral monism' – as opposed to idealistic monism and materialistic monism – is the theory that things commonly regarded as mental and the things commonly regarded as physical do not differ in respect of any intrinsic property possessed by one set and not by the other, but differ only in respect of arrangement and context.

Russell illustrates this idea by comparison with a telephone directory which has both an alphabetical and a geographical listing, so that every name appears twice, but in a different order. He goes on:

> The affinities of a given thing are quite different in the two orders, and its causes and effects obey different laws. Two objects may be connected in the mental world by association of ideas, and in the physical world by the law of gravitation. The whole context of an object is so different in the mental order

from what it is in the physical order, that the object itself is thought to be duplicated, and in the mental order it is called an 'idea', namely the idea of the same object in the physical order. But this duplication is a mistake: 'ideas' of chairs and tables are identical with chairs and tables, but are considered in their mental context, not in the context of physics.

It is important to recognize how heavily Russell's form of neutral monism depended on the fact that he was also a *constructionist*: he held the principle that, wherever possible, we should 'substitute constructions out of known entities for inference to unknown entities'. In other words, he believed that we should accept as basic only those things with which we are so well acquainted that we are in no doubt about their existence and nature; and that we should try to show how the more obscure things which we talk about, can be 'constructed' out of the basic ones. To 'construct' B out of A, in this sense, means to show how B can be understood in terms of A; so that acquaintance with A will, once we know how the construction works, allow us to understand statements about B without any trouble. Now the way in which we apply the constructionist principle will depend on *what* we take to be the kind of thing with which we are fundamentally best acquainted – physical objects, our own ideas, or whatever.

Russell thought what any person is best acquainted with is his own sense experience. He therefore sets about showing how both physical and mental things can be constructed out of sense experience. Sense experience is, of course, the private and immediate experience of an individual person. It is significant that, in his later neutral monist period, Russell allowed that the ultimate stuff out of which everything else is constructed includes not only our *own* sense experience, but also the experiences which it is reasonable to suppose that other people would have had, if they had, for example, been in a given place at a given time.

There are, then, two categories of things which we need to construct from sense experience: physical objects and minds. Physical objects present little problem, granted Russell's starting points. Minds are slightly harder. Russell begins by explaining that the 'self' which each of us is inclined to attribute to himself, is elusive. That is to say, if I try to capture what it is that I mean by my 'self', if I try, as it were, to 'turn the spotlight on itself', I am unable to discover anything in my own experience which corresponds to it. If we ask 'What are supposed to be the contents of the mind, or components of the mind?', we may regard them as falling into two categories. Into one category fall such supposed mental states as desire, belief, intention and the emotions. Now there are plenty of people who claim that we can do away with these, as far as counting them as genuine mental *states* is concerned; for there is nothing discoverable in us which corresponds to them (they have no *phenomenology*, as we say). An analysis can, however, allegedly be given in terms of behaviour: a dispositional account along the lines of Ryle. The other category is more difficult though, for into it fall sensations, feels, images: those things which constiture *one's own experience of* the world, the way things are 'from the inside'. But this is surely 'sense experience' itself. This, then, is what the mind is constructed out of, and what it is supposed to comprise. This shows how 'mental' and 'physical' things, in Russell's words, 'differ only in respect of arrangement and context'.

Neutral monism has some very attractive aspects. It prevents those of us who cannot swallow dualism, from having to choose between mind and matter as the more 'real', the dominant partner. However, it also has its drawbacks. Firstly, the way in which Russell presents it rather makes it sound as though, besides mind and matter, there is also some 'neutral stuff' out of which they are both constructed. If this were the case, all we would be doing would be adding a third category to those of mental and physical, and aggravating the problem. This is not what Russell intends, however. When we look at what it is that both the mental and the physical are constructed out of, on his account, we find that it is the very kind of thing which normally characterizes the mental: sense experience. For what else can 'sense experience' mean but things *as experienced*? In other words, our experiences themselves: our feels, sensations, call them what you like. In the next section, we will look at a view of mind and matter which has a great deal in common with Russell's, though perhaps it commits us to rather less.

double aspect theories

Those accounts of the mind-body relationship which are known as 'double aspect theories' trace their ancestry at least back to the Jewish Dutch philosopher Baruch (or Benedict) Spinoza (1632-77). Reacting against the dualism of Descartes, which we discussed in the last chapter, Spinoza thought it impossible that two substances as different as Cartesian mind and matter could interact with each other. For reasons of his own, which by no means all of us would wish to accept, Spinoza also thought that there could only ultimately be *one* substance. According to Spinoza this could be seen as Nature taken as a whole, or as God in whom everything exists. Having rejected the dualism of God and Nature, it was a reasonable step to reject the dualism of mind and matter. Yet once again Spinoza wishes to do justice to both, for he understands the claims of both. Thus he was led to a monism which came down neither on the side of mind nor of matter: a double aspect theory. Now a double aspect theory is one which holds that the mind and body of a person are two aspects of a single underlying reality, distinguishable from each other, but inseparable. As Spinoza himself expresses it, 'thinking substance and extended substance are one and the same substance, comprehended now through one attribute, now through the other'. Something of the same flavour as Russell's account comes across very strongly here.

But what is especially attractive about a double aspect theory is that it allows us to reject both the extremes of materialism and idealism whilst neither committing us to some third thing, nor threatening to collapse into idealism. Unlike Russell's neutral monism, a double aspect theory need not lead us, on the other hand, to postulate some neutral stuff out of which both mind and matter are constructed, nor, on the other, to regard the stuff out of which they are constructed as being mental stuff (which Russell comes perilously close to doing, though he does not wish to do it). The double aspect theorist need accept nothing more than the two aspects themselves. And if anyone says 'aspects of *what* – anything called an aspect must be an aspect *of* something', the double aspect theorist can claim that what there is to know about a thing is exhausted by the sum total of its aspects, and in particular that what there is to be known about persons is exhausted by their physical and mental aspects.

This is not meant to be a thoroughgoing defence of, or even elucidation of, double aspect theories. There is a great deal more to be said about this kind of view, and a great many varieties which such an account might take. This is intended only to make the point that the double aspect approach seems to be another step in the right direction, with regard to the way the exposition in this chapter has been developing. For it allows its adherents to reject the simple choice between mind and matter. No theory which forces us to make this false choice is going to do full justice to either. Although there are modern double aspect theorists, Spinoza remains the best known. Thus we seem at this point to have come, chronologically at least, full circle: for we began our look at the question of minds and bodies at the beginning of chapter 6 with Descartes, an older contemporary of Spinoza. But there is still one more kind of view to consider in the development of this exposition – that of Kant. The fact that it has been left until this point may be seen as reflecting both the way it fits into the structure of our argument, and also this author's sympathy with the Kantian position in general.

Kant and transcendental idealism

In some of what has gone before in this book, we have in fact been skirting around certain aspects of the Kantian philosophy without actually meeting it head-on; though the reader without much prior philosophical knowledge is unlikely to have recognised it. At the end of chapter 4 it was mentioned that Kant was the first person explicitly to identify certain arguments as transcendental arguments, a transcendental argument being an argument which begins from the facts as we know them to be, and proceeds to draw conclusions about what must further be the case in order for these facts to be possible. And earlier in this chapter we looked at the approach to the mind-body problem adopted by Strawson, whose own metaphysical views are derived partly from a certain understanding of the doctrines of Kant.

Immanuel Kant (1724-1804) lived his entire life in and around the University of Konigsberg, then in Germany, now the USSR. Kant is arguably the greatest philosopher of the modern period, sometimes being said to have synthesised and harmonised the major traditions of rationalism and empiricism which were current in the eighteenth century. As with most great and prolific writers, Kant's writings are not always easy to interpret, and it must be borne in mind that not everyone would agree with everything which will be said in the following sketch of his views which relate to the present topic. What is offered here can, however, be seen as a fairly orthodox account.

The Kantian approach to our subject must of necessity be approached a little obliquely, for Kant himself does not talk in terms of mind and bodies, much less of a 'mind-body problem' as such. Here the influence of Kant on Strawson is apparent in retrospect. The general metaphysical position held by Kant in his mature writings is known as transcendental idealism, a label coined by Kant himself. This position involves, initially, making a distinction between *things as they appear to us*, and *things as they are in themselves*.

This distinction is not as straightforward as it might appear on first sight. It is not simply that we are sometimes mistaken about the way things really are, as in thinking that something is green and discovering on closer inspection that it is blue. Rather, the way things appear to us, for Kant, is all that we can possibly know about them. Appearances which turn out to be in the ordinary sense untrue to reality, can be corrected only by reference to further appearances. The thing as it really is, however, can never be known to us at all, for the purely logical reason that all our experiences comes to us through the medium of our own faculties – sense organs, nervous system, and so on. A creature with a different sort of make-up (one of Nagel's bats, perhaps!) would experience the same object very differently, maybe not even by means of sight, sound, etc., at all.

If, then, there is a 'real' object underlying, and giving rise to, all the possible ways of experiencing it, then this 'object as it is in itself' must be independent of, or neutral between, all of these ways in which it presents itself to different kinds of percipients. And Kant believes that there must indeed be a 'real' object underlying the appearances. According to Kant, there can be no appearances without there being something *of which* they are appearances. Kant refers to the realm of appearances, or things as they appear, as the *phenomenal* world, and to that of things as they actually are in themselves as the *noumenal* world. It must not be thought, however, that Kant literally believed in two 'worlds': the phenomenal world is merely the noumenal world as it appears to us. And about this noumenal world nothing can be said, except that it must be postulated as necessary to explain the existence of the appearances, which is why the argument here is a transcendental one.

Where, then, do minds fit into this picture? Do they belong to the world of appearances or that of things as they are in themselves? If we have been following the argument so far, it will probably be clear that the answer is: neither wholly one nor wholly the other, since everything we are aware of has *both* aspects to it. Yet any given person only directly experiences one mind – his own. Nor (and this is crucially important) does a person even have experience of his own mind as it is in itself. In this respect, even one's own mind, insofar as one can know it, is just part of the world of experience, the phenomenal world. Thus Kant talks usually about the experience of one's own *self*, rather than of one's mind, lumping together everything a person can know about himself as phenomenal, as opposed to the noumenal self about which nothing can be known at all. (When what Kant has in mind is the traditional mind-body distinction he sometimes talks of 'inner' versus 'outer' experience.)

Yet although nothing can be known of the noumenal self, Kant regards it as indispensable if we care to make proper sense of things, just as he regards all other noumenal objects as indispensable. The chief reason for this is also based on a transcendental argument: for any experience to be possible, there has to be a subject which experiences as well as an object which is experienced. And the phenomenal self, being by definition an appearance, will not fill this role. Kant has two further arguments besides this for the concept of the noumenal self. One is based on the need to explain free will and moral judgement, but we will avoid going into this side of his work here. The other is rather obscure, and involves the claim that the existence, though not of course the nature, of this noumenal self accompanies all our experience, in the form of one's awareness of oneself as the subject of it.

Nothing, then, may be said about the noumenal self, except that it must exist, and possibly that it must be thought of as simple and indivisible, since it is what integrates and 'pulls together' all my perceptions, forming them into a unity – which is why my experiences, according to Kant, are able to present themselves as the experiences of the same person, rather than being mutually independent, disjointed and disembodied. We are now faced with two distinctions rather than the traditional one. For the phenomenal self is obviously closely related to the noumenal self, and stands with it over against the 'external world'; yet it stands with the external world, and over against the noumenal self, in that it is phenomenal, in common with everything else which can be experienced. The position seems, in other words, to be as follows:

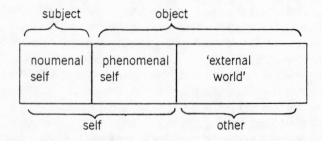

Figure 4

If we have understood the central ideas in the foregoing, we may now ask: what advantages, if any, does the Kantian position have over rival views, apart from the compelling force of Kant's arguments themselves? And how can it be of help to us here? Firstly, some of the unclarity of the physical-mental distinction are removed if we replace talk of mind and body with talk of subject and object – the thing which experiences and the thing experienced. Secondly, and partly as a result of this, we are able to retain the most useful insight of the double aspect type of theory, seen in the last section, whilst overcoming its greatest drawback.

To elaborate on this: the most attractive feature of the double aspect approach, as we noticed earlier, is the fact that it saves us from having to make a false choice between 'physical' and 'mental' and 'reducing' one of these to the other in such a way that only one of them turns out to be ultimately real. What we want is to be able to regard the mental and the physical as each possessing its own kind of reality. The drawback with a simple double aspect view, however, is that we are unable to answer the question 'Aspects of *what*?', for what we are left with is nothing but 'aspects', a position which Kant, at least, regards as untenable.

The way in which the Kantian approach can help us out of the dilemma is, perhaps, roughly as follows. By making the distinction between self and other cut across the distinction between subject and object, Kant shows, in effect, how we can retain the insight that the mental and the physical are somehow complementary rather than alternatives between which we have to choose, whilst at the same time allowing us to make a distinction between what is ultimately real and what is only appearance. For the wedge between self and other is driven in a different place from that between noumenal and phenomenal. Everything which can be an object of experience has, for Kant, a real, noumenal existence and also a corresponding appearance or appearances in the phenomenal world. This goes for ordinary physical objects. And since nothing can be said about the noumenal – about things as they are in themselves, the mental and the physical are, in this respect, on a par with each other: no question of choosing them arises. Of course, there exist other selves, besides what is, for me, the 'external world'. But they are all in the same position, and none is a part of the world of any other one – which ought to remind us of the reasons for which solipsism at first seemed inescapable in chapter 2. Kant's explanation of the necessity for other minds is different from Wittgenstein's, but is also based on transcendental arguments; we need not pursue it in detail here. It will suffice to say that Kant believes we must understand them by analogy with our own, but we should bear in mind that this is not the same thing as saying that we must *believe in them* because of any analogy with ourselves.

where do we go from here?

What bearing, then, does all this have on our main topic, that of the relationship between human mental life and the putative mentality of some machines? Firstly, the mind-body problem has to be taken seriously. If what we are after is a theory about the relation between the physical and mental aspects of machines, then this cannot be independent of some broader account of the relation between the mental and the physical in general. If, for example, we were central state materialists with regard to the human mind-body problem, this would give us a very different view of the conditions under which a machine could have a mental life, from that of a person who was convinced of the truth of Malbranche's occasionalism!

Secondly, it is hard to make convincing any view according to which either the mental or the physical aspect of a consciously thinking creature is 'really' only the other aspect under some different guise. In other words, it is hard to make either physical or mental reductionism plausible, since both appear to have features which are irreducible: the physical world seems to operate too independently of our wills and expectations for it to be 'all in the mind' (and in any case, whose mind, if we are not to be solipsists?); and the reality of the mental shows itself in the fact that no merely physical account of what is going on seems to add up to a description of the mental life as we experience it – any such physical account would be logically compatible with there being 'nobody at home', no consciousness present, at all.

Finally, it does seem that there exist ways of accounting for both mental and physical aspects of a thinking thing, without necessarily doing away with the distinction between what is ultimately real and what is secondary or merely apparent, though as we have seen, such an account is not going to be simple – and why should we expect it to be? If we are on the right lines in pursuing something like a Kantian approach to this issue, then we seem bound to accept this: that to be really consciously thinking is to have a viewpoint on the world, the nature of which is determined by the nature of one's own make-up. To be a subject, to have such a viewpoint, is to have a *particular* viewpoint, the nature of which is determined by the way in which one is able to experience. This fits in well with the earlier point, that the question 'Is this thing consciously thinking?' is the same as to ask 'Is there an answer to the question: what is it like to be this thing?' And, even if the argument from analogy for other minds will not suffice to guarantee their existence, yet if we are to accept other minds at all, we must understand them by analogy with our own, which gives us some justification for starting from our own make-up, and treating as good candidates for mentality just those things whose make-up is significantly like our own. It is to this, then, that we will be addressing ourselves in the next chapter.

9: the computer and the brain

To take stock of what has arisen from the foregoing, we may sum up as follows. The most attractive approach to the mind-body problem is one which does not force us to choose between mind and matter as two rival alternatives, but which allows us to recognize the different kind of reality of each, and give it its proper place. If we are not to end up as dualists, stuck with two different types of substance and a problem about how they can interact, we must accept that the mind and the body are not two things glued trogether, as it were, but two aspects of one thing, that the answer to the question 'What is it like to be that thing?' will depend on how the thing comes by its experiences. And the question 'Is there anything it is like to be that thing at all?' is only going to be answerable by comparing its channels of experience with those of creatures which we know to be capable of conscious thought – ourselves. Now one thing forces itself on our attention: there are some kinds of things which tend to exhibit the criteria for having a mental aspect as well as a physical aspect, and some which do not. Among those which *do* are human beings, and at least those species which are towards the top end of the phylogenetic tree. Among those which *don't* are tables and chairs, rocks, vegetables, and machines such as bicycles and lawnmowers. The next question is bound to be, where do the more 'intelligent' sorts of *computers* fit into this pattern in the light of this present position?

In order to bring us closer to answering this, we will next compare briefly the overall structure, function and composition of the typical computer, with that of the human central nervous system, asking what similarities and differences might reasonably be regarded as relevant to our question. We begin with a rough sketch of the working of a computer system.

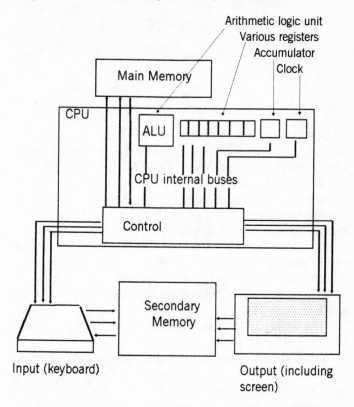

Figure 5: The main components of a conventional computer system

the mechanics of the computer

In one sense, there is no such thing as a 'typical computer', since computers come in lots of kinds, intended for different purposes and incorporating different patterns of construction (or 'architectures' as a computer scientist will say). However, it is possible to identify certain principles which are common to most machines, and certain fundamental components which any computer will contain in some shape or other. The five essential components of a computer (see figure 5) may be seen as:

(1) The central processing unit (CPU)
(2) The memory
(3) The input device(s)
(4) The output device(s)
(5) The communication path(s), or bus(es).

The CPU is the most important part of the computer and, in many modern machines, is contained on a single 'chip' (a small piece of silicon with an integrated circuit etched on to its surface). It controls and co-ordinates the operations taking place in all other parts of the system. The chief components of the CPU are: *the arithmetic-logic unit* (ALU) which actually performs the basic operations such as addition, subtraction, multiplication etc.; the *accumulator(s)*, which hold the number(s) currently in use by the ALU; the *clock*, which synchronizes those activities of the computer which need to be carried out 'in step' with each other by emitting a regular pulse; and the *registers*, which commonly include:

a *memory address register*, which holds the next memory address needed

a *memory data register*, which holds a piece of data recently brought from the memory

some *status registers*, which hold information regarding the present state of the system (e.g. whether or not we have to carry one from the last column of an addition)

some *general purpose registers*, which hold numbers needed soon or frequently by the CPU (since holding them in the main memory wastes time fetching them on each occasion)

a *program counter*, which keeps track of which instruction in a program is to be executed next

an *instruction register*, which holds the instruction currently being executed, and

a *stack pointer*, which indicates where the last item stored in the *stack* (a last-in-first-out storage space used by the CPU) is to be found.

The memory of a computer is obviously an important feature, since this is where most of the information is stored. Memory is divided into two kinds, *main memory*, and *secondary storage*. Main memory usually takes the form of a large number of 'cells' arranged in rows and columns. These cells normally consist, physically, of tiny electronic circuits on silicon, and each cell is capable only of holding one of two values (i.e. each can only hold a yes/no piece of information). The secondary storage is also contained in lots of yes/no units, but instead of being in the form of circuits constituting cells, it is usually retained by the magnetization of disks (hard or floppy), tapes, or cylinders, which can be loaded and unloaded from the computer, and stored quite separately when not required. Main memory may be lost when the machine is switched off, whereas secondary memory, of course, is not.

There are two other distinctions which ought to be made between types of memory. Firstly, *read-only memory* (ROM) is memory whose contents are a permanent part of the system, and cannot be altered by the user of the computer, wheras *read-and-write memory* (RAM) contains whatever has been put there by the user; main memory is partly ROM and partly RAM, whilst secondary storage is entirely RAM. Secondly, *random access* memory is memory which we can dive into at any chosen point (like putting a gramaphone stylus directly on to the track we require), wheras in *sequential access* memory we have to start at the beginning and work through until we come to the part we want (like trying to find a particular point on a cassette tape); main memory, disks and cylinders are random access, whilst magnetic tapes, of course, are sequential. The yes/no units of memory are known as *bits* (short for 'binary digits'). A group of eight bits is normally known as a 'byte'. Bits are also grouped into *words*, which vary in length depending on the machine in question, a common length being 16 bits (i.e. 2 bytes). A word is then the basic unit of information for that machine. Each word in the memory has a numerical *address*, that is a label for the particular location where it is to be found, identified by the rows and columns in which the memory is organized.

Input devices can be of various kinds. The most common is probably the keyboard, which receives messages typed in by the user by pressing keys corresponding to the characters of the alphabet, numbers, etc. Other sorts include, notably, those which bring information to the computer from some other device, such as a measuring instrument.

Output devices can be classified in a similar way. The most common sorts are the cathode-ray tube screen which is just like a television screen and is known as a VDU (visual display unit), and the printer; punched tape and cards used to be common, though they have now been largely superseded. Another kind of output is the transmission of information from the computer to control some other machine (e.g. to regulate a valve).

Here, a distinction should be made between *analogue* and *digital* representation of information. This is especially important with regard to input and output. We have already seen that a typical computer only handles yes/no questions (i.e. it only holds *binary* information), though in very large quantities. Clearly not all the possible input to the machine will be naturally of that kind. Of course, the input may consist of numbers alone, and numbers can easily be represented in binary form (by employing base 2 instead of base 10 for our arithmetic); but often it will be in other forms.

For example, suppose that the input is from a rain gauge, and that the computer is intended to turn on a sprinkler whenever the gauge falls below a given point. The information which forms the input does not naturally lend itself to being expressed as a series of discreet numbers, since it is a *quantity* which is constantly fluctuating: it invites not the question 'how many', but the question 'how much?' There are two ways in which a machine can handle this. On the one hand, it can incorporate some way of representing the information in a form analogous to that in which it naturally comes; this is, for obvious reasons, called *analogue* form, and a computer which employs such a method is known as an analogue computer. On the other hand, it can transform the information into digital form, by turning it into a series of discreet numbers (the readings being taken at intervals as close together as we wish); a machine employing this method is called a digital computer, and this is by far the most common sort. Clearly, the same considerations will apply, the other way round, in the case of output as in that of input. This distinction between analogue and digital methods of operation is crucial, and we shall be returning to it later.

To press on, *the buses* in a computer are the means by which one section or component of the machine is able to communicate with another. A bus consists of a number of lines along which messages can be sent, and buses tend to divide into: data bus (which carries the actual information we are dealing with at a given time), address bus (which carries information concerning where, in the memory, data is coming from or going to), and control bus (which handles information about what the system itself is currently supposed to be doing). The CPU will also probably have its own internal bus system.

Lastly, a computer will not run without *software* – the programs which tell the computer what tasks it is supposed to be performing. Apart from those programs which simply make the machine execute the specific task required by the user, two other pieces of software should be mentioned. One is the operating system, which oversees the total operation of the computer, enabling it to respond to users' programs, and doing 'behind the scenes' work such as memory management. The other is the compiler, which translates between the language the computer understands (consisting of the simple yes/no units) and the programming language used by the person who writes the programs; thus it allows us to 'talk to' the computer in a language tolerably similar to our own.

how the computer operates

In order to be clear about what is going on in the computer when it is in use, let us try to trace a single operation right through the system, taking as our example the operation of adding one number to another. It must be borne in mind that this is not a description of what happens in any given machine, but in some hypothetical machine which may be taken as typical. Suppose, then, that the instruction which the machine is to execute forms part of a program which has been loaded into the main memory, and let us take it from there:

(i) The program counter will hold the address of the next instruction, and send it to the memory address register.

(ii) A signal is sent to the memory telling it to read from the memory address register.

(iii) Suppose that the address which the program counter sent to the memory address register was address 200; the memory now sends the word in address 200 to the memory data register.

(iv) The memory data register now holds the instruction to be executed; for the purpose of the example, suppose that the instruction (held, of course, in the form of a binary number) decodes as 'add the contents of location 750 to the result of the last operation' and places the result in address 990.

(v) The result of the last operation will be in the accumulator, since that is where all results appear; suppose it is the number 3.

(vi) The number 750 is sent to the memory address register.

(vii) A signal is sent to the memory telling it to read from the memory address register.

(viii) The word in address 750 is sent to the memory data register.

(ix) Suppose that the word in 750 consists of the number 7; this number is sent to the arithmetic logic unit, which adds it to the 3 in the accumulator.

(x) Finally, the number 10, the result of the operation, is sent to memory location 990.

Notice that, though the memory has to hold two kinds of things – instructions and data – there is no *intrinsic* difference between them as they are stored. In other words, we can't tell simply by looking at a word in memory, what it is supposed to represent: the stored word 103478, for example, might mean 'add the contents of address 34 to the contents of 78', or it might just stand for the number one hundred and three thousand four hundred and seventy-eight. Which it actually means will be determined only by the context, which means by what has come before it in the program.

One reason why it has been thought desirable to go into a

little detail regarding the workings of computers, is that many people have a tendency to want to attribute 'real thought' to machines partly for the reason that they find something mysterious about how they work – just as there is something as yet mysterious about the way our own brains work. This temptation should be resisted. The first computers used cogs, gears and cards; and it is only for reasons of practicality that we cannot still build our immensely larger and more sophisticated systems in the same way. Few people would want to attribute genuine thought to a load of ironmongery; and yet electronic devices, being so small scale and their workings therefore hidden, have an unwarranted fascination for those who are quick to draw grandiose conclusions from every new development in the art.

from computers to artificial intelligence

What we have been looking at so far is computers, and a little of what it takes to make them run, the 'systems software'. But no computer considered by itself could possibly be said to be doing any thinking, even in a metaphorical sense. What makes the difference between mere computers and artificial intelligence is what we *do* with them. It is not the computer, but the whole *system*, including the programs which tell it what to do, which we call intelligent, or apparently intelligent. In this section we will look a little at some of the things people are doing, and have been doing, with computers, which constitute the discipline of artificial intelligence. First of all, however, we will have a brief glance at some of the tools of the trade for a worker in artificial intelligence.

Intelligent systems rely very heavily on *knowledge*. Leaving aside the question of whether we should put inverted commas round that word, we may divide up what the system needs in this respect into two parts: items of knowledge, and knowledge structures. The items are the individual things which the system is said to know something *about*. The designer of the system must therefore decide what kinds of things the system will be dealing with. Examples would be objects, properties of objects, relations between objects, numbers, geometrical figures, and so on. In some systems the concept of meta-knowledge is used.

Meta-knowledge is knowledge about what is known by the system itself (for example, being aware of just how much you know and how much you don't is a case of meta-knowledge).

But we also want to know how to put this knowledge together, and this is where knowledge structures come in. Probably the best-known form of knowledge structure is the state space. A state space is an arrangement of facts which allows the system to know where it can and can't go immediately from the state which it is currently considering. For example, the states might be arrangements of pieces on a chess board, and the state space would then be the arrangement of facts linking the different arrangements and telling the system which states can be brought about from which others. There are other forms of knowledge structure besides the state space. One is procedural representation, which allows the system to find its way around by an hierarchical arrangement of 'procedures', i.e. small chunks of a program. Another is production systems, which use a series of productions, which are rules, saying that *if* something is the case *then* such-and-such is to be done. A third is frames, which are, metaphorically, rather like arrangements of little pigeon holes.

Now the fact that artificial intelligence (AI as we shall henceforth call it, according to custom) relies heavily upon the idea of knowledge, has another consequence. Here we must make a distinction between two kinds of programming languages. Here we must make a distinction between two kinds of programming languages. Just as in English we have declarative sentences (or 'indicatives') such as 'The door is closed', and also imperative sentences like 'Close the door!', so there are two kinds of computer languages. One sort uses declaratives, telling the computer that something or other is the case, and the other sort uses imperatives, telling it to do something. The languages using imperatives are the older, and are referred to by the programmers and computer scientists as 'procedural languages' as opposed to 'declarative languages'. Declarative languages have, for obvious reasons, become increasingly important in AI. The two best known of these are PROLOG (whose name is meant to suggest that it is used for what is

known as logic programming), and LISP (which is also supposed to bring to mind the function of the language – list
processing). We now move on to glance at some of the areas
which make up AI, attempting both to get a panoramic (if
distant) view of the landscape, and also to try and understand
what kinds of claims are being made for it. We will take these
areas of interest in order.

natural language

It has long been an aim of workers in AI to produce systems
capable of learning, understanding and using natural languages
such as English, French or Dutch. In order to learn a language,
we need to learn implicitly or explicitly how to parse an expression in it; that is, how to recognize grammatical forms and
construct them for ourselves. On a computer, this is done by a
program called (not unreasonably) a parser. Parsers come in
two kinds: top-down and bottom-up. A top-down parser starts
by considering the rules for the 'goal symbol' (the symbol we
are trying to recognize, i.e. a properly constructed sentence) and
goes through the different ways in which it could be constituted,
until it finds one which matches the data it is given. A bottom-
up parser conversely starts from the symbols it is given as data,
and tries to find legitimate ways of combining them into larger
units, and finally into a complete sentence.

The syntax of natural languages is, however, notoriously
hard – much more complex that that of artificial languages –
and contains many ambiguities. When it comes to writing a
program which will not only understand but generate English
sentences, we face two difficulties. One is that it will need an
enormously large data base of facts, many of them just very
ordinary, trivial facts about the world, in order to stand any
chance of being able to take part in a dialogue with a human
language-speaker. We tend to forget the sheer quantity of
information which each of us carries around and which allows
us to communicate with each other. The second difficulty is
that of making the program sensitive to conversational
situations, which are of course social situations. How we
understand what is meant by something which is said to us

depends greatly on the context in which it is said. It was the failure to face both of these difficulties which led to the comical results generated by ELIZA, which we saw in chapter 5. An extension of language recognition is machine-translation, and many of the problems which have to be dealt with are similar.

expert systems

Expert systems are vast systems which hold a store of knowledge in a data base, and which can be consulted by users wanting a decision based on the vast amount of data such systems can hold, and exploiting their ability to access it and process it very quickly. An example would be a medical expert system designed so as to hold a store of information about symptoms and diseases, so that a doctor could enter a patient's symptoms and get a very fast opinion on what the patient might be suffering from. The information is, of course, initially entered by doctors who have learned it from experience or from other doctors, and new information may be entered. Thus the system is said to have two modes: consultation mode (when it is giving an opinion or a decision or a piece of information) and knowledge acquisition mode (when it is 'learning' something). A further aspect of expert systems is that their constructors have often designed them in such a way that the system can explain *how* it arrived at a particular answer – which might sometimes tell us as much as the answer itself. Besides being used for actual consultation, expert systems can also be employed as an efficient way of teaching a subject, for the novice can use it as a kind of encyclopaedia. The discipline of constructing expert systems is sometimes known as 'knowledge engineering', and employs many of the tools which will be discussed in a moment when talking about problem solving.

problem solving

Many aspects of AI involve problem solving techniques, and the subject is fruitfully studied in its own right. It includes such topics as problem reduction, searching, and deduction; all of which are aspects of the way in which an intelligent system goes about solving a problem. Problem reduction means breaking down the problem into smaller 'sub-problems', then breaking these down further, and so on until it sees how a solution is possible. Searching is an important topic in computing generally. It oftens happens that a program has to search a given collection of data in order to find the one which fits a particular requirement. For example, a chess playing program would have to search through a number of possible moves to find the one which would have the desired results and none of the undesirable ones. The total structure of possibilities is called the 'search space'. Deduction is, of course, reasoning; and in order for the system to be able to draw conclusions from the premises which it has, it must have at least the elementary rules of logic built into it. Just as we found there were two directions in which a sentence parser could reason, there are also two directions in which a problem solving program can reason. It can use *forward reasoning*, which begins with the given situation and tries at each stage to bring it nearer to fulfilling the goal condition, or *backward reasoning*, which starts from the goal condition and breaks it down into sub-goals, then breaks those down, and so on until all the final sub-goals are fulfilled by the given situation. Thus a bottom-up parser might be said to reason forwards, and a top-down parser to reason backwards.

Among the specialized areas within problem solving are theorem proving, which is of particular interest to logicians, mathematicians and, of course, computing scientists, and game playing. Computers can be programmed to play many games very well, even games as complex as chess, which was mentioned above (though there is no existing chess-playing program which cannot be beaten by a master). There even exist chess-playing programs which are capable of improving their own performance by learning from experience.

vision and pattern recognition

For some purposes it is necessary to have machines which can 'see', and which can recognize certain patterns in what they 'see' so that they can reidentify situations and behave accordingly. Seeing, in human beings, involves not just passively receiving stimuli through the eyes, but also a great deal of interpretation, most of which is done subconsciously. It is to be expected, then, that building a system which is capable of 'seeing' and making sense of what it 'sees', will be a complex task. It must be programmed to recognize certain configurations of lines and corners, in such a way as to allow it to pick out geometrical shapes. It must also be made to have some grasp of perspective – to interpret the input data as three dimensional objects, and to identify their relative spatial positions, which object is behind or in front of another, and so on. This is an aspect of 'pattern recognition', though there is more to pattern recognition than the identification of visual patterns – natural language programs, for example, may be said to employ pattern recognition in looking for certain configurations of words in the input data. Some aspects of visual pattern recognition are extremely difficult to program into a machine. The recognition of people's faces, for instance, which is very important in human life, and which we are quite good at, is almost impossible for an artificial device. One reason for this, is that we know very little as yet about how we ourselves do it. The importance of having real (as opposed to merely symbolic) input from the world, and being able to make sense of it, will be seen in the next chapter to be of great philosophical importance.

voice recognition

Another aspect of it is voice recognition, which of course is one aspect – the most important aspect – of the interpretation of incoming sound. Its significance for the future of interaction between human beings and intelligent machines is obvious. Research in this field began by devising systems capable of recognizing single words when spoken to them through a microphone. The next step was to get them to identify correctly connected sequences of words, which is especially difficult due to the way in which words run into one another in the spoken language, and the sounds of words alter depending on those of the surrounding words. Other difficulties are that the sounds which we give to words vary depending on individual speakers, on regional dialects, and on the social context and emotions of the speaker (whether said with surprise, delight, disbelief etc.). Some success has been achieved in this field, with systems having a vocabulary of around a thousand words. (Compare this, however, with the enormous vocabulary of a language such as Japanese.)

robotic control
Another aspect of interaction with the world, apart from the interpretation of incoming data, is the ability to manipulate the world – here the causal interaction is in the opposite direction. Robots are, of course, already extensively used in industry, in the manufacture of cars for example. These robots are very far from the quasi-human robots of science fiction. Most actual robots consist only of a single arm: the task of making such an artificial arm function intelligently is sufficiently difficult in itself. Amongst other things, it requires some of the techniques of 'problem solving' discussed above. The 'state space' for the robot will be a set of facts about its physical surroundings, known as a 'world model'. This will be given in terms of a co-ordinate geometry. What is also required is some equivalent of the kinesthetic sense in human beings: this is the sense which tells you where the parts of your body are, but 'from the inside', as it were, so that you know what position your own arm is in even with your eyes shut. The robot will, then, be rather in the position of a person with closed eyes, being told 'go left one unit, down two units, right one unit' and so on. Unless, of course, we combine machine vision with robotic control, so that the system discovers for itself where things are, and can then obey instructions about what to do with them.

learning
We saw above that there already exist, for example, some chess-playing programs which are capable of learning from experience and thereby improving their play over a certain number of games, as a human player does. This idea of building a learning faculty into an artificial system clearly has a large bearing on the enterprise of attempting to stimulate real human intelligence. We have already seen some successes in 'auto-

matic programs' i.e. programs which write programs, and some headway is being made with programs which are self-modifying – which can re-write themselves.

personal qualities

Many people feel that, even with all this intelligence, or 'intelligence', there is something about human beings which the artificial system fails to capture. Some work has been done on attempting to program personal qualities into a system – especially, of course, in natural-language-using systems which interact with human beings. Opinions vary concerning the success of existing attempts and the prospect for future ones in this direction. It is perhaps significant that the most convincing results have been achieved where the simulated personality was intended to be in a neurotic or psychotic condition characterized by a limited repertoire of behaviour.

Before considering the bearing of all this on the issues with which we are concerned, let us move on to the second topic of this chapter, which is meant to invite comparision with the above. This is an excursion into the physiology of the central nervous system.

the mechanics of human thought

What follows is an even rougher outline of the organization of the physical apparatus of thought in human beings, than that which was given above of the organization of the computer. It is intended merely as an indication of the basic structures and their functions, and not as a *vade mecum* of brain surgery! It must also be borne in mind that the workings of the human brain are far less well understood than those of the most sophisticated computer. With a computer, we work from man-made blueprints to the finished machine: with the brain, we start from the complete article and try, as it were, to reconstruct the blueprints.

The section of the human anatomy which is uniquely associated with thinking is the *central nervous system*, the chief components of which are the brain and the spinal cord (the chief pathway through the nervous system). Of these, the brain is by far the more important to us here. The building blocks of which organisms are made up are, of course, *cells*. In the nervous system, these take the form of *nerve cells*, or *neurones*, as they are usually called. Neurones have the special feature of being subject to a kind of electro-chemical event known as *arousal* of a neurone. When aroused, the neurone 'fires', i.e. discharges an electrical impulse. This impulse can cause the arousal of nearby neurones, thus being capable of setting up a chain reaction. The gaps between neurones are known as *synapses*, and the arousal of one neurone by another obviously takes place across the synapse.

The opposite of a state of arousal is a state of *inhibition*. If a region of the nervous system is inhibited, this means that the arousal of nerve cells is inhibited by a special mechanism: for example, if you thrust your hand close up to a hot fire, your nervous system will automatically inhibit the nerves tending to move the hand in the direction of the heat, so that your hand in involuntarily withdrawn.

This brings us to the distinction between the *autonomic nervous system*, and the part which is concerned with conscious thought. This distinction is of obvious significance for our purposes. The autonomic system deals with those functions of the body which do not involve conscious thought, such as breathing and the circulation of the blood (things we can do in our sleep). The non-autonomic part of the nervous system handles those functions which are subject to conscious control. It is not, however, easy to separate the physical areas of the brain into autonomous and non-autonomous categories.

When we begin to look at the division of structure and function within the brain, we find that it too falls naturally into five parts (see figure 6). These are:

(1) The cerebral hemispheres

(2) The interbrain, consisting chiefly of the thalamus and hypothalamus

(3) The midbrain

(4) The afterbrain, comprising the pons and the cerebellum

(5) The medulla oblongata.

Leaving what is probably the most important until last, we may very roughly sketch the main respective functions of these regions as follows.

The thalamus serves to integrate incoming nerve impulses from the sense organs, and relays them to the cerebral cortex (which we shall look at in a moment).

The hypothalamus deals largely with drives and their satiation (arousing and inhibiting as appropriate) including eating, drinking, sleeping and reproduction (by means of sex hormones), besides some aspects of emotional expression; it also controls the pituitary gland (the most important of the glands, which secretes hormones into the blood), and controls the balance of water in the body.

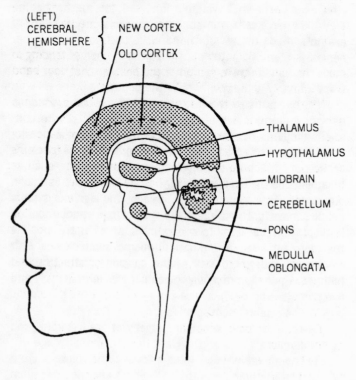

Figure 6 Structure of the human brain

The midbrain handles some simple reflexes concerned with seeing and hearing (for example the movement of the pupils of the eyes).

The pons contains the points of origin of some of the *motor nerves*, which are the nerves taking information from the brain to other parts of the body to initiate action (e.g. the motor nerves controlling bodily movement and posture originate in the pons); it also contains the terminations (i.e. the 'other ends') of some of the sensory nerves (which are the ones going in the opposite direction, taking information from the body to the brain), especially those to do with the sense of touch, with pain, with bodily temperature, and with hearing and the position of the head.

The cerebellum deals with the co-ordination of posture and locomotion (walking, running, etc.).

The medulla oblongata is really an extension of the spinal cord; it contains and integrates both sensory and motor pathways (of which there are many in the nervous system, all with specialized functions) and also handles the automatic functions of blood circulation and respiration.

The cerebral hemispheres are complex structures, dealing largely with perception and the interpretation of incoming sensory information, and with learning and memory. A hemisphere may be divided into two regions, each of which is known as a cortex. The *old cortex* is the simpler, and is found in many animals other than man. It regulates certain aspects of the body, and of the emotions, and includes a 'motor area', a 'sensory area', and an 'association area' which deals with associating and co-ordinating ideas to form coherent mental patterns. The *new cortex* only appears in this form in man, and is evolutionarily more recent, as its name suggests. It contains a number of 'lobes', notably:

the occipital lobes which are concerned with sight

the temporal lobes dealing with hearing and language

the parietal lobes which integrate sensory information from skin and muscles, and

the frontal lobes which are to do with movement and posture.

The new cortex also handles some associative functions more sophisticated than those in the association area of the old cortex, and which are still very imperfectly understood. Further- more, the new cortex *in the left hemisphere only* contains a *speech centre*. The cerebral hemispheres, then, form the area of the brain most associated with the activities which we think of as being intelligent and voluntary, and also with personality, disposition, temperament, and ethical thinking. It should also be noted, in passing, that the main connections between the left cerebral hemisphere and the rest of the body, are with the *right* side of the body, whilst the right hemisphere connects principally with the *left* side.

What we cannot do here, as we did in the case of the computer, is to trace a particular operation right through the system, and show in detail what is involved. We cannot do this, not simply from lack of space, but because it cannot be done: as was pointed out at the start of this section, we are only just in the process of 'reconstructing the blueprints' of the central nervous system. Prompted by this consideration, then, we will go on to ask what seem to be the major overall similarities and differences in principle between human thought mechanism and the working of a computer or intelligent system. This, it is to be hoped, will shed some light on the question of how far the physical make-up of (some) machines invites us to attribute a mental as well as a physical aspect to them.

some similarities

The most obvious, and seemingly trivial, similarity between machines and the human brain, is that they are both physical objects. Despite the apparent triviality of this observation, there is a point to it. For if we accept, as we have, that the seat of thought in a human being is the brain, then the answer to the question 'Is it possible to have a physical system which really thinks?' is already answered in the affirmative. And oddly enough, it is this question which has been a major source of contention between writers in the past. However, it is of course open to those who answer this question in the negative, to expand upon it by saying something like 'a *purely* physical system'. Thus, whilst admitting that the brain plays an important role in human thought, the anti-materialist may still wish to insist that real conscious thought is nevertheless impossible without some shadowy non-physical ingredient. And naturally, a person who wishes to insist on this will be very hard to answer, for reasons similar to those for which the solipsist was difficult to answer: direct evidence either for or against his position is impossible to come by (unless, of course, by 'non-physical ingredient' he happens to mean merely something like structures, patterns, rules or principles, in which case the argument will be of a rather different sort).

Further, it is clear that human brains and computers do some of the same jobs, though the extent to which even this is true is often exaggerated. For example, the exponents of artificial intelligence sometimes talk as though the creation of a computer system which matched the intelligence of a human being would be equivalent to simulating human intelligence, forgetting that human beings have many other qualities other than intelligence. Conversely, some of the things which machines are very good at (such as doing huge 'brute force' searches through masses of data) are things at which human beings are quite poor. This is perhaps a good point at which to emphasise the fact that we must beware of the idea of artificial intelligence as merely the mimicking of human intelligence, as though the whole purpose of designing intelligent machines were to create electronic replicas of ourselves.

But what most concerns us at this point, is the existence of some alleged similarities between the structure and operation of the two physical systems, i.e. the human brain and certain sorts of modern computer. One reason why this is important, is that if it can be shown that there are significant similarities of structure and function between them, this will strengthen the case of those who argue that genuine thought in machines is possible, and weaken the position of the sceptic who points out the lack of criteria for deciding how likely it is that this might be the case.

Firstly, it is easy for it to appear, on the surface, that both the brain and the computer use *language*. It seems, as we noted in chapter 4, that is is language which enables human beings to have the capacity for concept-formation, and hence for thought, that they have. It further appears to be the case that we have an inbuilt capacity for learning and using language, and to respond to verbal stimuli. And is it not also the case that the computer represents things to itself linguistically?

Unfortunately, this is not really true. For the 'verbal' abilities of computers are largely illusory. For a computer to 'recognise' a word, for example, it must go through the list of all the words it 'knows', and check the present one letter-for-letter against each. Compare this with the instantaneous recognition of a familiar word, of which people are capable. In the case of recognising faces, the difference is even more striking. Of course, it is possible that the same sort of thing is going on as in a computer whenever we recognise a word or a face, except unconsciously and very quickly. However, even this seems not to be quite right. We will have more to say about representation in a moment.

Secondly, and more importantly, it is often remarked that both the brain and the average computer, ancient or modern, work on the binary principle. That is, they are both composed of elements which have two states – 'on' and 'off'. In the case of the brain, these elements are the neurones, whilst in the case of the machine they are sometimes like electronic switches. All the 'higher level' operations of both, so the story goes, are built up in much the same way from essentially the same sort of ultimate components.

The trouble with this supposed parallel is partly that it seems not to be strictly true, since the neurones of the brain have been shown to operate partly on a binary digital principle, but also partly on an analogue (continuous rather than two-state) basis. It may be that the binary ingredient is the important one with regard to the way in which thought processes are brought about, and that the analogue element is subsidiary to this function. But moreover, the firing or non-firing of neurones in the brain does not really correspond to the opening and closing of switches, or 'gates' in a computer's circuits: the brain does not appear to use these binary operations in a way analogous to the way they are used in a switching network, as logical operations, but merely as ways of opening or closing various communication channels. Or at least, it has never been shown that there is a more significant resemblance in this respect.

However that may be, it does not affect the next point, which is that even if it were shown that this parellel holds, it would still be unclear what would follow from it. For, although we would be assured that, at bottom level, something like the same components were being used, the analogy would still be so general as to leave things hopelessly vague. Many things work on a binary principle besides brains and digital computers, and to argue the possibility of conscious thought in machines direectly from their binary nature would be a bit like arguing that a sufficiently sophisticated radio could be made to do the job of a spaceship, since both have transistors in them!

some differences

If the supposed similarities between the operation of a computer and that of the human brain seem much thinner than is sometimes supposed, the most obvious differences are comparatively profound. Perhaps the most significant of these (and maybe even so glaring that it is often overlooked) is the organic nature of the brain, contrasted to the inorganic, mechanistic character of a computer or computing system. Human nervous systems grow, whereas machines are built. Another, closely related, difference, lies in the material out of which brains and machines respectively are built: machines being composed of 'hardware' whereas our nervous systems are composed of what someone has christened 'wetware' i.e. organic tissue.

Yet the trouble with picking these things out as significant differences is rather like that of highlighting the supposed similarity of being based on the binary principle, which was discussed above. For it is seriously unclear what conclusions, if any, can be drawn from such a fact. The idea that this difference can be used to drive a wedge between the 'real' thought of human beings and the merely artificial 'thought' of machines, seems once again to be based on nothing stronger than the assumption that things are good candidates for genuine thought only insofar as they resemble us in certain ways. The problem here clearly lies in the question: *Which* ways, *which* resemblances are important?

Two things are worth mentioning here. Firstly, the structure of a thing would seem more important in this respect than the material out of which it is made. There seems to be no good reason why carbon-based creatures as such should have the capacity for thought whilst similarily structured creatures composed of other substances should not. Secondly, however, there is an important qualitative difference between organic and non-organic things, which lies in the capacity of the organic to interact with its environment in ways in which the inorganic cannot. This has been touched on already, and will be discussed in more detail in chapter 10.

One other result of the inorganic nature of machines, is that their parts can be swapped about in a way in which the parts of people cannot. Leaving aside such tricky issues as that of the implications of brain transplants, we may point to a feature such as the peripheral memory which computers have. Is there anything connected with human beings to compare with this? Can such things as books, libraries and tape recordings be regarded as human peripheral memory? The answer seems to be: not in quite the same sense. All of these latter are just part of the external world for a human being, whereas they are actually 'loaded into' a machine. The computer makes no distinction between those bits of software which are 'part of' itself and what is merely perceived or read from without. Even a machine's operating system which we can, perhaps, think of as the equivalent of a human being's personality, may be stored peripherally, and only loaded when required.

Another, and slightly more technical way in which the human brain has sometimes been identified as unlike a computing system, is to do with the fact that they seem to represent the objects of their thought in radically different ways. As we have seen, a computer is apt to hold a given piece of data in a particular location. Thus on the whole it is true to say that if we ask 'Where in this machine is the representation of Mr. Jones, or of Paris, or the Financial Times Index, held?', there will be some determinate answer to the question, in terms of particular chunks of the machine's memory. It seems characteristic of the brain, on the other hand, that representations are not localised, but 'distributed'. That is to say, we could surgically remove any given portion of the brain without necessarily destroying any individual representation – and not because there is a duplicate, but because that representation did not reside in any one specific location in the first place. This has sometimes been explained by reference to the example of the 'Grandmother Neurone': if representations in the brain were localised as in most computers, then there ought to be some cell, or maybe cluster of cells, which correspond to the concept 'Grandmother', such that, if we removed that cell or cluster of cells, the patient would be unable to think about his, or any other, grandmother! All his other concepts would remain in place, but that specific one would be lost, until he reacquired it by learning. This, however, is not the case – indeed, it is barely conceivable – which gives rise to the supposition that representation in the brain works on a different principle from representation in the kind of computer described above – the usual kind, in this respect.

Partly in response to this challenge, some recent workers in Artificial Intelligence have developed a kind of system whose operation with regard to representation (and therefore, importantly, to learning also) is claimed to resemble that of the human brain much more closely that any hitherto constructed, and to embody a qualitative difference of principle from that of the traditional computer. This departure is worth a special mention here, and we will conclude this chapter with a brief look at it.

machines that mimic the mind?
The kind of machines, or rather of machine 'architecture', which are currently in vogue tend to go under the generic heading of 'connectionist'. Thus connectionism, as it is known, has a claim to a special place in present-day thinking about the design of machines intended for use in the field of Artificial Intelligence. As suggested above, these architectures differ from traditional approaches to computer organization in the way they approach

the representation of the objects with which they are supposed to deal. Representation in connectionist architectures is meant to be 'distributed' (as it appears to be in the human brain) rather than 'localized' (as in the traditional computer structure).

What makes this possible, according to the exponents of this kind of design, is that, instead of having a single central processing unit (CPU), or a few similar processors, the connectionist machine contains a large number (potentially many thousands) of processors, which are correspondingly far simpler than those of the more conventional machine. The idea is that these 'processing units' should operate in parallel, each performing a very trivial message-passing function. The crux of the strategy is that, rather than an object being represented within some one element, or group of elements in the machine, the representation resides in the *connections* between the elements. These connections may have varying strengths, making it possible to build up a potentially enormous number of possible configurations. Once we see the representation of the object, or concept ('grandmother' or whatever) as being retained in the pattern of connections and connection strengths, we can understand how this differs from the conventional computer architecture, and at the same time how it can be claimed that such structures reproduce the way in which concepts are grasped and retained in the brain more faithfully than in any other kind of device hitherto developed.

It will also be fairly clear why proponents of the connectionist argument claim that machines constructed on these principles are actually able to *learn*, rather than merely spoon-fed with data. For concepts can be implanted gradually, an element at a time, each augmentation of a connection-strength rendering it easier for representations to be further built up along the pathways already established. As is apparently the case with human beings, the acquisition of concepts, or of associations between them, need not be an 'all-or-nothing', 'on-or-off' affair, but rather a matter of gradual building, strengthening, and, of course, adjustment where necessary. In other words, a process of genuine learning.

It seems, then, that whilst we have discovered the conventional computer and the human brain to be very widely different in their structure and functioning, there are signs that research may be moving in the direction of *rapprochement*. Whilst it is fairly clear that no currently extant machines look like good candidates for doing the same jobs (much less in the same *way*) as human nervous systems, there appears to be no reason in principle why machines should not be constructed which perform the same kinds of tasks by analogous means. Of this, more in chapter 11. For the present, however, we will pursue our discussion in the light of what has already been said, bearing in mind especially the considerations which were raised in chapter 5 regarding the significance of communication as a guide to what might or might not be 'really thinking'.

10: some further arguments

The last point is probably the most important of all. As we saw earlier in the book, the kinds of machines to which people are often tempted to ascribe conscious thought are commonly ones with no human-like qualities at all. We have noticed in the last chapter, however, that some machines in the area known as artificial intelligence do behave in a number of human-like ways. Now in chapter 5 we asked the question 'How could we get a computer to use genuine (as opposed to merely 'canned') language?', though no answer was given to this question. It is time to draw some of these threads together.

the importance of sentience
Might it be that the ability to do what some 'artificially intelligent' machines do, to play an active role in the world, to interact with and manipulate one's environment, plays a critical role in our ability to use language in the full sense? Most modern thinkers would certainly say this is so. The argument for it is, roughly, that it is in this kind of interaction and manipulation that we learn to apply the concepts which, taken together, make us into language-users. Here, we can also see what is wrong with the temptation to attribute real thought to a machine which does no more than sit on a desktop: there is no way (linguistic or otherwise) in which it could have *learned* the concepts which would have to be the tools of its thought. But having recognized that a static, inanimate machine has no way of acquiring concepts, we must not therefore assume that the only prerequisite for thought is animation, even if by that we understand

systematic movement, manipulation and so on. What will also be required is some form of perception, in other words *sentience*.

The reason for wanting to say this, is that if machines are to be supposed to think, there has to be something which they think *about*. Here, it is perhaps appropriate to take a slight detour via the concept which we met in chapter 3, of *intentionality*. We will remember that intentionality is the property of being about something, i.e. of having an *object*. It occurs in language, for sentences, speeches and books can be about something; and the reason why it can occur in language is that it occurs in the mind – our thoughts are thoughts about something. Now the philosophers who make use of the concept of intentionality tend to be divided over the question of whether all of what is mental is intentional or not, that is, whether there can be non-intentional mental states. Those who believe there can, point to such mental states as being in pain, which appears to have no object, whilst those who hold that the intentional is co-extensive with the mental argue that being in pain can be regarded as a state of mind of which the pain is the intentional object. Now although we have hitherto accepted mere sensations as being sufficient for mentality (for there being something it is like to be the thing in question), it is important to recognize that a creature which had nothing but 'raw feels' would hardly be a good candidate for being a thinking thing. And furthermore, it is thinking rather than feeling which machines are supposed to be good at. Either way, there is certainly a point to saying that true thought must be, at least sometimes, *about* something.

From this it follows that the feels and sensations, if not sufficient, are at least necessary to thought. For they form our link with the outside world, the world of things that can be thought about. If we are tempted to suppose that a non-sentient creature can nevertheless be doing some real thinking, we might like to consider the following example, the outline of which was invented by the philosopher John Searle. Imagine yourself to be alone in a small room, which you may never leave. The only communication between the room and the outside world is through a slot in the wall. You can't see out of the slot, but occasionally a card is pushed in from the outside, with some characters written on it in Chinese – and we will also assume that you do not know Chinese. But you have been taught what to *do* with the sequences of characters, in the sense that you know what response to give to a given sequence of characters. For you also have a pile of cards with Chinese characters on them inside the room, and you have been instructed which sequences to push out through the slot in response to a given sequence pushed in.

It ought to be clear that, assuming the above to be all that you know, you cannot be said to understand Chinese, or to be *saying* anything when you construct your Chinese sequence. You may, of course, be taking part in some activity, and even performing a very useful service. You might, for example, be a data base giving the name of the capital city of any given country when the name of that country is pushed through the slot. But then again, for all you know you may be giving someone the prices of drinks in a bar. The point is that in this situation you could not be said to *know* anything about the outside world at all, though the information contained on the cards may well be a source of knowledge to anyone who can decipher it.

The parallel with a simple computer should be obvious. It has symbols put into it, it manipulates the symbols, and it gives symbols as output; but nothing is going on which should lead us to suppose that the machine knows what they refer to. There is, therefore, no pressure to beieve that there is anything which the machine could be thinking *about*, unless it is the symbols themselves. And to say it is thinking about the symbols themselves gets us nowhere as regards the supposed parallel with human thinking, for it is analogous to saying that what we think about is configurations of impulses in our brains rather than things in the world around us.

The fact is that we learn the concept of redness, for example, by actually seeing red things. It may be objected that a machine could come to understand concepts by being given information (in its own code, of course) about the things to which they refer. For example, that a machine might know something about what 'red' is by being fed the information that roses are red. But this 'information' is just more of the same thing. It is true that we ourselves acquire some of our concepts by purely linguistic means (I am *told* that a black hole is a concentration of gravitational energy, and thus acquire the concept without ever having experienced one), but the way in which we get a grasp on all concepts learned in this way is ultimately via concepts which are *not* learned in this way. For the machine which is given the 'information' that roses are red, this is not actually information at all since, besides not knowing what redness is, it doesn't know what a rose is either. One cannot explain something which is obscure by linking it with something equally obscure, and in this case the machine will still end up not knowing a red rose from a hole in the ground – unless, of course, it can indeed have experiences in much the same way as we do. Otherwise, it will be just like giving the person in the Chinese room example the 'information' that Moscow is cold, by simply giving him the Chinese for 'Moscow is cold'. This is one important difference between the genuine use of language and the 'canned' variety: genuine language use 'hooks on to' the world via experience and learning.

on being an organism

From the above, we may conclude that a creature cannot be said to have thought unless it can be thinking *about* something, and that it cannot be said to be thinking about something unless there are channels through which it can acquire the relevant concepts. Now these channels must, for the same reason, involve direct access to the objects of thought, in the following sense: that the information about the objects does not come in the form of representations in some linguistic notation, but as the objects out of which linguistic concepts can be constructed. Think once again, for a moment, of the Chinese Room example. The reason why the person in the room cannot be said to possess the concepts which the Chinese symbols stand for, is that what he has are merely representations of the objects to which the concepts refer, but in a language which he has never learned – and that this stock of representations, along with the different permutations of them which he knows how to construct, exhausts the content of his world. Without direct access to at least some of the possible objects of thought, the machine's world, like that of the inhabitant of the Chinese room, is going to be devoid of any semantics (i.e. empty of meanings).

Now the possibility of direct access to objects, in the above sense, is going to be dependent on the possession of some sense organs, and of some arrangement of nerves, or the equivalent, by which information can be transmitted from the outside world to the central areas of the creature's controlling system. These need not be ears, eyes, nerves made up of electro-chemical nerve cells etc. In this case we may harmlessly adopt the functionalist strategy (see chapter 7) of saying that any things which stand in the corresponding causal roles will count as being the same kinds of things: they will qualify as being sense organs. And since we also observed that *acting on* the world is important for learning, as well as being *acted on* by the world, we will also require something corresponding to the organs by means of which we manipulate our environment; and this will also have to satisfy the criterion of directness outlined above. As far as artificial intelligence is concerned, these sensory organs and manipulatory organs take the form of sensory transducers and motor transducers – the devices which convert the external stimuli into digital electronic form, and the appropriate internal electronic impulses into physical action, respectively.

Note, by the way, that the fact that external stimuli have to be converted into digital form does not necessarily reduce the machine to the status of the occupant of the Chinese room. It is merely the form which the stimulus takes for the machine, and its role is purely causal: it is not meant as a representation of anything, in the linguistic sense, any more than the pattern of neural activity in my nerves is a linguistic representation of the stimulus which gave rise to it – I do not have to learn to interpret it as being a sensation of heat, or a blow on the head.

Of course, any amount of input and output via transducers is not going to guarantee that the creature in question is actually sentient. We have seen that, even in the case of human beings, there is not a logically doubtproof guarantee that other people are sentient. This was the point of formulating the requirement of directness above: it is meant as a necessary though probably not a sufficient criterion for sentience, which will have to serve our purposes at least for the time being, in the absence of a criterion which is both necessary and sufficient. However, what is not open to doubt about other people on the grounds of other minds scepticism, is that they are organisms. Being an organism is *par excellence* a functional property and not a mental one. Now it seems to follow from the foregoing that any artifact which is at all a candidate for possessing genuine thought, is going to be an organism. To say that something is an organism is, in fact, to say even less than that it has this directness of input and output with the world; plants, for example, are organisms, but they have no real nervous system. The proper conclusion, then, is that anything capable of actual thought is at least going to be an organism. The question which now suggests itself is whether something which is an organism can at the same time be a machine. We will not attempt to answer this question here, however, but will look first at another aspect of the background to thought in the full sense.

having thoughts and having purposes

Plants, as we noticed just now, are organisms, and yet they rate as poor candidates for thinking – even poorer than the lower animals. Why should this be, given that both are organisms but non-language-users? An obvious reason which springs to mind is that plants do not, in the normal sense, have a nervous system. There is, therefore, much less reason to believe that they actually feel anything. Another reason, however, lies in the idea introduced above, of ability to manipulate the environment. On the whole, this is something which animals do, and plants don't do. There are borderline cases, of course: amoebas are not very manipulative, but Venus fly traps are. These are not important. What is important is the fact that the ability to think – to use concepts – is not just dependent on having sensations, but also on the kind of interaction with the world which makes concept-learning a possibility. So far we have left this rather vague; it is now time to look at the reason for it in more detail.

It is now a platitude in educational circles that learning depends very much upon doing. Young children are taught by being encouraged to take part in activities, to interact with their surroundings. This principle is obviously sound. The only trouble is that many people take it to be an empirical principle; that is, something which has been discovered from experience to be true, but which might have been found not to be true. Such people talk as though being unable to manipulate the environment in any way would merely be a rather bad handicap. That this is not the case can be revealed by considering the position of a creature without the means for any such interaction – a creature which is only a passive receiver of incoming stimuli. How could the learning process ever get off the ground at all in such a creature?

To begin with, learning of any kind depends upon having mastered some concepts. The acquisition of concepts is logically prior to the acquisition of facts: one can't learn that roses are red without knowing how to recognise redness or a rose. The way we acquire most of our concepts is by learning the use of words. The response of others to our correct or incorrect applications of words teaches us when a concept is and is not applicable: it teaches us the *extension*, in other words, of the concept. There may possibly be some sense in which non-language-users can acquire concepts, but it may safely be assumed (for reasons discussed in chapter 4) to be peripheral. Now language, and the application of concepts, are *rule-governed* activities in the Wittgensteinian sense (also outlined in chapter 4). And to have mastered a rule is to have learned how to do something correctly, how to recognize appropriate applications from misapplications. From this we may deduce that any creature capable of mastering a rule-governed activity must possess a basic grasp of what it is to do something correctly; in other words, of the concept of correctness.

This might seem to some like too strong a conclusion. They might object that there is a difference between being capable of learning the distinction between the correct and incorrect application, say of a word, and possessing the concepts of correctness in general. And that only the former is necessary to make rule-governed activity possible. For example, it may be suggested that the mere fact of having been trained to respond in the right way to a given word is sufficient evidence that a rule has been grasped, without the trainee having the idea of what it is to be correct about other things, or of what it is that all cases of correctness have in common.

In response to such an objection we may ask where the motivation is supposed to come from, on the part of the trainee, to do those things which conform to the rule in question; if it is not the desire to do what is correct in the circumstances, what is it? Take the case of a rat which has been trained to jump through hoops. There are three possibilities to account for the success of the training:

(a) The rat possesses the concept of correctness, and wishes to learn the correct way to jump through hoops,

(b) The rat just likes jumping through hoops,

(c) The rat is rewarded with food whenever it performs the actions successfully, and that is what makes the training possible.

Presumably we may discount the first hypothesis in the case of rats, which is why we have used this example. And if the second is the explanation, then surely no real training is going on: I cannot be said to have trained a creature to do something which it would have done in any case. What about the last? It is true that a rat trained to perform a trick by being bribed with cheese, is nevertheless *trained*: the question is, does this add up to having learned a piece of rule-governed activity, in the required sense? And it seems that it does not.

To distinguish between mere training and rule-following, we must appeal to an important distinction, between *prescriptive rules* and *constitutive rules*. As the name suggests, a prescriptive rule prescribes something, in other words it tells us what to do. A constitutive rule, on the other hand, tells us what constitutes doing something. Thus 'keep off the grass' is a prescriptive rule – it tells us what we must do. The rules of chess, however, are not prescriptive but constitutive – they tell us what constitutes playing chess. 'The bishop can only move diagonally' does not tell us we must not move them any other way in the same sense that 'Keep off the grass' tells us we must not walk on the grass; nothing will happen to us if we do not, except that we will no longer be playing chess.

The significance of the distinction for us is this: rule-governed activity in our sense, has to do with *constitutive* rules – especially with the rules of language – and not with prescriptive rules. And rules which are only observed because they are enforced by rewards and punishments, are prescriptive rules only. What the rat is attempting to do is not to perform the hoop trick correctly, but to obtain food; and food-gathering, however sophisticated, is not a rule-governed activity in the appropriate sense. Only if some evidence were to emerge suggesting that the rat understood and took an interest in the activity as something independent from the reward, would we say that the rat knew what constituted doing the hoop trick correctly, as opposed to saying simply that it knew how to get food effectively. A creature which is really following a rule can be expected, for example, to reflect on what it is doing, especially in border-line cases, when it will be inclined to try and sharpen up its own conception of what it is that makes a correct application different from a misapplication.

Of course, a human being who has been taught to count, for example, might well have been trained initially by being bribed with sweets and suchlike. The difference between this case and the rat is that the human being will go on to understand the activity and its point irrespective of its association with the confectionary, and is likely to retain the concepts for an indefinite time after the training has ceased, which is not the case with such creatures as rats. People learn, for example, that the activity of counting is applicable in areas other than the one in which they acquired the skill, and can typically go on to expand their grasp of the activity in the absence of further training. It should now be clear why we cannot allow that the mere fact of being trainable to do a particular thing in the way which happens to be correct, adds up to an ability to be guided by rules. It has to be accepted, therefore, that what is required for the latter is at least some grasp of what it is to do something correctly in general.

Now to possess the concept of doing something correctly, what a creature must be further capable of is having purposes. To know what it is for a piece of rule-governed behaviour to be correct, is to know the distinction between achieving and failing to achieve a given goal, the goal of applying the rule in the right way. Thus any such creature must be able to engage in goal-orientated action. This is, of course, also something which tends to go along with being an organism.

We have come a long way in this section, and before moving on, it may be useful to recapitulate a little. It has been argued that genuine thinking implies the use of concepts, that the application of concepts is a rule-governed activity, that the possibility of mastering a rule-governed activity depends on possessing the concept of doing something correctly, and that the possession of this concept involves a knowledge of what it is to have purposes, or goals. In the next two sections we will look further at the idea of purposiveness, and its importance for the question of whether machines can truly think.

purpose as reflectiveness

The idea of purposiveness harks back to a topic which was raised in the first chapter – that of creativity, or originality. Remember that this was not intended to mean anything especially spiritual or artistic, but only to refer to some everyday capacities which all human beings and many animals have, such as being able to instigate interest in a particular topic or to do something for one's own reasons. This notion of reasons will emerge as important later. Another term for what we are talking about might be *self-motivation*. It tends to be typical of machines, even very sophisticated ones, that they are not self-motivated. Although we call certain kinds of machines 'automata' (because they are in a sense 'automatic'), what their behaviour is not, is autonomous. However 'clever' what they do might be, they merely do what they are programmed to do – no more and no less. What, then, is the difference between this and the way human beings behave?

Suppose someone were to argue as follows. Human beings have a particular repertoire of behaviour, in which they engage in more or less predictable ways. Every few hours they become hungry, and then they eat. At rather longer intervals they become tired and they sleep. They are also subject to the desire for relaxation, which they indulge when they are not either sleeping, or working to earn their food and relaxation. This account would, of course, need to be expanded in order to make it look anything approaching complete. But does it not seem intuitively plausible that an account of the human behavioural repertoire could, in principle, be given, which would show human behaviour as the kind of thing which might be describable by a computer-type program?

This is by no means an easy question, and threatens to embroil us in the whole problem of the freedom of the will, which we will touch on in the next section. That will be the second of two approaches to the above challenge. First, we will consider purpose in terms of that capacity which human beings have to *reflect* on their actions in an open-ended way. Reflection might be seen as a matter of taking one's deliberation 'one step higher', of examining one's own reasons from a detached point of view. An open-ended capacity for reflectiveness therefore involves being able not only to examine our own reasons, but to go on to examine the reasons which we use in assessing the first reasons, and then to examine *those* reasons, and so on without any theoretical limit. Take, for example, the following 'interior monologue':

> 'I am hungry, therefore I have good reason to eat.'
> 'But I am on a diet, therefore I should not.'
> 'However, dieting ought not to be taken to extremes.'
> 'But I promised I would keep to the diet, and the promise should be kept irrespective of the good or harm which comes of it.'
> 'Nevertheless, there are circumstances in which it is justifiable to break a promise in order to avoid harm.'
> And so on...

Notice that this monologue is not simply a case of 'On the one hand...' and 'On the other hand'. At each stage the reasons used to support the conclusion of the last stage are examined and criticised. What is important is the fact that there is no point at which the process of standing back from one's previous reason and assessing *it*, must stop. Theoretically it could go on for ever. Now this seems to be a feature which has not yet been captured by artificial intelligence, though this is not to say that it could not be. The trouble is that a lot of obscurity surrounds the question of what kind of capacity this open-endedness is, what it consists in. Furthermore, any creature which possesses this feature must also possess the further capacity to decide when to stop reflecting in this way and come to a firm decision, rather than deliberating indefinitely. This is not possible for a machine in principle either, however: a chess-playing computer, for example, has to 'decide' in a given situation how long to go on considering the pros and cons of a *prima facie* advantageous move.

At this point an objection might be raised to the whole idea that a machine could be capable of the sort of open-ended reflection discussed here. The objection goes as follows. The ability of a machine to reflect on what it is doing, is conceptually limited by the fact that the machine has itself been created for a purpose – a purpose which is not its own. And there is no 'going beyond' that purpose and asking how desirable a purpose it is. The machine logically cannot, on this view, bring into question the ultimate reasons why it does what it does, for they are not *its* reasons. A machine, for instance, which is built for the purpose of working out the series of prime numbers, may well be capable of deliberating up to a point. It may decide, say, to investigate a number which looks a hopeful candidate for being prime; and it might subsequently decide not to do so, on the grounds that if it investigated every number with the same degree of probability of being prime, the job would take too long. But what it cannot do is reach the point at which it begins to say 'What's the good of working out prime numbers in any case?' – for this purpose was not *its* purpose, and we can only deliberate about our *own* purposes.

This objection is very tempting, but in the end will not stand up. It is true that the machines which get built at present do not have the potential to say 'I'm going to stop diagnosing patients and have a game of chess instead'. This is the point about lacking autonomy. It is also true that a machine for diagnosing patients, or for working out square roots, cannot call into question the reasonableness of these activities. But we must be careful about *why* they cannot. It is not, in fact, because the purposes are the purposes of the designer or programmer and not of the machine itself. Rather, it is because it is a simple logical truth that a machine for working out square roots cannot call into question the reasons for its own activity: if it did so, it would be, at least partly, a machine for calling into question its own activity, and not a machine for working out square roots.

Consider a machine which is built for the purpose of simulating human thought. Here, there is no contradiction in supposing that it might question the reasonableness of its own behaviour. Of course, we need to be careful how we express what it is supposed to be doing: a machine which represented to itself its own purpose as that of 'simulating human thought' would be *eo ipso* a failure, since simulation of human thought means simulating what human beings do when they think – and what they do is not 'simulating human thought'! However, this is not a conceptual obstacle, since the only difference between 'simulating human thought' and simply 'thinking the way that human beings do' is what we call them – and the nature of an activity cannot be altered by what someone else calls it. If, then, the machine regarded its task as simply doing what human beings do, there is no reason why it should not bring that activity into question. Some human beings themselves do this: they typically go mad, or commit suicide, or write existentialist novels. This brings us to the second point which was to be discussed in response to the question of how human purposiveness differs from that of machines.

purpose as freedom of the will
If someone says 'How do you know you are not merely like a programmed machine?', it is possible that he intends the question to be synonymous with 'How do you know you have free will?' Freedom of the will is, after all, one meaning of

'autonomy'. A response which I might well make is to appeal to the experience of making a free choice. People have often talked, misleadingly, as though some psychological or sociological discovery might convince us that we lack a property, the property of free will, which we thought we possessed. In the words of another well-known limerick:

> There was a young man who said 'Damn!
> It is clear to me now that I am
> Just a creature that moves
> In predestinate grooves,
> I'm not even a bus, I'm a *tram*!'

The question of free will has often been approached in terms of the absence of constraints. If a person is not at gunpoint, or brainwashed, or whatever, he is free to act as he pleases, and this is what constitutes freedom of will – so the story goes. The application of this principle to the case of automata shows, however, what is basically wrong with the principle as applied to human persons. The mere absence of constraints is not sufficient by itself to make us suspect the presence of true self-motivation, or autonomy. One can imagine many an artifact which is in some way animated, and is not acting under any hindrance or abnormal influence, but is nevertheless a poor candidate for having an autonomous will. The absence of constraints can, then, be only a necessary, and not a sufficient condition for freedom of the will.

What is wrong with the attitude of the young man in the rhyme is that he is looking in the wrong place for the answer to the question about human free will. The person who takes this kind of position considers 'external' circumstances such as the fact that people are made of physical stuff, or that they undergo a process of socialisation, and comes to an absurd conclusion on the basis of them. Why absurd? Because anyone who has had the experience of making a free decision knows that this is what it is, and no amount of drawing attention to background and antecedents is going to alter the fact. To act freely is simply to make a choice. And the way we learn what it is to make a genuine choice – how we learn what the word 'choice' means – is by associating it with actions of just this kind. Nor does this involve committing ourselves to the idea that choice is an occult 'mental act', which many anti-mentalistic philosophers would want to reject, and which is certainly suspect. All we need to accept is that the word 'choice' has a legitimate use. We cannot then be denied the right to say that to experience the making of a choice at first-hand is to have been the agent, in a situation where the word 'choice' is rightly applied.

Two things ought to convince us that the idea of our not really possessing free will, though it seems to us that we do, is incoherent. Firstly, if I do not possess free will, what would it be like to be *really* free? Can we describe a kind of choice freer, say, than my recent choice of a cup of coffee rather than tea? Of course, we could say that a choice made without any causal influence would be freer, but, even granted that we could make any sense of this idea, how would that affect *me*? Hidden constraints which might or might not be there are no constraints at all. To insist nevertheless that I am not free, is like a person claiming that he is imprisoned, though he can't actually point to the walls, and they don't obstruct him in any way. Secondly, suppose that we *do* possess free will, but that we can never-theless make sense of the idea that we may have turned out not to do. What would this be like? Would we feel our legs and arms acting outside our control, suddenly carrying us where we do not want to go? This idea is equally absurd. But what is wrong with the whole picture, is the confused idea that some-how it is an open question whether or not we ever make genuine choices – that it might turn out one way or the other, and that it is possible to remain open to persuasion either way. The fact is, that if what I have got does not count as free will, then nothing ever would.

Now having – apparently – dispatched free will problem in a couple of pages, it is necessary to point out that this does not get us any further as regards explaining how free will is possible, or how it is brought about. The apparent short shrift given to the problem above was, in fact, *only* apparent; for the real question is this latter. Compare this with the way in which people often mistake the philosopher's question '*How* do I know there is a table in front of me?' for the question '*Do* I know there is a table in front of me?', and regard the philosopher as some sort of crank. What we really want to know is, then: how does it come about that human beings possess autonomy, that they can make genuine choices rather then merely apparent ones? And more acutely, how can we reconcile this with the fact that we are physical creatures living in a physical world obeying physical laws? This, unfortunately, is a perennial problem of philosophy on which there is an enormous literature but very little consensus. Notice also, that this problem is in some ways like that of other minds, in the sense that I have first-hand experience in my own case, but no direct evidence in that of other people: logically speaking, other people could be mere automata without free will, though once again there are *criteria*, though not indefeasible ones, for telling whether a person is really acting freely – and once again, certain things might follow regarding my own case, were I to adopt the sceptical point of view regarding others.

All this bodes rather ill for the prospect of explaining under what circumstances an artifact might be said to possess autonomy, or at what stage in the increasing complexity of machines we ought to be prepared to ascribe genuinely purposive behaviour to them. For on the one hand, the first-hand experience of free choice is one which is only accessible to the agent in question and to no one else: *direct* observation is out of the question. And on the other hand, we are so much in the dark regarding what it is that gives rise to free will in people, that we have little chance of understanding what conditions would give rise to it in artifacts: thus *indirect* evidence is also rendered next door to impossible. All we can do, it seems, is to conclude that the closer machines come to resembling our own structure and organisation, the more reason there will be to suppose them genuinely autonomous. Yet the function of artificial intelligence is surely not to produce an exact duplication of a human being. Nor is there any reason to suppose that *only* our own physical make-up is such as to give rise to the appropriate conditions for autonomy.

Some people have argued that an automaton could by its

very nature never be properly said to be acting autonomously, simply because it is by definition merely doing what it was intended to do by its designer. This, however, conflicts with the principle argued for above, which is that if one is acting freely, one cannot be mistaken about it: for it to be *exactly like* free action simply is for it to *be* free action. Because what this objection entails is that all that is necessary to discredit the idea that something is acting autonomously, is to show that it was designed for a purpose, by someone else, and that it is doing no more than fulfilling that purpose. But there is no contradiction in supposing that we were designed by somebody, with the intention that we should be doing exactly what we are in fact doing. Yet if we were right in thinking that freedom is ensured by the nature of the first-hand experience, then we appear to have a knock-down guarantee against such a discovery! This cannot be right. It seems that mere evidence of design, of derivativeness, is not sufficient to refute the ascription of free will. After all, most people who believe that we were designed, in some sense, by God, do not regard this as excluding the possibility of free will, but rather as the explanation of it.

Finally, if the nature of the first-hand experience of choice and decision – the action as it appears to the agent – is that in which free will ultimately resides, then it appears that only a creature capable of *conscious* thought is going to be a candidate for autonomy. Now it is interesting to see how the features we have been discussing appear to converge. It has been argued that thought, because of the need for concepts, rule-following, and therefore purposiveness, requires autonomy, and that autonomy requires consciousness. If all that has been said is true, we are now in a position to see how the ideas of thinking and consciousness, whose problematical relationship we observed in chapter 1, might be seen as connected. The pattern of entailment will look something like the diagram on the next page.

In the next chapter we will return to the connection between the capacity for genuine thought and the status of being an organism, and tie up some further loose ends from earlier chapters.

THINKING
|
CONCEPTUALISATION
|
RULE-FOLLOWING
|
PURPOSIVENESS
|
AUTONOMY
|
CONSCIOUSNESS

11: some conclusions

Continuing to draw threads together, we saw in the last chapter how a genuinely thinking creature would need to be sentient, purely in order to have anything to think about. We saw also that it would require the means to interact with and manipulate its environment. It has further been suggested that such a creature would have to be in the nature of an organism as a result of these preconditions. We will now look at another reason, arising out of the later sections of the last chapter, why this must be so.

more on organisms
If we accept that having purposes is an essential ingredient of the ability to form concepts, then it is appropriate to ask what might be the conditions under which it makes sense to ascribe purposiveness. Towards the end of the last chapter, we discussed two approaches to purposiveness, one in terms of the ability to reflect, and the other in terms of free will. Neither of these led us very far on its own, largely because the properties in question are not well enough understood in the case of human beings, let alone anything else. There is, however, something in addition that can be said on this topic, which is less abstract and more mundane, but which perhaps gets us further in the long run.

To have purposes is to have reasons for doing things. What kind of creatures, then, does it make sense to think of as having reasons? A plausible suggestion is that having reasons depends, at bottom, on having needs. It is hard to see how a creature without any basic needs could, for instance, go on to develop wants, interests and the like. This is not, of course, to say that all our wants and interests *are* really needs; that would be absurd. It is to say that the possibility of having these motivations which are, as it were, at one remove from the basic necessities of life, depends ultimately on being a living creature for whom some basic necessities exist.

Now the concept of needs is by no means an easy one. It enjoys somewhat vague and fuzzy relations with its neighbours, the concepts of *wants* and of *conditions*. For example, it is unclear whether it is correct to say that people need sexual activity as well as needing food, or whether it is something that they just want. They will not die without it, certainly, but it is nevertheless one of the basic stock of strong human impulses which will not go away, and pathological symptoms can result from its repression. On the other hand, a car can, in a sense, be said to need fuel. It will not run without it, and this is in some ways analogous to saying that a human being will not

The car itself is just as satisfied sitting in the middle of the road.

'flourish' without certain things being granted to it. However, it arguably makes more sense to say that it is *we* who need fuel in order to run the car. Fuel is not a need of the car in the same sense that food is a need for us, but only a *condition* of its functioning in the way we want it to. The car itself is just as satisfied sitting motionless in the middle of the road. The crucial difference between this and the case of organisms, is that the latter possess a kind of internal constitution which drives them to seek those things which are necessary for their flourishing. The needs and the drives are, in the case of organisms, internally related to each other, in the sense that the lack is recognized by its resulting in the drive, and the drive can be identified solely in terms of the thing whose lack it points to, and whose presence would be a fulfilment of it. Cars do not, in a sense, have drives – they are merely driven!

back to the original question
In the light of all this, then, what we are to say in answer to the main question which we set ourselves at the outset: *could a machine be really thinking?*

It should be clear that we have come a considerable way towards knowing what an answer to this question is going to look like. Having first asked the question in chapter 1, we went on in chapter 2 to see that it raises problems which have much in common with the traditional philosophical Problem of Other Minds, and that the two may usefully be treated together, which was what happened in chapter 3. In chapter 4 we gave what may be regarded as a fairly standard, present-day response to the Other Minds problem, along Wittgensteinian lines. In chapter 5 we drew out some of the implications of the Wittgensteinian concern with communication, and attained some understanding of what a machine would be required to do in the way of interacting with human beings, before it could be seriously suspected of harbouring a mental life.

At this point, it was decided to glance at various answers to the question of what, in general, is supposed to be the relation between a physical body and the mental life which it possesses – in other words, at the Mind-Body Problem. This we did in chapters 6, 7 and 8. Having reached a broad idea (only one among many defended by various people) of what kind of theory would be acceptable, we went on in chapter 9 to see, in the light of this, how man-made systems compare with human brains as candidates for supporting conscious thought. We will remember that at this stage it looked as though (a) no such system currently in existence would seem to be a very good candidate, but (b) there seemed to be no reason in principle why systems developed in the future should not be, provided we understand that they are still a long way in the future. In chapter 10, however, an argument was given to the effect that purposiveness, autonomy and free will all seem to come into the picture; and we have seen earlier in this chapter how any physical system which fulfils the conditions for genuine thought is almost certainly going to be some kind of organism, because of the apparent connection between purposiveness and the having of needs.

The question now arises: have we narrowed down the conditions under which we are prepared to entertain the idea that something is genuinely thinking, to the point at which machines are ruled out by definition? In other words, are we now committed to answering our original question in the negative, by saying 'No – nothing could be both a machine and fulfil these conditions'?

Frankenstein revisited
This question is not going to be so easy to answer, largely because the word 'machine', as used in this context, is not terribly well defined. We noted near the beginning that a question which can be answered simply by a stipulative definition in no real question at all – so the dictionary will not help us here. A better approach would be to ask: *what, if anything, would be the point of referring to something with the kind of thought-suggesting characteristics we have outlined, as a machine*? One answer might be, simply to record the fact that it is man-made, and not something that occurs spontaneously in nature. Yet plenty of things are man-made and yet are not machines. Another could be, to convey the idea that the thing

is non-organic. But in this case the answer to our question would now be trivial, for we have seen that a truly thinking thing is going to be an organism of some sort.

The word 'machine' is, however, sometimes used to signify that the thing in question exists for a purpose or purposes which are external to itself – that is, purposes for others, which are not the purposes of the thing itself (as in the example of the car above). Now on this understanding, it would seem on first sight that it is still going to be false that something could both be a machine and fulfil the conditions for genuinely thinking, since we have argued that purposiveness (involving self-motivation, having its own reasons, etc.) is one of these latter conditions. It is conceivable, however, that a thing should have both purposes of its own and also purposes for which it was designed and built by someone else, and that in such a case it would properly be describable both as a machine in the above sense, and as fulfilling the conditions we laid down.

But what could such a 'machine' be *for*? Surely the only possible kind of reason for creating a machine with purposiveness of its own – unless of course this self-motivation were just a sort of by-product – would be to see whether it could be done, or to find out how it would behave if it *were* done. And this is a somewhat trivial way of being a machine, since the 'machine aspect' of it cannot be described without making reference to its 'non-machine aspect' (i.e. it would be a kind of 'machine-for-being-something-other-than-a- machine'!).

Yet we might, after all, need to take seriously the idea of self-motivation occurring as a by-product. It may be that there could be good reasons for wanting machines which perform tasks which are so complex that any machine capable of performing them would turn out to be so sophisticated, and in just the right ways, that it would in fact be such as to have its own reasons, motives, purposes and so on.

At this point, however, it does look a little as if we are in danger of ending up merely juggling with words. This is not because the results of our enquiry are trivial, but because the real work has already been done. We have, as promised, ended up with an answer, and quite a substantive answer, to the question 'What kind of thing could we take seriously as a candidate for having genuine thought?' The further question of whether or not such a thing could ever be properly called a machine, does not have the same philosophical interest.

What is more interesting, perhaps, is the observation that such artifacts would be hardly anything like the things which pass for 'intelligent machines' at the present time. Even the kinds of system discussed at the end of chapter 9 are hopelessly crude by comparison. This is by no means an attempt to belittle the work done by researchers in Artificial Intelligence in recent years: it is only to point out that, if their goals are those discussed in this book, of creating conscious, thinking beings, then they are perhaps nearer the beginning of the road than the end. We have seen, however, that this is *not* at all the only possible (or actual) aim of Artificial Intelligence. Merely making replicas of ourselves would be at best a pointless, and at worst a perverse and grotesque, task to set ourselves. This is one of the *real* horrors of the Frankenstein story, as opposed to those of its stock Hollywood treatment. The sheer metaphysical audacity of wishing to do such a thing merely to prove that one can do it, is unattractive in itself. And research whose motivation is of this kind rarely results in anything genuinely edifying. Yet, as has been hinted, there may turn out to be perfectly respectable motives which in time will bear fruits in the form of conscious, thinking beings which are at the same time artifacts created by human beings. But this is mere speculation.

Whether or not it is the case, the philosophical questions retain their interest, and can if we wish be pursued as well for their own sake as for any light which they might throw on our technological future. We have, it is to be hoped, also found that in the pursuit of these questions many other interesting lines of enquiry present themselves, some of which are as much to do with ourselves and our own capacity for thought, as with that of our creations.

the indispensability of the philosophical questions
One more, fairly general, position which has been implicitly

argued for in this book, is the following: that a discussion of whether or not machines can be 'really' intelligent or can 'really' think, cannot, in the end, be carried on without reference to the question of whether or not they could be conscious. This is important, since it is often claimed that the questions about genuine thought and intelligence are independent of 'philosophers' questions' about consciousness and the like. On that view, the philosophical questions, though they may retain some academic interest merely for their own sake, are otherwise redundant. But if the argument in chapter 10 is correct, then the questions in which Artificial Intelligence researchers are interested *cannot* be divorced from those which the philosopher insists on asking. For, if we are right, anything which is a proper candidate for having 'real' thought (even in a fairly broad sense) must operate with concepts. And if it is capable of concept-ualisation, this presupposes the ability for rule-following, which itself seems to depend on the presence of purposiveness, which in turn appears to require the possession of autonomy. And we have seen that it is at least quite arguable that a creature can only plausibly be said to be autonomous in this sense if it knows what it is doing, in the fullest sense of this expression, i.e. if it thinks consciously, as opposed to merely 'going through the motions'.

Even questions about whether machines can think in quite weak senses of the word 'think', will tend to get us involved in the above sequence of reasoning. And if this in indeed the case, then it is no longer open for defenders of Artificial Intelligence as 'real', to maintain that the conceptual, philosophical questions can be ignored or shelved, safe in the knowledge that their own questions can stand independently.

suggestions for further reading

Chapter 1
For a variety of approaches to the question of machines and thinking, see Edward A. Feigenbaum and Julian Feldman (eds.) *Computers and Thought* (New York: McGraw-Hill, 1963), which is a collection of articles from various sources. Many other books on the subject are in print, some better than others.

Chapter 2
For more on solipsism and the problem of other minds, see for example the *Proceedings of the Aristotelian Society* supplementary volume 1946 which contains a symposium on the problem of other minds, in which the contributors are John Wisdom, J.L. Austin, and A.J. Ayer. Wisdom's is also reprinted in his book *Other Minds* (Oxford: Blackwell, 1952), and Austin's in Antony Flew (ed.) *Logic and Language*, 2nd series (Oxford: Blackwell, 1953).

Chapter 3
The main primary texts for the material covered in this chapter are as follows: Richard Rorty, *Philosophy and the Mirror of Nature* (New Jersey: Princeton University Press and Oxford: Blackwell, 1981); Daniel Dennett, *Brainstorms* (Montgomery, Vermont: Bradford Books, and Hassocks: Harvester, 1978) ch. 1; Thomas Nagel, 'What is it like to be a Bat?', *Philosophical Review* vol. 83 (Oct.1974), repr. in Nagel, T., *Mortal Questions* (Cambridge: Cambridge University Press, 1979); Bertrand Russell *Human Knowledge: Its Scope and Limits* (London:

Allen & Unwin, 1948); A.J. Ayer, 'One's Knowledge of Other Minds' in Ayer, A.J. (ed.) *Philosophical Essays* (London: Macmillan, 1954), reprinted in Gustafson, D.F. (ed.), *Essays in Philosophical Psychology* (London: Macmillan, 1967). The secondary literature is largely as for chapter 2.

Chapter 4
The primary text here is, of course, Wittgenstein's *Philosophical Investigations* (1953), and especially the part from section 201 to around section 265, where the Private Language Argument and related topics are to be found. A good secondary text is Fogelin's *Wittgenstein*, in the RKP *Arguments of the Philosophers* series. Also useful is Anthony Kenny's *Wittgenstein* (Harmondsworth: Penguin, 1973).

Chapter 5
The classic essay by Turing is contained in the collection edited by Feigenbaum and Feldman (see under ch. 1). On the issue of machines and programs which interact conversationally with human beings, see the relevant sections of Margaret Boden's *Artificial Intelligence and Natural Man* (Hassocks: Harvester Press, 1977) which is a good book for philosophical questions about AI generally, and does not presuppose any technical knowledge.

Chapter 6
The primary texts for this chapter are: Descartes, *Meditations* (1641); Malebranche, *De la Récherche de la Vérité* (6th edn., 1712); Leibniz, *Monadology* (1714); and T.H. Huxley, *Science and Culture* (1881). Annotated readings from the primary literature in the philosophy of mind can be found in Antony Flew (ed.), *Body, Mind, and Death* (London and New York: Macmillan, 1964). On Descartes a good introductory work is Anthony Kenny's *Descartes* (New York: Random House, 1968). On Leibniz, see George MacDonald Ross, *Leibniz* (Oxford: Oxford University Press, 1984). Good articles on the above philosophers, and on many others mentioned in this book, can also be found in F.C. Coplestone's multi-volume

History of Philosophy (London: Burns Oates, 1947-60).

Chapter 7

The primary literature here includes: D.A. Armstrong, *A Materialist Theory of the Mind* (London: Routledge and Kegan Paul, 1968); J.J.C. Smart, 'Sensations and Brain Processes' (*Philosophical Review* 1959); Gilbert Ryle, *The Concept of Mind* (London: Hutchinson, 1949); and Donald Davidson, *Essays on Actions and Events* (Oxford: Oxford University Press, 1980), particularly the essay 'Mental Events' (1970). Some original papers on functionalism are contained in Ned Block (ed.), *Readings in the Philosophy of Psychology* (2 vols. (London: Methuen, 1980)), and Block's introductions are particularly helpful. A good collection of articles, mainly on functionalism and related topics, is J.I. Brio and Robert W. Shahan (eds.), *Mind, Brain and Function* (Norman: University of Oklahoma Press, 1982).

Chapter 8

For this chapter the primary reading is: P.F. Strawson, *Individuals* (London: Methuen, 1959); Bertrand Russell, *Our Knowledge of the External World* (London: Allen and Unwin, 1914) and *The Analysis of Mind* (London: Allen and Unwin, 1921); Spinoza, *Ethics* (c.1666); and Kant's *Critique of Pure Reason* (1781) or his much shorter and easier *Prolegomena* (1783). Some useful secondary literature is: A.J. Ayer, *Russell* (London: Collins, 1972); Stuart Hampshire, *Spinoza* (Harmondsworth: Penguin, revised edn. 1962), and Ralph C.S. Walker, *Kant* (London: Routledge & Kegan Paul, 1978).

Chapter 9

On computers and how they work, a good introduction is Susan Curran and Ray Curnow, *The Penguin Computing Book* (Harmondsworth: Penguin, 1983). For a more advanced account of computer architecture, a classic is V.Carl Hamacher *et al.*, *Computer Organization* (New York: McGraw-Hill, 1984). On Artificial Intelligence see Avron Barr and Edward A. Feigenbaum (eds.), *The Handbook of Artificial Intelligence*

(New York: Pitman, 1981), also Deborah L.S. Sweitzer and Paul- André Schabracq, *Artificial Intelligence: The State of the Art* (Science Council of Canada, 1982). For a layman's introduction to the workings of the human brain, the best text is Colin Blakemore, *Mechanics of the Mind* (Cambridge: Cambridge University Press, 1986).

Chapter 10
For the Chinese Room example, and surrounding issues, see John Searle, *Minds, Brains and Science* (London: BBC Publications, 1986). On the question of sentience a particularly interesting (though perhaps difficult) paper is Daniel Dennett's 'Why You Can't Make a Computer that Feels Pain' in his *Brainstorms*, (q.v. ch. 3, above), ch. 11.

Chapter 11
For further reading on the general subject of this book, two good collections of articles are: J.R. Smythies (ed.), *Brain and Mind: Modern Concepts of the Nature of Mind* (London: Routledge and Kegan Paul, 1965), and Christopher Hookway (ed.), *Minds, Machines and Evolution* (Cambridge: Cambridge University Press, 1984).

glossary of names

Armstrong, D.M. (b. 1926)
Australian philosopher whose best-known work is *A Materialist Theory of the Mind*, in which he defends a form of Central State Materialism (see chapter 7).

Ayer, Sir A.J. (b. 1910)
The principal British exponent of Logical Positivism, a school of thought which was concerned to lay down criteria distinguishing the meaningful from the nonsensical. His book *Language, Truth and Logic* (1936) laid down a central thesis of Logical Positivism, which was that a statement is only factually meaningful if there is, in principle, some means of verifying it, i.e. of discovering when it is true.

Berkeley, George (1685-1753)
Emphiricist philosopher, who was also an Irish Bishop. Berkeley took empiricism (the school of philosophy which emphasised sense experience as the source of knowledge) to its limits, by arguing that there are only 'ideas' in the mind (e.g. sensations), and that material things have no real existence. This is a form of Idealism (see chapter 7).

Brentano, Franz (1838-1917)
German philosopher/psychologist who was the founder of that school of philosophy known as Phenomenology. In his book *Psychology from an Empirical Standpoint* (1874), he originated the concept of 'intentionality' (see chapter 3).

Davidson, Donald (b. 1930)
American philosopher, very influential since the late 1960s. His views are very difficult to summarise, but are largely contained in his books *Essays On Actions and Events* (1980) and *Inquiries into Truth and Interpretation* (1984).

Dennett, Daniel (b. 1942)
American philosopher of mind. His views are not easy to summarise, but are contained in his books *Content and Consciousness* (1969) and *Brainstorms* (1978).

Descartes, René (1596-1650)
French philosopher, probably now best known for his *Meditations*, in which he attempted to reconstruct the framework of human knowledge. In his philosophy of mind he was a dualist, believing mind and body to be two separate entities, or 'substances'. Among other things, Descartes believed that the existence of God could be rationally demonstrated.

Fodor, J.A.
American philosopher best known for his work in semantics with J.J. Katz, but who has also written on the philosophy of mind, taking a functionalist position (see chapter 7).

Fichte, J.G. (1762-1814)
German philosopher whose system of philosophy owes much to Kant, whilst departing from Kant's views in many important respects. In Fichte's account the primary source of knowledge is the self, or ego, which constructs the world for itself out of a collection of 'appearances'.

Hegel, G.W.F. (1770-1831)
Along with Kant (q.v.) the best-known of the German idealists. Hegel's vast and comprehensive system of philosophy is known as Absolute Idealism. His style is dense and obscure, making his work very difficult for a layman to approach.

Husserl, Edmund (1859-1938)
Along with Brentano, a founder of the school of philosophy known as Phenomenology, which attempts to proceed from closely and objectively observed data of consciousness, and working from these towards a general theory of knowledge.

Huxley, T.H. (1825-1895)
Scientist and philosopher whose main contribution to philosophy has probably been the theory of mind known as Epiphenomenalism (see chapter 6).

James, William (1842-1910)
American psychologist and philosopher, one of the chief exponents (along with Dewey and Peirce) of the school of philosophy known as Pragmatism. His theory of the relation between the mental and the physical, known as neutral monism, was taken up by Bertrand Russell (q.v.).

Kant, Immanuel (1724-1804)
One of the most influential philosophers of all time. Kant developed a system of philosophy known as Transcendental Idealism, which is laid out in his most celebrated work, the *Critique of Pure Reason* (1781). It is probably no exaggeration to say that all modern philiosophy owes something to Kant.

Kripke, Saul (b. 1942)
American philosopher, whose main work lies in logic, philosophy of language and metaphysics. He has argued against the materialist account of mind (see chapter 7).

Leibniz, Gottfried Wilhelm (1646-1716)
German philosopher, along with Descartes (q.v.) and Spinoza (q.v.) one of the three great Rationalist philosophers. Attempted to reconcile a mechanistic, scientific account of the world, with a teleological (i.e. purposive) theological understanding. He created a system of metaphysics in which the ultimate entities are non-interacting 'monads'.

Malebranche, Nicholas (1638-1715)
French philosopher, much influenced by Descartes (q.v.), but who espoused a theory of mind and body known as Occasionalism (see chapter 6).

Putnam, Hilary (b. 1926)
American philosopher, notable for his work in metaphysics and philosophy of science. His best-known works are contained in his volumes of collected papers. Putnam's large and fertile output has influenced many present-day philosophers.

Rorty, Richard
American philosopher who has advocated the rejection of much traditional metaphysics and philosophy of mind. Rorty's views are hard to summarise, but are to be found in his three main works: *The Linguistic Turn* (1967), *Consequences of Pragmatism* (1982), both collections of articles, and *Philosophy and the Mirror of Nature* (1980).

Russell, Bertrand (1872-1970)
The most famous English philosopher of the twentieth century. His most celebrated work, written with Alfred North Whitehead, was the *Principia Mathematica* (1910-13), an investigation into the foundations of mathematics. Later he went on to write in most branches of philosophy, and published many popular works besides those intended for the specialist philosopher.

Ryle, Gilbert (1900-76)
Influential Oxford philosopher whose best-known work is *The Concept of Mind* (1949), in which he attacks the idea of an immaterial mind, which he calls the 'myth of the Ghost in the Machine'.

Skinner, B.F. (b. 1904)
Behavioural psychologist whose work has frequently spilled over into philosophy. A believer in the value of deliberate behavioural conditioning of human beings, his most important work from a philosophical point of view is *Beyond Freedom and*

Dignity (1971).

Smart, J.J.C.
Australian philosopher who has written extensively on the philosophy of science and metaphysics. Along with Armstrong (q.v.), he is central state materialist.

Spinoza, Benedict or Baruch (1632-77)
Jewish philosopher who developed a system of metaphysics which he articulated in a deductive form, using axiomatic method as in geometry. Spinoza was a pantheist, believing God and nature to be ultimately identical, and was excommunicated from the Jewish religion as a result of his unorthodox views.

Strawson, Peter F. (b. 1919)
Oxford philosopher whose work is much influenced by Kant (q.v.). His major works are *Individuals* (1959) and *The Bounds of Sense* (1966).

Turing, Alan (1912-54)
More a scientist and mathematician than a philosopher, Turing was instrumental in developing some of the first computers, around the time of the Second World War. His reflections on minds and machines, especially the famous 'Turing Test' (see chapter 5) have, however, provided an interesting focus of discussion for philosophers.

Wittgenstein, Lugwig (1889-1951)
Possibly the most influential philosopher of the twentieth century. Wittgenstein's works are difficult for the layman: the best known of them are the *Tractatus Logico-Philosophicus* (1921) and the *Philosophical Investigations* (posthumus, 1953). Each of these works sets out a system of philosophy, though his views had altered considerably between writing the former and the latter.

Fal
the Boss

She's at his beck and call — day and night!

Falling for the Boss

A BOSS IN A MILLION
by
Helen Brooks

HIS SECRETARY'S SECRET
by
Barbara McMahon

SECRETARY ON DEMAND
by
Cathy Williams

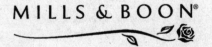

MILLS & BOON®

*MILLS & BOON and MILLS & BOON with the Rose Device
are registered trademarks of the publisher.
Harlequin Mills & Boon Limited,
Eton House, 18-24 Paradise Road, Richmond, Surrey, TW9 1SR*

FALLING FOR THE BOSS
© by Harlequin Enterprises II B.V., 2005

A Boss in a Million, His Secretary's Secret and *Secretary on Demand*
were first published in Great Britain by Harlequin Mills & Boon
Limited in separate, single volumes.

A Boss in a Million © Helen Brooks 1999
His Secretary's Secret © Barbara McMahon 2002
Secretary on Demand © Cathy Williams 2001

ISBN 0 263 84482 X

05-1205

*Printed and bound in Spain
by Litografia Rosés S.A., Barcelona*

Helen Brooks lives in Northamptonshire and is married with three children. As she is a committed Christian, busy housewife and mother, her spare time is at a premium but her hobbies include reading, swimming, gardening and walking her old, faithful dog. Her long-cherished aspiration to write became a reality when she put pen to paper on reaching the age of forty, and sent the result off to Mills & Boon®.

A BOSS IN A MILLION

by

Helen Brooks

CHAPTER ONE

'LONDON? Oh, Cory, don't. Don't leave. Things will work out for you here; I know they will. Just be patient.'

Cory Masters stared back into the face of her friend, her dear friend, the man she had known all her life and loved just as long. How could she tell him that the reasons she had just given for leaving her sleepy little rural home town nestled deep in the green folds of North Yorkshire were lies? The real cause of her intended flight to the anonymity of the metropolis was him, Vivian Batley-Thomas.

Cory smiled brightly, her deep sea-green eyes with their fascinating hint of purple determinedly clear and open and giving no hint of her inward turmoil. 'It's all arranged, Vivian.' She flicked back an errant strand of silky dark brown hair that had blown across her cheek as she continued, her voice cheerful, 'I had the interview a week ago but I didn't think I stood a chance of getting the job when I saw some of the opposition, but then this morning Mr Hunter's secretary phoned. I start in four weeks' time so I can have a few weeks with her showing me the ropes before she leaves to follow her husband to his new job in the States at the end of May.'

'But if you were thinking of something like this why didn't you *say*?' Vivian asked bewilderedly, his voice holding a slightly plaintive note and his boyishly handsome face set in a dark frown. 'And there's the wedding and everything; Carole was relying on you to help her with all the arrangements—she just hasn't got a clue regarding anything practical.' His voice was indulgent rather than critical and then it changed as he added, 'You *are* the chief bridesmaid after all.'

5

'I know.' The smile was being kept in place by sheer will-power now. If anyone knew, *she* knew. Chief brides-maid to the beautiful newcomer to the market town who had captured Vivian's heart from the first time he had seen her at one of the local barn dances. Carole James, with her long blonde hair and deep blue eyes, hourglass figure and the sort of legs that went on for ever. And she was nice too, Cory thought wretchedly. A bit giggly and helpless, and she'd definitely never win *Mastermind*, but neverthe-less nice.

'And I can still be Carole's bridesmaid so don't worry. Most of the arrangements can be sorted before I go—that won't be a problem—and you've already booked the church and the village hall with your uncle, haven't you?' Vivian's uncle was the local vicar. 'And I'll be home for the odd weekend before September if there's anything Carole needs help with,' she added soothingly.

'Of course there'll be things she'll need help with.' Vivian's voice was both anxious and irritated, and for a moment Cory's pain was swallowed in anger.

How could he be so…so *thick*? she asked herself silently. They had always lived in each other's pockets from the day they had first started kindergarten together, and with their families living only three doors from each other had spent all their childhood and youth in each other's homes. His parents were almost as close to her as her own. And even when they had gone to their respective universities and met other people none of their relationships had come close to what they had with each other.

Not that anything had ever been *said* exactly. But it hadn't needed to be. She had known he was the one for her and vice versa. Or so she had thought… More fool her, she added bitterly.

'Vivian, I know Carole has no family of her own but your mother will advise in any way she can.' Cory forced her voice to be calm and unruffled. 'The village hall is booked for the reception already and your mother knows the caterers your uncle suggested. There's really no problem. Everything is in hand.'

'But she was relying on your moral support—'

'She'll have you for moral support for goodness' sake!' It was a snap; Cory's patience only went so far. Her mother was a redhead and in a certain light the deep auburn highlights in her own dark brown hair bore testimony to the fact that she had a good number of her mother's vibrant fiery genes in her.

'So you really intend to go?' Vivian asked tightly after a small but very pregnant pause, his mouth pulling into a thin line.

'Yes, I really intend to go.' Cory's voice was equally tight. She'd go tomorrow if she could. She'd had quite enough the last few months of watching Vivian billing and cooing with the curvaceous blonde, and the engagement party the week before had been an ordeal she wouldn't wish on her own worst enemy. It was over six months to the middle of September, and she would never survive the course if she had to remain in Thirsk all that time. For some strange reason Carole seemed determined to make her her best friend.

'Then there's nothing more to be said,' Vivian said stiffly, and then, in repudiation of that statement, he continued, 'But why you couldn't have put your career on hold for a few more months and carried on working at Stanley & Thornton's I don't know. You say you want a change and that a new job and surroundings will stretch you, and I can understand that at your age—' she'd hit him, she really would, she'd hit him! '—but another six months wouldn't have made any difference in the overall run of things.'

'Perhaps at my *great* age I didn't think I'd got time to hang about,' Cory bit out sharply as Vivian walked towards the door. Carole, at just twenty years of age, was four years

younger than Cory and Vivian and had already pointed the
fact out several times in her cute, open-eyed way that made
Cory feel like Methuselah. 'Maybe I thought I'd got to grab
at life before it passed me by?' Even as she spoke the words
she realised there was more than a little self-prophecy in
them. She should have left Yorkshire years ago.

Vivian didn't pause in his retreat from her mother's
pleasant rose-coloured lounge, and after a second or two,
when she heard the front door bang behind him, Cory took
a long, deep, reviving breath and forced back the hot tears
that were burning the back of her eyes, blinking desperately
as she raised her chin high.

No more. *No more crying!* She willed herself to stand
perfectly still and for her heartbeat to return to normal. She
had cried enough tears in the last few months to fill the
ocean and she was tired of feeling so desperate. She was
leaving Thirsk in four weeks' time and even if the post of
secretary to the illustrious head of Hunter Operations didn't
work out—she hadn't mentioned to Vivian or her parents
that the offer was conditional—she wouldn't be back to
stay. She'd rather crawl through red-hot coals of fire.

All her dreams, all her aspirations since she had first
learnt to toddle, had been tied up with the tall, handsome
man who had just left the house so abruptly and she was
going to have to learn how to face the rest of her life without him, and, having learnt it, to carve a future for herself.
It wasn't the path she would have chosen, it certainly
wasn't the path that was going to bring her the sort of cosy
family joy and harmony she had foreseen for herself, but
there had been enough crying over spilt milk and she didn't
like the person she was turning into.

Her back straightened and her shoulders pulled back as
she emphasised the thought. *She wasn't a whinger.* She'd
never been a whinger, and enough was enough. She was
young, she was intelligent, and there was life after Vivian
Batley-Thomas…gorgeous as he was. No! The last thought

had crept in all by itself, and Cory frowned determinedly. She couldn't afford to think like that any more, even for a moment. Gorgeous he might be, available he wasn't. End of story.

'Cory, how nice to see you again, and please, call me Gillian.'

It was a cold April morning four weeks later, and, having taken up residence in her compact but attractive bedsitter the Friday before, Cory had just nervously entered the high-rise offices of Hunter Operations. The building was big, flamboyant and luxurious, and left the neat little offices of Stanley & Thornton's, Engineering Specialists, in the cold, but Gillian Cox's smile was warm and went some way to alleviating the panic Cory was feeling as she faced the chairman's secretary on this, the first morning of the new job.

'Hello, Gillian.' Amazingly her voice sounded nearly normal. 'It's nice to see you again too. How are you?'

'Rushed off my feet, half insane and heading for a nervous breakdown. Other than that, fine.' Gillian's smile widened. She had kindly come to Reception to welcome Cory personally and now walked her over to the lift, saying brightly before pressing the button, 'You must be dying to meet Max; it's not often one doesn't get to meet one's boss until the first day of employment, is it?'

'No.' Cory's voice was weak. She'd thought that herself!

'But he's back from that awful Far East session of conferences and tours, and it's proved very fruitful which is the main thing. And you'll get on fine with him, Cory, really. He's a boss in a million. If it hadn't been for Colin landing such a wonderful job in the States I'd never have dreamt of leaving Hunter Operations, especially after fifteen years with Max, but it's very important to Colin that we begin the cocktail round and so on as soon as possible. You know how these huge conglomerates work,' she added cheerily.

No, she didn't, but she didn't like to say so.

Gillian was still talking when the lift stopped at the exalted top floor and as the doors slid open to reveal lush thick cream carpets and brushed linen walls, the hushed calm was rudely shattered by a very irate, very male voice bellowing, 'Gillian? For crying out loud, woman! Where's that fax from Katchui?'

Cory's eyes shot to the doorway halfway down the wide corridor and to the big dark man filling it, but Max Hunter had eyes for no one but his cool and apparently unruffable secretary who, after a quick aside for Cory to wait in her own office directly opposite them, glided forward, saying calmly, 'It's on your desk, Max, where it's been for the last three days, but no doubt you've buried it under that mountain of paperwork you've been looking at all weekend.'

Gillian disappeared through the doorway but it was a moment or two before Cory could force her legs to take her into the other woman's office, which would soon become hers if this job worked out. Although, having now seen the formidable Max Hunter, she had her doubts about that very thing, she thought a trifle ruefully.

The man in the doorway had been big, very big—at least six feet four—and broad with it. He wasn't old; Gillian had told her Max Hunter's father—who had started the Hunter empire in the late fifties—had died fifteen years ago when his son had inherited at the tender age of twenty-three, but her glimpse of the hard male face and black hair dusted with silver had suggested a man some few years older than his thirty-eight years. And his manner…Cory breathed deeply as she sank into one of the plumply upholstered easy chairs dotted about Gillian's vast quarters. His manner didn't exactly tally with this supposed 'boss in a million' that Gillian had been so enthusiastic about at her interview.

'All's calm again on the western front.' Gillian was beaming as she bustled through the interconnecting door between her office and that of Max Hunter. 'He'd got Mr Katchui hanging on on the phone and Max hates to be anything less than one hundred per cent in control,' she said brightly. 'Typical man.'

Cory nodded without saying anything; she'd gathered that much for herself. She smoothed down the slim pencil skirt of the new navy blue suit that had cost her an arm and a leg, cleared her throat and had just opened her mouth to ask something intelligent when Gillian completely took the wind out of her sails as she leant forward and said, her voice urgent, 'Don't take any notice of how Max is, Cory—his manner and how he talks and everything. He really is a lovely man underneath it all. We've always got on great.'

'You have?' Cory needed every bit of reassurance she could get.

'Definitely.' Gillian nodded firmly. 'But he just takes a bit of getting used to. He's very sure about what he wants and even more so about what he doesn't, and he doesn't suffer fools gladly. Well, he doesn't suffer them at all actually.' She grinned at Cory who bared her teeth in feeble response.

'And he has very rigid views about people,' Gillian went on.

This was getting worse by the minute!

'I interviewed ten applicants on his behalf, you know, and, knowing Max like I do, you were the only one who met his criteria. Some of them were too officious and some not officious enough, one or two had a baby glint in their eyes and dealing with maternity leave and all that paraphernalia would drive Max mad; he's awful to temps. And he doesn't appreciate women who titivate all the time, or clock-watch, and he expects one hundred per cent discretion at all times of course.' She smiled sunnily, her face serene.

'Of course.' Cory gulped audibly. She had to take all this as a compliment that she was the one Gillian had thought fitting, she told herself desperately, but right at the moment it was hard. 'Well, you've told me what he doesn't like, Gillian,' she said carefully. 'Perhaps I'd better know the positive side too?'

And then a deep cold voice brought both their heads turning as it said expressionlessly, 'In essence the five Bs—brains, backbone, breeding, boldness and...' The pause was deliberate.

'And?' She had had to force herself to speak; close to, this man was positively devastating but she dared not let his effect on her show. She had been right in thinking his face was hard, but it was more than that, much more. The dark tanned skin was pulled tight over a chiselled bone structure that was disturbingly masculine, the aquiline nose and strong mouth increasing the impression of severity. But it was the eyes—amazingly beautiful tawny-gold eyes shaded by thick black lashes—which gave his gaze a ruthlessly piercing quality that was totally unnerving and more than a little formidable.

She had never in all her life seen eyes like this man's, and when added to his overall height and breadth—which she now saw was made up of muscle and bone and not fat—and the perturbingly cruel nature of his magnetic good looks the end result was almost paralysing. She couldn't believe this was her *boss*.

'And beauty,' he finished laconically, and in the split second before he smiled and moved forward to shake her hand Cory was conscious of that golden light shooting right down to her toes.

She recovered quickly, jumping to her feet and putting out her hand which was swallowed whole in his huge fingers, but she made sure her grip was firm and strong even if her answering smile quivered a little. She guessed he was joking about the beauty—Gillian was immaculately and expensively dressed, and her greying hair was expertly cut in the latest style, but not even her nearest and dearest could have called the homely-faced woman remotely beautiful.

'So you're the paragon Gillian was so delighted to unearth,' he said thoughtfully. His voice had a smoky, husky tone and a faint accent she couldn't quite place, and was utterly in keeping with the dynamic whole. It made her toes want to curl.

'I'm Cory Masters, Mr Hunter.' She had retrieved her hand as soon as possible; the feel of his hard, warm flesh was not improving the state of her nerves. 'It's very nice to meet you.'

'Likewise, and the name's Max by the way,' he returned easily.

Max. How on *earth* was she going to be so familiar as to call him by his first name? Cory thought feverishly. The thought was daunting.

'Short for Maximilian,' he continued imperturbably, only a slight narrowing of the brilliant gaze suggesting he was aware of the hasty withdrawal. 'My father liked to tell the tale that I was christened after one of his favourite film characters, Maximilian the robot, in the film *The Black Hole*?' Cory had never heard of it but she nodded anyway. 'But he admitted privately the name came from the Roman emperor Maximilian I, and that it is from the Latin maximum meaning greatest.' He eyed her lazily, his mouth quirking.

Robot or Roman emperor, the name fitted, Cory told herself with a faint touch of hysteria. He was easily the most overwhelming individual she had ever come across, and she had committed herself to work for this man as his secretary-cum-personal assistant. She must be mad! She was way, way out of her league here.

'Now, I understand from Gillian that for the next couple of weeks you are mainly going to observe and digest,' he said coolly. 'The following month you will assist and hopefully by the last week will have become autonomous. Ask any questions you like, dig, delve, call Gillian in the middle of the night if you feel so inclined, but don't bother me. I don't know how the office out here works and I don't want to; that's what I pay a secretary for. I expect you to be able to put your finger on anything I want at a moment's notice, and I never accept excuses. Is that clear?' he added smoothly.

'Perfectly.' There was something in his tone that had put Cory's back up although she couldn't have explained what, and now she found herself saying, before she could stop herself, 'I take it from this morning's incident that you expect your secretary to be as fully conversant with every item on your desk as she is of her own?' She had kept her tone pleasant, even conversational, and in the pause before he spoke again she could almost see the razor-sharp brain trying to assess exactly where she was coming from.

'Absolutely,' he agreed with apparent unconcern, but again the amber eyes had narrowed just the merest iota and Cory knew her little jibe about the buried fax had been received, analysed, and filed away under the correct heading of sarcasm.

Which made her crazy, she told herself in the next instant, when after a curt nod of his head he turned and disappeared back through the interconnecting door, shutting it sharply behind him. Why start off on the wrong foot right from word go? Oh, she should have kept her mouth well and truly shut! She was her own worst enemy. Her father was always saying the same about her fiery, volatile mother, and somehow in Max Hunter's authoritative presence all her father's calm, placid genes had died and all her mother's reckless ones had come rushing to the fore.

'Right.' Gillian's voice was neutral. 'Let's get you acquainted with all the companies under the Hunter Operations umbrella first. There's a breakdown on that desk over there with all relevant facts and figures. Most of it is confidential. I've also done a rough précis of the main people, both within Hunter Operations and without, whom you're likely to deal with, and any background—hang-ups, problems, difficult to communicate with or easy, that sort of thing—to help you along a bit. Could you destroy those sheets in the shredder once they're in your head because at least half of them would feel inclined to have me up for libel if they read them?'

'Thank you.' The other woman's smile was infectious and it made Cory feel a little better, although she found her hands were trembling when she took the seat at the desk Gillian indicated. Max Hunter was probably congratulating himself right now for the trial period stipulated in the job offer, she thought grimly, smoothing back a shining strand of dark hair which had escaped the prim French pleat at the back of her head, and she couldn't really blame him. But she intended to make sure that if, or perhaps she should say when, he decided not to make her a permanent offer he wouldn't be able to use the quality of her work or her dedication as the excuse.

Cory was deep in a very interesting and, she had to admit, somewhat aspersive review of Max Hunter's current main competitor when she heard the buzzer on Gillian's phone. 'Yes, Max?' There was a moment or two of silence and then, 'Oh, yes, that's fine with me. I'll just check... Cory?'

Cory lifted her head enquiringly to Gillian's slightly bemused voice, and saw the older woman was staring at her with a studiously blank face which gave absolutely nothing away.

'Max was wondering if you are doing anything for lunch? He suggests taking us to Montgomery's as a little celebration of your first day at Hunter Operations. I'm free, are you?'

'Montgomery's?' The name meant nothing to Cory—she had only been in London just over a week—but from the other woman's tone it clearly wasn't a fast-food restaurant. 'Yes, that would be lovely,' she managed faintly. And then, once Gillian had relayed their acceptance, she asked, 'What exactly is Montgomery's, Gillian?'

'It's a restaurant,' Gillian said carefully. 'A very...nice restaurant. I've been there once or twice before and the food is very good.' She was trying to be offhand but the message was clear.

'Right.' Cory's heart sank still further. No doubt men like Max Hunter took their secretarys to such places all the time, but she hadn't had Gillian's experience. She just hoped she didn't let anyone down. This was probably some kind of a test?

The remainder of the morning sped by as her brain tried to assimilate a hundred and one facts, and just before twelve, at Gillian's urging, she made use of the little pink and white cloakroom attached to the secretary's office to freshen up before lunch.

'What are you doing here, Cory?' She took a long breath as she stared at the wide-eyed girl in the mirror. The discreetly elegant hairdo, the circumspect make-up, the expensive suit and Italian leather shoes—this wasn't her. Who was she trying to fool? She wasn't going to carry this off, no way, no how. She should never have tried for this job— it was way, way out of her league. Huge, anxious, sea-washed green eyes looked back at her, and she gave a nervous swallow in the same moment she realised the palms of her hands were damp. Calm down, girl. Calm down.

She had to carry this off. She continued to stare into the mirror as she gnawed at her bottom lip, and then hastily splashed cold water over her wrists before re-touching her make-up and spraying a few drops of perfume on to cool skin. She had her bedsit now, and in spite of the fact that it was only one large room tucked away in an old house in Chiswick it was costing a small fortune. She needed every penny of her six-week probationary salary, but Gillian had stipulated a hundred per cent increase once the position became permanent, and that would be good money—very good money. Of course she could get cheaper accommodation, but she had fallen in love with the lovingly restored Victorian house with its gracious sense of the past, and her bedsit—right at the top of the house and affording a panoramic view over roaming rooftops and a huge expanse of light-washed sky—was an oasis of peace amidst London's bustle.

'Cory?' Gillian's voice just outside told her it was time to go, and she took a hard, anxious pull of air, smoothing down the fitted jacket of the linen suit and tweaking the collar of her jade-green blouse into place before she left the small sanctuary.

The two women had just slipped on their coats when the door to Max's office opened. He moved lazily towards them, his powerful body possessed of an animal grace that was entirely natural and all the more formidable because of it. There was no polite 'All ready?' or any other preliminary small talk; he merely gestured with one hand towards the outer door, his hard-boned face cool and closed, and as he did so Gillian's telephone began to ring.

'Leave it.' It was an order and Gillian nodded, but then, after her answering machine had cut in and just as Max was closing the door behind him, they heard a man's voice say after the beep, 'Gill? Gill, if you're there pick up the phone, love. It's urgent.'

'It's Colin.' Max had already swung the door wide again and as Gillian hurried to the phone with a muttered, 'I'm sorry,' he leant lazily against the outer wall in the corridor outside, his gaze switching to Cory with alarming suddenness and pinning her to the spot. She stared back at him, willing her nerves not to show.

'How was the first morning?' he asked in that husky dark voice that sent her nerve-endings into hyperdrive.

'Good.' She nodded in what she hoped was a brisk fash-

ion, and prayed he would put her burning cheeks down to
the central heating which was of the hothouse variety. This
was stupid, this was so *stupid,* Cory told herself angrily as
she frantically searched her blank mind for something to
say. She was supposed to be working for the man from
nine to five—or six or seven, whatever the day demanded—
five days a week, but at this rate she wouldn't survive the
day, let alone the first week.

She had been so composed and cool and calm at that
initial interview back in February. The pain and misery of
Vivian's engagement party two days before had been so
vivid in her mind that a kind of numb fatalism had guided
her through the ordeal of Gillian's hundred and one questions and practical tests; she'd felt then that the worst that
could possibly happen had happened, so what was the success or failure of a job interview compared to Vivian marrying someone else? In fact she'd still felt like that right
up until... When? *This morning at nine o'clock.* When
she'd looked into a pair of narrowed tawny eyes set in the
coldest face she had ever seen. And also the most attractive,
she added wryly.

'Good?' He drawled the word slowly with a hint of
mockery. 'Care to elaborate on that enigmatic statement?'

No, she wouldn't, and she wasn't mad about his supercilious attitude either. Funnily enough the thought brought
two of Max's aforementioned Bs—backbone and boldness—into play, and she heard herself saying, her voice
firm now and aiming at polite reserve rather than the cutting
coldness she would have loved to display, 'It would be
foolish of me to venture an opinion after just three hours,
don't you think? But certainly Gillian has been extremely
helpful and kind.' She raised her chin and straightened her
shoulders.

'It would be impossible for Gillian to be anything else.'
There was genuine warmth in his voice for the first time

and it made the smoky effect lethal. 'She's a secretary in a million.'

'That's just what she said about—' Cory stopped abruptly. She wasn't at all sure Gillian would appreciate her repeating her earlier comment, besides which, this man's ego was big enough as it was. But it was too late. He'd homed in like a nuclear missile.

'About?' he questioned softly, but she knew they were both aware of what she had been about to say. It was there in the eyes.

'About you,' Cory admitted grudgingly. 'She said you were a boss in a million.'

'And you doubt that very much.' The hint of laughter was unmistakable. Cory was too surprised to do anything but stare at him, her green eyes with their mercurial violet tinge wide and her full-lipped mouth slightly agape as she searched her mind for a response.

Max Hunter seemed to be enjoying himself. She watched him settle more comfortably against the wall, and there was a definite measure of satisfaction in the deep voice when he said, 'True or false?' as black eyebrows rose mockingly.

He was as unlike her previous employer as it was possible to be! The thought flashed through Cory's head and brought small, strutting Mr Stanley, with his formal, ritualistic working mode and almost phobic fear of any relaxing of office protocol or decorum, there in front of her for a moment. He would no more have a conversation like this with his secretary than fly to the moon! Mind you, she wasn't Max Hunter's secretary, not yet, and perhaps he never intended for her to be? Perhaps she didn't *want* to be? And she agreed with Gillian's statement—Max Hunter was certainly a boss in a million all right. It was just the way he'd earned the title she and his secretary differed on, Cory thought caustically.

It was the last thought that opened Cory's mouth and enabled her to say, with suspect sweetness, 'I'm sure

Gillian is absolutely right, Mr Hunter, when she says you're one on your own?'

'Max,' he corrected smoothly, 'and I've been insulted less prettily in my time. Do you work as well as you fence, Cory?'

She wasn't going to win a war of words with this man. For the second time in as many minutes Cory found herself with her mouth open and she shut it quickly with a little snap. 'Better,' she said brightly. This job was a non-starter. She knew it.

'Then we'll get on just fine.' He levered himself straight.

It was as he turned to face the doorway through which Gillian was walking that Cory noticed the scar on the right side of his neck. It was long and jagged, starting above his ear in his hair and disappearing down into the collar of his shirt, and spoke of a savage accident. The scar itself was silver but due to his dark tan it stood out quite distinctly from the surrounding skin, and for a moment or two Cory couldn't take her eyes off it. She had averted her gaze by the time he turned to her again, but it had really shocked her. What on earth had happened to him?

'I'm sorry I've kept you both waiting.' Gillian was flushed and flustered, and when her voice wobbled a little and she added, 'It's Colin—he's not well,' Max took the older woman's arm as the three of them entered the waiting lift.

'What is it?' he asked with surprising gentleness. 'What's wrong?'

'Oh, nothing, not really.' Gillian breathed in deeply. 'A touch of food poisoning, they think. Colin says it's not serious.'

'But you're missing him, and no doubt he's missing you.'

'Uh-huh.' Gillian nodded and then managed a fairly normal smile as she included Cory in her rueful grimace. 'Pathetic, isn't it? But the last eight weeks are the first time we've been apart in our twenty years of married life and it feels so strange. Still, at least Colin's found a gorgeous apartment out there and everything is going to be done when I arrive on the doorstep in six weeks' time.'

Six weeks. *Six weeks!* And then—if she was still here, that was—there would be only Max Hunter and herself and no comforting, homely Gillian around. Cory missed her step as she followed the older woman into the lift and immediately a warm firm hand fastened on her elbow. 'Careful.' He was just behind her and his six feet four towered over her five feet five as she turned to murmur her thanks. 'We don't want you breaking your neck on the first day, do we?' he added evenly. 'And certainly not in this building. I can do without a lawsuit for industrial injury.'

'I wouldn't *dream* of suing you for something that was my own fault,' Cory answered hotly as though the accusation were a reality.

'No?' It was blatantly cynical, his firm, cruel mouth twisting mockingly at the fierceness of her protest.

'No.' She stared up at him, her mouth very firm, and they were both unaware of the interested spectator watching the little drama in front of her. 'That would be positively immoral.'

'Immoral...' He considered the word lazily.

Cory was instantly aware she had chosen an unfortunate turn of phrase but it was too late to retract it. She'd have to bluff.

'And you are always...moral, Cory?' he asked quietly, with hateful butter-wouldn't-melt-in-my-mouth innocence.

'Always.' This wasn't going to work. This job *definitely* wasn't going to work. For some reason he didn't like her; there was veiled antagonism in his every word, his every glance, and she wasn't imagining it. He had been gentle, understanding even, with Gillian, but with her it was almost as though he was trying to catch her out all the time, Cory thought tightly. He was a cold, hard, macho *brute* of a man—everything she detested in a male, when she thought about it—and she hadn't made the move to London to live in a perpetual state of tension and stress.

'Then Gillian has chosen well.' It wasn't what Cory was expecting and she was eternally glad the lift chose that precise moment to open its silent doors and deliver them in Reception. 'Now, a nice relaxing lunch, I think?'

His voice was even and distant suddenly, and, ridiculous though it was, Cory felt as though the man now escorting Gillian and herself through the ingratiating smiles and nods in Reception was an entirely different creature from the one she had seen so far. He was cool and remote and self-assured, every inch the powerful tycoon and entrepreneur, as he strode through the hushed and immaculate surroundings and out through the gleaming brass and glass doors which one of the reception staff had fallen over themselves to open.

A blue and silver Rolls-Royce was parked at the kerb outside the building with magnificent disregard for yellow lines, and as Max led the two women towards it Cory had the notion she was taking part in a flamboyant movie, and any moment a director would be leaping in front of them and shouting, 'Cut! It's a take.'

The chauffeur had opened the rear door of the limousine the moment he had caught sight of Max, and now, as Cory followed Gillian into the rich leather interior, she wished there were a little more room in her skirt. Discreet, calf-length and prim it was, cut for scrambling in and out of breathtaking vehicles like this one it wasn't, and she was vitally conscious of Max Hunter just inches behind her and no doubt with his eyes on the material straining over her backside.

She was hot and pink by the time she was seated next to Gillian, but then, as Max joined them on her other side and his hard male thigh rested against hers, she knew what a pressure cooker felt like. He was her boss. He was just her boss. Say after me...

If her life had depended on it Cory couldn't have told anyone how long it took to reach Montgomery's, the route the Rolls took through the heavy lunchtime traffic or even what the three of them discussed *en route*. Every fibre of her being, every cell in her body was concentrated on not making the biggest fool of herself ever, but she must have sounded fairly coherent and behaved normally because Gillian's nice round face was quite cheerful and relaxed when the limousine eventually glided to a halt outside the sort of establishment that just reeked of class and wealth.

Of course the glass of champagne might have helped. When Max had leant forward and opened the polished wood cocktail cabinet in front of their seat Cory had determinedly stopped her mouth from falling open—twice in one morning was quite enough—but her eyes had widened all the same. The glasses were tall and exotic and chilled, the champagne was pink and frothy and tasted like all the summers she had ever experienced rolled into one, and Max's toast—'A welcome to the newest member of Hunter Operations'—brought the colour that had just receded from her cheeks flooding back again.

'I don't remember you doing this for me when we first started working together, Max?' Gillian had already said, with her first sip of champagne, that it would go straight to her head, and certainly as her employer helped both women out of the car Gillian was as flushed as Cory as she grinned at Max.

He smiled easily. 'I wasn't sure how to treat a secretary in those days, Gillian, if you remember. I've learned as I've gone along.'

Cory envied the other woman's quiet familiarity with their boss. Of course Gillian was a good few years older than Max and very happily married to boot, and she'd known him for years, but Cory just knew she would never,

never, be able to adopt the almost motherly approach that Gillian did so well and which, at heart, was the basis for all good boss/secretary relationships. He just scared her to death. He did what?

Immediately the thought formed she caught it in horror. She wasn't frightened of Max Hunter—she'd never been overawed by any man, even her old headmaster who was a tyrant of the first order and had scared everyone rigid. She was *not* frightened of Max Hunter! That was the most ludicrous, stupid, crazy notion she'd ever had! It was the champagne. It had to be the champagne.

'Cory? Is anything wrong?'

Gillian's gentle voice brought her out of the whirling maelstrom of her thoughts, and to the realisation that she was standing in the middle of the crowded pavement with people weaving around her. Hardly the pose for a young, dynamic secretary!

'Shall we?' Gillian gestured towards the building in front of them and as Cory's eyes focused on Max she saw he was holding open the door of the restaurant, an expression of great patience on his face, but it was the look in the beautiful and compelling amber eyes that bothered her. They were narrowed and intent and piercingly steady, and they brought to mind a wildlife programme she had seen just the other night, when a quite magnificent tawny-eyed lion had been watching his prey—a delicate and fine-boned wildebeest—with frightening and fierce single-mindedness.

And then he blinked and smiled, heavy lids and thick black lashes sweeping down, and when he looked at her again he was just an unusually arresting and powerful man. A man any woman would think worthy of a second glance, a man of intimidating intelligence and undeniable presence but, nevertheless, just a man.

The meal was simply wonderful, and seated as they were in a quiet and private alcove, where they could see and yet not be seen, Cory found herself relaxing enough to enjoy the good food. From the moment they had been seated Max had set out to be a charming and amusing dinner companion, keeping the two women entertained with a monologue of witty and slightly wicked stories, and by the time Cory had spooned the last delicious morsels of feather-light crêpe Suzette into her mouth she had been lulled into a comfortable state of false security.

So it made it all the more shocking when, Gillian having disappeared to the ladies' cloakroom a moment or two earlier, Max turned to Cory and held her eyes with his own as he said calmly, 'Well, Cory? Have you decided whether to turn tail and run or stay yet?' He raised those cruel black eyebrows again.

'What?' It was too loud—she knew her voice had been too loud and that was quite the wrong tack to take with this man. She needed to be calm, unflustered and in control, she thought feverishly as she watched him settle back in his seat and continue to survey her through slits of brilliant light that brought the poor wildebeest to mind again. Although at least on the plains there was somewhere to run.

He was the sort of man who was intimidating even when he wasn't intending to be, and she wasn't sure if he was intending to be now or not. He was so *big*, that was part of the problem—so masculine and uncompromisingly virile. Everything he did, every little gesture or movement, was so controlled and disciplined and it was formidable. He had an aura of authority, but not in a comforting or reassuring way—at least she didn't find it so, Cory told herself nervously. Hunter by name and Hunter by nature...

Oh, for goodness' sake, girl, pull yourself together! The rebuke was loud and angry in her head. She'd be crediting him with supernatural powers next and wouldn't he just love that?

The thought acted in much the same way as a douse of cold water on her fluttering panic, and Cory forced herself to take several silent breaths before she smiled and said, her voice as cool as she could make it, 'I really don't know what you are talking about, Max.'

There, she'd said his name without the slightest pause or hesitation, even giving it a slightly scornful intonation.

'No?' The gold was very clear around the bottomless black pupils. 'You mean to say you weren't considering whether you'd come back tomorrow or just call it quits?' he asked silkily.

'No, I wasn't.' And she hadn't been, not really. Admittedly she had wondered whether *he* would pull the plug on *her*, but she hadn't seriously considered leaving herself. Whatever else, she wasn't a quitter, and she said so now. 'I agreed to take the position for a trial period to see if things worked out and I would honour that whatever,' she said firmly. 'And it works both ways—*you* might decide I'm not suitable,' she added reasonably.

'I knew within the first five minutes whether you were suitable or not,' he said softly. 'In business you have to be able to determine the credibility of someone fast.'

'Snap decisions?' She raised disapproving eyebrows and hoped he hadn't guessed she was acting a part—his previous admission had sent her stomach haywire and churned up that wonderful lunch.

'No, measured appraisals due to years of hard experience and a natural distrust of my fellow man,' he corrected her swiftly, his tone faintly mocking. 'I never make mistakes, Cory. Not any more.'

'Oh, you used to be just like the rest of us, then? Human?' The second the words were out she was horrified. You didn't speak to your employer like that, she told herself silently—not if you still wanted him to remain your employer, that was. Mr Stanley would have had a heart attack on the spot! But Max Hunter wasn't Mr Stanley.

'You see?' There was a measure of amusement in the narrowed eyes and she knew her embarrassment was showing. 'I'd rather have you in my corner than someone else's.

Besides which...' He paused, swallowing the last of his coffee in one gulp before he continued, 'As my secretary and personal assistant you'll be working with me very closely and of necessity the days are often long ones— eleven, twelve hours. I couldn't stand anyone who didn't speak her mind and I don't like boring women, Cory.

'I can forgive anyone anything if they are honest and acting from the heart. I don't like deception or hypocrisy and I don't like prissy thinking along the lines of "the boss is always right." I *am*—' he eyes were gleaming with laughter now '—but if you thought so too, where would the spark be? And you don't have to like me, so don't worry your head on that score,' he added abruptly. 'Because you don't, do you?'

It wasn't a question, it was more of a statement, and one which Cory was utterly unable to answer.

He laughed out loud now at the look on her face and the sound was husky, rusty even, as though he didn't do it too often.

'Don't get concerned,' he said softly, his voice soothing. 'Believe it or not I look on that as another of your admirable attributes. Part of Gillian's amazing success all these years has been because she has her Colin whom she adores to distraction, and our working relationship has been just that...a working one.'

He was telling her he didn't want her fancying him! Cory didn't know whether to be relieved or furious, but she veered towards the latter. What an ego! What an outsize, monstrous ego!

'Power and wealth can be a potent aphrodisiac to some women. Now, whilst that's all to the good in certain situations—' the deep voice held a note that suddenly made her shiver as her nerve-endings sensitised '—at work it's just a damn nuisance and sometimes downright dangerous. You'll be party to some very confidential papers as my

secretary and the old adage of ''Hell hath no fury'' is still
alive and well, believe me,' he finished coolly.

'*Mr Hunter.*' She had probably been as mad as this previously in her life but she couldn't remember it. 'I would
no more dream of acting in the way you've described than
of…of flying to the moon,' Cory snarled angrily. 'Even if
I thought you were the best thing since sliced bread.'

'Which you don't,' he put in softly, his eyes gleaming.

'No, I don't!' she affirmed with furious emphasis.

'You see? The perfect solution for both of us. I get a
secretary I can trust and who—from the references Mr
Stanley among others supplied—is more than adequate not
to mess anything up with misplaced emotion. You get a
position which will only serve to further enhance your career, you get to travel a bit, see new places with the added
advantage of it all being paid for, and a handsome salary
to boot. Ideal, eh? And of course you're out of the little
home-town trap. Why exactly did you decide to leave
Yorkshire anyway?' he added with a suddenness that took
Cory by surprise. 'You were happy there for the last
twenty-four years.'

She stared at him a moment, getting a bland, expressionless gaze in return, and then forced herself to speak
quietly and calmly when she said, 'It was time to spread
my wings, that's all. My qualifications are excellent—' she
raised her chin slightly at this point; it didn't come naturally
to blow her own trumpet '—and at twenty-four I felt the
next stage of my career was overdue. I—'

'I'm not asking for a résumé of what was written on your
application form and CV.' He was terse. 'I mean the real
reason. Was it a man?' he asked with audacious coolness.

Cory was quite unaware of the shadow of pain that
passed over her face in the second before the fury hit, but
then her eyes were shooting bright green sparks and she
straightened in her chair, her chin thrusting out and her
hands clenched fists in her lap. 'I think I ought to make

one thing perfectly clear before we go on another minute,' she said icily, her voice belying the fiery colour in her cheeks. 'I do not discuss my personal life with anyone unless I want to. If you offer me this job permanently you will be entitled to all of my working days and the very best I can do, both for you and Hunter Operations, but you will not automatically have the right to take over my life. My private life is my own business and absolutely no concern of yours.'

So it *had* been a man. Max Hunter surveyed the taut, angry figure in front of him, his face betraying none of his thoughts. And she wasn't over him yet, not by a long chalk. 'You're absolutely right of course.' Gillian was making her way back to their table and now he stood, his voice merely pleasant and not at all put out as he added, 'I think we're all ready to leave? And Cory?'

She was in the act of rising, Max having pulled out her chair for her, and now, as she turned to face him, he was so close for a moment that she caught the scent of delicious aftershave on clean male skin and took an involuntary step backwards, bumping against the table and rattling the coffee cups. 'Yes?' she asked defensively.

'The offer *is* permanent; it was from five past nine this morning.'

CHAPTER TWO

THE next few weeks were something of a revelation to Cory, not least because she found, after the initial couple of days which passed in a tangled blur, that she was actually enjoying her job. No, enjoy was too weak a word. She was *loving* it; she couldn't wait to get to the office every morning, and that in spite of the million and one facts that were thrown at her every minute—or so it seemed—the hours flew by on winged feet.

She had had her good days and bad days at Stanley & Thornton's, and her position as secretary to the managing director had been both an interesting and extremely responsible one, but working for Max Hunter was something else. And that was the understatement of the year.

Nevertheless, on the morning of Monday, the seventeenth of May, when Cory awoke to clear blue skies and brilliant sunshine, and the realisation that from this day on it was just her juggling the hundred and one balls that Gillian had seemed to manage so effortlessly, she felt more than a little nervous and the butterflies in her stomach were going crazy.

Not that Max Hunter had been anything other than completely professional and detached from that first lunchtime, she reminded herself quickly as she flung back the covers and knelt on her bed to look out of the big picture window at half of Chiswick's rooftops. And patient when he'd had to be, calm, unruffled—at least with her. However, she suspected he'd made a special effort during her settling-in period, and with Gillian there—who practically seemed to read his mind and know what he wanted before he knew himself—he'd had no reason to be anything else. She had observed enough to know he was not a naturally patient man, also that his bark could be every bit as bad as his bite with lesser mortals who stepped out of line.

'Do…not…panic.' She spaced the words out slowly, her heart hammering. 'You're going to be fine, just fine.'

Of course, if she was being *absolutely* honest, it didn't help that he often worked at his desk with his jacket off and his tie loose or flung aside altogether. She nipped at her lower lip, shaking her head at her own absurd foolishness. It shouldn't matter, she *knew* it shouldn't matter—he was only her employer for goodness' sake—but the first time she had walked into his office, on her second day at Hunter Operations if she remembered rightly, and seen him frowning over a load of scattered papers on his huge desk, his massive shoulders and broad physique accentuated by the thin blue silk shirt he was wearing, she'd done a double take.

Thank goodness he had been more interested in the report he'd been looking at than her entrance, she thought now, as her cheeks flushed at the memory of how she had felt.

His tie had been hanging either side of his collar on that occasion and the first two or three buttons of his shirt had been undone, revealing a hard tanned throat and just the beginning of a smidgen of body hair below his collar bone, and she hadn't been able to believe what it had done to her.

Not that she was attracted to him. The thought was fierce and one which came into play several times a day without fail. Not in the slightest. It was just that after little Mr Stanley, with his bald head and paunch and unfortunate tendency to sniff all the time due to chronic catarrh, Max Hunter's particular brand of aggressive male virility was something of a shock. But she'd master what was after all nothing more than an animal response, a fleshly, purely physical thing. Of course she would. No problem.

She just hoped it would be sooner rather than later, she admitted to herself the next moment with a deep sigh. This stupid…awareness of him made her jittery and nervous, and although she was careful to hide it she was constantly on edge in his presence.

Cory breathed in and out a few times, her gaze wandering round the big light sun-washed room, and coming to rest on a huge cake tin perched on top of the small fridge in the minute kitchen in one corner of the bedsit.

She had been home for the first time this weekend, and before she had set off back to London, her mother had packed her faithful little Mini with enough food to keep an army for a month.

Her brow wrinkled as she thought of the two days she had just spent in Yorkshire. She had relished the time with her parents—she had always been close to the pair of them and they had had a riotous evening out on the Saturday when all three of them had eaten and drunk far too much— but meeting Vivian again for the first time in six weeks had been hard. Well, more than hard if she were honest.

As soon as he had spied her bright red Mini parked out-side the house on Saturday morning—she had travelled down late on Friday night after Gillian's farewell party— he had been knocking at the door, and it had been all of three hours before she could get rid of him. *Get rid of him?* The thought stopped Cory in her tracks as she made to walk across the room. She'd never want to get rid of Vivian, would she? She hadn't meant it like that, not really. It was just that she felt awkward now he was engaged to Carole— that was it—uncomfortable and unsure of how she should behave. And he had seemed so…unhappy? *No.* The denial was immediate. Of course he wasn't unhappy, just harassed with all the wedding arrangements and so on. And that was perfectly understandable; of course it was.

She shook her head slightly as she walked across the room. She was going to have a shower in the small bathroom across the landing directly opposite her door, and then fix herself toast and coffee before she got ready for work. She had plenty of time—she had woken a good hour before her alarm was due to ring—but she wanted to get into the office nice and early and have Max's post opened and ready for him on his arrival at Hunter Operations. She intended to start as she meant to carry on, and that would involve one hundred per cent commitment. But that was all right— certainly for the next few years at least. The last thing, the *very* last thing she was looking for after the heartache of the previous few months was a romantic involvement of any kind. Work was safe—you knew where you stood with career ambitions and the like—it was men who were the unknown quantity and liable to cause you heartache and grief.

A pair of hard amber eyes suddenly shot into the screen of her mind and she paused, her hand outstretched towards the big bath sheet on the little stool by the door, as she told herself that was different. Max Hunter was her boss, that was all, and any nervousness or flutters she felt about him were quite legitimate when you considered her financial security was in his hands. And that was the only reason, *the only reason*, that this magnetism problem was getting to her. It was. For definite.

Cory arrived at Hunter Operations at a quarter past eight, but when she walked into her office and looked through the open interconnecting door into Max's domain she realised he must have been in residence for half the weekend, from the amount of papers strewn about his desk and floor. The man was a workaholic!

'Good morning.' His voice was preoccupied. And she had opened her mouth to make the necessary response when he continued, 'Can you be ready to fly out to Japan this evening?' His tone suggested he was asking for nothing more unusual than a cup of coffee.

'Japan?' The therapy of a leisurely soak in hot bubbles followed by toast and coffee on her tiny balcony immediately vanished as she gazed at him in amazement.

'Uh-huh.' He didn't raise his head as he spoke but she saw he was frowning at the papers in front of him. 'This deal with Katchui is getting too complicated; I need to get over there and sort a few things out face to face. You can't beat flesh contact.'

He looked at her then, two piercingly sharp rays of golden light holding her to the spot before he lowered his head again. 'Two first-class tickets any time after three this afternoon; see to it, would you? And I need some coffee, black and strong, and a sandwich. Ham, turkey, beef—not salad or cheese. I need nourishment, not punishment,' he added dryly.

'Right.' She tried to make her voice brisk and secretarial rather than bemused and stunned, which was how she felt.

'And I need that tape on your desk typed up before midday; if we need to make any changes we'll have to do it before we leave.'

'How…how long do you expect us to be away?' Cory asked faintly. Talk about life in the fast lane; this was express mode.

'Five days, a week at the most.' Again the amber light raked her face. 'It's not a problem?' It was said in a tone that suggested it had better not be.

'No, no, of course not.' A week in a foreign country with Max Hunter for company? she thought weakly. And he asked if it was a problem? But it went with the territory and she had known that when she'd accepted the position; it was just that she had expected a few more weeks to get…acclimatised.

The morning sped by on winged feet, and once she had presented the report for Max's eagle-eyed scrutiny at just gone eleven Cory dashed back home and frantically threw clothes and other necessities into a case, dug out her passport, and was back in the office before twelve and straight back at work.

It was almost half past one when it suddenly dawned on Cory that she hadn't let her mother know about the trip, and she had just dialled the number and heard the receiver being lifted at the other end when Max chose that moment to put in an appearance with a sheaf of papers in his hand and a preoccupied expression on his face.

Blast! Cory heard her mother speak the number and didn't like to put the phone down. He *never* came to her; in all the weeks she had been at Hunter Operations the buzzer had invariably summoned Gillian into the inner sanctum. She spoke quickly into the phone. 'Hi, it's Cory. I'm just ringing to let you know I'm going on a business trip to Japan for a few days, so don't worry if you ring the house and there's no answer.'

'Japan?' Her mother was all agog. 'How exciting, dear. I'm glad it wasn't this weekend anyway; we had a lovely time, didn't we? It was wonderful to see you; your father and I so enjoyed it.'

'It was wonderful to see you too,' Cory said uncomfortably, vitally aware of the big dark figure on the perimeter of her vision.

'And Japan, you say? Well, well. Now make sure you take some travel sickness pills—you know how you are—and—'

'I'm sorry, I'm going to have to go.' She knew, without looking at him, that he was scowling. There were dark vibrations coming across the airwaves. 'And I'll look after myself, don't worry. I'll phone you as soon as I get back.'

'All right, darling, and thank you for letting us know. I hope everything goes well and that you have a lovely time. Love you.'

'Love you.' It had been their stock goodbye all through her days at university and since she had been in London and Cory didn't think twice about it. Until she raised her head and looked into Max's face, that was.

'Quite finished?' It was expressionless and even but she knew exactly how he meant it, and immediately she rebelled. He had told her in the first week that the making and receiving of private calls was quite acceptable, as long as she chose the appropriate time and didn't talk to her long-lost cousin in Australia every day, but this was the first call—the very first call—she had made. And she wouldn't have had to do that if he had given her more notice about the Japan trip, either! Well, he certainly needn't think he was browbeating her or making her feel guilty, she told herself hotly. Even Mr Stanley had allowed her more licence than this.

'Yes, thank you.' It was cold and curt and told him his attitude had been noticed and was not appreciated.

'Then perhaps you'd do a better job on these predicted sales figures than Mr Mason's secretary has. I can only just work out what they mean and I don't expect Mr Katchui to have to wade through columns and columns of unnecessary rubbish.' His voice was clipped and terse, as though she were the one at fault. 'Whatever we're paying the woman it's too much,' he finished on a growl.

'Right.' Cory's jaw was set as she took the proffered report. 'We will need to leave here no later than half past two; the flight is at four.' Her voice was as terse as his and just as cold.

She had been so busy concentrating on avoiding touching his hand that her grasp on the papers was minimal, and as the last page became adrift and began to fall she made a grab for it at the same time as Max bent to retrieve it. They didn't exactly make contact, but as her brow brushed against his and the warmth and smell of him encompassed her the effect on Cory was like a powerful electric shock, and the rest of the papers fanned out in a graceful arc about his bent head as she shot backwards.

'Oh, I'm sorry.' This time her lunge forward resulted in their heads cracking together with enough force to make Max see stars for a moment or two, and she was aware of her illustrious boss staggering a little and saying something extremely rude before he took a visible hold of himself and said, 'Leave them, leave them for crying out loud. I'll do it.'

Cory took a very long deep breath as she watched him bend his knees and gather up the pages, and she tried to ignore the way powerful shoulder muscles bunched under thin silk and the way the pose brought expensively cut trousers tight across lean thighs.

'Thank you.' It was succinct in the extreme but all she trusted her voice to say. She was just grateful it wasn't a croak.

'My pleasure.' He glared at her once on straightening before banging the crumpled papers on her desk and turning on his heel, disappearing through his door and slamming it behind him.

Wonderful, absolutely wonderful. Cory stared after him as she willed her heartbeat to return to normal. Not content with aiming to knock him out once, she'd had to go back for a second shot at the title! She bet she knew what he was thinking as he sat in there: Come back, Gillian; all is forgiven. The thought brought a weak smile in spite of her embarrassment. In all the six weeks she had been with Gillian she had never once seen the older woman anything but composed, placid and patient when dealing with her volatile boss. Well, they said variety was the spice of life...

Max didn't risk poking his head out of his office until ten minutes before they were due to leave and, as luck would have it, just as she typed the last number on the neat and concise sales figures she had displayed clearly enough for a child to understand.

'Just finished,' Cory said brightly as she pressed the print key. She didn't look directly at him; she just couldn't.

He walked across to her desk and stood waiting a moment without speaking, and then, as she handed him the first methodical and compact page of figures, glanced at it intently before raising his eyes and giving her one of his rare and devastating smiles. 'Excellent. You've checked it all?' he asked briefly.

'Yes.' She didn't add that she'd found several of the columns on the original report had been wrong and that she'd had to go back to Mr Mason to confirm what was what. She had an idea that his secretary wasn't going to last long anyway.

'Right.' He had put down the first sheet of paper and was fastening the collar of his shirt and pulling his tie into place as he said, 'Time to get moving, I'm afraid. You're all ready?'

Ordinary though his actions had been, there was a curious intimacy to them that Cory couldn't have explained but which made her cheeks flush, and now she busied herself tidying the other printed pages and handing them to him as she said, 'Yes, I'm ready.'

Was the rest of his body the same golden-brown as his face and throat and arms? With his great height and muscled lean frame he must look pretty sensational unclothed... A sudden shiver at the thought awoke her to what she was thinking, and she was weak-kneed with relief that he had turned and gone back to his own office to fetch his things, shutting the door behind him.

What was the matter with her? she asked herself faintly. Had she gone stark staring mad? She couldn't afford to harbour any thoughts like that about Max Hunter. It was all the more disconcerting because she had never, ever let her imagination run riot with anyone else, even Vivian. But Vivian wasn't like Max. The thought opened her eyes wide as she plopped down on her seat and then leapt up again to tidy her desk and fetch her suitcase and jacket from her washroom, all the time telling herself she was his secretary, his *secretary*, for goodness' sake, and she would be out on her ear if he so much as caught a glimmer of what she was thinking. He would misconstrue it, think she fancied him or something, and she didn't. She didn't. She *really* didn't.

Due to a last-minute call from the States and then one from Mr Katchui himself, Max didn't join her in the outer office until nearly three, but the drive from the offices in Brentford to Heathrow was straightforward and Max's chauffeur drove the car competently and fast through the heavy afternoon traffic.

The couple of package holidays Cory had been on in the past just didn't prepare her for the sort of treatment afforded the exalted first-class passengers, but she couldn't enjoy it to the full with every nerve-ending screaming. It was being *with* him like this. He was obviously the type of man who automatically took care of the woman he was with, and although it was nice—it really was—to be folded into him by his arm round her waist as he used his body as a barricade to protect her in the chaos of the terminal, not to have to carry her heavy case, to be whisked through the usual mind-numbing red tape in a way that made her breathless, it was disconcerting as well. In fact it was more than disconcerting if she was truthful.

And she was vitally aware of the little stir his presence caused among the female contingent too—not that Max seemed to notice. The older women and the very young ones weren't too bad—the former discreet and the latter somewhat awestruck, but there were a couple of predatory females in the VIP lounge in particular who were quite blatant in their appreciation. And it rankled. The more so because they totally ignored her as though she didn't exist.

Once on the plane—and never in her wildest dreams had she imagined air travel could be so luxurious—Max's jacket and tie were immediately discarded and he settled back in his seat with all the appearance of being utterly relaxed. 'Take your shoes off, loosen anything that needs loosening and prepare for a long journey,' he drawled lazily as the amber gaze took in her tenseness. 'We're nearly twelve hours in the air and the time difference means we land around midday Tokyo time. We're meeting Mr Katchui late afternoon, and it's going to be a long twenty-four hours whatever way you look at it. Once we've eaten try and catch a few hours' sleep.'

Cory nodded carefully. Yes, she'd try, and she would also aim to be the efficient, cool secretary a man in his position had the right to expect, she told herself flatly.

Sexual chemistry had its places, but the office was not one of them, she reflected soberly as she undid the buttons of her thin linen jacket and eased her court shoes off her feet. She just didn't recognise this side of herself when she thought about it. She had never considered herself to be a particularly sensual person; her love for Vivian had care and fondness and warm affection at its core, and of course she had thought he was a very attractive man, she added quickly. Very attractive. But there had been no stirring of her senses, a little voice in her head reminded her, or at least not in the same way as Max Hunter got under her skin.

'And don't look so worried.' He leant across as he spoke, his voice low and soft as Cory sat rooted in her seat. 'I would never have taken you on as my secretary if I didn't think you were up to the job. You may not have noticed but I'm not a natural philanthropist.' And then, when she just stared at him, 'That was meant to be amusing but don't feel obliged to smile just because I pay your salary,' he added with dry self-mockery.

'Don't worry, I won't.' It had been his nearness that had frozen her reaction—he had been so close she could see the little black regrowth of his beard beginning to show through the tanned smoothness of his chin and smell his aftershave, which was a subtle blend of something wicked, but now she forced a grin as she spoke and was rewarded by an answering quirk of his mouth.

'No, I didn't think you would.' He'd settled back in his seat and now the amber eyes narrowed, and he surveyed her for a good ten seconds before he added, 'Whoever he is, he isn't worth all the heartache, Cory. Take it from someone who knows.'

'What?' Her mouth straightened as her eyes widened in surprise. 'Who on earth are you on about?' she asked ungrammatically.

'This bozo who's been giving you the run-around.' His voice was quite without expression. 'Because he has, hasn't he?'

'I really don't have the faintest idea what you're talking—'

'What's happened?' he continued evenly, ignoring her interruption with his normal arrogance. 'Has he suddenly realised his mistake since you've been down in London and talked you round?'

'No one has talked me round,' she said indignantly.

'It doesn't look like that to me.'

What on earth was he talking about? she asked herself silently. He didn't know anything about Vivian, did he? Not that there was anything *to* know, she added bitterly. There never had been, not really. It had been a one-sided love affair in every sense of the word. 'Max, I'm telling you, no one has talked me round,' she insisted jerkily. As far as Vivian was concerned there had never been anything to talk *about*; she was just good old Cory, friend, comforter, confidante, mug. *Mug?* Where had that come from?

She didn't have time to explore the shock declaration her mind had thrown up before Max said, his tone astringent, 'Then why did you tell him not to worry about you and that you love him?'

'I told Vivian I *love* him?' The words were out before

she had got her brain engaged, but he seized on them like a dog with a bone, his eyes glittering and his mouth tight.

'Vivian? Is that his name?' It was magnificently scornful but he didn't seem as pleased that he was right as normal. 'I've always thought it far more appropriate for a woman than a man,' he said scathingly, 'but then I suppose it depends on the type of man.'

This was getting out of hand. Cory took a deep breath and prayed for composure. 'Max,' she managed to say quite calmly, 'I think we're getting our wires crossed here.' The phone call. The flipping phone call! 'I haven't talked to Vivian since the weekend and I certainly haven't told him I love him. If you're referring to earlier in the office I was talking to my mother.'

'Your mother?' He blinked once and she had the rare— the extremely rare—opportunity of seeing Max Hunter lost for words.

'Yes, my mother,' she answered, her tone tart, but inwardly the sight of her esteemed and authoritative boss literally gaping was really rather satisfying. 'You didn't give me much notice about this trip if you remember,' she continued coolly, 'and surprisingly I do have a life outside Hunter Operations, and there are people who might worry about me if I don't answer my phone for a week.'

He recovered almost immediately. 'Like the aforementioned Vivian?' he asked pointedly. 'The name did slip off your tongue.'

Why, oh, why had she been so foolish? She stared at him in exasperation as she wondered how much to tell him. He was watching her closely, observing her reaction in that big-cat, unnerving way of his, the pale amber shirt he was wearing accentuating the vivid gold of his eyes and increasing the impression of an animal about to spring. Oh, get a hold of yourself, woman! She forced herself to lean back easily in her seat as the thought hit. Max Hunter was a man who liked to hold all the cards—she had seen enough of

the way he operated over the last six weeks to know *that*—
and as far as he was concerned his secretary was an ap-
pendage of himself and therefore as much under his control
as his own right arm.

Gillian's life had been an open book—marriage at
twenty-five to her childhood sweetheart, and a mutual decision, on finding out that they couldn't have children, to
put all their energies into their careers—and that was
fine…for Gillian. But she didn't see that a baring of her
soul had any relevance to the way she conducted herself as
Max Hunter's secretary.

'Vivian is a friend,' she said at last, her voice flat. 'A
dear and old friend and I have known him for years. Okay?'

'No, it isn't.' And then, as her eyes turned a dark jade
and the violet tint was eclipsed by stormy grey, he added,
'I need to know you're with me, one hundred per cent with
me, Cory, and that's the bottom line. I don't need a secretary who's pining from unrequited love or anything of
that nature; it just won't do. It would affect your work and
you know it.'

'How dare you?' She glared at him angrily. This was too
much.

'I dare because it is necessary,' he said grimly, and never
had the dark, brooding quality to his powerful charisma
been more evident. 'I rely on my secretary too much to be
mealy-mouthed.'

'Look, Max…' She paused, biting back the hot retort
she had been about to make as several thoughts flashed
through her mind. He was paying her a very good salary—
an excellent salary—and the experience and credibility she
would gain as his secretary and personal assistant would be
enormous. There were hundreds of girls out there—probably just as well qualified as her—who would bite Max's
hand off if he offered them the chance of working with
him. All in all he probably had every right to demand that
one hundred per cent commitment, and it wasn't a problem

anyway. It really wasn't a problem! So why hadn't she bitten the bullet and told him so?

'Vivian is a childhood sweetheart who is marrying someone else,' she said flatly, 'and I am not—*I am not*—pining for him.' And she wasn't. The knowledge hit her like a ton of bricks and made her voice shaky as she continued, 'I want to make a success of this job, I really do, and you are going to have to take that as read because I am not going to beg and plead to try and make you believe me.' She looked at him straight in the eyes as she spoke.

'You don't have to.' Suddenly his voice was amazingly soft. 'Can I ask you one more thing?'

She nodded. She would have liked to have said no but her courage wasn't endless and the sooner this was finished the better.

'If he asked you for another chance tomorrow and meant it, what would you say?' he asked gently. 'And the truth, now.'

'I don't know.' His face was intensely sexy. It wasn't the moment to have such a thought but it was there and Cory just went with the flow. It was so strong, hard-boned, and the dusting of silver in his jet-black hair brought an experience to the magnetism that was lethal. How many lovers had he had in his time?

'You don't know?' He shook his head slowly, his mouth quirking. 'How long do you think you have loved this guy, Cory?' he asked quietly. 'This soon-to-be-wed childhood sweetheart?'

'Forever.' It probably wasn't tactful but it was the truth.

'Forever?' He echoed her words with another shake of his head. 'And yet if he came grovelling tomorrow, declaring undying love, you'd have to pause before you knew whether you would be prepared to take him on or not?' he asked pointedly. 'Is that right?'

Put like that it sounded awful. Cory stared at him, her green eyes mirroring her confusion as her creamy skin flushed with hot colour. Why did he have to twist things like that?

'Cory?' he prompted determinedly. 'Is that right?'

'You're twisting things.' It was weak but it was all she could manage through the whirling bemusement his probing had caused.

'Am I?' He smiled slowly, his eyes warm.

And then everything in her life before was reduced to nothing, and all her concepts of commitment, love, prudence, discretion were blown to smithereens as he leant forward and his mouth descended on hers, his gaze never leaving her face. His lips merely brushed hers in a light, momentary touch that was over before it had begun, and then he had reclined back in his own seat again and shut his eyes before she could say anything or even move, his voice very even as he said, 'The guy is an idiot who doesn't deserve you and you know it at heart. Forget him and get on with your life, Cory. You're young and beautiful and it's time to move up a gear and have fun. Work hard and play hard for the next few years; there are plenty of fish in London's pool and you don't want to splash around in the shallows forever.'

He had kissed her. Cory was eternally thankful that the shudders of sensation that continued to flow from that one brief embrace were hidden, but even so her face was scarlet and she was glad Max's eyes were shut. And yet you could hardly call that fleeting, transitory contact a kiss, she told herself in the next instant as the voice of common sense took over. Take hold, Cory.

He had meant it as an encouraging conclusion to their conversation, as his final words had proved, a positive statement for her future, and it had meant as little to him as a pat on the back. It wasn't his fault that she had found it…devastating. But she had. Oh, she had. She just couldn't help it.

She leant back in her own seat and shut her eyes, willing

her burning cheeks to return to normal. No, it *was* his fault, she told herself crossly some seconds later; he was just so totally *male*. There were some men whom women would find it easy to regard as friends or colleagues and have platonic relationships with, there were others who, due to their attractiveness or sexual charisma or whatever, made the comrade thing a little harder to achieve, and then there was Max Hunter. He was one on his own, there was no doubt about it, and it wasn't just she who thought so either, she comforted herself silently. She had seen his effect on the female of the species over the last few weeks and it was blistering. He reduced the most intimidating, hard-boiled businesswomen to purring pussycats when he *wasn't* trying, and when he was... Well, he was lethal. And he knew it and used it too.

She nipped at her bottom lip, finding it a relief to admit to herself at last that she was just like every other female and fancied him rotten. But he was her boss and therefore the main work colleague she would be dealing with day after day, and this attraction she felt—which was a purely physical thing and as such could be controlled with a little will-power—had to be kept strictly under lock and key. He had made it plain, ruthlessly plain, on her first day at Hunter Operations that all he wanted in a secretary was an efficient, pleasant and intelligent machine—any gooey feelings or romantic inclinations would mean she would be out on her ear faster than she could say Jack Robinson.

She nodded at the thought, feeling a surge of adrenalin that she now saw things so clearly. She had it all under control, of course she did, and that was good—very good. There was no need to panic or get alarmed. She could be as cool as the next girl.

The kiss having been put in its proper perspective and the little pep talk finished, her mind turned back to the disturbing revelation she had had about Vivian. Did she really think he had taken her for a mug? she asked herself with determined honesty. The answer was loud and clear. She hadn't been imagining all those times he had waxed lyrical about the future, their future, even if he hadn't been specific. And the kisses they had shared, his tenderness, his reliance on her. She had cosseted him and fussed over him, and when she had been at university and had had the odd date or boyfriend—something they had both agreed they would do—it had been as if he'd been there with her, as a silent and condemning spectre. He'd always gone quiet and hurt when she had spoken of other men, in spite of the fact he had been seeing girls himself, and she had *fallen* for it, she admitted now with silent wrath. She had, completely.

And he had still continued to manipulate her after he had shown an interest in Carole. He had behaved as though she was his protected baby sister from that point, turning things around and weaving his little threads of half truths until she had been convinced she had misunderstood their relationship in the past. How could she have been so *stupid*? She had to stop herself from grinding her teeth. She would have respected him much more, admired him even though she might have felt hurt, if he had come right out at the beginning and admitted he had fallen in love with someone else and out of love with her. She could have handled that.

She should have seen all this; she couldn't understand why she hadn't. Why had it taken a comparative stranger, Max Hunter, to point out the obvious? What was the matter with her?

'What a fierce little face.' It was cool and mocking.

Her eyes shot open and she turned her head to see the amber gaze casting its golden light over her face. 'I…I was just daydreaming.' She defended herself quickly. 'That's all.'

'I'm not going to ask what about,' he said with dry amusement. 'I've a feeling I'd rather not know. The stewardess has just left the menu for dinner; perhaps you'd care to take a look?'

Menu. They had a proper menu in first class? Oh, how the other half lived! Cory took the proffered menu with a smile of thanks and determinedly cast her eyes downwards.

Okay, so the more she *seemed* to know about men, the less she actually knew, but what the hell? This luxurious plane journey was a first and she was going to enjoy it with all her might. She wasn't at all sure about how her feelings stood with regard to Vivian, but one thing she did know— she had done the right thing in leaving Yorkshire and spreading her wings. Whether it had been right to fly into Max Hunter's particular net was another matter entirely, but only time would tell if she had jumped out of the frying pan into the fire.

She cast a sidelong glance at Max from under her eye-lashes and her stomach gave a little lurch at his closeness. There ought to be a law against one man having so much going for him, she thought winsomely, her mouth turning up at the edges. But at least she was safe from any weakness and temptation where he was concerned. He wanted a secretary. End of story. And she ought to be thanking her lucky stars that was so, because she wasn't at all sure she could have trusted herself should he have decided to turn on the charm. And Max was the eternal bachelor. She'd bet he'd broken hearts all round the globe.

'There is what could safely be called an enigmatic smile about those rather beautifully shaped lips.' Her eyes shot to his face and as far as she could tell he hadn't opened his eyes. The big body was quite relaxed, his limbs out-stretched and his breathing steady and controlled. 'Would it do me any good to ask what you were thinking about?' he drawled lazily.

'No.'

'I thought not.' He shifted slightly and she felt the move-ment in every nerve and sinew. 'Choose your meals and then settle back and relax,' he suggested evenly. 'You're too tense.'

Oh, how right he was!

CHAPTER THREE

THEIR plane touched down at Narita, Tokyo's international airport, just before midday, and they were through the green route system with the minimum of fuss to find Mr Katchui's car and chauffeur waiting to whisk them to their hotel to freshen up before they went on for the initial meeting at the Katchui building.

Cory had only indulged in the odd catnap on the journey—she had been too excited and nervous to relax into a deep sleep as Max had done—but nevertheless, in spite of the tiredness that was beginning to make itself felt, she was eager for her first glimpse of Tokyo once the narrow agricultural belt around Narita had vanished.

The city was huge; five million people travelled back and forth to work each day and it was not unusual for the tidal wave of humanity to spend four hours a day in travelling, Max informed her as he watched her drink in the vast urban sprawl.

'Four hours?' Cory stared at him aghast. 'The poor things.'

'In any other country there would be bedlam, but here patience and self-control are instilled in children from birth, and everyone treats everyone else with great respect.' Max sounded as though he approved, and this was borne out when he continued—leaning against her slightly as he gazed out of the window, which caused her some difficulty with her breathing, 'The city divides into self-contained little villages and towns, each with its own remarkable flavour and ambience, and the excellent subway system puts them all within minutes of each other. Everything is run with superb efficiency.'

'A city after your own heart?' Cory couldn't resist asking.

'When it embodies virtually no street crime and petty theft like this one, yes.' He had caught the faint trace of sarcasm in her voice and his voice was slightly curt as he relaxed back into his share of the seat, but he continued to fill her in on the background of the areas they were passing through.

It was as they passed the Shibuya district that their driver spoke in rapid Japanese, his head slightly bent their way, and Max answered him just as rapidly before turning to her and saying, 'He wants me to tell you the true story connected with the Shibuya station; everyone in Tokyo knows it. Hachiko, an Akita dog, used to walk with its master who was a university professor to the station each morning and meet him each night, but then one day he didn't return. He had been taken ill and died. The dog waited for the last train and then sadly returned home, only to repeat the journey every evening for seven years until it too died. The people of Tokyo were so impressed by the little dog's faithfulness that they paid for a bronze statue to be placed just outside the station.'

'Oh…' Cory stared at Max as a vision of the loyal little animal filled her mind. 'That's so sad.'

'In a way.' He was looking just beyond her out of the car window and although it might have been a trick of the light she thought his eyes were shadowed when he added, 'It's certainly an indictment on human beings' concept of fidelity.'

'Oh, I think most people are capable of faithfulness given the chance,' Cory returned lightly without really thinking much about what she was saying as she turned back to the scene beyond the car.

'Do you?' Now something in the tone of his voice brought her head swinging back to face him, and although his face was quite expressionless and his eyes clear the grimness was still there when he said quietly, 'I would have to disagree. Monogamy is one of the most spurious myths we higher animals perpetuate, and the enforcing of it causes more misery than all the wars in the world put together. People strive for the impossible and then blame each other when they can't achieve it.'

It was clear he meant every word and Cory was so taken aback for a moment that she simply stared at him, her large green eyes tinged with dismay before she managed to say, 'That's a hard way of looking at loyalty and devotion, isn't it?'

'Realistic,' he answered briefly, his eyes taking on a cold metallic stoniness. 'Where a man and a woman are concerned anyway.'

She knew she ought to leave it—they had been travelling for what seemed like for ever, and the May day was warm and humid and far from over—but it was beyond her. 'I don't think so,' she argued quietly. 'I know lots of couples who are perfectly content to be faithful and never look at anyone else.'

He shook his dark head slowly, his eyes never leaving her hot face. 'Now that has to be one of the most presumptuous statements I've heard for a long time; how on earth do *you* know whether they are content or not? And you certainly wouldn't know if one of them was indulging their more carnal appetites away from home, now and then. Most people do aim to be at least a little discreet,' he finished fairly irritably.

'So according to you the whole world is nipping in and out of bed with every Tom, Dick and Harry, or at least yearning to?' Cory asked heatedly, resenting the implication that she was naive.

He surveyed her without speaking for a moment, a touch of amusement in his face at her indignancy, which made her want to hit him, and then said, his tone lazy now and holding a smile, 'I don't know if "nipping" is quite the

word, and certainly I've never been tempted to indulge with
a Tom, Dick or a Harry, but the basic principle is there,
yes. Of course it is.'

'What utter rubbish,' Cory said pithily as his patronising
attitude hit her on the raw.

'Rubbish?' He couldn't have reacted more strongly if she
had reached out and slapped his face.

Well, at least he wasn't amused any more, Cory thought
a little uneasily as she saw the patronising expression replaced by sheer rage. She doubted whether too many people
had ever told Max Hunter to his face that he was talking
rubbish. But she stuck to her guns. 'Yes, rubbish,' she repeated a trifle nervously. He really was annoyed and the
space in the car had suddenly seemed to shrink by a few
feet. 'I admit that city life is different to the rural scene and
you are probably basing your opinion on your own set of
acquaintances and friends, but certainly in my home town
I know loads of people who have been married for twenty,
thirty years, and are as happy as Larry,' she finished defiantly.

'Leaving aside this Larry—' his tone was acidic in the
extreme '—are you honestly telling me that you can be
absolutely sure that these paragons of virtue are living in a
state of wedded bliss?' He eyed her grimly but she refused
to be intimidated.

'Yes,' she shot back sharply. 'I can.'

'Cloud-cuckoo land.' It was said with apparent resignation and sorrow that she could be so naive, and Cory found
she didn't trust herself to speak. Telling your employer he
was speaking rubbish was one thing; informing him that he
was a condescending, supercilious, male-chauvinist pig was
quite another. She turned back to the vista of grey ferro-
concrete offices, factories, warehouses and huge housing
developments outside the window and prayed for calm. She
couldn't lose her temper; it would accomplish nothing.

And then she thought of something and turned to Max,

her voice as flat as she could make it, and said, 'Do you know if this faithful little dog was a male or a female?'

Golden eyes held aggressive green, and she read the answer before a sardonic voice said, 'When the story was first told to me the animal was referred to as female.'

Cory nodded thoughtfully, her voice quite expressionless as she said, 'Yes, I'm not surprised.'

It was a tentative victory, but in the circumstances Cory was willing to take whatever she could get.

Their stylish hotel in Ebisu was part of a new leisure development on the former Sapporo Brewery site, and the richly decorated public areas and guests rooms were both luxurious and impeccably clean.

After all the hours of travelling Cory couldn't resist a quick bath in the exotic, beautifully tiled bathroom, and as she slipped on the cotton yukata provided for guests' use, prior to getting dressed, she glanced at herself in the mirror.

She didn't look tired, she reassured herself, before stepping forward and scrutinising the flushed, bright-eyed girl in the mirror. She had released her hair from its refining clip and now it rested on her shoulders in a thick, silky, gleaming mass, her creamy skin and sea-green eyes throwing her vivid colouring into warm prominence. Max had never seen her with her hair loose…

The thought came from nowhere and it shocked her into jerking away and moving into the bedroom where she dressed with record speed, before scraping back every strand of hair into an eye-wateringly tight knot at the back of her head which she secured firmly.

Max was in the next room, and when he knocked at her door some fifteen minutes later she had been ready and waiting for most of them. She was doubly glad she had had the time to compose herself fully on her first glimpse of him standing nonchalantly in the doorway. He had obviously taken the time to have a shower; his thick black hair was raked back from his forehead in its normal severe style but it was still damp, a small tendril or two curling forward and giving the hard masculine face an elusive touch of boyishness that was dynamite.

'All ready?' His brief smile was preoccupied.

'Yes, I'll…I'll just get my bag,' she said quickly.

Cory was hoping and praying she was up to the demands of this trip. The luxurious flight, the effortless efficiency with which they had been whisked to their hotel, the palatial surroundings had all further impressed upon her that she was up among the big boys where perfection was paid for and expected, and she was suddenly terrified was she going to let Max—and herself—down. Gillian had been so experienced and professional, she was never, ever going to rise to his previous secretary's standard, she thought with a sickening lurch to her stomach as she reached for her bag and thin linen jacket. And out here, in a foreign country, she felt so vulnerable.

'What's the matter?' Max's voice was quiet and direct.

When she turned to face him again he had stepped into the room from the corridor beyond and was looking at her intently.

'The…the matter?' It was soft and trembly and not at all the way an executive secretary-cum-personal assistant should talk, and Cory forced her voice into a firmer mode as she added, 'I don't understand. Nothing is the matter. I'm fine, just fine.'

'Liar.' For such a big man he moved very lightly, even fluidly, and the two or three strides to reach her side were made before she could blink. He lifted her chin with a determined finger, regarding her steadily for some moments before he said coolly, 'Are you nervous about the forthcoming meetings and all they entail, or me?'

Cory bristled; she couldn't help it. He was such a *know-all*; he thought he had her taped down to the last thought, she told herself crossly, and it didn't help that in this particular case he was right. But she would rather walk on coals of fire than admit it.

She drew herself up to her full five feet five, although with Max being nearly a foot taller it really didn't make much difference to the overall state of things, and stared up into his dark face. The confrontation was ridiculously like an angry little domestic tabby cat taking on one of its wild African cousins, but the analogy didn't occur to Cory until much later. 'Neither,' she lied again, her green eyes very steady. 'Why? Should I be?'

'So fierce.' It was a soft murmur, and the deep velvet note in his husky voice was so at odds with his normal curt tone that it made her knees want to buckle. 'Who, or what, has made you so prickly, Cory?' he asked as she took a step backwards away from him.

'Prickly?' It hurt; it really did. She had always regarded herself as well-balanced and generous of spirit. True, she could be fiery and emotional on occasion—she had always blamed that side of her personality on her mother's volatile genes—but she would hate to be labelled as touchy. She certainly hadn't been before she had met Max Hunter anyway, she justified quickly in the next instant. 'I'm not in the least prickly,' she stated sharply, her tone making the words a contradiction that was not lost on the man looking down at her. 'I'm not!'

'Of course you are not,' he agreed with dry sarcasm.

She had the amazing urge to stamp her foot at him—something she hadn't done since the tantrums of childhood—and checked it immediately, instead drawing on every scrap of composure and saying icily, 'I thought we had to get to the Katchui building?'

'All in good time,' he returned easily, with a coolness Cory found more than a little annoying. 'The car is coming for us in an hour; I thought we could have a cup of coffee downstairs first while we go over some of the facts and figures on that electro-ceramic report.' He raised his eyebrows questioningly, his eyes mocking.

'Fine.' She nodded quickly. The anonymity of a coffee lounge would suit her just *fine*. Anything was better than the intimacy of her hotel room. *Intimacy?* The word made her blush which in turn fuelled her irritation at herself. How was it her mind always seemed to turn in one direction with this man? She wasn't promiscuous for goodness' sake; in fact she had always tended to find the somewhat fumbling attentions from the males in her life to date definitely overrated, and had been quite happy to stop them before things got out of hand. Mind you, she *had* thought she was saving herself for Vivian. Saving herself... The term was as old-fashioned as she was, she thought with a touch of bitterness. Vivian must have had a good laugh or two at her expense in the past, and no doubt Max Hunter would split his sides if he knew he was looking at that rare oddity—a twenty-four-year-old virgin.

'Cory, I don't want to labour the point, and far be it from me to state the obvious, but I am *not* your enemy,' Max said coolly.

She had actually brushed past him and reached the half-open door when Max spoke, and when his hands touched her slender shoulders, moving her around to face him, she steeled herself to show no reaction whatsoever. 'I know that.' She tried to be very controlled and Gillianish but it wasn't easy. 'Of course I know that.'

'We are here on business,' he continued quietly, his eyes narrowed on her hot face, 'but if you are going to be so tense and on edge the whole week you'll run yourself ragged. I've great faith in you, okay? Take it as read. There will be nothing in the next few days you can't handle. Trust me.'

Oh, the irony of it. There was one six-foot-four thing she was beginning to think she was never going to be able to cope with. She had hoped, *desperately*, in the last six weeks that she would start to master this crazy see-saw of emotion that had started the first time she had ever laid eyes on Max Hunter, but it was getting worse if anything. But she'd rather die than let him know.

'I hope so.' Cory managed a fairly positive smile and was rewarded by a crooked grin that spoke of approval.

'I know so. Now…' He pushed her through the doorway and walked out after her, closing the door behind him. 'Plenty of black coffee first, I think—it wouldn't do for either of us to fall asleep on Mr Katchui, would it?—and then we'll go over a few matters before the car comes.' He had metamorphosed into successful tycoon again—even his voice was different—but Cory was more than happy to go along with the transition. Max Hunter, powerful mogul and multimillionaire she could cope with, but Max Hunter the man? That was where things got sticky.

In spite of her misgivings, Cory found she coped more than adequately with all that was expected of her. The drive to the Katchui building was an experience in itself. Most Japanese city roads, streets, lanes and avenues had no names, and those of Tokyo were no exception, but their host's driver knew exactly where to go in the vast maze and seemed determined to get there at great speed.

Max further impressed her when they arrived at Nagatacho. He seemed to understand perfectly the subtle matter of how deeply to bow according to age and status and other delicate matters, guiding her through the meeting and social intercourse tactfully and without any awkwardness so all was smoothness and nicely oiled wheels.

Mr Katchui and his personal assistant, a young man, both spoke good English and were charming, insisting the four of them eat out at a restaurant rather than allowing Max and herself to go back to the hotel once the day's business was concluded. The small but expensive restaurant specialised in the refined cuisine of kaiseki ryori, and the many small dishes of seasonal delicacies were mouthwateringly delicious, but by now Cory was so exhausted she could have been eating sawdust. But she smiled and nodded and kept up her end of the conversation as though she were as fresh as a daisy, until her cheek muscles ached and her head was thumping.

The three men had been drinking sake all night but Cory had opted for soda-water. Nevertheless, as they left the restaurant just before eleven o'clock and climbed into Mr Katchui's limousine, she felt as dizzy and nauseous as if she had consumed a whole bottle of Japan's innocuous-looking but somewhat potent national liquor.

Her head was swimming on the journey back to the hotel and her limbs felt like lead but she managed to make her goodbyes to their Japanese colleagues without disgracing herself. It was as she and Max walked into the hotel that she stumbled and almost went headlong.

'Are you all right?' Max had been a step or so behind her and caught her arm immediately, then, as he glanced down into her white face and shadowed eyes, he swore softly before saying, 'I should have realised sooner; you're exhausted.'

She really was feeling very peculiar… Cory wanted to answer him, to say something light and cool and finish the evening on an upbeat note before she could collapse into bed, but although her brain knew what it needed to say her mouth just wouldn't respond. She murmured something, some rubbish by the look on Max's face, but most of her concentration was involved in willing herself not to pass out at his feet. If she could just get to her room she'd be fine.

'Sit down there a minute.' To her horror he pushed her down in one of the big comfy seats close to the lifts in Reception and then pressed her head between her knees, but she was feeling so limp and helpless she couldn't fight him in spite of the worry she was making a spectacle of herself.

She heard him bark an order at one of the staff who had come forward to see if they could assist, and the young man immediately walked over to the lifts and held one of the doors open, presumably after pressing the button for their floor.

'I'm fine...please.' As Cory made to struggle to her feet Max swore again, his tone a low growl this time, and before she knew what was what she found herself caught up in his arms and carried over to the elevator as though she weighed no more than a child.

This couldn't be happening. The thought was there, but reality was being held firmly in muscled strong arms against a powerful ribcage with the faint, intoxicatingly sexy smell of him increasing her breathless confusion. His light grey jacket had been open when he had lifted her, and now, with her hot face buried in his shoulder, she could feel the measured thump-thump-thump of his heartbeat as he walked and the warmth of his skin.

Well, she had wondered what it would be like to be in his arms... She was so tired and defenceless that she didn't even try to deny the truth. Right from that first day at the office she had wondered, the more so as she had come to appreciate the ruthless accuracy of his discernment and razor-sharp intelligence that, when added to his overwhelming physical attributes, made him so hypnotically fascinating. And he was, as the number of different female voices who called him at the office testified to. He must have a different woman for every day of the week.

The last thought didn't help in the present situation and as Cory began to wriggle a bit a curt, deep 'Keep still, woman' made her protest, as she called on all her courage and raised her head.

'I'm all right now; I'm perfectly capable of walking.'

Scathing amber eyes met embarrassed green, and as he

recognised her discomfiture his own voice mellowed a fraction. 'You are not all right,' he stated impatiently, 'and I
have no intention of picking you up off the floor so just
relax, there's a good girl.'

'Please, Max, this is so embarrassing. I can—'

'*I mean it, Cory.*'

Said in that tone, there was no point in disputing the
matter any further, but the thought of being able to relax
when held in Max Hunter's arms was just plain ridiculous,
Cory acknowledged weakly. His hard-boned square jaw
was just two inches from her face, her left bosom was
pressed against his chest in such a way that she could feel
the faint roughness of body hair beneath the silk of his
shirt—in fact the whole sensual magnetism of the man was
increased about a thousandfold, she thought desperately.
The urge to move her head just the slightest bit and brush
her lips against the deliciously scented male chin brought
her out of the rapt contemplation of his face like nothing
else could have done, and she just hoped he couldn't sense
the trembling that had started deep in her lower stomach.

'I said relax, Cory.' As the lift glided to a halt and the
doors brushed silently open, Max's voice was slightly grim.
'I'm not about to take advantage of you, if that's what's
bothering you. You're my secretary, for crying out loud.
We're here on business.'

I know, I know. It was a wail from deep within her. She
hadn't even known this man two months and he had turned
her concept of herself and her own sensuality upside down.
Thank goodness he didn't know how she felt. She breathed
in deeply and prayed for calm. She would die with humiliation if he ever guessed; she'd absolutely die.

When they reached her door Cory found herself placed
very gently on her feet and it wasn't until then that she
dared open her eyes again, which had snapped tightly shut
along with the impulse to kiss him. 'Thank you.' She was
pleased with her voice; it wasn't half as fluttery as she'd

expected it to be considering the way her insides had reduced to melted jelly.

'My pleasure.' It was very dry. 'Let me have your key.'

'There really is no need,' she said primly. 'I can manage.'

'Your key, Cory,' he rasped irritably. 'Now.'

She gave him the key, and then, when he lifted her again
and carried her over to the bed after kicking the door shut,
she felt herself go hot all over. Talk about hidden fantasy
night!

'Right. Now I'm going to leave you in bed and I don't
want you attempting to walk until you've slept off some of
this exhaustion. If you can't give me your word on that I'll
sit by your bed all night.'

Cory stared up at him incredulously, totally taken aback
by the cool statement, her green eyes enormous and her
lips falling open in a little O of amazement before she nodded bemusedly. 'I won't move.'

'Do you need to go to the bathroom before I go?' he
added expressionlessly, although she knew she had caught
a little glimmer of amusement deep in the golden eyes.

'You're not coming in there with me?' she asked, aghast,
before she could stop herself, hot colour flooding her face
the next instant.

She thought she saw the hard mouth quiver suspiciously,
but he wasn't smiling when he said, his voice smooth, 'My
services would take you to the door only.'

'Oh, well, I don't need to anyway,' she managed weakly,
knowing her face was as red as a beetroot. Why did he
always make her feel so naive and gauche? she asked herself crossly. No one else ever had.

When he nodded slowly and then bent and eased first
one shoe then the other off her feet a wave of heat brought
her teeth clenching, and when he sat on the edge of the bed
and—taking one swollen ankle into his lap—started ex-

pertly massaging her foot Cory felt that the frissons of sensation must be frizzing her hair.

'You should have worn more sensible shoes for this afternoon,' he said disapprovingly, with a frown at her high-heeled elegant court shoes that had cost a bomb. 'A long flight like the one from England always causes problems with swelling.'

'My feet are fine.' And then, as he raised quizzical eyebrows at the swollen flesh in his wonderfully caressing fingers, she added quickly, 'Or they will be by tomorrow.' She wanted to jerk her feet away—she had never in her wildest dreams expected to be in such an achingly vulnerable situation with Max—but because she didn't trust herself or her feelings she didn't dare do anything which might arouse that incredibly astute mind to suspect that she saw him as anything other than simply her employer.

How would she react if it was Mr Stanley sitting there stroking her feet? she asked herself feverishly. The idea was so ludicrous that she found she couldn't even give it serious thought.

'I want you to sleep in late tomorrow.' He had carefully deposited one lucky little foot on to the covers and had started ministering to the other, his fingers deft and firm as they moved fluidly over the silky honey-toned skin. 'I've got a meeting at nine but I shan't need you for that, but the one at the Saito complex with Mr Katchui at three will be long and complicated, and I'd like you fresh and alert.'

'I can be fresh and alert at nine.' Cory stared at him indignantly. Would he have had to do without Gillian at the morning meeting? She doubted it very much, or that he would have suggested it.

He considered her dryly, his head to one side and his fingers still working their magic. 'I'm not criticising your efficiency,' he drawled with sardonic accuracy, his eyes gleaming like sun-touched water in the muted lighting and his face dark and shadowed. 'And I wouldn't have asked

Gillian to accompany me in the morning either,' he added impassively. 'You were wondering about that, weren't you?'

'Not at all,' she lied quickly, her heart thumping. He had read her mind again and it was happening too often for comfort.

'Little liar.' He placed her foot on the covers before standing up abruptly and Cory suddenly felt quite bereft. 'You don't lie well, Cory Masters, do you know that? Unlike most of your sex.'

For an awful, heart-stopping moment she thought he had guessed how she felt, and then her heart raced on like an express train as he continued, 'I know you are anxious to prove yourself, but you wouldn't be here if I thought there was any chance that you wouldn't come up to scratch. Believe me in that,' he added, with a slanting of those big-cat eyes that told her he was speaking the truth. 'And I never make mistakes,' he added lazily.

'Never?' The arrogance was back in full force and she didn't like it but at least it swept away any heart-stirrings.

'Never,' he affirmed imperturbably.

'Lucky old you.' She hitched herself up into a sitting position, and his power over her made her voice tart as she said, 'It must be wonderful to go through life without ever having made any mistakes, unlike the rest of the human race.'

'I didn't say that I've never made any, only that I don't now,' Max said in a distant tone that indicated he wanted to finish the conversation as he began to turn to walk away.

She was aware of the unspoken command, but a burning curiosity to know just a little more about this disturbingly charismatic man made her ignore it as she said, 'Your mistakes must have been pretty catastrophic to make you so careful these days?' Her voice managed to be both light and faintly sceptical rather than inquisitive.

He surveyed her for some twenty seconds without saying

a word, and then, as the silence stretched and tautened until Cory found she was holding her breath, he said slowly, and without any apparent emotion at all, 'If you call driving one innocent young woman to her death and allowing another, who was using both her sick mind and her beautiful body, to entrap you and turn black into white catastrophic, then you are probably right.'

'Wh-what? I…I don't understand,' Cory stammered helplessly, shocked to the core at the tangible bitterness that had turned the golden eyes into dark rust and was in striking contrast to the expressionless voice. 'I don't understand what you mean.'

Max stared fixedly at her for a long moment and then shook his head abruptly, his eyes clearing as he said, his voice rough, 'There is no reason why you should. Forgive me, I should not have spoken of it; it was a long time ago and is best forgotten.'

Forgotten? Cory tried to say something, to marshal some words past the whirling confusion in her mind, but the look on his face had frozen her thought processes and she was utterly at a loss.

And this state of helpless inertia was further compounded when Max remained looking down into her troubled white face for one moment more before he said, his voice dry with cynicism now, 'Like I said, forget it, Cory. We all make mistakes, like you with this Vivian guy who's given you the run-around after stringing you along for years. The worst ones are always the best in bed.'

She gasped out loud, she couldn't help it, fierce red staining her cheekbones at his audacity, and she was still searching her mind for some caustic comment to put him in his place—wherever that was—when he bent down and casually stroked a finger across the moist fullness of her bottom lip, his touch unbearably erotic, before turning abruptly and leaving the room without another word.

CHAPTER FOUR

CORY was in such a state after Max had gone that she expected to lie awake for hours after she had collapsed back on the pillows behind her, but she must have fallen asleep immediately because the next thing she knew a tentative dawn was casting pale mauve shadows about the room and she had awoken to the fact that she was still fully clothed and lying on the top of the bed, and that she was cold.

She rose gingerly, glad to find that the weakness and giddiness seemed to have vanished, undressed quickly, had a brief warm shower and brushed her teeth, and after pulling on her nightie climbed under the covers. She was asleep again as soon as her head touched the pillow, curled up in a warm ball like a sleepy little animal.

The sun was high and streaming in through the open curtains the next time she opened her eyes, and when she glanced at her little bedside alarm clock she couldn't believe it was midday. She had slept for a full twelve hours or more, but she felt so much better for the rest, she told herself as she flung back the covers and stretched like a small sleek cat, before padding through to the bathroom and running herself a scented bath.

She had just emerged from the bathroom—dressed in her own short white towelling bathrobe and not the hotel's cotton yukata—with her wet hair spread about her shoulders, when the knock came at the door and made her jump.

Max? She paused in the middle of the bedroom, panic catching her breath, but then as the knock came again, more impatient this time, she yanked the belt of the robe more securely round her slender waist and walked across the room, opening the door tentatively.

'Good afternoon.' It was dry and cool and very distant.

He was in business mode, utterly the cool, expressionless tycoon, and he looked absolutely drop-dead gorgeous, Cory thought weakly, her wide eyes taking in the green shirt and pale green and grey tie he had teamed with the light grey suit of the day before. He was holding the jacket slung across one broad shoulder, and his imperturbable glance didn't falter as it took in her state of undress.

But then it wouldn't, would it? Cory thought caustically. As far as Max Hunter was concerned she held as much interest as a tomato sandwich. Especially with her hair in rat's-tails and no make-up.

'Hello.' She managed a quick smile. 'I'm just getting ready; I slept late as you advised. I can be ready in ten minutes.'

'Good.' He nodded curtly. 'I just called by to say I've ordered lunch for one, if that's okay? The car is picking us up at two o'clock for the meeting so that'll give us plenty of time.'

'Right, thank you.' Cory felt very put out without knowing why and that annoyed her still more.

'So I'll call again in…' he consulted the solid gold Rolex on his left wrist '…twenty-five minutes?' he suggested coolly.

'Fine.' She didn't smile this time and her voice was as crisp as his as he turned away without another word.

This morning's meeting couldn't have gone particularly well. Once she was alone again she dried her hair quickly, her mind gnawing at the reason for Max's distinct coolness. Or perhaps it was because she hadn't been ready to go with him at nine? But he had *told* her not to, she reminded herself firmly, and she had taken him at his word. There was nothing wrong with that, was there? No, no, there wasn't. She nodded her head sharply and stared into the green eyes in the mirror for a few moments, before reminding herself she had to get a move on and be ready for when he returned.

Once her hair was dry she secured it in a clip at the back of her head and applied the minimum of make-up to her creamed face, merely a touch of honey-gold foundation, the merest suggestion of green eyeshadow and a coating of black mascara on her thick silky lashes. She dressed simply but smartly in a calf-length jade-green linen skirt—the slim fit relieved by the above-the-knee splits on either side—and a matching shirt-style short-sleeved blouse which she wore tucked in the skirt, the whole being complemented by a wide leather belt. Gold studs at her ears, high-heeled dark brown shoes in exactly the same shade as the belt, and she was ready.

Cool efficiency married with discreet femininity. She nodded to the faintly apprehensive reflection in the mirror at the same time as Max's authoritative knock sounded at her door. She would never give him any reason to think she was trying to make him notice her, she told herself firmly as she turned to answer the door. And the sexy little black dress she had brought along—just in case—was certainly not going to emerge from the wardrobe. She was quite content for him to see her as an extension of the office—more than content. She just wished it weren't accomplished with such ease.

He was lounging against the far wall in the corridor when Cory opened the door, and in spite of the stern pep-talk she had given herself when she was getting ready Cory's heart missed a beat or two as he levered his big body straight, raking back his hair lazily.

'I'm starving,' she said brightly, her tone determinedly cheerful.

'So am I.' He seemed to have found his normal cool equilibrium, so, whatever the difficulties of the morning, Cory assumed he had settled them in his mind as he added, his eyes narrowed, 'You look cucumber-cool and very

English with your clothes on. Quite different to the Aphrodite of half an hour ago.'

Aphrodite her foot! She'd left him cold. Cory smiled politely but said nothing as she shut the door and walked with him to the lifts.

They ate a light lunch and were sitting waiting in Reception some time before two o'clock, but although Max had kept the conversation flowing in his own smooth inimitable way Cory found herself wondering what he was really thinking several times as she caught the clear golden gaze.

He was an enigma. As Mr Katchui's car drew up outside the building and they rose, the thought was at the forefront of Cory's mind. Which was part of his subtle magnetism to the opposite sex, she supposed. But it was more than that; she couldn't imagine Max ever being small-minded or petty. Ruthless certainly, manipulative—when occasion warranted it—maybe, but he had been right last night when he'd said Vivian had given her the run-around, and she couldn't imagine Max Hunter stooping to such tactics to wriggle out of a commitment. Whatever Max was, he wasn't a wimp.

Was she saying Vivian was a wimp? Her eyes narrowed in the bright sunlight outside, but as she slid into the back of the limousine her mind was still worrying at the thought, and when the answer came it made her green eyes open wide. Yes, he was a wimp. She relaxed back into the seat in surprise. He had always been one; she just hadn't acknowledged it before, even through all the years of looking after him and nurturing him along. Her love for Vivian had been—she searched for the right words and found them— almost brotherly at heart, that was it. He'd been the younger brother she'd never had.

She gazed out of the window without seeing a thing. How could she have got it so wrong? she asked herself faintly. What did that make her? All the years of imagining he was the one for her, the tears and heartache when he met Carole, and now she was actually grateful for what she had to admit was a lucky escape. It would seem she knew herself even less than she had known the real Vivian.

'...if you'd like that?'

'I'm sorry?' She came back to the real world and the realisation that Max had been speaking to her and she hadn't heard a word, and now her face was flushed as she said quickly, 'I was daydreaming.'

'Right.' His voice was terse; he clearly didn't have too many women daydream in his presence. 'I asked you if you would like to visit a Japanese inn with me tonight that one of my colleagues has recommended; it's a taste of the real Japan and very different to the big western-style hotels.'

'Oh.' She blinked at him in surprise. 'Yes, thank you, that would be lovely,' she added hastily. 'I'd like that.'

'Tokyo is a long way to come without taking advantage of a little local colour,' Max said evenly as he looked into her heart-shaped face, 'and our itinerary is such that the rest of the trip is virtually programmed hour by hour, so the few hours available tonight is the only chance to have our minds broadened.'

Cory nodded again. He didn't have to spell it out, she told herself silently; she had never for one moment imagined that his invitation was in any way a date.

The meeting at the Saito plant went very well but it was still almost seven o'clock by the time things wound up. Max refused the offer of Mr Katchui's car and chauffeur for the evening and instead the two of them travelled by taxi to Akasaka in the south-west of the city. Max's colleague had given him a map with their destination clearly marked—essential in a city where building numbers generally related to the order of construction, not to position, and even the taxi drivers could rarely find anything but a big hotel, station or landmark from the address alone—and they reached the ryokan, Japanese inn, without too much trouble—a minor miracle in labyrinthine Tokyo.

'Am I dressed all right?' Cory was beginning to appreciate the hundred and one rituals that made up Japanese society, and as the taxi roared off down the narrow street, narrowly missing an old man in a cotton kimono who was clack-clacking his way home in wooden sandals, she knew a moment's panic as she stared at the attractive building in front of her. She wouldn't want to offend anyone.

'You're perfect.' As she glanced up into Max's face her stomach muscles tightened, but then he blinked and smiled, his gaze becoming almost remote, and she knew she had imagined the warmth in the golden eyes. 'And I'm hungry,' he added coolly. 'Come along.'

A path of flat rounded stepping-stones led through a pretty green garden complete with a small pool and floating water lilies, and into a neat stone-floored vestibule where a small and very beautiful middle-aged woman in a kimono was waiting. Max had telephoned the expected time of their arrival from the Saito complex, and now, as the woman smilingly indicated two pairs of slippers—one large, one small—Cory followed Max's lead and slipped off her shoes to replace them with the slippers.

Cory wasn't sure what she had been expecting—in fact the afternoon had been so gruelling and hectic she hadn't really had time to think about the evening at all—but as she and Max followed their host into the inn she was struck by the peaceful and next-to-nature ambience that the Japanese sought to create in their crowded land.

The room they were shown into was appealing in its aesthetic simplicity but small, and it was immediately clear it was not a dining room, although when Max shed his slippers before stepping through the open paper door Cory followed suit. The floor was of tatami mats, rice straw covered with finely woven reeds, the ceiling wood and the central table surrounded by floor cushions on which, Cory

presumed, one sat to eat. It was uncluttered and beautiful—
and intimate. Very, very intimate. And very different from
a crowded western-style hotel.

'I don't understand.' Cory glanced up from her contemplation of the surroundings to find Max's gaze on her bewildered face. 'We aren't eating in here, are we?' Perhaps
it was the custom that one waited in a room like this one
until their table was ready? she asked herself as the butterflies in her stomach went wild. 'Where's the dining room?'
she asked as steadily as she could.

'There is no dining room in a ryokan,' Max said quietly.
'All meals are served in the resident's individual rooms.
Why? Is that a problem?' he added silkily.

Was it a problem? *Was it a problem!* He expected her
to virtually lie on the floor with him in this romantic idyll
and share a cosy little meal for two, and he asked her if it
was a problem? A predicament of colossal proportions,
more like. 'No, not at all.' She managed a bright smile she
was proud of. 'I just wasn't expecting it, that's all. It's
very…Japanese.'

'Very,' he agreed solemnly, 'and rest assured that in spite
of the bedding in the cupboards beyond yon paper door—'
he pointed to a far corner where paper on rectangular pat-
terned frames of thin woodwork in the form of sliding
doors were '—we *are* here just for dinner, in case you're
wondering.'

'I wasn't.' It was true—Max Hunter, controlled, cold
king of his emotions and the world in general interested in
a little nobody like her, even for a brief interlude? No way.

'You'll never go to heaven,' he drawled lazily, crossing
his arms and staring at her flushed face with something akin
to amusement.

The fragile, delicate room with its low doorway—
through which Max had had to bend almost double as they
had entered, Japanese inns and houses not being set up for
a big six-foot-four westerner—and the pale light surround-

ings magnified the brooding quality of his dark maleness, and for a moment Cory was tempted to let him think what he liked, but she couldn't. 'No, I really wasn't.' She faced him determinedly, looking straight into his eyes without flinching. 'It didn't occur to me you'd try anything of that nature.'

'No?' He couldn't doubt she meant what she said, and she saw a frown brush his chiselled features before he searched her hot face. 'I don't know whether to take that as a compliment or an insult,' he said with a touch of acidity that suggested he was inclined towards the latter.

'Oh, no, I didn't mean it like that,' Cory said hastily. 'I know you like women! I mean, I'm sure your sex life… I didn't think—' She broke off, aware she was digging a hole for herself and Australia was already in view. 'I didn't mean it like that…'

'So we've agreed I'm a normal red-blooded male with my fair share of hormones,' Max said smoothly without taking his eyes off her hunted face. 'In that case why would it be so unthinkable that I might have less than pure thoughts for this evening?'

How on earth had she got herself into this? Cory stared at him without speaking for a moment or two, utterly at a loss to explain herself. Her heart was beating so hard it was threatening to jump out of her chest, and he must have sensed her agitation because he gestured towards one of the cushions, his voice soft as he said, 'Sit down before you fall down, woman. I'm not trying to pick a fight,' just as the door slid open again and the maid entered with their sake, Japanese rice wine, in a vase-like bottle standing in a bowl of warm water, and steaming handtowels in small wicker baskets.

As Max joined her on the floor, his big body amazingly adept at dealing with the intricacies of the Japanese style of eating, he said quietly, 'After wiping your fingers roll the towel up again and keep it for use as a napkin.'

Cory nodded, feeing desperately uncomfortable at her lack of knowledge of the country's customs in front of the exquisite little maid, and it was this feeling that prompted her to say, before she considered her words, 'We *are* going to eat alone, aren't we?' The smiling woman served them the sake in tiny glasses—no bigger than eggcups—and solicitously knelt at their side.

'You'd prefer that?' Max asked softly, his eyes glittering.

'I think so. I know so little about Japanese etiquette and so on, I wouldn't like to offend…'

'You wouldn't offend, Cory.' His voice was warm and as she blinked and looked at him he added, 'But if you'd be more comfortable…'

He spoke to the maid in rapid Japanese and she rose gracefully, bowing prettily before she left, but now Cory was regretting the fact that her hasty words had placed them in a more intimate position than if a third party had been present. He wouldn't think… She glanced at him from under her eyelashes as he refilled her glass with the fifteen per cent alcohol that tasted like delicious dry sherry. No, of course he wouldn't, she reassured herself in the next instant. She had never given him the slightest sign of a come-on, just the opposite in fact, and he found her as attractive as a block of wood.

'Now…' Max surveyed her easily from his position just inches away, and the fact that he had discarded his jacket and his tie and undone the first few buttons of his shirt was not helping her breathing, she acknowledged silently as she surreptitiously took another fortifying glass of sake. 'Where were we? Oh, yes, you were about to tell me why it would be so inconceivable that I might have ulterior motives for this little sojourn out of life's hectic rat race.'

He was enjoying this. As Cory stared into the dark male face she found she was angry. Angry at the position he had placed her in in pressing the issue, angry at his comfortable male arrogance and sureness that he was in control, but more than that—much more than that—she was angry at the fact that however much she tried to fight it she found this man so darned *attractive*. It was pure stupidity—and his morals, his lifestyle, his attitude to women was everything she disliked—but physically… Physically…

The adrenalin pumping round her body—along with the sake—enabled her voice to be both reasonable and cool as she played him at his own game. 'Because you are my employer of course,' she said with wide-eyed innocence, 'and naturally you are aware I could never look on you as anything other than a business colleague. That is the essence of all successful work relationships, isn't it?'

He listened without moving a muscle but nevertheless she had the feeling that his whole body had stiffened, and his stillness was further emphasised when she continued blithely, even managing a comradely smile, 'And of course you are an experienced man of the world, you've been around a lot longer than I have, and I'm sure your world is as different to mine as chalk to cheese. We've nothing in common, absolutely nothing—beyond work, that is—and although it might not be sophisticated to say so I could never indulge in the sort of casual affair that city folk seem to find so acceptable. My "cloud-cuckoo" mentality wouldn't let me,' she finished sweetly.

There was a long pause—a really long pause—where the air fairly crackled with electricity, and then she saw him take a deep pull of air. 'Quite.' It was smooth and silky and covered sharp steel and the mocking arrogance had quite gone.

If you can't stand the heat, don't come into the kitchen. It was one of her mother's favourite barbs but it fitted perfectly. She might be a little hillbilly from the wilds of Yorkshire in his eyes, Cory told herself with a touch of bitterness, as his comments the day before had made perfectly clear, but she had a mind of her own and she wasn't afraid to use it. How *dared* he laugh at her and treat her like some pet poodle? And that was what it had boiled down to. And she wasn't having it!

'More sake?' He refilled her glass and Cory swigged it with something of a 'what the hell' bravura, ignoring the fact that she hadn't eaten for some seven or so hours.

The meal, when it came, was very good. The seafood morsels, dipped in a light batter and cooked very quickly in boiling oil, were crisply delicious; the soup—drunk from the bowl as if it were a cup with the vegetables picked out with chopsticks—was subtle in flavour, and the rice and palate-fresheners and other dishes were all superb in their own right.

Max taught her that the slurping of the soup and noodles was a sign that the dish was being properly savoured, that rice was usually eaten by holding the bowl close to the mouth and using chopsticks—no mean feat in itself, Cory discovered as she shovelled the rice in—and that warm sake in between mouthfuls was wonderfully beneficial, if not actually etiquette in the strictest sense.

They were well on their way to consuming the second bottle of sake when Cory became aware of the warm sense of euphoria that was enveloping her like a rich blanket. She was comfortably replete, and in the last few minutes all the petty irritations, along with the pain and confusion of the last twelve months, had simply melted away.

Somehow, in the last half an hour or so, Max had drawn closer and now her shoulder was resting against his, but it seemed like the height of bad manners to move away. The height of bad manners... What sort of woman did he prefer? She contemplated him lazily from under her eyelashes as she finished her umpteenth eggcup of sake. Cool, sophisticated blondes? Voluptuous, warm brunettes? Volatile, fiery redheads? Probably all of them, she thought grumpily.

Gillian had told her that he had girlfriends—lots of girlfriends—but that none of them lasted more than a few months at most, and they all knew the score. 'He treats them well, spoils them rotten,' Gillian had said with a sightly disapproving edge to her voice, 'and then says goodbye with charm and generosity while everything is still sweet. It's Max's way.'

'Don't they mind?' she'd asked Gillian in astonishment.

'Max chooses like for like,' Gillian had said quietly. 'He doesn't want emotional involvement and neither do his women. His lifestyle is fast and wild and he works hard and plays hard. He puts all his commitment and energy into Hunter Operations; when he wants to relax he wants fun without any ties or obligations. That's how he is. That's Max—he makes it clear he can take it or leave it.'

Gillian had changed the subject then, as though regretting that she had said too much, but Cory had felt there was more unsaid than said. And after the disturbing conversation she had had with Max the night before she felt it all tied in with this catastrophic 'mistake' he had spoken of, which still clearly affected him very much although he would deny it. What had happened? The thought had been there in the back of her mind, nagging away all day. He couldn't really have been responsible for someone dying...could he?

'That was a wonderful meal.' Probably due to the nature of her thoughts Cory decided the silence was becoming uncomfortable and that she had to break it. Max, on the other hand, had been stretched out in apparent relaxation at the side of her, the slumberous dark attraction that he exuded as naturally as breathing emphasised by his lazy contentment and the delicate, almost feminine surroundings.

'Wasn't it,' he agreed softly, turning his head and letting his eyes stroke over her face as he spoke. 'Delicious...'

'What's that noise?' Cory had been conscious of a plaintive and somewhat poignant sound for the last few minutes, something far removed from everyday life and almost fairy-like, which perfectly fitted this step out of reality. 'I've never heard it before.'

'It's a soba seller, a street vendor of noodles,' Max said quietly. 'He announces his presence through the streets by blowing his tin flute to attract customers. It's a melancholy sound but one which everyone recognises.'

He had slightly shifted his position as he spoke and Cory, anxious to put some space between them, seized the opportunity to sit up straighter but in so doing caught the clip holding her thick coil of hair. As the clasp sprung loose and her hair fell about her face and shoulders in a soft veil of shimmering silk she made a faint sound of distress, reaching for the clip which had jumped under the table.

'Don't.' As her fingers reached the clasp Max's hand covered hers. 'Leave it.' Cory tensed, holding her breath until he leant back again and said, his voice wry with self-mockery, 'I've been wondering what your hair looks like loose for six weeks and now I know. It's criminal to hide such beauty.'

'I prefer to be tidy and neat for the office,' Cory protested as primly as the semi-reclining position and his dark presence would allow. 'Long hair would get in the way.'

'We aren't in the office now,' he said softly, his voice husky.

She was painfully aware that something had shifted and changed in the last minute or so, something indefinable but nevertheless very potent. Something that was making shivers trickle down her spine.

She knew he was going to kiss her, and she also knew it would be the height of foolishness to allow him to do so, but as she stared into his gold eyes which were coming closer—her green gaze wide and mesmerised like a small cat caught frozen in the powerful amber lights of an oncoming car—she waited for his mouth to touch hers with a breathless hunger that was paralysing.

His lips were warm and searching at first and he made

no move to hold her or draw her into him as the kiss deepened. She had known he would be able to kiss—the sensual expertise was evident in every movement and glance he made, even the way he carried the big male body with such confidence and authority—but she had never guessed a kiss could hold such mind-blowing sovereignty as this one. He knew just how to entice, to please, and he wasn't even *touching* her apart from his mouth on hers, she told herself swimmingly as a million and one nerve-endings became sensitised into one aching whole.

So this is what those other women enjoyed, she thought helplessly. But how, having once experienced Max Hunter making love to them, could they ever be content with any other man?

And then, her eyes shut, she ceased to think, abandoning herself to the eroticism of the sensations he was arousing in her. When she felt herself moulded into the strong male body it didn't even occur to her to object; she was fluid and felt molten heat as his lips moved to her ears, the hollow of her throat and then lower.

'So beautiful…' He was murmuring huskily in between the burning kisses. 'Your skin is translucent, do you know that? I've never seen such delicacy before, and your hair… Spun silk.'

Cory had lost all idea of time, along with every scrap of common sense she had ever possessed. She was in another sphere, a new dimension, where touch and taste and smell were heightened to an unbearable intensity and all that mattered was his lips and hands and what they were doing to her.

He was kissing her mouth again, passionately and intoxicatingly, fiercely, parting her lips with a dominant authority she didn't even try to resist, but the sensuality was exquisitely controlled too—even though his heart was beating like a sledgehammer against the softness of her breasts he wasn't trying to force her or go too quickly. It was heady, wonderful, and she couldn't get enough of it.

Her hands were on the broad thrust of his muscled shoulders and he was exploring her mouth in such a way that she was unable to disguise the shivers fluttering down her spine, the skilful plundering rendering her exposed and defenceless. His hands were caressing her body with a dexterity and knowledge that sent waves of desire coursing through her veins, and she found herself longing for his touch on her bare skin, their clothing a barrier that brought frustrated little moans deep within her throat. She hadn't imagined she could feel like this. She hadn't known...

Quite when she became aware that he was merely holding her—his mouth restrained as he brushed gentle little kisses on her forehead—Cory wasn't sure, but with the knowledge came a deep and humiliating awareness of just how completely she had submitted to him, the sounds of her own little inarticulate cries still echoing in her ears and her breathing uneven and ragged.

'Cory, I'm sorry; I shouldn't have done that.'

She couldn't believe what he was saying for a moment— that he had actually *stopped*—and then as she pulled away she was free immediately, Max's hands making no effort to hold her.

If she had glanced at him in that moment she would have seen a confusion and darkness in the beautiful slanted eyes that might have gone some way to alleviating her own embarrassment. As it was she fumbled with her clothes for some seconds before looking at him, and it was an imperturbable cold mask that stared back, and his voice was cool as he repeated, 'I shouldn't have done that; there's no excuse beyond the magic of this place.'

How did she handle this? She wanted to die with shame and mortification at his easy mastery over her, to scream at him that he was every low name she could think of and that she loathed and detested him, but that would only make matters worse. The facts were that he had leant across and kissed her and her response to that gesture had sent things escalating out of control, Cory thought wretchedly. She should have allowed his lips to rest on hers for a few moments and then pulled back with some light, easy comment that would have kept things on an even keel. He had *told* her the last thing he wanted was for his secretary to have any romantic notions about him; he'd dotted the i's and crossed the t's early on in that respect. He was a sophisticated man of the world—a kiss meant nothing at all to such men—and she'd practically *eaten* him.

She drew on all her resources and managed a smile that, if a little shaky round the edges, was the best she could do. 'The magic of the place and the sake,' she said as lightly as she could. 'The effect of it creeps up on you, doesn't it?' She had never felt so stone-cold sober in her life. 'I wouldn't have indulged quite so freely if I'd known,' she added, with another attempt at a smile.

'It's deceptive,' he agreed easily, and she hated him for the apparent effortless control. Here was she, feeling like something the cat had dragged in with her mind blown to smithereens, and the rat wasn't even hot under the collar, she told herself bitterly. How *could* she have been so incredibly, wantonly stupid?

They remained at the inn for another twenty minutes or so, which took on the torture of twenty hours as far as Cory was concerned. She didn't dare try to put her hair up—her hands were trembling so much she knew she would be all fingers and thumbs, and the last thing she needed was further humiliation—and if their little maid noticed it when she came to collect the dishes she gave no indication.

Max was his normal smooth and urbane self on the drive back to the hotel and Cory struggled to meet him halfway and keep her end of the conversation going, but it was difficult. Every fibre of her being seemed determined to recall how it had felt to be in his arms, the taste of his mouth on hers, the enveloping warm male smell of him that was the blend of his unique aftershave and his own bodily chemicals.

She knew the kiss had meant nothing to him, that it had been dismissed as a mistake the second he had let her go and as such disqualified from further thought. Max Hunter would never waste time on anything unimportant, she told herself bitterly as the taxi hurtled towards their hotel in the rainbows of light that was Tokyo at night, when ten thousand restaurants and drinking dens beckoned with flashing signs and glowing lanterns.

He was a cold, unfeeling monster! She risked a sidelong glance at him and saw the hard, strong face was perfectly calm and relaxed. She couldn't imagine any woman wanting to get involved with him, she really couldn't, whether they were of the same icy temperament as him or not. Thank goodness, *thank goodness* he had stopped before any harm was done. They'd just shared a kiss, that was all, just a kiss, and if nothing else it had awakened her to just what sort of a man he really was. She was glad this had happened; *she was*. In the long run it was probably the best thing.

The recriminations against both herself and Max and the downright lies continued to fortify her until they had said goodnight—a cool and very swift goodnight—outside her door, and Cory found herself in the sanctuary of her hotel room.

She sat on her bed without moving or making any effort to undress for a good ten minutes, her mind going over every word, every glance, every caress they had shared until she collapsed back against her pillows with a despairing little sigh. What a mess. What a twenty-four-carat mess. He had been aroused back there at the ryokan. The memory of his body, taut and hungry, pressed against hers brought hot colour into her cheeks. But then what man wouldn't be when it was virtually being offered to him on a plate?

No. No, she hadn't been that bad…had she? No, she hadn't. She nodded to herself abruptly as she rose up from the bed. And although he might have been surprised at her reaction to what he'd probably meant as no more than a brief peck, a man of his experience should have pulled back before things went so far. It wasn't *all* her fault. This time the nod was even more determined.

She padded through to the *en suite*, discarding her clothes on the way, and ran herself a warm bath, staying in the perfumed water until it was quite cold, after which she washed her hair and then wrapped herself in her towelling bathrobe.

Tonight had been a lesson she wouldn't forget. She stared at the anxious-eyed reflection in the mirror for a full minute, worrying at her bottom lip with small white teeth. But it had happened and she couldn't do anything about it now except learn from it. She would never, *ever* allow Max Hunter to kiss her again—not that he would be foolish enough to try after tonight, no doubt. But she wouldn't anyway. It might take a few days but then all this would become history and she could forget the humiliating part and just look on it as another thread in life's rich tapestry.

She shut her eyes tightly, opening them and seeing the ridiculousness of her declaration in the cloudy green gaze staring back at her. Forget it? How could she forget it? That kiss, everything that followed had been the most devastating experience of her entire life, and he had dismissed it as easily as blowing his nose! She wished she had never taken the job as his secretary. Tears were pricking behind the backs of her eyes and she blinked them away fiercely. But she had and she would make a success of it now even if it killed her.

CHAPTER FIVE

CORY got ready to go down to breakfast the next morning after a very careful make-up session aimed at hiding the ravages of a sleepless night. She had tossed and turned until gone three and then given up all thoughts of sleep, and rather than wasting the time doing endless post-mortems on the evening with Max had made a conscious decision to get immersed in work. She'd tidied up all her notes on her laptop computer, typed out two reports she thought might be relevant for Max for the day ahead, and generally got together all the facts and figures they had discussed with Mr Katchui and the others so far.

At six o'clock she had a shower and lay down on the bed for an hour to compose herself for the day ahead, and at seven rose and began getting dressed. She tried on every item of clothing she'd brought with her over the next half an hour—apart from the sexy little black dress—and, once she had discarded them all, repeated the procedure until she was thoroughly confused and over-warm.

She wanted to look cool, collected, self-assured and competent. But feminine. Feminine and attractive. And *definitely* not desperate for a man—or, to be more precise, Max Hunter. And from her response to his kiss he might be thinking just that.

She wriggled in front of the mirror, sighed deeply, and cast an eye over the heap of clothes on the bed. Oh, this was ridiculous! She grabbed an armful and replaced them in the wardrobe with savage haste, before dressing in a simple grey skirt and white blouse teamed with plain white high heels and white daisy earrings. Very secretarialish and restrained. It would do.

Discreet make-up had hidden the mauve shadows under her eyes and she fastened her hair in a neat, authoritative French pleat with no-nonsense firmness, ignoring the echo of his words the night before.

She was ready. She glanced at her watch and saw there were ten minutes to go before half past eight—the time she had arranged to eat breakfast with Max. Should she go down and be already seated when he made an appearance? He would no doubt knock on her door on his way to the dining room if she remained here, and perhaps it would be better to face him in a crowded room than in a deserted corridor? She nodded at the thought, her heart thumping crazily. Yes, that was what she'd do. Decision made, she couldn't grab her bag quick enough, and as she opened the door in a nervous flurry she was overwhelmingly relieved the corridor was empty.

And so it was that Cory was seated at a table for two, sipping at a small glass of fresh orange juice and nibbling on a slice of toast, when Max strode into the dining room some five minutes later.

She raised a cool, secretarial hand at his entrance and once he reached her side she was proud of the distant smile and her steady, 'Good morning, Max. I trust you slept well?' as she glanced at him.

'Fine, thanks.'

Yes, he looked like he had, Cory thought venomously. The dark tanned face was smiling and relaxed, the big body dressed as immaculately as always, and he just *exuded* tranquillity and self-control. She loathed him. She did, she *loathed* him. 'Good.' She forced the smile a kilowatt or two brighter.

'And you?' he asked easily as a waiter appeared at his side.

'Like a top, thanks,' she answered smartly.

Once the attentive waiter had taken Max's order, Cory indicated the folder on the table. 'I thought it might be an idea to put some facts and figures on paper, so I jotted down a few things before I came down to breakfast.' Well, it wasn't a lie. Three in the morning *was* before breakfast. 'Here.' She handed him the two reports as she spoke, and then busied herself pouring two cups of coffee, glad to give her hands something to do and her eyes something to focus on other than Max's face.

'Excellent.' The amber gaze flashed over the neatly printed columns before raising itself to her face.

Yes, they are excellent, you hard, unfeeling swine.

It was a thought that stayed with her for the rest of the day—or the hard, unfeeling swine part of it at least—and by the time they returned to the hotel for dinner Cory felt like a piece of limp lettuce—good for nothing.

Nevertheless, she determinedly prepared for dinner as though it was an important manoeuvre in a military campaign—which wasn't far from the truth—and after a warm shower and a change of clothes she sailed downstairs with Max for cocktails as though she hadn't a care in the world, bright and sparkling and as fresh as a daisy.

By the time he returned her to her room at just gone ten o'clock she was working purely on automatic again, but at least the long, exhausting day, followed by an even more exhausting couple of hours in Max's company over dinner, made sure she fell asleep that night as soon as her head touched the pillow.

And so it was for the next few days. Cory aimed to be the perfect efficient machine Max expected of his secretary-cum-personal assistant, and Max was his usual cool, controlled self. He hadn't once mentioned the evening in the ryokan, and Cory would rather be hung, drawn and quartered than bring it up herself.

She found the days quite easy to handle as it happened. Max Hunter, demanding, dynamic tycoon and human whirlwind, was one thing, but the evenings... The evenings were a different matter. He quite naturally slipped into the mode of attentive dinner companion then, and despite all the pep-talks she gave herself in the privacy of her room his particular brand of lethal sex appeal just tied her up in knots each night. Which was *so* pathetic…

He was perfectly correct of course. In fact everything he did and said made it clear he was treating her in exactly the same way he would treat any woman—from the age of seventeen to seventy—who had been forced on him by necessity. He was charming, polite, amusing and courteous, but each night she fell under that dark magnetism a little more. And resented it a little more too.

By the time their last morning in Japan dawned, Cory was just about on her knees—figuratively speaking. Throughout the protracted goodbyes with Mr Katchui and others she smiled until her face ached, made all the right noises and said all the right things. Mr Katchui had liked her, she'd sensed that, but she was still very surprised and touched when the hard Japanese businessman gave her a small gift on parting, along with a good deal of flowery compliments.

'You made a real hit there.'

Max's tone was appreciative as they sped through Tokyo's streets towards the airport, and she smiled briefly before saying, 'It was very kind of him to give me something; I didn't expect it.'

'Open it.' He gestured at the small gift-wrapped package on her lap, his tawny eyes stroking over her face for a moment.

'Oh, it's lovely…' The little box contained a tiny figure of Hachiko, the dog in the story, which had been worked in fine silver and was quite exquisite in its own way. The small accompanying note was simple: 'Faithfulness should always be rewarded.'

Cory wasn't quite sure if she liked being compared to a female dog, but she took the compliment in the spirit in

which it had been made as she showed the card to Max.
'Isn't that sweet?'

'Do I sense a message in there for me?' he asked dryly.

'Oh, I'm sure not,' Cory answered quickly. The close
confines of the taxi were a little too close for her comfort—
the waves of dark sex appeal were flowing hot and strong.

'Hmm, I wonder.' He eyed her somewhat morosely for
a moment before he said, his voice tinged with something
she couldn't quite place, 'And do you agree with that noble
sentiment, Cory?'

'That faithfulness should be rewarded?' she asked carefully. 'Well, in a perfect world that would be very nice, but
it doesn't always work out like that, does it?'

'Indeed it doesn't.' It was a little too abrupt—there was
a raw nerve showing somewhere—and her face must have
shown her surprise because in the next instant she saw Max
make a visible effort to relax, and his voice was less caustic
as he said, 'I'm sorry, it's just that I let someone down
badly once and I learnt there's not always time to make
amends. That's all.'

'Right.' It wasn't a question of 'that's all' by the look
on his face, Cory thought bemusedly, and she found her
heart was racing at the sudden glimpse of the real Max
Hunter. His eyes were dark again, and there was the same
look in them she had seen once before, that night in her
hotel room when he had spoken of this young woman he
had supposedly driven to her death. 'Well, we all make
mistakes.' Trite—too trite, she thought helplessly, but she
couldn't think of anything else.

'That we all do.'

Now his tone was both mocking and patronising and it
caused her to say, as she fired back without really thinking,
'I'm sorry, Max, I didn't aim to be flippant but I'm sure
you would prefer that to me asking questions? You're not
exactly easy to talk to at the best of times.' Conversation
with him was more like walking through a minefield.

'Aren't I?' He shifted in his seat as he spoke, turning to face her head-on, and she saw, to her secret amusement, that she had really offended him. He was so used to any woman he was with giving unconditional homage to anything he did or said, she thought a touch astringently, that he just didn't expect any come-back. Women didn't criticise the great Max Hunter—they fell at his feet in humble adoration.

And now he backed that theory as he added brusquely, 'You're the only person who thinks so.'

'Perhaps I'm the only person who has *said* so,' Cory argued calmly, her tone sweet. She could afford to be sweet—she'd rattled him and it felt wonderfully good after the torture of the last few evenings, sitting across the table from him over dinner, and thinking he must be the most attractive man alive.

He frowned, his strong jaw squaring and his eyes narrowing to golden slits of light. The expression did incredible things to her nerves, making him, as it did, about ten times more sexy. 'Look…' He paused again, and now she found herself totally disarmed when he said in quite a different tone that sounded almost boyish, 'Do you really think I'm hard to talk to? I'm sure Gill didn't. I think we used to talk about practically everything.'

Gillian didn't fancy the pants off you. She managed a shrug but speaking was beyond her for the moment. How could one man be such a combination of hard, powerful, ruthless macho man and charming, fascinating, sexy little boy-cum-black-hearted philanderer all in one package? And how could *she* have been so stupid as to agree to work for someone she'd never seen?

He continued to survey her for one more moment as the taxi hurtled along at breakneck speed, and then his scowl cleared and it was clear he had come to some sort of a decision as he settled back in his seat again and said, very quietly, 'The person I let down was my fiancée. I was set up to believe she'd been having an affair with someone else and I didn't believe her protestations of innocence. I dumped her, very publicly, and then immediately started an affair with her sister who had always made it clear she was willing and available. Saving face, I think they call it.'

Cory stared at him, utterly appalled, before she managed to pull herself together and say fairly steadily, 'And the sister was the one who…?' She raised enquiring eyebrows.

'Set me up, yes,' Max affirmed grimly.

'How…how did you find out the truth?' Cory asked faintly.

'A couple of weeks after we broke up my fiancée drove her car into a stone wall,' Max said dispassionately, but she could see the muscle working in his jaw and sensed the iron control he was putting on himself. 'The police said it was an accident—sharp corner on a lonely country road with an old barn least where you'd expect it—but Anne knew different and she confessed all to me in a paroxysm of remorse that was as shallow as she was. Within days she'd convinced herself Laurel had really had an accident and not taken her own life and she even tried to back-pedal on what she had said.'

'She might have been right?' Cory questioned carefully.

'Laurel was an excellent driver.' It was very cool and very final. 'Anyway, within weeks my father had had his heart attack and died and I'd inherited so there was no time for further regrets.'

No further regrets? He was eaten up with them.

'What did the rest of your family think about Laurel?' Cory tried to make her voice matter-of-fact and calm but it was hard. Very hard. Surely his mother or someone had tried to comfort him?

'There was no other family besides my father,' Max said shortly. 'My mother died when I was two and I was an only child, and my father never remarried. He wasn't a family type of man anyway.'

She was further aghast but she knew Max well enough by now to know that any show of sympathy would not go down well. But never to have known his mother... But all this explained a lot, Cory thought in the next instant. To have grown up without the softening influence of a mother in his formative years and then to have his faith in the female sex shattered so cruelly—it was little wonder that he had become so cynical and disenchanted. Of course the fact that he was wealthy beyond most folks' wildest dreams and had the sort of smouldering good looks and magnetic appeal that would give any star of the silver screen a run for their money couldn't have helped. He would have had women throwing themselves at him all his life. One click of his fingers and no doubt they were lining up.

The thought pierced her through, bringing, as it did, the night in the Japanese inn into vivid clarity again. He must have thought she was just like all the rest. She *had* been like all the rest!

It brought her sitting up a little straighter and her voice was quite brisk when she said, 'Well, I admit you might have more cause than most to be a little wary of the concepts of love and faithfulness, but that doesn't make them any less a reality.'

'You're not going to go on about this village of the good and pure where you were born again, are you?' he asked with cutting sarcasm. 'Because believe me you've done it to death.'

It worked like an icy shower on the lingering compassion his previous disclosures had produced, and now Cory glared at him, her eyes ablaze with green fire as she snapped, 'Really? It couldn't just be that you hate to be proved wrong, could it? I know hundreds of couples, my own parents included, who are very happy together. I'm sorry but I don't believe they've all got it wrong.'

'Hundreds...' he drawled laconically. 'It couldn't be that *you* are exaggerating now, could it?'

'And they are *real* people,' Cory continued with blistering determination. 'People who are prepared to acknowledge their mistakes and then get on with life rather than running away.'

The cool equanimity was wiped off his face in an instant, and in the same moment Cory reminded herself that this was her boss—*her boss*—and however liberal an approach Max encouraged with his secretaries she had gone just a touch too far. But she wasn't going to back down. No way, no how. He could dismiss her for all she cared! She had as much right as he did to say what she thought.

'Running away? I take it that was meant for me?' he asked with icy dignity, his face set and cold.

Her chin went up another notch at the look in the beautiful tawny eyes. 'What would you call it?' she asked tightly. 'You said yourself you were set up by this Anne, and if anyone is prepared to lie baldly enough they can be believable. You reacted perfectly understandably in the circumstances—'

'Thank you,' he interjected with lethal sarcasm.

'And therefore, in spite of the tragic outcome, you weren't really to blame for Laurel's death. Her sister was. And it might just have been that the accident *was* an accident anyway. Whatever you say, you don't know for sure,' Cory continued doggedly as she ignored the interruption. 'You aren't God, Max.'

He stared into the violet-splashed emerald pools for a long moment before he said, his tone very cool, 'If you love someone, *really* love them shouldn't trust be a basic ingredient of that emotion? In fact shouldn't it be the foundation stone?'

Cory looked back at him, and now her voice was wary as she answered, 'Yes…' Now what was coming? she asked herself silently.

'I thought I was madly in love with Laurel—I was planning to spend the rest of my life with her, for crying out loud—but I didn't believe her when she said she wasn't involved with someone else. Oh, Anne had set up an elaborate concoction of innuendoes and lies, but that was one of the things that Laurel flung at me when she was protesting her innocence. She said if I'd loved her, *really* loved her, I would have trusted her. And she was right.'

There was more coming and Cory waited for the punchline without saying a word, her eyes tight on his dark face.

'But I sailed in there like a gunboat with all guns firing, and do you know why? Because my pride had been hurt, that's why. And when you come down to it that's what this idealised emotion called love is all about. It doesn't exist, Cory, not really, not as we're led to believe by the poets and romantics anyway. Those couples that stay together do so because it suits them—career-wise, or because there's children involved or because they haven't met anyone else they fancy more—a million different reasons.'

Cory could see he meant every word and it was in that moment, for no apparent reason, that the thunderbolt hit. She loved him. *She loved Max Hunter.* A man who didn't know the meaning of the word.

'And all the divorces and broken families and the rest of it bear testimony to the validity of what I'm saying,' Max continued evenly. 'Love is just another name for sexual desire, physical chemistry, but most women—and some men too—can't engage in sex without it coming under the blanket of the name of love. They were probably repressed emotionally when they were young, or brainwashed, something like that,' he added with magnificent condescension. 'It happens all the time, unfortunately.'

She didn't believe it! Cory was still too shattered by the revelation of her own stupidity to respond to what he was saying. She'd fallen in love with this man—this powerful, incredibly wealthy, horribly attractive and wildly sexy man—who had had more women than she'd had hot dinners, and who looked for cool sophistication and unlimited sexual experience in his women besides them being beautiful and wealthy and gorgeous to boot. He would never look twice at someone like her, for goodness' sake.

And then, as though to prove her wrong, Max said, his voice even more bland, 'Take us for instance. I wanted you that night at the ryokan and I know you wanted me too, but it wouldn't have meant anything besides a brief satisfying of our carnal appetites, and it would certainly have interfered with our working together in the future. It shouldn't—assuaging the sexual hunger should be no more important than eating together or conversing—whatever—but the human race has been conditioned to think otherwise.'

Cory was aware she was gaping like a stranded fish, her mouth wide, and now she shut it with a little snap before forcing herself to say, her voice slightly shaky in spite of all her will being brought to bear, 'Are...are you saying you don't believe in love at all?' The subject of their wanting each other she ducked. There might be some women who could handle a live grenade but she wasn't one of them, especially when it was thrown by Max Hunter.

'Exactly.'

Cory felt an awful surge of temper at the overt self-assurance, but along with it there was a terrifying recognition of just how strong his power over her was, and it moderated her response as she said, her voice trembling, 'I don't believe that.'

'Of course you don't.' He was just plain patronising now and the anger increased. 'That's what I'm saying; you've been taught otherwise. You are a child of your environment after all.'

'I haven't been *taught* anything!' The secretarial college she had attended to get her excellent qualifications would be appalled if they could hear her now, Cory thought wretchedly as the echo of her shriek vibrated the airwaves. Screaming at one's boss was definitely a no-no. 'I'm a normal human being, for goodness' sake; it's *normal* to love! And to want to be loved,' she added more quietly. 'It's the most basic desire there is and stronger than lust.'

'I don't agree.' He eyed her coolly, quite unmoved. 'But I take it you're saying it was love, not lust you felt for Vivian?' And then, hitting way below the belt, he said, 'Now correct me if I'm wrong but I seem to remember that this great love that drove you to London, and had you all pale and wan beforehand, I'm sure, was the same love that some weeks later you weren't sure if you wanted or not.'

'What?' Cory stared at him angrily, her cheeks flushing.

'You stated you would be in two minds whether to take him back if he came crawling on bended knees,' Max stated triumphantly. 'Now, didn't you? This "most basic desire" can be a trifle capricious?'

How could you love someone and want to do them extreme physical damage at the same time? Cory asked herself furiously.

'And if you loved him in the way you think of love, you wouldn't have responded to me the way you did in the inn either,' he added firmly. 'You see? Love just doesn't stand up to the test.'

Oh, no, no, she could take so much and no more! The pig! The arrogant, self-satisfied, over-sexed, rotten *pig*! She called on all her considerable supply of will-power and prayed for the right words. They came. 'But you've already said that what we felt was just animal attraction,' Cory said sweetly. 'If I'd have gone to bed with you it would have just been like having a sandwich if I was hungry or going for a swim if I was too warm. It wouldn't have taken anything from Vivian because it wouldn't have mattered that much.' She clicked her fingers in his handsome supercilious face.

That face had to be seen to be believed. If anyone had told Cory she would have the satisfaction of seeing the great and imperious Max Hunter utterly lost for words she

wouldn't have believed them. But it was good. Oh, it was
so, *so* good.

And then the gratification was swept away and sheer
alarm took its place as he said, very softly and yet with
deadly intent, 'Cory, if I made love to you it wouldn't be
at all like having a sandwich or going for a swim, and it
would matter. Believe me, it would matter.'

She eyed him warily. He was mad. Oh, boy, was he mad!
'And if that was a challenge I'll give you something on
account to convince you,' he added silkily.

He had totally ignored her squeak of panic as he had
drawn closer, but stuck as she was on the back seat of a
taxi there was absolutely nowhere to go. She attempted
sweet reason as she quickly protested, 'It wasn't a challenge. It was you who said—'

The rest of her words were lost as his mouth took hers
in a kiss that was scalding hot and shatteringly experienced,
and in spite of all their previous conversations Cory went
down beneath it like dry ground opening up to life-giving
rain. His mouth was hard and sensual and she would never
have thought it could have produced such an instant reaction all over her body but it was happening. And Max
Hunter was a man on a mission—he was making sure it
was happening. She knew it, but she couldn't do a thing
about it.

She could feel her breasts swelling beneath the prim,
high-necked and sedately buttoned blouse she was wearing,
their tender, rose-tipped peaks growing hard and aching,
pressed as they were against the hard male chest. She felt
dizzy, disorientated, her head swimming even as her limbs
became fluid and her breathing nothing more than helpless
gasps, and overall, overall was a wonderful feeling of utter
pleasure that outdid anything she had experienced in her
life before. He was just so *good* at this!

He had curved her into him, his body covering hers as
he leant over her, and the smell of him was all about her

and it was intoxicating, delicious, like all the good things in life rolled up in one package.

His hands had stroked down to her slim hips, moulding her into him so she could feel every inch of his hard arousal, and it added to her excitement. She was burning, burning all over, she thought in wonder, and they weren't even in bed. They were in a taxi heading for Narita airport in the middle of a busy weekday morning.

The same thought must have occurred to Max because in the next moment she was free and he had settled back into his own corner of the seat, surveying her through narrowed amber eyes as he said, 'Well? Now tell me the egg and cress sandwich has it.'

She would have loved to be able to fire back with a barbed retort that would have put him very firmly in his place, but Max Hunter didn't have a place, she thought helplessly. Nevertheless she straightened her blouse and skirt carefully—she wanted to tidy her hair but she knew her hands were trembling and she'd never manage the pins that were holding the French pleat in place—and kept her voice as steady as she could when she said, 'This is sexual harassment, you know that, don't you?'

'Sexual…?' His voice trailed away but only for a moment. 'Cory, grubby little has-beens go in for sexual harassment. I most definitely do not!' he stated with grim ferocity, the self-satisfied expression he had been wearing just two seconds earlier no more. 'And you enjoyed that as much as I did. Be honest, admit it.'

'Enjoying it or not enjoying it is nothing to do with it,' she snapped back with equal ferocity. 'I neither asked nor wanted you to kiss me; *that* is the point. Just who do you think you are anyway? Being mauled on the back seat of a taxi is not my idea of enjoyment, let me tell you, Max Hunter!'

The silence was profound, but as the temperature of the atmosphere between them went plummeting to below zero

Cory held her ground as she stared back into the angry male face. He'd used brute force and that was unforgivable.

'I don't believe this.' It was a furious mutter, but underneath the rage was a very genuine echo of absolute bewilderment.

'I'm sure you don't.' She didn't allow herself to weaken in the slightest, and her voice was very tart. 'The trouble with you, Max Hunter, is that you've got used to snapping your fingers and having any woman you want slink to heel. Now, you might be quite happy with the sort of females who change their bed partner as casually as they change their nail varnish, but just take it from me—we're not all the same. Some of us employ a little discernment now and again, and some of us actually say no and mean it.'

'Really.' Black ice was making the airwaves freeze.

'Yes, really.' She continued to glare at him even as an image of the dole queue loomed strong. 'You are the last man, the very last man, I would offer a challenge to.' I've more sense for one thing, she thought wretchedly. You only have to touch me and I'm all gooey confusion. More fool me!

Now—in contrast to his cold, taut voice—the silence had begun to sizzle, and it took more effort than Cory would have believed possible to wrench her gaze from his and stare out of the window with as much cool as she could muster as she aimed for calm.

He might be the most spectacularly sexy man she had ever met—added to which she was head over heels in love with the rat—but that did not mean she was going to let him walk all over her, she told herself with a firmness she was proud of. And she didn't want to hear any other revelations about his past life either. She hadn't liked what his confidences had done to her. She'd wanted to fall into his arms, smother his face with kisses, convince him that there were still some good women left on the earth. But Max Hunter wasn't interested in *good* women, and the last thing

he needed was a female who wanted to comfort and cherish
him. Wear him out in bed maybe, but definitely not comfort
and cherish him, Cory thought bitterly.

Neither of them spoke another word until they reached
Narita airport, but Cory used the miles to claw back her
aplomb and sense of proportion and give herself a good
talking-to in the process.

It wasn't really Max's fault she had fallen for him, she
told herself with brutal honesty. In fact he had warned her
off in the first five minutes of seeing her. No, the fault was
all hers. She had no one to blame but herself for this mess.
And she shouldn't wage a war of words with him either—
she knew there could only be one conclusion if she did. He
was a ruthless opponent.

When the taxi drew into the airport confines she glanced
at him from under her eyelashes. They couldn't work together after this—the journey home was going to be a
nightmare as it was. Would he ask her for her resignation
now or later? she thought miserably. Either way she had
blown a fantastic job, but worse—a million times worse
than that—she would never see him again.

'I'm not going to eat you for speaking your mind, Cory.'
It was dry and mocking, and told her that her covert scrutiny had been noticed. 'And like I told you when you first
came to work for me, I don't like boring women, and—
whatever else—you're sure not that. I'm a big boy; I can
take it on the chin.'

She met the tawny gaze warily. The last few weeks had
taught her that Max was at his most dangerous when appearing calm and reasonable. That was the moment he usually went straight for the jugular, as many a savaged business colleague would testify to. 'I shouldn't have said all
that I did,' she admitted after a long pause when he surveyed her through lazily narrowed eyes.

'Why? Because you think you were wrong?' he asked
smoothly, his dark face giving nothing away.

'No, I do not think I was wrong!' It was very sharp and very swift. Eating humble pie was one thing but a whole meal quite another.

'Then I can only suppose you are following the adage of the boss is always right, and I've already told you what I think about that,' he said coolly. 'Don't be duplicitous, Cory. It doesn't suit you.'

'Duplicitous!' It was a splutter, and she had just opened her mouth to argue some more when he completely took the wind out of her sails by leaning across and depositing a swift kiss on her mouth a second before the taxi drew to a standstill.

'Out you get,' he said with silky satisfaction at her red face. 'And I want to dictate a couple of reports while we're waiting for the flight, okay? There are a number of things I need down on paper while they're fresh in my mind.'

He was back in boss mode and Cory had the wisdom to know when she couldn't win, but as she walked into the airport building, Max's hand on her elbow and his big body towering at her side, she found herself wondering how he could manage to sweep their previous conversation aside so completely and set things back on course with such consummate ease.

But she shouldn't wonder, should she? she told herself in the next moment, the warning voice in her mind distinctly acidic. If there was one thing Max Hunter knew how to handle it was women—be they business colleagues, maiden aunts, girlfriends or secretaries! She didn't know where she stood with him from one moment to the next and she had the feeling that was the way he liked it.

He was a control freak. She played with the thought, turning it over in her mind, and she knew she was right. He let people get just so close and then no more; the door was slammed shut and the drawbridge hauled up. She

wasn't quite sure if she had got the analogy right but she
knew what she meant anyway, she told herself miserably.
It could be summed up in one sentence. Max Hunter was
bad news.

CHAPTER SIX

THE weeks following the Japan trip were frantic and passed in something of a blur, although a couple of things stood out from the hectic pace. One was blonde and one was brunette.

The first time one of Max's girlfriends sauntered into the office Cory was quite unprepared, and the beautiful blonde—who was all emerald-green silk Dior and ice-cool perfection—made her feel frumpy, fat and fatuous in the five minutes or so before Max took Karin—a Swedish model, he informed her in an aside, and had she noticed the immaculate nail varnish?—out for lunch.

Cory had ignored the sarcastic reference to their altercation in the taxi with a regalness she had been proud of at the time, and when the lunch had stretched to three hours and Max still wasn't back in the office she had told herself she didn't care what he was doing. Determinedly. Over and over again.

The brunette was a week later and just as gorgeous, and this time Max hadn't come back to the office before she had left at five. She hadn't slept at all that night, even though she had told herself she was the most stupid woman in all the world and she had to pull herself together—and fast. This was going to happen over and over again and she had to learn to deal with it if she wanted to stay in the job.

But did she? This thought had remained at the back of her mind when the blonde and brunette had faded somewhat. And as the weeks went on and spring blazed into summer it hadn't gone away.

Gillian had been right when she'd said Max was a boss in a million, Cory told herself one Monday morning in July when she arrived at the office to find she was accompanying Max and two colleagues to lunch at a very swish restaurant in the West End—again. He might be a human dynamo but he treated his staff very well, and the perks to being his secretary were amazing.

The meal was one of several she had enjoyed that month at Max's expense, along with one or two days out visiting associates and business contacts, and the job itself was fast, thrilling and absorbing, but... She sighed, staring at the screen of her word processor as though it was going to provide an answer to her torment. She was tearing herself apart.

Not that Max had ever attempted another embrace since that time in Japan, just the opposite in fact. He had been utterly businesslike at all times, cool, amusing, considerate, generous—the perfect employer of Gillian's description in fact. She had seen him being ruthlessly cutting on occasion, aggressive when the circumstances warranted it, plain nasty once or twice—but never with her. There might be just a touch of satire now and again, but only enough to make her smile.

And all that should make her very happy, shouldn't it? So why couldn't she rid herself of the notion he was keeping her very firmly at arm's length, that she wasn't seeing the real Max Hunter at all now? And why, if it was true, should it bother her so much? She couldn't have continued working with him—feeling as she did—if he had followed up on their brief lovemaking, she knew that, so this was for the best. Absolutely. Without question.

And her state of mind hadn't been helped much by the weekend she had just endured, and endured was certainly the right word, she thought irritably, her mind winging back over the preceding forty-eight hours, which had been hellish. She had gone home primarily for her last dress fitting and that had been bad enough; Carole was a meringue and frothy lace person and that was fine—the clouds of sequinned chiffon and satin suited the giddy blonde—but the fact that the bridesmaids were attired in the same style— and in bright pink—was something else. The colour clashed horribly with the red tint to her hair and made her skin look like weak custard, and the fussy, over-the-top dress was more suited to a young child.

Even Cory's mother—who had been roped in by Vivian's parents to help with the arrangements after Cory's desertion to pastures new—had been unable to dredge up the required response as she had seen her daughter emerge from the village dressmaker's front room, and had stared at her with a look of helpless sympathy.

And Vivian... Cory found she was glaring into space now, and quickly forced her face into office mode. What on earth was the matter with Vivian? He had quite literally followed her round all weekend like a little puppy; she hadn't been able to get rid of him. Goodness knew what Carole and everyone else had thought, but she had found it highly embarrassing, not to mention acutely irritating.

Twice he had tried to get her alone and twice she had wriggled out of it, mainly because she didn't want to hear what he might say, she admitted with more than a touch of self-recrimination. If Vivian was regretting his engagement he had to sort it out with Carole, not her, and there was no way she was getting involved. No way.

She sighed deeply and then shook her head at her own meanderings. She couldn't think of all that now; she had a desk full of work to deal with and then lunch at Bloomsbury's with Max and two important business contacts. She needed to be bright, sharp and focused. Anything less around Max Hunter and you were in trouble.

The telephone rang when she was in the middle of a complicated and extremely confidential report, and she lifted the receiver to her ear without taking her eyes off the screen, her voice preoccupied as she said, 'Yes? Mr Hunter's secretary. How may I help you?'

'Cory?' It was Mavis in Reception and she sounded a little flustered. 'There's someone here to see you.'

'To see me?' Cory asked in astonishment. 'Personally, you mean?'

'That's what he said. A Vivian Batley-Thomas? He says he's an old friend and that he thought you might be expecting him to call in some time today?'

'What?' It had been too loud and Cory cast an anxious glance at Max's interconnecting door before she said more quietly, 'I don't believe this; I had no idea he was coming, Mavis. Look, I'm terribly busy this morning; I'm in the middle of urgent stuff that just won't wait. Could you explain for me, please? I'll hold on.'

'Right.' Mavis hesitated a moment before she added, 'But he was very insistent he see you right now, Cory.'

She could imagine, Cory thought grimly. Vivian had a way of expecting the world to revolve around him, and why she had never seen it when she'd lived at home she didn't know. Or perhaps she did.

A good forty seconds ticked by, and then Mavis's voice came again, saying, 'He says he's only in London for a few hours, Cory, and it can't wait. A matter of life and death.'

Life and death, her foot! Cory frowned ferociously at the receiver, and then, as Max's voice cut across the room with, 'What the hell is that face for?' her eyes shot up to see him standing indolently in the doorway, the amber gaze trained straight on her face. Oh, perfect; this was all she needed on top of everything else!

He moved far too quietly for such a big man, Cory thought crossly. She'd noticed that about him before.

'Well? I take it this face has something to do with that?'

He gestured at the receiver in her hand and belatedly Cory realised poor Mavis was still hanging on for her reply. 'I'll be down in a moment, Mavis.' She replaced the receiver very carefully—the urge to slam it down was strong and it would be a mistake.

'Problem?' Max asked silkily. 'Can I help?'

He wasn't going to go away. Why was it that he seemed to *feel* trouble? Cory asked herself irritably. And she suddenly had no doubt that Vivian was going to prove exactly that.

'Not really,' she prevaricated jerkily. 'Someone has called in to see me, that's all. I had no idea they were coming…'

'Someone?' he asked smoothly. 'Care to be more specific?'

'An old friend.' She could feel herself flushing and it made her furious with herself but there was nothing she could do about it.

'Hmm.' His eyes had narrowed, moving slowly over her anxious face, and then he took her aback as he moved swiftly to her side, drawing her up and holding her an arm's length away as his gaze locked with hers. 'It's him, this Vivian guy, isn't it?' he said coolly. 'I wondered how long it would take him.'

'Take him?' Suddenly, in the space of a few seconds, their whole relationship had shifted again and it had knocked her for six.

'To realise he's made a big mistake,' Max said evenly. 'And now he's sniffing about seeing how he can backpedal, eh? How do you feel about that, Cory? Have you got the sense and the guts to tell this creep to go to hell? Or would you like me to do the honours?'

His hands had tightened on her arms as he had spoken but that was the only indication of any emotion—his face and his voice were perfectly controlled and steady.

'I haven't even said it *is* him downstairs,' Cory protested weakly, her face glowing hotly. He was close enough for the smell of him to enfold her, its touch intoxicating on her senses, and as usual he had discarded his suit jacket and his tie as he'd been working. It wasn't the moment to feel a surge of desire but she couldn't help it.

Why did he always have to prance around half naked? Cory asked herself with wild exaggeration. Her nerves were quivering, her stomach muscles bunching, and the effect of him on her—her vulnerability where this man was concerned—made her voice sharper as she added, 'And it's none of your business anyway.'

'Wrong.' Now his strong fingers were actually hurting. 'Dead wrong. You start playing games with this guy and he'll tie you up in knots, and you'll be no good to me then. I want my secretary one hundred per cent dedicated and I pay for the privilege, as you well know. You knew what the job entailed when you took it on, Cory.'

The arrogance of it! Cory glared at him, rage surfacing in an overwhelming flood. He thought he owned her lock, stock and barrel, did he? Like some feudal lord keeping the peasants on his estate! She had never met anyone so full of their own importance as this man. Well, he could stuff his wonderful job—

'Besides which, I don't want to see you get hurt,' he finished more quietly, relaxing suddenly—something Cory felt was a definite decision on his part—as he said, 'I'm sorry, have I bruised you?'

'What?' She was staring at him, mesmerised by the change of tone and the softness apparent in the ruthless gold eyes. If anyone could tie her up in knots it certainly wasn't Vivian Batley-Thomas. 'Oh, yes, a little.' She rubbed at her arms, folding her hands across her chest and taking a step back from him. 'It's all right.'

'Cory, I've met a hundred Vivians in my time,' Max said softly, his gaze stroking her troubled face. 'At the bottom of him he is weak and that is why he is drawn to your strength. If you take him on now you will be carrying him for the rest of your life, you know that, don't you? He is not the one for you. Believe me.'

She knew *that*. If nothing else she knew that, Cory thought with a surge of hysterical amusement which she checked instantly. All this was going to drive her mad before she was finished. And then she spoke out the previous thought as she said, her voice as firm as she could make it. 'I know Vivian and I could never get together, Max. It's not an option as far as I'm concerned.'

'But he doesn't see it that way.' It was a statement, not a question, and the golden gaze was pinning her to the spot.

'Possibly not.' She wasn't going to be drawn into discussing this; Max had a way of eliciting far more information than people wanted to give at the best of times—and this wasn't the best of times, not with Vivian waiting in Reception.

'I bet he doesn't.' For a second the control wasn't absolute and she could have sworn there was a snarl in the male voice, but then he smiled, and amber eyes glowing a dark molten gold, as he repeated, 'I bet he doesn't,' his voice holding nothing more than mild irony now.

'No, well…' Cory found herself staring at him uncertainly, and she didn't like that. You couldn't be irresolute around Max. 'I'll just send him on his way, then.'

'You do that, Cory,' he said pleasantly.

She didn't know what it was—she couldn't have put her finger on it if it had meant her life—but there was something in the even dark tones that brought her head up a fraction and stiffened her back as she said, 'Don't worry, Max. I'll still get that report done in time and be ready to leave at lunchtime.'

'Damn the report.'

This time she knew she wasn't imagining the snarl, but in the next instant he had turned, strolling lazily into his office and shutting the door behind him with a gentleness that insisted she must have been wrong. But she hadn't been. She knew she hadn't been.

Cory spent another few seconds gazing at the door before she shut her eyes for an instant, screwing up her face before opening her eyes wide. And there was still Vivian… This

was going to be one of those days it would have been better
to have stayed in bed.

When Cory strode out of the lift at Reception she was
all set to send Vivian away with the proverbial flea in his
ear, but on her first sight of him as he sat, head down and
with a kind of desperate look about him, her resolve melted.

'Cory!' He leapt up as soon as he saw her, his handsome
face lighting up in a manner that would have once thrilled
her. 'I had to come, you know that, don't you? I had to see
you.'

'Hello, Vivian.' Cory was acutely conscious of Mavis's
interested eyes, and now she drew him over to a small sofa
sandwiched in between a prolific potted fern and a miniature palm tree. 'Is anything wrong?' she asked brightly,
forcing a lightness to her tone.

'Is anything wrong...?' He gazed at her, his brown eyes
velvet-soft and deep with liquid appeal. 'Cory, you have to
forgive me. Please. I've been such a fool, such a stupid,
mindless fool.'

This was going to be even worse than she had feared.
'Forgive you?' Cory smiled what she hoped was a brisk
smile before saying, 'What on earth have I got to forgive
you for, Vivian?'

'Oh, Cory.' It was almost a whine and everything in her
rebelled at the sound. He was like a boy, she thought won-
deringly, a selfish, spoilt brat of a boy, who had grabbed
at what he thought was the best gift on offer and been
presented with an empty box. But Carole wasn't an empty
box, she was a live, warm human being, and after losing
her parents when she was just a young child and growing
up with a maiden aunt who had had little time for her she
needed love and pampering and masses of attention. Which
Vivian was obviously finding hard to give. But that was
their problem, and they had to work it out together. She
couldn't help him this time.

'I don't understand.' She looked at him steadily. 'What have I got to forgive you for, Vivian?'

'For leaving you, for hurting you,' he said softly. 'What we had was so good, Cory. I was stupid not to realise it at the time.'

'What we had was friendship, Vivian, and we still have it.' Cory looked him straight in the eyes and her voice was very clear. 'I shall always count you and Carole as two of my dearest friends.' It wasn't quite true but she felt the circumstances justified a little embellishment.

'You don't mean that.' His face had reddened and now there was a sharper note to his voice. 'You love me, you always have. You know we were meant to be together. This thing with Carole… It's just made me realise how much I love you, that's all. And it's not too late, Cory, don't you see? I want things back as they were.'

She'd rather die.

'I'll tell Carole. I'll tell her that I've seen you and we've realised we want to be together, that the wedding is off and—'

'Vivian.' She didn't shout but something in her voice stopped him in his tracks. 'Please don't go on. You made your decision and I think it's the right one. We would never have been happy together, not in a romantic sense. We're friends, that's all. It's the wedding and all the arrangements that's making you feel like this; lots of people experience wedding nerves—'

'Don't patronise me, Cory.' His face had gone pale and there was a tightness to his mouth that reminded her of the tantrums he had indulged in as a boy when he couldn't get his own way. 'I know why you ran away to London; it wasn't because you really wanted to leave, was it? You just couldn't bear seeing me and Carole together. I saw your face that night we got engaged. You want me, Cory.'

'I always think it's a mistake to assume you know what someone wants.'

Cory didn't know whether to be relieved or horrified when Max appeared round the side of the potted fern. He was his usual cool, urbane self, dark eyebrows slightly raised and a polite, courteous expression on his handsome face that she didn't trust for a moment.

'I apologise for the interruption,' he continued smoothly, 'but I really do need you upstairs, Cory, if you've finished here?'

'Max…' She stared at him in amazement before recovering almost immediately and saying, 'Max, this is Vivian, an old friend of mine. Vivian, this is my boss, Max Hunter.' She found herself waving her hands in an exaggerated gesture of introduction and stopped abruptly.

It was a valiant attempt but neither man was having it. Vivian looked at Max, taking in the wildly expensive designer suit, the perfect grooming, the handsome face, and his eyes narrowed. Max was making no attempt to hide his contempt of the other man—every little bit of body language was screaming out exactly what he thought of Vivian Batley-Thomas and a worm under a stone would have pre-eminence.

'So that's it.' Vivian's voice was a low hiss. 'I see it all now. How could you, Cory? How could you?'

'Is this some kind of code you indulge in in the country?' Max asked with suspicious calm. 'Shouldn't we be saying, "how do you do?" or something equally facetious?'

'How long has it been going on?' Vivian asked Cory, his face as white as a sheet now. 'And don't lie to me, Cory.'

'If you are an old friend of Cory's then you would know she never lies,' Max said icily, moving a step closer as he homed in on Vivian in much the same way a hunter sighted its prey. 'In fact she is painfully honest at times,' he added with a touch of dark humour.

'Now look, you, I don't know who you think you are—'

It was a mistake, and one which Vivian tumbled to immediately, as Max said, his face grim now and his eyes chips of hard amber, 'I know exactly who I am, Vivian.' He gave the other man's name a connotation that was plain insulting. 'I am Cory's employer and the owner of this building, so if you have finished your business with my secretary I suggest you get the hell out of here.'

'And if I haven't?' Vivian asked sulkily with a glance at Cory.

This was getting out of hand. Way, way out of hand. Cory found herself beginning to wring her hands and she stopped herself at once, forcing her voice into its normal pitch as she intervened quickly. 'Vivian, this is a working day, surely you understand that? You shouldn't have come here without letting me know first.'

'I had to. Cory, you know how I feel. I *had* to.'

'Wrong.' In contrast to Vivian's mumble, Max's voice was rapier-sharp. 'You chose to. And I want you out of here now.'

This was the worst scenario she could have imagined. How on earth was she going to act as chief bridesmaid and the supportive friend and neighbour now? Cory thought savagely. She could have handled Vivian if Max had left them alone; she knew she could. She hadn't needed him barging in with all the finesse of a steamroller.

'I'm in London overnight.' Vivian was speaking directly to Cory and his voice was desperate. 'Can I see you later?'

At that moment she would have promised anything to get Vivian out of the building and to bring an end to the farce, so she nodded her head abruptly. 'Phone me later at the flat. You've got the number, haven't you? We'll talk some more then, Vivian.'

'I'm asking you nicely one more time before I throw you out.' Max's voice was liquid ice and he had kept his eyes trained on Vivian.

'I'm going.' Vivian cast one more imploring glance in Cory's direction and then he turned, walking swiftly out of the building without another word, his head bowed and his shoulders sagging.

There was a second of utter silence and then Max said, his voice mockingly cruel, 'And that's the man you were eating your heart out for? I'm disappointed in you, Cory. You could do better.'

She didn't need this! A second before she had been feeling shattered by the encounter, and now she felt the adrenalin pour in like fire and its heat enabled her to draw herself up, her eyes flashing as she said, 'He might not be perfect but at least he isn't afraid of commitment and love.'

'Granted.' It was lethal. 'But it would help enormously if he could make up his mind exactly where that commitment and love should be, don't you think?' Max drawled cuttingly. 'I trust someone has explained the concept of polygamy is illegal in this country?'

Cory flushed hotly. He was hateful! 'Vivian's confused.'

'You're telling me,' Max agreed bitingly. 'Now, if you've quite finished billing and cooing with love's young dream, perhaps you would come and do a little work? Incidentally...' he paused, fixing her with a cold stare '...does his fiancée know he's panting on the leash and that you're providing a warm and comforting shoulder?'

He was insinuating that she had encouraged Vivian to chase after her? Cory's stare was equally cold as she said, her voice extremely tart, 'I really don't know, Max. Would you like me to give you Carole's number so you can enquire yourself?'

Eyes as cool as a deep sea-green lake locked with clear amber, and Cory saw him take a long, hard pull of air before he said, his voice scathing, 'I think you've done enough damage already, don't you? The poor girl is probably going through hell as it is.'

She was trembling deep inside and if they had been anywhere else but in Reception—anywhere—no power on earth would have stopped her slapping that arrogant, cold face. But executive secretaries didn't indulge in hysterics, she told herself grimly, however much they were provoked. 'That was cheap and uncalled for, and I wouldn't even justify it with an answer,' she said proudly, glaring at him one more time before brushing past him and walking towards the lift.

He joined her a moment later and as the lift doors opened allowed her to precede him into the carpeted confines. She had expected some retaliation but they stood in grim silence until the doors opened again on the hushed top floor, and then his voice was icy as he said, 'I want to see that report as soon as it is ready,' before stalking into his office. This time there was a definite bang and, ridiculous though it was, Cory found the brief lack of control on Max's part comforting. It showed she had managed to prick that rhinoceros hide just the slightest bit, if nothing else.

Cory worked hard the rest of the morning and she concentrated totally on the tasks in hand without allowing her mind to wander for even one moment. She would examine the events of the morning later—once she was home—but for now she didn't intend to give Max the opportunity to criticise her professionalism whatever else.

Max's lunch guests arrived at just after twelve and by twenty past they had all left the building for Bloomsbury's in Max's chauffeur-driven Rolls with Cory acting the cool, efficient secretary.

Bloomsbury's was a restaurant of some standing—all crystal chandeliers, damask linen tablecloths, elegantly smooth waiters and subdued conversation, but Cory had visited several times in the months she had been working for Max and was past being overawed. She acted the perfect hostess for Max and he was—as ever—the gracious host, but underneath the small talk and sophisticated banter she could feel the tension between them like the effect of a lightning storm on a migraine sufferer and it was draining.

By the time they were all back in the Rolls at just after

three she found she was absolutely exhausted, although no
one would have guessed from her bright face and easy conversation.

They dropped Max's business associates off first, and
immediately the door of the Rolls closed behind them Cory
felt the atmosphere inside the car tighten and electrify. She
risked a sidelong glance at Max from under her eyelashes,
but the dark profile was as inscrutable as always. How
could one man be so *together*? she asked herself with understandable resentment. It just wasn't fair. She couldn't
ever imagine him losing control or letting his guard down;
he was one of the most unemotional men on the planet.

She settled back against the soft leather—they were still
some miles from the office and she had to relax or explode—and for the first time since the encounter with
Vivian allowed her mind to wander out of the tight confines
she had kept it in the last few hours.

Her first thought, which had been hovering uneasily, was
that Vivian had lied to her. He had supposedly called at the
offices because he was just in London for a few hours—
that was the message he'd relayed through the faithful
Mavis—but then once she had met him he had stated he
was in London overnight. She wasn't looking forward to
this evening... She wanted to shut her eyes and lay her
head back but such a show of weakness was unthinkable
with Max sitting beside her. What could she say to Vivian
that she hadn't already said this morning? she asked herself
wretchedly. Whatever way you looked at it the evening was
going to be awful, absolutely awful. Vivian knew how she
felt, deep down, but he'd fight it.

Her thoughts continued to ebb and flow, and mainly because of them and the physical exhaustion the nervous tension of the day had caused it was some fifteen minutes later
that Cory realised they were not on the right road. In fact
she wasn't sure where they were, she told herself with a

little start as she jerked upright in the seat and peered out of the window in alarm.

Max was lying indolently in his seat, his eyes closed and his breathing measured, but she knew instinctively the calm, relaxed pose was just that—a pose—and now her voice was sharp when she said, 'Where are we, Max? I don't recognise this area.'

He shifted slightly before opening his eyes, and once the piercing gold gaze met her anxious green one she felt her stomach turn over. He was up to something. 'We're in....' He sat up straight and peered out of the window. 'Pelham Street,' he said helpfully. 'It's just off Thurloe Square.'

Keep calm, keep calm, don't rise to the bait, Cory warned herself silently. She had seen this ploy of Max's with other people too often not to recognise what he was doing. He was contriving to rile her, to manoeuvre her into losing her temper while he sat back in apparent sympathetic—if slightly bewildered—benevolence, and to give him his due he'd had some spectacular results from what she'd seen. He reduced his opponent to teeth-grinding frustration, and then—when they were least expecting it—went in for the kill. *But not today, and not with her.*

'This is not the way to the office,' Cory stated grimly.

'No, no, it's not,' Max agreed genially. 'It's miles away.'

She bit down hard on her inner lip before she could manage, 'Then where are we going, Max?' And then, to avert further hedging, she asked flatly, 'Where is our ultimate destination?'

'I need some papers which are at home.' It was a cool statement and his face was deadpan. 'So it seemed opportune to call in.'

At home. Right, she could handle this. All she needed to do was stay in the car while he got the papers, that was all. Simple. She nodded abruptly, and then, when he shrugged off his jacket and indicated his tie with a 'Do you mind?' as he pulled it loose, she shook her head before turning to look out of the window.

Max's house was on the outskirts of Harlow, Cory had known that, but nothing had prepared her for the size of the grounds or the enormous mansion that came into sight once the chauffeur had opened the big security gates set in a stone-built, nine-foot-high wall and driven them up the winding pebble-covered drive.

'Cup of coffee?' The voice at her side was silky-smooth.

'What?' She drew her eyes away from the huge sprawling L-shaped residence that seemed to go on for ever, and then said hastily, 'Oh, no, thank you; I'll just wait here until you've got what you need.'

'I wouldn't hear of it,' he said easily. 'It will probably take a few minutes and my housekeeper would be mortified if I kept a guest waiting in my car that long without offering them refreshments.'

'I'm not a guest, I'm your secretary,' Cory pointed out.

'Mrs Brown wouldn't make that distinction.' There was a touch of steel beneath the smoothness now but Cory ignored it.

'I really would prefer to wait in the car,' she persisted politely.

'And I would prefer you to come in.'

She nerved herself to stare directly into the amber eyes and saw immediately he wasn't going to give in. Over the last months she had learnt to read most of his expressions and she knew this one quite well—it was dig-your-heels-in time. 'If you insist....' She allowed herself a resigned shrug and bored inclination of her head that suggested he was being tedious.

'I do, Cory.' His mouth curved into a sardonic smile and then he had opened her door, alighting himself and then reaching out his hand to help her out of the car, his dark face cool and expressionless.

She extracted her hand from his the minute she was

standing on the drive, but in the next instant he had taken her elbow, his fingers warm on her skin through the cotton material of the light summer jacket she was wearing and the scent of his body intoxicating.

'Come into my parlour said the spider to the fly.' It was a muttered aside as he shepherded her across the forecourt, up the semi-circular sweep of wide steps and then through the beautiful oak double front doors, and she ignored it. It wasn't difficult; she was having a job not to gasp out loud at what she was seeing.

The hall was majestic, there was no other word for it— from the beautifully polished wood floor to the high vaulted ceiling from which the bedrooms curved off balcony-style from the magnificent staircase—and just one of the exquisitely framed pictures on the brushed linen walls would have paid Cory's salary for six months.

'Come through to the drawing room.' Max led the way down the hall and into a room which was positively enormous and furnished in the sort of way most mere mortals just dreamed of. The carpet was cream-coloured and practically ankle-deep, the sofas and chairs a light honey and the scattering of fine antiques were tasteful and elegant and screamed unlimited wealth.

The huge French doors at the far end of the room, framed by long billowing cream silk curtains, led on to a beautifully laid out patio and beyond that there was a massive bowling-green-smooth lawn framed by mature trees with the glinting blue of a swimming pool in the far distance shimmering in the fierce July sun.

She shouldn't be surprised, Cory told herself silently as she gazed out at the sleeping garden. She had known he was a multimillionaire; he would hardly be living in a little three-bedroomed semi in the sticks, now, would he? But this… This really was beyond anything she had imagined. And quite overwhelmingly beautiful.

'Make yourself comfortable.' Max's voice was deep and

soft behind her, and as she turned, a polite compliment hovering on her lips, she found herself just staring into his eyes instead. He was magnificent. Her mind said it all by itself as she looked into the dark, handsome face. And perfectly suited to these surroundings. He was as far from her orbit as the man in the moon. 'Would you like that coffee? Or maybe something long and cool?' he asked evenly.

'I…I'm fine.' Oh, don't stutter, she warned herself irritably. At least *try* and act as though all this hasn't blown your mind. He was used to women who took all this opulence in their stride without turning a hair. 'I'll just wait here until you're ready to go if I can't help at all,' she said with office politeness.

'Ah…' Now there was a dark note and she sensed it immediately. 'Well, that might be some time.'

She dared not voice her suspicions and instead said brightly, 'No problem, you're the boss.'

'Yes, I am, aren't I?' he agreed musingly.

It wasn't reassuring, but she was determined he wasn't going to intimidate her. She stared at him, keeping her face bland.

'The thing is, Cory, I've decided not to go back to the office today,' Max said smoothly. 'It's really doesn't fit in with my plans.'

She continued to stare at him, her green eyes showing more of their violet tinge as she struggled to keep the panic from showing, and then she kept her voice very steady as she said, 'Okay, if that's what you want. Shall I call a taxi or will the Rolls take me back?'

'The Rolls has gone.'

'So it's the taxi, then,' she stated briskly.

'Not…quite.' And then he had the audacity to smile as he added, 'There are five guest bedrooms to choose from.'

Cory's heart took a flying leap against her chestbone and then subsided into fluttering alarm. 'I'm going back to the office, Max.'

'No, you are not, Cory,' he countermanded in the same tone, his voice silky. 'You are staying here until tomorrow morning.'

'Are you mad?' she asked unevenly. He must be!

'I might be.' He surveyed her through half-closed gold eyes. 'It's been suggested before, I must admit. But of the two of us you are the craziest. That guy is a liability, Cory. I'm not going to let you get involved with him again. You need protecting from yourself.'

'You're not...?' The magnificent mansion faded away, his wealth and power disappearing with it, and now Cory forgot he was her boss, that her extremely generous salary and the numerous perks that went with it were under his control, and she fairly spat out her rage as she snapped, 'Who the hell do you think you are, Max Hunter? How *dare* you try and tell me what to do? I'm leaving here right now and you know what you can do with your job too. Employing me as your secretary did not mean you had the right to my soul as well.'

'Now as it happens it's not your soul I had in mind.'

He had jerked her into his arms before she realised what was happening, and as she began to struggle he subdued her as easily as if she were a child, guttural sounds of irritation in his throat as he bent his head to capture her evasive lips.

His mouth was hard and sensuous and it made her heart pound even more wildly, a trickle of warm desire flowing through her blood in spite of her very real fury. His tongue searched for hers, the thrust of its erotic insistency insidious against her rage as it caused excitement to flow where anger had been a moment before.

'Cory.' He gasped her name as his hands slid down her slender shape. 'Sweet Cory. Sweet, angry, elusive Cory.'

She was unable to offer more resistance as his touch became delicate and wonderfully persuasive, the desire that had him in its grip as fierce in her. He had moved her further into his hard frame, his hands on her hips as his hot arousal spoke of his own need, and as the kiss continued in all its intoxicating wonder she felt her limbs become fluid until it was only his arms that were holding her upright.

'Now tell me you want to meet him tonight,' he whispered against her ear some long minutes later when his mouth left hers. 'Tell me he can make you feel like this. Tell me you need him.'

His whisper jerked Cory out of the world of colour and light and sensation his lovemaking had taken her into and into the harsh reality of the present like nothing else could have done.

She pulled free, her legs trembling and her cheeks burning, but her eyes were sparking as she hissed, 'At least Vivian has never forced himself on a woman. He always conducts himself like a gentleman.'

'Yes?' His mouth had tightened. 'That doesn't surprise me. He's the type who would be content to be led about by a ring through his nose all his life,' he said, darkly fierce.

'Oh, so you're saying it's macho to use brute force?' Cory spat furiously, aware she was using anger to cover up her burning humiliation and shame. How could she have submitted so completely? she asked herself desperately. How could she? After everything she had told herself over the last months...

'Of course I'm not saying that,' he bit back tautly. 'I have nothing but contempt for anyone—man or woman—who thinks brute force can get them what they want.'

'Oh, come on!' She was fighting herself now, and the terrifying control he had over her, but he didn't know that. 'You don't expect me to believe that, do you? Actions speak louder than words after all.'

'I don't care what you believe, Cory,' he said with sudden and sinister quiet, 'but it's the truth. I got this—' he indicated the scar at the side of his throat which his open-necked shirt revealed more clearly and which she had thought about many times since she had first noticed it '—because someone thought they could force me to agree to what they wanted by employing such methods. They didn't,' he added darkly. 'I'm not an advocate of physical violence.'

She stared at him, too taken aback by the sudden revelation to be tactful as she said, her voice shaky, 'Who was it?'

'A lady friend.' He smiled but it was a mere twisting of the firm mouth, and chilling. 'She hadn't told me one little fact about our relationship when it was developing— namely that she had a husband—and when I found out I dumped her. She objected.' He lifted wry eyebrows.

'And she did that?' Cory asked in horror. His experiences with the female of the species seemed to bear more similarity to walking through a minefield than anything else.

'Yes, she did.' His voice was cold. 'But first she tried the old feminine tactic of threatening to kill herself if I didn't continue with our affair, and when that didn't work she flew into a rage and started throwing anything to hand. A Victorian hand mirror can do considerable damage, as I discovered to my cost,' he finished smoothly. 'The consultant told me that just the merest fraction one way and I would have bled to death within minutes. As it was it meant a damn inconvenient stay in hospital but that was all, and at least it taught me to be more careful in the future.'

'That's...that's awful.'

Cory was deeply shocked and it showed, and now Max shook his head slowly, his eyes cynical as he said, 'Carmen was no better and no worse than the rest of her sex, just a little more fiery than most, perhaps due to her Spanish blood.'

'You think *any* woman would be capable of such deceit?' Cory asked hotly. 'Not to mention physical violence? You can't believe that.'

'Yes, I do.' It was unequivocal. 'The human race has two great passions—greed and desire—and when either one is thwarted there can be trouble, but both together—that's when the fur flies.'

For a moment the enormity of the situation—which seemed to have blown up out of nowhere—made Cory speechless, but only for a moment. And then she straightened proudly, her eyes very green and very direct as she stared him full in the face. 'Then all I can say is that I am sorry for you, Max,' she said quietly. 'More sorry than I can say.' She saw the shock of her reply register in the hard male face but she didn't pause as she continued. 'You might be rich and powerful and you might have your world at your fingertips, but in reality you have nothing. You haven't got a clue what makes nice normal people tick, have you? And they're out there, believe it or not.'

'There is no such thing as a nice normal person, Cory,' he said tightly after a moment's deafening silence. 'We all have our dark side just waiting to rear its ugly head; some people just hide it better than others, that's all. I preferred the honesty of Carmen's attack to all her efforts at sweet persuasion.'

'She was one sick woman, Max.' Cory's chin raised itself another notch. 'And perhaps if you associate with such shallow, conniving people you got exactly what you deserved. Water always finds it own level—I'd have thought you knew that.'

'How refreshing…homespun wisdom,' he drawled nastily. But she had seen the look in his eyes and the sudden paling of his skin under its tan, and she knew her words had hit their target.

'No, just basic common sense,' she shot back quickly, hoping the trembling in her stomach wasn't communicating itself to her voice. She had spoken the truth when she had said she felt sorry for him, but that pity added to her love made her want to smother him in kisses, to give herself wholeheartedly without any reserve, and she knew that would be fatal. He wouldn't understand such a gesture; to Max it would be purely a physical expression of desire. But still her heart bled for him—for the lost little boy who had grown up with all the advantages in the world except the one that counted most—a mother's unconditional love that could have mellowed and softened even the worst of life's experiences.

'Then apply a little of that common sense to your situation.'

She had forgotten, just for a moment, that she was dealing with a razor-sharp intellect and ruthlessly focused mind, but now, as he brought the conversation back to her proposed meeting with Vivian, she saw that Max was still controlling the shots.

Cory stiffened, biting back the hot retort that had sprung to her lips and forcing herself to take a deep breath and count up to ten before she said, 'I have no intention of getting involved with Vivian, if that's what you're implying. Not that it's any of your business.'

'A bit of soft soap and he'll have you eating out of his hand in minutes,' he mocked silkily. 'He's the puppy-dog type.'

If she hadn't loved him so much she would have hated him. 'I'm sorry your opinion of me is so poor,' she said tensely, 'but as it's *my* life and *my* decision I would like to go now.'

He shrugged. 'No can do, I'm afraid. Sorry.'

'I shall ask your housekeeper to phone for a taxi,' Cory warned tightly, 'and I shall tell her why if necessary. You have no right to try and keep me here against my will. It's…it's barbaric! Not to mention illegal,' she added as an afterthought.

'You know, I'd quite forgotten Mrs Brown was visiting

her sister overnight when I invited you here,' Max lied with careless ease. 'Silly of me. So it's just you and me, Cory.'

'You *planned* this?' She remembered he had been on the phone to his housekeeper when she had taken him a cup of coffee just after their morning altercation, and he had pointedly stopped talking until she had left the room. 'You did, you planned it,' she accused tautly.

'Of course.' The narrowed gold glare eyed her unrepentantly. 'You need protecting from yourself and there was no one else around.'

It was too much! The last straw! The final outrage!

'From myself?' The manipulating, devious, lying *swine*. 'You lure me here under false pretences, intending to keep me a virtual prisoner and try to get me to sleep with you, and you talk about *protection*?' Cory screeched angrily. 'You're unbelievable.'

'Sleep with you?' Max ignored the rest of her accusation with magnificent disregard. 'Cory, even among the shallow, conniving women I know it is customary to wait to be asked,' he said mildly. 'But of course I'm game if you are.'

'I'm not game!' she raged furiously, livid he had made her out to be some sex-crazy bimbo. 'I never will be. Not with you, Max Hunter, so you can forget it.'

'Pity.' He eyed her enigmatically. 'You tasted rather good.'

'I *insist* you let me leave,' she demanded autocratically.

'Don't be boring, Cory.' As he moved towards her again she tensed, but he merely took her arm, ushering her across the room as he said, 'Come and see your sleeping quarters and then change into a bikini. The pool is freshly cleaned and just waiting for us. And before you try, Mrs Brown unplugged and removed all the extension phones before she left and the master is in my study, the door of which is locked.' And he had the audacity to smile complacently.

'I wonder who could have possibly asked her to do that?' Cory snapped caustically. As if she didn't know!

'And there's a special code for the outside gate and the wall is unscalable, unless you've done mountaineering?' he asked mildly.

'You're unbelievable!'

'Thank you. It's nice of you to mention that again, especially as you haven't experienced all my attributes yet,' he murmured smoothly. 'Or not to their fullest potential, anyway, but of course we can rectify that any time you like. Now, I'm sure there will be swimwear to fit you in your quarters along with anything else you might need, so why don't you relax and enjoy the evening now you are here? A couple of hours relaxing by the pool followed by a good bottle of wine and a leisurely meal isn't *too* much of an ordeal, is it? You might even find you like me a little by the end of the night,' he added sardonically. 'Miracles do occasionally happen.'

If he only knew! It was that thought that silenced anything further Cory might have said, but as she allowed Max to lead her out of the drawing room and towards the stairs she was praying like she had never prayed before.

CHAPTER SEVEN

WHEN Max left her with a casual, 'See you in ten minutes downstairs,' after opening the door of what appeared to be a sumptuous guest suite, Cory stood for some moments just inside the room without moving. Oh, wow! Wow, wow, and treble wow, she thought weakly.

She was standing in an area which was obviously a small sitting room, and the normal furnishings were complemented by an ultra-modern flat-screened television, a hi-fi system complete with an extensive range of CDs, and what looked like a fridge and small bar. The decor was a deep dark rose and dull gold, like a dying sunset, and she could see the same colours reflected in the bedroom beyond, which was approached through a gracious arch at the far end of the sitting room. The *en suite* was in gold and cream marble and complete with Jacuzzi, and when she gingerly opened the walk-in wardrobe she saw enough outfits—all with designer labels—to kit out ten female guests. Guests? Lovers, she thought caustically.

But it wasn't the flagrant display of unlimited wealth that was making her heart thud, it was Max himself. She didn't understand this—the way he was acting—and neither could she quite take in that the world she had inhabited this morning had changed quite so dramatically in just a few short, action-packed hours.

This morning he had been merely her boss—Max Hunter, business tycoon and playboy extraordinaire—and in that capacity she could cope with her feelings regarding him, almost. But now... Now she wasn't quite sure what he was or how he saw her, and it bothered her more than she would have thought possible. Because she was weak where he was concerned—that one passionate embrace in the drawing room had confirmed it all too succinctly, and being alone with him like this was a recipe for disaster. And she didn't need it.

Why had Vivian appearing on the scene that morning got under his skin quite so fiercely? she asked herself now as she plumped down on the huge bed with a little sigh. He wasn't particularly interested in her—he'd made that quite plain over the last weeks since their brief lapse from boss/secretary mode in Japan. And even *that* had only been because he had thought she was available, she reminded herself miserably. Once she had spelt out how she felt he had left her well and truly alone. Her only redeeming feature, as far as he had been concerned, was that she wasn't boring, and he'd even accused her of that this afternoon!

What was she going to do? She sat for some sixty seconds more in the warm, faintly perfumed room, before jumping up from the bed and walking over to the wardrobe again. Well, if she wasn't going to sulk in this guest suite till morning there was only one other alternative, she decided bravely. She would go down to the pool as Max had suggested and act as cool and contained as any ice-queen.

Disdainful. As she surveyed the beautiful clothes she nodded at the word. That was what she would be. He had an ego as big as a barn door and she was blowed if she was going to be another notch on his belt. Two could play at the love-'em-and-leave-'em game!

She fetched out and discarded two or three minuscule scraps of no doubt wildly expensive material that were masquerading as bikinis, before her eyes alighted on a slightly more sedate swimming costume. The delicately shaded material flowed from dove-grey through to deep violet, and if it fitted she would feel somewhat less exposed in a one-piece, Cory decided as she quickly began to undress.

She felt a little less sure about the swimwear once she was staring at herself in the mirror some moments later, however. The costume was sensational but undoubtedly provocative. The cut of the legs went to waist level and the deep plunging neckline met it, with just a precarious ribbon of material holding the whole thing together. It made her somewhat small but full bust look great, she thought with a touch of pleasure despite the circumstances, and her legs went on for ever, but the thought of displaying her wares in front of Max was daunting to say the least.

She remained in irresolute silent contemplation for some seconds more, before a sense of 'in for a penny, in for a pound' bravura swept over her. The costume went hand in hand with a transparent silky shirt top of the same mate-rial—a beautiful thing on its own—and if nothing else the outfit screamed panache. And if ever she'd needed panache it was now. When she thought of the women Max was used to…

When she swept downstairs some minutes later no one would have dreamt her stomach was doing cartwheels and she was scared to death.

Max was waiting in the hall and in the second she caught sight of him before he raised his head Cory received a lightning bolt straight through her body. Normally his dark good looks were more than devastating enough, but nearly naked he was dynamite. The broad, hard-muscled shoul-ders, big lean frame and powerful legs were relaxed in ca-sual ease as he half lay sprawled in an easy chair at the foot of the stairs, and after her first glimpse of acres of hard, tanned, sinewy male flesh Cory kept her eyes on a point just above his head.

When her flip-flops reached the polished wood of the hall floor Cory nerved herself to meet Max's waiting narrowed gaze, and she saw his eyes were intent on her face as he rose to meet her, and he wasn't smiling. He was wearing just the briefest of swimming trunks.

'You look beautiful.' It was deep and low and made her shiver inside. 'Except…' He reached out and turned her round, loosening her hair from its pins and ignoring her protests. 'Now that's better.' There was a great deal of manly satisfaction in his tone as her rich, long dark brown hair tumbled about her shoulders. 'You should always wear your hair like that,' he added quietly as he turned her about to face him again. 'I've told you before.'

Cory shrugged in what she hoped was a sufficiently calm way to fool him into thinking she could have spoken if she'd wanted to, but in reality the closeness of that powerful male chest with its light dusting of black body hair had frozen her vocal cords and caused her legs to become liquid jelly.

'There's an ice bucket and champagne waiting for us by the pool,' Max said silkily as he took her arm and drew her towards the open drawing-room door. 'And strawberries of course. There is nothing nicer than champagne and strawberries on a lazy summer's afternoon, is there?'

She wouldn't know, Cory thought with a stab of pain, although she had no doubt this was a ploy Max had used with his women many times in the past. Although she wasn't one of his women, was she? She was his secretary. *That was all she was.* And she had better keep the fact at the forefront of her mind, she added caustically as they passed through the French doors and into bright sunlight, because she had the feeling Max wasn't going to.

They were halfway across the lawn when Max stopped, turning to enclose her lightly in his arms with his hands in the small of her back as he said, his tone reproving and faintly disappointed, 'How long are you going to keep the icy, silent approach up, Cory? I hadn't figured you for a poor loser.'

She knew exactly what he'd figured her as! The embrace in the drawing room and the champagne and strawberries spoke volumes! But it wasn't sulkiness that had kept her quiet, it was him, Max Hunter—although she would rather

die than admit to the desire that was snaking through her
limbs and making her fluid.

'Kidnapping is a criminal offence,' she said shakily as
she stared up into his face. His great height made her feel
as though she was tiny and delicate and utterly feminine
and it wasn't an unpleasant sensation, neither was the feeling that she was enclosed in steel coated with the veneer
of warm flesh.

'Then you can report me tomorrow,' he said silkily.

She could feel the hard thud-thud of his heart against her
fingers where they were resting lightly against the broad
chest, and smell the intoxicating fragrance of fresh male
skin and expensive aftershave, and it was heady.

'But for now...' He eyed her coolly, his gaze stroking
over the lovely flushed face framed by the glowing red-
brown waves that shone myriad shades in the white sunlight. 'For now you accept this is *fait accompli* and lover-
boy is going to go home to his faithful future spouse
disappointed, okay?'

Lover-boy? She had so completely forgotten Vivian that
it took a moment to understand what he was talking about,
and then it was guilt at her utter detachment from Vivian
and his troubles that made her voice tart as she said, wriggling a little now, 'What gives you the right to meddle in
people's lives like this anyway?'

'Nothing and no one *gives* me anything, Cory,' he said
smoothly. 'I take what I want. Isn't that the name of the
game when all is said and done?' He raised mocking, quizzical eyebrows at her cross face.

'*Your* game maybe.' She frowned up at him, her eyes
sparking, and then he cut through all her defences when he
grinned, his face relaxing and his rare smile lighting up the
darkness that was always hovering at the back of his eyes,
as he dropped a light kiss on the tip of her nose before
sweeping her up into his arms, saying, 'Come on, you stub-

born wench; a good dunking in the pool will wash away that pout and cool you down.'

'Don't you dare! Max! Don't you dare throw me in!'

She was struggling in earnest now but it had about as much effect as a tiny fly caught in a massive spider's web.

'You can swim?'

They had reached the edge of the pool now and for a moment she thought about lying but it was too late—he had read the truth in her eyes. The next moment she found herself flying through the air into the silky cold depths, and she just had time to hold her nose before going under the water in a tangle of arms and legs.

When she surfaced Max was treading water at the side of her, his mouth still curved in that grin that made him look like an overgrown boy, and it was that which made her voice weak as she said, 'You pig! That was really mean, you pig.'

'Careful.' He held up a warning finger, his eyes glinting with laughter. 'You're very vulnerable in here.'

She was very vulnerable anywhere if he was around, Cory thought as a surge of love made her wish from the bottom of her heart that things were different. But they weren't and they would never be.

'Can I at least put this on the side, please?' She tried to make her voice stern but it merely sounded breathless as she indicated the shirt top she was in the process of shrugging off.

'Of course.' His gaze was narrowed as he watched her swim with firm, strong strokes to the side of the pool and toss the sodden top onto the hot tiles, and his voice was approving when she swam back. 'You're an excellent swimmer; you swim like a man.'

'Is that supposed to be a compliment?' she asked mockingly. 'Women are able to do most things as well as—if not better than—men given half the chance.' She grimaced at him cheekily and he smiled back.

'Most of the women of my acquaintance are too worried about their hair and make-up to bother to learn to swim at all,' he said wryly. 'Pools are for posing by. Full stop.'

'I've told you before, Max, you mix with the wrong women.' It was too good an opportunity to miss, but Cory didn't wait for his reply, turning in one slender movement and cutting through the water with a powerful crawl to the deep end of the Olympic-size pool.

'Where did you learn to swim like that?' He had followed her but Cory had been pleased to see he hadn't been able to catch her up. 'I hadn't got you down as a woman athlete.'

'My father's a great swimmer, my mum too.' Cory raked back her hair from her face and grinned at him. 'The three of us did a course in scuba diving some years back, and once you've trained in a quarry in November in freezing cold water and taken your mask off ten metres under, and had what feels like a ton of ice hit you full in the face, anything else seems easy. My father and I continued with the advanced course but my mother had had enough by then.'

'Right.' He was surprised—she could tell by the expression deep in the gold eyes—but he was trying to hide it. It felt marvellously—*fabulously*—good to have taken him aback. 'Have you swum abroad?' he asked interestedly. 'Gone down in warm waters?'

'A few times, on package holidays—nothing elaborate,' Cory said evenly. 'Nevertheless the water was a good few degrees warmer and it was fascinating to swim down and see the different sea life to England. It's a whole different world down there.'

She launched off the wall of the pool as she finished speaking, glorying in the feel of the clean clear water on her warm skin, and this time Max was just behind her when she reached the shallows.

'A real-life water baby.' His eyes were warm and his

voice more so, and Cory didn't like what it did to her heart. He was too attractive and a darn sight too charming, she warned herself firmly as a little warning bell clanged shrilly in her brain. In fact Max Hunter was too much of everything! 'You obviously get on well with your parents?' he asked now, his voice probing.

'They're great,' Cory affirmed shortly. She didn't want to discuss her parents with Max; in fact the less he knew about her private life the better. She knew every little bit of personal information would be stored in that computer-like brain and analysed to his own advantage, and who knew when or how he would use it?

He nodded slowly, the drops of water moving like diamonds in the sunlight over his tanned skin and making her muscles clench. 'It's a great gift, a loving upbringing,' he said quietly, and for once there was no cynicism or amusement in the dark voice. 'My father loved me but he had no time to show it, and when there might have been a chance of us getting to know each other—after I'd left university— the time ran out.'

And then, as though regretting the brief opening of the window into his mind, his expression changed and the window was slammed shut and his tone was merely teasing as he said, 'I'll race you if you think you're up to it? You being a mere woman, that is.'

'Ha! I could beat you with one hand tied behind my back,' Cory challenged immediately.

She didn't, but neither did Max outdo her, and for a good few lengths—as they swam up and down in the blazing sunshine—they were neck and neck, until Cory found herself tiring. Max, it seemed, could go on for ever, and for some ten minutes after she had climbed out of the water and was sitting on the side of the pool he continued to cut through the clear blue depths like a machine. An incredibly sexy, live, warm, breathing machine who had a body erotic dreams were made of, Cory told herself ruefully.

She was no longer the same person since she had met him. It was frightening but true. And she couldn't imagine a world in which she didn't see him, watch him, feel him about her. And that was even more frightening. What she'd felt for Vivian…it just didn't bear any resemblance to this fierce, consuming emotion that was eating her up from the inside. But it was destructive and very, very dangerous.

'Right, a glass of champagne, I think.' He hauled himself out beside her and then stood in one lithe movement, offering her his hand as she continued to sit on the side of the pool. She had put on the shirt top as she'd sat watching him, and now she pulled the edges together, hastily fastening two or three of the buttons before she took his hand and rose to her feet.

'It's useless, Cory.' He eyed her intently, his skin gleaming.

'What?' His voice had been deep and husky, and she was painfully aware of the powerful body just inches from hers.

'Trying to cover yourself up,' he said softly. 'You could clothe yourself in black from head to foot and I'd still see those long, slender legs and tiny waist and wonderful breasts.'

'Max, don't do this.' There was a note of panic in her voice, and now his expression hardened, his eyes taking on the brilliance of liquid gold as he stared into her defensive face.

'Why?' His look was heated and angry. 'I want you, you know that, damn it, and you want me whatever you're telling yourself to the contrary. It's been slowly killing me the last few weeks, working in the same office, seeing you sitting at that desk with your hair hidden from view in those ridiculous buns. The times I've wanted to rip your clothes off and take you then and there on that same desk and to hell with the consequences.'

'That's lust, plain and simple,' she shot back tightly.

'It might be plain but it's sure not simple.' He scowled angrily. 'I'm sick of cold showers umpteen times a night.'

Cory was still battling with the image he had conjured up in her mind regarding her plain little serviceable desk—she'd never be able to look at it in the same way again—but she struggled to keep her quivering from showing as she said, 'I don't do cheap affairs, Max. I thought I'd made that clear. And you've told me yourself you aren't into anything else, so why are we having this conversation?'

'I *told* you I believe in enjoying a member of the opposite sex—and them enjoying me—without the illusion of happy ever after,' Max grated. 'That's why.'

'That's what I mean.' She faced him squarely, her eyes shadowed as she tried to keep her lips from trembling. 'Cheap affairs.'

'Hell!' His eyes had skimmed over her face and now he pulled her into his damp body with a roughness that spoke of inner turmoil. 'You're so damn stubborn you should have been born a man!'

She wanted to fight him but she just didn't have the emotional strength, and as she relaxed against him with a tiny stifled sob she felt him stiffen. He continued to hold her for some moments without speaking, the hot sun beating down on them, and then he said, still without moving her from him and with her face buried in the male, scented warmth of his shoulder, 'Why aren't you tough and hard like all the others, for crying out loud? Why are you tearing me apart inside? I eat you, sleep you, breathe you, work you…'

It was an unexpected confession and Cory was too dazed and bemused by his words—and his nearness—to even attempt to answer. He was like a fierce black whirlwind, sweeping everything it came into contact with into its orbit, she told herself tiredly, too shattered to think clearly. But if she gave in to him, if she let herself be absorbed into the swirling, spinning tornado that was Max Hunter, she would be drained and consumed of everything that was the real her. And she couldn't let that happen. Because it *would* end.

Max's fingers had started to stroke her back, their touch mesmerising, and now she arched back from him but he continued to hold her fast as he said softly, 'I can't help it, Cory. I want you all the time, I'm aching for you, and the thought of that insensitive, undeserving so-and-so pawing you about…'

'Vivian?' She raised her head now, too astonished at what she saw as his hypocrisy to watch her words. 'How have you got the nerve to call *him* insensitive when you are the world's worst on that score?' she asked in vehement outrage, thinking of the sleepless nights and constant turmoil she had suffered since she had first set eyes on this man. 'Anyway, you don't even know Vivian,' she added angrily.

'I don't have to.'

It was said with supreme arrogance, and then, as Cory opened her mouth to argue some more, his mouth took hers, his lips sensuous and horribly persuasive as his tongue began to fuel the fire.

He kissed her until she was gasping for breath and aching, her body betraying her completely as her breasts became full and swollen against the hard, solid wall of his chest, her nipples thrusting against the thin silk of the swimming costume and transparent top.

'You see, you do want me.' His hand brushed one full breast and she moaned out loud before she could stop herself, and then, as the sound echoed in her ears, Cory jerked away from him, her face scarlet. He had to prove his point. All the time, he had to be right.

'I don't.' It was a whisper but he heard it and his firm mouth twisted at the blatant lie, his eyes narrowing mockingly.

'Sure you do.' He smiled, but it wasn't the open, sweet

smile that had wrung her heart earlier. 'And you'll tell me that when you're ready. I can wait till then, Cory. I've never yet taken a woman who wasn't wholly and completely ready—mind and body—and I don't intend to start with you, however much I'm tempted.'

His body was providing ample truth of just how strong that temptation was and she shivered deep inside. She wanted to come back with some clever, witty retort, something to prove she was on a par with his other sophisticated, worldly women even if she didn't share their views on life and love, but she couldn't. If she had spoken at that moment she would have burst into tears. She loved him so much and this was all such a mess.

'Come on.' He took her elbow, his touch light and casual now, but as they walked over to the far corner of the area around the pool which was shaded by a massive willow tree she was vitally aware of every movement of that magnificent body.

There were loungers and small tables all round the pool at strategic points to catch some shade, but this tiny idyll was in a small semicircle of flowering bushes that smelt wonderful, their fragrance reminiscent of magnolia flowers and hot exotic nights.

Two cushioned loungers had been placed at either side of a low rectangular table holding a large ice-bucket in which a bottle of champagne nestled, and alongside were two tall fluted glasses of delicate crystal and an enormous bowl of strawberries. Two smaller bowls, spoons and even a dish of cream, again nestling in ice, were close by. Everything was perfect. Too perfect.

He really did think of everything. Cory eyed the cosy little setting with uncharacteristic cynicism and the champagne with definite wariness, glad of the substantial lunch they had enjoyed earlier in the day at Bloomsbury's. A master of seduction, no doubt. But this time all his careful arrangements would come to nothing.

Max thought she merely fancied him and that was all—his earlier comments had made it clear he wasn't even sure if she liked him very much—and he also thought she had slept with Vivian and probably other boyfriends in the past. Therefore, by his reckoning, a brief dalliance with himself was quite on the cards. No one would get hurt and he had been very careful to lay out the ground rules.

But she would get hurt. Cory sat down gingerly on one of the loungers and watched him as he flung himself on the other one, one lean muscled arm reaching out for the champagne a moment later. If she had merely been attracted to him as he thought, Max Hunter would have been a hard act to follow, but loving him as she did... It would destroy her when he tired of her body and decided enough was enough; she just wasn't tough enough to cope with it.

She wanted to give herself to him body, soul and spirit—to become one with him in the biblical sense, to have children, build a family and home—and he didn't even have any understanding of such a concept. And he'd laugh himself silly if it was suggested to him.

'Here.' She came out of the dark morass of her thoughts to find a glass of sparkling champagne under her nose, its effervescent exuberance mocking her misery. 'Eat, drink and be merry.'

'Because tomorrow we die?' She finished the old saying with a touch of whimsical amusement she was proud of in the circumstances.

He gave a sardonic smile that was so sexy it made her toes curl. 'Oh, no, Cory,' he said softy as he guided the glass to her lips with a firm hand. 'I wouldn't allow you to escape me like that. I want to teach you how to live.'

'I know how to live,' she objected quickly. 'I enjoy my life.'

'No, you don't, not yet, but you will,' he promised slowly. 'But for now...' The glass was again steered to her lips. 'Relax.'

It was wonderful champagne, Cory thought as she sipped at the fragrant, slightly strawberry-tasting liquid with very real pleasure. It knocked anything she had tasted before— which had masqueraded under the same name—into a cocked hat. But any sense of well-being it gave was short and transitory, as ephemeral as the morning dew on a summer's morning, and that was exactly how an affair with Max would be. As fleeting as a half-remembered dream.

The thought provoked her to say, as she placed the glass on the table and then turned to face the amber gaze directly, 'Correct me if I'm wrong, but it was you who said that an affair with your secretary would be nothing more than a nuisance at best and at worst downright dangerous, wasn't it?' she asked sweetly. She had never forgotten his words on that first day, or how angry they had made her feel.

He nodded slowly, his eyes smiling at her. 'You're the exception that proves the rule,' he said with audacious seriousness.

'And you really think that we could conduct an affair and still work together?' Cory asked quietly without an answering smile.

'Possibly.' He was watching her very closely. 'Yes, why not?'

'And when it ended?' she persisted quietly. 'What then?'

'We're two grown adults,' he answered calmly. 'If there was honesty between us from the beginning I don't see it being a problem. You are not the type to get all bitter and twisted.'

'Max, you don't have a clue what "type" I am,' Cory shot back tightly, stung beyond measure by his terminology.

'It was meant as a compliment.' He had immediately realised his mistake and now the charm was out in full force, Cory noticed irritably as he sat up straight and then leant across to take her hands in his. 'Truly, Cory, I think you're gorgeous,' he said huskily, releasing her hands to cradle her angry face in his hands. 'Utterly gorgeous and warm and sexy and wonderful.'

So this was how he was with his women, Cory told herself silently. It was a side to him she hadn't seen so far and it was absolutely lethal. And of course he knew it; he knew it only too well.

'And you were right, you know, when you said I got what I deserved with this.' He touched the side of his throat briefly. 'I've always gone for the packaging without bothering to unwrap the parcel; it was safer after the Laurel and Anne affair. That way no mistakes could be made.'

Oh, no, she didn't trust him like this. He could tie her up in knots with this little-boy-lost approach and she had the feeling he knew it. Her thoughts made her voice tart when she said, 'I'd consider the woman behind the hand that wielded that mirror something of a major hiccup in that thinking?'

He stared at her for a moment as she looked boldly back at him, and then he amazed her by throwing back his head and giving a bellow of a laugh. 'I walked into that one, didn't I?' he said with a rueful self-deprecation that made her love him more. 'Right, well, as I'm not going to seduce you by throwing myself on your feminine compassion, we might as well relax and enjoy ourselves, eh? A few strawberries, another swim, and then more champagne. No strings attached and no ulterior motives. How does that sound?'

'Okay.' It was tentative, and again the bellow echoed round the garden as she watched him in amazement.

'Cory, you're one on your own.' He had leant forward to take her mouth in a light kiss as he had spoken, and then he surprised her by stopping abruptly inches from her lips, his brow creasing in a slight frown as he continued to stare into the violet-splashed green eyes for long moments. 'One on your own,' he echoed softly.

'Max?' His expression disturbed her. 'What's the matter?'

'The matter?' He came back to her with visible effort, his face clearing as he noticed her worried face. 'What could be the matter?' he prevaricated easily. 'I've got the most beautiful woman in London at my side and the night is young.' But his eyes had hardened and his mouth had straightened—she had seen it—and now the charm was definitely forced. Something had happened.

She stared at him for a moment more but then he turned away to fill two bowls with strawberries, and when he turned back to her his face was clear and open, and she told herself she must have imagined the expression of what had appeared to be stunned comprehension.

They swam and dozed, and ate and drank, and then swam some more in the sleepy, sluggish air, until the heat of the day had been swallowed up in a mauve-tinged mellow dusk that filled the sultry garden with warm shadows and the scents of evening.

It was well past eight o'clock by the time they retraced their footsteps to the house, and in all that time Max had behaved with a circumspect correctness that Cory couldn't quite understand. But it was good, she told herself firmly as Max left her at the door of her suite after telling her to dress for dinner in an hour or so. It really was good. And this feeling of pique, even hurt, that had grown through the afternoon after their earlier conversation—that was just her stupidity of wanting her cake as well as eating it.

She ran herself a warm bath, and once she was lying in the foaming, bubbling water of the Jacuzzi she refused to let herself dwell on the feelings that were just pure self-indulgence on her part. She had told Max she didn't want to get involved and he had finally decided to accept it. End of story. If she was thinking of anyone it really ought to be poor Vivian, she told herself guiltily. He'd be ringing her bedsit all evening and wondering why she wasn't picking up the telephone. He'd think— Oh, she didn't care what he thought! And why was she thinking like this anyway? she asked herself.

She sprang out of the water and marched through to the bedroom, her face one big scowl. She was in a ridiculous position here, and Max had a lot to answer for, but the person who was really to blame was Vivian Batley-Thomas. How *dared* he slink down here and try to ascertain whether she was prepared to welcome him with open arms before he got up the nerve to give Carole the old heave-ho? Because that was what all this boiled down to, she told herself firmly. It wasn't a case of 'poor Vivian' at all! Poor Carole, more like.

She walked through to the sitting room and selected a CD of what she hoped was tranquil, soothing music, turning the volume up reasonably high as she went back into the bedroom to decide what to wear for the evening in front of her.

After choosing the least alluring dress she could find— not an easy task in the sexy contents of the wardrobe— Cory creamed her honey-toned skin and dried her hair, before standing stark naked in front of the long bedroom mirror as she scowled at the slender, dark-haired reflection in its misty depths.

Men! They were all selfish, egotistical, manipulating brutes at heart with just one thing on their minds. She looked at herself, her eyes moving critically over the long, well-shaped legs, the small waist and pert full breasts. Nothing special. She sighed, her heart aching, and shut her eyes a few seconds as she thought about the other females—the incredibly beautiful other females—who were falling over themselves to be seen with Max. She had no chance of ever changing his mind about life and love, she knew that, so why had today hurt so much? Why couldn't she accept things?

'Cory?'

For a moment she really thought her deepest longing had conjured up an echo of that dark voice, and she sighed again at her weakness, thinking wryly, First sign of madness, along with talking to yourself!

And then she opened her eyes.

The reflection in the mirror had changed. Now Max was standing in the arch that led to the bedroom from the sitting room with his eyes glowing like the eyes of a big cat as he stared straight at her.

CHAPTER EIGHT

'I KNOCKED.'

As Cory whirled to the bed, grabbing the scanty dress and holding it against her, the only thing that moved was Max's mouth.

'Get out.' She spoke through clenched teeth, trying to ignore the fact that the dress barely covered half of what needed covering. 'There's a name for men like you,' she hissed furiously.

'Misunderstood?' He had registered her outrage. 'I told you I knocked but with that damn music full blast you probably didn't hear me. What are you trying to do? Wake the dead?'

'Of course I didn't hear you!' She glared at him, her arms crossed against her breasts and the dress hanging down in front of her. 'And that still didn't give you the right to barge in here like this,' she spat hotly. 'Now will you please leave?'

'I didn't barge, Cory. I knocked—twice—and then I called as I opened the door.'

'Well, bully for you.' She had never been so embarrassed in her life and attack was the best defence. 'But for the third time of asking—would you like to leave now?' she ground out tightly.

'We both know what I would like to do.' It was dark and there was no humour at all.

'I'm warning you, Max. You lay a finger on me and—'

'You don't have to warn me, Cory,' he said tautly. 'I know your opinion of me is low but even I wouldn't stoop to what you're suggesting. Get some clothes on.' The last was said as though she had purposely paraded in front of him and it was thrown over his shoulder as he turned away. It made Cory so mad she couldn't contain herself and all her prudence was burnt up in the fire of anger.

She pulled the silk cover off the bed in one violent movement, sending the underclothes that had lain next to the dress flying in the air, and as she threw the dress to the floor she wrapped the cover round her sarong-style before leaping after Max like an enraged tigress. He was halfway across the sitting room when she bit out his name and he turned without a word, his amber eyes looking at her with what she was sure was contempt.

'I've had enough! Of you, this—' she flung out her arms wildly to embrace the beautiful room '—the whole situation, including your wonderful job!' She was so angry she was shaking.

'Do I take it you are offering your resignation?' Max asked with an unforgivable lack of emotion.

'I'm telling you I quit,' Cory shot back tightly. She couldn't take any more of this; she really couldn't. Seeing him every day had been bad enough, working with him, having to talk and laugh and act as though he meant nothing more to her than little Martin, the office junior, but now she knew how he felt... It was an impossible situation. Sooner or later she would give herself away and then her last defence would be gone. 'As of now.'

'You're under contract,' he reminded her coldly. 'You can't quit.'

'Then sue me.'

'You're being ridiculous,' he bit out, his voice sharp now.

'But *normal* people are ridiculous at times,' she shouted angrily, stamping her foot at his infuriating *togetherness*. 'We do crazy things, we make mistakes, we aren't perfect. We even love the wrong people sometimes.' She hadn't meant to add that bit.

'So you admit Vivian is the wrong person?' he grated tightly.

Vivian? She wasn't talking about *Vivian*, she thought desperately, if only he did but know it. 'Vivian is nothing to do with it,' she snapped furiously, 'not really. I'm saying that it's normal to lose control sometimes, to fail, to be *human*, for goodness' sake. But you, you're too darn scared to even dip your toe in the water of real honest-to-goodness emotion, aren't you? The original ice-man! All cool, macho love-'em-and-leave-'em and what the hell!'

She knew she was going too far—the blazing anger on his face would have told her that if nothing else had—but something had broken in the last few minutes and no power on earth could have stopped her now.

'You're just a coward at heart, Max Hunter,' she said bitterly. 'Lily-livered, as my father would say. You are terrified of emotional responsibility and so you've chosen to live in a deep freeze.'

He had reached her in two strides and for a moment—a terrifying moment—Cory thought he was going to hit her, but instead he pulled her into him with enough force to make her head snap back.

'So you think I'm an ice-man, Cory?' he rasped, so angry he had a job to get the words out. 'You think there is liquid ice in my veins instead of warm blood, is that it? You really don't know the first thing about men, do you? Although having seen Vivian I shouldn't be surprised about that.'

When his mouth took hers it was hard and savage and she knew—if she was anything like the heroine of a novel or a film—that she should now begin fighting like crazy. But—this was Max, and she loved him. She loved him beyond life. She didn't want to, she had never wanted to, but the more she'd found out about him—even the irritating, bad things—the deeper her love had become. Illogical, stupid, brainless—all those things could be thrown at her—but that was how it was.

She didn't know when his lips and hands stopped being punishing and became merely passionate, but it was far, far too late by then anyway. She was kissing him back, kiss for kiss, embrace for embrace, with an uninhibitedness that would have shocked her if she'd been capable of thinking about anything other than the sensations that were flooding her body with the fierceness of a stormy winter's sea crashing onto pummelled sands.

His kisses were drugging and sweet, his hands powerfully gentle and wonderfully understanding of what pleased her, and Cory was unaware the makeshift sarong had slipped to her waist until she felt the heat of his fingers on the velvet-smooth skin of her back. It was a sensual onslaught made all the more insidious by her innocence and she was too dazed and intoxicated by the wonder of these new sensations to think.

His tongue rippled along her teeth—she shivered. His hands worked magic on her silky skin—she arched in ecstasy. He let his mouth wander to her cheek, her ears, her throat, hot, burning kisses that evoked wild pleasure wherever they touched, and he took his time, nuzzling into the sweetly scented shadows of her collarbone as he murmured her name in a thick, husky voice that was an aphrodisiac in itself and druggingly erotic.

'Max. Oh, Max.' Her hands were clinging to his broad shoulders, her breath sobbing against his face. She was utterly his and they both knew it, and now he stiffened, his body language changing.

'Cory, listen to me. Listen to me a minute.'

'No.' As he raised his head she gave a little wail of protest at the different tone in his voice. 'Don't talk, not now,' she murmured frantically, and then, still in the grip of the tumultuous sensuality he had evoked, the wonder of being in the arms of the man she loved, the words that had been in her heart for so long just slipped out of their own accord. 'I love you, I do…'

She felt his reaction in every last fibre of her body although he didn't move or speak or even seem to breathe for some seconds. And then he slowly loosened her hands from his shoulders and took a step backwards, his face dark and closed and his body rigid.

'That's rubbish and you know it,' he said stonily; his eyes were hard on her face and there was something in them she couldn't fathom. 'You don't even like me half of the time.'

Cory fumbled with the cover, drawing it up over her breasts and tucking it tightly into the hollows of her armpits, her face scarlet, but she didn't take her gaze from his. She had a choice here, she thought wildly, even as she silently berated herself for her utter madness in the last few minutes. It had been bad enough to let him make love to her like that—after all she'd said, all her protestations of how she despised his lifestyle and morals—but to blurt out her feelings had been much, much worse.

She could say it had merely been a figure of speech in the circumstances in which she'd found herself—he'd understand that for some people it was almost a necessary formality preceding the act itself—or, humiliating and debasing as it would be, she could tell him the truth. The thought was crucifying.

One action would keep her in his life, if she chose to remain, and the other would definitely take her out of his orbit for good. The last thing Max Hunter wanted was a lovelorn secretary mooning over him across the filing cabinet or anywhere else for that matter.

Cory Masters, attractive and efficient secretary who was fun to chat up when he had nothing better to do, was one thing. Cory Masters in love was quite another. He'd run a mile. And then this thing, this wild, ecstatic, painful thing, would be finished. She knew which choice she was going to make before she spoke—it was the only one that would allow her to remain sane.

'No, Max, it's not rubbish,' she said with an icy calm that came from the utter numbness that had taken her over body and soul at the enormity of what she was about to do. 'I do love you; I've loved you for ages, although everything I've said about the way you conduct your life still stands.'

'But Vivian?' He glared at her, his voice as terse as if she had just slapped his face rather than told him she loved him. 'How can you say you care about me when you and him—?'

'There is no me and him,' Cory said dully. His reaction was worse than anything her darkest nightmare had conjured up. He despised her now—it was written all over his face—whereas before she had at least had his respect. But she couldn't have done anything else, she told herself bitterly in the next instant. Things had gone too far, much too far. 'There never has been, I realise that now. What I felt for him was affection, maybe love of a brotherly kind, but that's all. If I had married him, if he'd asked me, it would have been a terrible mistake.'

'He wants you, you know that. And perhaps you would be happy with him?' he said with a terrible lack of emotion, his face cold.

He was encouraging her to go to *Vivian*? It was the final humiliation and Cory knew nothing would ever hurt as much in her life again. He was so desperate to get rid of her now she had told him how she felt that he was throwing her at Vivian. Oh, she hated him. She did, she really hated him.

'I've told you how I feel.' She raised her head proudly now, her face white except for two spots of burning colour glowing dark across her cheekbones. 'And don't worry, Max, I know you are incapable of feeling the same and I don't want anything from you. I just thought it might help you to understand why I need to resign and leave immediately, that's all. I can't play at being the sophisticated, worldly type you go for; I just don't have it in me, and frankly I don't want to be like that,' she added bravely.

'This is crazy.' Max drew in a deep breath, his face set and frighteningly cold. 'I don't believe this is happening.' He raked back a lock of hair from his forehead, the gesture betraying his iron control was only skin-deep, before he added, 'Damn it, Cory, you never said, you never indicated…'

'I never would have.' She was determined she wasn't going to cry—whatever else she was *not* going to cry and add that to her list of failings in his eyes. 'And there would have been no need for any of this if you hadn't brought me here today.'

At least he couldn't blame her for orchestrating the whole miserable event, Cory thought painfully. From beginning to end it had been Max determined to get his own way as usual. Well, this time he had got a little more than he'd bargained for, she thought, with a black humour that put a touch of very necessary strength in her trembling limbs. A darn sight more, actually.

'So…' She raised her small chin, her eyes glowing like a fierce little cat's as she willed herself not to break down until he had left. 'If I get dressed now will you order me a taxi, please?'

She was still speaking when she heard the sound of a car drawing up outside and then loud, shrill voices, followed by the ringing of the doorbell. Oh, no, not visitors, not now, she thought desperately.

'Cory.' She had never seen Max stumbling for words but she was seeing it now. 'This is what I came to tell you—' He paused, and then, as the doorbell sounded again, said, 'I've invited a few friends round for the evening. I thought after all you said this afternoon that you would prefer that, and I did promise no strings attached and no ulterior motive. I thought a party might be just what we both needed to blow away the cobwebs.'

'I see.' There was a sick flood of despair flowing through her, but she kept her voice even as she said, 'A party sounds fine to me, Max. I'll get ready and then I'll see you downstairs, shall I?' She was *not* going to crumple; she was going to handle this.

Max looked at her and she stared back at him, hoping desperately that she was masking the agony that was making her feel as if she was shrinking into a tiny nothingness, and then he nodded abruptly as the doorbell chimed for the third time and yet another car pulled up outside, and with one swift movement he turned and then was gone.

She sank straight down on to the carpet the moment the door shut, her legs refusing to hold her up a second longer, and stared blindly ahead as she tried to formulate her thoughts in the chaotic whirl her brain had become.

She *knew* she had sensed something down by the pool, she told herself silently. There had been a definite withdrawal, a detachment from that point, even though he had been quite pleasant and amusing and fun to be with for the rest of the afternoon. He had decided to wash his hands of her then, she saw it now, and he had merely come to her room this evening to tell her that the cosy, romantic dinner for two she had been expecting was not going to happen. He had invited goodness knew how many friends to join them, and nothing could have stated his intentions to revert to their old boss/secretary status more clearly.

Oh… She swayed back and forth in an agony of pain and embarrassment. And then she'd allowed… She couldn't let her mind dwell on what she had allowed. And she had further compounded the whole disastrous scenario by telling him she *loved* him.

She had wanted to cry when he had been with her, but now her eyes were quite dry, the consuming despair that was churning her stomach and making her shake too intense for the relief of tears.

When it came to making a fool of herself she had excelled beyond most mortals' wildest dreams, she told herself bitterly. And how was she going to get through this evening? For a moment—just a moment—she contemplated sneaking out of the house and making a run for it. The gates were obviously now open—yet another car had driven up while she had sat in mute misery on the carpet—so she would have no trouble in escaping.

But then the fiery strength she had inherited from her mother's red-haired genes, along with the fighting spirit her father had instilled in her from when she was a small toddler and gone through a stage of being bullied at nursery by two slightly older little girls, sprang into play. She was *not* going to skulk away like a whipped puppy, she told herself tensely. Whatever, she would see this evening out with that sophistication and control he so admired in his harem, and then, come morning, she would walk out of this house and out of his life for good. She could do it; she could.

She sat for a few more moments as she did some exercises to regulate her breathing and bring her racing heart under control, and then she rose shakily, making her way across the room and back into the bedroom. She stared for a moment at the crumpled dress on the floor. Oh, no, no, that wouldn't do now. That dress had been chosen with a view to keeping the wolf at bay, but everything had changed now. When she walked out of his life she was going to do it with a bang not a whimper!

She scanned the wardrobe again but she already knew the little number she was going to wear. She had seen it earlier and she'd stroked the scarlet silk with an awed hand, wondering at the nerve of the woman who would dare to wear such a wildly sexy and undeniably wickedly provocative dress. She had noticed there was a pair of shoes in the same material as the dress—high, strappy sandals designed with a view to making the legs endless—and now she slipped them on anxiously. They fitted perfectly. An omen that this was meant to be. Cory nodded grimly at the thought. With a bit of luck this outfit was going to make Max's eyes stand out like chapel hatpegs!

The saying was one of her father's and for a moment it brought his comforting presence into the room, but then, as she felt the tears begin to burn the back of her eyes, she willed them away. No weakness, not now, not yet. She could cry buckets later but for now she was going to hold up her head and prove to Max Hunter she was just as sexy and desirable as any of those bimbos he ran around with! She shut her eyes tightly and took several long, deep breaths.

She had been virtually ready when Max had surprised her, but now she redid her hair, taking time to curl it into a mass of glowing waves that fell on to her shoulders in a gleaming curtain.

The cosmetics in the top drawer of the dressing table were amazing—all colours, all shades of absolutely everything—and Cory made up very carefully, accentuating the violet tinge in her green eyes with a deep blue shadow and plenty of mascara, and using a creamy red lipstick on her generous mouth.

When she slipped the dress and shoes on and then stood in front of the mirror she couldn't quite believe the reflection she saw was hers. The beautiful dress, with its flattering, low-cut neckline and fitted bodice, full skirt that ended just above her knees and swirls and swirls of red silk, had transformed her figure into something any red-blooded male would take a second look at. And Max was red-blooded; she had to give him that if nothing else. But it was the way it clung where it was meant to cling and pulled in and pushed out other parts of her anatomy that made it dynamite.

She would never say that designer clothes were a waste of money again, Cory promised silently as she sent up a prayer of thanks for the skill that had created such a confidence-builder. She might just get through this evening after all. No one looking at her tonight would believe she was harbouring a broken heart under this plunging neckline.

When Cory walked into the drawing room some minutes later Max was at her elbow in an instant, and she turned just in time to see the flash of desire that narrowed the amber eyes into slits of gold light before his expression changed and became bland.

'You look wonderful,' he said softly, but she heard the thickness he couldn't quite mask, and it gave her the shot in the arm she needed to be able to say coolly in response, 'Thank you, Max. You look pretty good yourself.' She forced herself to glance around.

Pretty good? He looked good enough to die for, Cory thought desperately. He must have been about to change when he'd come in to her earlier, because the shirt and trousers he had been wearing then had been changed for a dinner suit. The cream silk shirt was open at the neck, however, and showing a smidgen of dark body hair at the top of his chest, his bow tie hanging in thin strands at either side of his throat. He looked so sexy it made her knees weak.

She saw him raise one hand and in the next instant a waiter was there at her elbow with a tray on which reposed several sparkling glasses of champagne.

She took one with a smile of thanks to the waiter before again glancing at the assembled crowd, more than a little surprised to see there were already about thirty people present, with more arriving judging by the sounds in the hall. This was going to be a party and a half.

'You arranged all this on the spur of the moment?' she asked quietly. 'The waiters, the catering and everything?'

'I have a firm I use for such occasions; my housekeeper prefers it that way,' Max said coolly. 'They know me and they can jump at a moment's notice; they know I'll make it worth their while. As for my friends...' he waved a casual hand but there was a cynical twist to his mouth now '...they are avid party-goers, all of them, and they like to be in the right place at the right time.'

'And you are the right place at the right time,' Cory stated flatly. Of course he was; she should have known. How the other half lived... She thought of the wealth that engendered such power. She could see more uniformed waiters moving among the throng now, and in the garden, beyond the open French doors, there was a small band setting up. No doubt there was an army of caterers seeing to the food too. Clockwork. He paid for his life to move on instantly oiled wheels and that was what he got. He didn't need her—he didn't need anyone. He just clicked his fingers and the world came to obedient heel.

'*Sweety-pie*...' The tall, voluptuous blonde was hanging on the arm of another man but it didn't stop the sultry painted eyes from devouring Max. 'It's been absolutely *ages*, darling.'

'Three weeks to be exact, Adrianne,' Max said dryly. 'You and Frank were at Charles's fortieth if I remember right?' He shook the other man's hand as he spoke and then expertly manoeuvred Cory into the side of him with a dexterity that was formidable, before adding, 'This is Cory Masters, incidentally. Cory, meet Frank and Adrianne Peers. Frank and I go way back to university days.'

Adrianne managed something that could just about be called a smile, but her eyes dissected Cory with cat-like sharpness. 'Cory...' She held out an expertly tanned, red-taloned hand. 'How sweet.'

Cory wasn't sure if she was referring to her name or the fact that it looked as though she was Max's latest girlfriend, but she smiled back—coolly and calmly—as she said, 'It's always nice to meet the wife of one of Max's old friends.' And then to Frank, who looked a nice old thing although at least twenty years older than Max, 'It's nice to meet you.'

'Masters…?' Adrianne drawled the name slowly, running it over her small white teeth like a tasty titbit. 'We know a few Masters, don't we, Frankie? Are you one of Sir Gerald's daughters, perhaps?' she asked Cory as she turned to her again.

'No, I'm not.' This was some form of attack; Cory felt it in her bones and she kept her voice steady as she added, 'My father's Christian name is Robert.'

'Really?' For whatever reason, Adrianne made it sound as though Cory's grandparents had made a grave mistake in so naming their son. 'And you're from?' She paused, her painted eyebrows enquiring.

'Yorkshire,' Cory said politely, just as Max at the side of her shifted abruptly and said, his voice cold and almost cruel. 'And my parents lived in Essex, Frank's in Bournemouth and Adrianne's in the East End of London, so I believe?' His gaze had swept over the other woman and something in it made the ravishing blonde flush scarlet. 'So, we all know everything there is to know about each other, don't we?' he added pleasantly. 'Now, Cory, there are a couple of other people I'd like you to meet, so if you'll excuse us…'

He had moved her on before Cory could even say goodbye, but she had noticed the look in the other woman's eyes and she couldn't resist asking Max what the little scene had been all about.

'Adrianne's a snob of the first order,' Max said shortly, still frowning. 'She likes to put it about that her parents have their own business on the outskirts; in reality her father is a fishmonger in the East End where they've lived all their life and Adrianne is one of ten children who were brought up hand-to-mouth. Frank said the family is great, salt of the earth, but Adrianne won't even acknowledge their existence since she married Frank and moved into the fast lane. Her real name is Annie, by the way, but she considered it too ordinary for her new status. Adrianne puts a lot of store by names,' he added wryly. 'As you may have gathered.'

'You don't like her.' It was a statement not a question.

'She's the biggest mistake Frank ever made but he doesn't see it that way.' Max shrugged irritably. 'She's played around, she spends money like water, she's greedy and avaricious, with the morals of an alley-cat. Does that answer your question?' He turned to look down at her now, smiling derisively, but she didn't answer him.

How was she going to get through this evening if he remained at her side? she asked herself with bitter despair. He was torturing her; surely he must realise that?

The torture continued for a good few hours more, and it included forcing a plateful of food—which was no doubt delicious but tasted like sawdust to Cory—down her throat, chatting with all and sundry with Max's arm glued round her waist, dancing to the small band in the summer-scented shadows of the garden and much more. Neither she nor Max said a word about what had happened earlier—he was his normal cool, urbane self and she was determined that she could match him moment for moment or die in the attempt. It was horrendous, it was awful, but somehow—somehow—she got through.

And then it was gone three in the morning and gradually the guests were taking their leave, the beautiful women in their Guccis and Versaces and Armanis just as fresh and glowing as when they had arrived, and the men all seeming to have come from one wealthy, powerful, affluent cloning process.

Cory was so mentally, emotionally and physically exhausted she felt she could sleep standing up. As the numbers dwindled to the last ten or twelve and the band began to pack up, Max ordered for coffee and croissants to be served in the dining room.

'I'm going up to my room if that's okay?' Cory met Max in the vast hall where he had been giving last instructions to the caterers. 'It's been a long day.'

'Fine.' He nodded slowly, and then she tensed as he leant forward and lightly brushed her lips with his own as he said, 'We'll have to talk, you know that, don't you? But it's not important now.'

She wasn't important. She nodded in return and then, as one of the waiters came hurrying up and spoke in fluent French—a language that held no secrets for Max—she watched him listen for a moment before he turned back to her. 'There's a problem. You don't mind…?'

'No, you go.' Go, go, *go*!

And he went.

Cory had just taken half a dozen steps up the beautiful winding staircase, wondering how she could ever find the strength to reach the top and the sanctuary of her suite, when she heard her name spoken softly behind her. It wasn't Max's voice.

She turned to see Frank at the bottom of the stairs, his eyes tight on her. She had had a couple of conversations with Max's old friend during the evening and she liked him, very much. He was funny and sincere and witty but, more than that, he seemed kind, and kindness wasn't a trait she'd noticed much in most of the assembled company. They all seemed intent on outdoing each other in every respect.

He had gone to great lengths to explain that his wife was really insecure and unsure of herself; a 'lost child' was the way he had described Adrianne, whom no one understood. Cory couldn't help but be sceptical about this; Adrianne seemed about as unsure of herself as a shark in a feeding frenzy, but she had accepted his explanation for what they both knew was Adrianne's rudeness to her with a nodding head and a comforting pat on his arm, and the two of them had gone on to discuss everything from music to mythol-

ogy, which was Frank's hobby. They had discussed everything, in fact, except Max.

'Cory?' He joined her on the stairs and she saw he was
somewhat embarrassed about something. 'Can I ask you to
bear with me a moment if I'm a little presumptuous?' he
asked awkwardly.

'Presumptuous?' She stared into the velvet-brown eyes
set in a square face which reminded her of her father's.

'I just felt...' He took a deep breath and then said
quickly, 'It's about Max. Dare I ask you if you are in love
with him?'

It was on the tip of her tongue to evade the question
whilst gently indicating for him to mind his own business,
but she knew it must have taken him some time to work
up the courage to approach her, and so she said, after a
long pause, while her tired brain tried to judge how best to
answer such a loaded question, 'You must have a reason
for asking that, Frank?'

'I'm Max's friend and I think a hell of a lot of him,'
Frank said quietly, 'but you are one of the nicest people
I've met for a long time and I wouldn't like to see you get
hurt, Cory. Not without a warning anyway. You would
never survive with Max, not and emerge the same person
anyway. It isn't his fault but he's never satisfied for long;
he gets bored and then... But he normally chooses women
who know the score, and somehow... Somehow I don't
think you do.'

'It's all right, Frank.' His face had gone turkey-red and
she was finding she felt really sorry for him despite her
own embarrassment. 'It's not like that, really.'

'He's tough, Cory.' Frank had obviously braced himself
to say it all. 'He might have inherited a nice amount at the
beginning, but Hunter Operations has been built up to what
it is now by his hard work and dedication. He's ruthless
when he has to be and he doesn't take any prisoners. It's
just the way he is.'

'Frank, I told you earlier, I'm just his secretary,' Cory said quietly, and then, when he still didn't look convinced, she added softly, 'And between the two of us I resigned today, so really I'm not even that any more.'

'You've resigned?' There was definite relief in Frank's voice, and Cory found she really couldn't be annoyed at his interference.

'He needs another Gillian,' she said painfully.

'I know what he needs.' Frank looked at her for a long moment and his eyes were understanding. 'But he's too much of a damn fool to see it or too stubborn to admit it.'

She smiled, because it was either that or bursting into tears. Frank's unexpected concern had touched her more than he would ever know. And then she reached up and kissed him gently on the cheek as she said, 'Thanks, Frank, I don't suppose I'll see you again but Max is lucky to have a friend like you.'

He continued to stand at the bottom of the stairs as she climbed the treads to the big, balcony-style landing, and she turned at the top, raising her hand to him just once before she turned and made her way to the quiet scented tranquillity of her suite.

Although she didn't feel quiet or tranquil inside, she admitted bitterly as she closed the door of the sitting room behind her and stood for a moment against the varnished wood, her eyes tightly shut and her heart thudding. She doubted if she would ever feel those things again. She felt angry and hurt and desolate.

She walked into the beautiful bedroom and switched on the mellow wall lights before walking across to the mirror. 'Well, you got through, girl,' she told the vibrant, slender woman in the mirror. 'And you did it with style, I'll say that for you.'

And then she sank down on to the carpet by the side of the bed and cried as though her heart would break.

CHAPTER NINE

NERVES almost got the better of Cory the next morning when, after just a couple of hours of restless sleep, she prepared to go downstairs for breakfast.

She was dressed in the same clothes she had arrived in, but she had borrowed some underwear from the stacked shelves in the huge walk-in wardrobe, and she was sure the brief white lacy pants and bra—with their exclusive label—would have cost ten times more than the rest of her outfit put together. It somehow seemed to sum up the whole miserable state of affairs she found herself in, she thought ruefully as she checked herself one more time in the full-length mirror, her stomach turning crazy cartwheels and her legs feeling as though they didn't belong to her.

The reflection that stared back at her bore no resemblance to the exotic flame creature of the night before, but the will to walk out of Max's life with at least the remnants of her dignity wrapped around her was as strong, and it was this feeling that enabled her to pull herself together and walk out of the room and down the stairs a few minutes later with her head held high and her back straight. Battered she might be, broken she was not.

'Good morning.' The deep dark voice was relaxed and cool.

Max was already seated at the breakfast table and he was fully dressed for the office minus his suit jacket, his black hair slicked back from his forehead and his face freshly shaven. He looked wonderful. And lazy and untroubled.

'Good morning.' Cory managed to sound brisk and cool as she returned the greeting, her eyes moving to the laden table with very real surprise. There was enough food to feed an army.

As usual Max read her mind. 'Not my work,' he said quietly. 'Mrs Brown was back from her sister's at seven this morning; her sister only lives a few miles away.'

Cory nodded, contenting herself with one dry look at the handsome face before she sat down. He had obviously thought the seduction would have been complete by morning, she thought wryly, and hadn't intended to miss his normal routine which clearly included a massive cooked breakfast just because he had thrown his poor housekeeper out of her bed the night before. Typical man, or typical Max, more like. How she could love such a cold-blooded, manipulating so-and-so she just didn't know. But she did.

Mrs Brown—a small, stout personage with cheeks like rosy red apples—came bustling in in the next moment, and the following few minutes were taken up with introductions followed by the older woman filling Cory's plate with enough food for five secretaries. Although Mrs Brown didn't think she was merely Max's secretary, did she? Cory told herself silently once they were alone again. And after a woman had shared Max's bed for the night she probably came downstairs absolutely ravenous!

The thought took away any faint appetite Cory might have had, but she struggled manfully through several rashes of bacon and two large grilled tomatoes, although the egg, sausages, mushrooms and kidneys were quite beyond her.

After his initial greeting Max had disappeared behind his paper again—which suited Cory just fine—only emerging once or twice to refill their coffee cups and ask Cory if she wanted fresh toast or anything more from Mrs Brown.

It was just as Cory thankfully pushed her plate away, feeling she had eaten enough to convince anyone—even Max—that she was fine, that the paper was lowered and put aside altogether and she found herself staring straight into the level amber gaze. 'I want to talk to you.' It was cool and steady and so utterly Max at his most controlled and relaxed that she felt her hackles rise immediately. She hadn't even made the slightest dent in that rock-hard mind—all her anguish, all the torment of the last twenty-four hours was water off a duck's back as far as he was concerned. The rat.

'Yes?' Her eyebrows rose in what she hoped was an uninterested and bored gesture, and she wished she had left her hair loose so she could have tossed her head with a little more style.

'I don't want you to resign, Cory,' he said with quiet emphasis.

No, I bet you don't, she thought viciously. She had seen how money talked last night—an elegant and flamboyant party thrown together at a minute's notice in the same way most people would hold an impromptu barbecue—and Max had grown used to having his life flow on oiled wheels. His secretary leaving suddenly, without a trained replacement, would throw the side of life he valued the most—his work—into something of a hiccup.

'I take full blame for everything that has occurred,' he continued evenly. 'I should never have brought you here; it was totally unprofessional and a bad mistake.'

Double, triple rat!

'But there is no reason why everything can't go on as it has done. You are excellent at your job, and the things you said last night... You don't mean them, Cory, not really. You don't even know me, for crying out loud. All this with Vivian, the move to the big city and a new job—a new lifestyle—it's given you a false reading of your thoughts and emotions, that's all. In a few weeks, a few months, you'll find yourself laughing at all this.'

Right, that was enough. It was bad enough she had humiliated herself so thoroughly the day before, but to have to sit and listen to him suggest she had the emotions of an adolescent schoolgirl who had a crush on her teacher was too much.

Cory straightened in her chair, her back ramrod-stiff, and she allowed nothing of what she was feeling to show in her face as she said, very clearly and very coolly, 'The matter is not open for discussion, Max. I want you to accept my resignation as of today. I will, of course, stay until you have a replacement. It was foolish of me to say anything other than that yesterday, and I know how you hate temps. I'll stay and show my replacement the ropes.'

He swore, very succinctly but with great emphasis, before grating, 'This is not about me disliking temps, woman. I don't want you to leave!' He glared at her as though she were being obtuse.

Cory's heart turned over. The way he'd said that, the look on his face now—it was similar to that moment down by the pool when he had said she was one of her own; could it be that he had fallen for her, that he was beginning to think of her as something more than just a quick tumble in bed?

'Why?' she asked softly. 'Why don't you want me to leave?'

He stared at her for a moment, and she had never called on so much will-power as in this moment when she continued to look back at him without allowing the raging turmoil and soaring hope to show, and then the mask he could adopt at will slid into place and his eyes narrowed, his mouth thinning, as he said, 'I've told you, you are excellent at your job. And we get on well; I like having you around.' And he thought that would persuade her to stay?

'And I'm not boring?' It was flat and dull.

'That too,' he agreed expressionlessly.

Damn you, Max Hunter.

She rose from the chair, her expression as unreadable as his. 'Sorry, it's not enough,' she said quietly. 'Come four weeks from now I'm walking, Max, so you'd better get looking for my replacement because I'm not being strung along. I'll work with her to make the change-over as easy as possible—as many hours a day as you like—but that's as far as I'm going. Okay?'

'You won't just drop into another job,' he rasped impatiently. 'Surely you see that?'

'That's my problem, not yours,' she said stiffly.

'You intend to run home to lover-boy, is that it?'

'What I do or don't do is absolutely nothing to do with you, Max.' How dared he, how *dared* he suggest that?

He had been in the motion of standing but now he stilled, his eyes searched her closed face for one long moment before he straightened. Cory found she was holding her breath, her heart thudding, as they continued to stare at each other for what seemed an endless amount of time, and then Max nodded, his voice deliberately cold as he said, 'You're absolutely right of course. Very well, Cory, I accept your resignation. Perhaps you'd get on to the agencies we use once we're back in the office and get things moving. Weed out the best three they've got on their books and I'll do the final interviews.' He held her eyes one moment more and then turned.

'Fine.' Cory was pale and shaking as he marched from the room. He hadn't fallen for her—how could she have been so ridiculous as to imagine it even for a minute? she asked herself numbly. He would never fall for her. Oh, fancy her maybe, perhaps even enjoy her company—he'd said he liked having her around after all. But then people liked having dogs and cats and budgerigars around, she reminded herself harshly, but it didn't make them want to marry them. Not that she'd thought of marriage and Max being compatible anyway.

She continued standing there for a few moments more until the entrance of Mrs Brown moved her towards the open door leading to the hall. Once in her suite of rooms she collected her handbag and jacket and then went quickly downstairs to wait by the front door without glancing in the mirror.

He wanted her—or he wanted her body, to be more precise—but strictly on his own terms. End of story. End of job. And just at the moment it felt like the end of the world.

The next four weeks were harder than anything Cory had faced in her life before but she learnt quite a bit about herself.

The agencies fell over themselves to be helpful, but due to the fact that her replacement was needed immediately, and most of the women on their books were either in employment with a designated notice period to work out or not up to the calibre Max would demand of his secretary, the choice was limited.

However, within a few days of giving her resignation Cory had lined up three interviews—one with a twenty-six-year-old stunner who looked like a supermodel and had qualifications coming out of her beautiful ears, the second with an ice-cool blonde who looked as though she could handle Max Hunter as easily as blinking, and the third with a buxom, motherly type who was going on fifty and had just been made redundant after working twenty years for the same managing director when the firm had gone into liquidation.

The wild relief and joy Cory felt when Max chose the last applicant slowly trickled away as cold reason set in. It didn't matter whom he chose, not really. She would never see him again after she left Hunter Operations, she told herself on the Friday night of her second week of training the very able Bertha Cox, and soon all this would be just a memory. She had to be *sensible* about this.

After a wretched night's sleep she woke on the Saturday morning feeling she could be more sensible if she had some tender loving care, and by nine o'clock she had thrown her overnight bag in the back of the Mini and was on her way home to confide in her parents.

Her parents were wonderful, but she had known they would be. They sat and talked sense for hours, they kept all visitors at bay and they spoilt her rotten, but it was on the Sunday lunchtime, just as her father was carving the succulent roast, that he glanced across at Cory and said, 'I've got it! Of course. Aunt Mildred's cottage. It'd do you the world of good.'

'Aunt Mildred's cottage?' Cory stared at him and then winced as Vivian's unmistakable rat-tat-tat sounded at the front door. Since he had seen her Mini on the Saturday morning he had been round five times, and she had had to be quite rude to him the day before to get him to leave, telling him what she thought of him in the process.

'I'll get rid of him.'

As her mother scurried to the front door her father turned again to Cory, his voice lower as he repeated, 'Aunt Mildred's cottage in Shropshire,' as though that explained everything.

'What about it?' Cory asked patiently.

'She's on a cruise, for three months or so—wasting all her money, the daft old bat, but that's another story—and she said any of the family can use the cottage for a holiday while she's away. It's just what you need—a bit of peace and quiet and a chance to recharge the batteries.' Her father beamed at her.

'Dad, I don't think—'

'You said you wanted a break before you look for another job and the change will do you good. You've got enough money to cover the rent for your bedsit for a couple of months?' he asked quietly.

Cory nodded slowly. Her bank balance was very healthy.

'There you are, then; it'll be waiting for you when you go back to London after the wedding.'

Cory almost said, 'What wedding?' before she remembered and gave an inward groan. She'd need a holiday to stand that fiasco.

'Think about it, lass. You need a break, the cottage is free, and if you come back here Vivian'll give you no peace.'

Cory did think about it, but she only made her mind up about the cottage on her last day at Hunter Operations. It was the day she had been dreading, and for weeks her mind had played a hundred different scenarios as to how it would go, but the reality was ten times worse. A hundred, a million times worse.

Max had been nothing more than the original ice-man for days, which had made things terribly awkward more than once with Bertha Cox around—the other woman had taken to looking at them both very strangely—but up until five o'clock on the Friday evening Cory thought she had handled it all very well.

And then, just as she had slipped into her jacket preparatory to leaving the office with Bertha, Max put his head round the interconnecting door. 'I'd like a word before you go, Cory.' It was abrupt and cold and it sent the butterflies in her stomach—which had been having a whale of a time all day—into a fresh frenzy as he disappeared back into his office.

'I'll say goodbye now, Cory. I've got the family round for dinner tonight so I want to get away sharpish,' Bertha said quickly, giving her a brief hug and then scuttling out of the door before Cory could object, her grey hair bobbing agitatedly.

Brilliant. Thanks a bunch, Bertha. Cory's eyes were rueful as they stared at the fast closing door, but she really couldn't blame the other woman. Max at his coldest was formidable.

She took a long, deep breath, prayed that the heat staining her cheeks wasn't too obvious, and then knocked once on the interconnecting door before opening it wide. 'You wanted a word?' she asked formally.

The first thing she noticed was the bottle of champagne and two glasses. The second—the ice-man had disappeared and in his place was a warm, sexy hunk with a come-hither smile and eyes the colour of molten gold. Her heart gave a mighty kick against her ribcage and then bolted and her stomach turned right over.

'You didn't think I'd let you go like this, did you?' he asked softly, and then, as she continued to stand in the doorway, her eyes drowning pools of jade, he added, 'Come and sit down, Cory.'

'I don't want to sit down.' It wasn't true—her legs had gone to jelly but to sit down would mean she had agreed to listen to him.

'Please?' He had risen and taken the few steps to her side as he'd spoken and now he took her arm, his fingers gentle, and ushered her across to the seat in front of his desk, where he further compounded the problems with her breathing by perching nonchalantly in front of her, his trousers pulling tight across hard male thighs.

'Here.' He deftly poured her a glass of champagne, handing it to her with another devastating smile before turning slightly and pouring one for himself. 'A toast,' he said softly.

'To what?' She was hoping, desperately, that the impossible had become possible and he had discovered he couldn't live without her, even as the cold voice of reason warned her she was crazy.

'To us, of course.' His voice was low and husky and it trickled over her taut nerves like warm honey. 'You aren't my secretary any more, I'm not your boss. We're just two ordinary people who would like to get to know each other better. We can take it as slow as you like now, nothing heavy, you'll see. You can't deny the attraction between us, Cory, but in time you'll see it for what it is.'

'You mean I'll see I don't love you,' she stated quietly, her heart thumping. 'But I won't, Max, so what then? What will you say then? Sorry, Cory, but I did warn you of what to expect? Because you have, haven't you? You've laid it all on the line and given yourself the get-out clause way in advance.'

'It's not like that,' he said roughly, his eyes darkening.

'That's exactly what it's like.'

'Cory, listen to me.' He reached out for her glass and put it on the desk beside him before drawing her to her feet and into his arms. She didn't move and she didn't try to fight him, but she could have been a block of stone for all the response she gave as he moved her in close. 'I want you; I want you so badly I can't think of anything else,' he whispered huskily, 'and I know you want me too. It's crazy to deny us both.'

She wanted to remain still and distant, aloof from the frightening magnetic pull, but as the warmth of his lips found hers she shuddered helplessly. He was holding her so tightly she could scarcely breathe, her softness fitting into the hard frame of his body as though it were the last perfect piece in a jigsaw. His mouth crushed hers, the desire that had him in its thrall making him hungry for every little bit of her.

A wave of heat swept over her, burning up all the common sense and cool logic that had reiterated—time and time again over the last four miserable weeks—exactly why it would be nothing short of emotional suicide to get involved with Max. She loved him; she loved him so much. Perhaps it would be better to take anything he could give for as long as he could give it and not look to the future? Other women managed it and survived.

His kisses were becoming deeper and hungrier, his hands moving with controlled assurance as they touched and teased and brought exquisite frissons of pleasure wherever they roamed. She knew her body was betraying her need of him just as his arousal was doing the same, his manhood rock-hard against the soft swell of her belly. Her breathing had gone haywire; she was gasping and panting and the blood was singing through her veins like a warm flood, but there was something—some little echo of reason which had been born out of the misery of the last few weeks—that stopped her from capitulating fully to his unspoken demands.

He was offering her passion and an affair, not love and commitment, and he was determined it wouldn't be any different. The door to his heart was closed—it had been closed a long, long time now—and perhaps the key was lost for ever, but without his heart she had nothing. It wasn't that she wanted him to express declarations of undying devotion or ask her to marry him, Cory told herself silently. But she did want him to be open to whatever they might find together, that was all. But he wouldn't be. He *couldn't* be. She had to face it, let him go and get on with her life. So she had better open her mouth and tell him just that.

He sensed the change in her a few seconds later, raising his head to look down into her face from which all colour had fled. 'Cory?' he asked softly. 'What is it?'

'I can't be what you want me to be, Max, and I love you too much to try. Please, please don't contact me again because I won't change my mind.' She had to do this; she had to make it crystal-clear because if she didn't finish this now—cut off all avenues—he would keep trying to seduce her into his bed. And one day, in a moment of need and weakness, she might succumb.

'I don't believe that.' His voice was quiet but there was an edge of anger there too, and she understood why. He was so used to having his cake and eating it that he couldn't believe someone had taken away the spoon.

'You're going to have to,' she said softly as she pushed

away from him. 'Because I'm not going to change my mind.'

He let her go, his hands dropping at his sides as he stared at her with a most peculiar look on his handsome face. Bewilderment was there, along with irritation and surprise, but there was something else she couldn't fathom deep in the dark amber of his eyes. He thrust his hands deep into his pockets, frowning darkly.

'Do you think this is going to make me change my mind?' he asked coldly after a long moment when he had stood and watched her adjust her clothing. 'You can't blackmail me, Cory.'

'Blackmail you?' The pain and anguish that were tearing her apart were swallowed up in a fury that had her glaring at him as her eyes shot green sparks. '*Blackmail* you!'

'Yes, blackmail me,' he said tightly. 'What else do you call this? If you're holding out for a wedding ring—'

'*That's enough.*' It was a soft snarl and to give Max his due he had the sense to stop. 'You don't see, you really don't see, do you?' Cory said after a tense moment when she called on all her strength not to leap at him and bite and scratch and pummel that handsome face she loved so much. 'Max, I wouldn't marry you if you were the last man on earth,' she bit out painfully, her voice shaking. 'I love you, I think I'll always love you, but I'm not going to let you destroy me, and marriage with you would be a nightmare. Something in you has got distorted and warped; you are locked away inside yourself and you aren't man enough to come out into the light and take a chance like the rest of us. I'm not trying to blackmail you, I'm trying to tell you goodbye.'

She turned as she spoke, walking to the door and standing in the aperture where she turned to face him for the last time. 'The way you were brought up was hard, and what happened with Laurel was awful, but it was years ago, Max. Years ago. You are going to end up a bitter, lonely, forsaken old man if you aren't careful.' Her voice was devoid now of anger but very grim.

She was waiting for a come-back, one of the ruthlessly cutting remarks he was so good at or a verbal assault that would dissect and serrate, but he was completely silent and still, only the black fury in his dark face betraying his anger.

She didn't say goodbye; there was no point after all—their goodbyes had all been said that painful morning at his house weeks ago. She simply turned and stepped out into the adjoining office, shutting the door quietly behind her and then walking with careful measured steps out of the room and into the corridor beyond.

Right until she was outside in the busy London street Cory half expected him to come after her. It couldn't end like this, she told herself as she forced her legs to keep moving, hardly aware of the crowded pavements and the thick, sluggish August air. She *loved* him; how was she going to get through the rest of her life without him? And now he hated her; she had seen it in the glittering gold eyes and the way his mouth had pulled into a thin white line in the angry tautness of his face.

But perhaps this was the only way it could have ended? The thought was unwelcome but she knew it to be the truth. Nothing else could have convinced him to leave her alone. He had seen her as something of a challenge, she was sure of that, and added to that monstrous ego and razor-sharp intelligence was a very definite leader-of-the-pack type determination to subjugate and conquer.

She was walking blindly, her eyes desperate, and when she had bumped into three people in as many seconds she realised she had to get control of herself. She stood at the side of a shop doorway, breathing deeply and forcing the air into her lungs, and slowly the mad pounding in her head and buzzing in her ears lessened.

She would go to Aunt Mildred's cottage, she told herself

numbly as she slowly began to walk again. If nothing else it would give her a breathing space before the next hurdle—Vivian and Carole's wedding. And then after that... After that she would have to face the rest of her life. And right now she just couldn't imagine how she would do that.

CHAPTER TEN

IT WAS three weeks later, the middle of September, and Cory had spent all that time at Aunt Mildred's tranquil, peaceful retreat.

She had fled there the night she had left Max's office, her heart in shreds, and apart from a couple of telephone calls to her parents—Aunt Mildred didn't have a telephone: horrible, intrusive machines that embodied the worst of the twentieth century, according to her elderly aunt—and several excursions to the small village shop some three miles away she had spoken to no one. And it had been just what she needed.

She had spent warm, lazy days in the open air, tramping the lanes and open fields and valleys around her aunt's quaint little cottage, taking the paths by the river where water splashed in tiny natural fountains over time-washed rocks and where the rat-tat-tat of woodpeckers and their occasional lunatic cry could be heard.

She'd lain in green grassy meadows carpeted with daisies and cornflowers and wild orchids and campions, listening to the larks singing as they swooped and soared in the blue arch of the sky before she'd eaten the apple and chocolate she'd brought with her, then walked some more in the grass-scented air.

And then, as the evening shadows had begun to fall in the hedgerows and byways, she had made her way home to The Honeypot—Aunt Mildred's cottage—eating her evening meal of home-cured ham and salad, or chicken and new potatoes and vegetables, in her aunt's wonderful country garden, where honeysuckle romped up the trees and the evening resounded with birdsong, blackbirds, thrushes, robins, finches and a little jenny-wren—the noisiest of them all—all competing to sing the loudest.

Each morning had dawned sunny and warm and Cory had risen with the sun, looking with gratitude at the deep blue sky flecked with the cotton wool of fluffy white clouds as she had blessed the absent Aunt Mildred whose open-handed benevolence had allowed her such a sanctuary in which to lick her wounds.

At first she had tossed and turned the nights away, her heart sore and her mind heavy, but gradually the magic of the place had poured in a healing balm and she had begun to take each day as it came, not thinking too much, not contemplating the future, just being.

It couldn't last, she knew that, but it had been the safety valve she'd so desperately needed, and in this idyll, set apart from the rest of the world and normal life, she had managed to relax and step out of time. The sun had brought a honey-glow to her skin, deepened the rich red tints in her dark silky hair and softened the look of agony staring out of her eyes.

She had thought of Max—all the time at first and then, as the hot lazy days had worked their spell, just most of the time—and gone through the cycle of endless post-mortems that females were so good at, but within a few days she had come to the conclusion that she couldn't have acted any differently and remained half sane. And with that knowledge the peace had come. It didn't help the pain and loss, but it gave her the strength to relax, soak up the soothing ambience of the secluded haven and allowed her to prepare for the time when she would have to leave and go back into the real world.

And now that time was here.

Cory rose from the little garden bench surrounded by climbing roses and catmint and the hum of fat honeybees where she had eaten her breakfast each morning, and looked at the cottage garden dozing in the mild September sunshine one more time. Tomorrow was Vivian and Carole's wedding day and she couldn't delay any longer. Her holiday was over.

'You look beautiful, Carole. Absolutely beautiful.'

Cory had just put the finishing touches to Carole's head-dress and veil, tweaking the band of tiny fresh pink rose-buds nestled in green leaves and lace into place and making sure the clouds of chiffon that fell into cascading layers to the floor were securely gripped into the pretty blonde's fluffy hair.

'Thank you.' The other girl was already misty-eyed and weepy with emotion. The two of them were in Cory's bed-room at home—her mother had offered for Carole and the bridesmaids to leave from their home due to the fact that Carole had no family and was in lodgings—and now Carole leant forward and gripped Cory's hands as she said, her voice shaky, 'And thank you for not taking Vivian back, Cory. You could have, I know that, but once he realised you weren't interested we got things sorted. We'll be happy; I know we will.'

'Oh, Carole.' Cory hadn't realised Vivian's fiancée had known about his pre-wedding nerves, and now her voice was very firm and genuine when she said, 'I think he's very lucky to get you; I mean that.' And she did too. Whatever else, Carole loved her fiancé and she showed it unasham-edly. They would make the marriage work.

There was no time to say more; the other two brides-maids—a ten-year-old cousin of Vivian's and her teenage sister—bustled in in their layers of pink chiffon and it was time to leave for the church in the first of the two wedding cars.

The morning had been hectic, with a hundred and one little panics which hadn't been helped by the previous spell of hot weather having broken into drizzling rain, but now a weak sun was making itself felt and the air was warm and scented.

Cory had taken only the most perfunctory look at herself—the fussy bell-shaped dress with its flounces of lace and rosebuds and bows didn't suit her and she knew it—but now, as the car drew up outside the winding path to the church door, she forced a bright smile on her face for the waiting photographer.

It didn't matter that she looked faintly ridiculous, she assured herself in the moment before the car door was opened. This was Carole's day and she was every inch the radiant bride. Anyway, what was the ignominy of resembling a squashed meringue—and a pink one with rosebuds and frills to boot—compared to the fact that she would never see Max again? She would wear real meringue for the rest of her life if it would make him love her, she thought fiercely as she stepped out on to the pavement, clutching the round ball of flowers Carole had insisted the bridesmaids carry instead of the conventional posies.

And then she raised her eyes and saw the big dark man standing to one side of the church wall, and she froze.

'Come on, dear; it's supposed to be the bride who gets the jitters.' The photographer was nattering away but Cory didn't even hear him, and it was only when the other two bridesmaids pushed her from behind as they too scrambled out of the car that Cory moved on legs from which all strength had fled.

'We'll have a couple at the top of the path, near the church door, all right?' The photographer was all wide smiles and teeth. 'We want to show those lovely dresses off to the full, don't we?'

As the other two simpered and giggled Cory prayed the ground would open and swallow her. She looked awful, really awful, and although it hadn't mattered a minute ago at this second it was all she could think of.

'Cory?' His voice was deep and low and it made her shiver.

She had lowered her head and aimed to brush past Max and the rest of the crowd who had gathered at the perimeter stone wall of the church grounds, but now she felt a warm hand on her arm and she was forced to look up into his waiting eyes.

'What are you doing here?' she asked shakily, her heart kicking against her ribs with enough force to dislodge at least a ton of meringue. 'You shouldn't be here.'

'Waiting to see you,' he said softly. 'And yes, I should.'

'Max, this is crazy. We've said all that could possibly be said and this isn't fair...'

'I know,' he murmured quietly, his eyes eating her—meringue and bows and all. 'It *is* crazy and it isn't fair; you deserve far better than me. I've been looking for you for the last three weeks; did your father tell you? I've been going crazy.'

'My father?' She stared at him as though he were mad. 'You've spoken to my father?' This was turning into Alice in Wonderland.

'He wouldn't tell me where you were and he warned me off in pretty strong terms,' Max said wryly. 'I don't blame him; if you were my daughter I'd have done exactly the same thing. But I looked in your personnel records and saw when you'd requested a week's holiday for this wedding, so...I tried to be patient.'

'Max, I haven't the faintest idea what you're talking about,' Cory managed shakily. She knew she was trembling, she just couldn't control the shivers that were taking her over, but she hoped he—along with everyone else—would think it was bridesmaid's nerves. This finding her meant nothing, not really. She *knew* what he felt about her and love and commitment and everything. Nothing had changed. It was just Max unable to believe that he hadn't got what he wanted for once.

'Cory, we have to talk. You see that, don't you?'

'*Please,* dear.' The photographer had galloped back down the path from the church door where the other two bridesmaids were waiting, his round, effeminate face exasperated and perspiring. 'The bride will be arriving soon and I need to take some pictures. Can't you talk to this gentleman later?'

'This gentleman wants to talk to her now.' Max had rounded on the poor little man in much the same way as a panther who had had his tail trodden on, but the photographer wasn't having any of it. This was his art and he wasn't having anyone—even this big six-footer—messing it up. He glared at Max bravely.

'You're going to spoil the photographs,' he trilled tightly.

'Damn the photographs!' For the first time Max sounded like Max.

'Max, please leave me alone.' Cory cut into the exchange—which had drawn more interest and flapping ears from the crowd than ever a straightforward wedding could—her voice sharp now. 'This is Carole's day and you're going to ruin it, and I don't want to see you again.' Oh, my darling, my darling, my darling…

'Yes, you do.' No one was even breathing in their vicinity now. 'You love me.' It was soft and tender and very firm.

She stared into the painfully handsome, dear, dear face for one long moment, knowing she would never love anyone else the way she loved him, and then she said, her own voice firm now but with a catch in it that caused more than one female listener to sympathise, 'Stay away from me, Max. I mean it.' Then she allowed the photographer, who was positively dancing with agitation, to lead her away.

The wedding service was the sort of unmitigated nightmare Cory wouldn't have wished on her worst enemy but somehow she got through it, and no one—seeing her smil-

ing face and calm composure—would have guessed she
was falling apart inside. But that was what it felt like.

Why, oh, why had he come here like this today? Cory
asked herself a hundred times through the next half an hour.
She didn't dare turn round once and see if Max had followed her into the church. She wouldn't put it past him—
she wouldn't put *anything* past him, she told herself silently. She tried—she really, *really* tried—to work up some
healthy rage at his audacity, but the shock of seeing him
again, the wonder, the fierce stupid joy she had felt in the
split second she had met those beautiful amber eyes, got in
the way.

And it frightened her. It frightened her more than she
would have thought possible. *Nothing had changed.* If she
told herself it once she told herself it a million times during
the hymns and prayers and long—somewhat drawn-out—
address by Vivian's uncle. A relationship with Max would
be extremes of highs and lows, wild, ecstatic happiness or
deep, dark black despair, and when it ended—when *he*
ended it, she wouldn't know who she was or how to go on.
He would eat her up and spit her out and then simply go
on with his life as before. Impossible. Completely impossible. She would never survive him leaving.

But he *had* cared enough to come looking for her. She
caught and held the thought, shutting her eyes as her stomach turned over and she gripped the ball of flowers so hard
a few freesia heads dropped to the floor.

But that was just because he wanted her in his bed, she
reminded herself desperately the next moment, when she
opened her eyes as the last strains of 'Love divine, all loves
excelling' drifted away. When it came to satisfying their
physical desire most men's brains were situated a good deal
lower than their heads, and nothing in Max's history had
indicated he was any different. Just the opposite in fact.

Oh, it wasn't *fair* he had come today like this. Over the
last three weeks—if she had allowed herself the brief in-

dulgence of imagining them meeting up again—she had always pictured herself beautifully dressed and groomed, the very essence of cool femininity and elegance, and here she was dressed like the fairy on top of the Christmas tree with her hair frizzed and riddled with pink—*pink*—rosebuds and her face painted like a china doll. She felt utterly, utterly ridiculous.

Perhaps it would put him off? She found the thought wasn't as comforting as it should be. Perhaps he'd gone already? The pain sliced through her with enough sharpness to make her gasp. And still the service went on. And on. And on.

By the time a triumphant Carole swept down the aisle with her Vivian to the chords of the rousing 'Bridal March', Cory was working on automatic. She followed on John's— the best man's—arm, smiling, nodding and not looking to left or right, and once outside in the gentle September sunshine she went through the endless photographs without allowing her eyes to search the watching crowd. She simply didn't dare.

The reception was being held in the village hall, which was only a stone's throw from the church and didn't require the use of the wedding cars, and it was only as the last photographs were taken and most of the guests had already wended their way there to wait for the entrance of the bride and groom that Cory saw the pure lines of a deep red Ferrari parked on the far side of the church green. A Ferrari. Here. Today.

It had to be him. She didn't know where the Rolls was, but that just had to be Max. It was.

As Cory and the other two bridesmaids approached the car the door swung open and a long, lean body uncoiled itself from the leather interior. 'Cory?' he said softly. 'Wait a moment.'

The hall was just across the cobbled road, and Cory

pointed, clutching the ridiculous ball with one hand, as she said, 'I've…I've got to go in there. They're waiting.'

'I'm not going to go away.' It was cool and controlled and very calm. 'Not now, not ever. I mean it, Cory.'

She stared up at him, utterly unable to speak. There had been a note in his voice—a connotation to the words—that she dared not let herself believe was real but she wanted to cry.

The other two pink meringues shifted restlessly at her side and now Cory forced herself to say, her tone as steady as she could make it, 'Jennifer, Susan, this is Max— a…friend of mine. Max, this is Jennifer and Susan.'

'Hi.' He bestowed a brief smile on the two girls who were clearly smitten, and then, taking Cory's arm, he said, 'I'm borrowing her for a couple of minutes, okay?' as he whisked her aside.

'No, Max, it's not okay!'

As he pulled her away from the other two and frog-marched her firmly over the green to a small wooden bench set under a rich dark beech tree Cory was protesting strongly, and he looked down at her for one moment as he growled, 'Tough.'

'Who do you think you are anyway?' She was trying to be strong, she really was, but he looked so darn gorgeous, Cory thought bemusedly even as she spoke the words. The charcoal trousers and black leather jacket he was wearing accentuated his height and dark, magnetic appeal tenfold, but it wasn't that which kept her on the bench when he sat down at the side of her and began to speak. It was his voice—the slightly uneven note that betrayed the nerves he was trying to hide—and the fact that the look in his eyes was a reflection of the agony she had seen in the mirror so often over the last three weeks.

'Listen to me, Cory, please listen.' It was quiet and shaky and the rest of the world disappeared. 'I love you; I should have said that the first second I saw you again,' he said raggedly. 'But I've never said it before and it doesn't come easy.'

'No.' She shook her head as she spoke, dislodging one of the rosebuds which fell into her lap. 'No, you don't; you know you don't. Please don't say that.' *She wasn't going to cry.*

'I do love you, Cory.' His voice was fierce now, painfully fierce. 'Damn it, you have to believe me even if it takes me the rest of my life to convince you. I've known for weeks and I've been fighting it just as long, but I can't fight it any more. I want you, Cory. Not just for a week or a month or a year; I want you for the rest of my life. Forever.'

'No.' The anguish of all she had suffered was in her face as she whispered, 'You tried to make me go back to Vivian when I told you how I felt; that's not love.' It wasn't until this moment that she realised just how much he had hurt her when he had done that, and the pain was still as fierce as ever.

'I would never have let you.' It was a deep groan. 'I was still trying to convince myself you were just like all the rest. I was running scared, Cory, but I'd have killed him before I would have let him touch you. What I feel for you...' He drew in a hard, shuddering breath, shaking his head. 'It consumes me, it eats me up. I've never in all my life imagined feeling like this and I don't like it.'

The last was said with such bewilderment that for a moment she almost weakened. But she didn't believe him; she didn't dare believe him. She had seen him in operation— she had watched that ruthless mind bulldoze and manipulate and steer lesser mortals to his will too many times.

'How do you know it's love you feel?' she asked tremblingly. 'You don't believe in love, you told me. What's happened to make you change your mind?'

'You've happened,' he said softly. 'You happened and then you left me and that's when I knew I couldn't live without you. I can't, Cory, I mean it, but, like I said, it scares me to death. I'm not an easy man to be with, I know that, and I don't know how to handle this. I know what I feel, but the rest... I've never had someone of my own to love, I don't know *how* to, for crying out loud, but I can't be without you either. The last three weeks have been hell.' The words were a groan from the heart of him.

She looked into his eyes, into the golden orbs that could be so hard and challenging but were now desperate and wistful and glowing with something that melted her heart. Suddenly it was all so simple. He had come for her. *He had come for her.*

'I love you, Cory,' he said again, his voice shaky. 'I don't know how I'm going to prove it to you or make you understand. I want us to grow old together, to have children and dogs and cats and the whole caboodle, but it's like this great giant step into the unknown. Hell, I'm not saying this right.'

'Max—'

'No, don't say anything, not until you've let me convince you,' he interrupted passionately. 'You said marriage to me would be a nightmare and you might well be right, but all I can say is that I can promise you I'll never stop loving you. That's the one thing—the only thing at the moment— I do know. And I'd be yours, Cory—heart, soul, body and mind.'

'Max—'

'You can send me away but I'll keep coming back.' He was both winsome and pleading and fiercely aggressive in a way only Max could be. 'I've wanted women in my time and the wanting was easy but I'm ashamed to say it meant little. This loving...' His voice was unsteady. 'This is something else. This tears you apart inside and rips the guts out of you, but still the not having it is worse than all the pain.'

'Do you think I don't know that?' Cory asked softly.

'When you left the office that day I realised what a fool I'd been,' he said huskily. 'I went round to the flat but you weren't there, and then I suffered the torments of the damned thinking you'd gone back to him, that I'd driven you into his arms again.' His voice revealed a little of just what he'd suffered.

'There is no "again."' Cory knew he'd assumed she'd slept with Vivian, maybe other boyfriends, too, and she also knew he had liked his women experienced and well-versed in the arts of lovemaking in the past. She just didn't know how he would react to what she was going to tell him so she said it quickly, before she chickened out. 'Max, I never slept with Vivian; I've never slept with anyone.'

'You haven't?' She had astounded him—she could see it in the stunned golden gaze—but she also saw something else that made her heart leap. A fierce gratitude, a deep possessive glint that told her he was more than a little pleased with this latest development. It didn't matter! It didn't matter that she couldn't match those others in expertise.

'You're mine, Cory.' A muscle was jerking at the side of his jaw and his face was taut. 'I came here to tell you that, and that I love you, and…and to ask for your forgiveness.' He had been careful not to touch her since they had sat down but now, at the sound of her name being called out through the air, he took her face in his hands, his eyes urgent. 'You can't say no, Cory. Please, you have to give me another chance.'

She wasn't aware she was crying until his thumbs gently brushed the tears from her cheeks, and then she laughed shakily, her mouth trembling as she whispered, 'The boss is always right?'

He stared at her for a moment and she saw the shadow of uncertainty deep in the amber eyes, which made her love him all the more. 'Cory?'

'I love you, Max.' She answered him in the only way

possible. 'And I'll teach you how to show your love to me and to our children and to our children's children...'

And then she was in his arms and their mouths met, clinging together as their bodies strained and merged as though they were already one. The kiss was sweet and intense and—considering that they were sitting on a small wooden bench in the middle of the church green at two o'clock on a September afternoon—disgracefully intimate, but Cory didn't care. He loved her. He loved her! And he had looked for her and waited... Oh, Max.

'You'll marry me soon?' He had wrenched his mouth away just long enough to ask. 'Very soon?'

'Scared you'll chicken out if you don't get it over with quickly?' she teased huskily against the hard, firm lips that evoked such pleasure it was difficult to breathe.

'Oh, no.' The amber eyes glowed with enough love to satisfy her for the rest of her life. 'But I want the other wolves kept at bay. You are too beautiful and desirable not to have a gold band on the third finger of your left hand.'

Beautiful and desirable? Her mascara had run, her nose was probably the same shocking pink as the wretched dress and she could feel more curls and rosebuds coming adrift even as they spoke. But he thought she was beautiful and desirable. She smiled, her face glowing and her eyes shining in a way that made Max's heart thud.

He really was a boss in a million, but as a husband he was going to be pure dynamite...

And so it proved.

Barbara McMahon was born and raised in the south but settled in California after spending a year flying around the world for an international airline. Settling down to raise a family and work for a computer firm, she began writing when her children started school. Now, feeling fortunate in being able to realise a long-held dream of quitting her 'day job' and writing full-time, she and her husband recently moved to the Sierra Nevada mountains of California, where she finds her desire to write is stronger than ever. With the beauty of the mountains visible from her windows, and the pace of life slower than the hectic San Francisco Bay Area where they previously resided, she finds more time than ever to think up stories and characters and share them with others through writing. Barbara loves to hear from readers. You can reach her at PO Box 977, Pioneer, CA 95666-0977, USA.

HIS SECRETARY'S SECRET

by

Barbara McMahon

PROLOGUE

Karla Jones sipped her water and pretended to study the menu. In actuality, she was eavesdropping on the conversation at the adjacent table. The trendy Vancouver waterfront restaurant was crowded. It was almost one o'clock—the lunch hour just ending. Here and there checks were being paid, people gathering their things in preparation to return to work.

Recognizing several women at the adjacent table as secretaries from the company her friend, Pat, worked for, she idly listened to their chatter.

Karla liked to take her lunch break later than most, to avoid crowded restaurants. Already more and more tables were becoming vacant. In just a few minutes the women seated at the table behind her would disperse. The general din of noise would soften and her lunch would be more relaxed for it.

But now, she found their conversation fascinating.

"...heard he'd be closing the entire company down within the month," one woman said in hushed tones.

"That's dumb, why buy it if he plans to shut it down?"

"I heard he's going to move it lock, stock, and barrel to Toronto. And hire a whole new staff there."

"I heard Miss Evans gave notice today."

That comment startled everyone into silence. Karla almost jerked around to question the statement. Miss

Evans? Wasn't she the president's executive assistant? Karla was sure Pat had mentioned her more than once over the years.

Karla was surprised at the news. Almost as surprised as she'd been last week when she'd been told her own boss, vice president David Daniels of McCormick & Associates, was retiring almost immediately. She herself might be out of a job if Mr. Daniels's replacement wanted a different secretary.

"Well, it wasn't because Mr. 25-50 is into age discrimination—except in a reverse way," someone behind her said.

They all laughed.

"Don't worry, Suzanne, you're only twenty-four, still in the running."

Everyone laughed again as they divvied up the check and gathered their things. In only a few moments, they'd passed Karla's table without glancing her way, still talking about the mysterious new CEO of their company.

She watched them leave, wondering if any of the rumors had any basis in fact. Especially the one about Miss Evans. If she were leaving, was this fate's way of letting her know about a new job opportunity just when she needed it?

"Hi, sorry I'm late. The call of nature, you know." Pat Carns eased herself into the chair opposite Karla two minutes later.

"Can you fit?" Karla asked teasingly. Her friend was eight months pregnant and seemed enormous to Karla.

"Very funny. Just wait, one of these days you'll get married and the next thing you know—you'll be as big as a whale yourself. What looks good?"

"Everything on the menu. I'm having salmon."

"That sounds perfect, I'll have it, too."

Once their orders had been placed, Karla studied her friend speculatively. "Without breaching any confidences, can you tell me if your Miss Evans is really leaving?"

Pat blinked. "How in the world did you know that? She just gave notice this morning." Pat worked in the Human Resources Department of Kinsinger Electronics. The two friends had met in secretarial school eight years ago, hit it off instantly and remained close ever since. They rarely discussed business when they got together, however. Karla's confidential secretarial position dealt with a trade firm for Pacific Rim commerce while Pat's dealt with employee relations of an electronic manufacturing company. Neither were given to breaching confidences.

"It can't be a very big secret. There were several secretaries from your company discussing it before you came in. I overheard—as could almost anyone in the place," she said, glancing around. The tables were close together. Many were empty now, but earlier the place had been crowded.

"Someone should speak to them about the concept of confidentiality." Pat shrugged. "If it isn't a secret anymore, it won't hurt to tell you she gave notice this morning. She said she couldn't work for anyone else since Mr. Moore wasn't going to remain in charge."

"Was it she didn't want to work without Mr. Moore—or not work for the new guy?"

"I couldn't say, but I'm sure she's heard the rumors about Matthew Gramling—he's said to be a real slave driver. And the company is faltering, there's no denying that. Miss Evans was approaching retirement age anyway. Maybe she just didn't want to have to deal with a dynamic hotshot after her years with Mr. Moore.''

"Not deal with Mr. 25-50?"

Pat grinned. "Heard that part, too, huh?"

"I heard it. I don't get it."

"Well," Pat leaned closer—or as close as her protruding stomach would allow—and motioned Karla closer. "The rumor mill says he never dates women over twenty-five and never hires women to work directly for him if they are under fifty."

"Why?" Karla asked.

"Apparently women over twenty-five are worried about their biological clock and put a lot of pressure on a man. I take it our new CEO is definitely not in the market for a wife."

"Sounds like he has a monumental ego problem to me. Does he think every woman he dates wants to marry him? And the under fifty part?"

"Worried he'll train someone and she'll get married, have kids and leave him in the lurch." Pat sat back and laughed as she patted her stomach. "And he's probably right, look at me."

Karla smiled, but said nothing, her thoughts whirling. Her boss was leaving and her own situation tenuous. The secretarial slot for the CEO at another company was opening up. A perfect opportunity for her to move ahead.

"I want Miss Evans's job," she said.

"Didn't you hear what I said, the new CEO doesn't hire pretty, young women to work for him. He'd take one look at you and show you the door, certain you'd be on your way to the altar in no time.''

''But I'm not. And have no plans to be anytime soon, either,'' Karla said firmly. ''I've worked hard for eight years. Getting married anytime soon just doesn't fit into my plans.''

''Yeah, yeah, yeah. I've heard that. Once the right guy comes along, you'll change your mind.''

''Even so, it wouldn't necessarily mean I'd want to quit my job. I like working.''

''Whomever they promote to Mr. Daniels's place will love to have you,'' Pat said loyally.

''Unless they bring their current secretary with them.''

''Then you'll find something else. But not Miss Evans's job.''

''Am I not qualified for it?'' Karla asked bluntly.

''Of course you are. You have all the training and skills of a highly sought-after executive assistant. But you're forgetting Mr. 25-50's rule. No one under fifty for him.''

The waiter brought their salads and placed them on the table, effectively interrupting their discussion.

Karla thanked him, and began to eat, changing the subject.

But she wasn't finished with the idea. She'd find a way. This opportunity seemed too perfect to pass up. She'd been working since she was twenty, first for an ambitious manager, then a seasoned vice president. The next logical step was to a CEO's office.

And the perfect opportunity had just presented itself.

She'd just have to figure out a way to circumvent Matthew Gramling's convoluted notion of what constituted the proper age of an executive assistant!

CHAPTER ONE

KARLA pushed the button to the twentieth floor. She looked neither right nor left, but stared at the burnished-bronze elevator doors as the car swooshed quietly upward. She recognized one or two others from Kinsinger Electronics on the elevator, but, afraid they might realize who she was, she refused to look at them directly.

Granted the few times she'd stopped by to pick up Pat probably hadn't made an impression on anyone, still, she took no chances.

Butterflies danced in her stomach. She resisted the urge to check her hair again. Touching the natural-looking wig had the tendency of calling attention to it. Trying a small smile, she could feel the stage makeup pulling against her cheeks. Polly assured her the coating looked natural—though it wrinkled once she smiled or frowned— adding at least twenty years to her appearance. Or so she hoped.

Active in little theater productions, her friend Polly had a huge case of makeup aids. She'd been delighted to help Karla age herself—making her promise to call her as soon as the interview was over to let her know how the disguise worked.

The tinted glasses perched on her nose were annoying, but necessary. As were the staid, plain, classical designs of her business suit and low-heeled shoes. The wig was hot and made her scalp itch. It would all be worth it, however, if she got the job.

By the time she reached the twentieth floor, Karla was alone in the elevator. Stepping out into the quiet lobby, she instantly noticed the thick carpeting, the subdued lights, and the soft music. Quite a difference from the offices in which she'd been working. Of course, McCormick & Associates had been feeling the crunch of the Pacific Rim trade and was much more cost-conscious than Kinsinger appeared to be. She had enjoyed working for the firm, and would miss Mr. Daniels. But she had to look to her future.

There was no central set of desks housing staff on this floor. No hustle and bustle of a hectic work area. In fact, as she headed toward the office of the CEO, she wondered if she were alone on the floor. Surely someone else was around.

The quiet murmur behind one door assured her the floor wasn't deserted.

Entering the office with Miss Evans's name still on the door, she saw a huge wooden desk in solitary splendor— neat as a pin. Miss Evans had departed last Friday, according to Pat.

The door beyond stood ajar. Karla took a deep breath and stepped forward. Show time. Could she pull it off? Rapping sharply on the door, she reviewed all her plans. She thought she'd covered everything. The interview would show if she had or not.

"Come in." The deep voice touched her senses, sending a shivering spark of awareness skidding across her skin.

She pushed open the door and stepped inside the large,

corner office. Two walls consisted of tall windows, providing a beautiful panoramic view of the harbor with North Vancouver in the distance.

Spectacular as the view was, it was the man who rose when she entered that caught her eye.

Karla's heart skipped a beat and settled down to a fast pace. No wonder Matt Gramling had an uncomplimentary view of women throwing themselves at him. In his case, it was probably justified.

He was heart-stoppingly gorgeous. Tall with broad shoulders, he looked as if he should be advertising race cars or sleek yachts. His dark hair was styled perfectly for the boardroom, but for one startling moment Karla wanted to muss it up, run her fingers through it to see what it felt like. See it tossed by the wind, burnished by the sun.

She caught her breath. Was she losing her mind? She was here for an interview, not to get gaga over some man's outward appearance.

Yet when she met his blue eyes, her mind went blank. They were as deep a blue as the Pacific on a sunny day. Alert and intelligent, they fixed on her. She swallowed hard, a frisson of alarm darting through her. Darn. Mr. Daniels hardly ever looked at her. She'd thought for sure busy businessmen were too preoccupied to pay attention to their office staff.

Matthew Gramling seemed to be the exception. His gaze missed nothing, from her plainly styled hair, gray of course, to the sensible pumps on her feet.

Once again she resisted the urge to double check her disguise.

"Mr. Gramling? I'm Miss Jones. We have an appointment at nine."

"Come in, Miss Jones. You are actually a few moments early." He paused a moment and then smiled. "I like that."

Karla nodded and swallowed hard. His smile caught her by surprise. The white teeth gleamed against his tanned skin. And the smile softened his features, making him look that much more approachable. That much more appealing. And sexy as could be!

She took a chair quickly, hoping she sat gracefully and didn't collapse just because her knees had suddenly grown weak. That smile should come with a warning—lethal to a woman's equilibrium!

She handed him the folder containing her résumé and sat back, trying her best to look confident and competent and ignore the way her pulse raced. Nerves, that was all.

It was a high-risk gamble, she knew that. But—aside from her looks—everything was the absolute truth. She'd worked on her résumé over the last week, polishing it until it showcased her experience and talents. Mr. Daniels had written her a wonderful letter of recommendation. Of course she had not told him of Mr. 25-50's views on employment. Her old boss had apparently never heard of Gramling's philosophy, so had no reason to suspect it would be more difficult to get the job than any other. His letter made no mention of age.

Matthew Gramling scanned the résumé, then placed it on his desk. Leaning back in his chair, he studied Karla.

"You've been working only eight years?" he asked.

"I decided when planning to join the work force to take a secretarial course so I'd be better able to compete with—'' she hesitated just a moment, hoping she was playing this right ''—younger women.'' Tilting her chin, she dared him to comment.

"All your experience has been with McCormick & Associates, I see.''

She nodded. "A definite advantage wouldn't you say? I worked my way up, which shows they were pleased with my work. And I understand the ins and outs of Pacific Rim trade. I heard rumors you wish to expand Kinsinger Electronics into that arena. Mr. Daniels found me most valuable.''

"I plan to make changes in the firm, true,'' he said. He leaned back in his chair, but the pose was deceptive. Karla knew he remained alert to every nuance of their conversation.

"It would be odd if you didn't. I expect you have a lot of new ideas that will move the company ahead in the twenty-first century.''

"Moore ran it like a family business. I definitely plan to change that. Tell me something about your experiences at McCormick.''

The interview continued for more than forty-five minutes. Karla answered all questions honestly and with forethought. If he had asked her age, she would have told him without hesitation. He did not. If he thought she were older from the glasses she wore, the conservative clothing, the wig and the stage makeup that aged her skin, that was his problem.

She was convinced if she got the job, once he realized how competent she was, and that she had no intention of taking off on some romantic fantasy, he'd be willing to admit his odd notions of employee ages was faulty. But until then, she was willing to dress the part.

If she got the job.

"Do you have any questions?" he asked finally.

"You have covered everything perfectly. I would very much appreciate the opportunity to work for you."

He stood, offering his hand. "The Human Resources Department will be in touch one way or the other by the end of the week."

Karla shook hands briefly. His palm was warm against hers, his fingers long and strong. For a dazzling moment, her senses seemed to go into overload. She wondered what it would be like to have those fingers in her hair or stroking her skin.

She flushed, hoping color didn't noticeably stain her cheeks.

"Goodbye," she said abruptly and turned. She forced herself to walk calmly across the expanse of office when she really wanted to dash away and put some distance between them. She'd never felt so aware of a man before. And she'd better make sure she did not convey that awareness in any manner. She wanted the job. It sounded perfect—exciting, challenging, and affording the opportunity to work independently to a large degree. She could handle it. If she got the chance.

Closing the door behind her, she leaned against it for a moment in relief. The die was cast. Would she get the position or not? She'd done her best, now it was up to Matthew Gramling.

But, as she headed for the elevators, she truly hoped she'd be a part of the team he talked about building to lead this company into new areas and expanding it. What an exciting time it would be.

Karla was on tenterhooks all week. She had little to do at work with Mr. Daniels winding up his affairs. Helping out where she could in other departments, she noted nothing had been said about her own continued employment. She hurried home each afternoon to check her answering machine, having reprogrammed the outgoing message before the interview. It sounded staid and professional. Nothing like the usually irreverent jingles she changed weekly.

By Friday, Karla had given up. She knew from Pat—who had thought Karla was wasting her time by interviewing—that Matt Gramling had had a stream of applicants for the job during the week. Karla knew many of them would actually have decades of experience. Which didn't make her own eight years look so impressive. Hope was hard to maintain with nothing to feed it.

At three, the phone rang at her desk.

"The job's been filled," Pat said quietly.

Karla's heart sank. She'd so wanted it. Not only for the advancement of her career, but for the opportunities it had offered to learn a new business, be a part of the leadership forging new strategies for the next century.

"Oh. Well, thanks for calling to tell me."

"By you!" Pat shrieked. "I don't believe it, but he's hiring you! You're to start on Monday. How did you do it? I thought his 25-50 rule was firm. Wait until some of the other women in the company hear this!"

Karla felt almost giddy with reaction. She'd got the job! She'd done it!

Then what Pat said penetrated.

"Uh, Pat, wait! Don't say anything, please? I, um, actually, I think he believes I'm older than twenty-eight."

"Older? How much older?"

"I don't know. But at the interview, I, ah, had gray hair and a lot of wrinkles around my eyes and on my cheeks."

The silence on the other end stretched out for quite some time.

"You convinced him you're older?" Pat said at last.

"He never asked my age and I never volunteered it," Karla said, the first flush of excitement tempered by the knowledge she had to maintain that mature look for a while at least. Maybe for as long as she worked for him. Could she do it? For a moment the vision of twenty years of dressing older than she was danced before her.

She had to convince him, and quickly, that twenty-eight was a perfect age for an executive assistant!

"He'll know once he sees the employment papers, your age will be clearly listed there," Pat said slowly, as if having trouble taking in the situation.

"Ah." Frantically Karla tried to think. "Why does he need to see anything? You can just say Human Resources has taken care of everything. Impress him with your efficiency."

Pat giggled. "Good thing I'm leaving next week. I'd be out on my ear if he ever finds out. But why not? An unfair bias against age is wrong—whichever direction. I'll give it a shot. Anyway, congratulations. I guess. I hope you like the job as much as you think you will. I know you can handle it. That is, if you last the first day.

Honestly, Karla, this is the craziest scheme I've ever heard of.''

"It'll work. I'm sure of it. And I think I'll love the job,'' Karla said, then rang off, elated. She had done it! She started Monday morning as executive assistant to the new CEO of Kinsinger Electronics!

Now it remained to be seen if she could pull it off.

Matt Gramling loved a challenge, and pulling Kinsinger Electronics from the brink of bankruptcy and turning it into a dominant player in the Pacific Rim electronics industry was just the kind of challenge he loved. Some men had a talent for fishing, or acting or inventing. His was in turning around poorly run companies. And these days, he made sure he was the major shareholder before doing so.

He felt the familiar excitement build Monday morning. It was time to implement his ideas and strategies. See if he could pull the company from the brink of bankruptcy and make it a dominant player in its field.

He'd studied the reports generated by the department managers last week. They were in addition to the reports and projections his own people in Toronto had produced prior to the buyout. A firm grasp of the basic operation was crucial.

As was a good team. He glanced at his watch. It was still early. Today was Miss Jones's first day. He swiveled his chair until he could gaze out the window but didn't really see the waters of Coal Harbour dotted here and there with pleasure boats, or the dock where his floatation plane was moored with several others, or the tall trees of Stanley Park in the distance. The view of the Vancouver harbor was spectacular, but Matt ignored it, remembering their interview. He'd spoken with a dozen women last week, each more experienced and skilled than the last, it seemed. Yet there'd been something about the first one that had appealed to him. Her enthusiasm, maybe. Or her energy.

While she hadn't the breadth of experience some of the others had, she had worked at one firm her entire work career, which showed stability. If her boss hadn't retired, she wouldn't have been looking.

He wondered briefly what she'd done prior to that secretarial course. Raised a family, he'd bet. Had there been a divorce? Once the kids were grown, she'd gone into the work force?

It didn't matter. She was perfect—mature and sensible. She hadn't appeared the least bit flighty, and was too old to get moonstruck over some man. Or flirt with her boss. He'd be able to depend upon her as Daniels had. His letter had been straightforward and factual. Not the glowing testimony of some of the others, but solid. He trusted his instinct.

A noise in the outer office alerted him. Rising, he crossed to the door.

Miss Jones was putting away her purse. She looked up when he spoke.

"Good morning."

"Good morning, sir." She smiled. "Thank you for giving me the opportunity to work for you. I'll do my best."

"That's all I ask. When you've had a chance to settle in, bring a pad and we'll sort out how I like things run."

"Can I get you some coffee?" she asked.

"I picked up some earlier." He hesitated. Bringing coffee was something younger women objected to. He didn't need anyone to wait on him, but it was nice to have the offer made. "Do you want a chance to get a cup?"

"Oh, no, I'm ready now," she said, picking up two sharpened pencils and a pristine new notepad.

Matt held the door for her and stood aside as she preceded him into the office. It paid to hire the right people for the job. And here was someone who put work before coffee—ready to start even before eight! Strong validation for his choice.

She hesitated when she saw his desk. "Been working, I see," she murmured.

Matt walked around the desk, aware of the stacks of folders and printouts he'd been perusing since he arrived. He wanted her knowledgeable about the company as quickly as possible. She could review some of the reports as a kind of get-acquainted briefing.

"Some of this was from the weekend. I need to get up to speed as quickly as possible."

"I would have thought you'd know the company inside out before you bought it," she said, sitting in the chair opposite his and flipping open the notebook.

"I knew enough to know it was floundering and I could turn it around. In order to do that, now I need to know every little detail."

Matt sat in his chair and looked at her. Her gaze was on the notebook, pencil poised. She was going to be a gem!

"We'll start with my routine first. Then we'll get someone from Human Resources to give you a tour of the company. Introduce you around. Once you know the layout, you're welcomed to read some of the reports, to see what various departments do.''

''Perfect. Let me know what you expect of me, and what I can do to make things run more smoothly for you.'' She'd ask Pat to show her around. She'd get a lot of insider knowledge that way. She wished her friend would be staying at Kinsinger's, but she had already given notice, planning to stay home with her new baby.

He nodded. ''First you need to hire a typist to do the basics—for drafts of reports and correspondence, filing, that kind of thing. I need your skills for other tasks. Then arrange to get a newer computer than the former assistant had and have these programs loaded.'' He tossed her a sheet of paper with the programs he used noted.

Leaning back, he began to tell her how he liked his day structured. Realizing interruptions were part and parcel of daily operations, he still expected her to field as many calls as she could. He indicated which aspects of the office he expected her to handle and which he'd see to himself.

It helped periodically to review the way he ran things. The operation in Toronto was now managed by his chief operating officer, Ted Clyde. With Kinsinger Electronics, he was starting fresh once again. And could structure the operations the way he thought best.

His respect for Miss Jones began to grow. She was quietly taking notes, asking an intelligent question now and then to clarify things. She didn't seem overwhelmed with the tasks he was delineating. Nor did she protest at the amount of work he piled on. She was going to be perfect.

"That's it. I'll leave it to you to get started on scheduling the managers in to see me."

"No problem."

That had been her standard response for everything. Matt almost smiled. He hoped none of it would be too much, he found he liked being around her. She brought with her a sense of serenity. Would it last? Or once they reached their stride, would she become as harried as Sarah Marling, his secretary in Toronto, always seemed? Time would tell.

"One last thing," he said.

She looked up. For a moment he felt a hint of awareness brush across him. Her eyes sparkled with enthusiasm behind her glasses. No makeup—except what seemed to be powder. She was not plain by any means—her bone structure was good. If her hair hadn't turned gray and wrinkles covered her skin, she'd still be an attractive woman. Her figure—

He frowned. He didn't usually give much thought to the personal aspects of his assistants.

"The work week will be erratic starting out. I'll demand a lot of after-hours' time initially—until I get things going the way I want—as quickly as I can."

"No problem."

He did smile at that. "And what would constitute a problem?" he asked.

Her eyes narrowed slightly. "Nothing I can think of right now, sir. If I come up with something, I'll let you know."

"I don't go for so much formality. You can call me Matt. I'll call you—"

His mind went blank. He knew he'd seen her first name on the résumé, what was it?

"Miss Jones," she said primly. Then cleared her throat, smiling a little. "Or Jeannette."

"Miss Jones? Not married?" Why hadn't he covered this in the interview? Hadn't most women her age been at least married once? Maybe she had been and took back her maiden name after a divorce.

She shook her head once.

"Ever been?"

"How does that impact my work here?" she asked sharply.

"It doesn't. I was out of line, Miss Jones. Jeannette. I apologize."

Out of line, maybe, but curious. Had he hit a hot button? Not that it mattered. She worked for him now and that was what was important, not her private life.

"I'll see to this," she said, indicating the list of notes she'd jotted down.

He watched her walk from the office. For a moment he wanted to ask her to stay—to talk for a moment—to learn more about the woman he'd hired.

Time enough to learn more about her as they worked together. He already knew all he needed to start. But the curiosity lingered.

CHAPTER TWO

KARLA felt as if she'd been running a marathon by the end of work on Friday. Matt Gramling was a high-energy person from the get-go. No matter how early she arrived at work, he was already in his office—freshly attired and raring to plunge into the day's activities.

And she knew the description of slave driver wasn't far off. Yet, how could she complain when he worked so hard himself—harder than anyone else at the firm.

She stayed late three nights during the week, not getting home on Wednesday until well after midnight. Yet she knew he had to stay even later every night, with the fresh stack of work that always awaited her each morning.

She was tired beyond belief. How did he think an older woman would have kept up with his pace?

Not that she would ask. Or give any hint things weren't going along perfectly. She was determined to do her best with this job and prove to him his notions of employee ages were faulty.

And it appeared to be the only faulty thing about the man.

Besides incredible energy, he had exciting ideas to grow the business. New ways to view old techniques and policies—and innovative methods in dealing with personnel.

He engendered an excitement throughout the company

24

that was infectious. From the administrative offices to the plant on the outskirts of the city, morale was on the rise.

Department after department became caught up in the new wave of ideas and changes. Managers arrived at his office in trepidation—fearful of what he'd find wrong with their departments. They left refreshed and inspired by the new ideas discussed. For the most part, that is. Two managers were given notice, and one put on alert his department had to change for the better, or he'd be gone.

Karla watched daily, amazed she could actually feel the energy level throughout the entire organization rise.

She and Pat had time for a quick lunch on Thursday, but beyond that, she'd been at her desk nonstop. Except for the times Matt spent with her. Sometimes they'd get off topic and discussed philosophical aspects of running a business. He seemed to listen attentively to her views, which proved delightfully appealing when he had so much more success in business than she.

At five on Friday, she straightened her stacks of folders, wondering if she dare leave. She should check with Matt once more before taking off for the weekend. She had a date with her friend Kevin Fowler to attend a new musical. If she needed to cancel, she'd want to give him as much notice as possible.

Matt had mentioned to her earlier that morning that he was leaving for the weekend, so she knew there'd be no required work Saturday and Sunday. She planned to sleep in late tomorrow!

But did he have any last-minute tasks to take care of today?

Duty called.

She stepped into the open doorway to his office. "If you have nothing further for me, Mr. Gramling, I'll be leaving."

He looked up, then glanced at his watch. "No, nothing that can't wait until Monday. I'm glad you let me know the time. I have something going on tonight."

Karla nodded impersonally, wondering if it were a hot date. She had noticed during the week a certain number of calls he'd received from women that seemed to have nothing to do with business. He must be a fast worker, she knew he'd only been in Vancouver a couple of weeks.

Not that it was any of her concern.

He tossed down his pen and leaned back in his chair. "So how did your first week go?" he asked.

"I liked it. It was different from what I expected."

"And that was?"

"I didn't anticipate so much autonomy, for one thing. I appreciate your giving me the chance to make decisions right off the bat."

"Why not, you handled everything perfectly."

She smiled, taking pride in his compliment. "Not a problem," she murmured.

He laughed. "I'll wait for the day you announce a problem. Have a nice weekend, Miss Jones. I'll see you early Monday."

"And you, Mr. Gramling."

Despite his repeatedly reminding her to call him Matt, she wanted the barrier of formality between them. Sometimes he called her Jeannette, and she had to remember to respond. She was not used to answering to her middle name.

Their morning meetings worked to strengthen the bond growing between them. She knew in a few months she would be so attuned to his way of dealing with situations that she would be able to predict his reaction. Her hope was he'd feel the same about his executive assistant.

She hurried home and into the shower. Washing away the stage makeup each day was such a relief. And to be able to run her fingers through her short dark hair was also a delight she wouldn't take for granted anytime soon.

The shower refreshed her and she was ready when Kevin showed up promptly at six-thirty. They were grabbing a quick bite then going to the performance.

The musical had been playing to a sellout crowd. Kevin bragged about pulling in a favor to obtain great seats, near the center close to the front. Karla sat down with relief. For the next hour, she could sit and veg out— enjoy the entertainment and not have to be "on." Conversing with Kevin during dinner had been a strain despite their longtime friendship. Normally she liked spending time with him. But tonight, she was too tired. She should have begged off the evening, but knew he'd gone to a lot of trouble to get the tickets. And she'd been looking forward to seeing the show. If she could keep her eyes open!

Twice during the performance she caught herself in a huge yawn. Once, her head nodded as she almost dozed off.

Flicking a glance at Kevin, she was relieved he hadn't noticed. It wasn't his fault she was so tired.

She looked beyond him—and her heart stopped. Matthew Gramling was staring at her from two rows over.

Karla quickly looked away, her heart pounding. Fatigue fled. Good grief, what was he doing here?

What was she going to do? Had he recognized her? She lost track of the performance as thoughts tumbled around in her mind. Surreptitiously, she peeked in his direction again. He seemed engrossed in the antics of the actors on stage. The seat next to him was vacant. Then, as if he'd been touched on the shoulder, he glanced her way again.

She swung her head back to face the stage. Why was he looking at her?

She shifted a bit, her delight in the musical dimmed. Glancing casually over her shoulder, she met his gaze. Hoping she hadn't given herself away, she slowly looked away, wishing she could sink beneath the seats! He was staring at her! He must have recognized her. But how? Her hair, makeup, dress—everything—was different. It was dark in the theater, was he just suspicious? Or did he know for certain?

Could she plead a headache and get Kevin to take her home early? Escape before Matt had a chance to confirm his suspicions?

No, that wasn't fair to Kevin. He had every right to expect to enjoy the entire performance. What was she going to do?

After one week, Karla knew she wanted to work for Kinsinger for a long time. It was the perfect job! Was she going to get fired here at the theater a mere five days into her new career?

She let several minutes pass before peeking around. Matt was watching the show—no, he glanced her way and caught her gaze. Drat the man, couldn't he become engrossed in the musical? She looked straight ahead, wondering how long before she could escape.

At the intermission, Kevin offered to get them drinks.

"White wine?" he asked as they slowly moved up the long aisle, buffeted by the other theatergoers heading for the lobby.

"Just sparkling water tonight, please. I'm so tired I'd fall asleep if I drank anything alcoholic," she said. Glancing around the crowded lobby, she didn't see Matt. There were a lot of people—what were the odds they'd run into each other? Motioning to a quiet corner, she smiled at Kevin. "I'll wait there, if that's all right with you. I don't want to fight the crowd tonight."

"Good idea. I'll be back as quick as I can."

She cut across the flow of patrons and found the eddy of peace. What she should have done was stayed in her seat and taken a quick catnap. Or pleaded a headache and fled the theater to make sure she didn't run into her boss.

Another yawn came. She covered her mouth with her hand and gave in. She hoped she'd stay awake until she could get home. It wasn't fair to Kevin to be so tired he couldn't enjoy the evening.

"Can I get you a cup of coffee?" a familiar voice asked.

Startled, Karla swung to her left, and came face-to-face with Matt Gramling!

So much for trying to avoid him.

Stunned, she couldn't speak. What was he doing here? Had he deliberately sought her out?

"I, um," she stammered. Had he followed her? No, that was dumb—unless he *did* suspect and had come to uncover her deception.

"Sorry, I couldn't help notice you seem tired." Dressed in a dark suit and fresh shirt, he looked wonderful. Karla had to force her gaze away.

"I am a bit tired," she said shortly.

Scanning the crowd, he frowned slightly. "Weren't you with someone?"

She nodded, trying to capture some semblance of rationality. Taking a deep breath, she hoped she could calm her nerves. He hadn't recognized her—at least he hadn't instantly denounced her, or demanded an explanation. Was it just coincidence?

Swinging back to look at her, he smiled, and held out his hand. "I'm Matt Gramling. New in town. Are you enjoying the show, or too tired to appreciate it?"

She took his hand, releasing it as quickly as she could without causing comment. The same spark that she remembered from the interview seemed to flow up her arm. That same sexy smile had her knees feeling decidedly wobbly, and that same intensity he brought to bear on the job front showed as he gazed down at her as if they were the only two people in the theater.

"I'm, uh, Karla. And the show's great."

He'd think she didn't even know her own name the way she stammered. Better that than the truth—her nerves were stretched to the limit. Not only by the fear of exposure, but by the wild feelings that rose being so near him.

"Nice to meet you, Karla. Did you get stranded?"

"Stranded? Oh, no. Kevin went to get us something to drink. I didn't want to face the crowds."

"Coffee, I hope?"

She shook her head, glancing up to be caught by his

gaze, feeling mesmerized by his eyes. They remained focused solely on her. As a technique for making someone feel important, it was dynamite! Her heart raced and her thoughts spun.

So these were the plans he had for the evening. Good thing she hadn't told him of her own plans. She almost shivered at the close call.

"Are you here alone?" she asked, wondering how long it would be before some jealous woman came up and snatched him away. Yet the seat next to his had been vacant.

"My date came down sick just before we were due to leave, and I didn't want to waste both tickets. It was too late by then to call someone else."

He was alone—and trying to pick her up?

"Do you know me?" she asked warily. Was she reading the signs correctly? Any other time she'd have been delighted to meet such a personable man. Of all the luck.

"I don't know, do I? You look familiar. I saw you earlier in the theater."

Several times, she thought. Had he thought she was flirting with him?

"I'm sure I would have remembered if we had met before," she said, stalling for time. Where was Kevin? Things were getting complicated.

"While you appear to be enjoying the show, you also look tired. Tough day?" he asked.

"Tough week."

He tilted his head a moment as if listening more intently. His eyes narrowed as he studied her. "You look very familiar. Even your voice sounds familiar."

Oops, if he recognized nothing else, would he recognize her voice?

She lowered it slightly, rushing into speech, "Sorry about your date. The show is funny and I love the way that song at the beginning burst forth. I expect the CD sales will be terrific."

She glanced away as her mind went blank. What else could she say? Her heart raced. She had never in a million years expected to run into Matt without her disguise. Vancouver was a big city, what were the odds?

"How serious are you and the man you're with?" he asked abruptly.

She swung back, startled. "Kevin? We're friends. Have been for years."

"Do you ever expand your circle of friends?"

Slowly Karla began to smile. He was trying to pick her up. It gave her an entirely new view of her boss.

"It depends," she said.

He definitely hadn't recognized her! Of course with her own short dark hair, the lack of aging makeup, wig and glasses—not to mention the fun, flirty dress she wore—probably no one would recognize the staid Miss Jones.

He glanced around again—looking for Kevin? she wondered.

"I have to go out of town this weekend, but I'll call you when I get back," he said, bringing his focus back to her. "We could have dinner together one night this week." He raised an eyebrow in question.

Karla's mind went totally blank. She stared at him, wondering why fate had decided to give her the job, then snatch it away in such an unlikely manner.

"Karla? Would you have dinner with me one night this week?" he repeated.

Her thoughts whirling, she opened her mouth to refuse. Then snapped it shut and gave him a polite smile, feeling like her face would crack. "I, um, I'm not sure of my schedule."

"Busy lady," he murmured. "I'll call you and you can check."

Idiot, she told herself. You should have pretended Kevin was the love of your life. How was she going to gracefully get out of this mess?

"If you give me your phone number," he said when she remained silent.

Had he already asked her that? Hesitantly, she gave him the number of her cell phone. Was she playing with fire? She wasn't sure he'd call, much less that she'd go through with a date. She could say she was busy.

Then she almost laughed. Did he realize she was older than his dating limit? She'd often been told she looked younger than her age. Maybe she should mention she was twenty-eight and nip this in the bud.

"Karla, there you are." Kevin joined them, balancing two full glasses. He handed her one. "As requested."

He looked inquiringly at Matt.

"Kevin Fowler, this is Matt Gramling. A new… acquaintance," Karla said, with a provocative look at Matt. She was feeling much more secure. And it was unlikely he'd ever call.

"Matt." Kevin shook hands. "Enjoying the performance?"

"Very much, now," he said.

Karla sipped her sparkling water, aware of a tingling

sensation dancing across her skin. All thoughts of fatigue had fled. There was no denying just being around Matt—whether at work or in the lobby of a crowded theater—had her wide awake and alert.

And again very aware of him as a man. What would it be like to go out together? To spend some time talking about non-business topics. To learn more about the complex man who now headed Kinsinger Electronics.

The lights flickered, indicating time to return to their seats.

"I'll be in touch," Matt promised.

She watched him stride away, soon caught up in the swirl of bodies moving back into the theater. For a second the evening went flat. Then she smiled at Kevin. He was a nice man who had been her friend for years. She usually enjoyed going out with him, they had fun and there was no pressure. Neither felt any spark with the other, so their relationship was uncluttered by sexual overtones.

But something told her going out with Matt Gramling—if she dared—would not provide the easygoing companionship being with Kevin did. There were definitely sexual overtones—in spades. Was she the only one to notice?

Knowing Matt planned to be gone all weekend, Karla didn't expect to hear from him. When her cell phone rang early Sunday afternoon, she was surprised. Snatching it from her purse, she flipped it open.

"Hello?"

"Karla? Matt Gramling. I said I'd call."

"So you did." She sat on the sofa, a silly grin spreading on her face. "I also thought you said you'd be out of town this weekend."

"I was. Just got back."

And called her first thing? That gave her food for thought.

"Where were you?" she asked.

"I have access to a cabin up on Henley Island. I flew up to check it out. It'll come in handy to get away from the city when things get hectic at work."

She knew from the paperwork she'd seen during the past week that he owned and piloted his own floatation plane. If she had a view of the harbor, she might have been able to watch him take off or land this weekend. The shuttle planes routinely used the harbor, but private planes were rare.

"And is it nice?"

"It'll do. Are you free this afternoon? Since I got back earlier than originally planned, I thought you could show me around a bit and I'll buy you dinner."

Warning bells clanged. Karla knew better than to tempt fate. How long could she ever expect to keep two personas separate if she flaunted both of them at Matt?

But the idea of spending some time with him outside of the company tantalized. He was a fascinating and complex individual. Wouldn't it help at work to understand him better? And he wasn't asking for anything more than sight-seeing and dinner. She'd probably be home by eight.

"Okay," she said. "Where shall I meet you?"

"I'll come pick you up," he said.

Definitely not a good idea.

"How about I meet you at Canada Place? Do you know where that is?"

"Of course. It's near where I have my plane moored."

Canada Place was a landmark in Vancouver—the embarkation point for all the cruise lines that stopped on their way to and from Alaska.

"Say in thirty minutes?"

It wouldn't take her that long to get there, but she did have to change and do something about her hair!

"It's windy today, dress warmly," he said.

She clicked off the phone, giddy with anticipation. Darting into the bedroom, she flung open the closet door and almost groaned. What would be suitable for a casual afternoon, warm—and also be appropriate for dinner later?

If he was serious about seeing the sights, it wouldn't matter. She drew her shirt over her head and snagged a yellow sweater. Pulling it on, she fluffed her hair.

Makeup, definitely. She applied carefully, hoping she looked far, far different from Miss Jones.

And forget glasses—even sunglasses. She didn't want to give him a hint to remind him of her alter persona.

Ready in fifteen minutes, she let herself out of her flat and walked briskly toward the waterfront. The air was crisp and clean. The sun shone in a cloudless sky. The wind was cool, holding a tang of salt as it blew in from the water. As she drew near the rendezvous point, she could feel her heart rate increase in anticipation.

Karla spotted him long before he saw her. She watched as he leaned against the railing, studying the pleasure boats in the water. He checked his watch once or twice.

In the office he had the patience of Job. Was he impatiently waiting to see her?

She almost skipped with delight. Then stopped dead. Was she an idiot? She could blow everything with a careless word, or even a hint of similarity between herself and "Miss Jones."

Matt looked up and spotted her—his eyes narrowed as he watched her slowly approach. What was he thinking? she wondered. Then she forgot to think as his gaze drew her closer.

"Hi," Karla said when she drew near. The worry of exposure jumped to the forefront of her mind.

"Hi, yourself." His gaze traveled down the jacket, over the bright yellow sweater and down the long legs encased in snug black pants.

Karla let her own gaze drift over Matt. The thick cable-knit sweater lovingly encased broad shoulders, tapering to a narrow waist. His own dark cords added to the casual look. Glancing up, she smiled. His hair looked great wind-tossed and sun-burnished. Just as she'd wanted to see it. She just wished she could brush it with her fingertips—just once—to see what it felt like.

Feeling as if she were balancing on a tightrope stretched across Capilano Canyon, she threw caution to the wind. She'd have her afternoon, and do her best to make sure he never connected her with his superior secretary!

"So you want to see Vancouver, huh? Where are you from?" She hoped she didn't get her facts mixed up—in which persona she was learning things.

"Toronto most recently." He turned and they started walking along the seawalk. The wide pedestrian path was dotted here and there with others strolling in the balmy afternoon sunshine.

"I've never been there. I bet it isn't any prettier than Vancouver," she said, loyal to her birthplace.

"It's different. This is a beautiful city. Tell me what you think I should see first."

"You can't see it all in one day," she warned. "Especially starting out this late."

"Then maybe you'll take pity on me and offer a second tour."

She grinned. "I suspect pity is the last thing you ever need. You seem more the bold pirate type to me."

He took her hand and placed it in the crook of his elbow, covering her fingers with his. "I go after what I want," he said.

Her heart skidded, began to pound. She'd seen his business side, now she was getting a full blast from the personal side. The way his fingers caressed hers set her pulse pounding, her skin tingling and her mind doing somersaults. How could anyone keep things straight when going into sensory overload?

"Then we have something in common," she said. "I do, too."

She glanced up at him from beneath her lashes and smiled a slow, provocative smile. "Let's start with Stanley Park, shall we?"

"I'm in your hands."

She wished for a moment that was true. Hadn't she fantasized about being in his? Shaking off the memories of her daydreams, Karla began to relate what she knew about the famous park at the edge of the city. He stopped her after a few moments, saying he hadn't invited her out to be a tour guide.

"And what are you looking for?" she asked.

"I'll know it when I see it. How about just a friend for now."

He was flirting with her, that she could tell. She liked it even though it meant nothing. After today, if she were smart, she wouldn't see him again. She'd have to decide—her job or a flirtation with Matt Gramling.

Her career was too important to risk.

"So tell me something about Matt Gramling," she invited. Something I don't already know, she thought. Something special just for me.

"Born and raised in the east. Moved here two weeks ago. Though I've visited Vancouver in the past."

She looked up at him. "That's all? How succinct. No family, no ties?"

His face took on a hard look. "No family. No ties."

"Everyone has family—either a birth family or one made later."

"I don't."

"Why not?"

His expression grew cold. "My parents are dead. I had no brothers or sisters."

"So you've become part of an extended family with close friends, a wife, kids."

He shook his head. "It's never happened and it won't."

Karla grew quiet at the remoteness in his tone. Everyone had family, she thought. What had happened to shut him off from others? The closed look to his face ended her inquiries on that topic. But her curiosity rose.

Sooner or later, if they kept seeing each other, she'd open the topic again. She was close to her family, couldn't imagine anyone not having someone.

As the silence grew, Karla began to talk about inane things to fill the void. By the time they reached the Totem Poles in Stanley Park, Matt had thawed enough to ask questions. Things seemed on an even keel again when they stopped to examine the Indian carvings.

Karla was congratulating herself on the success of the afternoon when he looked at her and said, "I figured it out, you know."

Catching her breath, she looked at him, hoping her expression gave nothing away. "Figured what out? How the Indians carved them?"

"Who you are."

Her heart skidded, then seem to stop. Only one week, it wasn't enough. She loved her new job, had wanted to work there for years—not be exposed after only one week. It wasn't fair!

"And that is?" She hoped her voice sounded right—slightly interested, intrigued even. She'd go down fighting.

"Miss Jeannette Jones's niece."

She blinked. "Jeannette Jones's niece?"

"The resemblance is remarkable. It came to me after we parted at the theater the other night."

She swallowed hard. "Oh?"

He nodded.

"How do you know Jeannette Jones?" she almost stammered, stalling for time. What was she going to do? How much of a leap was it from that to the truth?

"She started work for me last week. And since she's

single and never been married, I figured you had to be her niece, right? The resemblance is almost uncanny. Of course, she's quite a few years older.''

Karla looked at the Totem Poles wishing they could provide her with the answer to his question. Did she go along with his idea, or confess all?

She definitely should not have accepted his invitation today.

''So you're the hotshot executive who's going to turn Kinsinger Electronics into a major player in the electronics field,'' she said, trying to bluff her way through. If she got home without discovery, she'd never risk it again!

''I plan to—with the help of people like your aunt. She's a great addition to the company.''

Karla forced a smile, wishing she'd never started this convoluted plan. And she was playing with fire trying to see him personally. Was she crazy?

''That's good to hear.'' She smiled involuntarily. Would he ever tell Jeannette that to her face?

''Come by the office next week. I'll take you and your aunt out to lunch.''

CHAPTER THREE

KARLA had a life-size picture of that! Quickly she tried to come up with an excuse—without clueing him in. Maybe she could say she was being transferred—to Nova Scotia. Or that she worked nights and had to sleep days. Or there was a family feud and she and her aunt weren't speaking.

"I'll have to see," she said when the silence had gone on almost too long to not be noticeable. The last thing she wanted was for him to suspect anything. "Would you like to see the rose gardens?"

"I'd rather head back toward Gas Town, and get an early dinner. I didn't have any lunch and the walk and all this fresh air has made me hungry."

"Gas Town, huh? Have you seen it?" she asked. The older part of the city was a favorite spot of tourists, and some of the more carefree of Vancouver's citizens. Full of trendy shops, pubs and restaurants, it was a favorite area of the city for Karla.

"The flat I've sublet for a few months is nearby. I've eaten in the district almost every night since I arrived."

"Maybe you need some variety."

"A home-cooked meal?" he asked. "I wouldn't turn one down."

"Then let's hope someone offers you one," she said, sidestepping the issue, and starting back toward the center of town. All she wanted to do was get dinner over

42

with and get back to the safety of her flat where she would swear off a dual existence forever!

"I thought you might be that someone," he said provocatively.

She shrugged, though the thought of him coming to her apartment, hovering over her while she prepared dinner, was tantalizing. "Maybe one day." When pigs flew.

Or when the masquerade was over and everything aboveboard.

"I'll hold you to that."

The wind from the sea had picked up as the afternoon waned. It was cooler walking back along the seawalk. As if in one mind, they both picked up the pace.

"Tell me about your seaplane," she asked as she spotted several moored in the harbor.

He looked at her sharply. "How did you know I have a floatation plane?"

"You mentioned it when I asked if you knew where Canada Place was. Have you had it a long time?"

"A few years. I bought it to get away to some of the remote spots in the Yukon. I can land on a lake and not have to worry about finding an airport."

"The Yukon? Do you hunt and fish?"

"Occasionally—but only to catch dinner. I fly to the wilderness to escape the trappings of civilization. Camping gives me a release. Ever try it?"

She shook her head. "It must be fun, a lot of people seem to do it." She was starting to feel a bit breathless with their pace. Matt's legs were longer than hers and she was hard-pressed to keep up.

"I don't know about fun, but it's the best stress reducer I know. Using the plane, I can fly into spots where no one has been in years. Hiking and exploring some of the last wilderness areas gives me a chance to relax. My best business ideas come at the end of a long weekend off by myself.''

''Man against nature?''

''You could say that. It hones skills most men have lost living in a city.''

''Doesn't it worry you that you'll get stranded or something catastrophic might happen so far from civilization?''

He shrugged. ''I like being challenged, and overcoming odds.''

She nodded—it figured. Hadn't she seen him as more than just a businessman? There was a latent restlessness about him. Being confined in the office every day wasn't his natural milieu. He appeared more real today, striding into the wind, with the sea beside him and the wind tossing his hair.

''Obviously no family in the picture,'' Karla murmured, thankful to spot the edge of Gas Town. The steam clock clearly visible in the distance. ''They'd be worried sick if you took off for long without a way to communicate.''

He shrugged. ''As I said earlier, none in the picture present or future.''

''You can't discount the future. Don't you plan to get married?''

''No, I don't plan to get married. How about you, anxious to tie the knot?''

She shook her head. ''Nuh, uh. Not for a long, long time.''

''That's surprising, most women I know can't wait to

get married—preferably to the man with the biggest bank account.''

''Wow, Cynics-R-Us. Maybe you're hanging around the wrong women,'' Karla said, taken aback at the vehemence in his tone.

''You're saying you wouldn't marry a man who had a big bank account?''

''I'm not sure a bank account is anything I'd care about at the onset. Don't you think compatibility and love should count somewhere in there?''

''Love? A purely feminine concept to cover the more honest emotion of lust. Which, once it moves on, leaves nothing!''

''Good grief, you *are* a cynic. Who burned you?''

He stopped at the traffic signal. Looking at her, Matt narrowed his eyes. ''Once a long time ago a woman promised love and devotion. We were planning to marry—until she found out the size of my bank account compared to a friend's. It didn't take long for her to correct her mistake. So much for love and devotion.''

''And you were so hurt you won't chance your heart again,'' Karla murmured.

''No. I was never in love, as you say. Celine and I enjoyed each other's company, she was good in bed. But once she showed her true colors, I moved on. Only this time, wiser to the ploys of women.''

''Sounds like you got a lucky escape. But not all women are like that, greedy for money and not the man. Most women marry for love.''

''I'd expect you to say that. Who wants to admit to being mercenary?''

''At least I didn't disappoint you,'' she retorted. ''So

because of one bad experience, you've sworn off women?''

"No. I like women. I enjoy being with them. I've enjoyed being with you today. I've sworn off marriage.''

"Do you want to grow old all alone?''

"If that begins to bother me in my declining years, I'll buy a wife. You're a fine one to talk. There's no wedding ring on your finger.''

"I didn't swear off marriage, but it's not something I'm looking for at the moment. Besides, I haven't met the right man.''

"You call me cynical. But with those rose-colored glasses you wear, I'm surprised you can walk around without bumping into buildings. How will you recognize *the right man?*''

Karla began to cross the street when the light changed, wondering how seriously Matt wished to hear her views.

"I would expect there would be some attraction between us.''

Like the instant attraction she seemed to feel whenever she was around Matt? Heck, she didn't have to be around him, she could just think about him and feel weightless.

That thought made her pause. "Of course we'd have to have a lot in common,'' she rushed to add. "Likes and interests shared, that kind of thing. And I think our goals should be the same—both want the same thing from a marriage.''

"And what if you meet some guy who's a bum, and there's that lighting strike of attraction? You're telling me you'd pursue it? I don't think so.''

She laughed. "Matt, I'm not going to find some bum and fall for him.''

"Because of his bank balance."

"Because I don't hang out where bums hang out. I also don't hang out where the really rich do, either. So the chances of finding and falling for a really rich guy are somewhere between slim and none. Get real."

He indicated a small restaurant, holding the door for her. Inside it was dark and modest, with few people occupying the tables. It was early, more tables would fill up later.

"It doesn't look like much, but the food's terrific," he said.

"I like pubs," she said, taking in the dark walls and large chairs. It didn't take long to be seated, and soon Karla was avidly studying the menu. The fresh air had caused her to work up an appetite.

Ordering shepard's pie, she looked at Matt, wondering if he planned to take up the discussion about matrimony again. His views were controversial, and a bit sad.

She wondered who the woman had been who had scorned him for his rich friend. And if she had any clue of the havoc she left in her wake. Was he protesting too much, or did he really not feel hurt any longer because of that woman's defection? Guys rarely expressed feelings like that. And she suspected Matt was more reticent than most.

He looked up and caught her gaze. "One of the things that caught my eye with you I saw at the play. You were with a date, but not hanging over him. Not trying to pretend you were the only person in the theater he should acknowledge."

"Kevin and I are friends, nothing more."

"Then I want us to become friends. But nothing more.

I suspected we might have something in common—a dislike of ties."

"I don't dislike ties."

"I phrased it wrong. You are not looking for a husband, right?"

She hesitated a moment. "Not now, at least."

"Knowing from the onset that there is no chance of a long-term relationship should keep things from getting sticky later."

She almost smiled. "You mean when we stop seeing each other?"

"I hate clinging women."

"And I would have said earlier that I disliked egotistical men. But I find you—" she tilted her head to the left, considering "—fascinating. You might want to work on that arrogance, however."

His eyes gleamed with humor.

"Want to work on it yourself?"

"Whoa, that's a tempting offer."

"Do we have a deal?"

She hesitated a moment. What of her commitment to stay as far from him as she could during non-working hours? Wasn't she playing with fire to see him again? But the afternoon had been so much fun—all from spending time with him.

"Deal. No entanglements for either of us! Friends only."

She dare not get too close—not if she wanted to keep her job with Kinsinger. He had nothing to worry about. Today would give them an idea of the limit of their involvement, she thought, as the waiter approached their table. They could talk, do things together, and share a meal. But nothing more!

"So, tell me how a closet woodsman became head of an electronics firm," she said once their orders had been taken.

He leaned back in his chair, stretching out his long legs beneath the table. He brushed against Karla. Deliberately? Awareness flooded through her at his touch. After he'd released her hand on their walk, she'd made sure they hadn't touched again. It was easier to pay attention to what was going one without her body going haywire from direct contact.

She didn't move, fearing he'd read more into the gesture than was warranted. Hadn't she tried to match his own detachment? But she was fully aware of the warmth emanating from his leg, of the tingling waves of excitement. Swallowing hard, she tried to focus on what he was saying and ignore the sensations that raced through her.

"I had to work my way through college. My sophomore year, I got a job at a rundown printing firm. They were barely making ends meet, and tried to cut corners by hiring the lowest-paid workers they could. One day, I made a suggestion to the manager. He thought about it for a while then implemented it. In less than two months, they started turning a profit for the first time in years."

She smiled, she was such a sucker for a happy ending. "So you were the hero of the hour. Had you studied business economics in college? Were you applying course work?"

He shook his head. "I was still in the basic breadth course work stage, hadn't had any business courses yet.

It was a gut feel, common sense, as I saw it. But it taught me one important fact.''

"And that was?"

"That not everyone in business has that common sense approach. And not a lot of people are willing to take risks on gut feelings.''

"But you are."

"I am.''

"So the company became a success?"

He nodded.

"Did you get a raise?"

Matt hesitated a moment, then a gleam shone in his eye. "Actually, I ended up getting partial ownership, and really studied the dynamics of the company. By the time I graduated from the university, I'd changed the entire way it was run, and it was making money hand over fist. It still brings in a hefty annual return.''

"So a businessman was born. What did you do next?"

He sat up when the waiter arrived with their meal, waiting until he left before looking back at Karla.

She missed the warmth from his leg when he changed positions. But at least she could concentrate more fully on what he was saying without the zinging electrical current zapping through her. She took a deep breath, hoping to keep her hormones under control. They were merely acquaintances who were sharing dinner. Nothing more. Matt had made sure his views were known. If a woman was foolish enough to think she'd get more, she had only herself to blame if he broke off early.

Karla knew she wasn't foolish enough to expect more than a casual date now and again. But that would be enough. She could learn more about her boss, and hopefully find ways to work more smoothly with him because of it.

And find ways to ignore the tingling attacks that happened only around Matt.

"There has to be more interesting things to discuss than my business background."

"Not to me," she said, fascinated by this glimpse of the man she'd been working with for a week. It gave her an idea of how he'd become so successful. The drive and determination were ingrained. She had a lot to learn from him. But more importantly, she wanted to glean every bit of knowledge she could about this fascinating man to satisfy her feminine curiosity.

"What do you do? I'll see if I can tell you some stories that would tie in with your own career."

Karla's mind went absolutely blank. She stared at him, conscious of the way his hair was still a bit wind-tossed, of the breadth of his shoulders in the sweater, of the focus of those clear blue eyes.

"I'm a secretary," she said finally. Please don't let him ask where.

"Like your aunt?"

She hesitated, then shrugged. Actually her only aunt was a veterinarian, but Matt didn't have to know that. He thought she was her own aunt.

"Where?"

"At a small firm near the financial district. I want to hear more about your career. You didn't just leave the printing firm for the electronics one, did you? What did you do between the university and now?"

She picked up her fork and took a bite of food. She couldn't talk if she were eating. She hoped he'd take the question seriously and tell her more. She liked listening to him talk. His voice was deep and dark. For a second, she wondered how it would sound whispering words of passion and love.

She choked on her food and quickly reached for her water glass. She refused to give in to fantasies about this man. Tonight was a one-off deal. Hereafter she'd do better to stick to work and not give in to temptation to spend personal time with him. If he ever even called again.

He began to cut the steak he'd ordered, glancing at her when she coughed. "Are you all right?"

She nodded, sipping the water to calm her throat.

"Tell me what happened after the printer's," she said when she could speak again. This time she'd keep her thoughts firmly on what he was saying and not daydream about hearing his voice in the dark!

"I found from that first place that I had an aptitude for turning around troubled situations. Once I had a bit of money set aside, I went looking to see if I could repeat what I'd done. Or if it were a fluke."

"It wasn't. I just bet you've been totally successful right from the start." She couldn't wait to hear the next success tale.

"Yes and no. The next venture was in sporting goods. A retail store in Toronto. That took a bit longer to turn around. And it was then I met Celine."

"Celine?"

"The woman I asked to marry me."

"Oh." Karla was dying to hear all about her. But hadn't a clue how to get him to talk without appearing blatantly curious.

She waved her hand dismissingly. "She sounds like a fool anyway."

"Why?"

"Choosing someone else over you."

He studied Karla over the table.

She looked up and met his gaze, feeling that same tingling sensation she'd felt when his leg had brushed against hers.

"What?"

"An interesting observation from someone who professes not to be interested in a long-term relationship—or marriage. Why was she a fool?"

She laughed. "Get real. I bet since she dumped you that you've made a mint. Nothing like wanting to better someone for strictly personal reasons to goad a person to achieve new highs. You probably out-earn your former friend hand over fist. If Celine knew, she'd be furious with herself."

"Not interested in bank accounts?" he said silkily.

"Come on, Matt, it's obvious. If you've done well in the first firm when you were so young, you probably did better in your next venture with experience behind you. Don't you think it only makes sense? You've done printing, sporting goods and security systems, now electronics. Obviously you know what you're doing, and with each success you can, and I bet do, demand a bigger piece of the pie. I know that much about how business works."

He put down his fork. "How did you know about the security systems?"

Karla's heart stopped for a second. "You told me," she said brazenly. He had, but not today, she realized.

She knew because he was still involved with the company in Toronto and, as Jeannette Jones, she'd had access to that information. "It's the firm you just left behind in Toronto."

God, she would never pull this off! He'd know instantly he hadn't mentioned it today. It wouldn't take him two seconds to guess where she'd learned it—then fire her on the spot.

Matt looked away, as if thinking. Karla took another sip of water, wondering how long it would be before he—

"I'm more tired than I thought. I don't remember talking about it."

"If you're tired from your weekend, we can eat quickly and call it a day," she said. What had started as a lark was proving to be more of a strain than she expected. Especially when she made a glaring faux pas like that one.

If she could just make it safely through, she vowed, she would not challenge fate again. It would be strictly business only from now on.

"I didn't think I was that tired," he said dryly. "At least I'm not yawning openly like you were last Friday night."

She cringed. "Please, let's forget that evening. I can't believe I almost dozed off during the production. I do try to get enough rest—like getting in early on Sundays," she said, trying to change the subject before he examined it further. "I have a busy week ahead and still have to get my clothes lined up for the week. I've had a great time this afternoon, but do need to go home soon so I can wash my hair and all." She was babbling, she knew it, but all she wanted to do was end the evening as quickly as possible before disaster fell.

Matt nodded gravely. "I can see that washing your hair would take a long time."

She blushed and began eating with gusto. Her short hair took no time to wash and dry. It was the easiest style to care for.

"Meet me for lunch tomorrow," Matt said.

"Can't, Monday's my busiest day."

"Tuesday, then?"

She met his eyes and shrugged. "I'll have to check my calendar at work. I don't get a long lunch hour." And if he pushed, she'd make sure she was busy every single day!

"Ask your boss for more time one day. It can't hurt. I'm sure your aunt would like to show off Kinsinger Electronics."

"Mmm." She was almost finished. Glancing at his plate, she almost groaned. He had over half his meal left. Was there any way to encourage him to eat faster?

Dodging pitfalls for potential exposure during the rest of the meal, Karla was relieved when Matt finally called for the check. She alternated between being fascinated with their conversation, and scared silly she'd say something stupid and blow her cover.

When they walked out of the restaurant, she smiled and held out her hand.

"Thanks for dinner. And this afternoon. I hope you enjoyed seeing Stanley Park."

He took her hand and tucked it in the crook of his arm, not shaking it goodbye like she wanted.

"I'm taking you home. We'll get a cab." He looked down the street.

"Actually, I don't live too far away, I can walk."

Raising one eyebrow, he shrugged. "If you like, but it's colder than earlier. I think a cab would be better."

"I can get home by myself."

"Is there a reason you don't want me taking you to your apartment? I didn't plan to invite myself in. What with you having to do your hair and all."

Karla bit her bottom lip. He was teasing her. She almost giggled. It did sound stupid. But she was afraid he'd remember the address that had been on her résumé.

"No reason at all," she said faintly. None she could give him.

He hailed a cab and in less time than she wanted, they pulled to a stop in front of her apartment building.

Matt climbed out and held the door for her. She didn't see any evidence of suspicion. He asked the driver to wait, which Karla took as a good sign, then went with her into the building.

Arriving on her floor, he walked her to the door of her flat.

"Thanks again," she said, fishing out her keys. "I had a great time." Inserting them in the lock, she opened the door and turned back one last time.

Matt was right there. He put his hands on her shoulders and leaned closer to brush his lips against hers. "Thanks for going out on such short notice, friend."

She nodded, incapable of speech. She thought her brain circuits had just been fried. Touching the tip of her tongue lightly to her lips, she imagined she could taste him.

With a soft groan, Matt pulled her into his arms and kissed her again. This was no brush of lips, but a full lips-moving-against-lips, tongue-tracing-the-seam, plunging-in-for-a-taste kiss.

Karla wrapped her arms around him and held on, thrilled with the excitement that exploded. His mouth was warm and electrifying, giving new meaning to the term kissed. His arms were strong, yet held her gently, sensually. His body was hard, pressing against her, making her conscious of her own softer curves and femininity.

When he broke the kiss, it was all she could do to remain upright. She'd never suffered from wobbly knees before meeting Matt Gramling. Now it seemed it was a regular occurrence. She was vaguely pleased to notice he was breathing as hard as she was. At least it hadn't been all one-sided.

"If you don't call by Tuesday, I'll call you," he said. Then he turned and headed for the elevator.

Karla watched until the doors slid closed behind him, then entered the flat. It was too bad he'd sworn off marriage—he needed to be locked up to protect the rest of womankind!

"Good grief," she said. "I'm in big trouble here." Dashing to the front window, she leaned her forehead against it to see the cab on the street below. In only seconds, Matt came out and climbed in.

"Don't go acting like some love-struck teenager," she murmured, watching as the cab drove away. "There is definitely no future in it!" Matt had made that clear.

But for a second, Karla thought it might be too late for such sage advice.

Turning from the window, she tried to come up with a way to refuse lunch without making an issue about it.

One of the things Matt Gramling had always prided himself on was the ability to compartmentalize his life. There was work. Business consumed most of his waking hours. He liked it that way. The challenges and problems to be dealt with gave him an outlet to be creative and innovative. The successful solutions gave satisfaction. Knowing he was building for the future, expanding and making a difference in the lives of hundreds of employees was fulfilling.

Of course when he took his wilderness trips, he closed off the business end and focused on nature, on the feel of the land, of the challenges living off the earth afforded. On the contentment he felt at the end of each day, falling asleep by a fire, knowing once more he'd pitted himself against the elements and won.

Rarely did he need to compartmentalize relationships. He dated casually, enjoying the company of women. Sometimes even developing an intimate aspect that lasted for months on end. But when apart, he had other things to think about.

Until this morning.

He threw down his pen and rose, walking to the window with the view of Coal Harbour and Vancouver's North Shore. He didn't see it, however. Before him danced an image of Karla Jones. He remembered her funny comments. Heard her laugh. Almost felt her in his arms again.

Had he been too long between women? Winding up his day-to-day involvement in the Toronto firm had been grueling. And plunging into Kinsinger Electronics, with a self-imposed mandate to turn it around as quickly as he could, was equally consuming. He hadn't had a date in months since the one planned for last Friday had not panned out.

Until yesterday.

He'd been up-front and clear with Karla. He wasn't looking for a long-term relationship. Fortunately, neither was she. That's just how he liked things.

While they had hit it off, she had not seemed excited for a second date. In fact, he had the feeling she was stalling. Deliberately not accepting a date in any way shape or form. Had he misread the signs?

Hearing a noise in the outer office, Matt turned and crossed to the opened door. Jeannette straightened after putting away her purse.

For a moment, he was able to observe her without her being aware of his presence. The resemblance between Karla and Jeannette was strong, but as he studied her, he could see the differences. Jeannette was a bit heavier, as was common with women in their fifties. And her hair was long, gray, pulled back into a tidy, neat bun, with never a strand out of place.

Karla's dark, glossy hair had danced in the wind yesterday.

"Good morning."

She looked up, startled. Then nodded gravely. "Good morning, Mr. Gramling."

He almost smiled. She persisted in holding to formality.

"I met your niece this weekend." He didn't need to tell her. But unless Karla had called her aunt after he left her at her flat, Jeannette wouldn't know. And for some reason, he wanted her to know.

"Karla?" she asked.

He nodded. "We went to dinner last night."

"Oh." She remained silent.

"Is there a problem?"

Shaking her head, she picked up a pad and two pencils. "No problem," she said.

One day he would find out something that was a problem for her. But thankfully his dating her niece wasn't one.

CHAPTER FOUR

EACH morning, Matt liked to meet with Jeannette first thing to prioritize tasks for the day. And to touch base. Then he let her get on with her own work. He liked that time before the frenetic pace of the day took hold. It had been his practice for years. Meeting with Jeannette was different from his morning briefings with Sara in Toronto, however.

Jeannette brought something more to the meetings. A fresh way of looking at things. A willingness to voice her opinions. And a sense of serenity that was oddly appealing to a man who thrived on the fast pace of business.

Once they were seated in his office, he reviewed the reports he'd read that weekend at the cabin—several needed more in-depth analysis from the managers and he directed her to obtain them. Two deserved special praise for being so complete and he asked her to draft a note to that effect in his name.

He glanced up and found Jeannette's gaze on his mouth. For a second he was startled.

She met his gaze and promptly dropped her own to the tablet. A hint of color stained her cheeks.

For an awkward moment, Matt felt nonplussed. Was she wondering if he'd kissed her niece? The memory of those kisses burned into his mind. He could still feel the effects twelve hours later and half a city away.

He glanced at Jeannette's mouth. There was a faint

sheen as if she wore some kind of lip gloss, but it wasn't the bright red lipstick Karla had worn. And her lips were tightened—with disapproval?

Hell, maybe it was going to be a problem dating her niece after all.

"You mentioned on Friday that you wanted me to set up a meeting with the Percell Group this week. I couldn't reach Richard Taylor on Friday, so will continue to try this morning," Jeannette said primly.

Matt tossed one of the reports across the desk. "That's the report by Myers about the Percell Group. Apparently they were one of our biggest customers a year or so ago. We dropped the ball and they went elsewhere. I want to get them back. You might want to read the report. I think this is a deal that with the right touch, will bring a major turnaround in the company. A lot of bang for the buck."

"You still want an initial lunch meeting?"

"Yes."

"Why?"

He looked up. "What?"

"I'm just wondering why you'd want a lunch meeting instead of meeting here where you'd be able to get facts and figures at the touch of a finger. At lunch, you'll be winging it."

He nodded. "This is the preliminary round. I want to meet the decision-makers. See what they are like. Find out what they want, then tailor a presentation to match their needs."

She looked thoughtful. "So you're not just selling them on how great we are now."

"We aren't great right now. It'll take time to turn the company around. And one way to do it is make sure we give the customer exactly what he wants. But we need to find that out, not assume we can make that determination based on what we think he should want.''

''So maybe I should do a bit more background work, myself,'' she murmured.

''In what way?''

''I could ask Mr. Taylor's secretary what his likes and dislikes are. Get a feel from that perspective.''

He nodded. ''Good idea. But don't push it if she's reluctant.''

''I'll be the soul of discretion.''

''I know I can count on you, Jeannette.'' He hesitated a moment, then added, ''Include yourself in for lunch. If you're going to be my right hand, might as well see this project through from the beginning. I want input from you, as well, if you see something I've missed. Or the managers haven't thought about.''

Not for the first time Karla wondered if what she was doing would end up in a total disaster. The ideal job, and she was playing fast and loose with her boss. For the first time she gave serious thought to coming clean with everything before he was convinced of her abilities.

It was after nine by the time Karla returned to her desk. Matt had reviewed plans and requested meetings and scheduled conference calls for the rest of the day. He'd also asked her to draft responses to most of the mail he'd received.

Even with a full day's work ahead, she almost danced to her desk. She loved the responsibility he gave her, relished the challenge.

After only a week, he was loading her up with important tasks, utilizing her skills and experience—and her own innate sense of business which she'd garnered under Mr. Daniels's tutelage. And already talking as if she was his right hand! She was going to show him how competent a twenty-eight-year-old could be.

In the center of her desk lay an envelope addressed in printed letters to *Miss Jones*. Placing the folders and correspondence from Matt's office down, she picked up the envelope and opened it.

A single typewritten sheet was inside with a very brief missive.

I know who you are. Don't you think Matt Gramling would find it interesting?

Karla sank onto her chair, rereading the words in stunned disbelief.

She rose and went to peer into the reception area, but the hallway was empty all the way to the elevator. Glancing over her shoulder, she was relieved to see Matt had not followed her to ask what she was doing. Who could have put the note on her desk? And why?

Folding the sheet, she slipped it into its envelope and slid it into her purse. What did it mean? Was someone planning to blow the whistle on her?

She definitely needed to speed up her schedule to let Matt know her age.

She took a deep breath and reached out to sort the work in front of her. Not yet, though. She still had to show she was indispensable before risking his knowing who she really was. Or rather, how old she really was.

Who could have sent the note? Briefly she toyed with various managers she'd met over the last week. Somehow it didn't seem like it could be any of them.

It took effort, but Karla gradually pushed away her

curiosity about the note and plunged into the work piled on her desk. She'd have to worry about that later, she had things to do.

She called Mr. Taylor's secretary at the Percell Group and forthrightly explained what she was interested in learning. After ascertaining his preferences, she asked to be connected to arrange a lunch meeting.

He'd been gracious on the phone, agreeing to a Thursday lunch. His wife would accompany him, he said. Karla knew that from the secretary's information. While not divulging anything of a confidential nature, the woman had told her she often thought Mrs. Taylor was the driving force behind the company.

After spending Sunday afternoon together, it proved harder than Karla had expected to ignore Matt during the workday. She could hear the murmur of his voice through the open door when he spoke on the phone. And she'd remembered his voice at dinner. She heard his laughter once, and her heart skipped a beat. She wished she could see his face. She knew she'd be mesmerized.

As when he'd been reviewing the day's schedule earlier, she'd practically been mesmerized by his mouth. Those lips had kissed her like she'd never been kissed before. For a moment she grew dreamy just remembering.

His catching her staring had embarrassed her, but the warmth from the memory of those kisses remained. She found herself anticipating briefing him on the Percell Group lunch plans—just to see him again.

She stepped in his office before lunch.

When she told him of the confirmed luncheon date, he jotted the appointment in his personal calendar. "Good work. I like the fact we'll be taking him to his favorite restaurant. That was a good idea to question the secretary.''

She nodded, reluctant to leave.

He looked at her for a moment. ''What would you do if someone called you to ask you the same thing?''

''Tell them what was available for public knowledge— to foster a feeling of cooperation. Unfortunately, I don't yet know which restaurant is your favorite here in Vancouver.''

''I'll have to try several, I can see. I invited your niece to lunch one day this week. I hope you'll join us. Maybe you or she can suggest a place I would enjoy.''

''I can call her if you like.'' Karla had a brilliant idea—she'd pretend to call herself and tell Matt the only day she could make lunch was Thursday. For a long-term solution, it only bought her a little time. But better than being put on the spot. If she had any sense at all she'd forget seeing Matt socially.

But common sense seemed in short supply today. Despite the pitfalls of last evening, she wanted to spend time with him. Wanted to see him away from the office. Maybe share another kiss or two?

She knew she should just tell him as Karla she wasn't interested. But there was no way she could lie that much. There was something very alluring about Matt Gramling. And the truth was she did want to see him again. He'd said he wanted to be friends. She could test the waters— see how it went.

The image of that note on her desk flashed into mind. For one crazy moment she almost considered confiding in him the next time she saw him as Karla. What did the sender plan to accomplish?

By the end of the day, Karla was having second, third and fourth thoughts about her brilliant plan. She loved her new job, relished working with Matt, but the strain of the whole scheme was beginning to wear. Especially with the threat of the letter writer hanging over her.

She'd told Matt in the late afternoon that Karla couldn't make lunch. He'd nodded and moved on to other topics. She couldn't tell if he were disappointed or not. Maybe he was only following up because he'd said he would and it really didn't matter one way or another. The thought left her a bit disappointed.

Karla had just stepped out of her bathroom where she'd scrubbed her face clean of all the heavy makeup a couple of hours later when her cell phone rang. Dashing into the living room, she scrambled through her purse to find it, flipping it open.

"Hello?" she said breathlessly.

"Busy all week?" Matt's familiar voice said.

"Uh, actually I had Thursday free, but I understand you're busy that day."

"Next week?"

So much for it not mattering. A warm glow settled in the region of her heart. She sat on the sofa and pulled her feet up, feeling free and excited. He hadn't let on in front of Jeannette, but he had wanted to see her!

"Why do you always ask when I'm not near my calendar?"

"Why didn't you anticipate I would ask and check your calendar before leaving work today?" he countered.

"I guess I didn't think you'd follow up," she said slowly.

"Why not? I thought you'd like to see where your aunt works."

"I'll make sure I swing by someday."

"Make sure you do it when I'm free. I want to show the place to you myself."

"Oh."

"Sure, so I can get your comment directly. I know I can trust a friend to speak the truth, right?"

"Oh, right."

"How did your busy day go? Eat lunch on the fly?"

"Something like that. It was hectic, but I love my job. And I didn't have to work overtime tonight."

Oops, would he associate that with his own executive assistant leaving on time today?

"Do you have to work overtime much?"

"Only as assignments warrant. And I don't mind. I want to be viewed as a team player."

"Your aunt said something like that last week. It's gratifying from an employer's point of view. And unusual in someone so young."

"Me?" she asked.

"I find older workers usually have a stronger work ethic and don't mind doing whatever is needed to get the job done. Younger workers are more self-centered and interested in doing what is best for them, not the company."

"I don't think that's an age assessment. It's more an individual thing," Karla countered, annoyed with his statement.

"In your vast experience?"

"Well, I have worked a number of years in the real world and have seen both young and old goofing off, and young and old putting out one-hundred-ten percent! Age had nothing to do with it. What do you plan to do, fire everyone under a certain age at Kinsinger and only hire older workers?"

"No, but I made sure my own personal assistant was more mature. No flighty young woman who is more interested in flirting than working."

"That's an unfair assessment. A lot of young employees work hard! You're saying you wouldn't even give a younger woman a chance to work for you?"

Ever? Maybe she would be stuck pretending to be twenty-some years older for her entire career. The thought had her close her eyes in frustration.

"It's a moot point, don't you think, Karla? Your aunt is settling in nicely. I won't have to look for anyone else, young or old."

"And what if she gets swept away with romance, gets married and leaves?"

"Do you think it's likely?"

She was silent a moment. "No." The only one she could imagine sweeping her away right now was her boss, and as far as he knew, she was twenty years older than he.

Maybe Pat had been right, it had been a dumb idea. One she was stuck with if she wanted to keep her job.

"Of all the things we could talk about, why discuss abstract theories about age and work ethic?"

"If my aunt left, would you hire me?"

The silence lasted several seconds. "Your aunt isn't leaving."

"But if she did and I applied for the job would you hire me? I've got good skills. I'm not flighty. And I could bring excellent references."

"No, I don't think I would," he said slowly.

"Gee, thanks a bunch."

"Probably not for the reasons you're thinking."

"How do you know what I'm thinking?"

"I wouldn't hire you because of the attraction between us," he said, ignoring her last comment.

Karla felt heat wash through her. That was blunt. Then it turned to a warm glow. The attraction wasn't all one-sided! Of course, she hoped for that after his searing kisses.

"I thought it was just me."

"Lady, you about set the world on fire just walking down the sidewalk. A man would have to be half dead not to notice. But I have definite rules against seeing staff members socially. So, no, I wouldn't hire you."

"Oh."

"But since you don't work for me, I have no rules against seeing you again."

"How nice for me," she said, that familiar bumping in her heart starting up again. Would she ever get used to it?

"So if lunch is out, how about dinner one night this week?"

"During the week?" she stalled, trying desperately to think of a reason to refuse. She wouldn't put it past him to invite himself over for that home-cooked meal he talked about.

"I want to see you again and I can't make it next weekend. I'm going up to the cabin again. In fact, I'm planning to ask your aunt if she can accompany me. We're working on a new proposal for a former client and I want to get it nailed down as quickly as possible. We can get a lot more accomplished away from distractions.''

A weekend at that remote cabin—just her and Matt? She'd better start thinking up excuses fast. There was no way she could pull off being the mature woman he thought her for an entire weekend. She had to wash that makeup off after a few hours to give her skin time to breathe. And she couldn't sleep in that itchy wig. Just her luck they'd have a fire or something and she'd run outside au naturel and he'd know instantly—

''Karla?''

''Huh? Oh, sorry. No, this week's not convenient for dinner.''

''Busy every night?''

''Usually I don't go out on dates during the week.''

''No date, just dinner with a friend.''

Oh, right, he wanted to be *friends*. Could she even entertain that idea? Somehow he and Kevin didn't fit in the same category.

''Come on, we both have to eat. How about we find a nice place, have a quiet dinner, and I'll have you home before ten.''

She laughed. ''You make me sound like I'm in high school.''

''You can't be long out.''

He *did* think she was younger than she was! She opened her mouth to tell him she'd been supporting herself for eight years, then snapped it shut. Good grief, she couldn't confess to matching her aunt's work record. He'd catch on instantly.

"Longer than you think."

"You can tell me over dinner."

She blew out a gust of air, her bangs flying every which way. "Sheesh, you're persistent. All right. How about Wednesday?"

"Shall we go out, or have dinner at your place?"

"I thought you were taking me out."

"I remembered the offer of a home-cooked meal."

"I never offered!"

"Mmm, I could have sworn—"

"Okay, fine! Dinner here. But not until seven." And heaven help her if she had to stay late at work that night!

"So what'll you cook?" he asked.

"Maybe I'll get take-out."

"I was looking forward to a home-cooked meal."

"People who invite themselves over can't be choosy."

"Damn! I was already anticipating something from an old family recipe."

She felt her bones melting. That sexy voice did funny things to her insides. If he continued along those lines, she'd promise him anything.

"Okay, pasta. How's that? With my grandmother's sauce, and French bread and salad."

"I'll bring some wine."

Had that been the only reason he'd called? Karla didn't want him to ring off. Wishing to keep him on the line, she came up with the first topic she could think of, "Tell me about your cabin. Will my aunt like it?"

"It's a bit rustic—log construction, but big and roomy. It's right on the water, so getting there and back is easy with the plane. And I have an office set up in one of the ground-floor rooms that almost matches the one at Kinsinger with equipment and communications capability."

"Mmm."

"And that means?"

"I'd think if you have a rustic cabin for a retreat from the stress and hectic schedule of work, the last thing you'd want was to be working."

"Ah, but this is a work retreat. When I really want to escape, I head for the wilderness."

"So tell me more about your wilderness adventures," she invited, settling back and closing her eyes. Listening to him talk to her about his last camping trip, she could envision the wild country he tackled. She wished she could see him tramping through the forest, building fires to cook and for warmth, fending for himself in the wilderness. But it didn't sound like her cup of tea. Listening was better.

Sometime later she realized they'd been on the phone almost an hour. The time had flown.

"I have to go," she said reluctantly. It was getting late, and she still needed to eat dinner before bedtime.

"I'll see you Wednesday."

She hung up, wondering if he would call between now and their dinner date. She wouldn't mind talking to him again before then.

Of course she would, she thought with a giggle. She'd see him tomorrow morning at eight!

By the next morning, Karla was a nervous wreck. First she had not come up with a convincing excuse to avoid a weekend trip with Matt. Second, she was having misgivings about his coming to dinner. How could she concentrate on work with so much else going on?

Promptly at seven Wednesday evening the bell to her apartment rang. Karla took a deep breath and went to answer it. She'd put on dark leggings and a bright blue silk top. Makeup on, cheeks smooth and unblemished, and her hair a silky dark cap, she was as ready as she was going to be. Butterflies danced in her stomach. She knew she was flirting with discovery. She swallowed hard, pasted on a bright smile and flung open the door.

"Prompt, I see," she said in greeting, her eyes going wide.

He looked wonderful! He'd changed since work. The charcoal-gray slacks were crisp, the white shirt, open at the throat, threw his tan into dark relief. The sports jacket emphasized his broad shoulders. And the smile that greeted her had her knees wobbling again. She hoped she wasn't drooling, but her mind seemed turned to mush. How could he look so different from the stern employer? A brief change of clothes wrought miracles.

He handed her a wrapped bottle of wine. "I said I'd bring the wine. You look lovely."

"Thank you."

He looked into the apartment, then back to Karla, waiting.

"Oh, come in." She stepped aside, wanting to smack her hand against her head. He'd think she was totally insane.

Glancing around, he waited as she shut the door. "This suits you. I wondered if you'd have lots of modern things. The country look is surprising, yet warm and inviting."

"Come in the kitchen while I finish fixing dinner. You can tell me all about your day."

He soon opened the wine and poured them each a glass, then leaned against the counter—much too close for comfort, Karla thought, wondering if having him in the kitchen was such a good idea.

She sipped her wine, then returned to cutting the fresh vegetables for the salad. The pesto sauce had been made, and the water was almost ready for the pasta.

"I'd rather you tell me about your day," he said.

She looked at him, caught by the intensity of his eyes.

"It was fine."

"Do you realize how reticent you are about your life?" he asked curiously.

"I'm not, I'm an open book."

"So tell me something you did today."

Stalling, hoping for inspiration, Karla turned back to the vegetables, dumping them into the large salad bowl. "My best friend had a baby today. She called and left word on my answering machine."

Pat had left a long message explaining that she'd wanted to call Karla at work, but hadn't dared. When Karla had returned the call, they'd spent thirty minutes excitedly discussing her new baby girl. Karla made plans to visit Friday evening—Pat and baby Brittany would be home by then.

She glanced at him and grinned. "Probably not something you want to talk about a lot, is it? Not being interested in marriage and all. But my friend and her husband are crazy about each other and thrilled to death with the birth of their first child."

"Someone has to perpetuate the species."

She laughed. "Confess, you're not as hard-hearted as you like to make out. Don't you like babies?"

"I've never been around them."

"Me, either. At least not a lot. But the few I've seen are precious."

"And does that make your own biological clock start ticking?" he asked.

She shook her head. "You have a narrow view of women. We do not spend every waking moment worrying about a biological clock!"

His eyes danced in amusement as he reached out to brush an errant strand of hair back. She drew in her breath. His touch was electrifying.

Matt let his fingers toy with her hair. It was as soft as silk. He heard her sharp intake and almost smiled, liking the fact she grew flustered. She had a similar effect on him, it was only fair to reciprocate.

His finger trailed along her cheek. Her skin was smooth and lightly flushed. She was lovely. And, thanks to her aunt, he knew exactly how she'd look when she was twenty or thirty years older.

The thought surprised him. Dropping his hand, he leaned back against the counter and studied her. He had never once thought about another woman twenty or thirty years ahead. Had she cast some kind of spell? He was not looking for long-term commitment. A few dates, some good times together, then they'd part and he'd find another companion.

He certainly wouldn't be around twenty years from now to care about how Karla had aged.

She turned and opened the utensil drawer. "Home-cooked meals come with strings. Here—'' She brought out forks and knives and handed them to him. "You can set the table while I throw the pasta in the water. It'll be ready soon and is best served hot and fresh.''

He took the utensils and headed for the table he'd seen in the alcove off the living room, glad to have something to do to take his mind off the disturbing thoughts of a future with Karla. He had his life just as he wanted it. And a complication with a woman wasn't in his plans.

He set the table, then checked out the view from her window. Not very inspiring, just other buildings, and a glimpse of the sky. Though at night he expected it was pretty with all the lights on.

When he found a permanent place, he wanted a view of the bay. For a moment he let his imagination envisiage a spacious flat with a panoramic view. He'd decorate it in country comfort and make it as warm and welcoming at the end of the day as Karla's flat was.

He jerked away from the window and the foolish day-dreams. He wasn't into country charm. He liked sleek, modern lines. Glass and chrome and leather. Glancing around, however, he couldn't help contrasting his place in Toronto with Karla's. He refused to admit hers had his beat as a place to wind down in.

Anyway, he was usually caught up with work. He didn't spend a lot of time at home—unless it was also working.

But would he, an insidious voice inside asked, if it was as welcoming as Karla's place? If Karla was there each evening to give him a choice between work and pleasure?

Now he was losing it.

She came into the room, carrying a bowl of bright

spring flowers. Placing it in the center of the small table, she tilted her head as she studied the effect. She smiled serenely up at him.

"I love flowers, don't you? I got these from a street vendor. I think they brighten up the place."

"You make it bright," he said slowly, reaching out to draw her into his arms. Time to worry about his careening thoughts later. Right now he wanted to kiss her.

CHAPTER FIVE

IT WAS as if she had been waiting for his kiss. Her body aligned perfectly with his. Her arms were warm and strong around his shoulders and neck. Her mouth seemed to be made for his.

Deepening the kiss, Matt relished the excitement holding her brought. His body hummed with energy and desire. Drawing her even closer, deepening the kiss, he wondered how long it would be before he could take her to bed. He knew she'd be explosive—look how responsive she was to a mere kiss.

Not that the embrace could be classified as a mere anything. He'd always scoffed at the romantic notion some people had given to desire. But there was something soft and almost sweet about the hot passion that sprang between them. Some of it had to be due to her own air of innocence—impossible though it was.

Vaguely he was aware of a dinging noise.

"Oops." Karla pulled back. "The pasta."

She turned and hurried into the kitchen, while Matt tried to get his rollicking emotions under control. The way he felt right now, they could skip dinner and head straight for dessert!

Waiting until things were under control, he followed her into the kitchen. Karla heaped pasta on their plates, concentrating on her task as if it were the most crucial aspect in world peace.

He leaned over and brushed his lips against the nape of her neck, revealed when she leaned forward. Her short hair was sexy. He thought he liked long hair on women, but that tantalizing exposure of her neck affected him as nothing else ever had.

"It's ready," she said brightly.

Recognizing temporary defeat when he saw it, he nodded and gave up on the kisses—for now.

"Want some more wine?"

"Yes, please." She sounded breathless. The surge of satisfaction that swept through him was astonishing. He always liked to please the women he was with, but with Karla it went deeper. He wanted to be the only one to please her, and satisfy her. To find out what she liked, and show her he could fulfill all her needs.

He wanted to find out more about her. What her favorite movie was, and did she have a crush on some movie star. Did she like to read, or listen to music? What was her preferred way to spend a Saturday afternoon?

Dinner was not awkward as he feared it might be after their kiss. She was more open and forthcoming than at any time since he'd met her. Asking the questions he wanted most to know about, he found out about movies she liked, about her family holidays at Okanagan Lake, about the mystery books she loved and the soft jazz she listened to. He was pleased to note she liked action adventure movies and there was no crush! Her love of romance novels threw him. But she teased him by saying she knew he wouldn't enjoy them—they contained the L-and C-words—love and commitment.

Once again Matt felt at home with a woman he'd recently met. Her demeanor reminded him of how he felt around her aunt. There was something about the Jones women that put men at ease. Maybe it was knowing neither saw him as husband material.

"Your turn," she said. "I've been talking almost nonstop. Tell me what your favorite subject was at the university."

He hesitated a moment, then nodded. It wasn't something anyone else had ever asked. "English lit."

She blinked. "Really? I would never have suspected it. I thought for sure you'd like something like Corporate Raiders 101."

"I took an English literature course each year. Initially to fulfill a basic requirement. But I found reading the classics a welcomed break from the analytical and mathematical emphasis of the business courses. And a way to get caught up in the action of a time and place so different from the one in which we live."

"You're a romantic," she said slowly, her smile breaking through. "A closet one, I hasten to add."

He shook his head, amused by her teasing.

"I bet you envisioned yourself as Sidney Carlton, saving a friend. Or Tom Jones, out for a rollicking time."

"I fancied myself the Scarlet Pimpernel," he reluctantly admitted.

"*That* was included in the syllabus? Your professor was also a romantic."

"Extra credit, and a great adventure."

She studied him through narrowed eyes. "Yes, I can see you as the Scarlet Pimpernel, swashbuckling and ready for adventure—risking life and limb for a cause."

"Maybe not that far."

"Of course you'd go that far. Don't you risk life and limb on your trips to the wilderness?"

He shook his head.

"What happens if you get sick, or attacked by a bear? You're miles from help, from human contact. You could be killed and no one would ever know what happened to you."

"There's no one to care what happens to me," he said gently.

Karla's eyes grew wide. He saw the realization hit, and then the softening as compassion filled her.

"I'd care," she said softly.

He felt the words like a kick in the gut. He'd been on his own for so long, he never thought to hear someone say that.

"I make sure I always come back."

"As the Scarlet Pimpernel always did. But don't forget, he had the help of a good woman at the end."

"So you'll come rescue me?"

Karla laughed. "Not unless you're tangled up somewhere in Stanley Park. That's about as wild as I go."

"You'll have to expand your horizons. Maybe spend a weekend with me at Henley Island. We can practice wilderness lifesaving tips there. Among other things," he said suggestively.

He was charmed by the wave of color that swept into her cheeks. She couldn't possibly be as naive as she sometimes acted. No modern woman living in such a cosmopolitan city as Vancouver could have remained innocent approaching her mid twenties. But it didn't matter. He, himself, wasn't without experience, why should he expect a partner to be?

But for one crazy moment, he almost wished she were as innocent as she appeared.

His comment threw her. Karla knew what going off for a weekend with a man entailed. Was he serious? Was she ready to take such a step? She loved spending time with Matt—whether at work or on their off hours. But she hadn't known him long. And it would comprise a huge step for her.

Still, imagine the two of them, with nothing to do but get to know each other better, and enjoy the outdoors. It was something she'd have to consider carefully. She didn't want to get hurt, or plunge foolishly into something beyond her control.

"Does going to Henley mean campfire cooking?"

"The cabin has a kitchen."

"And who cooks?"

"After this meal, I'd say you do. This is delicious."

"I'm happy you like it, but—" she wrinkled her nose "—I'm not sure my repertoire of meals would last a weekend." She was pleased when he asked for seconds on the pasta and sauce. He really did enjoy it.

"You don't cook dinner each night?"

She shook her head. "For one it's not worth it."

"But there would be two of us at the cabin."

She reached for her wine, took a sip. "Then no reason we can't share the responsibility, is there?" she asked.

"My experience is probably more limited than yours."

"Then there'll be things I can teach you, won't there?" She held his gaze, feeling reckless.

Matt laughed aloud. Karla smiled brightly, delighting

in the way the conversation sparkled. She wished for more evenings like tonight.

And if she got her wish, she'd have to decide how far to take this relationship—in light of Mr. 25-50's rule, and marriage phobia.

And in light of her masquerade at work. The thought threw a damper on the evening. Some of the zest vanished.

"Dessert?" she asked, rising to clear the table.

"Depends on what you have in mind."

He was doing it deliberately, she knew. He was so different from anyone she'd ever dated before. His sexy flirting keep her constantly on her toes. And she loved every moment.

"Chocolate mousse," she said, rising and reaching for his plate.

His hand caught her wrist, holding her loosely. "What if I want something different?"

Her heart caught in her throat. "I have some brandy?" She knew what he meant, and it had nothing to do with brandy.

His thumb caressed the soft skin of her wrist. She almost dropped the plate. Surely he could hear her heart pounding. The blood rushing through her veins sounded like a waterfall. Her gaze locked with his. She recognized desire—wondering if he saw a like expression reflected in hers.

Dropping her gaze to his mouth, she wanted to release the plates, drop on his lap and kiss him senseless. Or at least until one of them was senseless. And it probably wouldn't be him.

A hint of caution had her hesitate. There was something about Matt's never losing control that jarred. She was the one who seemed to lose control when he kissed her.

But what a glorious loss!

"Don't you like chocolate mousse?" she asked.

His hand tightened slightly, then released her. Rising, he took his own plate. "I like mousse."

"Sit still. I'll clear and get dessert."

"Just showing you how well things will work if we go to the cabin. Though my dessert might be different," he said suggestively.

She knew exactly what kind of dessert he had in mind.

By the time they'd had mousse, coffee and a small snifter of brandy in the living room, Karla's nerves were ragged. She knew she was toying with danger, but was fascinated—as a moth was to flame.

Everything about Matt was riveting—from the way his eyes crinkled when he smiled, to the strength of his muscles when he held her, to the wry sense of humor he rarely showed. Time had flown by and it was getting late, but she didn't want the evening to end.

If she had a lick of sense, she'd send Matt on his way and never see him again outside of the office. But she couldn't resist the lure of spending more time with him. If he asked her out again, she'd throw caution to the wind and accept. She never suspected she had this hidden flare for danger.

He checked his watch. "It's getting late—for a work night anyway. I'll be on my way."

Karla felt disappointed.

"I've enjoyed tonight, Karla. Thanks for inviting me. I wouldn't say no to another invitation. In the meantime,

I'll tender one officially. Next Wednesday evening? We could find a restaurant that has music, maybe dancing. I'd make it this weekend, but I'll need to work on the deal we're trying to consummate,'' Matt said as they walked together to the door.

''I'll check my calendar and let you know,'' she temporized. Next Wednesday? A lifetime away. Yet was she ready for another evening with Matt? At least in a neutral place like a restaurant, she would be better able to keep a rein on temptation.

He touched her cheek when they stopped by the door.

''I'm going to get you a pocket calendar so you can carry it with you at all times. If you do have something going on, it can't be that exciting that you can't remember it.''

''I don't usually date during the week. I'm a working gal, you know,'' she retorted honestly.

''Then we won't stay out late. Come to dinner with me.''

He put his hands gently on her shoulders, pulling her into an embrace. Lowering his head, he kissed with the passion that had been simmering all evening.

Karla let go of her inhibitions and returned the kiss with all the fervor in her. When in his arms, she didn't think. If he asked her now, she'd agree to anything as long as it included him!

''We're two adults who are attracted to each other. And who have no other commitments. We're not looking for forever. Dinner between friends. Maybe a dance or two. I'd like to hold you and sway to music. Say you'll come,'' he mumbled against her lips.

For a vague instant she rather thought she wanted commitment and a future together. But he was talking dinner. And a chance to spend more time with him. How could she refuse?

"I'll call you," he said, straightening. "Thanks again for dinner."

He cupped her neck and brushed his lips across hers again then turned and headed down the hall.

She watched as he strode to the elevator. Once the doors slid closed behind him, she turned and slowly reentered her flat. Sighing as she closed the door. She wished she knew what to do about the disturbingly masculine male who just left. And the raging hormones that engulfed her whenever he was near.

He'd made it abundantly clear he was not looking for any long-range relationship. But she wondered if her friend Pat had been correct—when Mr. Right came along, all her own protestations about wanting a career over marriage went out the window.

Mr. Right? Matt Gramling? She shook her head. When she fell in love, she wanted it to be with some man who would adore her in return. Not Mr. Burned-Once-And-Never-Committing-Again.

But as she washed the dishes and put them away, she wondered if she wasn't already a little too late in her caution. She was very much afraid she was falling head over heels for the man.

Time to put on the brakes.

No dancing. Dinner wouldn't be so bad—but definitely no dancing!

Late Thursday morning, Karla began to wonder if she'd imagined his saying he was inviting her aunt to the weekend retreat to work. He'd made no mention of it that morning. Did he expect to spring it on her as she was leaving on Friday afternoon?

She had dressed carefully that morning, in anticipation of lunch with Mr. and Mrs. Taylor. Her position at Kinsinger Electronics kept her isolated from the majority of the other clerical workers, so she hadn't worried too much about another woman seeing through her disguise.

But Mrs. Taylor would be spending a couple of hours with her in a close setting. Would the woman see through the makeup and question why she was pretending?

As the lunch hour drew closer, Karla wondered if she should plead a headache or something and excuse herself from joining them. She couldn't risk exposure—especially in front of a major prospective client.

Yet, she couldn't bring herself to back out and leave Matt in the lurch. She was a professional. If Mrs. Taylor showed signs of noticing something was wrong, maybe she could quietly explain and hope for her silence.

Sheesh, another dumb idea, she thought as she reviewed the notes she'd taken from the Percell Group report. She should be trying to promote the company, not discussing her own situation. It would make Matt look bad—that he hadn't recognized a masquerade when he saw one. And she would do nothing to jeopardize his relationship with these prospective clients.

Crossing her fingers for luck, Karla went to brazen it out.

She was looking forward to seeing Matt in action. She knew from his history he was good at turning things around. Today she'd see exactly how he did it.

She had to remind herself to focus on business. Twice during their briefing that morning, she'd caught herself gazing at him, remembering their kisses, their lively conversation from the night before. Fortunately, she'd glanced down at her notes before he'd discovered his staid, mature Miss Jones mooning over him. She gave herself a stern talking-to. She had to remain totally professional and forget about his arms holding her, his fingers brushing lightly against her cheek. His mouth devouring hers and leaving her breathless.

The Taylors were an older couple, already at the restaurant when Matt and Karla arrived. Introductions were made and they all were soon seated at a private table with a view of the city spread before them. The lighting was favorable, and Karla breathed a sigh of relief. Hopefully her makeup would bear up to scrutiny.

"So you've taken over Kinsinger Electronics, eh, young man?" Richard Taylor said heartily once their beverage orders had been taken.

"Now, dear, of course he has," his wife said, perusing the menu.

"Taken over, taken charge and moving it in a new direction. One I think you might be interested in helping me forge," Matt said easily.

"What? How could I help?"

"I'd like some insight into what went wrong when we had your account. And what you would have liked to have seen? What could the company have done to keep your business? One thing I don't want to do is repeat the past. We all know where that got Kinsinger."

"Very good plan," Mrs. Taylor said, joining the conversation. "So many times one's firm changes and its suppliers or customers can't keep up."

"And Mr. Moore was a bit old-fashioned," Matt said.

Mrs. Taylor looked at Karla, her gaze friendly. "And how do you fit into all this?"

"I'm Mr. Gramling's executive assistant," she said quietly.

"Ah." Mrs. Taylor smiled. "Then tell me something about his management style."

Karla looked at Matt. When he gave an almost imperceptible nod, she felt free to talk. "I find it open and aboveboard. I've just started working with him, but from what I can see, he takes time to gather information from which to make decisions—whether personnel related, customer relations, or from his management team. And he allows people to do their jobs. He's not one of these men who questions every decision people make. I think he feels if he hires responsible employees, he needs to give them the opportunity to be responsible. And do their jobs without interference."

"And do you think he can turn the company around?"

"Yes. And sooner than most people would think," Karla said enthusiastically.

"And I didn't even have to pay her to say all that," Matt joked. "One of the reasons I invited Jeannette to join us for lunch was to benefit from her insight. She'll be working on this project as well. She's lived here all her life, and knows Vancouver and any nuances we might face in dealing with another old city firm. She also has experience in Pacific Rim trading. I value her input."

"Nicely done, young man." Mr. Taylor smiled at his wife. "Women add an aspect we don't always pick up on. I always consult my wife in major decisions. She's a silent partner in the firm. And always has been a major asset.''

Matt met Karla's glance and his eyes twinkled. They already suspected something like this from her talk with Taylor's secretary.

''I'll tell you about our firms' dealings before. You aren't going to like a lot of it,'' Richard said.

''But I'm the one who can change it.''

''There is that.''

Taylor talked at length throughout lunch about the problems he'd experienced with Kinsinger. He and Matt discussed various ways to do business. And he was quick to let Matt know they were not displeased with their new vendor.

Karla watched as Matt was able to glean every bit of information he wanted. The older couple seemed pleased to have their opinion sought so assiduously. And at the end of lunch, when Matt asked if he could meet with them formally in the next week or so to present a new proposal, both acquiesced.

Matt and Karla bid the Taylors farewell in front of the restaurant, watching them climb into a cab.

''How about it, Miss Jones, care to walk back to the office? It's only a few blocks and the weather's warm enough,'' he said as the cab pulled away.

''I'd like that,'' Karla said, falling into step as he turned in the direction of the office building. ''I think it went well, do you?''

''Yes. Better than I might have expected. The order processing department really screwed up a couple of times. And that last batch that was substandard really hurt. I might not have found it so easy to remain as open-minded as they did. But nothing was settled today.''

''I realize that. You opened the door, however.''

''And I want to move quickly on this project. It could really give the firm a boost in the arm—not only monetarily. Morale would pick up with a major new contract.''

''And is morale poor?'' She had seen no signs of complaining or low morale—had in fact thought it on the rise. Of course, except for the new typist she'd hired last week, she didn't spend much time with anyone in the company except as they traipsed in and out of Matt's office. Her workload allowed no time for chitchatting with fellow employees.

''Not that I've noticed. But there is always uncertainty when a new person takes over.''

She nodded, matching her stride to his. She remembered their walk along the seawalk. And his kiss when he took her home after dinner. And last night. Heat washed through her and she wished she could reach out to touch him. Tell him how much she appreciated the chance to work with him. To get to know him. To know him even more than he suspected.

She cringed slightly, feeling guilty. She shouldn't be seeing him socially without being honest with him. Yet, he'd fire her in a minute at this stage. She needed to show him she truly could become invaluable.

But as the day's brightness dimmed a bit, she wondered how she could speed up her timetable to tell him. Maybe it would erase the guilt if she had a definite plan, and a deadline to meet.

''Something wrong?'' he asked. ''You're frowning.''

''No, just, um, trying to remember all I have to do this afternoon.''

''When we get back, have Henderson in accounting pull all the records concerning the Percell Group. And call Myers in to review his report. I want a meeting with department heads at three. You, too. Tell them to come with ideas to regain this account. Then do a quick scan and see whom else we've lost in the last year or two. We'll see if we can combine some strategies and regain more than the Percell Group alone.''

The office building was in sight. Karla wished for a moment that Matt had talked of something beside work. But why should he? To him, Jeannette Jones was the perfect executive assistant, and dedicated to work. No flights of fancy for her.

He stopped on the sidewalk in front of the huge glass doors leading into the building. ''We'll need to work through the weekend on this. I'd like to get back to the Taylors first thing next week. In addition to proposing changes, I want them to know how fast we can respond. Are you available for a marathon session this weekend?''

Here it was—the invitation to the cabin. ''Working Saturday?''

''And Sunday. I'll get all the data we need from the department heads. Saturday we can fly up to the cabin where we won't be disturbed. I want to hammer out this proposal completely by Monday. And I want total confidentiality. I want you to handle the typing, not Lisa.''

''No problem.''

''Good.''

Matt held the door for her when they entered the lobby

of the building. "Remind me to tell your niece another reason it makes sense to hire more mature workers."

"What?"

"We had a discussion the other evening about ages of workers," Matt said as he pressed the button to the elevator. "I should have added another advantage of the working relationship between me and a more mature worker—it doesn't bring the sexual tension or innuendoes working with a young secretary would engender."

"Oh?" Karla was puzzled.

"I couldn't take off for a working weekend with some twenty-something young woman. Think of the gossip and rumors."

"Of course." But because everyone thought she was fifty-something, working off-site would raise no comment.

But not everyone believed she was fifty, she remembered when she reached her desk. There in the center was another envelope with her name printed on the front.

She placed her purse over it and smiled at Matt.

"Thanks for including me in the lunch. I felt I learned a lot about strategy."

He nodded, pausing by the door to his office. "I appreciate the response you gave Mrs. Taylor about my management style. I think it went a long way in opening her mind to at least listen."

Karla wished she could bask in the glow of his comment, but as soon as he was seated behind his desk, she put her purse in a drawer and opened the envelope.

Matt Gramling has definite ideas on employee ages. What would he say to yours? For a favor, I won't be the one to tell him.

Good grief, it was blackmail! Karla stared at the note, stunned. What possible favor could someone want that she could grant?

They didn't know her as well as they thought if they believed she could be coerced to do anything wrong at work—even to keep her job.

She needed to find out who was doing this and stop it without causing problems. But where to start?

She didn't want to leave. If she refused to give in to the blackmail, would she have any choice?

Karla bought a few new clothes Thursday evening for her trip to Matt's cabin. Instead of the snug jeans or leggings she preferred, she bought loosely cut, tailored wool slacks. Her normal ribbed tops she eschewed in favor of tailored blouses also cut more fully than she normally wore.

And she bought a huge old-fashioned flannel nightgown that would cover her from neck to toes. Not that she expected a fire in the middle of the night, but she was taking no chances.

She loaded her overnight case with the theatrical makeup she needed. Hoping she didn't give the show away, she was as ready as she could be for the weekend. He'd offered to pick her up, but there was no way she could allow him to pick up Jeannette at Karla's apartment. So she arranged to meet him at the dock.

Friday evening she visited Pat and for a long time forgot the turmoil of her own making as she held and rocked the new baby girl. Holding the precious new child and the glow of happiness between Pat and her husband had Karla yearning for the first time for a family of her own.

Maybe a little boy with dark eyes that watched intensely, or a little girl like Pat's baby, to wrap her father around her little finger.

She refused to give a name to the father of those imaginary children—but Matt's face danced before her eyes.

CHAPTER SIX

PRECISELY at 7:00 a.m. Saturday morning, she walked down the floatation dock toward the moored seaplane. She had two small cases, one in each hand. The tailored slacks were comfortable, and she hoped baggy enough to disguise her figure. She was getting good at this, she thought wryly. Too bad it wasn't some kind of skill she'd need later in her career.

"Prompt as ever," Matt said as he climbed from the cockpit. He was dressed in dark cords, and the white cable-knit sweater he'd worn last weekend. His hair wasn't as immaculate as in the office, and Karla had that familiar urge to run her fingers through it, just to feel the texture, to connect with him.

That would shock his socks off, she thought, if his staid assistant made a move on him. For a moment she was sorely tempted.

He reached for her cases. "Ever flown in one of these?"

She shook her head, looking at the aircraft with a bit of hesitation as it bobbed on the water.

"A lot more fun than the big commercial planes. Hop aboard." He held his hand for her to steady herself, and motioned to the pontoon.

She could see the skid-resistant patch on the metal and carefully placed her foot on it. The plane tipped slightly when her full weight rested on the pontoon, but Matt quickly assisted her into the tiny cockpit.

She bumped her head on the low ceiling and immediately checked the wig to make sure it hadn't been knocked askew. Hoping everything looked normal, Karla sat in the seat indicated and gazed around with interest.

Matt released the mooring lines and climbed inside, closing the door. The space in the cockpit seemed to shrink. Karla watched as he eased himself into the pilot's seat and began throwing switches.

"When did you learn to fly?" she asked as Matt buckled the seat belt and reached for the earphones.

"When I first got out of the university. It was one of those challenges I couldn't resist. And it's proved beneficial over the years."

"For getting away to the wilderness," she murmured, fastening her own seat belt.

He glanced at her with a puzzled look. "Right. I told you about that?"

She nodded, once again feeling the breath of danger. He had told her, but as Jeannette or Karla? Sheesh, she was getting everything mixed up. How would she keep it all straight?

He started the engines and soon they were skimming over the water of Coal Harbour. Almost before she knew it, they were airborne. Vancouver spread out below them, like a miniature city. Karla was enchanted with the view. That feeling fled instantly when they hit an air pocket and dipped.

"Oh!" She clutched the armrests of her seat. "Are we okay?"

"Sure. No problems," he said with a look. "You've

lived here all your life, tell me what we're seeing as we head north.''

It was easier than she had thought to recognize landmarks from the air, and she was glad to have her mind focused on something besides Matt as they flew along. Not that she could help being aware of him every instant. His fingers were long and lean as he held the controls steady. She remembered how they'd felt caressing her cheek.

His head almost brushed the ceiling and his legs looked cramped. He was taller than she, but when he held her in his arms, the fit was perfect.

Karla could tell by the expression on his face, he loved to fly. And if he had been doing it for almost fifteen years, he must be an accomplished pilot.

Not that she could imagine him being anything but accomplished. If he undertook to do something, she knew he'd make sure he excelled at it.

Making their approach to Henley Island an hour later, Matt pointed out the small settlement where he stocked up on groceries. Making a wide sweep around the end of the island, he lined up the plane and gently set it down on the water, skimming across the surface to a small dock jutting out into the inlet.

''So how did you like it?'' he asked as they came to a halt just kissing the end of the dock.

''It was a lot more enjoyable than I expected,'' she said, her eyes shiny from delight. ''I'll look forward to the return trip.''

He made short work of tying them to the dock and unloading their bags. Karla reached for hers, but he shook his head.

"I'll take them up."

"Thank you." Turning, she followed the dock to land and then the pathway up the incline toward a log cabin.

When he'd said log cabin, she envisioned something early trappers might have had. Instead, while made of logs, there was nothing cabinish about the place. It stood two stories tall, with soaring windows and a wide front porch extending the width of the house providing plenty of room for sitting out on a warm summer's evening.

"Have you had this long?" she asked, following him up the shallow steps to the front door.

Matt put down the bags and reached into his pocket for the key. "It's not mine. I'm just using it. A friend of mine owns it. But he's in Europe for several months and this way I get a place to use and can keep an eye on it for him."

Inside the house was lovely. The furnishings were old-fashioned, with a warmth and welcome that immediately reached out to Karla. The door opened directly into the living room. She walked in and looked out of the huge window. It was almost as if the outdoors came inside.

Through the trees, she could see the sea. Just the tail of the plane was visible. She smiled and turned. Matt stood watching her.

"It's beautiful," she said.

"I think so. If Steve ever wants to sell, I told him I'll take it. The bedrooms are upstairs. I'll carry your cases up. Do you want to freshen up or anything?"

"I'll just check it out, then be ready to work." She needed to verify everything was in place. She couldn't have her wig tilting over one side.

"Steve has a room off the back I've set up as an office. We'll use that when you're ready," Matt said.

Fifteen minutes later Karla was seated opposite a huge desk from Matt. He plunged right into the task of drawing together a proposal to lure the Percell Group back as a customer.

Time flew by as they worked together—he requesting data, Karla quickly finding it from the various reports they'd brought. When Matt leaned back in his chair and asked Karla's opinion on one aspect, she gave him a thoughtful answer and was delighted when he said he liked it. His incorporating it into the plan made her feel a true team player.

She'd never been involved in strategic planning such as this before and relished every moment. They worked well together—despite her age.

He tossed his pencil down. "I'm getting hungry, how about you?"

"I could eat," Karla said, finishing up her notes. She glanced around at the several stacks of paper with notes on them. "Shall I type these all up this afternoon?" she asked.

"Let's take a break. Working uninterrupted as we've done, we're much farther ahead than we'd be if we were in the office. How energetic do you feel?"

"Very. Sitting all morning, I'd like to walk or something."

"I thought we could walk to town and get lunch at a small café there. The food's good and it would let you see something of Henley Island while you're here. Can't have you coming all this way and only seeing the cabin."

While it sounded like fun, she wasn't sure as Jeannette

how she should react. Shrugging her shoulders, she decided to just be herself. "I'd like that."

And Karla did enjoy herself. Primarily because she was with Matt. The late lunch they ate was delicious. She had chowder with fresh French bread. He had a shrimp sandwich that looked two inches thick.

While they ate, he told her something of the history of the island, how the first settlers, if they could be called that, had been stranded Russian traders. Their boat had been destroyed in a storm and survivors had washed up on the shores of Henley Island.

After lunch, they'd explored the single derelict wooden structure that was the last of the buildings remaining from the first inhabitants.

"I bet they wished they were here now," Karla said, wondering what it would have felt like to be stranded so far from home.

"Why?"

She smiled at him. "Think of the killing they'd make in real estate."

He laughed and Karla's heart hitched. Afraid he'd find it odd to have his secretary staring at him, she forced herself to look away. But the image of his happiness was imprinted on her mind. The day seemed brighter.

It didn't take long to see the entire town. Matt stopped at the small store and bought steaks and potatoes for dinner. Karla teased him about the fare being so typical of what men cooked.

"Never learned the fine nuances of cooking," Matt said. "If you'd rather prepare us a feast?" His look was hopeful, but she laughed and shook her head.

"No, thanks. I love steak."

When they reached the cabin, Matt put away the groceries while Karla headed for the office. She had a lot of things to get typed. Once the first draft was done, they could fine-tune it. By the end of their stay tomorrow, the proposal should be almost complete.

Matt stuck his head into the office. "I'm going down to refuel the plane and run a maintenance check. Do you need anything?"

"No, I have plenty to do," she murmured, not even looking up from the keyboard. She was halfway listening to him and halfway thinking of another way to present this particular concession to make it seem even more important.

Karla lost track of time as she worked. She'd been right to go after this job. After only a couple of weeks, she felt like she was making a contribution—and learning a great deal.

It didn't hurt that she liked her boss. She just wished she didn't have to wear thick makeup and the blasted wig! She had to tell him soon. She hoped he'd admire her boldness for going after what she wanted—and not fire her on the spot.

When the warble from her cell phone first sounded, she wasn't sure what it was. Glancing around, she didn't see Matt anywhere, so reached for her purse.

"Hello?" she said. She should have turned the thing off. What if he came in and she was talking—

"Karla?"

It was Matt!

"Yes."

"How's your weekend going?"

"Fine." Her heart beating, she rose and went to the

door, shutting it firmly. "Where are you?" she asked, knowing he wouldn't tell her precisely enough for her to locate him, but she couldn't take the chance he'd hear her talking.

"I'm at the cabin. Your aunt and I have been working all day on the proposal for a new client. I would have rather stayed in Vancouver to see you."

She walked to the window and gazed out at the lovely scenery. No sign of him on the path to the plane. "That would have been nice," she said.

"Only nice?" Was his voice taking on a more intimate tone?

"Very nice?" she offered.

"Better. What are you doing today?"

She glanced around the office, leaning against the wall. "Catching up on things."

"And what do you plan to do tonight? Do you have a date?"

She knew she didn't imagine the roughened edge to his tone.

"No. I plan to just hang around and maybe work a bit."

"On?"

"This and that. How does my aunt like your place?"

"She likes it. And she continues to be a terrific asset. Didn't waste any time settling in. We took a break at lunch, walked to town and ate there for lunch. Since we've been back, she's been typing up the notes we made this morning."

"Is it a big town?" It was hard to keep straight what she knew and what she wasn't supposed to know.

"No, we walked from one end to another in about five minutes."

"Different from Vancouver, then."

"I'll bring you up some weekend and you can see it for yourself."

Her heart rate sped up. Matt was talking again about bringing her up for a weekend—and not a working weekend like this one was, but definitely a date kind of weekend.

"That would be—" she searched for a word besides the insipid *nice.*

"There's not much nightlife, however. I have to warn you about that."

"I'm sure we could find something to do in the evening. Watch TV maybe?"

"No TV."

"Ah, that is rustic, no matter what you think."

"There is music. We could always dance. I'd like to hold you in my arms."

She swallowed hard. "I like to dance," she said blandly, already imagining them entwined, swaying slowly to sensuous mood music.

"With the right partner."

She smiled. So she might be the right partner?

"We're friends, right?"

"Close friends," he said.

Oops, wasn't that what she'd promised not to do? Not get involved. She couldn't play with fire and not get burned.

"Board games are fun, too," she said. Was she seriously considering going off with a man for the weekend?

No, not any man—Matt.

"Is it wilderness there?" she asked, gazing at the soaring trees that marched to the sea. Not a high-rise building in sight.

"No. Country, but not wilderness. There are some hiking trails. We can walk along the sea. Plenty to do."

"Mmm. Then what are you doing there this weekend working? How do you manage with the lure of the outdoors calling?"

"It isn't easy. The walk to town today with your aunt helped. Want to talk to her? She can let you know her impressions."

Karla almost yelped. She spun around and raced back to her seat, listening intently. Don't let him walk in and find her on the phone!

"No, I don't need to talk to her," she said quickly. "If she's working, she won't like being interrupted."

"Time she took a break."

She could hear him now, in the hallway.

"I've got to go. Um, someone's at the door. 'Bye." She flipped off the phone and plunged it into her pocket. Placing her hands on the keyboard, she was looking at the screen when the door opened to the office. Her heart raced a hundred miles an hour. Matt stood in the doorway, gazing at a phone in his hand, a frown on his face.

Had he heard her voice through the door? She tried to look innocent.

"Hi. How's the plane?"

He dropped his hand to his side and walked to the desk, dropping the phone on top.

"Fueled up and checked out. How're you coming?"

"Almost finished. I've printed out the first section, want to review it now?"

"I'd rather wait until morning. It'll seem fresher for having a break." He seemed distracted as he moved a couple of files to one side.

"Is anything wrong?" The weight of her phone seemed to pull on her slacks. She swallowed, hoping it was fully hidden in her pocket and didn't fall out.

He looked up and caught her eyes. "I guess I didn't think this through. There's not a lot to do around here in the evening."

"I brought a book. I don't expect to be entertained, Mr. Gramling."

He almost smiled, amusement danced in his eyes. "Glad to hear that, Miss Jones. But I don't expect you to shut yourself up in your bedroom when not working."

"I wouldn't mind an early night," Karla said, turning back to the computer. Truth to tell, she couldn't wait to wash her face and take off the wig. Her entire head itched, from her scalp to her cheeks.

As she watched Matt prepare dinner a couple of hours later, Karla wondered how she could bring the topic around to younger employees. His comments during earlier conversations had shown her his bias, and she was at a loss to know how to change his mind. She felt she'd painted herself into a corner and it wasn't going to be easy to get out.

Before she could say anything, he poured her a glass of wine and slid it across the counter to where she sat on one of the bar stools.

"You're easy to be around, Miss Jones."

"Why, thank you." His comment caught her by surprise. "Do you usually surround yourself with people who are not easy to be around?"

He shrugged, taking a glass for himself and sipping the wine. "Not intentionally. But young women seem to like to fill the air with chatter. I find it entertaining for the most part. But there is something to be said for quiet companionship."

She sipped her wine and nodded, hoping she looked wise. She wouldn't mind filling the silence with chatter, but not at the risk of exposing her deception. It was hard to be herself, and not. Yet she wouldn't trade this time with Matt for anything.

"Is that combination of seasonings you anointed the steak with an old family recipe?" she asked.

"Hardly. Any old family recipes I'm likely to have would be beans on toast. My mother died when I was very young and my old man wasn't exactly a gourmet cook."

"You could have learned," she said, wondering what his childhood had been like. How awful to lose a parent when young. Or at any time. She made a note to call her folks when she got home, just to touch base.

"Not my field of interest. And now that I've made a success of things, I can afford to buy my meals."

"Don't you get tired of eating out all the time?"

"Yes. In fact, your niece invited me for dinner this week. A home-cooked meal I didn't have to prepare myself."

"You seem to be interested in my niece," she said slowly.

"Do you disapprove?" He leaned against the counter, keeping an eye on the steaks.

"It has nothing to do with me. I just thought—" Careful, she warned herself. Which one had he told his views of dating?

"Thought?"

"That you weren't interested in a long-term commitment."

"Neither is your niece."

She nodded once. She couldn't tell him at this juncture how being around him had her questioning her long-held beliefs. Maybe there was more to life than getting ahead in business. And while she wasn't truly worried about her biological clock at twenty-eight, if she didn't do something in the next ten years, she would start to worry!

"So tell me a bit about growing up in Ontario. Any siblings?" she asked. Jeannette wouldn't know that, would she?

"No siblings. No family to speak of when I was growing up except my old man. And I left home as soon as I turned eighteen."

"Is your father still living there?"

"No, he died ten years ago." Matt stared into his glass of wine for a long moment. "We were never close. He hit the bottle pretty hard toward the end. I think the booze finally killed him."

"I'm sorry," Karla said, her heart touched by how alone he must feel. No wonder he didn't expect commitment. Not only had Celine let him down, his own parents had done so as well. What would it take for him to change such ingrained beliefs?

Karla excused herself shortly after dinner was finished. She claimed she was tired and wanted an early night, but she couldn't wait to wash her face and take off the hot wig!

Once in the sanctity of her room, she ripped the wig off and threw it on the bed. Heading for the adjoining bath, she soon had the wash cloth in hand and was scrubbing off the theatrical makeup.

"This feels great," she murmured, glad to be back to normal. She donned the long flannel nightgown and slid into bed. She'd read for a while before going to sleep.

But she had just opened the book when her cell phone rang.

Scrambling out of the covers, she ran across the room to her clothes, trying to find the phone before it sounded again. Matt was just downstairs. He'd hear it for sure.

She snatched it up and flipped it on. "Hello?" she said breathlessly.

"Karla, it's Matt."

"Hi."

Tiptoeing to the door, she eased it open a crack and listened. She could hear his voice from the living room, as well as in her ear. Quietly she closed the door.

"No one at your door this time?"

"At this hour?" She crept back to the bed and slid beneath the covers. "Actually, I was getting ready for bed."

"It's only nine-thirty."

"I've had a busy day." She almost laughed, thinking of him downstairs and her up here. She hadn't wanted to leave him after dinner. If she had had his number, would she have called?

"Yeah, me, too."

"Doing?"

"Thinking, drafting up a proposal, entertaining your aunt. She's easy to have around. Not like some people I know."

"I'm easy to be around," she said indignantly.

"Not with the sparks you throw off."

"Sparks?"

"Mmm, remind me to demonstrate when we have dinner next Wednesday."

"If you need reminding, it can't be that obvious."

"Maybe only to me."

She snuggled down in the covers, and reached out to switch off the light. She'd dreamed about hearing his voice in the darkness, now she could.

"So tell me more about this island of yours," she invited.

"I'd rather tell you what we could do when you come to visit. Ever been in a flotation plane before?"

Prior to today? she almost asked. "No."

"We'll fly up along the coast so you can see the mainland from the air. Circle Henley Island to give you an overview of the place. Then land by the cabin. What would you like to do first, go hiking or visit the town?"

"What would you suggest?"

"Ah, a woman who puts herself completely in my hands."

She blinked. Those hands she'd stared at in the plane that morning? What would it be like to be totally in those hands? To have them caress her skin, thread themselves through her short hair and hold her for another searing kiss? She grew warm all over.

"Well, maybe not totally," she said breathlessly. The images dancing before her eyes set her pulse to racing.

"And I thought you were daring."

"I am. In certain areas."

"But not all?"

"Tell me more about this island trip."

"We'll go for a hike first. Walk through the trees until we come to the highest point on Henley. From a meadow on the mainland side you can see almost three hundred degrees. On a sunny day, the sight is breathtaking. I'd kiss you there."

Karla sunk down farther on her pillows. She could almost feel his lips against hers again. Almost taste him, almost reach out to touch him.

"Karla?" His voice was so deep, so sexy. She wished she'd never embarked on this adventure. Would she still have met him at the theater? Would they have found something in common without the problem of work threatening?

"Karla?"

"Hmm?"

"What would you do?"

"Kiss you back, of course. Good night, Matt."

CHAPTER SEVEN

KARLA set her travel alarm early enough to make sure she would have enough time to don her makeup before Matt awoke. She was dressed and ready to descend when she heard him go downstairs. Opening her door, she followed, only to find the place empty. Glancing out the window, she saw him walking toward town.

Wandering into the kitchen, she soon had coffee brewing. Had he gone to get something for breakfast, or should she rummage around and see if she could find something and start preparing the meal?

A hasty glance in the refrigerator assured her there wasn't anything but condiments. He hadn't been kidding when he said he ate out a lot.

When the coffee was ready, she took a cup and went to sit on the porch. It was still cool and she was glad of the thick sweater she'd worn. The wig was like a warm cap, holding in the heat.

The setting was tranquil and serene. She could hear birds chirping in the trees, smell the faint tang of salt in the air. The sun sparkled on the water, and she could just make out the tail section of the little plane. Otherwise there was nothing of mankind to interrupt the flow of nature. No wonder Matt liked getting away. There was a dramatic appeal about the setting.

He had not returned by the time she finished her coffee, so Karla went to the office to double check the proposal they'd drafted. Today they'd fine-tune it and once back at work she'd have time to polish it up for presentation—including the charts and visuals he'd annotated in the margins.

Lost in thought, she didn't hear Matt. But something— a sixth sense almost—alerted her. She looked up to see him leaning against the doorjamb, arms crossed casually over his chest.

"You didn't have to start work so early," he said. "I went for breakfast. I didn't think you'd be up yet."

"I'm a morning person," Karla said, "I always get up early. There's coffee in the kitchen."

"I smelled it as I came in. There are also croissants and rolls in there as well. Care for breakfast?"

"Yes, I'm starved. Your cupboards are practically bare."

"No sense leaving food up here to spoil," Matt said as he led the way to the kitchen.

Their conversation was pleasant and innocuous as they enjoyed the fresh-baked rolls. Nothing like the phone call of last night, Karla thought. She was getting a rare view of how a person reacted with different people. And she liked everything she knew about Matt Gramling.

Matt was critical of the proposal as they reviewed it after eating. He paced the office, challenging everything. Karla tried to remember their strategy and always turned the answer to the best interest of the client, jotting notes in the margin when something didn't come off as strongly as Matt wanted.

At one point he contested a fact and Karla stood, with hands on hips, and gave him the perfect response. He appeared startled for a moment, then swooped in and hugged her, crushing her against his hard frame.

"That's perfect. Absolutely perfect!" Instantly aware, he stepped back, arms dropping to his side. Tilting his head slightly, he looked at her. "Sorry, I got carried away."

Color flooded her cheeks, she knew, but she tried to carry it off with aplomb. "I'm delighted I was able to provide some assistance." Jeez, she sounded like a prig. But, she hoped, a fifty-year-old one.

"We make a great team, Jeannette. You'll be with me when we do the presentation. If you can think as fast on your feet there as here, we won't be stopped."

Pride filled her. She was good at her job, and had a firm grasp of important business goals. Too bad Matt wasn't willing to be as open-minded about younger executive assistants.

It was early afternoon when Matt asked if she could be ready to leave shortly.

"I need to get back to Vancouver," he said, packing his briefcase. Glancing up, he continued, "And you'd have something left of your weekend. I appreciate your help, Jeannette. We finished faster than I thought we would."

"Thank you, Mr. Gramling. I want to be a team player."

He stared at her a moment, then nodded. "I'll be ready to go in about fifteen minutes. Whenever you're ready—"

"I'm already packed. Fifteen minutes will be fine."

She went to get her bag with mixed emotions. She had enjoyed the weekend, especially spending so much time with Matt. And she'd learned more about him, about his family, about what made him the man he was.

But she'd come no closer to finding a way to change his mind about his employee rule. Maybe she could concentrate on that the rest of the day.

She double checked her cell phone to make sure it was off. She didn't want to risk it ringing in the plane.

Feeling like a seasoned traveler, Karla had no qualms about getting into the plane from the dock. The return trip seemed faster than the outward bound one and in virtually no time, they were tying up to the dock in Vancouver.

"I'll have the proposal corrected first thing in the morning," she said, as Matt handed out the suitcases.

"Can you schedule a meeting with department heads as soon as you're finished. I want to review everything and make sure we can live up to our promises. If that goes well, then we'll schedule a meeting with the Taylors. I'll give you a ride home."

Karla had known he'd offer. "Thanks, but I have a couple of errands I'd like to run now that I'm already out. If you could just get me a cab?"

He didn't seem to question how she planned to do errands encumbered with two suitcases, and within five minutes she was safely ensconced in a cab—alone.

Once clear of the dock, she gave the driver her address and leaned back, feeling the relief wash through her. She'd pulled it off! A weekend in close proximity and he'd never suspected!

The relief was twinged with guilt, however. She hated not being as forthright with him as he was with her. Please, let him forgive when she told him. Let him admit his ideas about age were outmoded and she was a perfect executive assistant.

Beyond that, she refused to think. Would he want to count her as a friend once he knew?

Matt entered his apartment and tossed the duffel bag on the floor. He'd unpack later. First he wanted to see if Karla was free.

Punching in the now familiar number, he was disappointed to hear the phone was not in service. Had she turned it off? Or let the battery run down?

He refused to give in to the disappointment. He'd come home as early as he could in hopes of seeing her. Not that he'd given her a hint of that plan last night.

Heading for the kitchen, he pulled a cold bottle of soda from the refrigerator and went to sit on the sofa, legs stretched out in front of him. Sipping the beverage, he thought about last night's conversation.

Her responses had been fresh and forthright. And reminded him of how much he'd enjoyed being with her last Sunday afternoon and Wednesday evening. He wondered if she would really go off for the weekend with him. Could he guarantee it would remain as platonic as the weekend with her aunt?

Restlessly, he shifted on the couch. He did not want to remember his giving Jeannette a hug. Or the reaction his body had felt. For a moment there had been something there. He'd never felt attracted to older women before. It was the excitement of having her nail that particular aspect so strongly. Nothing more.

He took a long pull of the soda, frowning. At least that's all it had to be. He wanted to be able to work with the woman for a long time. He refused to let anything get in the way of that.

But the memory of her feminine body lingered. And the feeling of sexual desire that had filled him disturbed him.

By Wednesday morning Karla felt as if she'd already worked a week. The conferences with the various managers had gone well. Wanting to strike quickly, once Matt learned the Taylors had been available on Wednesday, he'd set the meeting for immediately after lunch.

Today's agenda was all business. The meeting was about to commence. She had her fingers crossed the one o'clock starting time would allow them to wrap things up well before the end of the business day. She had to get home and change before Matt picked her up for dinner at seven.

As she slid into her seat at the polished conference table, she glanced his way. He'd been distant all week, opting for the formality she'd originally tried to instill. She wasn't sure why the change, but it gave her the space she wanted, so she didn't question it closely.

"So nice to see you, my dear," Evelyn Taylor said as Karla sat down.

"Nice to see you, too, Mrs. Taylor. I hope you are ready to be convinced Kinsinger Electronics is the best vendor in town."

"If your enthusiasm is found in the other departments, maybe we will be."

The presentation could not have gone better, Karla thought as the afternoon unfolded. Matt introduced several key managers, brought up each point of contention, and proceeded to demonstrate how the company would deal with each issue. When one or the other of the Taylors had a concern, he often let others handle the response. When Karla answered a particular one and received his smiling nod, she was thrilled.

By four they'd covered everything. Mrs. Taylor looked at her husband. "I think we've seen more than enough to help us make our decision. Shall we be back in touch next week?"

Matt smiled broadly and nodded. "That would be perfect. And in the meantime if any other concerns crop up, please call me or Miss Jones."

Evelyn rose and smiled at Karla. "Thank you, my dear. This presentation has shown me as nothing else could have how much the management of the company has changed with Matt being in charge. I look forward to speaking with you frequently."

Karla almost danced around the room once the Taylors had left and the managers returned to their respective offices.

"Did you hear what she said, Matt?" she asked, her excitement spilling over. "She looks forward to talking with me *frequently*. That has to mean they're going for it, don't you think?"

"Yes, I do. The delay is merely window dressing— and maybe to wring another concession or two from us. Which we factored in. But I think this one is nailed." He stood at the head of the table for a moment. "Would you care to join me in a celebratory drink after work? You did a lion's share of the work on this project."

She was torn. Drinks would be great. Cementing the bond between them. And she had done a lot of the work.

But she needed the time to get home and change.

Noting her hesitation, he picked up his folders. "Never mind, Miss Jones. Another time, perhaps."

"I'd like it another time. But tonight, I have an appointment. I really need to leave at five."

"I understand." He nodded formally and left the conference room.

Picking up the rest of the notepads and folders, Karla knew she'd blown it. He'd never understand. Not unless she confessed all—which she was not about to do yet. Yet how much longer could she continue? Wouldn't it be easier to forgive the sooner the deception ended?

She almost walked into his office to confess all that moment. She'd done well on the project. He had to recognize her skills. And he knew better than anyone she wasn't getting interested in another man. He had no worries about her taking off on some romantic adventure.

But she hesitated. Not yet.

Once the contract was signed. That would be the best time. He'd already given her credit for her part in the project, he'd be in the best mood possible when they signed. She'd wait just a bit longer.

For once fate seemed to be on her side, Karla thought that afternoon when Matt left early. She dashed off for home with extra time to get ready for their dinner date. Her spirits rose now that she'd definitely decided to tell him once the Percell Group deal was signed, sealed and delivered.

She could enjoy their evening without the constant nagging remorse. Not that she could relax her guard, but at least she knew the end was in sight.

He'd be angry, probably. But he had to admit she was an excellent executive assistant, and she was counting on that to enable her to keep her job. That and the aspects she'd contributed to this project.

The flirty dress she donned after her shower was bright red, flaring at the knees, but hugging her where it counted. She carefully applied makeup, fluffing up her short hair and grinning at herself in the mirror. She couldn't wait to see him again.

Watch it, she admonished, trying to rein in the anticipation that soared. She needed to keep control of those emotions. He was a *friend,* someone to share a meal with. At this stage, that was all!

When the doorbell sounded, she almost floated to answer. Matt stood there—a huge bouquet of spring flowers in his hands. She raised his gaze and raised her eyebrows in question.

"For you. I thought the flowers from last week might have wilted by now."

"Thank you." She reached out for the bouquet, her heart somersaulting in her chest. She loved flowers. He'd remembered from dinner last week.

"Come in. I'll put these in water and then be ready. Do you want a drink before we go?"

"We don't have a lot of time. I booked a table at Balcomb's in North Vancouver. I thought we could take the ferry over."

"Sounds great," she called from the kitchen. Finding a suitable vase, she soon had the bouquet arranged to suit her. Carrying it carefully so not to slosh the water, she returned to the living room, placing the vase in a place of honor in the center of her coffee table. Stepping back, she admired the flowers—daisies, tiger lilies, carnations, and several others she didn't recognize. Their bright colors blended beautifully.

"I love flowers," she said softly, her blood humming through her veins when she looked at Matt. How could he look better than he had at the office?

She reached up to kiss his cheek in thanks.

"If I remember, the dock isn't far, and it's still warm outside, want to walk? Or I can get a cab if your shoes aren't suitable," he said, glancing down her legs to the high-heeled shoes she wore.

"Walking's fine. These are comfortable shoes." Just in case there was dancing, though she refused to let the thought linger.

The ferry from downtown Vancouver to North Vancouver was crowded with business people returning home at the end of the day, some still working, others talking on cell phones, and others just sitting. Tourists crowding the rails, excitedly pointing out sites they recognized.

Matt found them a place inside—away from the wind and salt spray, but with a view from the huge windows. He smiled at the elderly woman seated beside them, then turned his attention to Karla.

"Have you been to Balcomb's before?"

"Once or twice. It has the best Italian food in the area, I think."

"It came highly recommended by Richard Taylor."

Karla started to comment, then caught herself. As Karla she wouldn't know Richard Taylor from a hole in the wall. "Is he a friend of yours?"

"New client—I think."

"The big deal you're working on?" she guessed.

"The big deal I think we've cinched." He told her about the presentation and the reaction of the Taylors. Karla listened, touched when he gave her credit for several aspects. He also mentioned the managers who had contributed ideas and data. He might be a turnaround manager, building on the incompetence of others, but he didn't hog the glory. She was fascinated by his persistence in recognizing the contributions in others.

When they reached the dock in North Vancouver, most of the people on board made an immediate surge to exit.

"If we wait a bit, the crush will pass and we can walk off like civilized people," Matt commented, eyeing the crowd.

"I like the way you think. I'm not much for pushing through crowds."

"I remember that from the night at the theater. So we'll wait."

As apparently was the elderly woman beside them. In fact, she was watching the crowd with something like apprehension.

When the majority of passengers had departed, Matt rose and offered his hand to Karla.

"Excuse me, sir," the elderly woman said, rising unsteadily. "This is the only stop here, isn't it? If someone is meeting me, this is where I would get off?"

"Yes, ma'am. This is the terminal in North Vancouver. Is someone meeting you?"

"My grandson," she said proudly. "He and his wife are taking me to dinner for my birthday. I said I'd come here to meet them. They work so hard, they didn't need to come to Vancouver."

"Why not walk out with us, and we'll make sure he finds you," Matt said.

"Thank you."

The three of them slowly made their way off the ferry and to the busy terminal. Passengers were already in line for the return trip.

It was more than fifteen minutes before a harried young man and his wife dashed over to them.

"Grandma! I'm so sorry." He gave her a hug. "Traffic was terrible."

"Hi, Grandma." His companion hugged her and smiled down at the older woman. "We were so worried about you. Did you think we weren't coming?"

"No, this nice young man and his friend kept me company."

Introductions were made, and then Matt and Karla bid the others goodbye and headed for the restaurant.

"I almost thought she'd been stood up," Karla commented once they were on the sidewalk.

"Much longer and I was considering asking her to join us for dinner."

"You had no responsibility for her," Karla murmured, touched he'd already gone out of his way to keep Mildred Williams company as they had. She tried to think of another man she knew who would have done so.

Matt might argue against ties and a family. He might come across as a hard-nosed businessman, dedicated to work and getting ahead. But he had a heart. He'd probably deny it to doomsday, but she knew.

Karla also suspected she could fall for the man in a big way—and she didn't have a clue what to do about it.

The restaurant was not crowded. They were shown to a quiet table which afforded plenty of privacy. Ordering the same entrée, veal scalopini, Matt commented on the fact.

"Great minds run alike, don't you know?" she replied, toying with her water glass. She studied him across the table, her heart catching slightly when his eyes met hers. She felt as if she'd been touched. Her internal temperature soared, staining her cheeks red, she knew, but she couldn't look away.

"So tell me about your day, I've already talked your ears off about mine," he said.

"It was a great day. I got kudos from my boss, and got to leave on time."

He smiled. "And that makes it great? He must be a regular slave driver ordinarily."

"He's a terrific boss," she said seriously. "And I'm learning a lot from working with him."

"Loyalty. A nice trait, Karla."

"So are you renting a flat? Buying a house? What?" she asked, changing the subject before she threw herself into his arms and demand he sweep her away. All from a smile?

"Renting a flat temporarily. I'd like to find a bigger one. With a view of the water, if possible."

The conversation moved easily from Matt's plans for the future, to the musical where they'd met. He casually mentioned seeing another one together soon. Karla liked the fact he easily made plans. He liked being with her, she knew that. As much as she enjoyed being with him?

They were sipping coffee at the end of the meal when he formally invited her to the cabin.

"The one on the island?" she asked, stalling for time. He'd mentioned it before, but now he was asking about this weekend. He wanted her to spend Saturday and Sunday with him on Henley Island. Just the two of them!

"I'll have to check—"

"—my calendar," he finished in unison with her. "You do that and call me tomorrow."

It was hard to concentrate on the conversation after that—when the decision about the weekend loomed. But Karla did her best. The time flew by and it was with reluctance when he mentioned leaving she agreed.

True to his word, they returned to her apartment before ten. He walked her to the door.

"Want to come in for coffee?" she asked, not wishing to end the evening so early.

"I'll take a rain check, if I may." He brushed the backs of his fingers against her cheeks again and gazed into her eyes. "Thank you for spending the evening with me, Karla."

"I had a great time." He was going to kiss her, she knew it. Slowly his head came closer. Seconds before his lips touched hers, she could almost feel him, taste him.

Impatient with his pace, she stood on tiptoes and pressed her mouth against his. The sensations that washed through her filled her with delight. When his arms came around to hold her closer, she relaxed into his embrace, knowing it was almost heaven on earth.

How long could they remain friends? Even good, close friends?

Thursday morning there was another cream-colored envelope in the center of her desk.

"I'm almost expecting them," she murmured as she picked it up and slit it open.

A small favor to keep a big secret. The old boys' network has its referral program, time we did, too!

Karla stuffed it back into the envelope and slipped it into her purse. She thought about asking Lisa if she'd seen anyone that morning, but didn't want the new typist to start speculating why she'd ask. From the last comment, she now knew the sender had to be a woman. But who?

Karla had three choices. First—do nothing. Second, confess to Matt now and hope he was satisfied enough with her work to waive his 25-50 rule—at both ends. Or, third, try to find the person who was sending the messages and make it clear she was not going to cooperate. Her loyalty to the company and to Matt was complete.

And on top of this worry, she still had to decide what to do about the weekend. She spent all day every day with the man, surely it wouldn't hurt to spend a weekend together at the island. The personal time they spent together enabled her to learn precious tidbits of personal information that she alone knew.

And indulge her own desires to be with him. She had never felt so special, so feminine as she did when with Matt. Did he have any idea of the effect he had?

Confessing would probably change everything, she thought morosely. Matt had been very clear he didn't date women who worked for him. Even if he allowed her to remain as his executive assistant once he knew her age, which she fervently hoped he would, he'd stop seeing her socially.

That was enough to give a person second thoughts

about confessing even when she knew it was the right thing to do.

And she had no doubts he'd follow through with his no dating rule. That wasn't even an edict she would argue with him. Office romances could become so tangled.

So this might be the only time she'd have to spend a weekend with him.

She grabbed her cell phone and headed for the stairwell. Checking to make sure no one was using the stairs, she punched in his private number. He answered on the second ring.

"It's Karla," she said, straining to hear if anyone was approaching. It would never do to be caught.

"Did you check your calendar?"

"Yes. I'm free. I would be delighted to go with you to the island this weekend." The die was cast!

"Good." There was a wealth of satisfaction in his tone. "We'll leave early Saturday morning. I'll pick you up at seven."

"Sounds great. See you then." She clicked off the phone, relieved she'd gotten away with the call without anyone using the stairs—not that there was too much risk. Being on the twentieth floor, most people used the elevator.

Focusing on work, Karla decided to ask Pat's advice about her mysterious letters when she went to visit with her and the baby again tomorrow evening. There wasn't anyone else to ask. She just hoped the sender didn't pick up the pace and demand the payoff before Friday.

After dinner, Karla put on the TV and tried to settle in to watch a sitcom. But her mind wandered to the forthcoming weekend. She was about to give up and go do something constructive—like clean her closet—when there was a knock at her door.

Opening it, she was surprised to see Matt.

"I took a chance you'd be home," he said.

"Come on in. I told you I rarely go out on work nights, so it wasn't too much of a chance I'd be here."

"Am I interrupting something?" he asked, quickly scanning the living room.

"No. I was trying to get interested in TV, but it wasn't working. Did you come for that rain check?" She didn't much care why he'd come, she was glad to see him. "I can put water on for coffee."

"Want to go out for a quick dessert? It's warm outside, maybe we could go for a walk along the seawalk, stop for coffee at one of the cafés along the way."

"Sounds great, let me get my jacket." Almost giddy with happiness, Karla was ready to leave in less than two minutes.

"I should have called," Matt said as they headed toward the bay.

"I like spontaneity."

"Good." He took her hand, lacing his fingers through hers. Karla caught her breath, the tingling sweeping through her, making her more aware of everything, from the deepening colors of the sunset, to the feel of the breeze caressing her cheeks.

"I didn't want to wait until the weekend to see you again," he said. "Want to have dinner tomorrow night?"

"I can't. I already have plans."

Matt seemed to withdraw a bit. Stiffly he nodded once. "A date?" As an attempt to sound casual, it failed.

Karla hid a smile, shaking her head. "Not really. I'm going to see my friend and her baby again." Her spirits soared. He cared if she saw someone else. Despite being only friends, he didn't like the idea of her dating! She stepped closer, tightening her hold on his hand and smiling up at him. "I'm glad you came by tonight."

At seven on Saturday morning the doorbell rang. Karla hurried to answer it. She'd packed last night after returning home from visiting Pat and Todd and little Brittany. Rising earlier than usual, she'd dressed quickly and waited impatiently for Matt to arrive. She was excited about the possibilities of the weekend. Two glorious days in his company. It would make up for missing dinner with him last night.

"Good morning," she said with a wide smile, her heart skittering in her chest at the sight of him.

"Good morning to you," Matt said, leaning over to kiss her.

Startled, Karla was swept up into his embrace, opening her mouth to his sweet assault. She'd only caught a glimpse of him—dressed in a black sweater and dark pants. But even a glimpse was enough to convey the sexy, masculine image Matt always transmitted.

He ended the kiss slowly, as if reluctant. Then rested his forehead on hers. "You look lovely."

"How could you tell? I open the door and you give one of your killer kisses."

"Killer kisses?"

"They kill all my good sense."

He smiled slowly, and Karla felt her bones melt. She

was falling in love with the man. What was she going to do?

"I like that."

"Mmm, I bet you do. Are you in a hurry to leave? Want some coffee first?"

"Coffee would be great. I brought breakfast. You didn't eat yet, did you?"

She shook her head. "I don't usually eat much at breakfast."

"You'll love these." He gently urged her into the apartment and closed the door.

"Good grief. Good thing it's early, or there would have been spectators in the hall." She couldn't believe she'd forgotten to even shut the door.

"I knew we were alone," Matt said, heading for her kitchen as if he'd been there a dozen times.

Karla had made a pot of coffee and went to pour them each a cup. The fragrance of fresh-baked bread filled the room.

"Something smells great," she said.

He found a plate and placed the croissants and rolls on it. "If you have jam we'll be set."

They sat at the small table, the morning sun streaming in, his flowers in the center—still fresh and colorful. It was cozy and domestic and almost like a fairy tale, Karla thought as Matt spread jam on his croissant.

One she had best not plan on repeating.

But for today, she'd enjoy the moment. And have the memories forever.

"No morning paper?" she commented, taking pleasure in watching him eat, memorizing his ritual of spreading jam, taking a bite, then a sip of coffee.

"Why would I want to read the paper if I could look at you?"

She laughed. "Do you stay up nights practicing lines to hand out?"

"Only if I think the lady involved would be susceptible."

"And am I?"

"You tell me."

Slowly Karla shook her head. It was a lie. She was as susceptible as the next woman as her fluttering heart attested. But it would never do to let Matt know it. His ego was enormous as it was.

And she must never forget this was but a moment out of time for her. For this moment, she would savor the words and pretend she would change his mind and together they could build a future.

She did have it bad, she thought as she quickly rose to refill the coffee cups.

CHAPTER EIGHT

KARLA felt like an old hand at flying when she stepped
into the floatplane an hour later. She balanced easily on
the pontoon, and slipped into her seat. The cabin again
seemed to shrink when Matt joined her. She could feel
her tension rise a notch when his leg brushed against hers
as he settled into his seat. Deliberately she'd be willing
to bet.

Two could play that game, she thought. Reaching forward to take the earphones he'd shown her how to use
last time, she brushed against his shoulder.

"Are these for me?" she asked, leaning forward
slightly until her face was only inches from his.

The amusement in his eyes showed he was on to her.
But he merely nodded, his gaze dropping to her lips.
Karla felt as if he'd touched her. She placed the earphones on her head, her gaze holding his. Slowly Matt
leaned closer. Closing the distance, Karla kissed him. Her
eyes drifted closed while she enjoyed the texture and
temperature and taste of his lips against hers in the gently
rocking plane.

"A pilot isn't supposed to drink or take drugs before
flying," Matt said, pulling back. "Kissing you is about
as intoxicating. If we want to get anywhere today—" he
touched her lips with his index finger "—mark my place
and we'll take it up again later."

She pursed her lips and kissed his finger. "I've never been intoxicating before."

"Oh, lady, I bet you have. The other guy just didn't tell you. It's a dangerous thing to give a woman a weapon like that."

"But not for you?"

"I love danger."

Karla could understand that. She discovered recently she loved danger as well. Wasn't that what this entire weekend was about?

Feeling almost too keyed up to sit, Karla sat back and tried to enjoy the hour's flight to Henley Island. She had a glorious view of the western border of Canada as they flew north. And a glorious view of Matt when she'd sneak peeks in his direction. She hoped he didn't notice. He seemed caught up in his flying.

When they settled on the inlet near the cabin, she felt a new wave of excitement. This time it was the two of them—with no work to occupy the hours. The enforced intimacy was thrilling. She knew they'd go hiking, maybe have lunch at the café in town. And later—

"Welcome to Henley Island," Matt said, as the plane gently bumped the floating dock. "Hold on a sec, I'll tie up and you can get out."

The air felt balmy against her cheeks as she stepped out of the plane. Matt's hand was there to take hers.

"I hope you have a good time this weekend," he said in a low voice.

Even if they stood all day on the dock, as long as he held her hand, she knew she'd have a great time.

"We'll take the bags to the house, I'll show you

around then we can walk to the village. They have a nice café there where we can get lunch,'' he said.

"So my aunt said."

"Did she tell you a lot about the island?"

"You might say I saw it all through her eyes," Karla said daringly.

"Then you'll have to give me your impressions as we go along, and see how they compare."

He showed her to the same room she'd had last time and told her to come downstairs when she was ready. Did that mean he had no plans for the dessert he'd alluded to during their dinner on Wednesday evening? Or was he giving her the choice?

Knowing what to expect from the village, Karla had dressed more appropriately to exploring old ruins than she had the last visit. Jeans and sturdy shoes were perfect. The light yellow sweater was enough to keep her warm, without getting hot.

Matt seemed to take as much enjoyment in the exploration as she did. He even stopped in the small general store and found a paperback pamphlet extolling the history of the island. Together they read various sections, and tried to find the original sites discussed.

By the time they stopped for a late lunch, Karla knew a great deal about the stranded Russians and the hardships they'd faced.

"Glad it wasn't me," she said as she began to eat the thick roast beef sandwich she'd ordered.

"Glad it wasn't you what?" Matt asked. He'd ordered the same and was slathering horse radish on his.

"Stranded here."

"It wouldn't have been so bad. There was game, fishing, plenty of firewood."

"There speaks a true outdoorsman. Drop you anywhere and you'd survive."

He nodded, his expression pensive. "I believe I could. Doesn't mean I ever want to put it to the test."

She nibbled the sandwich as she envisioned him striding out boldly into the wilderness. He fit in that setting as much as in the boardroom. She had never met another man who would.

"So after we eat are you taking me up to that meadow with the terrific view?" she asked.

He raised an eyebrow. "Is that what you remember about the meadow—the view I spoke about?"

She nodded, knowing she fibbed. The primary memory was of his promising to kiss her there.

"I remember something more," he said softly, teasing lights dancing in his eyes.

"Are you suggesting your memory is better than mine?"

"Perhaps a bit more selective. I can refresh yours if you like."

"Maybe." She peeked up at him from beneath her eyelashes and caught the intensity of his gaze. She had no doubts about the meadow and how he'd refresh her memory.

Walking up the hiking trail sometime later, however, Karla wondered if she'd live to reach the meadow. The trail was steep in parts, rocky throughout and narrow. Tall lodgepole pines rose on each side, giving her the feeling she was walking through a roofless tunnel.

But she wouldn't complain for anything. Matt strode

ahead as if on the seawalk in Vancouver. He wasn't even breathing hard! She knew he'd be at home in the wilderness—while she was gasping for breath, and hoping her heart didn't rupture from its rapid pace.

"You all right?" he asked at a bend in the trail. He stood with one foot resting on a rock, the sleeves of his dark sweater pushed up on his arms. His hair was mussed, his eyes sparkling in the sunshine.

"If I live to get to the meadow, I have no doubts I'll find it worthwhile," she said, trying to breathe normally.

He reached out and pulled her up the last few feet. "You could have said something. We can take a rest if you like."

He brushed back a strand of hair, almost caressing her cheek in the process. "We're not in a race. If we want to take it slowly, we can."

"*We* don't need to take it slowly, *I* do," Karla said, surrendering her pride. She took in a deep breath, another. It was good to just stand still for a few moments.

"We're almost there," he offered.

She glared at him. "This had better be spectacular."

He laughed, his head tipped back. She caught her breath, her heart racing for a totally different reason. It wasn't fair that one man had so much charm and appeal. Especially one who reiterated that he was not interested in a relationship.

Lowering his head until he almost touched hers, Matt narrowed his eyes, gazing into hers. He blocked the sun, the trees. Karla could see nothing but Matt, and the power in his gaze.

"I promise I'll do all I can to make sure you find it spectacular."

"The view?"

"Oh? Were you talking about the view?"

Her eyes locked with his, she tried to think of something that would set his blatant sex appeal back a notch or two, but nothing came to mind—except an image of the two of them kissing on the hilltop with the sea around them, and the mainland in the distance.

His finger tipped up her chin, until her mouth was only a scant inch or two from his. "We don't even have to go all the way to the meadow if you don't want."

She could feel the warmth from his finger seep into every cell. Her lips actually tingled in anticipation of his. Did he know the effect he had on her?

"I want to see the view from the meadow," she said firmly. Taking another deep breath, she filled her lungs with the scent of pines, dust, and Matt. It was a heady fragrance that did nothing to ease the tension winding tightly in her body.

"That's all?"

She smiled saucily. "You're the tour guide, surprise me."

The remainder of the hike up seemed easier. In no time Karla walked out into the center of the large meadow. Wild grass grew almost knee-deep. Here and there a brightly hued clump of wildflowers shone in the sun. She could see the sea, the tall trees on the lower slope and in the distance, the Canadian mainland. It was as beautiful a spot as Matt had said.

For a long time, she soaked up the sights and sounds. The hush of the breeze, moving over the grass, causing it to undulate in a mirror image of the waves on the water. Sparkling lights danced on the water. And the quiet was tranquil and serene.

"It's lovely," she said.

Matt stood at her left. He nodded. "I thought you'd like it."

"Is this what you see when you go on your wilderness treks? No signs of mankind anywhere?"

"Usually. Sometimes I discover an old mining camp, or a place where hunters stopped and didn't clean up after themselves. But usually it's just the land the way God made it."

"Wow, no wonder you take off every so often. This is amazing." She wondered if she'd ever get her fill of the view. He'd been right, it was spectacular.

"Want to stay here a little while?" he asked.

She nodded. "Maybe forever."

Matt sat on the grass, stretched out his long legs and leaned back on his hands. "Gets cold at night."

Karla sat down beside him. "You could build a fire."

"Mmm. There are other ways to stay warm."

Tearing her gaze from the view, she looked at him. "And I bet you know them all."

"I know a few. Shall I share?"

Do or die time, Karla thought. She leaned closer. "Yes, share."

Matt pulled her into his arms and lay back in the lush green grass. One hand cradled her head as he brought it in position to kiss her. His mouth was warm and firm and moved against hers with gentle persuasion.

Unnecessary persuasion, Karla thought in the last fleeting seconds of rational thoughts. She reached out to encircle his neck and let the kiss take its course.

Heat to rival the sun swept through her. Passion and desire mingled and grew. She loved this man, loved what pleasure his touch brought. Time seemed to stand still, or spin wildly. She wasn't sure which.

He rolled them over until Karla lay on the sweet-smelling grass. She tightened her hold on him and savored the touch of his hands in her hair, running down the side of her body, pressing her closer to him.

She knew the blazing internal fires he generated would have kept them warm in the most severe blizzard. In the balmy afternoon sunshine, she was burning up. For Matt. With Matt. She'd never felt like this before. It was heaven, it was glorious.

He raised his head and looked at her. She stared into his eyes, seeing the rampant passion he couldn't damp down.

"I want you, Karla, more than I've ever wanted anyone. Are you going to spend the night with me?"

Karla set the table in the cabin, listening to Matt moving in the kitchen. They were having steaks and baked potatoes. His menus weren't too varied, she mused, but delicious all the same.

She studied the table, checking that she had everything. Outwardly she was functioning normally. Inside she was a mass of nervous energy. It was as if her mind was processing at two levels—normal everyday functions, and focused on Matt's question. Was she going to spend the night with him?

She had not given a definitive answer in the meadow. And, instead of being angry, he'd seemed amused. Or was that a cover to hide his own uncertainty?

Hardly. Matt Gramling had not had an uncertain moment since he was five, she'd bet. The man had definite goals, views and opinions and wasn't slow in sharing any of them.

Instead of getting angry, he'd acted as if nothing out of the ordinary had been said. The walk back had been much easier—being downhill the entire way. Conversation had been friendly, and she'd even picked some wildflowers.

Then, they'd checked the plane and she'd helped in the refueling.

When she offered to help with dinner, he'd firmly told her to sit and keep him company but he'd handle everything.

She liked being treated so royally. Kevin had never had her to dinner at his place, they always ate out if they shared a meal. Nor had any of the men she'd dated over the years invited her to their apartments for a meal.

Not that there'd been that many. She had spent a lot of time on her career, and social activities with groups of friends. She knew Pat despaired of her ever falling in love. Wouldn't her friend be shocked to discover Karla had—and with whom?

Last night hadn't been as helpful in solving her dilemma as she had hoped. Taken with the new baby, Todd hovering nearby, Karla had not been able to share everything with Pat as she'd planned. Not that it mattered. In the end, she was the only one to decide what she would do.

Karla touched one of the wildflowers that now graced the center of the table. Glancing around, her gaze was drawn outside. She loved this place. No wonder Matt had come three times already since moving to Vancouver. When his friend returned, would Matt look for a similar retreat?

Seeing him today in the outdoors had given her a new view of the man. She wanted to know everything about him, but realistically knew she'd never see him in his wilderness mode. Still, the things he shared today had given her insight into what he probably was like on his own—man against nature. Strong, calm, resilient and capable. Just about the perfect male.

If only he didn't have that quirky rule about ages!

"Ready to eat?" Matt asked from the doorway to the kitchen—a plate in each hand. In no time they were seated at the table enjoying the meal he'd prepared.

"You are very versatile," she said, slathering butter on her baked potato. "What else, domestically speaking, do you do?" Karla asked.

"This is my limit."

"Surely you don't eat steak and potatoes every night when in the wilderness."

"There, I usually eat what I hunt—small game, or fish. Of course, I always carry a few dehydrated food packs, just in case."

"Have you ever used one?"

He shook his head.

"If you could live any life you chose, would you live in the wilderness all the time?" Karla asked.

"No. I like the challenge of business, the dynamics of turning a faltering concern into a profitable one. And—" he raised an eyebrow "—I think I mentioned, I like women. I don't know any who would relish spending

time in the Yukon without any of the amenities we normally take for granted. Would you?''

"Probably not." Though if anyone could make it exciting while safe, it would be Matt.

"What would be your ideal life?" he asked. Holding
the bottle of wine, he hesitated over her glass until she
nodded. Filling it again, he replenished his own glass and
waited for her reply.

"I like the life I have now," she said slowly. "I have
a lot of friends to do things with, a job I love, and parents
near enough to visit without feeling like they're smoth-
ering me."

"But no steady man."

She shrugged. "Is that another misconception you harbor? That women are sitting around waiting for a man to
sweep them off their feet?"

"A *rich* man, yes. Want to argue the point?"

"I certainly do! I make a good income, have a nice
apartment, and plenty of activities and friends to fill my
life. I'm not waiting for some man to come along and
change all that!"

"Unless he was rich," Matt said smoothly.

"Will you get off that kick? You were burned once.
That's too bad. But not all women are like that. Don't
you worry about growing old all alone? No family around
you? Work can only fill so much of a person's life."

Matt toyed with his glass a moment, then took a long
pull of the wine. "I don't think about that. If I get to the
point where I think a family would be something I
wanted, then I'd do what I needed to get one."

Karla stared at him for a moment. He was serious. Her
heart melted for him. What a sad state of affairs. "Don't

do that, Matt. Don't settle for someone who doesn't adore you. You deserve happiness and love.''

He looked uncomfortable. ''I'll keep that in mind.''

''Just because you haven't fallen in love yet doesn't mean it can't happen.''

''Are you in the running?''

She shook her head, trying a smile. ''No thanks. Carefree and liking it that way,'' she said firmly. It was cowardly, but she couldn't tell him how she felt. Even though she wondered what he would say if she told him.

''Ready for dessert?'' he asked.

She felt a kick of adrenaline. Did he mean—

''I can't make a chocolate mousse, but the café in town makes a terrific apple pie. And I picked up some ice cream so I can offer it à la mode.''

''Sounds lovely.''

By the time they finished their dessert, and had some coffee, it was growing dark outside. Matt rifled through a small stack of CDS and placed one in the player.

The soft music filled the house as he held his hand to her. ''Dance with me, Karla.''

She rose with alacrity, delighted to be in his arms. The tempo filled her and she gave in to the swaying her body wanted, moving with Matt, safely held in his embrace.

Song after song played as they danced around the large living room, lost in a world of two.

When the CD ended, he still held her. ''I need your answer now, Karla. Come upstairs with me and stay the night. I want you.''

She looked into his eyes and saw the truth, the sincerity, the passion and desire. No one knew the future. But

Karla knew no matter what it held, memories of a night with the man she loved would always be special.

"Yes," she said softly.

"I'll turn off the lights and lock up," he said, a husky edge to his voice.

"I'll run up and, mmm, change," she said. Her legs would scarcely hold her as she climbed the stairs and headed for her room. Quickly she drew the nightgown she'd brought from the drawer—not the flannel one from the last trip. Trying not to think, to ignore any doubts and second thoughts, she pulled the sweater over her head and in only seconds was ready for the satiny nightgown.

Ivory in color, it was cool as it slid over her skin. The thin straps held it up—but barely. Skimming over her breasts, it fell to just above her knees, a mere slip of a gown, shifting to caress and reveal her body as she walked.

She peered into a mirror, startled to see the glow on her skin, the sparkling lights in her eyes. She already looked well loved.

Spinning around, she took a deep breath and crossed the room to open the door.

Matt leaned against the wall waiting. He didn't know what he was doing, only that he wanted Karla more than he'd ever wanted anyone. She was different from anyone else he'd known. Her laughter seemed to fill him with sunshine. He groaned softly. Did he have a touch of sunstroke? He was sounding as sappy as some damned poet.

She was fun to be with. That was all. And caring. She'd been as concerned for the lady on the ferry as he had.

Loyal. Great, now he made her sound like a favorite dog.

She was— His thoughts fled when she opened her door.

She was beautiful and sexy and slim and satiny soft and smelled like a million flowers. The light in her eyes, the radiance of her smile humbled him. He swallowed hard and pushed away from the wall, drawn to her like a magnet homing north.

His gaze ran down her like a caress. He wanted to touch that silky hair, feel the velvety texture of her skin, slip that barely-there gown from her shoulders and kiss every inch of her.

"You are so beautiful," he said as he reached out his hand to take hers.

He led the way into his room almost wishing the bed was small instead of large. That they'd have to sleep together whether she wanted or not. Would she like to be held all night? The darkness was complete outside, but he could catch the glimmering of stars. He didn't turn on a light, using only the dim illumination from the hallway to show the way.

They should make love outside. He'd love to seek her skin in the starlight. Maybe on another visit—if the summer grew warm enough. He'd wanted to make love to her in the meadow, their meadow, with nothing but the stars to cover them.

Stopping by the bed, he turned her and looked into her eyes, placing his hands on her shoulders. His warm palms heating her cool skin. Taking a deep breath, he held his breath a moment, savoring her special scent before lowering his head to kiss her.

* * *

The fragrance of coffee slowly filtered in. Karla rolled over in bed and frowned. Coffee? She opened her eyes. The room wasn't familiar. Then she recognized where she was.

The telephone rang.

She sat up, holding the sheet in place when she realized she no longer wore her nightgown. It had been discarded long ago. Matt was no longer in bed.

Was that her phone? It sounded a second time—and was answered. She looked at the clock on the bedside table. It was only seven, not late. She slid out of bed, looking wildly around for her nightgown. Finding it at the foot of the bed, she put it on. Still feeling exposed, she dashed out to the hall and across to her room.

Quickly snatching up a change of clothes, she headed for the bathroom and a shower.

Dressed a short time later, she sat on the edge of her bed. What was she going to do? Last night had been special. Matt so attentive and loving. And she wasn't really having regrets. Only wishing his feelings for her were as strong as hers for him.

But the morning after was awkward. Did she march down there and greet him like they were longtime lovers? Or wait until she saw how he acted? Should she have stayed in bed waiting for him? Or was he glad she was already up and ready for the day?

They could go hiking again. Maybe have lunch at the café before heading back to Vancouver.

She rubbed her palms over her slacks, knowing she needed to go downstairs, reluctant to move.

Matt rapped on her door. ''Karla? Are you dressed? I

have to get back to Vancouver." Urgency sounded in his voice.

She opened the door. "What's wrong?"

"There's a major problem with my company in Toronto. I need access to my fax and computer. I may have to fly back there if I can't get things straightened out from this end. Sorry to cut the weekend short, but I need to get to Vancouver as quickly as possible."

"I can be ready in no time," she said, already turning away to pack her bag.

He caught her arm and stopped her, swinging her back gently. "This wasn't how I pictured this morning," he said, lowering his mouth to hers briefly.

"It's okay. I understand business demands," she said. "I'll be ready in five."

"Coffee's ready. Get a cup before we leave." With that, he turned and headed for his room.

At least the awkwardness of the morning was mitigated, she thought, as she folded her jeans and sweater and placed them in the suitcase she'd borrowed from Pat. She had not wanted to take the chance Matt would recognize her own from Jeannette's weekend.

Karla placed her suitcase by the front door and went into the kitchen to get a cup of coffee. She'd have something to eat when she got home. Disappointment about their weekend welled. Yesterday had been so much fun, the two of them shared a lot of interests. Now work intervened.

A thought struck. Would Matt want Jeannette to help out? Good grief, he might have already called to ask her to meet him at the office!

She poured a cup of coffee with shaky hands. There

was no way she would be able to go into the office today. Not after last night. If he had left a message, she would just not respond and make up an excuse tomorrow morning.

"Ready?"

"Yes." She finished the coffee and rinsed the cup. He unplugged the machine, dumped the rest and rinsed it with water, leaving it to drain on the side of the sink. With a quick look around in farewell, they headed for the plane.

In no time they were airborne and heading for Vancouver.

CHAPTER NINE

KARLA stared out the window, at the sea, at the scattering of smaller islands that dotted the expanse of ocean. A jumble of emotions swirled around inside. She closed her eyes in memory of last night. Matt had been so incredibly tender—and so amazingly sexy she couldn't believe it. Their lovemaking had been fantastic—and had topped off her love with feelings so strong she wondered if she would ever get over the man.

She knew last night's memory would always be special. The wealth of love she'd poured out, the kisses that had been so potent, his caressing hands, her own. His scent, and taste and touch. All were burned into her mind for all time.

"You're quiet today. Regrets?" he asked.

Opening her eyes she looked squarely at him. "None. You?"

"Only that our weekend got cut short. We'll have to go away again."

She nodded, smiling warmly. "I'd like to see the meadow again. But before next time I'm practicing so I can climb up there without going into cardiac arrest."

He nodded, reaching out to take her hand, resting their linked fingers on his hard thigh. "I appreciate your not throwing a fit at the way the weekend turned out."

"I understand business demands, Matt." What had his

other women been like if they threw a fit when a crisis
arose?

"I hope the crisis at your company is easily resolved."

"We'll see. I need to get all the facts before proceed-
ing."

She could almost see him click into business mode.
She gazed out the window, feeling dismissed, yet linked
by their hands. His palm was warm, firm against hers.
His thumb absently caressed the back of her hand. A
small thrill raced through her. His touch was still potent,
and sexy. She wished the business problems had not
arisen. She felt cheated of their day together.

When they docked in Vancouver, she took her small
bag and walked along the pier with him. "I'll get a cab
home. You can head right for work."

"I'll take you."

"No need. I know you need to get in and start the ball
rolling on that problem." She stopped and looked up at
him. "I had a great time."

He smiled. "You sound like a proper little girl being
polite."

"I was properly brought up and I am being polite. And
honest. I had a great time."

He brushed his fingers against her cheek and caught
the nape of her neck, caressing gently, his palm warm
and firm. "I don't want this to be our only weekend."

She smiled and nodded, afraid to speak. How many
could they have? She felt another twinge of guilt. Before
she went again, she'd make sure he knew everything. It
wasn't fair to Matt or to her to continue they way they'd
been. And it was up to her to make everything right.

He kissed her gently. "I'll call you."

"Okay."

He signaled for a cab and put her inside, handing the driver some bills.

Karla glanced out the back window as they pulled away, Matt was already striding down the street in the direction of the office building. Business came first.

When Karla reached her office Monday morning, Matt was already on the phone. She waved through the open door and went to her desk. Lisa arrived a short time later and Karla heard her starting work.

Reviewing the things she had left from last week, Karla kept an eye on the phone. As soon as Matt got off, she'd go in for their routine morning planning session. She was impatient to learn what had happened in Toronto, and if she could help.

But the minutes ticked by and he remained on the phone. Was the call connected with the problem in Toronto? It had to be. At least he hadn't had to go east to deal with it.

When Karla's phone rang midmorning, she answered it unsuspecting.

"Are you going to grant a small favor?" an unfamiliar voice asked.

"Are you the one sending me anonymous notes?"

"I know who you are and the stunt you're pulling. But if you help me, I don't have to blow the whistle."

"What is it you want?"

"The job available in Human Resources."

"Pat's job?"

"Yes. They're considering two other people. But a few good words put in by you, and I bet Mr. Matthew

Gramling will throw his weight my way. At least you better make sure he does.''

"Who are you?"

The hesitation on the other end was noticeable. Finally the woman said, "Alice Sawyer. I've been here for six years. It's time I was promoted to department head. You fix it and I'll keep quiet." She hung up.

Karla replaced her phone and glanced around guiltily. Matt was still on the phone and from the sound of typing in the outer office, Lisa was fully occupied.

Quickly Karla dialed Pat's home phone.

"Hello?"

"Pat, this is Karla."

"What are you doing calling me at this time of day? Boss out of the office? You're lucky I was home. Brittany and I are venturing out today for the first time. For a doctor's checkup. I guess it's okay, or they wouldn't have scheduled it, but she's so tiny and—"

"Pat! I need some information and I can't talk for long."

"Oh, okay. Shoot."

"Do you know an Alice Sawyer?"

"Of course, she worked for me when I was at Kinsinger. Why?"

"She wants your job."

Pat laughed. "Yeah, she's wanted to be promoted from almost the first day she started. The problem is she doesn't retain anything. She's all right for filing and some basic work, but try to explain benefit procedures, or retirement options or general labor law to her and it's like talking to a wall."

"She thinks she can be head of Human Resources here."

"She's wacko. How are you involved?"

"She knows I'm not a fifty-something woman working for the big boss and is threatening to blow the whistle unless I fix it for her to get the job. She seems to think Matt would be swayed by my opinion."

"Whoa. Karla, that's bad. If she's trying something like blackmail, she can't be trusted in the department."

"You don't think I would recommend her, do you?" Karla asked.

"No. Wait a minute, I'm thinking. I bet she got your age from the personnel records. She does our filing. Guess she's bored enough to read the applications. But she's supposed to hold things like that confidential."

"Well she's threatening to tell, but maybe she won't— it could be all bluff. Anyway, I thought I'd check with you about her. I'll have to find a way to tell Matt the truth before she makes good her threat."

"Karla, I can't believe you got away with it for this long. He's going to go ballistic when you tell him."

"You might be right. I'm just hoping he'll listen with an open mind. I have done a great job—he can't deny that. Damn, this timing stinks. I wanted the Percell Group deal signed first."

"Call me when the dust settles and let me know how it went."

"Okay. Kiss the baby for me." Karla hung up.

Now what? Try to find a moment to speak to Matt to spike Alice's guns? Or should she try to talk to the woman once more?

Matt stood in the doorway to his office. "Jeannette,

call the Taylors and see if they've decided about the proposal and if so schedule a conference for tomorrow morning if they can make it. Then get me a flight tomorrow afternoon to Toronto—return on Sunday. Cancel anything I have scheduled for the rest of the week.''

"So you have to go?" she said.

He nodded. "You heard?"

Karla looked away, forgetting his secretary hadn't heard, his date had.

"From Karla," she said.

"I'll need a car and a place to stay close to the office there." He turned back and before she could ask him about getting together to review things, he was back on the phone.

She called Mr. Taylor, but he was unavailable. Leaving a message, she jotted herself a note to follow up later in the day if he didn't call back.

Karla watched the rest of the morning for an opportunity to speak to Matt, but he remained incredibly busy. Faxes poured off the machine in Lisa's area and she dutifully brought them in instantly. Karla knew Matt was directly linked to the Toronto office on his computer and with the phone constantly at his ear, he was unavailable for anything else.

She took a late lunch and returned to the office to find Lisa back at her desk, but Matt gone.

"Mr. Gramling went out for something to eat," Lisa said. "I have most of those papers done he wanted. But he gave me two tapes to transcribe this afternoon, so I can't get to that other project."

"He knows his priorities. Don't worry about the project, it'll keep."

She stepped into her office and stopped. A young woman of about thirty was sitting in the guest chair. She glared at Karla.

"Alice, I presume," Karla said, wondering if she should shut the door between her office and Lisa's work area. She never had—would it cause comment? How much could Lisa hear if she didn't close the door? The sound of the keyboard rattled behind her. Hopefully Lisa was fully occupied with her tapes.

"I can see how he was fooled," Alice said, standing. She wasn't very tall, and her attire was casual for business. "Are you going to tell him I'm the best for the job?"

"I can't do that," Karla said. "I spoke with Pat Carns after you and I talked this morning. She says you aren't qualified."

"I've been working at that job for six years! I know everything that goes on around here. I had you figured out, didn't I?"

"There's more to the position than that. What about payroll regulations, labor law, benefits, things like that."

"There are a lot of people in the department, each one specializes in one aspect. I would be the manager. I don't need to know it all, that's what they're for!" Alice said hotly. "I want that job and you can help me get it."

"No, I can't. Even if I thought it would do any good to recommend you, I couldn't do it. It's not right."

"What you're doing isn't right. It's lying and cheating and wrong. But you went ahead anyway. Why are you standing in my way? *I want that job!*" Alice was almost yelling.

Add emotionally instable to the list, Karla thought

wryly. And her own experience wasn't so extensive that she knew how to defuse the situation.

"Shh. Yelling about it won't change anything."

"I'll yell if I want! You had better help me or I'll make sure Gramling knows everything there is to know."

"And that would be?" Matt asked from the doorway. Lisa stood behind him, peering in, her eyes wide with shock.

Karla spun around in horror. How much had he heard? Alice glared at him.

"Perhaps we should take this discussion into my office. I could hear you from the elevator."

"I can explain," Karla began.

"I can do my own explanations!" Alice said.

"Inside my office, both of you." Matt's tone would not be denied.

He waited for the two women to precede him, followed, and closed the door. Moving to one side he folded his arms across his chest and looked from one to the other.

"I don't know you," he said to Alice.

"Alice Sawyer, from Human Resources," she said grudgingly, glaring at Karla.

"What's the problem?"

"There wouldn't be any problem if Miss Jones would recommend me for the manager's position."

"The opening in HR?" he asked.

Alice nodded.

Karla could only stand, dreading the explosion that would erupt if Alice didn't keep quiet.

"Aren't there channels to go through to apply for a job? Why come to my executive assistant?"

"She owes me," Alice mumbled.

"I do not!" Karla said.

"Why is that?"

Alice looked at Karla. "Are you going to recommend me?"

For one second Karla wished she could. Wished she could do something that would stop the tidal wave that threatened.

Slowly she shook her head. "I can't do that."

With a sly look Alice shifted her gaze from Karla to Matt.

"That woman is an imposter. I don't know how she's fooled you all this time, but she isn't any more fifty years old than I am. A wig, makeup and dowdy clothes don't mean she's who you think she is." Her triumphant expression made Karla want to slap her. She'd done it. She'd told Matt!

Matt looked at Karla.

She met his gaze, startled at the anger that flared. He stepped forward and looked at her hair, reaching out to pull the wig from her head.

"I can explain," she said quickly.

He snatched the glasses from her nose and tossed both on his desk.

"Karla Jones. Not Jeannette." The coldness in his expression was frightening.

"If you'd listen to me for a minute, I can explain everything."

"No explanation necessary. Not from you. Nor you, Miss Sawyer."

He opened the door. "Lisa!"

She appeared instantly. "Yes, sir."

"Call security to escort these women from the premises."

"Matt, no!" Karla said, horrified. "Let me explain."

"As of this moment, you no longer work for Kinsinger Electronics. Either of you. You're both fired."

Matt closed the door behind the departing contingency several moments later feeling furious. He strode to the desk and snatched up the offending wig, balling it tightly he flung it across the room.

He was seething with anger.

He stalked to the window, hoping the sight of the sea would sooth somewhat. But he could still feel the shock of discovery.

Jeannette was Karla.

Or vice versa.

And some woman in the Human Resources department tried to blackmail her for advancement. God, what a mess!

Unbelievable.

How could she have done it!

And how could he have not seen it?

Which made him more angry, he wondered dispassionately, the fact she'd pulled it off, or that she'd tried to begin with? Or the fact he'd believed in Jeannette?

There was a light tap on his door.

"Yes?" He turned as Lisa poked her head inside.

"There's a call for Miss Jones. I didn't know whether to take a message or not."

"Who is it?"

"Oh! I don't know. I can ask."

"Never mind, I'll take it." He reached for the phone

as she closed the door. He'd never noticed how timid Lisa was before. Of course, she worked for Jeannette—Karla, would she be able to run things as smoothly?

"Gramling."

"Hello, Matt, Evelyn Taylor here. I was trying to reach Miss Jones. She called earlier about setting up another meeting."

"Miss Jones no longer works for the firm. I need to go out of town on business this week, but wanted to touch base with you and Richard before I left—to see if there were any other aspects of our proposal you had questions on. I'm hoping you are ready to sign."

"What happened to Miss Jones?" she asked.

He scowled and turned back toward the window, hoping the anger didn't show in his tone. "She was dismissed today."

There was a moment of silence on the other end. "Fired?"

He couldn't believe it himself. He rubbed his forehead. "Yes."

"Why?"

What possible business was it of a possible customer to know about the personnel problems at his firm? Not something conducive to instilling confidence. Still, he could hardly tell her it was none of her concern. That'd go over well.

"Turns out Miss Jones wasn't quite what she purported to be. She is not in her fifties, but somewhere around twenty-five."

"So?"

"So I hired a mature woman, and got an imposter."

"What were her reasons for the impersonation?" Evelyn asked, curiosity obvious.

"I don't know."

"What was her explanation?"

"There was none. I didn't need to hear any cock-and-bull story to mitigate the damage. When I discovered the deception, she was history."

"You fired her on the spot and gave her no chance to explain?" Evelyn's voice cooled noticeably.

"Exactly." Why did hearing it from Evelyn make it sound like a poor decision? He was decisive. When he made a decision, he didn't second guess it after the fact.

"I see."

"As I said, I have to leave town tomorrow, but would like to schedule a meeting with you and Richard before I go. Or if that won't work, how would next Monday suit?"

She was quiet for another moment, then spoke again, "I'll talk to Richard and we'll be in touch. Goodbye." She hung up.

He opened his door and called for Lisa.

She rushed in, looking flustered. Similar to the way his secretary in Toronto often looked.

Neither had the calm demeanor Jeannette—Karla—had always shown.

"Get the head of the HR department up here to discuss this situation. Check on my reservations, I'm leaving tomorrow afternoon for Toronto and should have an open ticket so I can return when I'm ready. Make sure I have an updated version of the Taylor project folder to take with me."

"Okay." She looked positively petrified. "Where is the Taylor project file?"

"Look on Miss Jones's desk."

He watched her for a moment, scrambling the neat piles Karla had stacked on the surface. Impatiently, he crossed to the desk and found the folder in only seconds.

"Sorry. I'll call HR." She fled for her desk.

Matt knew it was going to prove a long afternoon. For a second he almost questioned his rash act. But seeing the glasses lying on his desk strengthened his resolve. She'd played him for a fool—at work and in their personal lives. He wouldn't forget.

The next Monday afternoon, Karla entered her apartment, more tired than she had been a couple of weeks ago after a long day at Kinsinger. Interviewing was hard work. She kicked off her shoes and padded in her stocking feet to the kitchen to get a glass of water. She refused to let herself become discouraged. It had only been a few days.

Of course she'd spent that first day alternating between rage and tears. Angry that Matt had not let her explain, and upset and sorrowful he'd let her go like that. Not caring enough to even ask why. She sure had him figured wrong.

She glanced at her answering machine as she walked back into the living room. The message indicator light was flashing.

A callback maybe from her Friday interview? That one had gone well. She pressed the button and caught her breath when a familiar voice sounded.

"Karla, Matt Gramling. Call me."

There was a second message. "Karla, Gramling here. Call me. I'm at the office."

And a third. "Karla, where the hell are you? Call me."

All three calls since nine that morning.

"Well that's surprising," she murmured as she crossed to the sofa and sat down, sipping more of her water. He kicked her out last week without a chance to explain and now called her and almost ordered her to contact him. Didn't he realize he was no longer her boss?

"So what's up, Mr. Gramling, that you're calling me? Had second thoughts and want to hear my side? Missed your effective executive assistant?"

Karla stared at the answering machine as if it could give her answers to her questions.

She could call and find out. But was she ready? Tears filled her eyes and she blinked them away. He'd been so harsh and unapproachable. To refuse to give her a chance to explain was inexcusable. She'd expected more of him. He'd been fair to others, why not to her?

"You can just wait a bit longer, Mr. Gramling," she told the machine. "Until I'm good and ready to talk to you. Or hell freezes over, whichever comes first!"

Rising, she went into the bedroom to change into casual clothes.

The phone rang. Karla's heart leaped, but she remained in the bedroom, straining to hear the machine.

"Karla, Gramling here. Call when you get in."

There was definitely impatience in that tone, she thought wryly. The head of Kinsinger Electronics was used to people jumping to do his bidding. She almost laughed. He didn't like being kept waiting.

"And I don't like being blown off like you did. You

should have given me a chance to explain,'' she said, walking back into the living room and erasing the messages on her machine.

On to the kitchen, she tried to decide what to prepare for dinner. Tomorrow morning she had another interview scheduled and wanted to make an early night of it. Not that she'd sleep. But she could make the effort.

Twice more during the evening Matt called. The final time his tone changed.

''Karla, I know you have to be home by now. Pick up…Please.''

She knew the word please had been an afterthought. Hesitating, she heard him continue.

''I need your help on the Percell Group project.''

She lifted the receiver.

''So because you need some help on a project, I should forget the way you treated me last week and leap at the chance to come to your assistance?'' she said.

She heard his indrawn breath as if he were trying to find some patience.

''Evelyn Taylor has this bee in her bonnet that if I'm so ruthless I wouldn't even listen to an explanation, I'm not the kind of businessman they want to deal with. There are other deals out there, but this one would be immediate, and show the employees we are turning things around and moving forward. We worked hard on it. I want this deal consummated.''

''So?''

''So I need your help. The Taylors have agreed to another meeting to hammer through things—but only if you are also there. You owe me.''

''You're kidding.''

"No, dammit, I'm not."

Karla could almost feel the seething rage in his answer. She did not owe him!

"So how does my being there help?"

"It'll show them I'm flexible. The company will respond to their concerns in a rapid fashion. I don't know, she just won't come unless you're there."

For a moment Karla wondered why Evelyn even cared. "I'll consider it on one condition."

"And that is?"

"You give me a chance to explain and listen to me— really listen to me."

"After the deal is signed."

Once that had been her timetable as well.

"No, after the meeting—win, lose or draw with the Taylors—you listen to me." She wasn't going to be blown off a second time.

"Deal. Can you be here in the morning at ten?"

"Is that when the meeting is scheduled?"

"Yes."

How like him to schedule it and then see if she could make it. She'd have to postpone her interview, but for the chance to tell Matt why she'd pretended it would be worth it. "Okay, I'll be there at ten. But I'm warning you, I'm coming as Karla. You still have my wig."

"I trashed it."

Great, now she owed Polly a new wig. Maybe she'd request Matt pay for it.

Good grief, she must be growing giddy with the thought of seeing him again. There was no way in the world he'd pay for the wig. She'd be lucky if he'd give her five minutes to listen to her explanation.

Would it change anything? Would he offer her the job again? Invite her to dinner one night?

"I'll be there by ten." She hung up before he could say anything further.

So Matt needed her to clench the Percell Group deal. What was Mrs. Taylor up to?

Right before ten the next morning, Karla pressed the button for the express elevator. She wished she'd listened to Pat at that fateful lunch several weeks ago and not considered it fate when she'd learned of the open executive assistant's position. Then if she and Matt had met at the theater, she could have considered that fate.

And been no farther ahead, she thought, her heart speeding up in anticipation of seeing him.

Hope was hard to kill.

When the elevator reached the executive floor, Lisa was waiting. She greeted Karla with relief.

"Oh, Miss Jones, I'm so glad you could come. He's been absolutely horrible. So demanding, and I can't find anything! I'm glad to do all the typing, but you always handled everything else."

She led the way to Karla's office, talking as fast as she could, as if to dump all her aggravation on Karla in the short distance and span of time she had.

"Do the best you can. Surely he's interviewing for my replacement," she said with a pang when she saw her desk. It was *her* job. She'd given it her all, and loved it.

And, if nothing else, she had planned to see Matt through the years at work, knowing a long personal relationship was impossible. It would have been enough. Maybe.

"Not yet. He was in Toronto until yesterday. But I can tell you, another day like yesterday and I'm history!"

Matt opened the door to his office. Lisa gave a small yelp and scurried away. He glanced at her, then at Karla, his gaze tracking from her short sassy hair, down the fitted navy dress, suitable for office wear, yet nothing like the staid clothes Miss Jones wore.

"She might be a great typist, but she can't do anything else."

"That's all she was hired for." Karla slowly took a deep breath, trying to calm her roiling nerves. He looked tired, as if he hadn't slept in days. Her heart lurched.

"How are things in Toronto?" she asked.

His expression tightened. "None of your business."

She should have expected it. Placing her purse on the desk, she faced him. "So what do you want me to do for this meeting?"

He rubbed the back of his neck. "I don't know. Look like you work here again. Tell Mrs. Taylor that we've ironed things out and I'm flexible and willing to listen."

"Lie to her, you mean?"

He glared at her, "Why not, you're good at that."

She raised her chin. "I never lied to you. Everything I said was truth. Check my application form."

"You said Miss Jones was your aunt."

Shaking her head, she responded, "No, you said that, I didn't correct you."

"A technicality. And not the issue I need to deal with first. The Percell Group account takes priority."

"But you and I will talk afterward," she said firmly.

CHAPTER TEN

"MISS JONES?" Lisa peered around the door. "The people from the Percell Group are here. I put them in the conference room."

"Thank you, Lisa. We'll be right there," Karla said calmly. She glanced at the desk then back to Matt. "Do you have the folders and spreadsheets you need?"

"In my office. Took Lisa half a day to find it all."

Karla kept quiet, knowing he could have called her or had Lisa call her, to find whatever they needed. Sometimes stubborn pride deserved hardship.

"So I pretend I'm your executive assistant for the duration of the meeting. That all?"

"That should be enough."

"Fine." She gathered a notepad and a couple of pens and headed for the conference room, conscious of Matt's gaze fixed on her until she left her office.

Evelyn and Richard Taylor greeted her warmly when she joined them in the conference room.

"How nice to see you again. Oh, my, what a difference," Evelyn said, as she took in Karla's changed appearance.

Karla flushed at the scrutiny, embarrassed to be caught out by this nice couple. "It is easier to keep up," she said weakly.

"You haven't met our son, Ashbury. He's going to be taking the reins one of these days. I thought he should be in on our meeting,'' Richard said, stepping aside so a tall young man could offer Karla his hand.

"Delighted to meet you, Miss Jones. I understand there has been some problems with your employment.''

"I can't wait to hear why you thought dressing up as if you were an old lady was necessary to get a good job,'' Evelyn said. "I spend a fortune each year trying to look younger than I am.''

"It was because of the twenty-five/fifty rule,'' she said just as the door opened again, admitting Matt.

"I don't believe I know that rule,'' Evelyn said.

Karla moved to take a seat down from the head of the table. "I'll explain later,'' she murmured, hoping Matt hadn't heard.

Once greetings had been exchanged, and Matt had met Ashbury Taylor, everyone sat and the meeting began in earnest.

Richard Taylor questioned certain aspects of the proposal as presented and Matt easily cleared up the concern. He and Ashbury Taylor discussed delivery dates and contingency plans if problems arose. Evelyn said nothing, merely watched from the sidelines.

The meeting wound up before noon, with a promise of a major contract to be signed as soon as the attorneys drafted it—incorporating all the points agreed upon.

Karla wondered what her purpose had been. She, like Evelyn, had said very little. But she'd noticed Matt's gaze more than once. And Ashbury Taylor's.

As the Taylors were preparing to leave, Ashbury came over to Karla.

"Are you free for lunch? I'd like to discuss a possible

position with our firm. Unless I'd be stepping on toes somewhere?''

''There are no toes to step on,'' she said. ''But, um, you might hesitate if you knew the full story about my employment here.''

''I can't wait to hear it, but anyone who goes through all my mother talked about to land a job shows determination and gumption. Something we value at Percell Group.''

Matt heard. His glower could almost be felt.

Karla ignored him, smiling brightly at Ashbury. ''I'd be delighted to have lunch with you.''

''May I see you a moment,'' Matt said, taking her upper arm in a grip that wouldn't easily be broken. He practically marched her from the room into the hallway.

''What are you doing?'' Karla asked in startled surprise.

''I thought you and I were going to have an explanation session. Now you're flirting with a customer?''

''I'm not flirting,'' she hissed, pulling herself free. She glared up at him. ''It won't take five minutes to give you an explanation. And if there is a possible job opportunity, I need to investigate it. He's not my customer—unless you're offering me my job back here?''

Matt shook his head once. ''Not a chance, sweetheart.''

''I didn't think so. That makes me free to seek other employment. And you can't stop me.''

''Mr. Gramling,'' Lisa said behind Karla. ''Your assistant in Toronto is calling. She says it's important. I told her you were in a meeting, I didn't know you were already finished. But she said I should get you. Can you take the call?''

''Of course I can take it, tell Sarah I'll be there in a second.''

''Don't let me keep you,'' Karla said.

''And your burning desire to give me that explanation?'' he asked silkily, his eyes narrowed in frustration.

''It's waited a week, what's a little more time.'' Karla knew no matter what, he wouldn't change. Hadn't his last comment proved it? Did it matter if she told him why she'd tried to look older. It wouldn't alter anything.

''Wait here. I'll see what Sarah wants and then I'll take you to lunch.''

She blinked in surprise. ''Why would you do that?''

''Damned if I know.'' He stepped around her headed to his office.

Karla watched him walk away, puzzled by the invitation. Longing to accept, she thought she'd do better to explore new opportunities. ''I can't,'' she said softly to the empty hall. ''Much as I want to, I can't.''

She turned and reentered the conference room. The Taylors were ready to leave, and when Evelyn pressed her into joining them for lunch, Karla accepted. They were nice people and they might offer her a new position somewhere.

Despite her best intentions, Karla regretted not waiting for Matt. Lunch was delightful. And Ash, as he'd asked her to call him, had come through with a job opportunity. She was going to the Percell Group offices in the morning for a formal interview, and to see their offices.

Evelyn had been totally entertained with the reason for

her acting older, and asked Karla if she minded if she told some of her friends.

"I'd rather you didn't," Karla said slowly. "I wouldn't do anything in the world to jeopardize Matt's image in the business community."

"Loyalty is a valuable commodity. I wonder if Matt realizes he still has yours?" Richard asked.

He had more than her loyalty, she thought, he had her love. But he wanted neither.

After lunch she'd taken a brisk walk along the seawalk, enjoying the fresh air and the breeze that danced across the harbor. She tried to ignore the memories of walking with Matt. Just over a week ago they'd had dessert at that little café.

She sighed and tried to forget. It wasn't easy. But Vancouver sparkled in the sunshine, and her spirits gradually rose.

By the time she returned to the apartment, she felt better than anytime in the past week. She changed into old jeans and a T-shirt. Going barefoot into the kitchen, she rummaged around for something to eat. Living alone, she didn't often cook for herself, but ate her main meal at lunch to get at least one good meal a day.

She'd been disappointed when she first entered the apartment to notice the answering machine had no messages. She'd hoped Matt had called. He'd have been angry at her, no doubt for standing him up for lunch. Which would have been the perfect reason for him to call—if only to yell at her.

Glancing at the clock, she saw it was almost five. Too late to call him to arrange a time to give her explanation.

She'd phone first thing tomorrow, before heading out for her interview at the Percell Group.

The knock on the door startled her. Wondering who it was, she crossed to answer. Opening the door, she was totally dumbfounded to see Matt Gramling.

"We need to talk," he said, pushing his way into the apartment. "And you're not walking out this time."

Karla closed the door and leaned against it. Thinking of all the other outfits she had she could have worn, why was she in faded jeans and a baggy old T-shirt? Her lipstick had worn off and she knew her hair was tousled from the wind.

"Thanks for the advance warning," she mumbled, pushing off from the door. Matt had slung off his jacket and tossed it across the back of the sofa, sitting on one end as if he owned the place. Karla crossed the room and sat gingerly on the edge of a chair.

"What warning?"

"If I had known you were coming, I'd have— Never mind." She wasn't about to tell him she cared how she looked. No telling what he'd think with such a confession.

But it wasn't fair. He looked terrific. A bit leaner than she remembered, and tired. But the same intensity shone in his eyes. The same broad shoulders she'd once thought could hold the world filled his shirt. The same fluttering in her heart told her immunity against him was a long way off.

"I told you I'd take you to lunch," he said.

She shrugged. "I decided to go with the first invitation."

"Did they offer you a job?"

"Is that any of your business?" she asked, still hurt from his brusque response to her question about the Toronto problem.

"I'm making it my business. In fact—" He took a breath, rose and paced to the window. Turning, he looked at her. "In fact, if things go the way I want, I'll make a lot of things my business."

"I don't know what you're talking about."

"Sometimes I think you've cast a spell. Other times I wonder if it's something in the water in Vancouver. Whatever, and despite everything that's happened, I still want you."

Her heart kicked into high gear. She stared at him, her thoughts tumbling. "Want me?" Visions of their night at the island filled her mind. She'd thought she'd never see him again, and he talked of wanting her. Had she entered an alternate universe?

"I want to see you, spend time with you. Hold you. Make love to you. How many ways do you want it spelled out?"

She stared at him, totally at a loss. It was the last thing she expected to hear.

"I'm twenty-eight," she blurted out.

"So, I'm thirty-four. Is that too old for you?"

She shook her head quickly. "No, but I thought you didn't date women over twenty-five."

He frowned. "Where did you get that idea?"

"Mr. Twenty-five/Fifty."

"What does that mean? I heard you say that to the Taylors earlier."

Karla rose and stepped around the chair, putting it between them, holding on for support. "Before I even met you, your reputation preceded you. A man who didn't hire women to work for him that were under fifty and didn't date anyone over twenty-five.''

He stared at her for a long moment. ''That's what all this has been about? Some damn-fool notion that I wouldn't hire a woman under fifty?''

She nodded. ''I wanted the job. If you didn't hire younger women, I didn't have a chance. So I aged myself a bit. But if you'd look at the application sheet, you'd see I listed my age accurately.''

''I never saw it.''

She kept silent. No use implicating Pat if she didn't need to.

''You don't look twenty-eight, either.''

''I figured you thought I was younger—or you wouldn't have asked me out. That night at the theater I thought you recognized me.''

''You kept looking over at me, I thought it was a pickup.''

Karla almost smiled. ''I thought you were picking me up.''

''I did.'' There was satisfaction in his tone.

''I'm good at my job.''

He nodded once. ''I've missed the no-problem response to every request. Even Sarah in Toronto gets flustered, and she's worked for me for years.''

''She's over fifty, I bet.''

''Yes, as a matter of fact, but I inherited her when I took over the firm. Who was this authority who told you about that dumb rule?''

She flushed a little. ''Actually I heard a group of secretaries talking at lunch one day.''

"Based on gossip, you came up with this elaborate scheme?"

"It worked."

"Did you plan to retire in fifteen years when I thought you were sixty-five?"

"I planned on telling you everything once I thought you were convinced at how indispensable I was. Actually, my timetable was once the Taylors signed. I thought you'd be in a more receptive mood then."

"And what did you expect my reaction to be?"

She shrugged. "I don't know, angry at first, but unable to let me go. Convinced I was the best for the job."

She gazed at him, wishing they were back on the island, or in the office. Wishing Alice Sawyer hadn't changed her world.

"I'm convinced," he said slowly, his eyes hot with desire. "And unable to let you go."

Hope flared. "I have my job back?"

He shook his head. "I'll find another executive assistant. There were one or two others I interviewed that were on the short list."

"Then I'm not indispensable." Her heart sank. Where was this conversation going?

"Come here, Karla," he said.

She looked at him suspiciously, then slowly came around the chair and walked over to him. Tilting her head back to look into his eyes, she wondered at the intensity of emotions displayed.

"I want you," he said again. "And I suspect you want me. Am I wrong?"

She licked suddenly dry lips.

He slowly lifted his hand to brush her cheek, to sweep back her hair, tangling his fingers in the silky tresses.

When he lowered his head to kiss her, she was ready, eager even for the touch of his mouth against hers, for the tidal wave of heat that swept through her. With a soft inchoate sound, she threw her arms around him and held on. He pulled her tightly against his strength and deepened the kiss.

Was it even sweeter that before, for having gone through the fear of never seeing him again? Was it more sensuous because she knew where such kisses could lead? Was it more loving because she loved him so much her heart felt as if it would burst?

He ended the kiss and looked at her. "I'm glad that's settled. Are you going to invite me to supper?"

"What's settled?" she asked, her heart racing, every nerve in her body tingling in reaction to his kiss. She was wrapped in a warm glow of love and desire and having a bit of trouble concentrating. She wished he'd kiss her again.

"We'll continue seeing each other," he said.

She disengaged herself, feeling like a pail of cold water had been thrown at her. "What do you mean continue to see each other? What about my job? I don't think anything's been settled."

"That kiss said a lot."

"What exactly did it say?" she asked, growing more wary.

"That you want me as much as I want you."

"I want a lot of things, that doesn't mean life is settled and planned out. I want that executive assistant's job. I was good at it, you have to admit that."

"We'll plan to see each other as much as our other commitments allow. But the job's out. I don't mix social and business."

"So we see each other—when?" she asked, feeling chilled by the vision his comment evoked. Where was she going to fall on his priority list? After everything else had been seen to?

"As whenever we want."

"For how long?"

"For as long as we want."

"What if I want forever," she said daringly.

Instantly his expression changed. "I don't do forever."

"Why not?"

"I've explained that. You told me you weren't in the running for the matrimonial stakes. Another lie?"

When Mr. Right comes along, you'll know, Pat had said. Karla was certain she knew. But it didn't appear Mr. Right knew. Or maybe for him, she was not the right one. The thought was depressing.

"Things change," she said slowly.

"Some things don't," he returned.

"For a man who is used to taking risks in business, and even in life with those wilderness treks, you sure are running scared in the personal aspects."

"I'm not going to listen to your pop psychological assessment of my life because I'm not changing it to suit you. We have a lot going for us, could have a lot of fun together. But not forever."

"Impasse," she said, amazed at the calmness of her tone. She wanted to rant and rave and *demand* he love her as much as she loved him. But she knew it wouldn't change anything. Now her only hope was that she could carry this off with a bit of pride.

"Dammit, Karla. I'm not getting married. I thought I made that perfectly clear at the beginning."

"Perfectly," she said, walking over to the sofa and picking up his jacket. She hugged it for a second, breathing in his special scent. She was going to miss him so much. Turning, she held it out.

"You need to go, Matt. Thanks for letting me explain why I pretended I was older. I wish things had worked out differently. I really liked working for you and being with you."

"I'm not leaving."

"Yes. I need for you to leave. I don't want a fling, a casual affair that ends with me heartbroken and eaten up with regrets. Better to part now while we can be friends of a sort."

He strode angrily across the room, and took the jacket. "I have never looked on you as a *friend*," he almost snarled.

"Maybe that's part of the problem. I would have been your best friend as well as lover, and more. If you had given us a chance."

"We can still spend time together."

Did he sound almost desperate? Or was it just wishful thinking on her part?

She shook her head. "I need to make a clean break. Goodbye, Matt. I wish for you all the best life has to offer."

She held her head high, hoping the tears wouldn't fall until after he left. Her throat ached. What kind of gesture would it be if she fell apart and began sobbing?

She opened the door and tried to smile. Her lips trembled and wouldn't cooperate. So be it.

"Karla."

She shook her head, refusing to meet his eyes.

He walked out and hesitated in the hallway. Gently, Karla closed the door. The tears spilled over, tracing down her cheeks. She leaned her head against the cool wooden door, the longing so intense she thought she'd scream with the pain.

Her heart was breaking, she could feel it. How could she have fallen for the man? She knew he was hard and remote—unreceptive to even the thought of a relationship. Blithely she thought she could match his attitude.

But she couldn't. She loved him, wanted to be with him, share her life. And bits and pieces weren't enough. She refused to settle for less than his love and commitment. A lifetime commitment.

The heart doesn't necessarily choose wisely, it just chooses. And it was up to her to pick up the pieces and move on.

She went to bathe her eyes in cool water. Listlessly, she went to heat water for tea. She wasn't hungry, but maybe the tea would soothe. The universal remedy, her mother always said. Even for heartbreak?

The knock startled her. Who was it this time? she wondered. A neighbor? Maybe she wouldn't answer it. No use trying to explain red eyes to a neighbor.

It sounded again, more forcefully.

"Okay, I'm coming," she mumbled, going to the door. Opening it, she was startled to see Matt. His jacket was slung over one shoulder, hooked on his index finger. His tie loosened.

"Matt! I thought you left. What are you doing here?"

He pushed his way into the apartment and reached around her to close the door.

"I got as far as the elevator."

"You've been in the hallway all this time? You left more than ten minutes ago." She didn't get it. What had he been doing for all that time?

He brushed his fingertips along the top of her cheeks. "I never wanted to make you cry," he said softly.

"I'm fine," she said quickly, stepping back. His touch sent pure delight skittering through her. She wasn't sure she could handle the roller coaster of emotions.

His hand encircled the nape of her neck, feeling warm and sensuous. His eyes gazed into hers.

"Well, I'm glad one of us is, then. I'm not."

"What do you mean?"

"You were right."

"About what?" Was she hearing correctly?

"About us. I don't want a casual affair." He took a deep breath. "I want a best friend. I've never had one. And I want a lover who delights me in bed like no one else ever has. A woman who is loyal even when she has no reason to be. A woman who will give a man a second chance. And maybe even a third if he needs it. I want you, Karla."

"I don't get it."

"I'm not sure I do, either. But this last week has been hell. I had a crisis in Toronto, that mostly I wanted to say to hell with since I had more trouble with a certain executive assistant who'd been playing me along. I couldn't believe it. I never in a million years would have guessed your reason. I spent more time envisioning hearing your explanation than dealing with the problem in Toronto. I thought of industrial espionage, of revenge, or just plain craziness.''

"Which maybe it was. I mean, pretending to be fifty just to get a job?''

"A job which you do effortlessly, competently, and enthusiastically. I've never worked with an assistant like you before. You're the best I ever hired.''

She blinked. She wasn't hearing right. Had his touch short-circuited her senses so she imagined things?

"Even if I'm only twenty-eight?''

"I never voiced that rule.'' He looked thoughtful. "But if people are so concerned with things like that, I can see how the rumor got started—except for the printing firm, all my secretaries have been older women. But in almost every case, they were already working for the company when I bought into it.''

"And the women you date?''

"Younger women are not as interested in settling down. I didn't have a rule about it. But maybe I did have a tendency to date young. The question is now, will you marry me?''

"Marry you?'' Karla's breath whooshed out. She stared at him. *"Marry you?''*

"Say yes.''

"What happened to you were never getting married? To the belief all women were after your bank account?'' Her heart pounded so hard she could hardly hear over the rushing of the blood through her veins. She drew in a ragged breath, her eyes never leaving his. Was he making a joke? *Was it possible he was serious?*

Amusement showed in his eyes. "If you want my bank account, you can have it. But I go with it."

Exasperated she glared at him. "I don't want your bank account."

"But you want me?"

She was imagining things. For a second she thought she glimpsed vulnerability in his eyes when he asked if she wanted him. It couldn't be, not her strong, risk-taking, intrepid Matt Gramling.

Slowly she realized it wasn't imagination. He was uncertain of her response.

As if there were any doubt.

She threw her arms around his neck. "Yes, I want you. I love you, Matt Gramling. I didn't mean to fall in love, but you are irresistible."

His arms tightened around her. She felt as if she'd come home.

"I don't think so, but if you want to think that, hold the thought as long as possible."

He kissed her. Molding her body to his, she could feel the ragged beat of his heart pounding against her. His lips moved persuasively, his tongue dancing with hers, bringing new heights of awareness and desire. Karla floated on a balmy sea of sensation, happiness filling her.

The kaleidoscope of colors behind her lids soared and sparkled. Her breath was gone, but who needed to breathe? She had Matt. Or he had her, it was hard to tell where one left off and the other began he had her wrapped so tightly against him.

Karla didn't have a complaint left in her. Questions, yes, but no complaints.

It was some time before he pulled back enough to gaze

into her eyes. Slowly she opened them and gazed into his.

"Tell me you love me, too," she said. "It's customary, you know."

"I do, Karla Jeannette Jones. I felt as if a part of me had been amputated this last week."

"Next time, give a person a chance to explain. Though as angry as you seemed, I'm not sure you would have listened last Monday. I've felt guilty for weeks, and then when I could explain you wouldn't even let me!"

"I was afraid I was falling for you, fighting it every step of the way," he said slowly. "Then to find out you'd been pretending something that wasn't real, it hit me as hard as Celine's betrayal. I was blindsided. I never expected such a thing. And I could only think of getting away, from you, from the situation." He shook his head. "I never knew I was a coward before."

"You're not! Lisa said you spent all last week in Toronto."

"Good excuse to convince myself I was dealing with business, rather than running away."

"I'm sorry," she said, kissing his chin. Her eyes were sincere. "I planned to tell you as soon as the Taylors signed, honestly. I wouldn't have done it except I wanted the job so much."

"And dating?"

"That I couldn't resist, not after I realized at the theater that you didn't recognize me. You're too potent to refuse."

She gazed at him with all the love shining in her eyes. "So how did we go from you'll never let me come back to work at Kinsinger to a proposal in less than a half hour?'' she asked, snuggling closer, delighting in the feeling of intimacy that wrapped them together.

''I was angry when you kicked me out.''

''No, duh!''

''Don't interrupt. While I waited for the elevator, what you said about risk struck me. Then it opened and was empty. For a second, I saw my life like that. I have no one at home waiting for me at the end of the day. No one to share successes with. No one to completely be myself with. And I saw that empty life down the years. I'm thirty-four. If I want a family to leave the businesses to, or even just a partner to share life with, I need to do something about it.''

''So I'm an old-life alternative.'' She couldn't have imagined a half hour ago she'd ever be teasing him.

He squeezed her. ''I said, no interruptions.''

She tried to look suitably contrite, but she knew the happiness that filled her spilled over.

''So I asked myself how I was going to feel never seeing you again. That put it all into perspective. I'd already had one week without you. I didn't want another, much less a lifetime. If I stopped fighting my age-old beliefs, I suddenly realized you are the perfect woman for me. Look how you took to the island. Look how you took to the job—we could discuss ideas and strategy and you had as many good ideas as I did. Those morning planning sessions became the highlight of my day. I just didn't realize why at the time.''

''Gee, you make it sound so romantic. Morning planning sessions?''

''We'll get to the romantic part in a minute. I'm explaining how I came to my senses.''

"And doing a wonderful job, darling. I love you, Matt."

He looked into her eyes, seeing the warmth and love shining so true. That was all that counted.

"I love you, Karla."

"Partners forever?"

"Forever," he affirmed. He hesitated. "So I don't have to explain any more? You'll marry me?"

"Yes. I'll marry you." She reached up to kiss him long and deeply. Explanations could wait. Or be ignored. The important thing was the end result—a lifetime of happiness for them both.

"I make a great executive assistant, too," she said sometime later, safely wrapped in his arms as they sat side by side on the sofa.

"No! Definitely not. I don't allow family members to work together in my companies. It's not good for business."

"Trust me, Matt, we'll make it work beautifully. No problem."

He did trust her. She held his heart, happiness and hope for the future in her hands. He had been taking risks for years—but this was a sure thing. No problem.

Cathy Williams is originally from Trinidad but has lived in England for a number of years. She currently has a house in Warwickshire which she shares with her husband Richard, her three daughters Charlotte, Olivia and Emma and their pet cat, Salem. She adores writing romantic fiction and would love one of her girls to become a writer, although at the moment she is happy enough if they do their homework and agree not to bicker with one another.

SECRETARY ON DEMAND

by

Cathy Williams

CHAPTER ONE

'GUESS who's here, Shannon!'

Shannon paused for a second to look up at her friend who was contributing to the general chaos of the kitchens by balancing a large circular tray, laden with empty crockery, precariously above her shoulder on the flat of her hand.

'Who?' She flexed her fingers and grinned which was an open invitation for Sandy to deposit her tray on the stack of paperwork on the desk and lean forward with a conspirational gleam in her eyes. Sandy did amateur dramatics twice a week and devoutly believed that there was nothing in life that couldn't benefit from elaborate gestures. She would never make it to the big screen.

'Guess!'

'I would if I thought that Alfredo would let us get away with playing a few guessing games when it's pandemonium in here.' On cue, Alfredo yelled something threatening from across the kitchen and was blithely ignored. 'The Queen?' Shannon hazarded. 'A famous Hollywood star interested in sampling a more down-market venue in fashionable Notting Hill? Someone from the Lottery Board coming to present you with a cheque for several million pounds?'

'*He's* here!' Sandy straightened up with a smug smile of satisfaction.

'What on earth is *he* doing here at this time of day?' Shannon felt a sudden little swell of excitement.

'Watch it, kid, you're going red in the face.'

'Who is he with?'

'No one. *At the moment*...' Sandy allowed the tantalising titbit to drop. 'But *he's requested two menus*!'

'We're sad people, Sandy.' Shannon stood up and smoothed down her calf-length black skirt. 'Wasting our time speculating on someone we don't know from Adam...' Which wasn't entirely true. They *did* know him, in a manner of speaking. The man had been coming in regularly to grace their eating establishment every morning, no later than seven, for months. In fact, almost as long as Shannon had been living in London, and there was a pleasurable familiarity about the routine.

Of course, they had both given in to wild speculation about him.

He was too aggressively good looking to ignore. His hair was very short and very dark and the sum total of his features added up to an impression of understated power that made their spectator sport of watching him virtually irresistible.

'Where are you going, my little Irish friend?' Sandy asked tartly. 'Don't you have a spot of important typing to be getting on with?'

'I'll just have a quick peek at him. See if he looks the same at lunchtime as he does first thing in the morning.'

'You mean you think that his mascara might have smudged? Lippy worn off a bit? Facial T-zones looking a bit greasy and in need of a dash of Almond Beige pressed powder?'

Shannon ignored her and quickly grabbed the cream and blue apron folded in the corner of her desk. She'd originally been hired as Alfredo's secretary, to look after his books, do his typing, take phone calls and generally make sure that the nuts and bolts of the restaurant were well oiled and running smoothly, but the plan had gone pear-shaped on day three when one of the waitresses had failed to show up and she'd been requisitioned to help serve tables. Since then, Shannon had combined her well-honed secretarial skills with her newly discovered waitressing talents, donning an apron whenever the situation demanded, and always in the morning when the paperwork could be left for a couple of hours.

By the time she had quickly slipped the apron over her head, Alfredo had appeared in all his five-feet-four, seriously corpulent Italian glory.

He was one of the few men in the entire world, Shannon was sure, whose lack of height made it possible for her to address him on an eye-to-eye level.

'Just taking over serving, Alfredo…' Shannon looked meaningfully at her friend who was hovering to one side like a spare part. 'Sandy's hurt her foot.'

'Don't you tell Alfredo anything about the hurt foots, missy! The foots looked just fine when she came a running over to whisper to you when it is madness here and I am not paying her to have the little cosy chats when she should be taking orders! Don't you two little missies think that Alfredo does not have the eyes at the back of the head! I see everything!'

The hurt foot had been a good idea. It released Sandy's barely contained lust for drama and she instantly shot into wounded mode, removing one shoe and tenderly touching her ankle as though it might explode at any minute if too much pressure was applied.

Shannon took the opportunity to scuttle through the kitchen, pausing to glance at the orders stacked on the counter, then hustled outside into the restaurant.

Yes, so what if she was sad? A sad twenty-five-year-old girl who had fled Ireland in a welter of misery and had grasped at the giggling normality of fantasising about a mysterious customer who had fired her imagination. Didn't her imagination deserve to be fired after what she had been through? It was all a silly game but silly games had been just what her depressed soul had needed.

She walked briskly over to his table and appeared to be startled at finding him there.

If she had been Sandy, she would have been far more elaborate when it came to playing startled. Instead, she smiled with consummate politeness and said, 'Oh! What a pleasant surprise to see you here at lunchtime, sir! Shall I take your order or are you waiting for someone?'

'Oh! And what a pleasant surprise, seeing *you* at lunchtime, and, yes, you may take my order for a drink but I am waiting for someone.'

He had a deep, slow voice that had a disturbing tendency to curl around her nervous system, which was what it was doing now. He leaned back in his chair and looked at her with amusement.

'I thought your little blonde friend was serving me.'

'Oh, Sandy's hurt her ankle. She's sitting for a few minutes.'

'In that case, I'll have a bottle of the Sancerre. Could you make sure that there's ice in my glass? I like my white wine very cold.'

'Of course, sir. Will that be all?'

'Now, there's a leading question,' he murmured, and Shannon's colour rose. *Was he flirting?* No. Impossible. The man might be terrifyingly good-looking but he was also highly conventional. Didn't he wear impeccably tailored suits and read the *Financial Times* every morning?

She cleared her throat and met his dark eyes steadily. 'Perhaps I could bring you a little appetiser to sample while you wait for your friend? One of our chefs has prepared some delicious crab and prawn pastries.'

'Tempting.'

'Or you could wait until your partner arrives.'

'My partner?' he drawled with lazy amusement. 'In what context would you be using the word "partner"?'

Shannon looked at him in confusion. She'd assumed that his lunch date was with a woman. Maybe even his wife, although he didn't wear a wedding ring. Or maybe, she thought sheepishly, she had just been fishing for information.

'You blush very easily. Has anyone ever told you that? And when you blush, you look even more like a schoolgirl, especially with those braids on either side. What sort of partner do you think I'm meeting for lunch? A female partner, perhaps?'

'I'm very sorry, sir. I just assumed...perhaps your wife...or maybe a female friend...'

'I don't have a wife, actually, and *a female friend...*' He let his voice linger on the description for a few seconds while he continued to watch her gravely. 'What an extraordinarily quaint way of putting it. Alas, though, no female friend on the scene either.'

Her surprise must have registered on her face because he laughed softly and raised his eyebrows. 'Yes, I'm one of those sad old men who is still waiting for the right woman to come along and make an honest man of him.' Disconcertingly, the mildness in his voice seemed to encourage a response to this, but for the life of her Shannon couldn't think of a thing to say. She got the distinct impression, in fact, that the man was trying to tease her.

'I'm sure that's not the case,' she replied tartly, shoving the order pad into the pocket of her apron and doing something pointless with the cutlery on the table because she was rather enjoying the feeling of being watched by those incredible eyes.

'What makes you say that?'

'If that will be all, sir, I'll just go and fetch your wine.'

'You mean you're leaving me in the middle of my unanswered question?'

'I'm very busy at the moment, sir.' She drew herself up to her full height of five feet three and looked down at the darkly amused face. 'I'll return with your drinks order…'

'And some of the delicious crab and prawn pastries…'

'What? Oh, yes. Right.'

It was the strangest conversation she'd had with him since he'd appeared through the door months earlier and she found that she was shaking when she returned to the kitchens. Let that be a lesson to her not to indulge her curiosity! She'd been bitten by the speculation bug and he'd returned the favour with panache, deliberately playing verbal games with an air of complete fake gallantry. She would be better off getting back to the work she was paid to do.

'Your foot's completely better,' she informed Sandy, when she managed to eventually corner her, 'and table four wants a bottle of Sancerre. A bucket of ice on the table as well.'

'Oh, dear. I take it your curiosity has been satisfied?'

'The man,' Shannon said loftily, 'is not quite the paragon of politeness we thought he was.'

Sandy's eyes gleamed with sudden alertness. 'Ooh… Tell me more… Was he rude?'

'No.' Shannon sat down and rustled lots of paper into a stack then she pushed a button on her computer so that the screen lit up. How was she supposed to get any work done when her desk was stuck here off the end of the kitchens without even a partition to separate one from the other? It was noisy and disorienting and she felt giddy.

'Oh. Did he make a pass at you, then?'

Shannon's eyes shot to her friend's with horror. 'He most certainly did not!' she denied vehemently.

'Then what did the man do?'

'He...he... Nothing really, I suppose,' she said lamely. 'But you can carry on serving him, and you'd better hurry with his wine before he marches in here to find out what's going on. Oh, and he wants some of those crabby pastry things as well.'

She would take no further interest in him, or his lunch companion for that matter.

So when, ten minutes later, Alfredo announced to her that she would have to help out with the serving, she point-blank refused. Albeit in a pleading tone of voice and sheltering behind the excuse of having to catch up on her paperwork.

'Are you disobeying me, missy?' Alfredo's jowls wobbled and he folded his arms expressively. He had an array of menacing gestures which routinely failed to work because his jolly approach to life was always too near the surface. He was a sucker for giving leftovers to their little coterie of down-and-outs who stopped by every night at closing time and sometimes he would force them to comment on some of his concoctions. How could anyone resist Alfredo?

Which was why Shannon ended up sticking on the apron again with a little sigh of frustration. As luck would have it, table four needed their order. She decided that it would be good practice at smiling brightly and acting like a sophisticated Londoner who could handle most things without batting an eyelid, which was the image she was steadily trying to create. On no account would she allow the man, still nameless, to think that he had thrown her into a tizzy with his word games.

She approached his table with the plates, studiously avoiding eye contact, and gently deposited the halibut in front of him. Then she decided to further test her *savoir-faire* by asking him whether his wine was all right.

'Enough ice, sir?'

'A bucket is more than enough,' he agreed in a murmur. 'And the little crab pastries were truly exquisite. My compliments to the chef.'

'I'll pass on the message,' Shannon said, rather proud at her self-containment.

'Very obliging of you.' He looked at his food and she had a sneaking suspicion that there was something resembling a smile lurking at the corners of his mouth.

She turned to his companion and the practised smile froze. She could feel the colour drain away from her face.

'You!' she whispered, clutching the plate of food. 'What are *you* doing here!' Her fragile mastery over her emotions crumbled spectacularly away in the face of Eric Gallway, who was sitting back in his chair, looking at her with smiling, polite blankness. He was as blond-haired and blue-eyed as she remembered, with the plastic good looks of someone who had spent a lifetime cultivating their outward image to the detriment of everything else. He'd captured her with his looks and then used every ounce of smooth charm at his disposal to try and get her into bed with him. Goodness knew, he might have succeeded as well in the end if she hadn't found out about his wife and his children and the whole life he had conveniently concealed while promising her happy-ever-afters and wedded bliss. Only then had he turned vicious and the mask had slipped away to reveal a small man with a nasty, cruel mind.

'Excuse me, do I know you, miss?'

In retrospect, it was the worst thing he could have said. In retrospect, Shannon liked to think that she wouldn't have done what she had if he'd acknowledged her. Looking at her coolly and blankly and pretending that he didn't have a clue who she was, it sent all the vanished colour rushing back into her cheeks. Her frozen hands began to tremble with rage.

'Maybe you don't. How disappointing,' she agreed. She heard her mother's voice telling her to always count to ten because her temper would get her into trouble one day, and made it to two before she removed the plate from the tray and tipped twelve ounces of medium-rare steak, dripping with Alfredo's special sauce, accompanied by potatoes and vegetables, straight onto the pristine jacket and well-tailored trousers.

It was intensely satisfying to hear Eric Gallway's yelp of pain as hot food hit the thin covering of expensive wool. It reverberated through the restaurant like the crash of breaking crockery in a china shop. He stood up and frantically began wiping the food with his napkin, while everyone in the restaurant stopped eating and positioned themselves the better to look at what was going on.

'How dare you?' he growled. 'How *dare* you throw a plate of food over me? I don't know who the hell you are, miss, but I'm damn well going to make sure you're sacked! Get me your boss! This instant!'

Shannon had a strong urge to laugh and covered her mouth with her hand. No need to get her boss. Alfredo was hurrying over towards them while trying to encourage the other diners to carry on with their meals. Perhaps pretend that this was nothing but some simple Italian jollity.

'What is going on here?' Alfredo ignored Eric's frantic cleaning-up process and stared at Shannon who hung her head. Hopefully, he would interpret that as a gesture of shame instead of an insane desire to stifle her mirth.

'What,' snarled Eric, 'do you think the problem is? This…this…*so-called* waitress of yours has dumped a plate of food all over me and let me tell you right now that unless she's sacked immediately, I'll sue you for everything you possess! I'll personally make sure that this restaurant is out of business!'

'It sort of fell, the plate,' Shannon said, her green eyes wide and luminous. If he could pretend not to know who the hell she was, then she could pretend that it had all been an unfortunate accident. 'Sorry.' She grabbed a serviette and made a flicking motion, which was venomously brushed aside. 'I think some of the carrots oozed into your pocket, *sir*…and there are a few mange-tout on your left shoe…'

Eric seemed incapable of responding to the helpful observations and stared at her murderously as Alfredo launched into a profuse apology, ending with assurances that any dry-cleaning costs would be covered.

'Oh, dear, your lovely patent leather shoes seem to be ruined,' Shannon observed with extravagant seriousness.

'Please, allow me to offer you a full replacement for your suit and your shoes.' All eyes followed a path down the soaked trousers to the ruined shoes under discussion. Someone burst out laughing a few tables away.

'You sack this *creature* immediately, my man, or you won't be able to afford your next loaf of bread, never mind my clothes. And let me tell you something, I happen to know quite a number of people in high places!'

'I think it's time you took yourself off to the bathroom and cleaned up,' drawled a familiar voice. 'You're making a spectacle of yourself.'

For a minute, Eric looked as though, now in his stride and regardless of the state of his clothes, he was more than prepared to stand his ground and continue his litany of threats, but after a few seconds he nodded and walked off, watched by everyone in the restaurant. Someone yelled for an encore and Shannon felt a rush of appreciation for the bawdy clientele who frequented their establishment.

'I hope your friend will calm down,' Alfredo began worriedly. 'Of course, it was a dreadful accident, but all these threats of closing down my restaurant…well, I have a family to support! Perhaps I better go see what is happening in the bathroom, hope he listens to reason…' He extracted a handkerchief from a pocket to wipe his brow and then hurried off towards the direction of the bathroom.

'Sit down.'

Shannon slowly turned to look at the man, who seemed to be the only person in the restaurant unaffected by what had just taken place.

She slumped into a free chair and rested her head against her hands.

'Feel better?'

She looked at him for a while in silence. 'Not really, no, but thank you for asking.'

'What was that all about?'

'I'm very, very sorry that I ruined your lunch.' She stared at the congealing halibut on his plate. There was nothing funny about what had just happened, she realised. Alfredo had had nothing to do with anything, but he had taken the brunt of it and it had all been her fault.

'Forget the lunch,' he said drily.

'Poor Alfredo,' she said miserably to herself. 'I shouldn't have dropped the plate of food all over your friend. It was wrong of me.'

'He's not my friend. You certainly know how to create a scene, don't you?'

'Were you very embarrassed? I'm very, very sorry.'

'Will you stop apologising? And, no, I wasn't embarrassed. It would take rather more than that little incident to embarrass me. Tell me what you're going to do now.'

'Resign, of course.' She stood up and his eyes followed her thoughtfully. 'What choice do I have? Alfredo will never trust me with another plate of food, and I couldn't blame him. Who needs a waitress with a talent for flinging food over customers?' Besides, she *knew* Eric Gallway and she knew that he was more than capable of doing his utmost to get what he would see as just revenge for his humiliation.

'Resign, reds? And who will serve me my morning coffee and bagel?'

He was trying to be nice. In the midst of her misery, she realised that he had called her 'reds', a reference, she assumed, to her bright red hair, and the softly spoken intimacy was almost as powerfully unsettling as the prospect of her future without a job.

'I'm going to pack up my things,' she said glumly. 'Thanks for being so understanding.' She reached out to shake his hand, for some unknown reason, but instead of a shake, he casually linked his fingers through hers and squeezed her hand gently, then he reached for his glass of wine and sipped some, with his fingers still interlinked with hers. He rubbed his thumb idly against hers and she felt a curious sensation of prickling down the back of her neck. Then he released her.

'I don't suppose you'd like your meal replaced?' she joked half-heartedly, and he raised his eyebrows, appreciating her attempt at humour.

Funny, during all their speculations about him, she had never noticed how strongly the curves of his mouth spoke of compassion and humour. Or maybe anyone would have seemed compassionate and humorous alongside Eric with his infernal vanity and monstrous self-absorption.

'Strangely, I appear to have lost my appetite.' He gave her a little half-smile.

'Well.' She heaved a sigh. 'The halibut was very good. Trust me. Much better than the wretched steak.'

She walked the long walk back to the kitchens, and by the time she'd told Alfredo she was resigning, said her last goodbyes to everyone and cleared her desk of what belonged to her, her usual buoyancy was back with her.

She would find something else. She wasn't fussy. Hadn't she ended up enjoying Alfredo's even though initially the early start had put her off and the hours were often longer than her contract demanded? She would find something else and she would enjoy it. And if she didn't, then couldn't she always head back up to Dublin?

True, it felt good to be away from the claustrophobia of having all her large family around her but if she did decide to go back to Ireland, she knew that she would settle back in without any real difficulty. And after all this time, they would have at least stopped oozing sympathy about her wrecked love life and making endless remarks about adulterous men and young, impressionable girls.

Things would work out. She had a sudden, wild memory of the man with his fingers entwined with hers and felt a little shiver of regret. One face lost to her for ever. For no reason whatsoever, the thought depressed her, and she was so busy trying to analyse the foolishness of her reaction that she didn't notice him until he was standing in front of her. Towering over her, in fact. Shannon just manage to stop before she collided with his immovable force and it was only when her eyes actually trailed upwards that she recognised him and gave a little gasp of surprise. Mostly because he seemed to have materialised from the sheer power of the thoughts in her head.

'How did it go?'

'What are you doing here?' She wanted to reach out and prod him to see if he was real.

'Waiting for you, as a matter of fact.'

'Waiting for me? Why would you be waiting for me?' It wasn't yet four-thirty, but the light was already beginning to fade and there was an unholy chill in the autumn air.

'To make sure that you were all right.'

'Of course I'm all right.' She stuck her hands in her pockets and stared at his shoes. She hadn't realised how big a man he was. Not just tall, but broad-shouldered and powerfully built. 'Why shouldn't I be?' She raised her eyes to his and made fleeting contact.

'Because, reds, you looked pretty shaken up back there in the restaurant.'

Shannon debated whether she should tell him to stop calling her 'reds' and decided, perversely, that she liked the nickname.

'Did I?' she said airily. 'I thought I handled myself very well, actually. I mean, losing a job isn't the end of the world, is it?' Bills. Rent. Food. Not the end of the world but not far off.'

'Look, it's cold trying to hold a conversation out here. Why don't you hop in my car. I want to talk to you.'

'*Hop in your car?* I'm very sorry but I can't do that.'

'Why not?'

'Because I don't know you. You could be anyone. Don't get me wrong. I'm not saying you're an axe-wielding maniac, but you *could* be for all I know.'

'An axe-wielding maniac?' he asked, bemused.

'Or a fugitive from the law. Anyway, my mother told me never to accept lifts from strangers.'

'I'm not a stranger! You've been serving me breakfast every morning just about for months! Nor am I a fugitive from the law. If I were a fugitive from the law, wouldn't I be hiding out somewhere less conspicuous than a busy Italian restaurant in the middle of crowded Notting Hill? Your imagination is obviously as vivid as your temper, reds.'

'And stop calling me *reds*.' She'd decided she didn't care for the appellation after all. It was insulting.

'Then accompany me, please, for a short ride in my car which is just around the corner. I want to talk to you.'

'Talk about what?'

'Oh, good grief,' he groaned. 'Let me put it this way, it'll be worth your while.' He turned on his heel and began walking away, expecting her to follow him, and she did, clutching her coat around her and half running to keep up.

'I don't even know your name!' she panted in his wake. 'And where are you planning on taking me for this little talk that will be worth my while?'

He stopped abruptly and she cannoned into him. Instinctively he reached out and steadied her. 'Kane Lindley,' he said, 'in answer to your first question. And a little coffee-bar two blocks away in answer to your last. We could walk but my time on the meter is about to run out so it's as easy for us to take the car and I'll find somewhere else to park.'

She realised that he was still holding her by her arms, and he must have realised that as well because he politely dropped his hands and waited for her to respond.

'Kane Lindley…'

'That's right. Have you heard of me?'

'Why should I have heard of you?' Shannon asked, puzzled.

He said swiftly, 'Absolutely no reason. I'm not a celebrity but I own Lindley publications and I'm now in charge of a television network.' He zapped open his car with his remote after a short mental tussle. Shannon hurried over to the passenger side and slipped in, slamming the door against the stiff cold.

'I haven't heard of Lindley publications,' she told him as soon as he was sitting next to her.

'It doesn't matter.' His voice was irritable. 'I'm not trying to impress you. I'm merely trying to put you at ease in case you think I'm not to be trusted.'

'Oh. Right. Well…' She stared out of the window. 'I'm Shannon McKee. How long were you lurking around, waiting for me to come out, anyway?'

'I wasn't lurking around, reds,' he growled. 'As a matter of fact, I went to buy some ties at a little shop tucked away around the corner and then dropped back here. Coincidentally, you were leaving.'

The coffee-bar really was only a couple of streets away and they got a parking space instantly. It felt kind of nice to be the one sitting at the table and being waited on for a change. Meals out had been few and far between since she'd moved down to London, where the cost of living had hit her for six and relaxed cups of coffee in trendy coffee-bars, as this one was, had been even more of a rarity.

He ordered a cafetière of coffee for two and a plate of pastries and then proceeded to look at her with dark-eyed speculation. 'Now, tell me a little about yourself. I know you don't like football, like the theatre even though you never get there, loathe all exercise except swimming and are self-conscious about your hair, but what are you doing in London?'

Shannon blushed. She never would have guessed that her passing titbits of information had been stored away. She would have assumed that he had more important things to think about than the details of a waitress's life. 'I am not self-conscious about my hair!' she snapped, a little disconcerted by this regurgitation of facts.

'Then why you do always wear it tied back?'

'Because it's convenient. And I'm in London be-cause...because I wanted a change from Ireland. I lived in a little village about twenty miles outside Dublin and I guess I wanted to sample something a little different.' Now that he had mentioned her wretched hair, she found that she couldn't stop fiddling with it, tugging the ends of the braids. She had to force herself to fold her hands neatly on her lap.

'I wish you'd stop looking at me,' she said after a while. Here they were, one to one, no longer in the roles of waitress serving customer, and their sudden equality made her feel breathless. She felt as though those un-readable, considering eyes could see straight past the dross and into all the secret corners of her mind that she preferred not to share with anyone.

'Why? Does it make you feel uncomfortable?' He didn't labour the point, though. Thankfully. Instead, once their coffee and pastries were in front of them, he began asking her about her work experience and what she had done in Ireland and what she had done since moving to London, tilting his head to one side as she rambled on about her education and her first job and her secretarial qualifications.

'So,' he said finally, 'you did secretarial work, but really you'd call yourself quite adaptable.'

'I can turn my hand to most things.'

'I'll get to the point, reds. Sorry, Miss McKee. I feel very badly about what happened today. I've been coming to Alfredo's for months and I know that you're good at what you do. I suspect you enjoyed working there and the fact is that if I hadn't chosen to go there at lunchtime with that particular person, you would not now be out of a job.'

'It's not your fault.'

Kane relaxed back and folded his arms. 'That's as maybe, but the fact remains that I would like to make amends by offering you a job…working for…me.'

CHAPTER TWO

'YOU want me *to work for you*?' Shannon asked incredulously. 'But you don't know me! Not really! You don't even have any references! You've seen me wait tables at Alfredo's for a few months, and we've chatted off and now, and now you're offering me a job as your secretary because *you feel obligated*?' Her eyes dropped from Kane's face to his big hands, cradling the sides of his mug. Somehow the thought of working for this man frankly terrified her.

'And are you qualified to throw job offers around willy-nilly?' she pressed on, frowning. 'What will your boss say?'

'I *am* the boss. I own the company, lock, stock and barrel. I told you that already. Everyone in the company reports to me, reds.'

'I told you to stop calling me by that name,' Shannon said absent-mindedly. 'Anyway, aren't there more suitable candidates lining up for the job? And how come you've coincidentally got a position vacant?' She chewed her lip, mulling over this wildly improbable development and trying to read between the lines to the hidden agenda. Because there must be a hidden agenda. Job offers involved interviews and references and procedures. They didn't land like ripe plums into your lap without there being one or two glaring catches.

'I mean, top executives are never without a secretary. Someone is always available to handle things like that, to make sure that vacant positions get filled.' If he owned the company, he need only snap fingers and there would be someone on the scene, saluting and racing off to make sure that a suitable secretary was located pronto. He wouldn't be lounging around, making do on the offchance that someone might show up at some point in time.

'Oh, dear. In that case, perhaps I'm lying. Perhaps I don't own Lindley publications after all.' He laughed with genuine amusement and gave her a long, leisurely and far too all-encompassing a look for her liking. 'Don't worry, reds, you're asking all the right questions. The job exists because my old secretary retired to live in Dorset with her widowed sister two months ago and since then I've been using a selection of secretaries, none of whom has been particularly suitable. My only alternative at the moment is to usurp one of my director's personal assistants who *would* be able to cope with the workload, but it's not an ideal choice because it would entail leaving someone else facing the same problem. Aside from that obvious problem, there are one or two other considerations that need to be met, and I assure you, not that I need to, that the lady in question would be unable to meet them.'

As far as Shannon was concerned, the situation was getting more and more bizarre by the moment. 'What other considerations?' she asked slowly. She nibbled one of the pastries and looked at him steadily as she did so.

'Before we get to those, just tell me whether or not you're interested in the job.'

'Naturally, I'm interested in getting *a* job. Having just been forced into early retirement from the last one.'

'Well, shall we skip the arguments for the moment so that I can try and establish what sort of secretarial experience you possess? Obviously, if your experience is insufficient, you can be slotted in somewhere a bit lower down the scale, although working for me is more than a matter of relevant secretarial experience. I'm looking for an attitude and I think you've got it.'

'Because I've been so successful as a waitress? Except for today when I flung a plate of hot food over a customer?'

'I particularly liked the way you pointed out the stray mange-tout he had missed on his shoe.' He gave her a crooked smile, then before she could respond he leaned forward and casually brushed the side of her mouth with his finger. 'Pastry crumbs,' he murmured. 'So, run your background by me.'

'All right. What do you want to know?' She had to clasp her hands very tightly together to stop herself from touching the spot where his finger had been.

'A brief job history would be nice. Details of what your actual jobs involved.'

'School, secretarial college, several temporary positions and then, for the past three years, a permanent job working for a radio station just outside Dublin. A local radio station that focused on good music and gossip. Generally speaking, I did all the office work and also updated their computer programs to accommodate their growth. They were in a bit of an administrative mess when I arrived, actually, so it was a challenge to get things straight. It was a fantastic job,' she added wistfully. 'Never a dull moment and the people there were great fun.'

'So, bored with the personal satisfaction of it all, you decided to leave…'

'Not quite.'

'Then why did you leave?' He looked at her evenly. 'I'm not asking out of morbid curiosity, but as your potential employer I have to establish whether your abrupt departure might influence my decision. I mean, did you leave for the pay?'

'I left...for personal reasons,' she said, flushing. Passing conversations with him had not prepared her for his tenacity.

'Which might be...what?'

'I don't see that that's relevant.'

'Of course it's relevant.' He drained his cup of coffee. 'What if you left for the personal reason of, let's say, theft?'

'Theft!'

'Or...flamboyant insubordination. Or immoral conduct...'

Shannon burst out laughing. 'Immoral conduct? Oh, please! What kind of immoral conduct?'

'Stripping at the office party? Smoking on the premises? Sex in the boss's office when there was no one around?' His voice was mild, so why did she suddenly feel her skin begin to prickle? She imagined herself lying on a desk in his office, with those long fingers touching every part of her body, and she shrank back in shaken horror from the image. It had been as forceful as it had been unexpected.

'I have all my references back at my bedsit,' she told him primly.

'At your *bedsit*?'

'Correct.'

'You *live* in a bedsit?'

'It's all I could afford. Anyway...' she paused and reluctantly flashed him a wry smile '...a bedsit is the height of luxury after you've grown up in a house with seven siblings.'

'You have...' He looked green at the thought of it.

Hates children, she thought smugly, perversely pleased that she had managed to shake some of that formidable self-control. Probably an only child. She and Sandy had never actually speculated on his family background but she would have bet money that he was the cosseted son of doting parents who had given in to his every whim, hence his unspoken assumption that he could get whatever he wanted at the click of a finger.

'I know. That's how most English people react when I tell them that. My mother maintains that she wanted each and every one of us, but I think she just got a bit carried away after she was married. I suppose you're an only child? Only children are particularly appalled at the thought of sharing a house with lots of other brothers and sisters.'

'I'm…well, we're not really here to discuss my background, Miss McKee…'

It didn't escape her notice that he had reverted to a formal appellation now that he was no longer manipulating their conversation. 'Oh, it was merely a question. Are you an only child?'

'Well, yes, as a matter of fact, I am.'

'I thought so. Poor you. My mum always said that an only child is a lonely child. Were you lonely as a child?'

'This is a ridiculous digression,' Kane muttered darkly. 'We were talking about your living arrangements.'

'So we were,' Shannon agreed readily. She took a small sip from her coffee, enjoying the sensation of sitting and having someone else do the waiting for a change. Their cups had been refilled without her even noticing the intrusion.

'And your decision to leave Ireland and come down here?'

'I thought we'd already talked about that. I told you that I had references and that you could see them. My last company was very pleased with my performance, actually,' she continued.

'Did you leave because of Eric Gallway?'

The luminous green eyes cooled and she said steadily, 'That really is none of your business, Mr Lindley.'

'No, it isn't, is it?' he said softly, but his eyes implied otherwise. 'Now, there are one or two other minor considerations that come with this job,' he said slowly, resting both his elbows on the table and leaning towards her. He had rolled up the sleeves of his white shirt so that she had an ample view of strong forearms, liberally sprinkled with fine, dark hair.

'Minor considerations?' Shannon met his thoughtful, speculative look with a stirring of unease. What minor considerations? She didn't care for the word 'minor'. Somehow it brought to mind the word 'major'.

'There are a few duties connected with this job that will require some overtime…'

She breathed a sigh of relief. She wasn't afraid of hard work and clock-watching had never been one of her problems. If anything, she'd often found herself staying on to work when she could have been going home.

'I'm fine with overtime, Mr Lindley,' she said quickly. 'Alfredo will vouch for that.'

'Good, good.' He paused and his dark eyes flitted across her face. 'These duties, however, are possibly not quite what you have in mind.'

'What do they involve, Mr Lindley?' Shannon asked faintly, for once lost for words in the face of the myriad possibilities filling her imaginative mind. She hoped that he wasn't about to spring some illegal suggestion on her because she'd just become accustomed to thinking that gainful employment was within her reach and to have it summarily snatched away would be almost more of a blow than the original loss of her job.

'I have a child, Miss McKee...'

'You *have a child*?'

'These things *do* happen as an outcome of sexual intercourse when no contraception has been used,' Kane said with overdone patience. 'As,' he added mildly, 'you are probably aware.'

Shannon failed to take offence at his tone. 'I—simply never associated you with a child,' she stammered, realising belatedly that her admission might give him the idea that she had been speculating wildly about him behind his back.

'And may I ask why?'

'You just don't look...the fatherly sort...' She shrugged helplessly. 'I mean,' she said hurriedly, as his eyebrows slanted upwards, 'you were always at the restaurant so early... I just assumed that you weren't much of a family man... How old is your child?'

'Eight and it's a she. Her name's Eleanor.'

'Oh, right.' Shannon paused long enough to digest this piece of information. 'And if you don't mind me asking, what does all this have to do with me?'

'At the moment I have a nanny in place to—'

'You have *a nanny in place*?' She gave a snort of derisory laughter.

'Would you do me the favour of not interrupting me every five seconds?'

'Sorry. It's just the expression you used.'

'I have a nanny in place who takes Eleanor to school in the mornings and brings her back home. Under normal circumstances, I would have a live-in nanny but Carrie has always insisted on having the evenings to herself and I've been loath to replace her because she's been there since Eleanor was a baby.'

'What about your wife? Does she work long hours as well?' Shannon's voice was laced with curiosity.

'My wife is dead.' He glanced down and she felt a rush of compassion for him and for his child. She tried to imagine a life with no siblings, no mother, an absent father and a nanny—and failed.

'I'm sorry.' She paused and then asked curiously, 'When did she die?'

'When Eleanor was born, actually.' There was a dead flatness in his voice which she recognised. She'd heard her mother use that tone whenever someone asked her about her husband. She'd used detachment to forestall questions she didn't want to answer. 'The pregnancy was fraught, although the birth was relatively simple. Three hours after Eleanor was born, my wife haemorrhaged to death.'

'I'm so very sorry, Mr Lindley.'

'So occasionally I might need you to act as babysitter, for want of a better word. My old secretary was very obliging in that respect but, as I said, she now lives in Dorset. Naturally, you would be paid handsomely for the inconvenience.'

Shannon cradled the cup in between her hands, rubbing the rim with her thumbs. 'Looking after a child could never be an inconvenience,' she said quietly.

'So.' He signalled for the bill and she could sense his eagerness to be off the subject of his child and back into the arena of discussing work. 'When would you be able to report for work?'

'Whenever you want.'

'What about next Monday morning? Eight-thirty

sharp. And, naturally, I needn't tell you that your first month will be a probationary one.'

'On both sides, Mr Lindley,' Shannon told him, just in case he got it into his head that she would somehow feel obliged to work for him even if she hated the job, simply because he had offered it to her out of duty.

'I wouldn't—' he graced her with such a powerful smile that her heart seemed to stop for a few seconds '—dream of expecting otherwise.' He stood up and politely offered her a lift to wherever she was going. When she declined, he nodded briefly in her direction before ushering her out of the coffee-bar.

The fresh, cold air whipped around her and for a few seconds, she had the unreal sensation that it had all been a vivid dream. She had always been particularly good at dreaming up improbable scenarios. Perhaps this was just another one. But, of course, it wasn't. She had quit one job and then Fate had smiled on her and decreed that she land another within hours of losing the first. Wasn't that just like life? Things, she had always thought, were never quite as black as they seemed. All you ever needed to do was leap over the first sticky patch and, sure enough, things would right themselves. There was always room for healthy optimism.

The healthy optimism stayed with Shannon for the remainder of the week and right into the weekend, which was spent with Sandy who seemed agog at the turn of events. She kept referring to 'the luck of the devil' and the way that Irish blarney could get a girl what she wanted until Shannon was forced to point out that the man was obviously impressed by all the secretarial potential he had spotted in her while she had waited tables.

'Ha! Perhaps he spotted *other potential*,' Sandy whispered darkly over their celebratory pizza.

But even that failed to quench her optimism.

She dressed very carefully on the Monday morning, making sure that everything matched and that there were no unknowing eccentric touches which had always been permissible at the radio station and at Alfredo's but most certainly would not be in most normal working environments. She looked regretfully at her floppy hat as she left the bedsit, and at her flat black lace-up shoes which were her faithful companions whether accompanied by skirt or trousers. Neither would do. Blue skirt, white blouse, blue and black checked jacket, which unfortunately was the only one she possessed and as a hand-me-down from one of her sisters didn't fit quite right, and, of course, her coat, one of her more expensive purchases from her working life at the radio station.

Her hair had presented a bit of a problem. Braids didn't seem right for a secretarial job in a normal office environment, but wearing it loose wasn't an option because as far as she was concerned, it was just too *red*, too *beacon-like*, so she tied it into a low ponytail which she held in place with a large, tortoiseshell barrette.

Shannon decided, as she caught the underground to the address Kane Lindley had written down for her, that her mother would have loved her outfit but her brothers and sisters would have fallen over laughing. Although she wasn't the youngest in the family, she was the last girl and so her elder sisters had mothered her. She was the only one in the family with red hair and somehow the red hair had always made her look much younger than her years. Thank heavens she had tied it back. Severely. She was about to embark on a severe career path, she decided, working for a man who would certainly not tolerate too much gaiety within the four walls of his office.

Her first taste of exactly how different her job would be compared to the last two was when she arrived at the office which turned out to be in a building all smoked glass and, as she entered, marble floors and plants in the foyer. Mr Lindley, she was told by the receptionist who was separated from the public by a large, smooth circular desk, was waiting for her and that if she took the lift to the fourth floor, she would be directed to his office.

By the time Shannon was standing outside his door, she was fast losing faith in her office skills. They had certainly done nicely in her previous two jobs, but did radio stations and restaurants really lend themselves to the sort of top-class working skills needed in a place like this? Somewhere with thick carpets and enclosed offices and people hurrying like ants from computer terminals to fax machines and photocopiers? Her carefully thought-out clothes seemed hideously informal next to the smartly dressed women she had spied, who seemed to be in a uniform of grey suits and black pumps.

She tentatively knocked at the door, which was opened by a middle-aged woman with iron grey hair and sharp eyes.

'I'm sorry,' Shannon stammered. 'Actually, I'm looking for Mr Lindley's office. The girl at Reception—'

'Should have called me to come and fetch you,' the woman said, interrupting her nervous explanation. 'I shall have to have a word with her. Step inside, Miss McKee. Allow me first of all to introduce myself. I'm Sheila Goddard. I don't normally work for Mr Lindley, although it has to be said that he hasn't found a suitable replacement for his previous secretary for…well, frankly, months, and I've spent quite a bit of my time covering. Most inconvenient.' She gave Shannon a look

that seemed to imply that this inconvenience was somehow her fault.

'This will be your office. As you can see, Mr
Lindley's office is just beyond the inner door. Now, my
dear, I must confess that we were all a little surprised
when Mr Lindley informed us that he had found himself
a permanent secretary…'

Not as surprised as I was to be offered the job, she
thought. 'I'm on one month's probation,' Shannon
pointed out quickly, as she looked around the large outer
office with its walnut desk and swivel chair and discreet
company advertising pictures framed on the walls. Her
optimism was fading fast in the face of all this sterile,
hygienic space. No one around, no one to occasionally
chat to. She might very well go mad within the month.

'Naturally,' Sheila said. 'You may join the line of
unsuitable candidates, which is why I did suggest to Mr
Lindley that it might have been a bit *rash* to take you
on full time rather than as a temporary.'

'If you don't mind me asking, why exactly has there
been a long line of unsuitable candidates?'

'Mr Lindley,' Sheila said ominously, 'is a demanding
boss. Anything less than first rate never satisfies him.'
She knocked respectfully at the imposing door separating the two offices, giving Shannon ample time to accommodate the prospect of trying to work for a monster
who would attack at the first sign of a typing error.

The monster, waiting for her behind his desk, was on
the telephone when she entered and he carried on talking, his voice clipped, while Shannon looked all around
her, taking in the even more sterile surroundings of his
office, unbroken by any hint of personality. Not even a
picture or two of his daughter in sight. When there was
nothing else to look at without doing damage to her neck

muscles, she finally rested her green eyes on him. As he spoke, he leaned back in the leather chair, nodding at whatever was being said, answering solely in monosyllables.

'Right,' he said, as soon as he had replaced the receiver. 'You're here.'

'With my references,' Shannon agreed. 'But I must be honest, Mr Lindley, you were very kind to employ me but I don't think this arrangement is going to work out.' She pushed the references over to him and he began scanning them, then he sat back and looked at her.

'Why not?'

'Because this isn't the sort of working environment I'm used to at all. I really don't think I'll be suitable for the position.'

'Why don't you let me be the one to decide? Would you like some coffee? Tea? While I explain what your specific duties will involve?'

'No, thank you.'

'You're nervous.' He sat back and looked at her with his hands loosely folded on his lap. 'I'd never thought it of you, reds.'

'I'm not nervous.' Pointless, she thought, trying to tell him to use her full surname. 'It's just that…this is all a bit too formal for me… I wouldn't want to waste your time.'

'Very considerate of you,' he said drily. 'Your references are excellent. You're computer literate, you're willing to accept responsibilities… What makes you think you'd be wasting my time?'

'Apparently you've run through quite a number of unsatisfactory secretaries. Well, either the recruitment agencies have all been failing to do their jobs, or else you're a difficult man to work for.'

'I set high standards, if that's what you mean. Now, stop wittering about letting me down and let's start getting down to business. When I'm finished going through one or two clients with you and explaining what we do here, you can trot off to Personnel and sign your contract of employment.' He stood up, and glanced down at his watch, flicking back the cuff of his sleeve to expose dark hair gently curling at the strap.

'I have meetings this afternoon, but I shall leave you to do the basics. Some letters, faxes, e-mails. You can fence incoming calls by taking messages and I'll get back to them later. Sheila's always down the corridor if you run into difficulties.' He could see doubt stamped in her wary green eyes and he wondered, in passing, whether she realised exactly how appealing it made her.

'Look, if you really don't want to work for the company, I won't force you to stay. I can't force you to stay. The door's there and you're more than welcome to walk right through it and keep on walking until you get to an agency that has vacancies for interesting jobs in exciting, informal environments. Clearly you think that all this is just a little too stuffy for you. Perhaps you think that bosses should just lounge around all day in garish clothes with their feet on the desk, making as few demands as possible on their staff so as not to interrupt the enjoyment of it all. But,' he said, 'I can guarantee that your pay will be more than double what you were earning at that restaurant. And that's excluding what you'll personally be paid by me for anything you do involving my daughter.'

Shannon gave him a wry look to match his own. 'I'll give it a go. I'm as open to bribery as the next person.' Their eyes tangled in perfect mutual and amused understanding before she looked away.

She preceded her new boss into her office and sat down at the desk. He watched as her skirt rode a few centimetres higher, exposing slim, pale thighs through her tights. She'd disposed of the coat and the peculiar jacket, revealing a blouse that fitted snugly over her small breasts.

'Clients.' Kane Lindley cleared his throat and frowned in concentration as she flicked on the computer and waited for him to pick up the sentence. 'Accounts. Yes. Well, you'll be expected to update accounts and everything has to be filed in alphabetical order.' He leaned forward so that his forearm rested on the desk, almost brushing her bare skin.

'A lot of business is conducted overseas, so it would be helpful if you knew the money markets. Not in any great detail, but it would give you some idea of what is likely to be profitable and what is not. Now the media group I've just taken over...' He leant past her to flick back to the main menu so that he could begin running through details of the finances of the various companies under the one umbrella and as he did so she felt him brush against her breast. She drew away, a little shaken at the fleeting contact.

'Generally speaking, you won't be needed to accompany me to meetings.' He moved away from the desk and chose instead to pull up a chair so that his eyes could remain safely fixed on the same level as hers. 'However, you *will* need to check every e-mail I get when I'm not in the office and I get quite a number. In time, you should be able to deal with a good proportion of those.'

Shannon, turning to look at him, was a little disconcerted to find him quite so close to her. Close enough for her to distinguish the various shades of dark brown and black in his eyes and to breathe in the musky scent of male body, unimpeded by any colognes.

'Now,' he said finally, sitting back and pushing himself away from the desk, 'any questions?'

Shannon swivelled her chair to face him. 'About work?'

He looked at her wryly. 'No. I thought we might just have a general discussion about world affairs.'

'Don't you get a little lonely stuck out in this office on your own?'

'*Lonely?* Don't I get *a little lonely*?'

'Yes. You know…surely you don't spend the entire day focused on work. You must need to chat now and again…'

'*Chat?*'

'To people? Maybe when you break off to have a cup of coffee?'

'When I break off to have a cup of coffee, reds, I actually normally remain at my desk and more often than not I devote my attention to paperwork while I'm having it,' he said crushingly, and she nodded.

'Then how do you know what's going on in your company? You know, if you don't get around and hear the gossip on the ground floor?'

'*Hear the gossip?*'

'Well, you *did* ask me whether I had any questions,' Shannon trailed off, when he continued to stare at her as though she were crazy. 'As far as the actual *work* goes, I think I can handle it. I might be a bit slow to start with, of course. Until I find my feet.'

'I shouldn't think it'll take you very long,' he said. 'I've told Linda in Personnel to expect you some time before lunch.' With a swift, graceful movement, he stood up and eyed her blandly. 'Right now I shall be busy with meetings, so I probably won't see you until tomorrow. Linda will fill you in on all of this, but if you're interested, there's an office restaurant on the ground floor. I suspect that's where all the chat and gossip occurs.'

'Perhaps *you* should eat there more often in that case,' Shannon said with a slow grin.

'Actually,' he threw at her over his shoulder, as he slipped on his jacket and adjusted his tie, 'I do. Whenever I get the chance.'

He walked towards the door, then paused before turning to look at her. 'I think it might be a good idea if you met Eleanor. Carrie's been staying on late to accommodate me over the past two months, but now that you're here we can work something out so that she can get back to her social life.'

'I thought the babysitting arrangement was more on an...occasional basis,' Shannon faltered. 'And what about *my* social life?'

'Oh.' He walked slowly towards her, rubbing his chin with his hand as though startled at the concept of her having a social life. 'I thought you had come to London to nurse a broken heart. Don't you spend all your free time pining?'

Shannon flushed at his blatant and cheerful disregard for boundaries. 'Actually, if you read any self-help book, you'll discover that women with broken hearts immediately rush off to cultivate new and exciting social lives,' she replied tartly. She wondered whether dinner dates with Sandy constituted a new and exciting social life. Having come to London, she had quickly realised that the novel taste of freedom from her brothers and sisters and extended family members also carried a downside. Namely, that there was no handy cushion to protect her from her nights spent on her own. She went out with Sandy and with some of the other staff who worked at Alfredo's and was gradually building up a social life of sorts, but it was hardly humming.

'Well,' Kane conceded, 'I normally return home by eight, so your exciting social life shouldn't suffer too much.'

'By *eight*? When do you ever get to see your daughter?'

'I usually try and keep weekends free,' he muttered, turning away as a dark flush spread up his neck. 'Do you know your way around London?' He bent over and scribbled his address on a piece of paper. 'No, forget that. I'll get my driver to come and collect you, say, Friday evening? Around seven-thirty? Eleanor usually stays up late on a Friday as there's no school on a Saturday.'

'I'm sure I can find my way to your house, Mr Lindley.' She looked at the address and wondered how far it would be from an underground station. She wasn't averse to walking but walking at night, freezing cold and potentially without any real clue as to where she was heading, wasn't her idea of fun.

'I wouldn't dream of it.' He smiled briefly. 'After all, you're the one who will be doing me the service.'

'What is she like?' Shannon asked curiously, folding the piece of paper and stuffing it into her bag.

'Small, blonde hair, blue eyes.'

'Actually, I meant her personality.'

'Oh, Eleanor is…very quiet.' He frowned and seemed to be thinking of some other way he could find of describing her. 'Doesn't give any trouble at all.'

To Shannon, that hardly sounded like a great description of an eight-year-old child. I mean, she thought, if you can't get into a spot of trouble when you're eight, then when on earth *can* you? She had spent most of her formative years getting into trouble! When she'd left school at sixteen, she could remember the headmistress telling her mother that never in the history of the school had one parent paid so many visits.

'Right,' Shannon said in a subdued, reflective voice.

'Don't forget, if you run into anything you can't handle, and I'm not around, Sheila will help you out. She knows as much about this business as I do, probably.' He moved towards the door and stopped to say with a gravity in his voice that was only belied by the glint in his eye, 'And don't forget the office canteen. It's a hot-bed of gossip and intrigue. Let me know if you hear about any insurrections I should beware of.'

She could have sworn she heard a chuckle as Kane shut the door behind him and she was left with the computer, a stack of letters to type and the prospect of dinner *en famille* in four days' time with a man who was reluctantly beginning to intrigue her even more than he had when she'd been serving him his coffee and bagels.

CHAPTER THREE

KANE LINDLEY'S house was as far removed from Shannon's expectations as it was possible to be.

She'd expected something modern and austere, perhaps a penthouse suite in a renovated building with thick white carpets to drown out the noise of an eight-year-old child, whom she imagined wandering forlornly amid the luxury, searching for places to hide from a largely absent father.

But when the chauffeur-driven car turned into a pair of wrought-iron gates, the house confronting her was an ivy-clad Victorian house with neatly trimmed lawns. The outside lights revealed mature trees shading some swings and a slide.

She rang the doorbell, feeling her stomach muscles tense. Kane Lindley was proving to be a very good boss, so how was it that she still felt a little quiver of alarm every time she saw him? In fact, even when he was working in his office and out of sight, there was still a part of her that seemed tuned in to his presence, waiting for him to emerge. She assumed that it was all wrapped up in the usual nervousness of being new to a job.

She might have surmounted this initial nervousness if he'd been out of the office much, as he'd implied he would be at their first interview, but, in fact, he was in a great deal. Through the partially open door, she was always aware of his clipped voice as he conversed on the phone or else his steady silence as he worked through paperwork and on his computer. Ever so often he would call her in and dictate something, and then he would swivel his chair away from his desk and talk fluently and smoothly at her, frowning as he spoke, while his fingers lightly drummed his thigh. And he never failed to peer in at least twice a day just to see how she was progressing.

She couldn't really see why he hadn't been able to find a suitable secretary. It was hardly as if he was prone to dramatic mood swings or unpleasantly critical behaviour, and she could only think that his pace was maybe too fast for someone with too little experience. If nothing else, working at Alfredo's and at the radio station had promoted a healthy ability to think quickly and react without confusion to abrupt changes of routine.

A rotund, middle-aged woman answered the door, introduced herself as Mrs Porter and informed Shannon, without preamble, that Kane was waiting for her in the sitting room.

'And where's Eleanor?' Shannon asked, anxious to make sure that the object of this evening visit hadn't done something unfortunate, like gone to bed. A cosy little dinner with only Kane Lindley for company, while his daughter innocently slumbered upstairs, wasn't an appealing prospect. But Eleanor, she was told, was in the sitting room with her father and was, she was also told in a confidential whisper, eagerly looking forward to meeting Shannon.

'If you ask me,' Mrs Porter said, her voice sinking lower so that Shannon had to strain to hear what she was saying, 'Mr Lindley should have remarried a long time ago. A child needs a mother figure. No stability, that's her problem, poor little mite. Young Carrie is fine with her, but she really needs someone permanent. Not these women friends who seem to drop in one minute and out the next.'

Shannon nodded, loath to continue talking in this manner about someone else's private life yet avidly curious to find out more about Kane. Women friends? He had women friends? Of course he had, she thought, wildly trying to imagine what this long line of inappropriate women friends was like. He always seemed so controlled that the idea of him flinging himself passionately at a woman, growing weak at the knees whenever she came into the room, was beyond the powers of even *her* imagination.

Fortunately, the temptation to elicit more information on this suddenly raunchy side of Kane Lindley was abruptly halted by Mrs Porter pushing open the door to the sitting room and then stepping aside so that Shannon could enter.

'I'll be off now, Mr Lindley, if that's all right with you. The food will just need heating up, but the table's all set.'

'Heating up?'

'I can help, Dad.' There was a childish eagerness to Eleanor's voice that made Shannon ache.

'Eleanor, this is Shannon, my new secretary. You're going to be seeing a bit of her when I'm not around.'

'Hello.' She smiled briefly, then turned to her father with a pleading face. 'But, really, Dad, I can help. I know what to do. Honestly.'

'Eleanor, darling, you're far too young to be doing anything in the kitchen. Most domestic accidents originate in the kitchen, did you know that? There are knives, fire, pans of boiling water—'

'She can do a bit, Mr Lindley,' Shannon interrupted, growing impatient with his listing of danger points which made the average kitchen sound like a death trap. 'When I was Eleanor's age, I was already doing a few basic things.' She sneaked a glance at Eleanor who was gaping at her with shy gratitude. 'You just have to make sure that there's supervision and—'

'*You* may have been preparing three-course meals at the age of eight, but Eleanor didn't have your sturdy upbringing.' He turned to his daughter. 'Shannon comes from a family of seven children.'

'*Seven?* Wow!' The revelation had turned her eyes into saucers. 'How lucky! I wish...' Her voice trailed off and her eyes flitted across to her father.

'I'll make sure I supervise her, Mr Lindley,' Shannon said hurriedly, before the telling sentence could be completed. 'I mean, Eleanor, don't you do home economics at school? A bit of baking and stuff?'

'Not really,' Eleanor admitted, frowning.

'There, you see! Even the school realises the limits of letting children loose with dangerous objects.' His eyebrows rose with the satisfaction of someone who has proved a point, and Shannon flushed hotly.

'Actually, Mr Lindley—'

'Kane. It's ridiculous for us to be on such formal terms. And I can see from the indignant expression on your face that I'm about to be subjected to a lecture on the importance of teaching young children how to play with fire.'

'I wouldn't dream of lecturing you on anything of the sort,' Shannon informed him in a huffy voice, 'but what I'm talking about here is a wooden spoon, a bowl and a bit of stirring perhaps. How many young children do you personally know who have fallen victim to a sharp cut from a wooden spoon? And how many serious domestic accidents have been caused from a bit of stirring?'

'We do woodwork at school,' Eleanor interrupted helpfully. 'Don't we, Dad? Do you remember that box I made for you a few months ago? The one with the lid that could open and close?'

'Yes, of course I do.' But Shannon could tell from the vague expression on his face that the last thing currently stored in his memory bank was a box with a lid that could open and close.

'I hate to criticise you,' Shannon muttered as they walked towards the kitchen with Eleanor eagerly leading the way like a proud, albeit diminutive, hostess, 'but do you take any interest in what your daughter does at school?'

'And I hate to criticise *you*, reds' he muttered back, 'but I hope you're not going to launch into a load of psychobabble about workaholic fathers.'

'So you admit you're a workaholic.'

'I don't admit anything of the sort,' he said, *sotto voce*. 'And just in case the ground rules of this contract have escaped you, you're employed to look after Eleanor for a few hours a day after you leave work, not to analyse me.'

'Smells wonderful in here,' Shannon exclaimed, ignoring his remark.

'Mrs Porter always does the cooking when Dad entertains his women friends at home,' Eleanor said. 'I laid the table. I wasn't too sure where the soup spoons went, so I thought I'd just stick them in the bowls.'

'Excellent!' Kane said heartily, avoiding eye contact with Shannon. He moved over to the stove and flicked on the fire, looking dubiously inside the saucepan as though not too sure what his next move should be.

'I think you're meant to pour it into the bowls,' Shannon said, and Eleanor gave a stifled giggle. 'Surely, with all those women friends you've been entertaining, you must have got to grips with the basic food-serving procedure.'

'Oh, Mrs Porter usually does all that,' Eleanor informed her earnestly. 'Doesn't she, Dad? She had to leave tonight because her son is poorly. He's twelve years old and he twisted his ankle in a game of rugby at school.'

'A dangerous sport. I'm surprised schools allow it,' Shannon said piously. 'On the whole, I'd say it was a darn sight more dangerous than home economics, actually.'

'Or woodwork, even,' Eleanor replied, tucking into her soup and licking her lips after every mouthful. 'Last week, Claire Thompson hurt her finger when her bowl dropped on her hand.'

Shannon made tutting noises under her breath. The soup was delicious. No wonder he used Mrs Porter whenever he entertained at home. All those hundreds of women who probably flitted in and out of his life like ships in the night. Did they know, she wondered, when they started dating Kane that they would end up as a ship in the night?

'And I can remember getting a paper cut once at school,' Shannon mused in the startled voice of someone putting two and two together and suddenly arriving at the correct answer. 'Perhaps schools should ban paper.'

Eleanor started to laugh. 'Or food at lunchtime, in case someone spills some over themselves and gets burnt!'

'Or desks! A child can get a nasty bang on the edge of a desk if she's not careful!'

'Oh, shut up, the two of you,' Kane said, smiling at his daughter. Her face was flushed. 'And you can start on your home economics course,' he added, wiping his mouth with his napkin and sitting back in the chair, 'by clearing away these bowls to the sink.'

By the end of the meal, Eleanor was becoming more what Shannon envisaged an eight-year-old child should be like. Her voice was less of a whisper and she was laughing as she related things that had happened at school, what people had said, what games they played at break.

'When are you going to be coming to stay with me?' she asked Shannon, pausing on her way out of the room to hear the answer.

When Shannon looked enquiringly at Kane, he said, raising his hands in mock surrender, 'I'll be a bit late home next Monday. Can you make it then after work? Carrie will collect Eleanor from school as usual and then she'll leave when you get here to replace her.'

So that was settled. It was only when Eleanor had been escorted upstairs by her father, and Shannon was left alone in the stillness of the kitchen, that she felt a sneaking suspicion that she had somehow been manipulated. She also had the uneasy feeling that she was being drawn into a family unit which would somehow undermine her bid for freedom.

Part of her mission in coming all the way to London, aside from the obvious reason of physically distancing herself from Ireland and its nagging, unpleasant memories, had been to try her feet at walking without the aid of her family around her. So what was she doing? Getting involved with another family.

'She likes you.' Kane's voice snapped her out of her worrying speculation and Shannon turned to him with a bright smile. 'Some coffee in the sitting room?' He moved over to the kettle and switched it on.

'I really should be heading back, actually.'

'At nine-thirty? On a Friday night? We need to talk about how often you're prepared to take over from Carrie,' he told her bluntly. 'Eleanor...' He perched against the kitchen counter and folded his arms thoughtfully. 'To be honest, I've never seen Eleanor respond so quickly to anyone.'

Shannon had a sharp mental picture of Eleanor in the presence of the mysterious line of women, which had been preying on her mind more than she was willing to admit, shyly retiring, insecure, mouse-like, seeking her father's approval even though the furthest thing from his mind would have been the attention-seeking of his daughter.

'I always knew that having so many brothers and sisters would come in handy some day.' She followed him into the sitting room and sat in the deep chair closest to the fire, curling her legs underneath her like a cat.

'Shall we scrap the coffee and have a nightcap instead?' Kane moved over to a wooden cabinet in the corner of the room and clicked open a concealed door to reveal a healthy supply of glasses and drinks. 'What would you like? I have pretty much everything. What about a brandy? Or a glass of port?'

'I'll have a port,' Shannon told him. 'You have a lovely house, Mr Lindley...Kane. How long have you lived here?'

'My wife and I bought this house when we were first married...'

'And you stayed on after...?'

'After she died?' He strolled over to her and handed her a glass of red liquid, his fingers brushing hers as she took it from him. Then he sat on the sofa and crossed his legs, resting his hand lightly on his knee. 'I thought about moving, but only briefly. I like the house and, at any rate, you can't run away from your memories. They'll follow you to the end of the earth. You just have to learn to cope with them. Now, what did you think about Eleanor? It's not an ideal situation, leaving work to come immediately here, and I expect you to be honest and tell me now if you don't think you'll be able to do it on a regular basis.'

Shannon took a sip of port and it rushed down her throat like fire. 'By regular basis, you mean…?'

'Every day after work,' he said lazily, 'but, of course, that's open to negotiation.'

'Don't you get back early *any* evening?' Another sip of port. This time the fire seemed slightly less potent, although her head was now beginning to feel fuzzy. Her new-found freedom and aspirations towards a exciting, cosmopolitan lifestyle hadn't included nurturing a taste for alcohol. She still only drank wine, and in small amounts, and the port was like a bullet being fired into her brain.

'Some evenings. And I always make sure that I keep the weekends free.'

'Hmm. That's big of you.' She could grow to quite like this drink, she thought, swigging back the remainder in the glass and making a poor show of refusing a refill. Over dinner, with Eleanor present, Shannon had been a model of perfect behaviour. Aside from her brief debate on the relative safety of kitchen gadgets, she had chatted amiably to Eleanor about school and friends and hobbies, but after the glass of port she could feel the polite veneer beginning to slip a little.

That had always been her problem. She'd never been able to resist saying exactly what was on her mind, even though she'd had many an occasion to regret her lapses.

If she'd had ten pence for every time she'd spoken without thinking, according to her mother, she would have been a millionaire by her eighteenth birthday.

'I mean…' she said, deciding to go easy on the second glass of port. A little honesty was often bad enough but an overdose of it could be lethal. In fact, might lose her job, which she was already beginning to enjoy, despite her initial reservations. 'You ask me about Eleanor…'

She frowned in the manner of someone focusing on a knotty problem when, in fact, she was simply struggling to gather her thoughts together so that she could formulate a sentence or two that made sense. 'I feel a little sorry for her, to be honest. She's so desperate to get some of your attention.'

'Desperate to get my attention? She has my attention whenever I'm around! And whatever she wants, she gets.'

'Have you noticed that every time she says anything, she looks to you for approval? It's as though…' As though *what*? Time, she thought, for another sip of the yummy burgundy liquid that was really very helpful when it came to clarifying her thought processes. 'As though…she doesn't want to put a foot wrong in case she disappoints you!'

'How on earth could Eleanor disappoint me?' He shot her a wry look and said mildly, 'Are you sure your observations aren't originating from two glasses of port?'

'Of course not!' Shannon laughed merrily. 'Actually, I've always been able to hold my drink! You asked me about what I thought of your daughter, and I told you. In my opinion…' she leaned forward and grasped the collar of her coffee-coloured blouse which was, she had thought earlier, the perfect outfit for a prospective childminder—babysitter meeting her charge but was now revealing an offputting tendency to gape and expose the lacy top of her matching beige coloured bra… 'Shannon needs a mother.'

'Oh, that's your opinion, is it?'

Why did she get the impression that Kane was humouring her?

'Yes, as a matter of fact, it is. Girls need mothers, it's as simple as that.'

He appeared to give this statement a bit of thought. Then he said in an infuriatingly amused voice, 'Well, at the risk of disappointing you, there's no mother substitute in the picture at the moment.'

'Not even from the long line of women who flit in and out of your life?'

'Ah. I wondered when you would bring that up. I caught that expressive little flicker in your eyes when Eleanor was talking about Mrs Porter and her handy knack of whipping up meals for all these women who come and go.' He settled back comfortably on the sofa and linked his fingers behind his dark head while his eyes continued to survey her face with lazy amusement. 'Now, Shannon, tell me truthfully, do I look like the kind of man who has a queue of women lining up to go out with him? Hmm?'

That compelled her to look at him. Out of his impeccably tailored office suit, he looked less conservative, but only slightly less so. His khaki-coloured trousers and green short sleeved shirt and brown loafers were all traditional garb. His black hair was raked back from his face and there was no stubble to suggest anything wickedly decadent about the man sitting in front of her.

'Out of the mouths of babes…' she said weakly.

'You haven't answered my question.'

'All right. Then the answer is yes!'

'Because I'm exciting and sexy?' he asked drily, enjoying the flush that was creeping steadily up her cheeks and the nervous fluttering of her fingers as she slipped them around the stem of the glass and drained the remainder of her port.

'Because,' Shannon said, 'Eleanor would have no reason to lie. Anyway,' she said defiantly, 'perhaps you're too fussy when it comes to women. Surely you've felt the need to remarry, settle down, perhaps have more children…?'

'I haven't found the right woman. I told you, I'm a sad old man who will probably end up on my own with no one to look after me but my faithful housekeeper who knows how to cook five-star meals.'

He grinned boyishly at Shannon and she went a little pinker. She suspected that if she felt round the edge of her bra, she would find a thin layer of nervous perspiration. For a man who never raised his voice, at least not at work, ever, he still had the ability to make most people feel flustered. It was something to do with the laser-like sharpness of his eyes. Right now her port-clogged mind was feeling very flustered indeed.

'But still you keep trying.'

'As you must.' The smile was still playing at the corners of his mouth as if her unwarranted intrusive line of questioning was a source of enjoyment rather than discomfort. 'How else will I ever find Mrs Right?' he asked in a sanctimonious voice.

'Is there any specific routine I should stick to with Eleanor?' Shannon asked, reflecting weakly that her crisp tone of voice was a little late in coming. It also wouldn't last very long, not with two glasses of port swimming around inside her. She tilted her head to one side to lend more authority to her tone and felt a little giddy in the process.

'I believe Carrie makes sure that homework is done, food eaten, bath taken and some reading done before bed. Sometimes I make it home by book-reading time but, as you've seen for yourself, it's impossible to stick to any kind of timetable in my line of work.'

'And would you prefer it if you could?' Shannon asked curiously.

'Of course,' he answered, not that she believed a word of that. She doubted whether Kane Lindley ever consulted his watch when it came to leaving work behind. Well, as his secretary, she could very well arrange a more sociable timetable for him when it came to seeing his daughter more regularly. In fact, she decided that she would make it a top priority.

'So, how are you finding the job so far? As invigorating as the restaurant business?'

'More concentrated, if anything,' she admitted. 'Alfredo never had much of a conscience when it came to relieving me from secretarial duties when there was a shortage of waiters. He said that it was the typically Italian way of running things.' She grinned. 'Actually, he had a reliable habit of blaming most things on his Italian temperament. I think he expected us to fall in line because his temperament, according to him, was volatile but basically non-negotiable.'

'And you never questioned that?'

'I'm accustomed to volatile people!'

'And aside from the temperamental Italian, we poor Londoners must seem very tame in comparison.'

Shannon was unsure how to deal with this informal, teasing question. Within the confines of the office, Kane was formal and utterly self-controlled. She had seen how he dealt with other members of staff. Polite, courteous, the epitome of the professional man, not given to chit-chat. She realised that in accepting the job of babysitting his daughter during the week, she had opened a door to a less predictable side of him. Less predictable and more disconcerting.

'Have you made any friends in the company yet?' he asked, relieving her of the task of answering his unanswerable question, even though she would have been more relieved if he'd ended all conversation by standing up, yawning and saying goodnight. 'I've more or less left you to your own devices. What have you been doing at lunchtimes?'

'The canteen, actually. Sheila felt sorry for me and took me down on my first day and introduced me to some of the people who work in the other departments. In fact, did you know that there's something called the Lottery Club?'

'The Lottery Club?' He looked at her with a bewildered expression.

'Yes!' She leaned forward, pressing her hands against the sides of the sofa, and stared earnestly at him. Or, at least, she hoped that her stare was earnest. If a little unsteady at the edges. 'Apparently lots of people are on it. They all put in money to do the lottery and then on a Friday they go down to the pub to celebrate the fact that they probably haven't won! In fact, I would have been there now if I hadn't been, well…here instead. But next Friday they're all going to a club in Leicester Square and I've been invited to go along. It'll be fun!'

In fact, she couldn't wait. This was what she had come to London for, she decided. Fun with a capital F! Despite her exuberant personality, she was more of a homebody than she would have ever cared to admit to anyone, and she had eschewed clubbing in Ireland for the more mundane activities of going to the movies with her friends or having a meal out at the local pizza place or Chinese restaurant. The first she'd tasted of a more glitzy lifestyle had been during her brief and traumatic fling with Eric Gallway, and even then, she thought sourly, she'd been more interested in running around behind him like a pet pooch than enjoying the nightclubs he had taken her to. It had been one of his many angry criticisms of her when the whole thing had blown up. That she was boring and unsophisticated. That she was like a teenager, but without the sense of daring.

Daring was something she was currently striving for, and next week's fun at a club would be the first step.

Unfortunately, Kane was looking at her with a concerned expression, as though she had inadvertently informed him that she intended to become a lap dancer for the evening. Perhaps, she thought crossly, he was wondering whether she was a suitable candidate after all to look after his child for a handful of hours every week. Perhaps, on top of the children-should-be-allowed-in-the-kitchen attitude, an admission of wanting to go to a nightclub in Leicester Square was confirmation of her juvenile tendencies.

'Sounds like a bundle of laughs,' he said drily. 'Even though you don't look too convinced.'

'I happen to be very convinced,' Shannon informed him, tilting her chin up.

'And you've been to clubs before, have you?'

'Of course I've been to clubs! Dublin is very well stocked with them, in case you didn't know. And what makes you think that I haven't been to any? I may not be a Londoner born and bred, but I'm not exactly green round the ears!'

'I do apologise if I've given you the impression that that's what I thought,' he said, in an unapologetic voice, 'but for some reason I got the impression that you were a family person, perhaps even rather sheltered.'

'I used to be,' she corrected him firmly, breaking off to ask for a top-up, just to prove that wild and daring was the woman she was and not young and uninitiated, which had been Eric's opinion of her. Young, uninitiated and therefore ready for a little corruption. 'But we all grow up, don't we?' Her head was beginning to feel a little chaotic, and for some strange reason she had the maddest urge to shock him. He always looked so *unshockable*. If a mushroom cloud had gathered over his house and there had been a two-minute warning going off, she doubted whether he would have been galvanised into panicky action. She wondered madly what he would look like roused.

'And you've decided that now is your time to grow up.'

'I'm certainly looking for adventure,' she confided, leaning forward to retrieve her glass of port and recklessly not bothering to clasp the top of her blouse so that her small breasts could be tantalisingly glimpsed. No wonder he was pursued by women, she thought. They probably were all falling over themselves to rise to the challenge of making him lose control.

'Would this have anything to do with your experience in Ireland? Before you came down here?'

'What experience?' Shannon dodged, frankly glugging the port at this point.

'With Eric Gallway.' He stretched out his long legs in front of him, crossing them at the ankles, and proceeded to fix her with an unblinking stare.

'Nothing happened between Eric and me,' she muttered feebly.

'Which is why you threw hot food all over him.'

'Anyway,' she said with sullen resistance, 'as I've already told you, it's none of your business.'

'But in a way it is. The fact is, we're thinking of hiring him…'

'What? To work in your company?' Her stubborn expression was replaced with horror. She would pack in the job tomorrow if the alternative was running into Eric Gallway round every corner!

'Yes, as a matter of fact.'

'Then you can accept my resignation as of now.' She teetered to her feet, alarmed at how unsteady they felt, and hovered there, hoping that she could make it to the front door without losing either her dignity or, for that matter, her sense of balance.

'Oh, sit down! He won't be working where you are. He'll be working for my newly acquired media group, in front of the cameras. I gather the thought of that rather appealed to his vanity.'

Shannon sat back down. Sitting felt distinctly better.

'And the reason I want to know what happened between you is that I want you to tell me if there's any reason why we shouldn't hire the man.'

'Any reason like what?' She was beginning to feel vaguely cornered by this subtle battering of her defences.

'Oh, I don't know. Perhaps you uncovered something about him…'

'Oh, I uncovered something about him all right,' she said bitterly, 'but nothing that would make him unemployable.'

'And what was that?' His voice was a silky whisper and he leaned forward, resting his forearms on his thighs and staring intently at her. She sincerely wished he wouldn't do that. It made her feel giddy.

In the short, taut silence that followed his question, she could feel a reckless urge to confess everything to the man sitting in front of her. And why shouldn't she? It wasn't as though it were some dark, horrifying secret. In fact, it would be a relief to tell someone, someone unconnected with the whole affair. Since coming to London, she had maintained a rigid silence about the unfortunate episode, preferring to be accepted as the person she was now, and not judged in any way by what had happened in the past. But wasn't it more in keeping with the varnished exterior she was cultivating to laugh the whole incident off with a casual shrug and a knowing smile?

'I had an affair with him!' she confessed gaily, ruefully realising that her glass was once again empty just when she could have done with a bit of morale bolstering.

He nodded and failed to look nonplussed. 'How did you meet in the first place?'

'He came to the radio station to do an interview with my boss about the differences between working in Ireland as opposed to working in England. How things differed in the area of media and suchlike. Also our radio station was up and coming because it was small and really only dealt with local gossip.'

'And you fell for his charms, did you?' He stood up and watched patiently and expressionlessly while she wobbled to her feet, then he helpfully took her arm to steady her. 'I gather you're not accustomed to drink?'

He couldn't even be bothered to hear her out! He was too busy being paternalistic about the state of her intoxication! This was the Big City and confessions of affairs and broken hearts were a dime a dozen.

'Yes, I fell for him!' Shannon snapped, reluctantly grateful for the support of his arm because without it she had a sneaking feeling that she would plummet to the ground in an inelegant heap. 'He was a smooth talker. He took me places, promised me a future and then I found out that he was married!'

'Oh, dear,' he said sympathetically, as they made their way slowly towards the hall, where her coat was perched in the downstairs cloakroom. 'It must have come as quite a shock.'

'Married with two children!' Shock was a mild way of describing what she had felt at the revelation. She had felt the world collapse around her. 'And when I confronted him, he laughed! Said that I needed to grow up! Told me that married men had affairs all the time and that I would realise that if I wasn't too busy being a baby! He said that he was glad to be rid of me because I wouldn't…wouldn't…you know…'

'Wouldn't what?'

'Wouldn't sleep with him,' Shannon said. She felt a little tear of self-pity gather in the corner of her eye and she blinked several times, taking her time as she allowed him to slip her into her coat and telephone for his driver to come for her.

'He was a cad, reds,' Kane said gently, inclining her face to his with the pressure of a finger under her chin. 'He didn't deserve you. Forget him.'

'I have. I only brought up the subject because you asked.'

'Good girl.' He tapped her nose with the tip of his finger and smiled. Frankly, it was insulting. Next, he would say 'chin up' and tell her that she was only a kid after all.

'And I've seen the error of my ways,' she told him, all self-pity banished by sudden, swift anger at his response.

'Go for the good guy next time.' He nodded in a soothing way.

'Oh, just the opposite, actually,' she threw back at him. 'At my tender age, I've already discovered how men use women, so why not apply some of the same medicine to them? Starting,' she added, for further credibility, 'next Friday.'

CHAPTER FOUR

'AND...? How did your wild and exciting evening on Friday go? Was it everything you expected?'

Kane had finished briefing Shannon on what he wanted done and now he sat back in his leather chair and looked at her with a little smile. They had settled into a working routine that included a cup of coffee first thing in the morning in his office while he flicked through files, passing over what he wanted her to do, what meetings needed to be scheduled, what meetings needed to be cancelled and what clients needed to be contacted in order of priority. On the trip into work, she now found herself looking forward to that half-hour. In a strange way, it seemed to set her up for the rest of the day.

Shannon gathered up the files from the desk and rested them on her lap.

'It was scintillating,' she lied, casting her mind back to the pub where they had all met at eight for drinks, followed by a nightclub which had turned out to be a cramped dark space somewhere in Soho where the music had been too loud, the atmosphere too smoky and the crowd almost entirely composed of nineteen-year-old kids dressed in way-out clothes.

Having expected something a little more sophisticated, Shannon had settled at a table in the corner with three of the women from work and had spent the remainder of the evening comparing notes on how young the people had seemed to be and trying to identify the music which had not so much blared as throbbed with a steady bass beat that had been very good at promoting headaches. She'd had the odd dance with one of the guys from the company but there had been so many people on the dance floor that it had been difficult to move, never mind dance properly. By the time she had got back to her bedsit at one-thirty, her dress and tights had smelled of cigarette smoke and had born the telltale patchy spots of spilled drinks.

'Scintillating… Where did you go?'

She gave him the name of the club, safe in the knowledge that the last place Kane Lindley would have heard of would have been a nightclub for wild, young things—most of whom hadn't looked old enough to earn a living, never mind be in possession of the money needed to have a good time for hours in a nightclub in central London.

'You went *there*!' He sounded horrified and she felt her hackles rise at the tone of his voice. Now, more than ever, she was determined to drive home to him what an exciting evening it had been. 'I don't suppose you realised that that place has a reputation for illicit drugs? Not exactly fertile ground for meeting new people. Well, not unless you're interested in meeting boys who probably haven't started shaving yet! What would your mother say?'

'My mother isn't here!' Shannon declared icily, 'so she isn't going to say anything, is she? And,' she continued, fixing him with a gimlet stare, 'how do you know about this place? Don't tell me you go there on a weekend to live it up!'

'Why not? Can't you picture me slugging back pints of lager and gyrating on a dance floor with eighteen-year-old girls?'

Actually, Shannon found it easier to picture herself growing five arms and three legs overnight. There was a quiet gallantry about Kane that resisted any notion of him misbehaving in any way in public. Or in private for that matter. She doubted if he had ever lost his self-control. He just wasn't that type of man.

'Frankly, no.' She rustled the files on her lap, waiting for his invisible signal that it was time for her to go, but he carried on looking at her, smiling.

'Maybe you're right,' he conceded in a low, amused voice. 'Eighteen-year-old girls don't interest me. And I can think of better ways of dancing than flinging myself around and bashing into everyone else.'

His voice left her in no doubt what form of dancing he had in mind and she felt faintly unsettled at the thought. She had a vision of him on a dance floor, his strong arms engulfing the woman with him, his body pressed erotically against hers, hips grinding against hips, face and hands buried into hair. Losing that iron self-control. His body trembling slightly in anticipation of what was to come. His voice thick with desire.

She gulped and shuffled the files a little harder.

Every so often a rogue thought would enter her head—that his innate gentlemanliness disguised something wild and dangerous, lurking suggestively beneath the surface.

'Can't you?' he prompted, and she looked at him with an addled expression.

'Can't I what?'

'Think of better ways of dancing?'

'Oh, yes,' Shannon said crisply. 'The foxtrot can be quite a laugh. And, of course, there's Irish dancing. You can't beat it for burning off calories.'

He gave a wry laugh and then said lightly, 'And I can

think of better ways of doing that as well. Eleanor,' he said, changing the subject before she could dwell on what he had said, 'seems to be quite taken with you. She tells me that you're fun. How are you finding it? Is the travelling too much of a hassle? It's dark by the time you leave and really I don't care to think of you traipsing through London on the underground to get back to your flat.'

'Oh, it's fine,' Shannon said airily, thinking of the dark, isolated walk once she left the underground and was heading back to her bedsit. The Victorian house which had been converted into bedsits was in a leafy, residential area but a residential area that only just managed to creep into the category of savoury. In the daytime it was fine, because there were always people around, leaving for work, but on one or two occasions she had walked the pavements back to the house on her own and then the sound of her footsteps clattering on the tarmac had made her nervously turn her walk into a semi-run. Good job she didn't suffer from high blood pressure or it would have been through the roof by now. And with winter swiftly descending, the nights would get darker earlier and eight-thirty would seem like midnight. She would have to make an effort not to think about it. 'I like the exercise,' she lied feebly. 'And the fresh air.'

'Because I could always arrange for Jo to drive you home.'

'No!' She was already indebted to Kane for her job, which was far more highly paid, she was sure, than she could have got somewhere else, and for the babysitting which she enjoyed and which, incidentally, further boosted her income. She didn't need to be further reliant on him for her transport. 'I mean, thanks very much but, no, thank you.'

'Why not?'

'Because it would…confuse my arrangements.'

'What arrangements?'

'Arrangements to go somewhere else once I leave your place!' Shannon insisted in a shrill voice, racking her brains to think of any arrangements she had made recently that had involved her not returning in a semi-run back to her dreary bedsit.

'You mean like another fun club,' he said gravely, and she bristled at his patronising tone.

'I shall have to try out quite a few before I find the right one!' she declared defiantly. 'I'm new to the area, after all.'

'A club crawl at nine p.m. on a weekday every time you leave my place. Sounds hard work. Are you sure you're going to be able to fit all this in with getting up in the morning to come to work?'

'I would never let my personal life affect my working life—' Shannon began swiftly, only to be cut down in mid-self-righteous explanation.

'I'm surprised you can say that after your fling with Eric Gallway, which ended up in your leaving your last job and fleeing Ireland.'

That, she thought, was hitting below the belt and she could tell from Kane's sudden flush of discomfort that he was aware of that as well.

'Which is why I shall always make sure that the two sides don't meet,' Shannon retorted. 'Now, will this be all?' She cocked her head to one side in a businesslike manner and he grinned and lowered his eyes. There was a certain wickedness to his grin, she thought absent-mindedly, that belied the stern appearance. Was he aware of that or was it just some characteristic he had been born with? Like some people were born to have dimples when they smiled?

'For the moment,' he agreed, back to his usual highly professional and unreadable self. 'Dennis Clark and one of our accountants will be here in an hour. Make sure there's coffee, would you?'

'Of course, sir,' Shannon said in a docile voice. 'Anything else? Some biscuits perhaps? I could rustle something up from the canteen.' Me secretary, you boss. This was more like it. At the risk of overplaying her role, she was tempted to launch into a selection of various other secretarial duties he might avail himself of, but instead she headed back to the safety of her own office and decided to banish all thoughts of Kane Lindley the man by working fast and furiously and keeping her eyes fixed on the computer screen in front of her.

She was the perfect secretary until lunchtime when she bolted down to the canteen, later than usual because the meeting, in which she'd been asked to sit and take notes, had lasted until after one.

A bowl of soup, some bread and fruit and a cup of coffee, she thought, sitting at one of the many empty tables, would revive her enough for the afternoon. Working for Kane outside work hours had seemed easy enough when she'd accepted the job. How had she known that she would begin to feel a little too submerged in him and his personal life for her own sense of well-being? Eleanor was a joy to look after, but she chattered about her father, whom she adored, and Shannon was finding herself going down the slippery slope of piecing together all the intriguing facets of Kane's personality that emerged during their girlish conversations together after school.

The fact that the women he had brought back to the house, far from being a heady stream of dizzy blondes, had all been, as far as Eleanor had been concerned, boring and formal. Which Shannon shrewdly interpreted as career-women who had found it difficult to accommodate an eight-year-old. The fact that Carrie had developed a crush on him and it had been his idea to relieve her of some of her hours rather than the other way around, which was what he had initially implied.

'How on earth do you know that?' Shannon had laughed.

'I could tell,' was Eleanor's implacable reply. 'She started giggling whenever he was around and finding all sorts of reasons to stay later than she needed to.'

Shannon learnt that Kane rarely took holidays, and when he did he was always in contact with his office, which made her feel acutely sorry for Eleanor, but was firmly told, as a follow-on, that he couldn't help working so hard because it was all to do with looking after her.

She was reflecting on all of this, drinking her soup and relaxing, when a familiar voice said from behind her, 'Mind if I join you?' Before she could answer, Kane slid into the chair opposite her and deposited his plate of salad in front of him and his glass of water.

'What are you doing here?' Shannon muttered, looking around her nervously, relieved that there was no one she recognised left in the canteen. Little did he know that there were quite a few young girls in the company who considered him a heartthrob, and the last thing she needed was the job of fending off their curiosity should they see them together, having lunch.

Then she decided that she was being utterly ridiculous because there was nothing meaningful about sitting at the same table at the same time by chance. Bosses frequently came down to the canteen at lunchtime and most of them sat at whatever table was available, usually at the ones where their secretaries were sitting, which was an instant gossip-quencher but did promote a healthy informality in the company.

'Eating lunch,' he said mildly, pausing in mid-mouthful to look at her. 'And don't look so shocked. I do occasionally manage to slip in a mouthful of food some time during the day.'

'But *here*?'

'If you recall, you suggested I eat here now and again so that I could be on the ground floor when it came to seeing and hearing what's going on in the company.' He gave her one of those bland smiles which she was sincerely coming to distrust. 'Not that there's anyone around to speak of,' he said ruefully. 'Bad timing, I suppose. You're not eating your soup. You can't afford to lose weight. You'll disappear. So eat up.'

Shannon reluctantly swallowed a mouthful of soup while he dug with hearty enthusiasm into his salad, spearing the tiger prawns and making favourable remarks about the quality of the food, finally hinting that maybe he should make the time to frequent the canteen a bit more often, and when it was more crowded.

'You can't!' Shannon squeaked.

'Why not?' His dark eyes were unrevealing which, she thought sceptically, meant that he would somehow try and worm a response out of her by feigning innocence. Since she wasn't about to comply, she started talking briskly about work, meanwhile drinking her soup as rapidly as she could without spilling the lot in the process.

After she had concluded her five-minute monologue on various assorted topics, ranging from the filing sys-

tem to computer programs, he looked at her calmly and
said, 'I get the impression that you're a little on edge. I
hope I haven't unsettled you in any way by joining you
for lunch.'

'Unsettle me? Of course not!' She laughed to further
the impression that it would be impossible for him to
unsettle her, then laughed again just in case he hadn't
received the first message. 'Why on earth would I be
unsettled by you?'

Kane shrugged his broad shoulders and continued eating. If he was at ease with the silence stretching like
elastic between them, she certainly wasn't. What on
earth was wrong with her? She could hear herself babbling about everything under the sun until she finally ran
out of steam, at which point he surprised her by asking
about Christmas.

'Christmas? What about it?' Shannon asked, bewildered.

'What are you doing about it? Going back to Ireland?
Staying here? The reason I ask is because Eleanor would
like you to spend Christmas with us if you're at a loose
end.'

Spend Christmas with them? He really must feel very
sorry for her! Fortunately, she had already planned on
heading back to her family for Christmas so she could
reject his offer in all truthfulness.

'I really would have enjoyed that,' she told him, laying it on thick, 'but I've already told my mum that I'll
be back home for Christmas. The family have never
spent Christmas apart, not even when Francis was away
studying in Paris. I'm sorry. I'll explain it to Eleanor, if
you like.'

'No, I'll do that. She'll be disappointed, of course.'

'Haven't you got…grandparents? Aunts? Cousins?'

'We're a small family. Pretty much the opposite of yours. Now. Back to work, I suppose. Although I rather fancy playing truant at the moment.' He chuckled at the thought of it.

She said, startled at the personal aside, 'I can't imagine you playing truant.'

'It seems there are quite a number of things you can't imagine me doing,' he said, ticking them off on his fingers. 'Playing truant, gyrating on a dance floor, eating lunch...would you like me to tell you what I can't imagine *you* doing?'

'Not really,' Shannon said hurriedly, alarmed at this sudden turn in the conversation, and he laughed as though her response had been exactly as he'd predicted. He was no psychic but he had a knack of seeming to second guess her reactions which she found a little unnerving. Either he was a sharp judge of human character or else her human character was so bland and transparent that he could read her like a book.

'I just couldn't imagine what,' she informed him coldly, 'you would do if you did play truant. Go to the park and feed the ducks? Take in a sneaky afternoon movie? Head for the nearest junk-food place and gorge yourself on hamburgers?' There. That sarcasm should put him in his place if nothing else.

'I like the park option,' Kane said slowly, undeterred by her tone of voice. He stood up, waiting till she clambered to her feet, then they strolled back to the bank of lifts, with Shannon looking shiftily around her just in case someone she knew appeared in front of her like a rabbit from a magician's hat. 'A leisurely walk in the park...'

'It's freezing outside,' she pointed out with crushing pragmatism.

'True. Point taken. Then perhaps in a cabin some-where in front of a roaring fire.'

The image sent a little shiver down her spine as her imagination took flight once again into the land of no-go.

'I never thought truants liked skipping work for that kind of thing,' she told him, watching as he punched a button to the side of the lifts and they waited for one to arrive. 'Anyway, why don't you just take some time off and go away somewhere with Eleanor?'

The lift arrived and they stepped inside. As the door shut, Shannon had a sudden trapped feeling and found herself pressed against the back, staring fixedly ahead of her but very much aware of the man slightly in front.

'Time is the one thing I never seem to have enough of,' he commented drily.

'Which would make a depressing epitaph,' she said lightly. 'Why don't you do something about it? In fact, in a couple of weeks' time Eleanor's class is putting on a play. Nothing formally to do with Christmas...' Shannon smiled as she remembered this particular con-versation '...since there are several religious denomi-nations to be considered. It's at two in the afternoon, before school finishes. She'd be thrilled if she knew you were going.'

The lift finally arrived at their floor and as the doors opened Kane leant against one so she could slide past. Out of the claustrophobic confines of the lift, she could feel her treacherous breathing return to normal.

'Were you planning on going to this play?' he asked, and Shannon blushed.

'I might have the afternoon off,' she admitted. 'It broke my heart to think of the little mite in a play with no family or friends to watch. At eight, children get so excited about things like that. It's a shame.'

'What else does Eleanor get excited about that she fails to mention?'

A good eight inches shorter than him, Shannon had to walk at a brisk pace to keep up with his long, easy strides, and by the time they were back at her office she was slightly out of breath.

She shrugged noncommittally and sat down, putting on her supposedly stern secretarial mask. But instead of going away, he swung her chair round so that she was facing him and placed his hands squarely on either side of her. The jittery claustrophobia she felt now made those few minutes in the lift seem like a run in the open countryside by comparison.

'Care to answer my question?' he pressed, towering over her, his tie falling forward to brush against her blouse.

'Oh, just the usual. She's got a starring role in this production. Apparently, it's a great honour not to be sidelined into playing one of the animals. She's thrilled because she has a speaking part and Jodie, the class big-mouth, is playing a camel.' Shannon grinned. 'She's also excited because she's now in the top group in maths and her poem was read out day before yesterday at assembly in front of the lower years.'

Kane looked bemused by this array of accomplishments.

'It's not my fault I have to work all the hours God made,' he objected roughly, as if she had criticised his parenting. A bad case of guilty conscience, she decided, and well deserved as well.

'It *is* your fault, actually. You could make more time

for Eleanor, and don't tell me about your weekends. You constantly get business calls on a Sunday, anyway!'

'Business calls! On the weekend!' He was virtually spluttering.

'Yes,' Shannon said smugly. 'Eleanor told me. Girls' talk.'

'And what else do you girls talk about when I'm not around?'

'I can make sure that you're free for the play. Will you be coming? As I said to you, Eleanor *would be thrilled.*'

He pushed himself back from her chair and appraised her with his eyes. 'I wouldn't dream of missing it, now that it's been brought to my attention. Nor,' he added, shoving his hands into his pockets and smiling with satisfaction, 'would I dream of letting you miss it. Not after you had planned on going. I think this mighty corporation could do without us for a couple of hours, don't you? We can watch Eleanor in the play and then afterwards we can take her out for something to eat somewhere. Settled?' He flashed her one of those smiles that indicated there was no room for manoeuvre.

One week later, Shannon was feeling even more hopelessly ensnared. Ensnared on a stake of her own making. And helpless to protest because Kane's new-found determination to put her advice into practice and see more of his daughter was all to the good. At least all to the good as far as Eleanor was concerned. She was probably seeing more of her father during the weekdays than she had for her entire life. Shannon left him working at five only to see him again at six-thirty when he strolled through the front door to delighted squeals from his daughter. And more disastrous to her mental health than that, he always insisted that she join them for supper.

'She's so thrilled at you being here with us,' he'd told her depressingly on the first evening of his run of early homecomings. 'She really almost considers you to be one of the family.'

'But I'm *not* one of the family!' Shannon had protested vigorously, her hands on her hips, glaring at him as he'd divested himself of his jacket and moved away, tugging at his tie to remove it and drape it over the banister. 'I happen to have my *own* family!'

'But they're not here, are they?' he had countered smugly.

'I'm not looking for a family substitute!'

'And I'm not offering you one. I'm merely suggesting that it seems so important to Eleanor, and what's important to Eleanor is important to me.'

Which had silenced her. He'd seemed so sincere, almost vulnerable in the admission, but a healthy sceptical streak in her read that as a cunning move to get what he wanted and there was no denying that it was easier for him when she was around. He could relax, have a drink and whilst he was bombarded with Eleanor's accounts of school and what had happened that day, a fair amount of time was spent comfortably watching his daughter and Shannon play games, cook tea and exchange ideas while he sat at the kitchen table, making the occasional remark and half reading the newspapers.

The domesticity of it frightened her, but when she tried to dig deeper into the reasons for that, she came up against a brick wall.

Now, as she slung on her coat and braced herself to face the brisk walk to the underground and the tube journey back to her bedsit, she couldn't help looking at him accusingly from under her lashes.

'What?' he asked, walking her to the front door and

muttering that he didn't care for the thought of her journeying back to her bedsit in the dark.

'I didn't say anything.'

'You don't have to. You're like an angry little bull terrier waiting for a leg to bite. My leg, I get the feeling.'

'I'm not *little*,' Shannon told him through gritted teeth. 'And I'm not a child either.'

'You look like a child with those pigtails. Why do you tie your hair back all the time?'

'It's practical,' Shannon said uncomfortably. She self-consciously took one of her ridiculous braids in one hand and played with it. Lots of women wore their hair tied back! 'And I can't wear it tied back in a bun because it's not long enough. Not that I have to explain my hairstyles to you.'

She thought of one of the company lawyers who made a habit of popping in unannounced and insisting on seeing Kane with important business. A tall, glamorous blonde with fashionably short hair. She doubted whether Kane had ever mentioned to her that she looked like a tomboy with such short hair!

'I suppose I could have it all chopped off, like Sonya Crew,' she added waspishly. 'Would that be mature enough for your liking?'

He gave her a long, leisurely and very thorough look which sent shivers down her spine, and she edged back against the front door. 'Anyway, I've got to go,' she said in confusion. 'I don't want to be getting back too late.'

'Which has been my point all along,' he said mildly, still looking at her with that shuttered expression that sent her nervous system into panicky overdrive. 'How long will it take you to get back?'

'Oh, about half an hour, I guess. Maybe a little more.' If she pushed any harder against the wooden door she would go right through it, but for some reason she felt threatened by Kane's proximity and, worse, excited by the thought of it.

He stepped back. 'Right. I'll see you tomorrow, if you're sure you don't want to be driven back.'

Shannon heard herself squeak out a stuttering refusal.

'And tomorrow there's no need for you to come after work,' he continued. 'I'm going to be back late so Carrie's staying on for the night. You can catch up on your social life which must have gone into a bit of decline with the hours you've been putting in here.'

'Oh, no. As I said, I leave here early enough to go out afterwards!'

She felt disproportionately disappointed to be missing that little illicit taste of domesticity which she now found she had become pleasurably accustomed to. Reactions like that wouldn't do and she immediately decided that she would go to the pub after work with some of the girls from the office. She couldn't afford to pander to her instincts to behave like the homebody she naturally was. She would just find herself slipping into another rut, this time involving a family that wasn't hers.

She was young and living in the Big City! It was crucial that she remind herself of the fact, and of the fact that she should be out there enjoying all the wonderfully exciting things that London had to offer after dark. One brief foray into a second-rate nightclub didn't really qualify her to join the ranks of the young and free, did it? And cosy meals with Sandy didn't count either. Starting from next week, she would dictate the days she babysat for him and start concentrating on herself.

'In fact,' she said boldly, pleased with the various options she had now opened for herself, 'tomorrow suits me. I'll go to the pub with some girls from work, maybe head for a club after—'

'Head for a club? On a Tuesday?'

'That's right!' Shannon snapped. 'I can party till dawn and not feel the effects!'

She gave him a challenging look and then considered that she had scored a point when he was the first to look away, opening the door for her with his usual gentlemanly politeness. She'd discovered that he belonged to that old-fashioned and sadly fast-disappearing breed of men who still believed in treating women like ladies.

The opposite of Eric Gallway, in fact, who had once remarked, sniggering at his own sense of dubious humour, that women shouldn't expect to be treated any differently from men since they all seemed to make such a fuss about being equal, and since when did he ever open doors for men? It hadn't occurred to her at the time to counter that by asking him why, then, he bought her chocolates and flowers.

But maybe, in the throes of her infatuation, she might not have cared for the obvious answer, which would have been that chocolates and flowers were groundwork for getting a woman into bed.

'Lucky to be so young and carefree,' he murmured blandly, giving her one of those smiles that suggested the opposite of what he was actually saying but left no room to argue the toss.

'I think so!' she threw back carelessly. 'Now, if you don't mind…?'

But the following day, Shannon couldn't help but wonder whether she'd had a victory over him at all. She also found that going to the pub wasn't the attractive option she had banked on. In fact, a malicious inner voice told her, it was decidedly inferior to babysitting

Eleanor and waiting in tense expectation of Kane's arrival.

At eight-thirty, she found that she was restlessly looking at her watch and rather than continue to cradle her glass, she drained it, made her excuses and began the journey back to the bedsit.

It was now dark by four in the afternoon and by nine it was dark enough and cold enough for her to think that she was walking down some street in Siberia. A stiff, steady breeze whipped against her, making her ears and face and fingers feel numb.

From the underground to her place was no more than a matter of fifteen minutes' walk. She made it back in under ten, racing along the pavements, her arms tightly drawn around her body to conserve some heat.

It occurred to her that when she had decided to flee Ireland and head for another life in London, she could just have easily have headed abroad. Somewhere hot. She could have got a job doing a spot of nannying somewhere where the sun shone until eight in the evening. Or, frankly, somewhere where the sun shone and didn't pay occasional visits like a guest with better things to do than hang around in one spot for too long. The Italian Riviera might have been nice. She might have had to learn Italian but it would have been a small sacrifice for glorious warm days and glamorous movie-star-style nights, flitting from one venue to another.

The fantasy was enough to sustain her sense of humour until she made it back to her bedsit, clambering up the three flights of stairs to the shabby door to her room. She couldn't wait to feed the meter and get some heat crawling back into her.

What a dump, Shannon thought, looking around her despondently. She was sick and tired of trying to see the good things about it. The fact that it was fairly central and not too far from the underground. The fact that the fridge and stove and oven actually worked. The fact that, unlike most bedsits, this one had its own bathroom. Was it any wonder, she asked herself fiercely, that she was so willing to work extra hours, babysitting?

It was nine-thirty by the time the room had warmed up sufficiently for her to relax. She'd had a shower and changed into her maiden-aunt night attire of flannel nightdress and fluffy bedroom slippers. She'd had nothing to eat but the thought of doing anything that required more effort than it took to make a mug of hot chocolate wasn't worth thinking about. Another thing, she thought sourly, that she had become accustomed to. Hot food, the shared pleasure of making it with Eleanor.

To begin with, Mrs Porter had left casseroles for them to eat, but after a couple of days they had both found it more fun to try their hand at cooking dinner themselves. There were always masses of fresh vegetables and the freezer was well stocked. Mrs Porter, who did all the shopping, was as expert in her purchasing as she evidently was in her culinary skills.

She switched on the television and was half watching something on the news when there was a knock on the door. Three sharp knocks, actually. Since Shannon couldn't imagine who it could be, and there was no way that she was opening the door to some drunken lout who had come to see someone else in the building and had mistakenly lurched his way to her door instead, she remained where she was, cradling her mug with her hands, her feet curled under her, waiting for whoever it might be to stagger off to their correct destination. When the knocking continued, but more urgently, she finally stormed to the door and flung it open. Or rather flung it open the few inches that her chain lock permitted.

'Mind letting me in?' Kane asked.

She didn't. She was too shocked to see him. 'Who's with Eleanor? What are you doing here?'

'Mrs Porter. Let me in.'

'How did you know where I lived?'

'These and other questions to be answered shortly. Just as soon as you open this door and let me in.'

CHAPTER FIVE

'WAIT a minute.' Before Kane could say anything, Shannon slammed the door in his face and rushed to get her bathrobe.

She reappeared at the door several seconds later with the bathrobe drawn tightly around her. The bedroom slippers, a previous Christmas present from one of her brothers, would have to stay on.

'Come in, then,' she said reluctantly, pulling back the chain and allowing him to enter.

'How,' she asked, leaning against the door with her hands behind her while he took the few steps needed to get to the other side of the room, 'did you know my address?'

He was so damned big that her bedsit seemed to have shrunk to the size of a matchbox, and his masculine aroma, a fuzzy mixture of clean, cold air and the remnants of aftershave, filled her nostrils like incense.

'I know everything, reds. Haven't you realised that already?' He grinned. 'Actually, I had a look in your personnel file. Believe it or not, that's what they're there for. Useful information. And stop standing by that door and shivering. Why don't you offer me something to drink? Like a good hostess would.'

'It's late. I really am tired.'

'I thought you said that you could party from dusk till dawn,' he pointed out, using her own frivolous aside to bludgeon through her feeble excuse. 'Mind if I take my coat off?'

Shannon shrugged in a non-answer and he removed the trench coat, folding it in half and then placing it on one of the two chairs in the room.

'Ah. Hot chocolate,' he said, spying the half-empty cup on the table. 'It's been years since I had hot chocolate. I used to love it when I was a kid. A cup would be great.' He gave her a slow, implacable smile and Shannon reluctantly unglued herself from the door and sidled past him, muttering along the way that he might as well sit down and make himself comfortable.

She returned a few minutes later with a mug of hot chocolate to find him browsing unashamedly among the array of family snapshots which had been the first thing to decorate her bedsit when she'd first moved in.

'Who's this?' he asked, holding up a framed picture in one hand.

'My family,' Shannon said, handing him the mug but keeping her distance.

'Brothers and sisters?'

'Yes.'

'What are their names?'

So she had to take a few steps closer to him to peer at the picture and point to each member of her family, listing them by name from the eldest Shaun down to the youngest Brian. As she spoke, he sipped his hot chocolate and she could feel his breath as he exhaled very gently on the top of her head. When she had finished, he carefully placed the picture on the ledge exactly where he had found it, but continued to scan them all, asking her questions about where they were now and what they were doing.

'You must be very close to them.'

'I am.'

'Which is probably why you're such a natural when

it comes to Eleanor. You've grown accustomed over the years to sharing your time with other people. What about your father?'

'He died a few years ago.'

'I'm sorry to hear that,' Kane said quietly.

He moved back but instead of sitting in the required docile manner on the chair so that she could begin quizzing him on what he was doing in her bedsit at this time of the night, he surveyed the rest of the room, even having the nerve to check the kitchen, before saying with a frown, 'Where's the bedroom?'

'Why?' Shannon immediately asked with sudden, mounting panic. 'Why do you want to know where the bedroom is?'

'*Bedroom* I said, not *bed*.' He gave the chair in the corner a doubtful look, as if unsure as to whether it would take his weight, and then gingerly sat down.

'There is no bedroom. The sofa is really a single bed. I just fling the sheet on it when I'm ready to go to bed and use the big, square cushions for pillows. It's very comfy, actually.'

'You sleep on a chair?'

'Sofa,' she corrected, bristling at the incredulous contempt in his voice at her living arrangements.

'Surely we pay you enough to find somewhere a bit…' he looked around him and she could see him searching for the least offensive description to apply '…bigger?'

'Places are very hard to come by in London,' Shannon informed him, following his eyes and looking around the poky room herself. 'It was a bit of luck getting this in the first place, as a matter of fact.'

'Yes. A bit of bad luck.' Kane drank some more of the hot chocolate. 'How was your evening at the pub?'

'Don't try to distract me with lots of questions. What are you doing here?'

'I was in the area and...'

'You thought you'd drop by for a cup of coffee and a chat?'

'Not exactly, no. I thought I'd take a drive to see how far you have to walk once you get to your underground station here.'

Shannon gave an exasperated sigh.

'And I wanted to check out the area,' he expanded, making her feel even more cringingly helpless.

'Is there any chance at all that you might stop acting as though I'm too young or too stupid to take care of myself?' Realising that she was still standing up, Shannon tucked herself back into the sofa and folded her arms imperiously.

'If that's the impression I've given you, I apologise,' he said in a voice that didn't sound very apologetic, 'but when I think of Eleanor living in a place like this, my skin crawls. And if, for some reason, she found herself forced to, I'd be bloody glad if there was someone around who took an interest.'

'You mean someone like you.'

Kane shrugged and raised his eyebrows.

'In other words, I should be grateful for you nosing around in my private life.'

'Does your mother know about your living conditions?' he asked shrewdly, and Shannon squirmed a little bit, whilst trying to hang on to the liberated, twenty-first-century veneer she was in the process of creating.

'Of course she does,' Shannon lied. It was, in fact, such a vast lie, that she amended slightly, 'Well, she knows I don't live anywhere grand...' She had an uncomfortable feeling that her mum thought she was living somewhere small but charming, a bit like a smaller version of her own house, in fact. Somewhere with more than two rooms and an atmosphere of cosy homeliness. She would have an instant heart attack were she to know that the small but charming place in her head was in reality a charmless dump in a borderline part of the city.

Shannon could imagine her mother swooping down to London on a bedsit inspection tour and she would probably drag her daughter back off to Ireland the minute she clapped eyes on her rented accommodation.

'I take it you've been economical with the truth.'

'I had to,' Shannon grumbled defensively, 'for her own good.'

He didn't say anything for so long that she finally blurted out, 'Look, I haven't eaten yet, so would you mind leaving? I'm tired and I'm hungry and I'm not in the mood to argue with you. I'm not your child, you don't have to look after me and when I can afford something better, I shall naturally move out. I don't see why you're complaining. I do a good job for you at work and I don't complain about travelling back here in the evenings.'

'Why haven't you eaten?'

Oh, Lord, here we go again, she thought. More lectures, this time about the importance of nutrition.

'Because I was having such a brilliant time at the pub that I just didn't give it a moment's thought!'

'Well, we'd better rectify the situation.' He stood up and Shannon scrambled to her feet in pursuit.

'"We'd" better rectify the situation?'

'That's right.' He began rummaging through her cupboards, then he opened the fridge and scanned the contents with a critical eye.

'Not much here, is there?'

'Do you mind?' Shannon spluttered to his back, finally slipping past him and slamming the fridge door shut.

The fridge, as she had known, was virtually bare. No cheese, just some butter and some milk, but whoever heard of spaghetti and milk? Or spaghetti and chocolate mousse? With a few mouldy onions thrown in for good measure?

She closed the fridge door and faced him with quiet dignity.

'I may have forgotten do go shopping recently,' she agreed loftily, catching his amused eye for a few seconds then looking away. 'As a matter of fact, I've never been one of these people who is obsessed with food.'

'I wouldn't call having more than three items in a fridge being *obsessed with food*,' he murmured. 'Go and get changed, reds, and we'll go out and have a quick meal. 'I'll turn my back while you get dressed, if you like,' he added gallantly, and she snorted with laughter.

'OK, then, I won't.' He looked at her slowly, from her feet upwards, taking his time, arms folded, until every nerve in her body was vibrating with tension.

'I don't suppose you'll just go away?'

'Now, why would I do that when I can stand here and watch you change?' He smiled at her blushing outrage as she pulled open the door to the small wardrobe, wretchedly conscious of the man peering curiously over her shoulder. She extracted the first things that came to hand and stormed into the bathroom, locking the door behind her.

'No need to lock the door, you know,' his voice came from very close to the door indeed. 'Don't you trust me?'

'You're a man, aren't you?' Shannon retorted, struggling out of one set of clothes and into another—this time jeans, a long-sleeved green jumper and a pair of thick socks.

'Now, why do I get the feeling that underneath that liberated, feminist remark is an incurable romantic?'

'Because,' she said, yanking the door open and, as she'd expected, finding him standing two inches away from it, 'you don't know me?'

Instead of answering, Kane located her coat hanging from a hook behind the door and held it out for her. The brief contact of his fingers brushing against her arms felt strangely like an invasion of her privacy and she stepped away, fumbling with the buttons, aware that in her haste to get dressed she had omitted a bra, so that now her breasts felt heavy and her nipples tingled against the rough grain of the jumper. She had a fleeting reckless thought that he might very well be aware of her bra-less state, and hot on the heels of that came the even more reckless thought of his hands caressing her bare breasts under the jumper, seeking out her sensitive nipples, playing with them with his fingers. Just imagining it, it made her body feel hot and feverish.

'I hope I'm well dressed enough for this little meal you've insisted on taking me for.' She had thought that a sparky comment from her might re-create some vital distance between them but, instead of rising to her bait, he smiled and raised his eyebrows in an unnervingly knowing way.

'It makes a delightful change to see you out of work clothes,' he said, opening her door and then politely stepping back so that she could fiddle with her key.

'*Delightful?* Isn't that taking courtesy a bit far?' she asked feverishly.

'Don't you like being described as delightful?' His

eyes were shuttered. 'What adjective would you rather I used? How about sexy? Mmm. Yes, sexy might be more apt. Those freckles, that ivory white skin and flaming hair. Not obviously sexy, but discreetly so. Like a woman in jeans and a man's shirt, not thinking she's flaunting anything but arousing all sorts of illicit thoughts anyway.'

His words made her feel limp.

'I don't arouse illicit thoughts,' she squeaked.

'How do you know?'

'Because...' she spluttered helplessly.

'Would it turn you on if you thought you did?'

'No!'

'So...should I keep my illicit thoughts to myself, then?' He dropped his eyes so that she couldn't see whether he was being serious or not. No, of course he wasn't being serious, she thought hotly.

'You haven't got any illicit thoughts, so you can stop playing games!'

'You're very suspicious of the opposite sex, aren't you?' he said, letting her off the hook and allowing her to lead the way down the narrow flight of stairs to the front door, but stepping forward once they were in the hall to open the door for her. 'Not really surprising, I suppose. One sour relationship can have a knock-on effect that lasts much longer than we expect.'

'Oh, you speak from experience, do you?' Shannon asked sarcastically, stepping past him, her head held high just in case he got the notion that anything he said might actually be absorbed and stored for inspection at a later date.

'Not really, no,' he admitted, walking towards the high street, his hands in his pockets and his coat flapping around him, brushing against her legs. They walked with their heads down, instinctively pushing against the bracing wind that had sent the temperatures dropping.

'Was that what Gallway asked you to do? Trust him?' he quizzed her shrewdly, and Shannon could have kicked herself for her momentary slip of the tongue.

'Isn't that what *all* men say when they're intent on getting a woman into bed?' Shannon retorted heatedly.

'No, actually.'

'*You're* different, I suppose?'

'Very different,' he murmured. 'Look. There. A Chinese restaurant. Shall we try it?'

'OK,' she said grudgingly. 'I never noticed before, not that I spend much time on the high street.'

'Too dull?'

'Way too dull for someone as sizzling as I am,' she answered brashly. 'Not enough…pubs and wine bars and swinging clubs.'

At which Kane had the insufferable temerity to burst out laughing, and she felt a smile reluctantly tug the corners of her mouth. Like it or not, she was enjoying his company, even though he had dragged her out of the warmth of her room at an ungodly hour, kicking and screaming, more or less.

'London isn't just about pubs and wine bars and swinging clubs,' he pointed out. 'What about the theatres, the operas, the restaurants, the art galleries, the museums?'

'What about them?' Shannon shot back airily. She decided that she would get some fun out of the remainder of the evening after all and play him at his own game of being patronising. She brushed past him as he held open the door for her to enter the restaurant, which was not quite empty but nearly.

'What do you mean ''what about them?'''

'Well…' She allowed herself to be relieved of her coat and then waited until she had sat down at the small table. 'Yes, there *is* the theatre,' she agreed, ticking off option one on her finger. 'But if I could afford constant trips to the theatre I would have enough money to move out of that hole I call home away from home, wouldn't I?'

'So you *do* admit that it's a hole.'

'But I never said I didn't like living in holes. Some people do, you know.'

'Ah, I see. Or do I?' He grinned and waited for her to continue.

'Then the opera. Well, really. I would have to save three months' pay to afford a seat at an opera.'

'Not quite three months.'

'Besides, I hate opera.'

'Have you ever been?'

'No. So that's the opera taken care of. Then the restaurants. I worked in one so actually going to one always felt like a busman's holiday.' She ticked off that particular option. 'Then the art galleries and museums. Very interesting, I'm sure. Very cultured and refined, but—'

'Don't say it—you're a wild young thing with no time for culture and refinement…'

'I'm glad you noticed! Perhaps,' she added wickedly, 'when I'm older and more mature…'

'Like me…'

'If the cap fits…' She smiled smugly at him and then proceeded to inspect her menu. A pointless exercise as she allowed him to order the food rather than wade her way through everything on the menu. 'I mean…' she leaned towards him with her elbows resting on the table '…in between your operas, theatres, museums and art galleries, don't you sometimes just long for the hectic buzz of a club?'

He appeared to give that some thought, stroking his chin with one finger, looking at her with a pensive expression that didn't quite conceal the humour lurking just beneath the surface. 'Is there a hectic buzz in a club? I thought it was all loud music and drunken youths.'

'See!' Shannon exclaimed triumphantly.

'What am I supposed to have seen? Oh, I know. That I'm an old fuddy-duddy? A stick-in-the-mud? I *do* manage to get out now and again to the old club, actually. Sorry to disappoint you.' He sat back to allow the waiter to pour them both a glass of wine while Shannon digested the image of Kane Lindley flinging himself around on a dance floor in hip-gripping snakeskin trousers and garish top. It was almost easier to imagine him in a black frock and dog collar preaching from a pulpit.

'You go to clubs?' she asked, guzzling her wine like water and giving him a patronising, incredulous smirk.

'Admittedly not the kind of clubs you probably have in mind.'

'Oh, you mean dreary gentlemen's clubs where you all sit around little table sipping glasses of sherry and discussing politics…'

'Not quite.'

'Then what kind of clubs are you talking about?' The cold white wine tasted glorious, although with nothing in her stomach Shannon could feel the alcohol racing through her bloodstream and shooting straight to her brain.

'Jazz clubs, for the most part.'

'Oh, jazz.'

'Another piece of culture you find you have no time for, by any chance?' He refilled her now empty glass and sat back to look at her. How was it possible for anyone still dressed in their working garb to look so cool and unflappable at this time of evening? Not to mention bright-eyed and bushy-tailed?

'Not really exciting, are they? All slow music and sensible conversation...'

'Depends who you go with.' He raised his glass to his lips and looked at her with amusement over the rim while she went a delicate shade of pink.

'I doubt that very much,' Shannon declared robustly, uncomfortably aware that the image of Kane dancing very slowly, cheek to cheek, with a woman at a jazz club made her feel more bothered than she would have admitted in a million years. There had been no evidence of any women in his life, at least not since she'd been around, working for him, and he'd been increasingly at the house whenever she'd been there in the evenings during the week. But what did that say? His weekends could be spent anywhere. He could have a woman for every weekend for all she knew.

'Do you? Why? Don't you think that listening to good music and dancing to it can be a very erotic experience?'

'I prefer dancing to quicker numbers myself,' Shannon told him quickly, relieved that their food had now arrived, conveniently marking an end to this particular line of conversation, even though she knew that she had generated it in the first place. She watched him surreptitiously as she helped herself to food, ravenously hungry all of a sudden.

'Have you ever been to a jazz club?' he asked, once they had begun eating.

'Not really.' She manoeuvred her chopsticks around a mouthful of cashew chicken and noodles and hoped that the food would soak up some of the wine which had made her feel pleasantly but unreliably light-headed.

'What does "not really" mean?'

'It means no, actually.'

'Oh, dear. No jazz clubs, no opera, nothing that smacks of culture.'

'As a matter of fact, I would *love* to go to jazz clubs and theatres and I might even be persuaded to try the opera…' Unlikely, that last one, she thought, but who could tell? 'But these things cost money which I haven't got at my ready disposal. Unfortunately.' She could feel herself warming to her theme of misplaced cultured person, just in case he imagined that she was a bimbo whose only interest was to go somewhere where the maximum amount of sweat could be worked up in the minimum amount of time. In fact, the few nightclubs she had frequented in her lifetime had left a lot to be desired. That, however, was a little titbit she would not be sharing with him.

'I can't think of anything more exciting,' she ventured, realising with some surprise that she had drunk three glasses of wine and eaten enough food to keep her going for a month, 'than going to…the Tate Gallery, followed by an evening at a quiet, refined club. Just grabbing an exquisite meal somewhere along the way, of course! It would be wonderful to…' Her mind was beginning to feel decidedly fuzzy.

'To…?' Kane prompted silkily.

Where was she? Oh, yes. She was in the middle of conjuring up an alternative lifestyle as befitted someone whose proclivities were more in tune with culture, and not culture of the youth variety. 'To really wear something fancy to go out…a little black number…or maybe something elegant…and backless…in dark green…'

'You have little black numbers and elegant, backless dark green frocks?'

'*Frocks?* No one uses that word nowadays.'

'You fall for it every time, don't you,' Kane murmured, watching her from under his lashes. 'Have you?'

'Have I what?' *Fall for what every time?*

'Got fancy dresses with no place to wear them?'

Having embarked on this road, Shannon suspected that ignominiously admitting a complete lack of any such thing would make all her protests of wanting to absorb culture like the proverbial sponge appear hollow if not a downright lie. And for some perverse reason she wanted to impress him. She wanted to prove that she wasn't just his secretary who was adept at handling his work and good with children, whose only source of amusement were pubs and the odd foray into clubbing. Neither of which had lived up to her expectations anyway.

'Yes,' she lied.

'Mmm. A little black number...'

'That's right! Very little and very black as a matter of fact.'

'The mind boggles. Sure that isn't the wine talking?' he asked with a straight face.

'Quite sure.' Shannon scowled.

'In which case...' He signalled for the bill and looked at her pensively. Too pensively for her liking. She began to feel a little rattled by the lingering silence.

'In which case...*what*?' she demanded impatiently.

'In which case,' he murmured, 'it seems a shame not to have the opportunity to use your glamorous outfits, doesn't it?'

'Just what I've been saying.' Shannon shrugged ruefully, rather pleased with the image she had succeeded in creating for herself. She'd always been the cute, chatty one in the family. The easygoing member upon whom her mother could always rely. Willing to help out in the house, happy to look after the younger ones when her sisters had been too busy rushing about, getting into mad flaps over boys and dates and party dresses. She'd been privileged to have lots of friends of the opposite sex, simply because she'd always been one of the lads. Now, with a few choice phrases and white lies, she had become, she thought gleefully to herself, a woman of mystery and intrigue. She didn't currently feel too mysterious or intriguing in her get-up of jeans and sweater, but in a small, black number she was certain she could be.

'Are we ready to go?' she asked, surprised because she had been having such a good time. When she stood up, she felt slightly giddy and he took her arm.

'Feeling steady enough to walk back?'

'Of course I am. But,' she added slyly, 'if I wasn't, would you do the gentlemanly thing and carry me?'

'That wine has definitely gone to your head,' he muttered under his breath, guiding her along the pavement which was now deserted so that the sound of their footsteps echoed on the concrete.

'You're avoiding the question! Would you carry me?'

'Of course I would,' he said drily, and Shannon laughed.

'And risk three slipped discs in the process?'

'You look as though you'd be as light as a feather,' he told her huskily, and she felt her body flooded with sudden, furious heat at the tone of his voice. 'Would you like me to prove it to you?' He moved round so that he was facing her, and in the darkness she could see mocking challenge in his eyes. He couldn't be serious, could he? It was difficult to tell, especially when the streetlights were throwing his face into sharp angles, making it impossible to decipher any expression.

'Believe me, I weigh more than you think.' Shannon felt her breath catch in her throat. 'It's cold, isn't it? If we don't run back I think I might get frostbite.'

'Backing away, Shannon?' he whispered softly, but he moved aside and fell into step with her so that she wondered whether she had imagined all those various disconcerting tones in his voice. More than likely, considering the way her imagination had taken flight after the wine. On impulse, Kane scooped her up in his arms and carried her to the front door while she protested wildly against his chest and tried to flail her arms and legs, to no avail.

'Put me down!' she wailed eventually, when they were at her front door.

'All in good time. Now, why don't you get your key out of your bag and open up the front door for us?'

'I can't like this!' She was clutching her bag to her chest, using it as a flimsy barrier between herself and his broad chest.

'Give it a try.'

She frantically unzipped her bag and pulled out her bunch of keys, which he promptly took from her with one hand so that he could open the door without putting her down. Moving against him made her skin burn with a strange, restless heat, and where his arms curled behind her back, reaching to grasp around her behind the bent crook of her knees and her chest, it made her want to writhe in a useless attempt to escape. His fingers were splayed only inches from the curve of her breast and her head was consumed with graphic images of them touching her soft flesh. Even if only accidentally.

'That's quite enough,' she protested giddily, as he mounted the stairs. 'And don't blame me if you suffer irreparable back damage!'

'Oh, I might blame you for lots of things, reds, but I won't blame you for that.' He laughed and they arrived at her door without him appearing to have broken sweat. Then he finally stood her up and looked down at her.

'OK,' she bristled furiously, 'so you proved that you're a big strong man! Was that the object of the exercise?'

'No,' he answered, leaning against the doorframe as she opened the door. 'Want me to tell you what was?'

They stared at each other and Shannon felt her mouth go suddenly dry because there was no teasing glint in his eye to rescue her from her wild alarm. In fact, his stillness just sent her nervous system into further overdrive.

'No,' she whispered, and he laughed harshly.

'Why? What are you afraid I might say?'

'I really must get to bed now...' she answered desperately.

'And being the perfect gentleman I am,' he said in his deep, caressing voice, 'I wouldn't dream of intruding on your beauty sleep. And being the perfect gentleman that I am, I also wouldn't dream of allowing you to return to Ireland for Christmas with no tales to tell your family of this wonderful city of ours and all it has to offer. So I've decided to take you to my personal favourite jazz club for dinner and an evening of less frenetic fun than you seem to think is necessary for a good time...'

'*You've* decided?' Her body was taking time to recover from its proximity to his. As was her breathing.

'That's right. *I've* decided. Next Saturday. How does that sound?'

'It sounds—'

'Good. I'll pick you up at seven forty-five and don't worry, you'll have a good time.' He leant so that his mouth was almost touching her ear. Her highly sensitised ear. 'Trust me.'

CHAPTER SIX

THE following few days saw a feverish and panicky assault on all the reasonably priced clothes shops in Central London. Shannon couldn't help but marvel at how the cost of clothes, in particular clothes that required the least yardage of fabric, had sneakily crept up almost when she'd had her back turned. One minute she could afford one or two things in Ireland, nothing designer but nothing shabby either, the next minute she was to be found gaping incredulously at price tags that would have brought her bank manager out in a sweat.

What had possessed her to lie? Didn't she know that lying was nothing more than the laying of foundations for future regrets? If she hadn't, then she knew now because she spent most of her waking time regretting her reckless blunder.

It helped on the one hand that Kane was abroad and so couldn't witness her frantic lunchtime forays into increasingly unsuitable shops. On the other hand, his absence gave her ample opportunity to build up feelings of nervous apprehension. When she thought of him carrying her back to her bedsit, his arms engulfing her body, she felt a sick flutter of dismayed panic but then she couldn't understand why because he hadn't touched her, at least not in any way that could have been construed as suggestive.

'Dad phoned last night,' Eleanor said casually, as they were washing dishes on the Friday evening.

'Oh, did he?' Shannon trilled, before clearing her

throat and trying to assume a less sinister tone. 'How is he? Is he having a good time in New York?'

She communicated daily with him by e-mail, but the subjects covered didn't stray from the work arena.

'He's back tomorrow morning,' Eleanor told her brightly. 'He says he's bought me something but he won't say what.'

'Mmm.' Shannon thoughtfully finished washing up and squeezed the sponge of soapy water. In ten minutes Carrie would be coming to take over. 'And have you got anything planned for tomorrow night? Perhaps a special father-daughter bonding thing? Over some chicken nuggets and chips?'

Eleanor gave her one of those looks that implied wisdom beyond her years. *'Father-daughter bonding?'*

'It *does* happen, you know.'

'But Daddy's too...' She spent a few seconds rooting around for an adequate description of her father. 'Too absent-minded when it comes to stuff like that.'

'You two could share a meal,' Shannon persisted, taken with the idea of wriggling out of her unwelcome dinner date, about which she had been reminded only that very morning by e-mail, due to circumstances over which she had no apparent control. 'Carrie will be here with you in the morning. You two could go and do a shop, buy whatever food he likes most, prepare something special...' Her voice trailed off at the wry look being shot at her from the diminutive creature at her side.

'He's taking me to tea,' Eleanor said, 'and, besides, aren't you supposed to be going out with him in the night?'

'Ah, yes!' Shannon forced herself to give a hundred-watt smile. 'Forgot!'

'How could you forget?'

'I just did.' She shrugged as if forgetting dinner dates was an affliction from which she routinely suffered.

'Have you got your little black dress?'

'And how,' Shannon asked curiously, 'did you know that I was wearing a little black dress?' She faced her eight-year-old sparring partner with hands on hips. 'Spill the beans, miss,' she said, waggling one finger at her. 'Or else your pudding days are over!'

Eleanor giggled and looked unthreatened at the prospect.

'Oh, Daddy mentioned it on the phone yesterday. He said that he hoped you hadn't forgotten about your date and that he was dying to see your little black dress. I can't imagine you in a little black dress,' she tacked on undiplomatically, and Shannon only just managed to refrain from agreeing. 'Nor can Dad,' Eleanor continued with ruthless frankness. 'You're always wearing those funny, boring suits.'

'My suits are not funny!' She laughed. 'If they were, they wouldn't be so boring. But you wait until you get into the big, bad world of work. You, too, will find that your wardrobe is limited!'

'What's your dress like?'

'Very small and…well, small is about all there is to say about it.' In fact, it was the smallest dress she had ever owned in her life, but the shop assistant had said it looked great, and on the fifth day of fruitless shopping, with desperation yapping at her ankles, Shannon had cheerfully believed her.

'Is this a work thing, then?' Eleanor asked, dropping her eyes, and so fortunately missing the colour that flooded into Shannon's face.

'That's right! Work-related,' she confirmed. If only.

It was unlikely, however, that an eight-year-old child would understand an invitation that had stemmed from a combination of pity for the poor woman whose knowledge of London was obviously lacking, curiosity to see what she looked like in the small black number which she had somehow made sound wildly exciting and sexy, and sheer devilry at the tacit challenge behind Shannon's inebriated teasing.

'So…not a date…'

'So…not really…'

'Because,' Eleanor said in a rush, 'I wouldn't mind. I mean, it's not as if you're like the last woman Dad brought home for me to meet. She was awful.'

'Hideous, do you mean?' Shannon asked, briefly tussling with her conscience which was telling her not to try and get information out of a child, particularly information that was none of her business, and losing. 'Unappealing? Perhaps spots?'

'Oh, no, Claudia was beautiful, but…you know…'

'Dull?'

'Too clever and full of herself.'

Beautiful, clever and self-confident, Shannon thought with a stab of emotion that felt suspiciously like jealousy. Only a child could have read disadvantages into such a description.

Beautiful, clever and self-confident was not how she felt on Saturday evening at seven-thirty, with fifteen minutes to go. Having decided that she wouldn't get overwhelmed and stupidly dress in her finery with hours to spare, she now found herself frantically putting on her make-up in front of her mirror and anxiously looking at her watch in a race to get herself ready and presentable before Kane rang the doorbell and she had to hurry down to meet him.

The dress, which she had been told made her look sexy, felt like cling film and left so little to the imagination that she couldn't fathom why she'd been persuaded to buy the thing in the first place. Ten minutes of temporary insanity and here she was, stuffed into sausage skin with far too much leg showing for comfort. The neckline was modest enough but, then, Shannon thought, inspecting herself in the small mirror on the wardrobe door, it would have to be if only to compensate for the plunging back that made wearing a bra out of the question.

Thank goodness it was winter and she could hide behind her thick coat at least for the duration of the drive to the club.

The red hair at least didn't seem too overpowering. She'd had it trimmed into a bob a few days earlier and it swung nicely around her face, if with somewhat glaring intensity. There was nothing that could be done about that. She experimentally swung her head from side to side and was quite pleased with how it looked. Better than tied back into something puerile and unattractive which was how she normally wore it.

It will be a subdued evening during which I shall try very hard not to gabble. I will refuse all drink on some pretext or other and will act like a mature and sophisticated woman instead of an eccentric, unpredictable one.

By the time her bell buzzed from the downstairs front door, Shannon was ready to face Kane. She took her time slipping on her coat and gloves and greeted him five minutes later with a controlled smile.

'You've done something with your hair' were his opening words, which sent a little rush of pleasure through her. He was lounging against the doorway in his black coat, with a cream silk scarf draped casually around his neck.

'I've had it trimmed.' She tossed her head back in the manner of a film star. 'Do you like it?'

'It's very nice,' he said. 'Very chic.'

In the darkness, Shannon looked at him narrowly, wondering whether there was some hidden meaning in his remark to which she should take immediate offence, but the contours of his face were bland, and there was nothing remotely smug in his voice as he began talking about his trip to New York.

'Have you ever been to New York?' he asked, as he manipulated the car smoothly along back roads she wouldn't have recognised in a thousand years.

It crossed her mind that it would have been glorious to have swapped notes on life in the Big Apple. Unfortunately some lies just couldn't be countenanced.

'You could rephrase that,' Shannon said tartly, 'to ''Have you ever been anywhere except London and Ireland?'''

'You've *never* been anywhere else?'

'I know. Shocking, isn't it? I've never even been on a plane! Just one of the many things I never seemed to get around to doing!'

'Now you sound very brittle and you're not a brittle person, are you? How have you managed to live your life without setting foot on a plane in this day and age of cheap air travel?'

Shannon chewed her lip, wondering whether she should counter his kind curiosity with something trivial and vague, but in the end she said thoughtfully, 'I guess that, growing up, there was never the money to go around. Don't forget how many of us there were, and Mum would never have taken a few on holiday and left the rest behind. So we went on holidays to the beach, camping, to the countryside. And by the time I started working, well, I never seemed to have any lump sums of money around that I could use for a holiday some-where hot.'

'You must have saved something from working,' he persisted wryly, 'if you lived at home with your family and had no astronomical rent to pay. Or did you spend it all on clothes? Warn me now so that I have an idea of what to expect when Eleanor gets older and insists on augmenting her pocket money with a weekend job! Tell me she won't blow the lot on shopping!' He flicked an amused sideways glance at her then looked back ahead of him, his mouth curved into a slight smile.

Why did he group her and his daughter together? It was ridiculous. Shannon suddenly felt perversely pleased that she'd worn the skin-tight number after all.

'Actually, I usually ended up buying stuff for my younger brothers,' Shannon said reluctantly. Of course she had bought clothes for herself and gone out with her friends, but she had also paid rent to her mother and it was true that pay days had always been a source of treats for the kids. It had always seemed natural to share.

'That's great,' Kane said warmly, and she grimaced.

'I don't suppose Eleanor will run into that particular problem,' she pointed out. She'd just succeeded, she thought wryly, in making herself sound like a prosaic goody two-shoes! 'She'll probably blow all her money on clothes and shoes and holidays and will leave poor old Dad picking up the tab!'

'Maybe.' Kane turned around in his seat to manoeuvre the car into a parking space, his arm splayed along the back of her seat behind the headrest. 'But then again, maybe,' he said, facing her but with his arm still behind her seat, 'she'll grow up with other siblings and shed out all her money on treats for them. Who knows?'

'You mean you want another family?' For some reason, the thought was shocking. It also made her wonder, uncomfortably, whether there was another woman on the scene somewhere. A prospective Ms Right, discreetly lurking in the background. Very discreetly, since she had seen nothing of her, but, then, Kane Lindley was a very discreet man, wasn't he? If he wanted to hide something, he would do it with the utmost tact.

'Not,' she added hastily, 'that it's any of my business.'

'You sound astounded. Isn't the desire to procreate as natural as breathing?'

They walked into the jazz club which was small, intimate and reassuringly dark so that he couldn't see the flush that had spread across her cheekbones.

'Your coat?' He reached to help her out of it and Shannon resisted the urge to cling tightly to the comforting barrier of wool concealing her scantily clad body.

'I might be cold.'

'I doubt it. It's pretty warm in here and after a couple of dances you'll be hot.'

'A couple of dances?'

'If you can slow your tempo to accommodate an old man.'

'I wish you'd stop referring to yourself as an old man,' she grumbled, relinquishing her coat with reluctance and refusing to wilt under his thorough inspection. 'You certainly didn't seem old when…when you…'

'Swept you off your feet? Well, thank you very kindly. I trust that was a compliment?' He glanced down at her, very slowly.

'The little black dress,' he murmured. 'It *is* little, isn't it? I hope the men here can stand the strain on their blood pressure.'

Her own blood pressure appeared to be soaring through the roof as he continued to gaze at her with her coat draped elegantly over his arm.

'Do you know,' he said with a low laugh, 'I didn't quite believe you when you told me that you possessed a little black number?'

Shannon gave a tinkling laugh. Tinkling and, she hoped, mildly amused at the suggestion herself. 'Didn't you? I have a wardrobe of them back in Ireland!'

'Have you now?' They handed their coats to the girl at the counter and were given a disc which Kane slipped into the pocket of his jacket.

'Oh, yes. Of course, I couldn't bring them all down here to London. I knew I wouldn't have the space to hang them.'

'What a complex little creature you are, reds,' he said, as they were shown to their table which was tucked away at the side. Very cosy, very intimate, very nerve-racking. 'How to equate the girl who spent her hard-earned money buying presents for her siblings with a provocative woman with a wardrobe of daring numbers?' He called a waitress over and ordered a bottle of champagne and then resumed his inspection of her. 'Perhaps I'm a typical man who naturally puts women into categories, and the category of someone who's obviously so good with children doesn't seem to slip into the category of a woman who willingly flaunts her charms by night.'

Flaunts her charms? Well, on the one hand, he *was*, she thought with heady pleasure, admitting that she had charms to flaunt. On the other hand, the woman he was describing didn't seem to bear any relation to her at all.

'That *is* a typical man,' she agreed in a smoky voice.

In the presence of this man, she was discovering another side of her which hadn't existed before. Someone sensual and responsive, far more sensual and responsive, in fact, than she had ever felt in the company of Eric Gallway, whose pursuit had made her feel giddy enough, but giddy in the manner of a teenager. She'd enjoyed his attention, but most of all she'd enjoyed the sensation of feeling herself to be in love. Well, she wasn't in love now, but Kane certainly had the knack of making her feel like a woman.

Perhaps, at long last, she was finally breaking out of her chrysalis to spread her wings and fly free from the cheerful girl next door she had always been. Just the thought of this new woman emerging sent a racy thrill through her body.

At the back of her mind, she recalled that she *was* his secretary, but the boundary lines were blurred, particularly as she saw him so regularly out of work, even if it was still in the controlled setting of his house with his daughter present.

'Or maybe,' she mused thoughtfully, 'you've always mixed with women who slotted into one role or the other. Beautiful career-women, for example, clever and self-confident but unable to cross the barriers into normal, boisterous family life...?'

'Maybe I have...' He sipped his champagne and continued to look at her over the rim of the glass. 'So do you think I've been playing it all wrong?'

'I think so!' Shannon said airily. Funny stuff, champagne. It felt as though she wasn't drinking at all.

'What do you think I should do to correct my preconceptions?' he asked meekly.

'Look beneath the surface.' Shannon gave him a wise look from under her mascara-tipped lashes.

'I'll try my best,' he replied gravely.

There was a sudden flurry of activity on the slightly raised circular platform towards the back of the room and then the jazz band appeared, eight men dressed in black who then proceeded to give a spirited rendition of a recognisable Gershwin piece, which was heartily applauded, followed by a more subdued and atmospheric number which saw couples flocking to the dance floor.

Shannon turned to show her appreciation of the music to Kane just as a tall, dark-haired beauty materialised at his side and tapped him on his shoulder.

She leant over him so that her long raven hair rippled along the back of his shirt, exposing in the process, Shannon noticed viciously, a bird's-eye view of a very ample cleavage. She could feel her heart beat savagely inside her and gulped down some of the champagne so quickly that she had to stifle an undignified coughing fit. She couldn't hear what was being said but she had no need to be an expert lip-reader to see, from the body language of the slender arm casually resting along Kane's shoulder, that they were more than just passing acquaintances.

'Would you mind,' the woman said, leaning over Kane to address Shannon, so that the generous breasts which seemed intent on bursting forth from the tight-fitting red top rested tantalisingly close to his face, 'if I drag this gorgeous beast up for a dance?'

'Be my guest,' Shannon responded through tightly clenched teeth, thinking that she could drag the gorgeous beast backwards through a holly bush for all she cared, but Kane was having none of it. He made his apologies with a rueful smile and a shrug of his broad shoulders and the woman departed with a 'Maybe later' promise between them.

'My apologies for not introducing you,' Kane said, standing up and extending his hand for Shannon's so that she had no option but to ungracefully submit to a dance, 'but the music was a bit loud and I didn't want to keep Carole from her dinner companion...' Another slow, soulful jazz number was being played, and he pulled her close to him, cupping the small of her back with one hand while the other clasped her own hand which felt ridiculously small engulfed in his.

'She didn't seem all that bothered to keep her dinner companion waiting,' Shannon pointed out coolly. Her cheek was resting lightly against his chest and she could feel his heart beating.

'Well, perhaps I thought it rude to keep *my* dinner companion waiting,' he said into her hair, and Shannon drew away slightly to look at him.

'It didn't bother me one way or another.'

'Didn't it?'

Her green eyes were unable to sustain the glitter of his dark ones and she was the first to look away. It was impossible not to feel vulnerable and disadvantaged, she thought, when she had to crane her neck upwards to look at him, like a woman arching up to receive her lover's kiss.

'No.' Shannon's voice was resolute. 'I was more than happy to sit on my own and listen to the music.'

'I wouldn't dream of letting you do any such thing.'

'Because you're too much of a gentleman?' she heard herself sniping, and he smiled.

'Possibly.'

His ambiguous reply sent a flare of dangerous excitement coursing through her body which was instantly quenched by the memory of the glamorous brunette who, from all appearances, would have ditched her dinner companion for the sake of an evening with Kane.

'So,' she asked after a short silence, during which his body against hers seemed to burn with increasing heat, 'who *is* she, anyway? Feel free not to answer if you don't consider it any of my business.' Her voice implied that whether he chose to answer or not was a matter of supreme indifference to her because she was merely making convenient small talk.

He pulled her fractionally closer to him so that their bodies were now grinding against one another, as though engaged in a slow mating ritual. Shannon shivered.

'She *was* a business acquaintance and…personal friend…'

'*Was* a personal friend?' Shannon asked innocently. 'Oh, dear. Friendships are so valuable. Did you fall out?'

This time it was his turn to draw back and look down at her, catching her wide green gaze with enough of a dry smile to make her very aware that he knew what she was playing at.

'We concluded our relationship,' he said. 'And if you want to find out precisely what kind of relationship we had, why don't you just ask?'

Shannon flushed and stared at the button on his shirt for a few seconds. When she was sure that her expression was composed, she looked back up at him and smiled sweetly. 'I take it that it was an intimate relationship and I assure you I'm not in the least interested in prying for details.'

'Shall I give them to you anyway? To satisfy whatever faint shreds of curiosity there might be playing around in sweet little head of yours?'

'If you like.'

'I met her through work. She's a lawyer, and we got

to know one another earlier this year over a period of a few months, but time showed that we weren't suited at all and we mutually agreed to call it a day.'

'*She* looked as though she might be persuaded to re-kindle the affair,' Shannon said, feeling horrible because the remark was so obviously catty, but he didn't appear to take any offence.

'Possibly. But...' He tucked her hair behind one delicate ear and whispered, 'Once I've decided on something, I don't change my mind.' Which was just the sort of remark to egg on her already seething curiosity to further unprepossessing heights. Fortunately, before she could launch into yet more questions, the number ended and she used the brief respite in the music to mention food.

And for the next hour they chatted about non-threatening topics. Safe discussions about music and Ireland and celebrities and Kane's massive experience of other countries, while Shannon's champagne-fuddled brain tried to pinpoint precise things he had said to her while they had been dancing. The brunette did not reappear, although halfway through their *crème brûlée* Shannon spotted her on the dance floor in the arms of a tall, attractive, fair-haired man who seemed to be having a whale of a time, his hands roaming over every inch of her body within respectable limits.

'Having a good time?' Kane leaned towards her and Shannon gave a merry laugh.

'Fabulous food...great music... Of course I am!' More than that, she felt wonderfully alive, burning with energy, in fact.

'In that case, care for another dance?'

'I need one,' she said breathlessly, 'if only to burn off some of the calories of the food I've just eaten!'

'Nonsense, you don't need to lose an ounce of weight.'

'You haven't seen me…seen me without…' The observation, which had started off impulsively enough, trailed off into an embarrassed silence.

'No, but I've felt you.' He rescued her from the no-entry road down which her conversational impulse had foolishly taken her.

'You've *what*?'

'Felt the shape of your body through that very minute dress you're wearing, and believe me when I tell you that you don't need to watch what you eat.'

Shannon narrowed her eyes at the open, innocent expression on his face. 'Well, it doesn't matter how much I eat, I'll never attain the proportions of the lovely Carole,' she said nastily, falling into step with him once again and feeling as though their bodies were in perfect sync.

'She is rather tall and well-endowed, isn't she?' he said with a low laugh that brushed against her cheek like warm breath.

'And clever with it,' she couldn't resist adding.

'And very clever with it,' Kane concurred. 'Just the sort of woman I should be steering well clear of, in fact. Too one-dimensional.' He gave another low laugh which made Shannon wonder whether he was being condescending at her expense but her suspicious eyes met another of those bland, innocent looks with which it was difficult to find fault.

'Eleanor didn't care for her anyway,' he added, which gave Shannon a treacherous stab of satisfaction. 'And I'm old-fashioned enough to want approval from my daughter for any woman I choose to have a serious relationship with.'

'That's not old-fashioned, it's considerate and compassionate. I know my mother would never have contemplated settling down with a man who didn't get full approval from all of us.'

'A tall order for any man,' Kane said with a groan, and Shannon giggled.

'I know. Not that we wouldn't want our mum to have every chance of happiness...'

'But to appeal to seven! I take it your mother never remarried?'

Shannon shook her head. 'She's had quite a few dates. She's still an attractive woman considering we should all have put a thousand lines on her face over the years, but she's always said that her hands were too full to contemplate settling down and adding a man to the list of people to take care of.'

'Worries about you all, does she?' He unclasped one hand to place it at the back of her neck so that her hair fell over his fingers. She could feel every touch of every individual finger like a branding iron against her flesh. Thank goodness he was unaware of her reaction, she thought jerkily, because he would laugh his head off if he knew. In fact, in the cold light of morning and without the effects of champagne drifting like incense in her brain, she would, no doubt, laugh her head off at the memory herself.

'Of course she does,' she said. 'Don't all mothers? No, that was naïve of me. Of course they don't all. We were lucky with Mum and I guess we sometimes take that for granted. But *you* worry about Eleanor, don't you?'

'Oh, inordinately. As you say, it should come with the territory.'

They danced in silence for a while and in fact, the

snippet of conversation lay semi-forgotten at the back of Shannon's mind when, on the way back to her flat, he raised it once again via the circuitous route of quizzing her more about her family. If he seemed suddenly fascinated by her background, Shannon didn't notice. The champagne had taken its toll and she was on the verge of falling asleep, even though she kept forcing herself to open her eyes every time she felt herself beginning to drift off. She had a vision of herself slumbering peacefully against the door of his car, blissfully unaware of everything, mouth half-open, and it didn't make a pretty picture.

But she could barely answer his questions without yawning, so when he slipped his vital question in, she was almost unaware of the implications. She assumed it was yet another family-type question until her brain deciphered his message and she sat up abruptly and asked him to repeat what he had just said.

'I merely said,' he obliged, talking very slowly and keeping his eyes fixed to the road ahead, 'that you should consider leaving that hovel you're renting in view of the anguish it would cause your mother, if nothing else, and move in with me.'

'Move in with you.' It was such a ludicrous suggestion that Shannon nearly burst into laughter at the thought of it. 'Are you crazy? What sort of offer is that?'

'A perfectly reasonable one, as it happens.' He slowed down as they approached her building and managed to find a space for his car directly outside, but when she turned to open the car door, he swiftly reached across and stopped her by placing his hand over hers.

'Reasonable?' Shannon shrieked.

'Just listen to me for a minute.' He let go of her hand and sat back with one arm resting loosely on the steering-wheel. 'That bedsit of yours is no place to live. In fact, your landlord should be shot for carving up the house into such small rooms just to squeeze more money out of gullible young people...'

'I am not gullible!'

'And as you agreed earlier on, your mother would hit the roof if she knew your living conditions...'

'Well, she doesn't!'

'So what better solution than for you to move in with me? My house is more than big enough to accommodate an extra person. In fact, you'll have a suite so that your privacy won't be invaded in any way whatsoever, and it would ease my mind if I knew you didn't have to endure that walk back to this dump every evening. Naturally your working hours with regard to Eleanor would remain unchanged, and if you wanted to go out in the evenings, Carrie would babysit as she always has in the past...'

Shannon felt as though she had been cruising blithely along only to suddenly find herself on a mad roller-coaster ride.

'No, wait just a minute—'

'Of course, the situation would only stand until you find somewhere else, and as I won't charge you any rent, you would be able to save all the more quickly for just that...'

'No, it really is out of the—'

'Think about it overnight.' Kane stepped out of the car and opened her door for her. She nearly fell out.

'We'll discuss it,' he continued implacably, 'first thing on Monday morning.'

And before she could utter another word of protest, he was back in his car, patiently waiting to make sure she was safely inside before driving away.

CHAPTER SEVEN

NO WONDER Kane hadn't offered to see her up to her door, make sure she travelled the two flights of stairs without being accosted five times on the way, checked under the sofa for possible snakes. Discretion had overcome valour! He must have known, Shannon fumed, that she would have clobbered him over the head with something very large and very hard!

She'd never heard such a ridiculous suggestion in her whole life and she knew why he'd made it. Because life would be infinitely easier for him if he had her in place as nanny and his over-developed protective instincts would be satisfied, knowing that she didn't have to scurry like a fugitive along the dark streets leading to her flat every time she left his house.

Did he really imagine that she would relinquish her freedom and be grateful for the opportunity?

Her bedsit might be the last word in undesirable, but it was hers and she had no one looking over her shoulder every time she sneezed!

Shannon tried to imagine life under Kane Lindley's roof but when she did her mind was overwhelmed by suffocating thoughts of never being able to escape him. It was bad enough trying not to be aware of his presence when she was at his house with Eleanor for three hours after work. It was bad enough constantly crossing that line between secretary and babysitter, without having to endure it twenty-four hours a day! Never mind his logic about saving up to rent somewhere halfway decent!

Logic, she thought sourly, might rule his life, but it certainly didn't rule hers!

'It's a very thoughtful offer,' Sandy told her treacherously the next day over lunch. 'London's not safe at night. I mean, don't you feel worried having to walk back to your flat in that part of town?'

'You're supposed to take my side, Sandy,' Shannon complained, toying with the pasta on her plate.

'You could always share a house, like me. It means I can afford a room in a much nicer area...'

'And have four people breathing down your neck! I need my privacy!' Sandy shared a large house on the outskirts of Hampstead with four other girls, and whenever Shannon was around, there always seemed to be people bursting through doors or having loud telephone conversations in the room next door, or else opening fridge doors and speculating on who had stolen their food. Sandy might enjoy the constant hum of activity but Shannon suspected that it would drive her crazy.

'Well, he said you would have all the privacy you wanted...'

'And pigs might fly. What's this?' She stabbed a peculiar object in her plate of pasta and held it up for examination.

'Oh, Alfredo had one or two scallops going spare so I flung them in.'

'It's a strange addition, don't you think?'

'Not for anyone with refined tastebuds. Anyway, you're changing the subject. If his house is that big, you won't even have to see him at all.' There was a sudden flurry of activity as the kitchen was invaded by several people who all seemed to be hunting out scraps for lunch, stopping to chat *en route* and dip into what was on offer in the dish in the middle of the table. Having a conversation was impossible in Sandy's house.

'And as he pointed out,' Sandy continued, oblivious to the chaos, 'you'll be able to save lots of money and put a deposit on somewhere a bit more upmarket. In fact, you'd probably only have to stay there for a couple of months and your finances would be sorted out. Stop playing with that food and eat up. You'll fade away to nothing.'

No help from that quarter, Shannon thought, but after delivering a long lecture on the role of friends who should always support one another and not try to introduce counter-arguments which only clouded the issue, she allowed herself to be diverted into their usual gossipy chat about what was happening to whom and why.

After all her weekend seething and fulminating, it was almost an anticlimax to get into work the following day, only to discover that Kane had been called away on urgent business and wouldn't see her until possibly later that evening, if not the following morning. No mention of what they had spoken about on Saturday night, and she wondered whether he had forgotten the whole thing already. Maybe at the time he'd been roaring drunk even though he'd seemed as sober as a judge. Perhaps he just hid it well and was, in fact, one of those people who seemed to suffer no effects from alcohol except inexplicable memory loss the following day.

The thought cheered her up. By five o'clock she had come to the comforting conclusion, having spoken to him twice on the telephone during which he had mentioned nothing of what had been said, that he had decided to drop the whole issue. He had probably sensed that under that open, cheerful and seemingly malleable exterior there beat a heart of steel.

Or maybe, she thought to herself, he, too, had realised the implications of his offer. That he would see more of her than he might find palatable. Judging from the beauty at the jazz club, he had a life of his own to pursue and maybe he had reached the conclusion that one Irish girl with a tendency to be too outspoken for her own good might just be a fly in his ointment.

She was due to be at his house to supervise Eleanor by five-thirty but it was nearly six by the time she arrived, to find Kane's car sprawled on the driveway. Before she could ring the bell, the door was open and he was standing in front of her, dressed casually in a pair of cords and a rugby-style sweatshirt that made her hurriedly avert her eyes. Too much masculinity at too close a range.

'I thought you said you were away on urgent business,' she greeted him, as he stood aside to let her enter.

'One thing I admire about you,' he reflected drily, shutting the front door, 'is your talent for bypassing social niceties.'

'Well, I didn't expect to find you here,' Shannon told him by way of apology. 'You said you'd be away until tomorrow morning.'

'I said I *might*.'

'Where's Eleanor?' She tried to peer past him but failed.

'Actually, spending a night with her friend.'

Shannon looked at his coldly. 'In which case, why didn't you inform me?'

Kane, infuriatingly, grinned. 'You're very cute when you try to be cutting. Perhaps because it's so out of character.'

Trust him to leave her speechless. She recovered quickly. 'I won't be needed in that case.'

'Now, whatever gives you that idea?'

Lost for words twice in the space of as many seconds, Shannon contented herself by glaring icily, and he relented with a mock gesture of surrender.

'OK. You're still needed...' he let the words linger tantalisingly in the silence between them '...because I have a visitor to see you. Waiting in the kitchen, as a matter of fact.' He strode off, leaving her to hurriedly get out of her coat and trip along behind him while she frantically tried to work out who this so-called visitor was. Only a handful of people knew where she lived.

'What visitor?' she managed to hiss before they reached the kitchen, and he stopped so abruptly to face her that she nearly staggered into his chest.

'No introductions will be needed. That's all I'll say. Wouldn't want to spoil the surprise.'

He stood dramatically aside for her to precede him and then waited behind as Shannon walked into the kitchen and her visitor stood up with arms outstretched.

'Mum! What are you doing here?' She was aware of Kane standing behind her and she didn't have to look at his face to know that he was the arch-manipulator behind her mother's sudden appearance on the scene. Arch-manipulator with a specific purpose in mind, and the purpose, she suspected wildly, had nothing to do with a tender reunion of mother and daughter for a cup of tea and a cosy chat.

By way of response, her mother engulfed her in a hug, then stood back and inspected her from arm's length.

'Shannon, you've lost weight.'

Her mother was a slender woman with short brown hair and a habit of looking ferocious when she chose. Right now she was looking ferociously at her daughter and Shannon quailed and stammered out something in-articulate by way of denial.

'Don't you try and tell me I'm wrong,' her mother countered with a voice that precluded any further debate on the subject. 'You've lost weight and your lovely gen-tleman friend had every right to be concerned.' She gave the lovely gentleman friend a warm conspirational look and Shannon controlled the insane impulse to spin around and sock him on his gloating jaw.

'He's not *my lovely gentleman friend*, Mum. He's my employer and *he has no reason to be concerned about me*. I *have* told him that,' she said in a voice laced with the promise of retribution, 'so *I hope he hasn't made the mistake of fetching you all the way from Ireland over nothing!*'

'I don't think my baby's welfare is *nothing*,' her mother said reprovingly, so that Shannon wanted to groan. 'You led me to believe that everything was a bed of roses down here, Shannon. I thank my good Lord that this young man of yours had the sense to call me up and let me know one or two facts!'

'He's not *my young man*.'

The young man in question finally saw fit to sidle past Shannon into the kitchen and offer her a cup of coffee.

'Or something stronger, although it *is* a little on the early side for wine...'

'Oh, my Shannon doesn't drink. A good, strong cup of tea for the both of us would be a delight. Then we can have a nice little chat about things.'

'Very sensible,' Kane agreed, ignoring the killing look that Shannon directed at him.

'Things?' Shannon said weakly. 'What things?'

'Why don't you two ladies go to the sitting room and I'll bring the tea through?' Kane said, giving her a soothing smile that made her want to breathe fire. 'And some of those lovely home-made shortbread biscuits you brought with you, Rose.'

Rose? *Rose?* So now he and her mother were on first-name terms? She watched aghast as her mother gave him another warm smile, the warm smile of someone who had fallen victim to Kane Lindley's charm. Shannon felt herself hustled out of the kitchen by her mother tugging her along and only had a fleeting opportunity to glance backwards over her shoulder at Kane who was busying himself with a tin on the counter, presumably home of the lovely shortbread biscuits.

'What a beautiful house, wouldn't you agree?' Rose said, looking approvingly around her as they passed through the hall and into the sitting room. 'Kane gave me a guided tour of the house and I must say it's beautiful. So quiet in the midst of all this noise and pollution. A haven, if that's the word I'm looking for.'

'He gave you a *guided tour*? How long have you been here, Mum?'

'Oh since around eleven-thirty this morning, darling. You *really do* look gaunt, Shannon. You haven't been eating properly, have you? And I thought you were old enough to look after yourself down here. I should have known better! Didn't I tell you that it would be a mistake, coming here to London? On your own? Away from your family?' She was shaking her head as she said this and Shannon felt as though various lifelines were slipping away, out of her grasp, leaving her defenceless and gasping for air.

'Mum…'

'Now, don't you "Mum" me, Shannon.' She sat down and primly folded her hands on her lap.

'Kane had no right to get in touch with you.'

'He had every right, my girl. It's a blessing that there's someone in this godless city who cares about your welfare. He explained how worried he was at the state of your living quarters—'

'My living quarters are fine, Mum!' Shannon protested feebly. 'Adequate, at any rate.'

'Well, my girl, I'll be the judge of that. Kane suggested that the best thing might be if I go with you to have a look for myself.'

Shannon's last remaining wall of defence crumbled in the face of the implacable steamroller now looking at her, and there was a minute of respectful silence while she contemplated the outcome of any such impending visit to her bedsit. There was no opportunity to vent her fury at the instigator of it all until much later that night, after her mother had been ensconced in a bed in one of the guest rooms.

'You...you...*rat*!' Shannon spluttered, stamping into the kitchen to confront a cool, calm and collected Kane who had managed to spend the evening further ingratiating himself into her mother's good books by saying all the right things, making all the right noises and behaving in the sort of gallant manner calculated to overcome all maternal obstacles.

'Coffee? Nightcap?'

'Don't you *coffee* and *nightcap* me!' She looked at him with withering rage. 'How *dare* you bring my poor mother all the way here just to suit yourself?'

'Sit down. You look as though you're about to explode,' he said with his vast mastery of understatement. He indicated a chair at the kitchen table facing him and Shannon flung herself into it, making choked noises under her breath.

'Now, why don't you get a grip and we can discuss

this like two adults?' He was drinking a glass of port and appeared utterly serene in the face of her blistering gaze. 'Sure you won't join me in a glass of port? My little teetotaller? Tut, tut, tut, fancy letting your mother think that you hated the demon drink…'

'I'll join you in a glass of port,' Shannon informed him through gritted teeth, 'if you'll allow me to pour it over that conniving head of yours.'

He shook his head and poured her a glass. 'Now you're being childish. You have to admit that your mother saw my point of view completely, and aren't you happy that she felt confident about giving you her blessing to shelter under my roof until you found somewhere more respectable to live? I told her all about Eleanor, of course, and she was delighted to think that you would be joining in a family instead of living on your own.'

'My life is none of your business! You had no right—'

'You don't want to accept help, but accepting help sometimes can show strength of character. If you're nervous about sharing my house…'

'Nervous? Why on earth should I be nervous?'

'I don't know. Perhaps you think that things might be different somehow if you moved in. Less of an employer-employee situation…'

'I don't think anything of the sort,' Shannon told him frigidly, distracted from her argument by his sweeping assumption that his presence might affect her somehow. Did he imagine that at closer quarters she might develop an unlikely crush?

'Then what's the problem with accepting a helping hand for a month or two until you find somewhere else? Your freedom won't in any way be curtailed. I'm not going to take advantage of your good nature…' He paused and stroked his chin reflectively. 'Well, perhaps good nature is a bit strong,' he murmured slyly. 'Put it this way, you can come and go as you please.'

'How did you manage to persuade my mother to come here? How did you know where she lived?'

'Your next of kin on your personnel file in answer to question two. And in answer to question one, I simply appealed to her good sense to come and see how you were.'

'Ugh. Sickening.' She knew that she would get precisely nowhere if she continued ranting and railing. Her mother had been pathetic enough over Mrs Porter's superbly prepared dinner, treating Kane as though he was the impersonation of everything wonderful and even having the cheek to slide her the odd glance or two indicating how much she approved of him.

Her mother, who had always been a dragon of embarrassing, inquisitive questions when it came to her boyfriends, had melted in the face of Kane's studied thoughtfulness. She had treated Shannon's stuttering, wrath-filled protests over the washing-up with incomprehension, pointing out that she should be grateful to have found such a considerate employer who was responsible enough to take an interest in her well-being. After half an hour of this, Shannon had felt like flinging herself over the edge of the nearest precipice.

'Your mother didn't seem to think I was sickening.'

Shannon eyed him narrowly. 'She's probably suffering from undiagnosed senile dementia.'

'In fact, she thought I was a very responsible, thoughtful kind of guy…as she herself said on several occasions if my memory serves me right…'

Shannon wondered how she was ever going to spend even a week in the company of someone who had a tendency to get under her skin like a worrisome burr without going mad. But move in she would because she had been left no option.

Her mother had been predictably appalled at the bed-sit, peering at everything, checking her fridge, clucking her tongue, shaking her head and generally acting as though the mere fact that her beloved daughter had lived in such a place without informing her constituted a mortal sin. She had implied to her trailing daughter that she had somehow been rescued by her saintly employer from a vicious fate of assault at knifepoint and had then proceeded to deliver a scathing lecture on her poor eating habits. As though the loss of a few pounds were somehow inextricably linked to her living arrangements.

'Well, if I move in here—'

'When, you mean.'

'I intend to lay down a few ground rules,' she continued, ignoring Kane's smug interruption. 'First of all, I don't work as an out-of-hours secretary if you have anything that needs typing. Secondly, I don't want anyone looking over my shoulder at what I'm doing—'

'Will you be doing anything that might tempt me to do that?' he asked mildly.

'And, thirdly, I don't intend to clock in and out and ask permission to breathe. Oh, and, fourthly, I have to give you some rent money.'

'Absolutely no rent money,' he said forbiddingly.

'I don't like the idea of accepting favours,' Shannon informed him stiffly.

'Why ever not? Sometimes it's important to see the big picture or else we end up missing valuable opportunities by getting entangled in the little things. One of the most important pieces of advice I can give you is to have long-term vision.'

'I didn't realise that I had asked for any important pieces of advice.'

'I wouldn't be here today if I hadn't accepted a few favours along the way.'

Shannon looked at him suspiciously. 'I can't imagine *you* accepting favours from anyone,' she muttered.

'Hmm. For a confirmed non-drinker, I must say you've managed to finish that glass of port in record time. Can I pour you another?' Kane shot her a grin that was wickedly amused. 'Didn't you drink at all when you lived in Ireland?'

'Of course I did! I just didn't…drink in the house.'

'And what other little secrets have you been keeping from that delightful mother of yours?'

Shannon thought that she might hit him at any moment.

'I mean, does she know about the wild and irresponsible life you've been leading down here?'

'I haven't been leading a wild and irresponsible life!' She had nightmarish visions of her mother quizzing her on her after-work activities, making dubious leaps of the imagination and coming to the wrong conclusions. 'And stop interfering,' she added as an afterthought.

'You're right.' He stood up and flexed his muscles. 'I'm nothing but an interfering old busybody.' His smile was a devastating mix of rueful apology and old-fashioned charm.

Did he expect her to buy that nonsense? she wondered. His words implied that he was nothing but a harmless senior citizen whose nosy interference she should indulge, if only to humour him. Ha! His self-effacing description couldn't have been further from the truth, as they both very well knew.

'True,' Shannon said sweetly in agreement. 'And I

personally can't think of anything worse than an interfering old busybody.'

Kane didn't care for that. She could tell from his
frowning expression, and her saccharine smile grew
broader.

'I suppose,' she mused, 'when a person gets old
there's very little left to amuse them but interfering in
other people's lives. They bustle about, poking and prying, and don't even realise how irritating they are.'

'You have a point,' Kane conceded. But before she
could rest on her temporary victory and enjoy the taste
of it before it evaporated altogether, he added, *sotto
voce*, 'Next time I see Rose I must ask her whether she
ever considered me an interfering old fool with nothing
better to do.' He laughed softly to himself, as if remembering a particularly pleasant thought. 'Perhaps she
might see it as her duty to try and patch up my poor,
wounded ego.'

While Shannon was trying to find a suitably cutting
retort to this, he sauntered towards the kitchen door and
paused, to throw over his shoulder, 'Oh, forgot to mention. I told your mum that you'd take a couple of days
off work to move and show her around a bit. And before
you thank me, there's absolutely no need.' Then he was
gone before she could launch a few well-deserved verbal
missiles in his direction.

'I don't know how you could let yourself be conned into
believing Kane Lindley,' Shannon grumbled to her
mother two days later in the airport lounge, where they
were waiting for Rose's flight to be called. Trust him to
finish her mother's trip with flourish. First-class air fare
back to Ireland. Excessive and flamboyant, she thought
to herself, although when she'd tried to share this hum-

ble opinion with her mother, she'd immediately found
herself in the dubious role of small-minded daughter suffering a bad attack of sour grapes just because she hadn't
got her own way.

'Now, don't be silly, Shannon. I wasn't conned into
anything. Kane has chosen to take you under his wing
and I must say I have utmost trust in him.'

'Why?' Shannon cried. 'Why?'

'Because he's a dying breed, my girl. A true gentleman.'

'When it suits him.'

'And Eleanor is a charming little girl. I can see how
fond she is of you.' Her mother smiled warmly at her
daughter. 'You always did have a gift with the little
ones. It'll do you the world of good, living there for a
little while, give you time to eat properly, get your
money together for somewhere better to live.'

'Just so long as you don't go into a state of shock
when I tell you that I'm moving out,' Shannon warned.
'And you might as well know that I'll never be able to
rent anywhere like Kane's house. I'll still only be able
to afford somewhere small.'

'Small doesn't have to be dangerous and dingy.'

Her mother. Brainwashed. It was enough to make a
girl ill. But Shannon had to admit, as the days rolled by,
that Kane was true to his word. Carrie still collected
Eleanor from school, and on the very first evening had
asked Shannon to let her know what nights she planned
to be away so that she could come over to babysit. There
would be no question of her being trapped in a full-time
nanny role.

Neither had she found herself obliged to politely accept lifts to work with Kane in the mornings. He left
before seven, giving her an hour to get herself together

before having to leave the house. And at the office he was utterly professional. However long the situation lasted, there would be no intrusion into her personal space.

Amidst the general upheaval, she had almost forgotten about the Christmas play until Eleanor reminded her one morning before she was about to leave for school.

'I hope you haven't forgotten about this afternoon' were her opening words as she went into the office to find Kane sitting at her desk and riffling through her in tray.

'Have you seen that Jones file? I'm sure I had it on my desk before I left work yesterday.'

'Have you checked your briefcase?'

'Good point.' He abandoned the abortive search and focused on her. 'What about this afternoon?'

'Eleanor's play?'

'Damn. Damn, damn, damn.'

'I'm afraid she'll be terribly disappointed if you don't turn up,' Shannon told him quietly. 'I specifically arranged no meetings for you this afternoon after one-thirty and that meeting shouldn't overrun. I have to tell you that I'm really disappointed. I just can't believe that you could have forgotten about it. She's shown us her routine often enough, for Pete's sake!' As soon as the words were out she realised how cosily domesticated they made them both seem. Like a traditional couple playing at happy families instead of a boss and his secretary who had found herself in the unnatural situation of living under his roof.

To hide her burning cheeks, she began flapping around the coat rail, then spent a few seconds busying herself by dusting down her coat, as though it had somehow accumulated grit on the journey to work. When she turned to face him, she was less flushed.

'Joke,' Kane said, standing up and spinning her chair round to face her but keeping both his hands on the back of it.

'What?'

'Joke. Of course I remembered about the play. A few months ago I may have forgotten about it, but I've come a long way since those days of absentee father.' He waited until she had primly positioned herself on the chair before swivelling it round to face him and leaning over her with his hands on either side of the chair. 'Now I find our domestic little routines quite appealing, just as you seem to.'

Shannon was beginning to feel faint at his closeness. 'We don't have a *domestic little routine*,' she denied, shakily, which made her sound as though she was guiltily denying some earth-shattering, self-evident truth.

'Of course we do! You and Eleanor do homework and chat, and then you both prepare some food and I get home in time to catch up on the last half-hour of family chat…'

'Family chat! Don't be ridiculous!'

Kane raised his eyebrows expressively before pushing himself away. 'We'll leave at three. Will that give you enough time to change before we go to the school?' Having wreaked havoc with her nervous system, he had now resumed his role of thoughtful employer and was looking at her with his head inclined to one side, patiently waiting for her to answer.

Shannon could barely stammer out an affirmative and even the demands of the job, which were usually constant enough to take her mind off everything but literally what was in front of her and needed attention, failed to deliver. Her mind refused to keep to the rails and insisted on breaking its restraints and merrily galloping down Avenue Wild Imagination.

The drive back to the house seemed unnatural at three in the afternoon, when they should both have been at work.

'I feel like a truant,' Kane said, reading her thoughts, and Shannon relaxed enough to smile.

'So do I,' she admitted.

'Do you think we'll get found out and the boss will have us for dinner?'

Shannon laughed at that. Wasn't this what she found most disconcerting? His amazing ability to make her laugh when it was usually his fault that she was in a grumpy mood in the first place? However huge his personal assets were, literally and metaphorically, he still retained a sense of self-irony that could reach out and find the humour behind most things.

'We might,' she said, playing along with the game. 'What do you think we should do if it happens?'

'Throw ourselves at his mercy and beg for forgiveness?'

'Or maybe pretend that our watches were both showing the wrong time and really we thought that it was five-thirty?'

'Ah, we'll be all right.' He gave her a sidelong, teasing look. 'After all, our boss is known to be the fairest, most generous man in London. A paragon amongst the male sex, in fact.'

'Funny. I thought you might reach that conclusion.' She laughed again, and the remainder of the trip back to the house passed by in pleasant silence, broken only by quiet, easygoing conversation that skirted from topic to topic, never resting long enough on any one for it to meander down dangerous byways.

And it was oddly gratifying to dress for a school event. She had been to her brothers' and sisters' various school plays and awards evenings and sports days but she had never attended a school event in the capacity of adult spectator. She wore a green and black checked skirt and a bottle green jumper and her high boots, all fairly new acquisitions since she'd started working for Kane and seen her pay packet considerably increased. She brushed her hair until it shone and then swept it away from her face, pinning it back on either side with two tortoiseshell clips, and was inordinately pleased when Kane told her that she looked absolutely perfect.

And the play was perfect as well. Eleanor remembered all her lines, not that there were that many to remember, and the animals and trees all behaved themselves.

Afterwards, over a fast-food dinner, Shannon recounted her various experiences of school plays and all the disasters that had befallen the various members of her family. When she talked about her past, she could feel it come alive, could feel her excitement as a child as she'd dressed in Nativity costume for a ten-second starring role in the class play. Her eyes sparkled and once or twice, when she looked at Kane, it was to find him staring at her, seemingly enthralled at her recounting of old times. He even joined in with the reminiscences and gave amusing thumbnail sketches of things that had happened to him as a boy.

Eleanor looked gratified but astounded to hear that he'd had a boyhood. Like all children, she probably assumed that her father had mysteriously emerged, fully grown and mature, from his mother's womb.

So it seemed natural, when they had got back to the

house and Eleanor was settled and asleep, to continue the trip down memory lane. And it seemed natural to mention Kane's wife over a cup of frothy coffee. Shannon almost expected him to refuse to answer, but he did, startling her with the length and breadth of his explanation. They met and it had been, he told Shannon, an instant attraction.

'But really,' he said, caressing his coffee-cup thoughtfully, 'when I look back, I wonder whether our mutual infatuation would have matured into something stronger. I don't normally, I assure you, bore people with details of my private life but…' their eyes met and tangled and Shannon's pulse accelerated '…what can I say? We rushed headlong into a relationship and within a year Annette was pregnant. In retrospect, I wonder whether we really ever knew one another that well.'

'What makes you say that?' Shannon asked.

Kane looked at her broodingly. In the muted light, his face was all angles. The shadows lent him a remoteness that was at odds with his frank discussion of his dead wife. 'She was distraught at being pregnant. It wasn't planned and towards the end I could tell that she was terrified that her party days might be over. She was also upset at how her body changed. I always assumed that women found pregnancy enjoyable.' He focused his attention on her, as though indicating that she might be able to provide an answer to this, and Shannon shrugged.

'Not all do. I would, though.' She smiled mistily. 'I can't imagine how wonderful it must be to have a baby growing inside you, feeling it, waiting for it to make its appearance…'

'I thought that might have been your way of looking at things.' There was a lingering silence during which she became aware of the breeze rustling against the window-panes, blowing through the leaves on the trees.

'There's something girlish yet womanly about you.'

'Girlish yet womanly...? What does that mean?' She laughed to dismiss the thick atmosphere between them but found that she couldn't tear her eyes away from his and the laughter died in her throat.

'I guess another way of putting it is...sexy.'

Sexy, sexy.

Sex.

With the man sitting just next to her at the kitchen table.

Shannon licked her lips and Kane watched the unconscious gesture of nervousness, which made her even more nervous. Nervous but excited. Unspeakably excited, in fact.

Then he leant across the few inches separating them and she closed her eyes as his cool lips touched hers.

CHAPTER EIGHT

THIS was what Shannon had been waiting for. The realisation hit her like a bombshell the minute Kane kissed
her. It was a slow, lingering kiss. He was tasting her,
exploring her mouth with his tongue as his hand reached
behind her head, pulling her to him, and Shannon allowed herself to be directed. She was barely aware of
the smooth wooden table between them as she leant towards him and into him, drowning in the depths of his
mouth. When he finally drew back, she found that she
was trembling.

How could he stop? She opened her eyes and saw that
he was looking at her.

'What? *What?* What's the matter?' She leaned across
and closed her eyes, but he placed one finger very gently
on her mouth and her eyes flicked open again.

'We need to talk about this.'

Talk? How could he be contemplating discussion at a
time like this?

'Why?' she cried. 'Why do we have to talk about it?'

He sat back in the chair and folded his hands behind
his head.

'Look, if you don't want to…if you… I don't turn
you on, so what's the point…?' Shannon could feel herself on the brink of tears, but she wouldn't give in. It
was obvious. One moment of impulse was now being
considered in the harsh glare of reality and found wanting. If he really wanted her, like she really wanted him,
he wouldn't have been able to pull back, never mind sit

138

there looking at her through shuttered eyes and telling her that they needed to talk.

She stood up and he said quietly, 'Sit back down, Shannon.'

'And what if I don't?' she flung at him, gripping the edges of the table so fiercely that her knuckles were white. 'What are you going to do? Stop me? So that you can tell me that we need to talk? Drag me back to the kitchen table, kicking and screaming?'

'That,' he said, 'is precisely what I would do.'

By way of reply, she pushed herself back from the table and stalked across the kitchen, her eyes glazed and aching from the effort of not bursting into tears from sheer humiliation. How ironic to think that Eric Gallway, the man she had once idiotically considered the love of her life, had never been able to stir a response like this in her. His seduction had been intense, brief and polished, and his techniques for trying to get her into bed had been much on the same level.

But the stronger he'd tried to fan her flames, the more she'd pulled back, believing that years of indoctrination had given her principles which she couldn't overcome. She had really believed that she couldn't commit to sex before marriage.

If he could see her now! Not a principle in sight. All her principles had vanished over the face of the horizon and she knew, with mounting dismay, that they had vanished because what she felt for Kane Lindley was nothing like what she had felt for Eric Gallway. What she felt was true and strong and right because she was in love with Kane.

The realisation brought a choked lump to her throat. Her eyes were stinging.

She felt his steel-like grip on her wrist before she even realised that he had covered the distance between them.

Shannon stood frozen to the spot, aware of the futility of any physical battle between them. 'Go on, then! Talk! If you want to talk, talk! Get it off your chest.'

'Not here.'

'Why? What difference does it make?'

'In the sitting room.' He didn't give her time to answer. Instead, he pulled her along while she ineffectively tried to wriggle out of his vice-like grip.

The sitting room was in darkness but instead of switching on the overhead lights he flicked on a lamp with one hand while the other remained firmly superglued to her wrist. Then he pulled her along to the sofa and only released her when he was sitting right next to her, close enough for any idea of a quick sprint to the door to be out of the question. Not, she thought, that it mattered. The short distance between the kitchen and the sitting room had been enough for her to consider her options. They were basically limited to two. Attempt a pointless flight from the situation from which she would emerge with her dignity even less intact than it was now, if that was possible, or brazen out her mortifying rejection with as much cold self-possession as she could muster.

'Why don't we just forget what's just happened?' Shannon suggested, staring at the fireplace. She could feel the pulse in her neck beating and she drew in a long, steadying breath. Rallying her defences would be so much easier if she could just ignore the man sitting next to her. He wasn't in her line of vision, but unfortunately she was still intensely aware of his eyes on her. She was also, unfortunately, all too aware of what he was seeing. A woman with heightened colour, her breathing shallow and gasping, hands clammy and shaking. Hardly a vision of cold self-possession, she thought bitterly. More like a vision of total collapse.

'Why would I want to do that?'

'Because we're both adults and adults should be able to deal with mistakes.'

'You're presuming,' Kane said drily, 'that I consider it a mistake.'

'And don't you?' Shannon swung to look at him. Having initially breathed a sigh of relief that the room was in semi-darkness, she now wished that it was bathed in fluorescent light which might have enabled her to read his expression. As it was, his face gave her no clue to his thoughts and she felt like a swimmer, thrashing around in the dark in pursuit of the nearest piece of land. 'Why did you stop, then?'

'Because I need to know that this isn't going to end up being a mistake for you.'

'Very magnanimous of you, Mr Lindley,' Shannon said cuttingly. 'And what about you? What if it turns out to be a mistake for you?'

'I can handle myself.'

'And I can't?'

'Not if your experience with Eric Gallway was anything to go by.'

There he goes again, Shannon thought despairingly. Even on the brink of passion, his wretched sense of consideration took over. Was he like this with all the women he hopped into bed with? Or had he just singled her out as incompetent when it came to taking care of herself? Maybe he was trying to warn her off him. Was that it? Her madly whirring brain tried to deal with every possible hidden meaning behind his attitude and eventually appeared to short circuit.

She gave a short laugh and said sarcastically, 'You certainly know how to kill passion.'

'Oh, is that what I've done?' His dark eyebrows rose beguilingly. 'My passion still seems to be very much alive.'

'Oh, it does, does it?'

'Why don't you find out for yourself if you don't believe me?'

The full extent of her inexperience hit her like a blow and she let out a strangled squeak.

'Sorry, what was that?'

Shannon cleared her throat while her body resisted all attempts at sophistication and went up in flames at the thought of touching him. He was less alarmed at the prospect and he gently took her hand in his and placed it on his lap so that there was now no mistaking the throbbing arousal that told its own story.

'Do I prove my point now?' he asked huskily, and she nodded.

'P-perhaps we should t-talk,' she stuttered, which was rich considering, she thought, that she could barely make her vocal cords get it together to form a sentence, never mind string sentences together to form anything halfway coherent. Every part of her body was actually vibrating, like an engine waiting to race away from the starting post.

'You want to make love with me, don't you, my little flame-haired beauty? I know. I can feel it. I can *smell* it. And I want to make love with you, but if we do, once isn't going to be enough. Not nearly enough.'

His words swam in her head, muffling her thoughts, and she had to fight to concentrate on what he was saying.

'You mean you want to have an affair with me?' she whispered.

'More than that.'

For the merest of split seconds, she was overcome by a swooping sensation of elation as the prospect of marriage flashed on the horizon. Marriage to Kane Lindley, weeks and months and endless years of sharing her love, having his children, basking in the blissful knowledge that they would grow old together, two trees forever entwined.

'I want you to enter into this knowing that we'll be lovers.'

'Lovers? For how long?'

'That's a question without an answer, Shannon.' His voice was gentle. 'I can't and won't make you rash promises of wedding bells and happy-ever-afters and I know you might find that impossible to accept.'

Disappointment was like a wave crashing over her, and it took her less than a second to make her mind up. 'Yes,' she said, closing her eyes. 'Yes, yes, yes.'

'Yes, yes, yes...what? Yes, you find it impossible to accept?'

Shannon opened her eyes to look at him and felt the breath catch in her throat at the thought of all the things they would never share, but they would share enough. He was right, life was hard and there were no happy-ever-afters. All she could hope to do was snatch her piece of happiness while she could and let her dreams take care of themselves.

'Yes. I'll be your lover.' Because I love you, she added silently to herself. Those were dangerous words that would have to be contained, but she could do that because the alternative was turning her back on what her heart needed and yearned for.

Kane smiled and brushed the hair away from her temple. Shannon held his hand, leaning into his palm with her cheek.

'Are you quite sure, my darling?'

'Quite sure.' She leant towards him and opened her mouth against his, taking the initiative to still any further questioning on the subject. This was enough because it would have to be enough, and she could deal with the consequences.

This time there was sweet savagery as his tongue clashed with hers, and when she pressed her hand against him, she could feel him stirring against her, his urgency matching her own. As his mouth left hers, she arched back, groaning as he trailed a path wetly along her neck with his tongue, pausing to tease the tender flesh behind her ears and to tickle her ear with the tip of his tongue.

'What do you like, Shannon?' he asked in a deep, uneven voice. 'What feels good for you?'

'I don't know,' she whispered back. 'But this feels... nice.'

'Just *nice*?' He laughed softly into her ear and his breath sent a shiver through her.

'Well, maybe...wonderful... Would that do?'

'For the moment.' Kane slipped his hand underneath her jumper and delicately traced the outline of her bra, running his fingers along her rib cage, then down to her flat stomach, stopping at the waistband of her skirt. Then he resumed his explorations, down to where her skirt was rucked up against her thigh and then underneath so that the barrier of her flimsy tights felt like iron cladding separating his fingers from her bare flesh.

'But right now,' he murmured, 'I want you to get undressed for me. Very slowly. I want to feast my eyes on every inch of you.'

Shannon stood up and watched him as he watched her. Did he want her to perform a striptease? Instead of feeling nervous at the prospect of that, she felt wantonly erotic. She slowly tugged the jumper over her head and then dropped it to the ground, then undid the zipper of her skirt and stepped out of it, kicking it aside. Then her boots, bending over to release the laces until she could ease them off. No one had ever seen her naked before, not like this.

The excitement was pulsing inside her like waves of hot lava and as she removed her tights she looked up at him and their eyes clashed. Now she was bare other than the lacy flesh-coloured bra and her underwear. She reached behind her, unclasping the bra and letting it fall to join the rest of her clothes. Her instinct was to cover her exposed breasts with her hands, a gesture of modesty, but the naked hunger on his face was an immense turn-on. Instead, she walked towards him and he pulled her to sit on his lap, so that the pointed tips of her nipples were on a level with his mouth.

With a soft sigh, Shannon curled her fingers into his hair and looked down to watch as he suckled at her nipples, drawing first one then the other into his mouth, rubbing his tongue over the sensitive tips until she could barely stand the explosion building up inside her.

'Don't worry, I'm going to take things nice and easy with you...'

As he continued to suck her ripe nipples, hard and engorged now and slick with the wetness of his mouth, his hand moved along her rib cage and he stroked the flat planes of her stomach. Then he slid his hand down beneath the silky elasticised waistband of her underwear, cupping her, and with gentle pressure he rubbed the sensitive mound between her thighs with his palm. Shannon gasped and began to move against his hand, throwing her head back, her mouth half-open as she moaned her pleasure.

'Do you like me touching you there?' he groaned unsteadily into her ear. 'I know you do. You're wet for me.' He eased her off him, laying her flat on the sofa, and she watched as he stood up and began to remove his clothes.

He was as beautiful as she'd imagined he would be. As he stripped off his shirt, she noticed, with feverish excitement, how defined his muscles were. The breadth of his shoulders emphasised the narrowing of his waist and hips and as he stood, finally, in proud nudity for her to absorb, her eyes were drawn to the dark hair curling tenderly at his groin, framing his thrusting erection. She wanted to touch it so badly that she reached out and felt a shudder of heady power as it moved beneath her hand, responding to the lightness of her stroking.

He curled his fingers into her hair and she sat forward to obey his silent command, taking his hardness into her mouth.

'Yes, my darling, just like that.' He controlled the rhythm with his hand on her head. He gave a shudder and tilted her face upwards so that he could look down at her.

'Now, where did you learn to do that?' he asked with a soft, shaky laugh, and Shannon stretched back along the sofa, her arms provocatively raised above her head to hang limply over the edge of the soft cushions.

He pulled her underwear off but, instead of joining her on the massive sofa, he remained standing to stare intimately at her fully unclothed body and Shannon obligingly parted her legs just slightly, enough to afford him the briefest glimpse of her scented womanhood.

They devoured each other with their eyes and when she could bear her mounting need no longer he knelt down and eased her towards him, parting her thighs still wider, then he blew gently between her legs and she whimpered involuntarily.

'You tasted me,' he said, catching her eye and laughing softly as she blushed at the directness of his statement. 'Now it's my turn.'

Kane peeled aside the softly swollen lips sheathing her femininity to expose the small nub, then ran his tongue over it, applying a delicate pressure that made her cry out and buck against his mouth. Her fingers scraped along his shoulders, curled in frenzied passion into his hair, and the delicate pressure became firm strokes.

He eased himself into her so fluidly that Shannon felt not the slightest twinge of discomfort. Her body was ripe and ready for him and his slow thrusts, building up as he moved quicker and faster, brought her to a shuddering climax that seemed to go on for eternity.

Her body was still alive and he gently stroked the flanks of her thighs, as if he were soothing an excited horse. Then, tentatively, he traced the outline of her breast, spiralling his finger in small circles until he was feathering her pink, engorged nipple.

'I think I've developed a taste for you,' he murmured huskily, and she gave a shuddering sigh.

'Is that good or bad?'

'Perhaps I ought to remind myself of it to find out.' He laughed under his breath, a dark, sexy laugh that made her head spin.

Then he pulled her so that she understood what he wanted, easing her along him until his flared nostrils could breath in the musky scent positioned provocatively above his mouth. From her advantageous position, Shannon could see his tongue flick out to touch her sensitised womanhood. Just those delicate flicks were enough to make her arch back and her legs stiffened as his finger moved inside her to touch her deepest depths while his tongue caressed and rubbed until she had to close her eyes, gasping as another orgasm shuddered through her body, as powerful as the first.

This time, as she finally lay beside him, she felt drained. Beautifully drained. There were no thoughts in her head and she might have dozed off if he hadn't spoken, with infinite gentleness.

'I think it's time for bed.'

'Already?' She sighed languorously.

'My bed,' he said gravely, and she gurgled her pleasure.

'But what about Eleanor?'

'Asleep and oblivious. As I'm your boss, it's your duty to comply with my orders.' He cupped her breast in his hand while his thumb stirred her resting nipple into upright alertness.

'Are you saying that I have no choice?' she teased, wriggling on the sofa.

'Correct.'

She giggled and obediently complied. Trusting in the darkness, they grabbed their clothes and hand in hand headed for his bedroom, their footsteps making soft, padding sounds along the carpet.

She had never felt so whole in her life before. The thought that this was simply the start of an affair, no strings attached and no promises given for anything beyond that, was not enough to quell the bubble of joy that had spread through her.

'Are you taking anything…?' he asked, chucking his

clothes on the deep two-seater sofa by the window, and Shannon looked at him blankly.

'Anything like what?'

'Anything like contraception?' he asked.

She hadn't given that a moment's thought. She knew enough about the biological workings of her body, however, to realise that the chances of becoming pregnant were pretty slim. 'I'm in a safe period,' she said quickly. 'Why? Do you think I should go on the Pill? I'm not sure I like the thought of—'

'Shh.' He took her in his arms and cradled her head against his shoulder. 'It's my responsibility as much as yours. If you don't want to take the Pill, I'll make sure I use the necessary protection.'

Shannon closed her eyes and smiled. How could she ever *not* have fallen in love with this man? He made her feel safe, as if his presence could cocoon her against everything unpleasant in the world.

'Don't you mind that I'm so...'

'So what?' He led her towards his king-sized bed and then covered them both with the sprawling duvet, wrapping his big body around her small one so that they were nestled into one another.

'So...hopeless,' Shannon said. 'I mean...well, I bet all the other women you've slept with in the past were on the Pill. I bet you didn't have to worry about accidents happening...'

'You mean apart from my wife...'

'Well, yes.'

He absent-mindedly stroked her thigh and she covered his leg with her own.

'I've always been careful,' he told her thoughtfully. 'It's better to be in control of a situation than to discover down the line that the situation was in control of you...

As to you being hopeless…maybe I like it…' He nuzzled her jawline and then raised himself on his elbows to look down at her. 'You bring out the caveman in me…hadn't you noticed?'

'Mmm. Not sure I like the sound of that…'

'Maybe I mean protector…'

'Oh, yes, I can see that,' Shannon said wryly. 'My mother's surprise visit was proof enough.'

'And how pleased she would be to know that I'm going to carry on protecting you,' he told her smugly. 'Keep my eye on you, stop you from straying off the straight and narrow…'

'Thrilled, I'm sure,' she said with a laugh.

But, she thought to herself, that was a little piece of information she definitely would be keeping to herself.

More difficult, she thought three weeks later as she walked into her office, was keeping it from all her friends at work. No one had said anything, but Shannon was sure that they'd noticed the difference between herself and Kane. For a start, he came to the office canteen for lunch whenever he happened to be in the building, and instead of discreetly sitting at a distant table, out of sight, he always made sure to sit where she was, seemingly oblivious to any abrupt silences that greeted his arrival. Lunching with the head honcho reduced even the most garrulous to awed, stuttering silence.

'People will suspect,' Shannon had told him the week before.

'Suspect what?' He had moved across to perch on her desk and idly played with a strand of her hair.

'Suspect what's going on.'

'Why?'

'Because you never used to go to the canteen before?

Because you always come and sit where I am? Because most people can add two and two and get four?'

'I'm just a good boss,' he'd said soothingly, 'taking an interest in what's going on on the ground floor.' And that had been the end of that.

'Christmas,' he said, as soon as she walked into his office with his ritual cup of coffee, very strong and black.

Shannon was now well accustomed to his lack of preliminaries when it came to conversation.

'Two weeks' time.' She sat primly in the chair, facing him, and felt that familiar stirring as he leaned back in the swivel chair and looked at her from under his lashes.

'I want you to stay here with me. With us.'

'I can't,' she said with a little sigh. 'Mum would hit the roof.'

'We could go away. Somewhere hot. Two weeks in the Maldives. Wouldn't it be nice? Making love on a beach every night?'

'Every night?' She blushed and he pushed himself away from the desk and patted his lap invitingly.

'I bet you've never done it on a bed of sand before...'

'You know I haven't.'

'Come and sit closer and tell me why you won't consider it.'

'We can't...not here, Kane...not in the office... What if...?'

That was another thing she had become accustomed to. The deceptively chivalrous nature that fooled you into thinking that all his actions were ruled by an inner code of good behaviour. In public perhaps, but in bed, he threw off that mantle and was thrillingly primitive in his love-making. He was also thrillingly inventive.

'You worry too much, my sweet,' he said, crooking

his finger for her to come to him. 'The outer door is closed, isn't it?'

'Well, yes, but...' She glanced nervously over her shoulder and obediently sidled around the desk to be yanked down forcefully on his lap.

'But nothing, woman. Can't you see how much you turn me on? I can't see you without wanting you. I amaze myself by even being able to work fairly normally when I know you're only a matter of a few feet away.' He unbuttoned her decorous blouse and groaned when he saw that she wasn't wearing a bra. 'Was this for me?' he asked, cupping her breasts in both his hands, weighing them and then opting to lick and suck her left nipple while she cradled his dark head in her hands.

'My bras don't seem to fit any more,' Shannon said in little pants.

'Good. Get rid of the lot. Mmm. And your nipples look bigger as well. Maybe they're responding to frequent use...' He demonstrated his definition of 'use' by virtually making love to her breasts until she was squirming on his lap. 'For a lady who was so concerned about being caught in a compromising position,' he told her huskily, 'you've managed to shed your inhibitions pretty quickly. Not, my little wanton hussy, that you have any inhibitions...'

He paused to reach into his drawer and Shannon scolded him reprovingly but indulgently as he withdrew a condom, shifting her so that he could unzip his trousers and slip it over his hardness, already fully erect and hungry for satisfaction. He had been true to his word. After the first time, he'd taken no chances of any unwanted pregnancy; no sex without protective measures.

But before Kane could slide into her, he raised her skirt, pulled her underwear to one side and inserted his tongue into the apex between her thighs, doing there what he did so well, driving her insane with desire as his tongue flicked and explored and delicately probed the pulsating, acutely sensitive nub. It was agony having to be pleasured without moaning out loud but heaven only knew what the fall-out would have been if someone had happened to innocently open the outer door to the sounds of elevated groaning coming from the direction of Kane's office!

Then he sat her on him and gripped her firm buttocks as they lost themselves in the furious business of wild gratification.

'Will that be all, Mr Lindley?' Shannon whispered into his ear, head on his shoulder, eyes half closed with pure happiness.

'Why, I do believe my perfect little secretary is going to corrupt me with all of this. Quite unorthodox, my dear.'

'You only have yourself to blame. I learnt from the hands of a master.' She blew into his hair and he clasped his arm more tightly around her waist.

'If you insist on abandoning me for Christmas,' he said softly, with little-boy petulance that made her want to laugh, 'then at least go for the shortest time possible.'

'I *am* allowed a fortnight's leave from work, sir, according to company policy...'

'Are you now?' He looked at her as if disbelieving the source of her information. 'Actually, I only work it out as a week...'

'Uh. I'll think about it.' Shannon reluctantly straightened herself, at the end of which she still felt wickedly debauched.

'And I expect phone calls every day.'

'Or else what? Sir?' She resumed her correct position

at the chair in front of his desk and inclined her head curiously to one side.

'Or else you may find an unexpected and sex-starved visitor at your mother's door...' At which he saw fit to conclude the conversation with a glimmer of a smile on his lips and begin proceedings for the day.

It was only three days later, after a Christmas tree had been mounted amid much excitement from Eleanor, that something occurred to Shannon.

She hadn't had her period recently. Her timekeeping when it came to her periods tended to be lax but she was sure that something should have happened already.

By the following morning, as she slunk into the nearest chemist's during her lunch hour, she was in a state of thinly suppressed panic. Once. They had made love once without protection, and by her calculations it hadn't been during a fertile period. She didn't think. She hoped.

She bought the pregnancy kit and secreted it in her office, relieved that Kane was tied up in meetings and nowhere to be seen. She waited in gut-wrenching anxiety until five o'clock rolled around and she could straighten her desk and head back to the house.

Actually taking the thing out of the bag and using it brought Shannon slap bang into the darker side of reality which she had blissfully spent the past few weeks ignoring. The fact that, however much she loved Kane Lindley, the love was one way only. Even at the heights of passion, when men, she had once read, were wont to make declarations of a love they didn't feel, he had remained silent on the subject. He wanted her, he lusted after her, he enjoyed her company and he had no hesitation in telling her as much. But love?

In the silence of her bathroom, while Eleanor was downstairs doing her homework, she sat and watched while fate came home to stay. She was pregnant. The clear blue line in the pregnancy box was unequivocal.

Shannon hadn't expected it. She'd bought the kit, she'd played with the vague notion but, looking at that determined blue line, she realised now that she hadn't expected to be pregnant at all.

The unexpected accident had happened and all the time they had been blithely making love, using protection, she'd been pregnant. She felt as though somewhere up in the heavens, the gods were watching her and snorting with laughter.

She felt a wave of nausea replace shock. What would Kane say to this sudden development in what was supposed to be a light-hearted affair with no strings attached? Pregnancy wasn't merely a string. It was a thick rope and she tried and failed to picture his reaction. He would want to take responsibility. That was the type of man he was. He might even ask her to marry him. The prospect of a marriage made under these circumstances was enough to make her blood run cold. She couldn't think straight while she was under his roof. She needed time to work out some kind of plan before she broke the news to him.

It wasn't yet six o'clock and she knew that he wouldn't be back for at least another hour, probably a bit more.

Shannon picked up the telephone and after a shaky phone call to Carrie, who wasn't best pleased at the favour being asked of her, she went downstairs and explained to Eleanor that she had to leave on important family business. When she said that she would be back as soon as she could, she made sure to superstitiously cross her fingers behind her back. Carrie, she said, was on her way over.

Eleanor listened and then said, 'Are you feeling all right? You don't look very well. You're not ill, are you?'

The smile Shannon offered Eleanor in response to this question was glassy and unfocused.

'No! No, of course not! It's just...' she mumbled. 'Mum, actually. Bit of an accident around the house. Vacuuming. Broken ankle. Fell over the, um, vacuum.'

Eleanor looked perplexed at this explanation but let it go. 'What shall I tell Dad?'

'I'll call him. You just tell him that I'll be in touch.'

CHAPTER NINE

SHANNON lay on her bed and stared up at the ceiling. It was something she had been doing quite a bit of over the past three days. Her mother had given up asking her what was wrong since the standard answer Shannon supplied was, 'nothing, Mum.' She had also, thankfully, stopped asking how 'that nice young man of yours' was. If she was disturbed at her daughter's vague responses as to how long she intended to stay in Ireland, she kept her unease to herself.

But Shannon knew that her mother was worrying. And she thought that she would have plenty more to worry about if she only knew the full extent of the situation. One pregnant daughter, one 'nice young man' who would promptly turn into a monster the minute she knew that he was the father and one job in London which would be no more.

She sighed heavily and felt her eyes begin to well up again. Crying was also high on her list of sudden idiosyncrasies. If it weren't for the fact that she had to maintain a cheerful façade whenever she was with her family, she seriously reckoned that she would be crying all the time. Her bedroom would become a swimming pool. And she still hadn't managed to work out what she was going to do.

Returning to London wasn't an option. Naturally, she would have to tell Kane about her condition, but when she thought too hard about that she could feel herself braking violently at the prospect and cravenly telling

157

herself that there was no need for immediate revelations. She would get a job first, find somewhere to live because living under her mother's roof would be impossible and then present him with a *fait accompli*. Except, what job? She couldn't think offhand of any employers who would hire a pregnant woman with open arms. Not unless they were mad. Which would mean temp work. Which would mean no money. Which would mean no independence. The sigh became a groan of despair.

From downstairs she became aware of her mother calling her and Shannon heaved herself up from the comfort of her bed and reluctantly went to her door and shouted.

'I'll be down in a minute, Mum! I'm just...' What was she just doing? Meditating? 'Cleaning up my bedroom!' She looked around her and decided that she would really get her act together very soon and actually do something about the state of it. Her bed was unmade and her brother, who had been ousted amid much protest, had not seen fit to tidy up his clothes and neither had she.

'Well, come down now!'

The voice had come nearer. In a minute, knowing her mother, she would come and fetch her down. Shannon grudgingly went downstairs and trailed limply in the direction of the kitchen, bypassing the small lounge which the family used as a television room and from which came boisterous noises of her brothers who seemed to spend most of their free time playing weird games on the television with their friends.

'You have a visitor.' Her mother appeared in front of her with a rolling-pin in one hand and a bowl in the other.

'Who?' At six-thirty in the evening, she couldn't think

of anyone who might be visiting her. No one knew she was around, apart from her family.

'You haven't been sleeping again, have you?' her mother asked suspiciously, and Shannon went pink.

'Why would I be sleeping at this ridiculous hour, Mum? I told you, I was cleaning the bedroom. It's a tip. You have to tell Brian to move his clothes out. I can't find anything.'

'There seems no point to that, Shannon, when you haven't deigned to tell us how long you're going to be here.' She looked as though she might say more, but she had already said it. On a number of occasions. Usually with a level of concern in her voice that brought on an instant attack of crippling guilt.

'Well, who's my surprise visitor? Can't you tell them that I'm not well?' She hung back from the kitchen door, alarmed at the prospect of having to be sociable when all she wanted to do was curl up like a ball and hide.

'No, I can't. You do your own dirty work, Shannon.' With which she strode away, with her daughter following miserably in her wake. 'And let me tell you right off that I'm sick to death of you moping around this house as though the sky's fallen in. You put a smile on your face, my girl!'

Shannon grimaced.

'That's better. Not much, but better.'

Shannon was still sporting the sinister grimace on her face when she pushed open the kitchen and froze in her tracks. Her legs refused to propel her any further and her heart seemed to do something funny.

'Your visitor,' her mother introduced triumphantly, doubtless, Shannon thought numbly, expecting her to be pleased, thrilled, over the moon. After all, hadn't the 'nice young man' whose name Shannon had refused to mention, followed her all the way from London to Ireland?

Kane was sitting at one end of the long, weathered kitchen table with a cup of tea in his hand, while her mother rolled pastry at the other end. A cosy scene. He looked perfectly at ease in a pair of black jeans and a thick, black jumper, the sleeves of which he had pushed up to the elbows to accommodate the warmth in the kitchen. Shannon felt her heart begin to do a panicky quickstep.

'Well, aren't you going to say hello?' Her mother paused in her pastry-rolling to shoot Shannon a lethal look that spoke volumes.

'Uh, hello,' Shannon said, hovering uncertainly by the door. Her hands began to stray guiltily to her stomach and she clasped them firmly behind her back. 'How are you?'

'Fine.' He spoke at last. It was bad enough seeing him but she dreaded hearing that deep voice.

'Cup of tea, love?' her mother asked, and Shannon shuffled into the kitchen, managing to somehow walk sideways, like a crab, towards the kettle.

'So, what are you doing here?'

'I came to see how your mother was.'

'How *I* was?'

'Apparently,' Kane drawled, not taking his cool eyes off Shannon's flushed face, 'you broke your ankle, tripping over the vacuum.'

The lie rebounded off the walls of the kitchen and then subsided into deafening silence.

'Ah.' Shannon cleared her throat. 'As you can see, Mum's fine.'

'What's going on here?' Rose asked. She stopped rolling altogether and proceeded to dish out one of her spectacularly penetrating glares at Shannon. 'What's all this nonsense about broken ankles and vacuum cleaners?'

'Oh, dear,' Kane said in a voice dripping with false innocence, 'have I put my foot in it?'

'Shannon, you look at me. Have you been telling untruths?'

'Sort of.' At which point the kettle began whistling furiously and she busied herself with making a cup of tea, taking her time, while two pairs of eyes were focused on her conscience-stricken back.

'You seem to have a nasty habit of sort of telling untruths, don't you, reds?'

Shannon swung to look at him and found him standing right there beside her like a dark, avenging angel, which was crazy because he didn't know anything. *Go and sit back down,* she wanted to yell. *Go where I don't have to breathe you in.*

'You shouldn't have come here,' she whispered shakily.

'Why should I leave you to crawl away? I've done you a favour, reds. There's guilt stamped all over your face. If I hadn't shown up, you would have been living with your guilt for ever.'

'I have nothing to be guilty about!'

'And is that another sort of untruth?' He removed the bottle of milk from her shaking hands and poured some into her cup.

She was temporarily saved from the necessity of having to enlarge on that explanation by the thundering sound of boisterous young boys who pelted into the kitchen and stopped in their tracks.

'Oh, hi,' Brian said, looking at Kane with devouring curiosity. 'Mum, when's tea? We're hungry.' His three friends shuffled about in the kitchen, peering around for anything edible on offer. 'And the computer's crashed.'

'Who's the visitor?' Brian asked.

'Kane Lindley.' Kane was looking at the assorted, badly dressed heap of fourteen-year-old boys with amusement. 'Your sister's employer.'

'When is she going back to London? She's in my room.'

'No, Brian, I'm actually in *my* room.'

'It's not your room any longer.'

His friends began hooting and jeering and making disgusting noises, and heaven only knew how long their juvenile antics would have carried on if Kane hadn't stood up and informed them that he would have a look at the computer.

All four pelted out of the kitchen in a reverse stampede, followed by Kane who paused only to say to Shannon, 'I'll leave you to chat with your mother, shall I? You probably have one or two things to say by way of explanation.'

'So,' her mother said, once the kitchen door was shut. 'What's Kane doing here?'

'He said you vanished without notice and he came to find out if anything was wrong.'

'You see what I mean!' Shannon cried out, clutching her mug. 'Didn't I tell you that this would happen the minute I made the mistake of taking him up on his offer to live under his roof while I looked for somewhere else? Didn't I tell you?'

She thought of Eleanor, who had enjoyed every minute of her company, and the pleasure she had shared with Kane before circumstances had taken a turn for the worse, and felt herself flush with guilt. It was easier to deal with him, though, if she could work herself up to a fury so she doggedly fanned the little spark of self-righteous anger until she was feeling suitably hard done by.

'I don't need anyone chasing me up here to find out what's going on when nothing's going on! I was due to have some holiday leave anyway! I didn't choose to move to London so that I could end up in a situation with someone checking on my every movement!'

'He said you disappeared without any explanation. Apart from this nonsense, presumably, about my broken ankle, tripping over a household gadget. Did something happen there that I should know about? Sit down, Shannon and stop hovering there by the counter. Sit down and talk to me.'

She finished putting the pastry over the chicken pie which she popped into the oven, then she wiped her floury hands on her apron and sat down.

'The last time I spoke to you on the phone, you sounded very happy. So what happened to you in the space of one week?'

'Nothing. I just…needed a bit of space…'

'So you flew back here, where there's no peace and quiet to be found with those mad brothers of yours stamping through the house like elephants. Spin me another fairy-tale, Shannon.'

'I felt homesick,' Shannon said.

Now was the perfect time to tell her mother everything. She would be shocked and disappointed at first, but she would also be supportive. There was nothing to fear in that respect. But she just couldn't. The conditions, she decided, were not optimum. She needed to have her mother to herself for her confession. It couldn't be done when Kane was outside and four adolescents were waiting to burst into the kitchen again in another feeding frenzy. She would take her mother out for tea, perhaps tomorrow, when Kane had gone, and she would tell her everything then.

'It gets lonely down in London,' she elaborated, playing loosely with the truth, 'especially at Christmas. I mean, Mum, Christmas is special here at home. All of us together. I just gave in to a fit of nostalgia. You could say.'

'Why didn't you tell Kane that? Instead of having the poor man rush up here, thinking you'd been taken ill?'

'He thought I'd been taken ill?' Shannon asked anxiously. 'Did he tell you that? That I was sick?'

He couldn't suspect anything, could he? No, she thought, men's minds didn't operate like that. And there had been no signs. No sudden bursts of unexplained nausea, no strange food cravings, nothing suspicious. Just as well she'd found out early, before she'd begun to put on weight. Just as well she hadn't gone on the Pill after all after that first time. Shannon considered the consequences of that and shuddered. She'd accepted the fact of the baby inside her from the very first moment of discovery, and what she felt wasn't a sense of despondency or of hopes shattered but, strangely, one of rapture that she would now have something to show for her love, a child she could treasure, a lasting memory of the only man she would ever love.

'Not in so many words, but he was obviously concerned.'

'I did contact him after I left,' Shannon said truthfully. Actually, she'd left a message on his answering machine at home when she'd known he would be at work, telling him that she was very busy but would be in touch as soon as Christmas was out of the way. 'Did he say when he would be leaving?'

'He didn't. And I didn't see fit to ask him. I wouldn't want him thinking that he was unwelcome here after all that he did for you.'

'Well, it won't be overnight. He has to get back to Eleanor.'

'Why don't *you* ask him, then?'

'Ask me what?'

Typically, Kane had given no advance warning of his reappearance in the kitchen. He hadn't even knocked! So much for exquisite, gentlemanly good manners. Shannon looked at her mother to see whether she had noticed that oversight, but her mother was smiling. Lord, did this man know how to worm his way under people's skin!

'Shannon was just wondering how long you were going to be here,' her mother said guilelessly, 'because she wanted to take you to a new Italian restaurant that's opened just outside Dublin. Very near here, in fact. Give you two a chance to talk. There'll be no opportunity here, that's for sure.'

'Oh, was she now?' Kane murmured. He shot her a telling look and smiled. 'Well, you're in luck, Shannon, as it happens. I booked to stay overnight in a hotel and it would be my pleasure to be taken out for a meal.'

'Well...I...' Shannon stalled.

'I know,' her mother said, reaching over to pat her hand, 'you're worried about lack of transport. Well, love, you're welcome to my car. It's only an old thing,' she explained to Kane, 'but it goes and it's very reliable. And taxis can be very unreliable at this time of year unless you book one in advance. Of course, you'll have to change, Shannon. You look a state in those clothes. Whatever possessed you to walk around the house in those faded jeans and great, baggy jumper?' She clucked her tongue reprovingly.

'Shall I make a reservation? For, let's say, eight?'

'I'll just fetch the number for you.' Her mother inspected various assorted cards attached by magnets to the fridge door and pulled one off. 'Very handy that I kept this, wouldn't you agree, Shannon? Hilary went there only last week and was so impressed that she gave me the card. Not that an old woman like me gets to go out to fancy places.'

Shannon felt like a cornered rabbit.

'In which case, I'm sure Kane wouldn't mind if you came with us!' she said, inspired.

'I wouldn't dream of it.' Her mother firmly squashed any such hopeful suggestion. 'I wouldn't leave these young lads in this house unsupervised if my life depended on it. Don't know what the state of the place would be when I got back! No, love, you two go and have a good time. Now, you get upstairs and do something with yourself, there's a good girl.'

So, left without a choice, Shannon stamped upstairs, pausing *en route* to look in on Brian who gave her a thumbs-up because evidently the computer had been fixed.

'He's pretty cool,' Ronan said, winking conspirationally at her. 'Better than the last cretin you went out with.'

'Thank you, Ronan,' Shannon scowled, 'but when I want the opinions of a minor, I'll ask.'

Which resulted in the predictable roaring of four adolescents with nothing, she thought, better to do than make loud, suggestive noises at the slightest opportunity.

When she reappeared half an hour later it was to find

Kane and her mother ensconced in the sitting room, poring over photo albums.

'My fault,' Kane said, standing up and countering her sour glance with an unrepentant grin. 'I begged your mother to take a trip down memory lane.'

'Not that I needed much persuasion!'

'What a wonderful way to pass the time,' Shannon said with a little scowl. She was wearing an old, long-sleeved, black woollen dress, one of the few items in her wardrobe not in need of ironing thanks to Brian's cavalier treatment of all her clothes which had been bundled up into a trunk in the corner of the bedroom.

'And informative,' Kane added, walking towards her and helping her on with her coat.

She muttered cattily under her breath, 'Especially to nosy people like you.'

'Now, now,' he whispered silkily into her ear, 'you won't get rid of me by being nasty. I'm a persistent guy. I thought you would have known that by now.'

In retrospect, she thought as they drove through icy weather to the restaurant, his persistence was the one factor she hadn't reckoned on. She thought that he would have waited for her to contact him, but she should have known that Kane Lindley didn't wait for people to do things. If it suited him, he would simply intervene and would then proceed to bludgeon through all obstacles until he got what he wanted.

The drive was completed in silence. She'd demanded silence because she'd said that she would need all her concentration to get them to the restaurant in an unfamiliar car in wintry driving conditions. Obligingly, he said not one word, even though her fertile imagination conducted a conversation of its own, formulating imaginary questions from him and then sifting through the various answers she could give him.

The restaurant, when they arrived twenty minutes later, was pleasantly crowded. With snow predicted, the weather had kept some people away so that it wasn't packed to the rafters, and they were shown to a table at the back. It didn't have the elegance of some of the London restaurants, but there was a pleasing informality about it. In fact, it reminded her of Alfredo's.

'So, reds,' Kane said, after he'd ordered some wine and mineral water, 'have you missed me? You look a bit peaky. Have you been pining?'

She hadn't expected that question for an opening gambit. In fact, she thought that he might have gone immediately into accusatory mode, with her mother no longer around to put a brake on his self-control, and had consequently prepared a mental list of all possible answers to deal with accusations.

'I don't feel peaky,' she hedged, pretending to give the menu her full attention.

'That's not what I asked.'

'Don't tell me that you flew to Ireland to find out whether I was missing you or not.'

'Why? Is it that inconceivable?'

'Yes, as a matter of fact.' She snapped shut the menu and linked her fingers together on her lap. 'I'm going to have the soup, followed by the cannelloni. What about you?'

He ignored her weak attempt to steer the conversation out of choppy waters. 'Why? Don't you think that your sudden absence might have left a dent in my life?'

'I think it may have left a dent in your ego,' Shannon told him. 'Look, perhaps I shouldn't have run out like that. I know it was rude but, um, I suddenly got cold feet. Anyway, I did leave a message for you on your answering machine. Didn't you get it?'

'Oh, I got it all right. I just wasn't too impressed with it.'

'Why not? I told you I'd be in touch.' When he didn't say anything, she rushed on, 'Maybe I should have spoken to you in person, but I didn't think at the time. I just felt as though I had to get away...'

'In which case, why did you lie and tell Eleanor that your mother had tripped and broken her ankle?'

'Well, I wasn't about to tell her that her father and I had been lovers, was I?' The words sent a warm flush spreading across her cheeks and she gratefully watched the progress of the waiter towards them. Any distraction to relieve her of her cross-examination.

They ordered their food and Kane waited in polite silence until wine had been poured and glasses filled with mineral water.

'You're blushing,' he commented mildly. 'Does it still make you go hot under the collar when you think about us making love? Does your skin still tingle when you think about me touching you?'

'Why are you asking me these questions?' She felt herself go a deeper, brighter shade of red. 'Why don't you just get to the point? I know you're angry with me.'

'Do I look as if I'm angry with you?'

Shannon sneaked a look at his face. No, he didn't look angry, but he must be. In fact, she desperately hoped that he was because it would make her life a whole lot easier.

'How do you think I felt when I got back home to find that you'd disappeared? Eleanor was upset. She didn't understand and she didn't believe you when you told her that lie about having to rush back to Ireland to see about your mother's ankle. She may only be eight, but children are very clever when it comes to reading between the lines.'

'Yes, I know, and I'm sorry about that.' Shannon's guilt was fast reaching overwhelming proportions. 'I just couldn't think of anything else to say.' She thought of Eleanor's trusting face and felt a pang of excruciating misery. 'I wasn't thinking straight at the time.'

'Why not?' he moved in swiftly, his eyes narrowing. 'That's what I don't understand. Why you suddenly felt the need to run away. If you wanted to tell me that you weren't happy with...us, why couldn't you have waited until the morning instead of rushing out of the house in a panic?'

'Because...because...' Shannon thought wildly, wondering what she could come up with that would turn desperate, irrational behaviour into something reasonable.

'Take your time. I'm in no hurry.'

'Why can't you understand that some people act on impulse?' she cried desperately. She daren't meet his eyes. She hardly dared look at him, in fact, because there was no part of him that didn't fill her with memories. 'Not everyone thinks things through and then behaves in a rational manner! Some of us just do things on the spur of the moment! It's just another reason why you and I are so ill suited, why we have nothing in common. *Nothing!*'

'I can think of quite a few things we have in common.'

'And I'm not talking about sex!' Shannon attacked swiftly.

'Nor am I!' He leant forward and forced her to look at him, forced her to meet his glittering black eyes. 'I can't imagine how little Eleanor and I meant for you to just disappear like a bloody thief in the night, woman!'

'What's the point trying to defend myself when you won't even try to understand?'

'I understand that you're a coward...'

As she was feverishly trying to come up with an answer to that, the waiter produced their starters and she fell on hers with the enthusiasm of someone saved by the bell.

'So, reds, want to pretend that everything's all right? Fine. Let's behave like civilised adults and pretend, shall we? Make polite conversation for a while?' He gave a mirthless laugh. 'How does it feel, being back in Ireland?' He sighed, as though he couldn't help himself, and ran his hands wearily over his eyes.

Shannon didn't care whether he was humouring her. She grabbed the lifeline with alacrity.

'Weird.' Her voice was high and unreal. He looked shaken. Was he hurting? She wanted to reach out and stroke his hand, make believe that everything was going to be all right. Instead, she took a few deep breaths and concentrated on her garlic prawns. 'Also, Brian had taken over my bedroom and he was put out when I turned up because now he's sharing with Ronan again.'

'Sometimes it's hard to return to the family nest when you've flown it, isn't it, reds?' he murmured roughly.

Shannon relaxed and told herself that perhaps the worst of their confrontation was now over. When she tried to think ahead, she wondered how he would react when he learnt of the pregnancy. If he could follow her to Ireland simply because he wanted one or two questions answered, what would he do when he discovered that he was going to be a father? She would have to delay the revelation, she thought. For his sake.

'And what have you been doing since you got back? Going out much?' There was a curiously flat inflection to his voice, but his expression remained watchful.

'Now and again,' Shannon said vaguely. 'I've felt a bit…tired recently, so I've been staying put quite a bit.'

'Tired?'

'Just lethargic,' Shannon said hurriedly, intercepting any possible questions about her health. 'Must be the weather. Winter is awful for making me want to hibernate. Is Carrie with Eleanor?'

Kane nodded and sat back to allow his main course to be placed in front of him. Roast cod, surrounded by vegetables. He almost always ate fish when out. It was an unimportant titbit of information that made her feel suddenly nostalgic. How much else had she stored away in her memory about him that would jump out and surprise her over the years to come?

'So you'll be heading back…in the morning?'

'Around lunchtime, actually.'

'Oh.'

'And what about you?'

'Me? What about me?'

'When do you intend to head back to London? Or do you intend to head back at all?'

Shannon tried to feel infuriated that he was pinning her down when she should have the freedom to make her own choices, but she couldn't. She just thought about him leaving and her having to cope on her own without his sense of humour and intelligence and conversation to carry her along.

'I don't know if…' she said weakly.

'I hope you wouldn't let me put you off coming back, because it was well within your right to kill our affair.'

'I didn't want to kill anything,' Shannon blurted out,

reddening as he digested her outburst without saying anything.

'No,' he agreed softly, 'you didn't, did you?'

Shannon shook her head and gave a long, resigned sigh. Well, it had worked. She had fallen straight into his ambush and it had worked a treat. He had been so nice, so understanding to have stopped quizzing her about her abrupt departure that she had dropped her guard, and it was only been a matter of time before he got the truth out of her. She knew him but, conversely, he knew her, too. He knew her well enough to realise that arguing would have put her back up so he hadn't argued. She was overcome by a feeling that none of it mattered any more anyway.

'So tell me why you concocted that story about getting cold feet. You don't have to have any secrets from me. You can share what's really on your mind. I'm not going to punish you so there's no need to feel as though you have to run away. Problems don't evaporate because you choose to run away from them. In fact, it's been my experience that the faster you run from a problem the larger it looms on the horizon.'

'I *did* get cold feet, Kane.' She knew that every word he was saying was true, he didn't know how true, but she just couldn't face him with the full truth. 'I didn't *want* to end it, but I...' She placed her knife and fork very precisely together and then rested her elbows on the table and stared down disconsolately at the uneaten food on her plate.

'I realised that I'm not cut out for an affair after all. I thought that I would be able to handle it, but I can't. When I went down to London, I was determined to grow up, I guess. I mean, I'm hardly a teenager any more, am I? That's what happens, I think, when you grow up in a family as large as mine. You're so cushioned against everything that you just don't have to mature as quickly as other people the same age as you.'

'Or maybe it's just easier to go with the flow. You don't have to make decisions if there are other people around who will make them for you. London must have been a shock for you, Shannon.'

She shrugged. 'At any rate, I thought I could behave like the sophisticated woman I never will be so, yes, I ran away.'

'So if you don't want an affair, what *do* you want?'

'Some coffee?' She laughed nervously.

He allowed the flippancy to pass and ordered two cups of cappuccino which arrived with a little plate of interestingly shaped chocolates and biscuits.

'You haven't answered my question.'

'Yes, I have!' Shannon squirmed in the chair and then spooned some of the milky froth into her mouth. 'I told you why I ran away like I did. I wanted to be one kind of person but I'm not.'

'But I know all that,' Kane said gently. His gentleness was unnerving. He should be hurling criticism at her, not sitting there making her believe that he understood.

'What do you mean, you know all that? You don't know me at all!'

'Oh, yes, I do. I know you better than you know yourself.'

'Trust you to say something like that.'

'You mean I'm predictable?' He laughed softly. 'We'll have to do something about that, then, won't we?'

Shannon's heart gave an unhealthy flutter of excitement. He reached out and lightly covered her hand with his, stroking it with his thumb.

'We will?' she found herself weakly compelled to ask.

'Oh, yes. Why do you think I travelled all this way?' He sipped his coffee and looked at her narrowly over the rim of the cup. When Shannon took her own cup in her hands, she could feel her fingers trembling.

'Because you were annoyed that I left without any explanation?'

'We're back to this dented ego thing, aren't we? I didn't come here because I was mad with rage and suffering from wounded pride because you walked out on me. I came here to take you back where you belong.'

'You haven't heard a word I've just said!'

'I've heard every word, reds. Of course, I'm still waiting for the three you haven't said. Those three little words that made you run away like you did.'

'I...' Shannon looked at him sulkily. 'I...I love you, Kane Lindley.'

'Now, that wasn't so hard, was it?'

'I'm still not coming back to London to be your mistress,' Shannon said hotly.

'And I wouldn't ask you to. I've come to take you back with me so that you can be my wife.'

CHAPTER TEN

'YOUR wife?' Shannon looked at Kane incredulously.

'That's right.' He signalled for the bill and then smiled at her, a smile that sent her fluttering heart soaring upwards, somewhere in the region of the heavens.

'Shouldn't that proposal be accompanied by three little words?'

'Rather more than three.' He stopped talking to sign the credit card slip, then leant across the table towards her. 'But I'll just start by saying that I love you.'

'But you can't. Can you? Really? Are you...sure?' She looked at him anxiously. If there was a fly in the ointment, then it was important that she find out sooner rather than later. 'But you said that an affair with me was no promise of a wedding ring, you told me that it was a relationship without commitment.'

'And I believed it at the time, I assure you.' He shook his head, as if marvelling at the way events had altered the course he had originally planned. 'But,' he told her as they walked out to the car, 'I was wrong. By nature, I have always been a considered man. You know that, don't you? I've been accustomed to using my head rather than my heart, especially after my last marriage when I realised, somewhat late in the day, that impulse has a nasty habit of backfiring when you least expect it.' He switched on the engine but, instead of pulling away, he turned to her, resting his arm along the back of her seat. It had begun to snow, light flurries like powder than brushed against the windscreen. Stray people on the streets hurtled along, heads bent, hands clutching tightly at their coats in an attempt to protect themselves from the freezing weather. Inside the car, with the engine on, it was warm.

'I thought I could handle anything. I thought that marriage was a step I wouldn't take until I was one hundred per cent sure it would be the right step. I failed to realise, until you ran out on me, that I had been one hundred per cent sure for longer than I cared to think. Do you know that you were the reason I kept coming back to Alfredo's every morning?'

'Me?'

He laughed softly at the incredulity in her voice. 'You. I was on my way to a breakfast meeting at a client and I stopped in for a quick coffee and a chance to look over some files. And there you were, with your red hair and your Irish voice and that way you had of looking as though any requests for a refill of coffee might result in a heated debate. In the end, I didn't get through nearly as much work as I'd anticipated, and I found myself going back the next morning and every morning after that, even though the damn place was hardly convenient. I began to look forward to seeing you in the mornings, before my day had begun, bursting with vitality, always ready to make comments on my choice of newspaper or some item of news that might have captured your interest. There were times I caught myself wondering what you did for the rest of the day, where you went, who you saw, what the quality of your personal life was like…'

'You never said…'

'On a conscious level, I don't think I was aware of it myself at the time. But I do know that when you threw that plate of food over Gallway, I felt myself want to laugh in a way I couldn't remember wanting to laugh in a very long time.'

'But you didn't.'

'No, I didn't. I offered you a job instead.' He brushed her hair back with his fingers and then gently pulled her towards him. When his mouth found hers, she was powerfully aware that this was where she belonged. Wrapped up and possessed by this big, strong man who could admit to feelings most men might want to hide, to being vulnerable in a way that assumed unswerving trust in her response.

'And it was the best damn thing I ever did,' he murmured into her mouth, before resuming his kiss. 'I should have thanked that arrogant little twerp for handing me the opportunity to have you near me. Although if I'd known your connection with him at the time, I might have been tempted to kill him on the spot.'

He slipped his hand under the lapels of her thick coat and moaned huskily as he found the mound of her breast, primly concealed by the woollen dress but, even so, responding to the hot touch of his hand.

'Is there a law in Ireland against making passionate love in the back seat of a car?' he demanded, nibbling her ear lobe. 'Because if there is, I have a rather nice hotel room booked and we have some catching up to do…'

'Kane…'

The fly in the ointment, which had been dormant during his heady, blissful protestations of love, now began to buzz. Gently at first, but then with increasing vigour. A nasty, frightening thought lodged in her mind. What would he say when he discovered that she was pregnant? How would he react to knowing that she'd concealed it from him and, as far as he was concerned, might well have carried on concealing it unless he'd sought her out?

Could fate be so cruel as to offer her everything her heart desired in one hand, only to yank it back with the other?

'Shannon...' he murmured, his breath warm in her ear while his hand continued to caress her breast. Her nipples were erect, like soldiers standing to attention, and as he rubbed his thumb over the swollen bud protruding through the lace in her bra she knew that he could feel it.

Shannon took a deep breath. 'Look, there's something else I have to tell you,' she said awkwardly.

'Something else? Apart from your declarations of undying love? Now, what could that be, I wonder?'

'I can't think straight when—' She gasped as his wandering hand left her sensitive nipple to sweep beneath the hem of her dress. Just as well the car had been parked away from any streetlamps. He pressed his palm between her thighs and she squirmed against the steady, hard pressure, rubbing herself against him with half-closed eyes.

'When you're turned on?'

'Yes,' she said unsteadily. Her breathing sounded thick. 'And we can't do this here...'

'Then let's go back to my hotel room.'

'What would Mum say if she found out?'

'Why would she find out? I'll make sure to deliver you back safe and sound before the cock crows.' He laughed at the unwitting suggestiveness behind his remark. 'So tell me what you have to tell me.'

'I'm...'

'Yes?'

'I'm...' She tried desperately to recognise the importance of what she was about to say, but her mindless body was too busy responding to his hand which pressed rhythmically against her tights, already dampening at the erotic contact.

'You're not pregnant by any chance, are you?' He detached himself from her and tilted her face to his. 'Is that the revelation? That you're carrying my baby?'

She nodded mutely. 'And now you're going to walk away, aren't you? You're angry with me for not telling you sooner, aren't you? I don't blame you,' she cried, agonised, 'but what was I supposed to do? When I found out, the only thing I could think of doing was running away as fast as my legs could take me. And don't tell me that running away never solved anything!'

'I don't have to tell you, Shannon. I think you've discovered that all by yourself. And as for being angry with you, well, I wondered when you were going to tell me.'

Shannon looked at him in bewilderment. 'You *knew*?'

'I suspected,' he answered drily, and when she didn't say anything, he continued, 'I'm not a fool, my darling. I can add up as good as the rest of them, and I worked out that you hadn't had a period for well beyond the normal limits.'

'Why didn't you say anything?'

'Because I wanted you to,' he said simply. 'When you left, my first urge was to rush up here and confront you with it, but I knew what would happen. You would back off like a scared rabbit, and then, if I told you that I wanted to marry you, you would jump to the conclusion that I was proposing for all the wrong reasons, that I just wanted to fulfil my responsibilities. So I lost sleep for three nights and told myself that it was for the best because it gave you time to think. And then I told you how much I loved you because, my darling, I can't bear the thought of not being with you. Night and day. And the fact that you're having my baby is the icing on the cake.'

'It is? Am I dreaming?'

'If you are then so am I. Shall we continue with our pleasant little dream…in a hotel not a million miles away?'

At four in the morning, her body still tingling from hours of love-making, Shannon crept into the dark house, feeling like an adolescent terrified of being caught in the act of disobeying parental orders.

Kane would be coming around later that morning and she had made him promise to let her do all the talking.

'My mother might have a heart attack if she knew what we were up to,' Shannon had said to him. 'I don't think she suspected for a minute that you were anything but a nice man who had my welfare at the top of his mind.'

'Which I was,' he'd pointed out, as he'd stroked her thighs, his fingers as delicate as butterflies brushing against her skin. 'A kind hearted gentleman innocently taken advantage of by a wanton and abandoned young woman with a fabulous body and eyes that could drive a man crazy.' When he'd said that, his strolling fingers had begun stroking the bulging nub that made her groan in anticipated ecstasy, spreading apart her legs in eager arousal, and that had been the last coherent sentence for a while.

She hoped, as she surfaced from a dreamless sleep at ten o'clock that morning, that he remembered her instructions to leave the talking to her.

At ten-thirty, she rushed to answer the door and flashed him a warning look with her eyebrows.

'Don't forget,' she whispered, 'let me handle this.'

From behind his back he produced a startling bunch of lilies with the flourish of a magician pulling a rabbit from a hat.

'For me?' Shannon beamed.

'For your mother, actually,' he replied gravely, and she giggled behind one hand.

'Creep. Anyway, I've managed to clear the house of children and family, apart from Mum. I thought you might get distracted by lots of—'

'Computer-crazy adolescents?' He grinned and kissed her lightly on her lips. 'Mmm. Slightly swollen lips. Do you think it's the pregnancy or an overdose of love-making?'

'Shh!' Shannon laughed and dragged him through to the sitting room.

'Mum!'

'Well, Kane, I thought you might have been on a flight back to England. Come and sit down for a moment. I'm taking a rest from Christmas preparations.' She patted the chair next to her, flushing when he handed her the flowers. 'So, did you two children have a good time last night?' She looked shrewdly at her daughter. 'You must have. You didn't get back until well past three.'

'How did—?'

'Having children makes light sleepers of us all, Shannon. I take it the restaurant was an all-night one?'

'Well…' She glanced helplessly at Kane who smiled serenely back at her.

'We…have something to tell you, Mum.' Shannon reached out for the flowers and placed them on the cof-fee-table, then she sat down, leaning forward with her elbows on her knees.

'I'm sure you do. When is it going to be?'

'We haven't set a date as yet,' she said, gaping in disbelief.

'I didn't realise,' her mother said, frowning, 'that you could set a date for a birth. Technology must really have advanced without me noticing.' Then she saw her daughter's expression and laughed.

'I knew the minute you came back all in a rush, my girl, that you were in the family way. Just as I knew the minute I saw the both of you together that you were in love. There was no point in preaching to you about saving yourself for the right man because you'd found the right man and I expect you'll be married. *Won't you?* So. Where's the good in giving long lectures and trying to bolt the stable door after the horse has gone? Just tell me, how long have I got to do my knitting? And how much time do I have to look for a suitable hat?'

EPILOGUE

'YOU are the most exquisite creature in the world.'

Shannon looked drowsily at Kane and smiled. She watched as he tenderly picked up the eight-pound-three-ounce baby girl sleeping in the crook of her arm and watched as the tiny newborn figure stirred and stretched with closed fists and made small gurgling sounds before settling back into her new sleeping position.

She felt as fragile as a piece of china, Kane thought as he circled the small hospital room with his baby in his arms. A family. Eleanor, Sophie, Shannon and himself. Nothing else mattered.

For years work had been his driving force but now that he'd delegated much of it to his various directors it seemed natural to slide into a less frantic schedule. In a short while he would drive back to the house to collect Eleanor so that she could meet her sister for the first time, and as soon as Shannon was ready they would be moving out to the country and leaving London to the Londoners. He looked at his wife and felt a burst of gratitude and love.

'Have you called everyone on the list?' Shannon asked, and he went to sit by her on the side of the bed.

'You forget that you're speaking to the most organised person in the world.'

'Oh, is that right? Would that be why you forgot my overnight bag when I went into labour?'

'Ah, but you have to admit that I made sure it was packed weeks in advance.'

'How was Mum?'

'A bag of nerves,' Kane said drily, 'as you can imagine. They're all coming over tomorrow, so expect a hectic day of showing off our daughter. Your mother will be in her element considering you deprived her of a big, white wedding...'

'My mother has ample opportunity for big, white weddings with my sisters. Not that she's a big, white wedding kind of lady. Anyway, she said that she couldn't have hoped for anything more. Family only for the register office and then a reception in the grandest hotel in Dublin...'

Shannon closed her eyes and knew that even if the photographer hadn't been present, recording everything from every angle, she would still hold that memory in her heart for the rest of her life. The joy as she'd turned to Kane and kissed him chastely for the first time as his wife, her mother dabbing her eyes with a handkerchief, Eleanor bursting with the thrill of it all, and then the reception in Dublin where every friend and relative had showed up with good wishes on their lips.

She'd had her cream silk dress dry-cleaned and one day soon she would sit Eleanor down and tell her how much it meant to her, how powerful a symbol it would always be of her great happiness. When she looked at Kane, she saw him smiling at her, understanding what was going on in her head, the way he always did.

He placed the baby back with Shannon and watched in fascination as Sophie uncurled her fists and wriggled about. 'Now, reds, I feel you should get some rest before Eleanor comes to visit.' He leant over and kissed her on the tip of her nose. 'She's bursting with excitement at the thought of seeing you and our baby. Not forgetting your family...'

'They did kind of adopt her, didn't they?'

'They certainly did, Mrs Lindley.'

'Mrs Lindley.' She savoured the words and smiled at him. She wondered whether it would take her a lifetime to adapt to the fact that dreams could come true.

'My Mrs Lindley.' He raised her hand to his mouth and kissed it. 'And I would be no one without you.'

'Good,' she said comfortably. 'Because you're always going to have me.' She kissed their baby's downy head and thought how their love would only grow stronger over the years, a safe, secure haven she would never leave.

Modern
romance™

THE SHEIKH'S INNOCENT BRIDE by *Lynne Graham*

Desert Prince Shahir has three rules: never sleep with
a virgin; never get involved with an employee; never get
married. But rules are made to be broken! Kirsten Ross
is a lowly cleaner, but the sexy Sheikh can't resist her...
now she's pregnant with a royal baby!

BOUGHT BY THE GREEK TYCOON
by Jacqueline Baird

Greek multimillionaire Luke Devetzi will go to any
lengths to get Jemma Barnes back in his bed for a night of
blistering passion. He discovers her father is in financial
trouble and in need of cash. Luke will provide the money
– if Jemma agrees to be his wife...

THE COUNT'S BLACKMAIL BARGAIN
by Sara Craven

For Italian Count Alessio Ramontella, seducing women
comes naturally – so bedding innocent beauty Laura
Mason should be easy. But Laura seems to have a future
with another man. Should Alessio leave well alone, or
ruthlessly pursue Laura until she succumbs...?

THE ITALIAN MILLIONAIRE'S VIRGIN WIFE
by Diana Hamilton

Mercy Howard has had a sheltered upbringing, so her job
as housekeeper to Italian businessman Andreo Pascali
means a new way of life. She soon sees that her dumpy
image must be changed. Andreo realises he no longer has
a mouse for a housekeeper – but a fox!

On sale 6th January 2006

*Available at most branches of WHSmith, Tesco, ASDA,
Borders, Eason, Sainsbury's and most bookshops*

Visit www.millsandboon.co.uk